Laurie Lee

The Well-loved Stranger

VALERIE GROVE

VIKING

VIKING

Published by the Penguin Group
Penguin Books Ltd, 27 Wrights Lane, London w8 5tz, England
Penguin Putnam Inc., 375 Hudson Street, New York, New York 10014, USA
Penguin Books Australia Ltd, Ringwood, Victoria, Australia
Penguin Books Canada Ltd, 10 Alcorn Avenue, Toronto, Ontario, Canada m4v 3b2
Penguin Books (NZ) Ltd, Private Bag 102902, NSMC, Auckland, New Zealand

Penguin Books Ltd, Registered Offices: Harmondsworth, Middlesex, England

First published 1999
10 9 8 7 6 5 4 3 2 1

The publisher would like to thank the following for granting permission to use copyright material:

Pam Matthews for the letters of Tom Matthews; Peter L. Potts for the letters of Molly Smart; Rachel Mooring
Aldridge for the letters of Wilma Gregory; Lady Selina Hastings and Roland Philipps for the letters of
Rosamond Lehmann; Miles Huddleston and Charles Osborne for the letters of John Lehmann; Jill Balcon for
the letters of C. Day-Lewis; Betty Farmer (née Smart), Celia Goodman, Georgina Hammick, Val Hennessy,
Emma Smith, Julian Bream and Brian Patten for their own diaries and letters; Valerie Eliot for the letter from
T. S. Eliot; and U. A. Fanthorpe for the poem 'Dear Mr Lee', from A Watching Brief, Peterloo Poets, 1987.

Insets: Unless otherwise stated, all the photographs are from the Laurie Lee collection

Endpapers: These are from Laurie Lee's diary for 17 April 1942

Set in 12/14.75 pt Monotype Bembo
Typeset by Rowland Phototypesetting Ltd, Bury St Edmunds, Suffolk
Printed in Great Britain by Clays Ltd, St Ives plc

A CIP catalogue record for this book is available from the British Library

ISBN 0-670-88177-5

To Mr Smart

Contents

List of Illustrations

Section 1

1. Laurie's father, Reg Lee
2. Laurie's mother, Annie Emily Lee, *née* Light
3. The infant Laurie ('a frail lifeless lump'), with elder brother Jack and sister Frances
4. Laurie aged five
5. Annie's cottage (now Rosebank) in Slad
6. Slad School: Laurie and his cousin Rosie Green
7. Peace Day fancy dress parade in Slad: Laurie as John Bull, with Rosie Green as a fairy
8. Laurie in Slad Wolf Cubs with his brother Tony
9. A couple of swells: Jack and Laurie in their plus-fours
10. Molly Smart with Laurie, June 1932
11. Betty and Molly Smart, the girls from Gloucester, 1933
12. Cleo of Whiteway, in 1934
13. Sufi Rogers, the girl from Buenos Aires who taught Laurie to say '*Un vaso de agua, por favor*'
14. Laurie, photographed in Southampton, having just walked out one midsummer morning
15. Laurie in Toledo, with Mary (*née* Garman) and Roy Campbell, 1935
16. Wilma Gregory, benefactress and self-styled 'aunt'
17. Laurie in Martigues, with six-year-old Kathy on his knee, 1937
18. A bronzed Laurie and his fiddle in Málaga, 1935
19. Lorna Wishart, mistress and muse
20. Laurie bound for the Spanish Civil War, 1937
21. Laurie, his fiddle, and his two-year-old daughter Yasmin, Sussex, 1941
22. Portrait of the poet by Bill Brandt, Bognor, 1942

Section 3

Preface

A note about NAMES: Laurie made the rules about people's names. He was always Laurie (Lol to intimates), never Laurence. His wife was baptized Katherine Francesca – her mother was reading Tolstoy just before she was born, and thinking of Katerina – and as a girl she was Kathy. Laurie's first published reference to her was as 'Kati' (in *A Rose for Winter*) but privately he had by then decided that the letter C was softer and more feminine, and after he married her, he called her Cathy. (She said that his changing her name 'tells you everything you need to know about our marriage'.) For many years, she signed her name with an ambiguous K/C – i.e. with a C separated from the stalk of the K, so friends could choose which form to use. But since Laurie's death she tells me she has decided to reclaim her own name, and be Kathy again. So I have referred to her in my text as Kathy – except when quoting directly from Laurie's diaries, notebooks and letters (and those of some friends) in which she is 'Cathy' or 'C'.

Jessy was baptized Jesse – not Jessica – but Laurie decided later that Jessy was nicer, so Jessy she is in this book.

Acknowledgements

Kathy Lee's warm hospitality and help were beyond the call of any dutiful keeper of her husband's flame, and I thank her with all my heart. I also particularly thank Laurie's three closest blood relations, without whom this story could not have been told: his daughters Jessy Lee and Yasmin David, and his surviving brother Jack, a sprightly eighty-six, in Sydney. It was a stroke of fortune for me that my editor was Annie Lee, Jack Lee's daughter-in-law, whose insights and familiarity with the story made working on the finished text a pleasure. I thank the trustees of the estate of Laurie Lee – Margaret Pollock, Patrick Kernon and David Long – for permission to use Laurie's invaluable papers. And I am grateful to Pat Kavanagh, Laurie's literary agent as well as my own, for proposing to Laurie in 1996 that I should do this book; also to Tony Lacey, Laurie's last publisher, for wanting to publish it; and to Peter Stothard, editor of *The Times*, for giving me time to write it.

The letters of Wilma Gregory lent to me by her niece Rachel M. Aldridge were absolutely vital, revealing episodes in Laurie's life that were otherwise unknown and unrecorded. So were those of Betty Farmer (*née* Smart), and her late sister Molly. Three women – Roy and Mary Campbell's daughter Anna Campbell Lyle, Kathleen Epstein's daughter Kitty (the Hon. Mrs Wynne Godley), and Anne Dunn Moynihan, former wife of Michael Wishart, were immensely helpful about the Garman family background, as was John Byrne, literary executor of Michael Wishart (and proof-reader extraordinaire). Mavis Nicholson's two televised interviews with Laurie evoked him at his best. And I am thankful that the late John King, whose BBC films of *As I Walked Out One Midsummer Morning* and *A Rose for Winter* are masterpieces (the like of which will probably never be filmed again), was still able to talk

to me about Laurie with great perception, six months before he died.

I am indebted to many others who had preserved their letters, or their family's letters, from Laurie: his sister-in-law Nora Lee, Lt-Col. Val ffrench Blake DSO, John Fuller, Clare Francis, Christopher Fry, Celia Goodman, Georgina Hammick, Lady Selina Hastings, Val Hennessy, Elizabeth Jane Howard, P.J. Kavanagh, Pam Matthews, Lady Monson, Alan Ross, John Ward and Antonia Young. I thank Emma Smith for lending me her wonderful Indian diary of 1946, Brian Patten for sending extracts from his diary, and the Devas family for letting me see their precious Holiday Books. Without Dr Barry McLoughlin's Russian-speaking expertise and trips to Moscow to furnish me with documentary evidence I could not have broached the Spanish Civil War episode, and without Richard Rogers of Buenos Aires, and his surprise visit to Slad in the summer of 1998, we might never have identified 'Sufi' and her Spanish phrases. Michael and Helga Still's Castillo San Rafael, and the nearby home of Tom and Celia Read, in the almost unaltered hills above Almuñécar, provided the perfect base from which to experience the Spain that Laurie loved.

My thanks also to: HRH The Prince of Wales; Dannie Abse; Bill Alexander; Jill Balcon (Mrs C. Day-Lewis); the Revd David Barlow; Virginia Barrington; Adrian Bate; Barney Bates; Anne Olivier Bell; Rt Hon. David Blunkett MP; Michael Bott; Lord Bragg; Julian Bream; Paul Burroughs; Judy Campbell; Mavis Cheek; Douglas Chisholm; John Clive; Christopher Cook; Johnny Coppin; Simon Courtauld; Sean Day-Lewis; André Deutsch; Prosper Devas; Bob Doyle, Jr; Michael Eaude; Viscount and Viscountess Esher; U.A. Fanthorpe; William Feaver; Mary Fedden (Mrs Julian Trevelyan); Jim Fern; Jock Gallagher; Stephen Gardiner; David and Judy Gascoyne; Roberta Green: Jill, Duchess of Hamilton; Jeremy Hayes; Daphne Hardy Henrion; Jill Hepple; Susan Hill; Jeff Hoare; Jennifer Hovmand; Christopher Howse; Dr Jim Hoyland; Lord Hutchinson of Lullington; Martin Jarvis; Rebecca John; Anne Kidman; Pam Kirby; Bobby Kok; Chris Eldon Lee; Lynda Lee-Potter; Jeremy Lewis; Bob Light; Charles Light; Roger McGough; Iain Morley;

Sir John Mortimer; Andrew Motion; Clare Moynihan; John Moynihan; Rosaleen Mulji; Michelle Newell; Philip Oakes; Mary Omond; Katie Paltenghi; David Parker; Jill Paul; Alan F. R. Payne; Henry Porter; George Pownall; David Queensberry; Paul Robinson; Jeremy Robson; Kay Rogers; Diana Roper; the late Jim Rose and Mrs Pam Rose; Richard Ryan; Jeremy Sandford; Vernon Scannell; Kate Searle; Anne Sebba; Laurence Seidler; Anthea Sharp; Monica Sims; Adam Sisman; Natasha Spender; Sir Roy Strong; John Summers; Malcolm Tarling; David Tarratt; Joy Thacker; Gwyneth Thomas; Revd C.E. Leighton Thomson; Helen Thornton; Joanna Trollope; Rosemary Trollope; Alan and Joan Tucker; Lady Tucker; Claudia Wolfers Vasquez; Freddie Vasquez; Ted Walker; Johnny Wallace; Michael Watkins; Brian Wharton; Edward Williams; Professor Peter Wilson; Joan Winterkorn; Anne Wintle.

I was lucky to have the nonpareil of indexers, Douglas Matthews; while Nina Drummond's diligent sleuthing managed to unearth even the lost newspaper files of sixty years ago.

And I send undying gratitude to Mr Neville Smart, my old English master, who started it all with Micky Thumps.

1 | Annie Light of Sheepscombe

Prologue

When Laurie Lee's friends gathered at St James's, Piccadilly, in October 1997 for a service of thanksgiving, the men had their say. We heard Laurie's voice, on tape, and we listened to him playing 'Andalucía' by Granados on his violin. Words and poems of praise were spoken, by twelve good men. Not one female voice was heard. Laurie was a pub man and a club man, so he might have seemed to be a man's man; but in fact his life was dominated by women: mother and sisters, girlfriends and lovers, wife and daughters, and indispensable women friends.

From boyhood, he was under the influence of women, and he needed them. They saw, he said, a hunger in his face. In youth he made women want to care for him, advise, nurture and soothe him. Without the women in his life, without their loving him, tolerating and believing in him, the boy who left school at fifteen uncertain about what kind of artist he would be could never have become the Laurie Lee of legend.

Not that Laurie ever quite acknowledged this. It was often said about him (and he said of himself) that he loved women – but he never paid tribute to their influence on him as mentors; only as cosseting, embracing, accommodating creatures. He liked women, but in their place.

The woman he did acknowledge, and immortalize in *Cider with Rosie*, was his mother, Annie Emily Light . . .

★

The Bloom of Candles, Laurie Lee's second slim volume of poems, was dedicated to 'Annie Light of Sheepscombe'. He should have put 'Annie Light of Quedgeley', she reproached him in a letter. 'I *wish* you had said Quedgeley. That's where my love of beauty &

of books & of solitude in my own "little wood" was born, and where my beloved old schoolmaster Mr Beacon encouraged me.' As a girl Annie used to get top marks for composition, and music, which fired her imagination; but Mr Beacon had to spend hours with her after school over her sums. 'He was very good to me Laurie. But I turned away then from books and started working as they would not let me stay at school . . .' As the eldest child of John and Emma Light, and the only girl, Annie was needed to help bring up her five brothers, Charlie, Sid, Tom, Ray and Fred: 'a responsibility she discharged somewhat wildly'.[1]

Quedgeley, now a suburb of Gloucester, was a village in 1879 when Annie was born. Her mother (*née* Morse) was from a yeoman farming family. Annie's father, John Light, had been coachman at Berkeley Castle. The Light family view is that their grandfather John had an air about him, and 'could have dined with the kings of England' in the words of Laurie's cousin, Charlie Light. Moustachioed, dandyish in checked waistcoat and buttonhole, John Light is pictured in 1902 at the Coronation celebrations in Sheepscombe, cutting a dash.

Laurie did investigate his family history. An exercise book labelled 'Roots' among Laurie's papers painstakingly listed all the local seventeenth-century Lights and Morses – yeomen, butchers, gentlemen – who might have been his antecedents. 'But whatever the illicit grandeur of her forebears,' as he wrote, 'Mother was born to quite ordinary poverty.'[2] Two of her brothers went off to fight in the Boer War; all five were cavalrymen in the Great War. Laurie saw the returning uncles as 'bards and oracles . . . the horsemen and brawlers of another age, whose lives spoke of campaigns on desert marshes, of Kruger's cannon and Flanders mud'. Three came back eventually to Gloucestershire, Ray went to Birmingham; Fred, the youngest, wounded in 1917, went to live in Scotland, and prospered in insurance.

When the brothers left home in their teens, Annie went into service in stately homes, which gave her a lasting respect for the gentry (she would curtsey, Laurie said, to the Squire's governess) and a refined taste for the accoutrements of the Quality: good china

and porcelain; feather beds and linen sheets; silver cutlery, old paintings, inlaid walnut furniture, tapestry hangings, leather-bound books. Among prim housemaids and imperious butlers and cooks – about whom she would write satirical verses – the scatty Annie 'was something beyond their ken', Laurie wrote. She was pretty, however, and often told her boys that she had once entranced a whole regiment of soldiers when dressed in her Sunday best on a street corner in Aldershot.

Then her father left Berkeley Castle and took a pub, the Plough at Sheepscombe, and when her mother died, at fifty, Annie came home dutifully to help her father behind the bar: 'a lonely young woman, mysteriously detached, graceful in face and figure' but also volatile, witty and adept at handling drunken customers. More durably than anyone else Laurie wrote about, it is Annie's warmth, optimism and courage that linger in most readers' minds.

She obviously liked children, or she would not have answered the advertisement placed by a widower, Reg Lee, manager of the Co-op grocery in Stroud, in the local paper, seeking a housekeeper for himself and his family of four children. Annie was just thirty, short and shapely with a bright, intelligent face, when she arrived on the doorstep of his redbrick terraced house in Stroud. Reginald Joseph Lee was six feet tall, precise in manner and immaculate in dress. Annie fell in love at first sight. A few months before, the paper had reported the death in childbirth on 15 April 1910 of Reg's first wife, the beautiful Catherine Maude Critchley, under the headline 'Sad death at the Uplands'.

A painful sensation was created in the Uplands by the death on Saturday evening under peculiarly sad circumstances of Mrs Lee, wife of Mr R. J. Lee of Uplands Road, Stroud and manager of the local branch of Stroud Co-operative Society, with whom the greatest sympathy is felt. Mr Lee, who is well known and greatly respected, formerly resided at Brimscombe, and for a great many years had been organist at Holy Trinity Church. He was also conductor of the Stroud Co-operative Glee Society.

Deceased, who gave birth to twins on the evening of her death . . . leaves seven little children.

In that last sentence is summarized the lot of the Edwardian bride. Catherine had produced Arthur Reginald in 1901, Marjorie Winifred in 1903, Dorothy Clair (one of twins, the other being stillborn) in 1904, Phyllis Maude in 1906, Harold Mortimer in 1908. The newborn twins died on 24 June 1910, six weeks after their mother.

The bereaved Reg stayed a while at Burleigh House, Brimscombe, with the children's grandmother Critchley. The children were sent briefly to various relatives, and the eldest boy, Reg junior, remained with his grandmother, to be taken into the family business, Critchley Bros, making knitting needles and safety pins in the Chalford Valley.[3] So there were four children – Marjorie, Dorothy (Doth), Phyllis and three-year-old Harold – to be taken on by Annie.

Reg's wreath at his wife's funeral had said 'Looking forward.' Did he mean reunion in heaven? Or 'to the next wife'? He married Annie a year later, on 11 May 1911, and they lost no time in starting a new family. In 1912 a daughter, Frances, was born. Jack (Wilfred Jack Raymond) followed in January 1913; Laurie (Laurence Edward Alan) in June 1914; and Tony (Anthony Lisle) in January 1916. Laurie was baptized at, and named after, Stroud's parish church, St Laurence.

Laurie's birthplace was in Slad Road, Uplands, Stroud – at 2 Glenview Terrace. Here Reg installed Annie and the brood in the crowded house where the sisters created a vortex of fun and laughter – and screams, when Jack tumbled down the steps, fracturing his leg on one occasion. When Laurie was born, Jack had scarlet fever; and Laurie was sickly from birth. He wrote of lying seriously ill for many months, still and silent, staring at the ceiling 'for a year' he claimed, 'in a motionless swoon' – and was being laid out as dead until Annie, arriving home, revived him. 'I must tell you if I never have,' wrote Annie to Laurie, in 1947, 'that your Dad helped me to nurse you very patiently when you were ill & through that careful nursing you are alive today.' Laurie could recall, from those infant days, the prismatic light from a spinning glass ball that hung over his pram, the start of a lifelong obsession with light.

After the outbreak of war, Reg left to join the Royal West Kent regiment. He would be back, Annie thought, when hostilities were over. In 1917 Reg arranged for his family to move to a cheaper cottage in the village of Slad, two miles east of Stroud in a winding valley, then 'a place of long steamy silences, punctuated by horses' hooves and mowing machines, sleepy pigeons and mooning cows'. This was the move with which *Cider with Rosie* so memorably opens. Laurie was just three. 'I love you for that story,' wrote Annie. 'You brought back so many things to my memory so vividly. How when you first got out of West's cart & was placed at the top of the bank and the grass was so long & high, how frightened you were & how you cried . . .'

The oak-beamed three-storeyed cottage, 'with rooks in the chimneys, frogs in the cellar, mushrooms on the ceiling, and all for three and sixpence a week',[4] still stands, in its half acre, down a steep bank in the centre of Slad. It was a T-shaped farmhouse of Cotswold stone, known as Bank Cottages (now 'Rosebank'). The Lees were in the downstroke of the T, and two old ladies – 'the grannies', actually Mrs Waldron and Mrs Tyrrell – shared the crosspiece, one living above the other in perpetual enmity. The windows, deeply recessed in thick walls with upright mullions, were screened by beech and yew trees outside. Only shafts of sunlight lit the dim interior. By night there were shadowy pools of lamp and candlelight.

'Well! You ask where did we all sleep when we came to Slad first,' wrote Annie to Laurie late in 1945, when he had started writing about his childhood. 'Tony slept in his cot, as he was quite small 1 year & 8 months, & my double bed was in the same room. There were three beds in the attic Marjorie & Doth slept in one, Phyllis in another & you & Jackie in another. Harold slept in the sitting room on a nice little camp bed placed under a book case. That is the big bedroom now: we made it into a nice sitting room at first. An old lady of 70, Miss Scotford, came to help settle us in & she stayed a fortnight. She was a wonderful help & so fond of you little boys & we had many a bit of fun.

'Yes, when we went to that house in June 1917,' she told him, 'I

had so many happy brave young people to help me and it was *beautiful* weather – hot, sunny & dry & the flowers in the garden were blooming, oh it was lovely, syringa, lilac, roses & pansies & in a few days your Daddy (as he was then) came & hung up the pictures. Then he went to France, where after a few months he was invalided home [Jack Lee says his father never saw action in France] & was at a Hospital in Yorkshire & when better sent home to us at Slad. I met him at Gloucester as he wrote and asked me to. He looked very ill then, but seemed glad to be with us all again and *we* were glad to have him. After he had been home two or three weeks he was recalled to his regiment in Kent & would have to go on at his old work in the Army Pay Corps & report at the War Office.'

Reg never did come back to his family. After the war, he stayed in London, joined the Civil Service in Customs and Excise, and would visit Slad only once or twice a year. He sent Annie £1 a week ('Dear Nance – Herewith the usual – Yours, Reg'). His picture – 'trim, haughty, with a badged cap and a spiked moustache: I confused him with the Kaiser,' Laurie said – hung over the piano. Jack has no doubt that Reg was too fastidious to tolerate the messy household he had left behind. 'You can imagine the chaos of Annie's cottage. He would have been driven mad by it. I don't think the life in Slad was grand enough for our father.' Marjorie, in her eighties, remembered their father as 'a straightforward man, quite clever, who took the Civil Service examination in his late thirties to better himself'.[5] But he had by then also become involved with Mrs Reynolds, known as Topsy, his landlady in the southern suburbs of London; Jack, who visited them once, recalls a woman with straggly hair and a husband in carpet slippers. Reg was the lodger who took over when her husband died.

Annie's three boys grew up loving her family, the Lights – solid, robust yeoman stock – and intensely disliking the Lee side, who were originally from Dorset. Reg's mother, Emma, kept a little greengrocery and confectionery shop in Wallbridge, Stroud. Uncle George, Reg's thin, whiskered brother, known to locals as Tansy, sold newspapers: Jack says if they heard his voice crying 'Citizen!' they would pretend they hadn't seen him.

The pivot and focus of the boys' lives was Annie. 'Mad, but hilarious,' says Jack. She was scatty, garrulous, emotional. 'She was too honest, too natural for this frightened man,' wrote Laurie, 'too remote from his tidy laws. She was after all, a country girl: disordered, hysterical, loving. She was muddled and mischievous as a jackdaw. She made her nest of rags and jewels . . . and couldn't have kept a neat house for her life.'[6]

Everyone who remembers Annie mentions her mismatched collection of pretty china pieces from salerooms, and the wild flowers in vases which filled her kitchen. Picking flowers for Annie was something all the village children did. She couldn't sew or cook: her porridge was lumpy and her lentil soup was 'like eating hot, rusty buttons', Laurie said. But what she lacked in housewifery she made up for in artistry. 'She taught us to love and appreciate books, which we did,' Marjorie said.[7] From Annie came the creativity of Laurie and Jack. She made Laurie an observer of skies and spring leaves, and a lover of music and rhymes, stories and songs.

She was known for her curiosity and neighbourliness, her obsessive letter-writing on tiny scraps of paper (she would spend hours in Stroud post office, which had a table and chairs for this purpose), her enthusiasm for picnics and her hopelessness with money. Every six months a cheque known as 'the Critchley money' – dividends from the first wife's family business – would arrive and save them from desperate straits. Laurie and Jack grew up with a horror of debt, having so often had to walk to Mr Dover's to pay the rent, promising, 'We'll send the rest in a fortnight's time.' They also became fiercely punctual because of 'the misery I endured when she sent me to hold the bus while she found her corsets', Laurie said. Helen Thornton, daughter of the Slad vicar Cyril Broadley Hodson, remembers: 'Everyone on the bus looked out for Mrs Lee, scrambling up the steep grass bank with the hook of her umbrella held aloft – so it would be seen before her head emerged – in a long black coat with a fitted waist, and black hat. She was known and loved by all – driver and passengers alike.'

Helen's mother, the vicar's wife (who was incidentally Great-aunt Muriel to Joanna Trollope), befriended Annie. Both loved reading.

'Mother would find Mrs Lee spreading newspapers over the wet kitchen floor, and as she couldn't resist reading them, I think my mother sometimes had to finish the floor for her.' But in the evenings, the boys would collect firewood and they would crowd round the fire, and Annie would read or sing in the glow from the paraffin lamp. The death of her only daughter Frances, at four, made her sentimental for ever about little girls; brothers and sons being 'her lifetime's lot'. Once the three helpful stepdaughters had gone (they all married in 1927), her shrieking increased; Laurie's teenage diary is peppered with references to 'Mother's tongue'.

Diana Roper, Marjorie's daughter, remembers visiting Annie's cottage as a child: 'We'd arrive from Stroud on the bus, down the bank through the overgrown garden, and there'd be a squawk: "I'm not expecting you!" but she was always welcoming, in a navy or black soft dress with a white fichu or piece of lace, a silver chain, a scarf, a cameo. She smelled of Eau de Cologne. The house was filled with the scent of flowers and greenery.' Inside was a clutter of tables all littered with books, vases, candles. She surrounded herself with things: piano, harmonium, piles of newspapers. 'She always had something of interest – a newspaper cutting, a picture for her scrapbook, a piece of old netting so that I could dress as a bride. She was never dull.' She gave Diana a *Pilgrim's Progress*, a book about Oliver Cromwell, and a Royal Academy catalogue of Dutch paintings with a note: 'Study them all dear, specially Vermeer and Jacob Maris.'

Marjorie, Dorothy and Phyllis were comfort-givers and figures of fascination. They inherited the beauty of their mother, Catherine Critchley, and would sail past the infant Laurie 'like galleons in their busy dresses . . . How magnificent they appeared, those towering girls, with their flying hair and billowing blouses . . . At any moment one was . . . swung up high like a wriggling fish to be hooked and held in their lacy linen.' 'Marvellous women,' brother Jack says. Only the girls' younger brother, Harold, awkwardly placed between his sisters and the second family, cared little for their feminine fussing: 'Oh how I hate women,' was his refrain.

The ending of the war seemed to Laurie inexplicable: 'Oh the

end of the war and the world! . . . and Mother had disappeared,' he wrote of his infant panic. When Laurie's account was published in *Orion* magazine in 1947, twelve years before it became the first chapter of *Cider with Rosie*, Annie read the article with maternal pride, but was stung by the reference to her absence, which might sound like negligence. She sat down and wrote Laurie her own account of why she had been away in London on that day in 1918 – ten closely written pages in which every moment of her absence was remembered in minutest detail. Her letter gives the flavour of her personality, and her narrative skill:

'As fortune would have it, in November 1918 I had a telegram from Auntie Hilda at Sittingbourne in Kent saying Uncle Fred my youngest brother was very ill in a hospital there & asking me to go to see him. Your Dad said Yes, of course Nance you must go, & travel up with me tomorrow, which I said I'd do, tho' I felt a compunction about leaving you children alone. So I went with Dad and he left me somewhere on the journey & I went on alone, but was met by Hilda at the station, we went straight to the hospital, and I saw poor old Fred, but by that time he was on the mend, I *was* glad to see him & he was delighted to see me.

'I heard from your father, we had letters on Sundays then, to meet him by the Fountains at Trafal. Square midday on Monday. There were rumours in the hospital of what was going to take place on the Monday . . . I arrived at Victoria Station exactly at 11 o'clock & my dear old Uncle Tom was outside the barrier waving his hat on his stick & three officers were on the platform walking along arm in arm & singing, and Uncle was beaming & he said, "It's over Annie, it's over! The war's over my girl come along" so he took me under his wing and *what* we saw when we got away from the station takes some describing. He took me to his home at Covent Garden, where was my dear Auntie Nell & Cousin Bess & we went to meet your Father at Trafalgar Square. It was lovely. My Uncle said "Look! the fountains have not played during the war": but there they were playing once more. We went about seeing crowds and crowds of cheering people & in a minute or two your Dad came up to me. There were men selling flags & I bought one a

french one, oh I hope it is not destroyed, as I am not sure myself where I put it . . . Your Dad took us to the Stoll Theatre in the evening & we heard speeches & wonderful music & patriotic songs, one being "Land of Hope & Glory" another the Marseillaise, Dad, Bess & myself joining in – oh my heart the Tears start at the memory of it all. But I felt I *must* tell you *why* I was not at Slad with all you dear children. I wanted to be, but I was involved with them, Uncle, Aunt, Bess, travelling back to Stroud next day Nov 12th. I had sent a wire to Marjorie to ask her to meet me, with Eyers Waggonette. I said, "Order Eyers." Well, you *all* came to meet me, & I had a lot to tell you, and how glad I was to see all you dear little ones again & Marjorie had been so good. And Dorothy too. I often thought how cruel it was of me to leave you all – but I went to see poor Uncle Fred, that is how it all came about. So dear Laurie forget that bit. I would *never* have left you all otherwise, then I should have seen the happenings in Slad. Never say or think bad of me Laurie. I tried to be good, but there I'll say no more. God bless you Ever Your Loving Mother.'

'She waited for thirty years,' Laurie wrote, of Annie's desertion by Reg. 'I don't think she ever knew what made him desert her.' But she certainly knew about Mrs Reynolds, since Reg eventually brought her to Stroud with him when he visited his son Harold during the Blitz. Marjorie's daughter Diana knew her as 'Auntie Topsy'. She remembers that Reg brought a silver half crown and a tube of silver Nestlé coins for the grandchildren.

'When I think Laurie of his cruel mean ways & how cruelly he treated you boys & neglected you all again & again, I could wring his neck. Yes I could . . .' wrote Annie in 1945. 'I cannot think how he can have the cheek & the impertinence to bring "Tots" or "Toots" to Stroud – dear Laurie enough of this.' But when Reg died she was all forgiveness. 'I grieve about him passing on before I ever could be reconciled to him, or to hear him speak kindly to me, for I always loved him.'

Jack recalls Reg's visits. 'He wore a flat cap and pince-nez, and white canvas tennis-style shoes we called Daps. He would go down to the Co-op to lord it over the old colleagues with whom he'd

worked before going to his not very glorious war. We rather despised him for leaving Mother with all his children, not only us but the first brood as well.' Laurie had no affection for his father either, and recoiled when he later visited his new ménage in Morden.

But Annie usually preferred to remember that there had once been happy days. It was she who recalled all the details of life in Slad, the folk tales, the neighbours, the children's songs, the way to make plum and blackberry wine – and furnished Laurie with these details when he needed them. Her letters to him in the 1940s often contained oddments: 'Mother sent me an assortment of cuttings – Borotra's secret of youth, a picture of Painswick, and a ten-year-old article on Lloyd George.' Annie had all the maternal virtues in abundance, but also the maternal deficiencies: she was increasingly needy and clinging, indulgent and sometimes self-deluding.

When *Cider with Rosie* came out in 1959, every critic singled her out as the dominant portrait. 'Laurie Lee's mother will be remembered long after Whistler's mother has sunk into oblivion,' wrote one. 'It is to Mrs Lee – haphazard, lackadaisical, fanatically unselfish, tender, extravagant, with her love of finery, her unmade beds, her litters of unfinished scrapbooks . . . her remarkable dignity, her pity for the persecuted, her awe of the gentry . . . that this book belongs, rather than to the Rosie of the title.'[8] One critic 'would willingly have swapped both my mother and my life for his mother and his life. He became a poet. How could he help it with a mother like that?'[9] All agreed that Laurie had been 'splendidly and richly mothered'.[10]

'I wish more people had known her,' Laurie wrote to a friend in 1959,[11] 'and I wish for her own modest sake that she had known how many "figures" she had admired at her village distance – Harold Nicolson, V. Sackville-West, Cynthia Asquith, Priestley etc. – had picked her out in their reviews of the book for a particularly affectionate mention. This would have knocked her sideways.'

Annie lived just long enough to see her two elder sons distinguish themselves: Jack as a film director, Laurie as a writer, 'my Poet

son'. When Laurie sent her *The Bloom of Candles*, dedicating it to her, 'like a dear blind idiot' she wrote, thanking him: 'It was sweet of you & a tribute of love to your silly old mother who never could see an inch beyond her nose, or it would have been different for all of you – in fact there'd never have been a you or any of you – but there you are in the world, and though to me it does not seem true that you and your brothers have accomplished what you have, I'm thrilled and proud of you, bless you! You were such a dear little boy, loving & dreamy.'

2 | A Steep Cotswold Valley
1918–31

Slad, or The Slad, originally the Slade, meaning stream, is an odd village. The eponymous stream once divided the Domesday villages of Bisley and Painswick. Slad was never picturesque in the postcard sense, being half-hidden from view on the road from Birdlip to Stroud, now signposted 'Scenic Route', which rushes through the middle of it. But it is certainly 'greener, and more exotically lush than is decent to the general herbaceous smugness of the English countryside'.[1]

Reminiscences of English country childhoods are riddled with idylls; Laurie often said he had never wanted to romanticize rural life. 'I was poor,' he said. 'Everybody was poor. It wasn't all rising fields of poppies and blue skies. A large part of it was lashing rain; chaps walking round dressed in bits of soaking sacking, and children dying of quite ordinary diseases like whooping cough.'[2] He did not name Slad in his book, but its identity was soon known. The stories he told – about the murder of the braggart from New Zealand, the escape of Jones's goat, 'huge and hairy as a Shetland horse', the Browns' sad ending in the workhouse – were village legends. The schooldays he described were every village child's. They all went haymaking in summer and carol-singing in the snow; played hop-scotch and tag, bowled hoops and whipped tops. They played quite safely in the middle of the road; they could see a horse and cart coming a mile away. 'When we were kids,' says a note in one of Laurie's notebooks, 'we used to light fires in the open and bake sparrows in coffee tins after first stuffing them with shredded coconut. They tasted chiefly of burnt feathers and coffee dust.'

There had once been prosperous cloth mills in the valley, until steam-driven machinery relocated the woollen business to the coal seams of the north. The 1880s had brought unemployment, poverty, emigration. Slad's last mill, in the corner of the village called the

Vatch, employed 600 men, women and children until the 1890s when its chimney stack fell. What remains is a scattering of houses and farms on the valley's slope. There was no road through the valley until 1801. When Laurie was born, Lewis Eyers kept horses in stables next to the Woolpack inn, and his cart could take you to Stroud, two miles along the road. The first weekly bus arrived in 1924; soon there was Thorpe's daily motor-bus. There was no gas or electricity, no drains or piped water; every cottage had a well.

There was a church and a chapel, a post office, two pubs – the Star and the Woolpack – and the Hut for penny dances, whist drives and mothers' meetings, dominoes, darts, cards, billiards, and the Slad Players' performances of comic songs and sketches. Slad's one substantial house – Steanbridge House, originally Jacobean – was occupied by a benevolent squire, Samuel Gilbert Jones, who opened his garden for Sunday School treats, and his ponds for skating and fishing. A village woman acted as midwife, another would lay out the dead; there was a grave-digger, a pig-sticker and a dry-stone waller. Families often intermarried. Villagers bottled fruit, kept pigs and hens, trapped pigeons, collected kindling, fermented flowery wines, and bartered home-grown vegetables, eggs, rabbits and game. There was a heroic village cricket team. Life was intensely communal, with choir-outings, concerts and harvest festivals. Once a year the entire village went by charabanc to spend the day on the tidal muds of the Severn. Otherwise they just amused themselves. Laurie's diary often records that he and Jack 'hovered' or 'lurked'.

Laurie always said he was lucky to land here at the age of three, in a village community with a way of life still dominated by the horse, in a valley where 'life was a glass-bottomed boat, you could see through to all the details of life, animals, neighbours, and nothing was concealed, nothing got between us and the history of our neighbours, both tragic and comic, and we only had each other for entertainment'.[3]

Laurie said he was born with a careworn face and developed into a tubby, square child with little red eyes, who stared and sniffed and was covered in warts and whose teacher called him Fat-and-Lazy. In

fact the photographs show an average-sized, wart-free small boy who looks, like most small boys, adorable. But he suffered from the chronic ill-health that was to dog him all his life; and he learned early to use it as a weapon.

When Laurie was thought lost in Spain during the Civil War in 1938, Jack sent him a letter reminiscing about their childhood haunts: 'Do you remember how we used to float logs down "Joey" stream as far as the "whirlypool" and how we stopped up the drain by trying to float Harold's boat through it? And those walks over to Painswick Beacon to lie on our stomachs and, shading our eyes from the afternoon sun, look out across the Glo'ster plain to that lovely line of the Malverns? . . . Sunny days those were. Strange and sad to think that those simple irresponsible joys (I deliberately forget the unhappy days) will never occur for us again.'

Framed in Laurie's study is his first letter written to his mother at the age of ten in 1924, when she must have been away:

'Dear Mother: How are you going on. The ride to Weston yesterday was lovely. When we got towards Bristol, we saw two "Bristol fighting Aeroplanes". We had a lovely day there, except in sometimes the wind brought spray up from the sea. I bought some rock for the girls and daddy, and I got some for you when you came back. My legs pained ever-so when I came home. We saw the docks at Bristol three times. I went in Bristol Cathedral. While I am allright I think we shall have to stope here, or it will be to late for post.

From your loveing son, Laurie. XXXXXXXXXXXXXXXX.'

A year later, Laurie was winning a prize in a Bird and Tree competition[4] with an essay on 'The Dabchick', alias the grebe. He described how he watched a pair of grebe building a nest of reeds and 'in a few days five white egges were layed'. Slad School's headmistress, Miss P.M. Wardley, encouraged pupils to observe wildlife and enter this contest each year. Laurie's sister Dorothy told him in 1949 that Miss Wardley said Laurie 'had a marvellous brain but never got enough rest – rushing up and down that bank all hours of day & night – came to school each day with little pink eyes, and as soon as the room got hot fell fast asleep'. Laurie said,

of Slad School: 'We learnt nothing abstract or tenuous there – just simple patterns of facts and letters, portable tricks of calculation, no more than was necessary to measure a shed, or read a swine-disease warning.' But that basic grounding enabled Laurie at eleven to write clear, well-punctuated script.

The three Lee boys sang in the choir, acted in plays at the church hall (the vicar's daughter, Helen Thornton, remembers them in a sophisticated whodunit, in raincoats and trilby hats), and all spoke well; Annie saw to that. She did not allow dialect or slang.

At twelve, Laurie went to the Central Boys' School in Stroud. Jack had gone the year before, but found it uncongenial, and Annie, who thought he was the bright one, accorded Jack the common privilege of the eldest son and sent him instead to the Marling School, a traditional grammar school on the Cainscross Road with a Latin motto over the front door. It was founded by the Marling family, owners of Vatch Mill. 'Jack was at Grammar School, and his grammar was excellent,' as Laurie drily wrote. Jack says: 'It started a great rift between us that went on, really, the rest of our lives. We never recovered from it. We had been so close, slept together, were in the Wolf Cubs and the choir, played around the place, since birth.'

Jack was in the sixth form when Erinoid, a factory at Lightpill, near Nailsworth, which made plastics from dried milk, asked the school to recommend a smart young man. So in March 1930 he embarked on a career in factory management, cycling three miles home at three in the morning after the night shift.

Laurie's notebook for 1928, when he was fourteen, the year at which his famous boyhood memoir ends, is the commonplace book of a schoolboy who might easily have become an artist or a musician instead of a writer. It contains drawings and caricatures, poems by Keats and Tennyson, and a scene from *Macbeth*. There are pages headed 'Books in my possession' and 'Books I have read'. He had long outgrown Annie's collection of Penny Readers, and the days when, lent a book by a neighbour, he was astonished at the idea that he might read it: 'I used it as a tunnel for my clockwork train.'[5] Now he was reading almost exclusively Edgar Wallace. He lists

fifteen pages of Wallace titles – *Sanders of the River, Barbara on Her Own, The Four Just Men, The Man Who Knew*, etc. An extra list of Wallace's 'Criminal Books' enumerates the murders in each. He practises Wallace's signature. He lists his sets of cigarette cards. There are two short stories of his own, one about life in the trenches, one an account of helping a neighbour, Mrs Robinson, to fetch water from the spring as she is 'having a stockbroker to tea'.

Another list is significant: 'Concert and Dance Appointments'. Laurie at fourteen was in demand to play his fiddle at dances: twenty-two engagements between the autumn of 1928 and January 1930, mostly in Slad Hut, a recreation hall given to the village by the Misses Bagnall, who lived at the Old House with their donkey. Laurie's trio, with Harold Iles on piano and Les Workman on drums, earned five shillings a night with free lemonade and buns. The boy Laurie Lee was not quite the 'turnip-faced grinning oaf' he later alleged, but musical and artistic, good-natured, and very keen on keeping lists.

Laurie left the Central School at fifteen when – he claimed – Miss French said, 'Off you go and I'm glad to get rid of you.' But she taught him English, his best subject. Forty years later Laurie presented Miss French with a copy of *Cider with Rosie* at the Linden School, Gloucester, when she retired as head. She later wrote in the school magazine: 'Our Speech Day this year, was quite an event, as we were honoured by the presence there, of Mr Laurie Lee, the Gloucestershire author and poet, who, incidentally, was an old pupil of mine.' Laurie annotated this comma-crazed sentence in the margin: 'My English mistress – hence my trouble with punctuation.'

Laurie's life from fourteen to eighteen was dominated by his violin, known as Claude, which he later changed to Fritz, 'after our old friend Kreisler'; and his bicycle called Oscar. His boyhood diary is full of rain-soaked cycle rides, often with a puncture 'as wide as the mouth of a frog'. He had been taught the violin by a music teacher named Travis Cole who would cycle round the villages, selling lessons for sixpence. Jack remembers his starting refrain – 'Up bow!' – and 'Don't give your bow a penn'orth – give

it the whole shilling's worth.' Laurie practised every night. 'My three lovely half-sisters were very tolerant, but sometimes I used to hear a voice downstairs saying "Oh Mum does 'e 'ave to, 'e's been on all night" and it was time to wrap it up in my silk scarf and put it away. But they wouldn't dream of knocking on the door . . . Those dear girls would never question my liberties.'[6]

Two weeks before his sixteenth birthday, Laurie started work. 'A pretty eventful year on the whole,' noted Laurie of 1930, promising that if he continued the 1931 diary past March (last year's record) he would treat himself to a bottle of Moët & Chandon at 17s 6d. A nephew and niece had been born; he had been to Worcester at Easter ('bit of a washout') and had visited Uncle Ray near Malvern. He had ordered a new nib for his Conway Stewart fountain pen, and *Melody Maker* monthly from Smith's. 'But the greatest event happened in June, the 12th to be exact – I started work. Messrs Randall & Payne, Chartered Accountants, 4 Row-croft, Stroud is the firm that has been fortunate in securing my services.'

At the back of the diary Laurie noted: 'I have met the following through the office's medium: In order of importance they are:

Walter Richards Payne FCA – the Guv'nor.
Mrs Payne – his wife.
George Percival Leslie Hudson – junior partner.'

The list continued through articled clerks down to caretaker.

Laurie was the office boy at 10s a week. His immediate boss in the mahoganied, gas-lit office was irascible Teddy White, ex-Army Pay Corps, who terrorized the staff. 'Teddy White gave Laurie a hell of a life since he could not stand anyone with an artistic outlook,' says Alan Payne, son of the chairman, who joined the firm in 1933 as an articled clerk. Laurie's poems on scraps of paper also infuriated the obsessively tidy White.

Laurie would arrive on his bike every day, violin slung over his back. Sometimes he was towed uphill by the bus on the ride home, and he was constantly lashed by rain. As office boy he had to run

errands, organize the post, make tea and write up the ledgers in a neat, cursive hand. The first Thursday each month was 'postal orders, Directors' Receipt book, green envelopes and gas company cheques. A busy morning raking in the shekels. Worked like the devil today.' Sometimes he would be sent out to get a signature. 'Mr Payne having an attack of liver did not come to the office at all this afternoon. I had to go up to his house at five o'clock with some letters. I was shewn in by Cook, and after picking my way through divers leopard skins lying about the floor I knocked at Mr Payne's room. He was sitting in front of a roaring fire in the comfortable drawing room. It has pictures, prints, & china plates hanging on the walls & it is sparsely but tastefully furnished. Myriads of small dogs were rushing about the room. If this is the way Chartered Accountants do themselves I shall have to see about it.'

'Mr Payne is a gentleman,' he noted Pooterishly. 'I saw him in Gloucester and he put himself out to wave to me.' But after a few months there Laurie considered himself 'not a very good business person because I think of too many damn things at once: I am so made that I seek out individuality . . .' 'A hell-of-a-day today. I left the office feeling like a depression over Iceland.' If the books did not balance, he had to stay behind and chase up the missing money – 'one of Fate's buffets'.

'How does anything exciting happen in a blasted office?' Laurie asked himself. Miss Lewis prattled of an aunt who read fortunes in tea-leaves. Colleagues argued about the merits of chapel-going. One of the clerks suggested that they design an office crest: 'Mr Hudson proposed three pencils rampant on a field of blue ink.' There was excitement on 23 October, however. 'Mrs P.R. Goddard, wife of the fellow who won the £1,000 Crossword Puzzle in *The People*, came into the office and brought his cheque. I had the job of cashing it.'

After work he could double his salary by teaching the fiddle to villagers. He had three students: Mrs Twining, Mrs Munby and Kenny Oakey, a young lad with a good ear. And he was always practising for the next concert or church bazaar with Harold and Les. 'Out all evening to play dance music. Started off with "William

Tell" and we did let it rip. Our best tune is "You will remember Vienna".' Afterwards he would roll home with the moon, Oscar and Fritz. He also bought a ukulele, 'as much in need of a second instrument as a good dinner is in need of a second vegetable'. On the crystal wireless set he listened to Henry Hall and the Savoy Orpheans, Jack Payne and other big bands, and Albert Sandler's classical concerts (Laurie wrote for his autograph). He discovered Schubert and Beethoven. A Wagner prom cast him into a blank depression, but *Der Rosenkavalier* from Covent Garden impressed him, though he could not understand a word. 'After tea wrote a little, read a little, drew a little. Listening as I write to a beautiful selection of Mendelssohn.' He saw and enjoyed his first opera, *The Pirates of Penzance*. He and Jack went into Stroud to buy an HMV gramophone: 'Mother signed on the dotted line and the thing was ours. There were a couple of records thrown in which I chose with great felicity: Dances from Henry VIII by German, and Haydn's Serenade played by Albert Sandler.'

The eighteenth of November 1931 was an auspicious date. He went to the White Horse Inn at Painswick to audition, and was engaged by Arthur Swain and his Blue Rhythms, for two dances. Laurie analysed his fellow musicians: Arthur the pianist 'a good fellow, not overloaded with intellect, but musical ability brilliant', Alvin the tenor sax 'superior to the others where the grey matter is concerned', Ernie on trumpet 'quite a stout fellow but will never suffer from brainstorms', and Tony on the banjo 'the blight, the prize wart of the show. Excessively presumptuous.' That meeting at the White Horse Inn was to prove significant.

Like any teenage boy Laurie was not disposed to lyricize the colourful qualities of his mother. ('I gave her a lot of silence in my teens . . . didn't talk to her enough, or listen when the others had gone away in her life,' he later said.⁷) 'Mother has been talking at full speed for the last hour. It does get on your bally nerves.' Annie would shriek and scream whenever torrential rain swept down the bank. It is a very sheer drop, at the mercy of floods, and Jack remembers quaking with fear as water, leaves and twigs hurtled

down. But in the garden Annie could 'order the earth to bloom with a royal wave of her hand while we boys did the heavy digging', Laurie recalled.[8] She also got them to hang wallpaper, 'one of the world's worst jobs', grumbled Laurie. 'The house was most uncomfortable. What with the weather, the muddle, my stiff neck & mother's tongue it was hell!'

There was in the tiny cottage, even with only four occupants after Harold had gone and the sisters all married, considerable commotion. They had a dog called Rover that kept running away; the water did not always boil for the tin bath, so Laurie would have 'a cold one, which is fashionable'. 'House and mother in a state of chaos. She was getting ready to go to London, and she had about four hours work and about thirty minutes to do it in. I tried to help but things got worse so I oiled out. Mother invariably breaks things when she's flustered.' 'Mother was involved in a verbal scrap with T[ony]: old Mrs Driver next door listening to everything . . . she's as shameless as a Hottentot.' 'Had a hell of a row with J[ack] this morning & let him have a few home truths. He is a damn prig at times & thinks he's so superior with his big talk.'

At weekends Annie and her boys would visit the sisters, aunts and cousins for tea or Sunday dinner: 'a lively meal (Sunday dinners mostly are) at Auntie Alice's – about half a hundredweight of potatoes, three or four gross of Farrows, marrowfat peas, and some slices of ham cut thick. I have never been so fat in my life.' When they visited Uncle Charlie, the forester, they admired his tree nursery where hundreds of tiny beech, ash and larch trees were planted in close rows 'like radishes'. Today, Uncle Charlie's giant beech trees overhang the winding road from Bulls Cross into Slad. In the winter of 1930–31, cousin Charlie (also a forester) says, they planted 34,000 trees.

Laurie was receptive to the natural scene, the call of the cuckoo and the state of the moon, a lifelong fascination. 'The sun shines shame-facedly from an imperial sky mottled with small fleecy clouds . . . But it deserves some homage, for like the hand of an invisible artist it touches the trees with a riot of burning copper . . .' 'Cycled back over Horsepools & strove to appreciate the serene majesty of

the plain. It is peerless just now. Ridges of trees veering away to the blue distance and the coppery Malverns.' He adopted the descriptive style of whichever author he had borrowed from the public library, where he was charged a penny a day on late returns. He had yet to discover Dickens, Lawrence and Joyce. He found Priestley's *The Good Companions* engrossing; it is touching to read his analysis of Priestley's skill in conjuring up a smoky industrial town when, twenty-five years later, Priestley was the critic loudest in praise of *Cider with Rosie*. Marjorie lent an engrossing book called *Stories of Blood and Cruelty*, but mostly he loved Jeffery Farnol, Sax Rohmer and Warwick Deeping. 'Deeping is a master of similes,' he discovered, and promptly began incorporating similes in his prose. 'I woke up feeling as sleepy as a library lizard this morning' . . . 'I'm as miserable as Inge the Dean, but so is the weather' . . . 'found that the bike tyre I had mended so judiciously yesterday was as flat as a biscuit' . . . 'The depression increases as I feel as misplaced as a stick of garlic in a cherry trifle.'

'Under the influence of *All Quiet on the Western Front*,' he writes, 'I am going to write as an experiment in the tense of that story. This morning I go for a walk up Scrubs way . . . This afternoon a man comes up from the Infirmary to tell Mother that Grandfather is very ill. Jack sets off to Woodchester to tell Uncle Tom, while I cycle up to Uncle Sid's. Cycle down the Painswick Rd to the bowl of the valley where I explore a ruined manor . . .'

(His grandfather Light died the next day; Uncle Tom came into the office to tell Laurie. 'That's hard luck on mother because she was going up to see him today.')

When the cinema came to Stroud and Gloucester, Laurie went every week. He saw Douglas Fairbanks Jr in *The Dawn Patrol*, Jack Buchanan and Jeanette MacDonald in *Monte Carlo* and Rudy Vallee in *The Vagabond Lover*. He decided that his favourite film actress was Madeleine Carroll. 'She is my idea of the perfect Jeffery Farnol heroine. It's a pity they can't film his stories.'

He wrote letters to a girl called Pat Robinson, a friend of his sisters, who became a kind of mentor. She lived with her elderly mother in Birmingham and sent him *The Hunchback of Notre Dame*

for his seventeenth birthday in June, a month of rain: 'Bengal climate: sodden grass, mud, dripping trees, and June the month of roses and sweet-smelling hay is turned to a month of November-like gales, of postponed cricket matches and washed out fetes.'

As Laurie later said, the village was small, in half a mile of valley, but the details of its life seemed enormous. On 28 April 1931 the first telephone was installed in the Slad post office, and on 13 May Laurie recorded: 'This lunchtime I did something that I have never done before. I had vocal intercourse with an inhabitant of Slad, without being at Slad. In short, I rang Mrs Oakey.' On 26 April, 'We filled in the Census form tonight. An historical event.' In May a new vicar, the Revd Cyril Hodson, arrived. On Election Day, 31 October, when the National Government was formed, 'Mother polled for Perkins (Con) whose majority was 16,500.'

They watched Farmer Webb catching rabbits with a ferret; were awakened at 4 a.m. by the bloodcurdling howls of foxes from the garden; went to a rummage sale and got 'a Slazenger tennis racquet, a good pair of skates, an operatic record and a couple of tennis presses for one and sixpence'. They played whist and quoits for penny stakes. One night a policeman stopped him for not having his bicycle lamp on: 'First time in my life I got to grips with the law.' On summer evenings Laurie and Jack would play strenuous tennis 'with Eileen and other gentry'. They cycled to fairgrounds and air shows. If it rained Laurie painted 'a fair lady from a Farnol novel' or 'a portrait of Jack which I shall call Adonis reclining'. On the day of the Whitsun treat, Laurie had tea with the vicar and other locals: 'I consider this event to be a desirable social success.' Mostly they just loitered with other boys at Bulls Cross, a mile up the road, and 'spouted rot'.

Nothing much happened, but life was crowded with incident. On 26 May Laurie saw his first elephant, from a local circus. 'It was a flabby worn-out looking thing rather like a perishing bicycle tyre, but it was an elephant.' On 19 September he saw giraffes, gorillas, lions and bears, on the chara outing to Bristol Zoo. On Derby Day, 3 June, in the office sweepstake Laurie drew the favourite, Cameronica, and won six shillings for a sixpenny stake.

He purchased, as he put it, a new suit of clothes. 'The waistcoat is a glorious thing, double-breasted with lapels. The trousers are long and baggy. The coat has one button and is also very natty. Each day I feel conscious of the saw that Hepworths publish in its truth – "Clothes make the man." J and I went to church this morning, rather staggered Lionel Ballinger with our sartorial glory.'

And then there were girls. On 10 March he gave a résumé of 'the maiden situation': 'The Clarks lass is a nice girl although a trifle fast which of course to the uncynical is no handicap. The one in Woolworths merits closer attention by the connoisseur but is a trifle childish. The two Aldridges from the typewriting school are in every way eligible but unresponsive. And there are a few miscellaneous ones hanging about who would go like fire at a little attention – such fields to conquer.'

He was half envious of Jack who was bold enough to take girls to the pictures: 'An awfully prosaic idea of love-making don't you think so brother Farnol? But still under the influence of a glance of coquetry or at the sight of red lips and a trim waist we all do it.' Jack would 'make love' – flirting and lovemaking meant the same thing in those days – to the Hogg sisters, who could throw seductive over-the-shoulder glances like Pola Negri, and would call at the Lee cottage on the slightest pretext. ('A fine thing, a sofa,' Laurie discovered.) But Laurie prided himself on being extremely selective. He lived in hope of a billet-doux from an elusive one. Girls would inquire for him at the office, but he was indifferent; one was described as 'like the scentless carnation and I don't think I shall pick it'. On 31 March an invitation came from a girl named Peggy for Easter weekend; Laurie danced a jig with the stool in his office. But it was 'an abortive visit'. Laurie and Peggy played ping-pong. 'I may as well hermetize,' he concluded.

'I think the wish to attain the unattainable, to reach the ripest fruit which is forever out of reach, is the uppermost quality in this pot-pourri of affection,' he wrote in his diary. Such sentiments came from Jeffery Farnol romances, which taught Laurie all about the joys of 'yearning'. 'As I strode along between the dark hedge-rows feeling the gritty road crunch beneath my feet . . . a great

longing seized me to attain "the Ideal" – and then an owl hooted and this mournful sound seemed to accentuate the seeming hopelessness of my yearning.' There was no mention of a Rosie – but then, as he explained later, Rosie was just a composite of several village girls.

In July, father Reg arrived for his twice-yearly visit, looking older and balder, and 'more of the irritated cynic than he used to be'. Laurie played music with him and decided: 'Dad is not so good as I had thought he was. His sense of harmony is warped . . . Honestly I can't see eye to eye with Dad's musical taste. Later he and Mother had the inevitable row which showed a weak spot in both their characters, though I think D is principally to blame.' Reg set about repairing Annie's wireless set. 'He cursed its condition, scraped & twisted, & finally declared that it was fifty per cent louder. Personally I consider that he's bugged it up more than improved it.'

The next day Laurie visited his father 'and listened to platitudes & texts and flowery squiffy squaffy "advice on life" till I'm afraid I yawned'.

That summer, too, Laurie first found the Whiteway Colony, two miles from Slad, between Sheepscombe and Miserden. The colony had been founded by the Tolstoyan Anarchists, a group of liberal-minded young schoolteachers, clerks and shop assistants who bicycled out from Croydon on a hot summer's day in 1898, inspired by Leo Tolstoy's Utopian ideals. In Gloucestershire they could buy land at £7 an acre. They ceremonially burned the title deeds and built wooden houses, each in one acre with no fences.

The colonists did not believe in marriage. They buried their own dead, grew fruit and vegetables, made sandals, threw pots, knitted and wove, organized camping holidays, and ran a school which 'encouraged initiative and natural abilities'. The women wore white smock dresses, the men sandals, shorts, beards. In 1901 one of the colonists, a young baker named Sudbury Protheroe, appeared at Stroud court charged with indecency, having been out on the highway in his shorts when he unluckily met the disapproving vicar of Bisley, the Revd Herbert Edgecumbe Hadow. The

Whiteway Colony was much visited by left-wing intelligentsia, including Malcolm Muggeridge; and descendants of the original colonists still flourish, in the much-improved wooden houses.

At Whiteway Laurie was invited to vegetarian suppers and watched the sandal-shod colonists doing folk dancing and ballet. This took place at Whiteway's elegantly colonnaded village hall (once Cranham sanatorium, dismantled and rebuilt in 1924). It was also the venue for Esperanto classes, play readings, lectures, and meetings of the Peace Pledge Union: during the Spanish Civil War, Whiteway accommodated a dozen Republican refugees. Laurie joined the Whiteway Club and often went to their gramophone recitals to hear Richard Tauber or Paul Robeson, and played at their Saturday dances, for which he designed posters after the style of Picasso. Whiteway gave him his first smattering of politicization. It was there that he met the composer Benjamin Frankel, and the mysterious 'Cleo' who was to feature in *As I Walked Out One Midsummer Morning*.

Laurie was not the untravelled youth he later made out. (In 1992 in a radio interview he claimed he'd never even been to Tetbury, eight miles away, until he was nineteen.) In fact he cycled long distances – Birmingham had 'the biggest Woolworths I've ever seen' – and motored with an uncle and aunt in a car named 'Matilda' to Stratford, Warwick and Leamington Spa. On 23 August he set off to cycle to Oxford: 'At work Maurice bet me a shilling I couldn't get to Oxford in under 3 and a quarter hours . . .' He reached sister Dorothy's in time for dinner. Jude-like, he went to the Cathedral service the next day, visited Worcester College and Magdalen Tower, sketched New College and St John's, went to the Radcliffe Camera, and to the Electra to see Marie Dressler and Wallace Beery in *Min and Bill*. In the Parks he found 'each tree labelled in the correct museum manner', and at the Cadena he heard 'a five-piece orchestra with a violinist who I think was a top-liner. I remained until 5 p.m. appreciating them and drinking in their wisdom. Then to the Scala to see Greta Garbo in an MGM film.' He left Dorothy's with an invitation to return the following year.

The day after his seventeenth birthday ('Meagre post') he

reported: 'Self clearly at a dead end. The range of hills, low, breathing mystery; the rolling plain, stretching away to the blue haze in the Midlands, emitting Romance & a poignant suggestion of what might have been.'

The 1931 diary broke off briefly in October because he lost his pen and 'principally it is because of the absence of any motive power to force me, in fact there is now no personal being to inspire. I suppose such a happiness will not come my way.'

But Boxing Day 1931 'will go down in my history as a day of varied experiences. Of sport, rustic boredom, middle-class bliss, domestic complications and moreover an idyll.' He had watched Earl Bathurst's hounds meet, seen Cirencester beat North Cerney 2–1 at football, walked on the 'blasted heath', and after 'some homestead discord' he 'was presented to the Simpsons & spent the rest of the evening with Hilda & family. It was about 11 o'clock that the idyll was enacted. It was an experience that I shall never forget.' (Was this Laurie's first kiss?) 'This week has made history but such history that I can keep to myself.'

Two items in his 1931 diary are worth remarking. 'There was a fire along London Road yesterday,' Laurie noted, 'and the owner came in to claim today as expected for their monthly fire. The insurance money will carry them on for a bit I suppose & then the can of petrol will be brought out again.' (This is an eerie foretaste of the contentious 'piano factory fire' in *Cider with Rosie* that caused Laurie to be sued for libel thirty years later.) And on 15 April he reported on 'the Spain trouble'. 'King Alfonso abdicated & left Spain in a warship for an unknown destination' . . . 'Learnt that Alfonso has gone to France & there's a hell of a row in Madrid, but more scrapping is going on at Barcelona.' These were the earliest rumblings of the unrest that developed into the Spanish Civil War.

One other event from Laurie's childhood, recorded in *Cider with Rosie*, must not be overlooked. He was knocked down by a bicycle, one dark night in 1924, which may have been what triggered his epilepsy. Of all his many childhood ailments, the two-day concussion after the accident had the deepest impact. 'That blow

in the night,' he writes, 'scarred me, I think, for ever – put a stain of darkness upon my brow and opened a sinister door in my brain, a door through which I am regularly visited by messengers whose words just escape me, by glimpses of worlds I can never quite grasp, by grief, exultation, and panic . . .' At that time, epilepsy was untreatable and regarded as a mental illness, carrying a stigma of enduring shame for those afflicted by it. Epilepsy is common, mysterious and, even today, frightening. Even though Laurie's was manageable, much of his secretive behaviour could be explained by his anxiety about imminent oblivion and loss of control, which he feared more than anything.

Laurie's affliction – Julius Caesar's 'falling sickness' – was shared with many writers of genius: Byron, Dr Johnson, Flaubert, Dosto-evsky (who described the 'state of startling illumination and euphoria' before an attack) and Edward Lear, who kept his 'terrible demon' a secret except from his diaries. Edward VIII's and George VI's youngest brother John was an epileptic, kept away from his family and out of public view. Those close to Laurie knew about his epilepsy, but throughout his life he strove to keep it a secret from the world at large.

On 11 June 1931 he had noted: 'I have been at work just one year. M.E.P. says I've changed a lot during those twelve months – I hope I have, because if I'm still the green, egotistical youth of Summer 1930, I must be a whelp. I know one thing, I've learnt more in this one year of the things that matter than I did in five years of school life.'

3 | 'The well-loved stranger'
1932–4

'I did pretty well,' Laurie said, looking back fifty years. 'I had a golden blond, vulnerable, idealistic face. Women cosseted me. I had an open face which said "love me" and I was enveloped by love.'[1] He liked to describe girls as voluptuous (a favourite word), comforting. Like many men of his day, he found intellect unnerving in the female. Yet the girls who were drawn to him were intelligent, well-read, and keen to encourage a poetic youth, and to tell him he could do great things.

At seventeen Laurie was considered good-looking in a vaguely artistic way: less exquisite than Rupert Brooke, but of that fair type, with a heavy lock of hair always falling over the forehead and a wide, full-lipped, sensual mouth. He also had an effortless charm. 'And you, you darling,' wrote a devotee, 'striding along in your plus-fours (your pipe inevitably out) and your hair blowing in the wind, I could hug you.' His brother Jack found him a hard act to compete with. 'He could paint, he could write, he was a musician and a damn good one. And I was none of these things. He was a poet. It gives you a romantic aura, doesn't it, to be a poet. It was very tough for me, plodding away at my factory. Laurie lived on a wave of effervescence.'

With Laurie, girls felt free to talk about the moon rising from behind a hill, or the scent of rain-washed lilac. 'It's beautifully easy to write to you!' wrote one, waxing lyrical about a springtime walk through the Golden Valley, with its mist of bluebells, and banks bright with primroses. Laurie matched in kind their pantheistic outpourings. 'You who can see beauty & put down what you feel about it, should offer praise to Heaven for those gifts,' they told him.

This chorus of encouragement came from two bright sisters, Molly and Betty Smart. They were cousins of Arthur Swain, the

jazz pianist whose band Laurie had joined in 1931. They lived in a semi-detached villa named Annesbrook in suburban Gloucester, with their parents, older brother Roy, younger sister Joan and, later, a baby brother called Beverley John. It was a happy, cultivated family; their mother, known to everyone as 'Lady', was invincibly cheerful; their father was quiet, an avid reader and an excellent musician. Molly, black-haired and green-eyed, and five years older than Laurie, wrote: 'I think you & I are going to be very firm friends – fellow conspirators.' She taught in the village school at Hillesley, and wrote poetry herself. She sent him her verses for his critical comments, addressing him as 'Laurielee' because 'your names together make music & separately they don't. I love musical names, don't you? . . . PS What does Laurie E.A. stand for?' (She was relieved that he was Edward Alan: 'I was dreadfully afraid you'd be Ernest Albert.')

But the irrepressible Betty was the first to fall in love with Laurie. She wrote, during a Latin lesson at her school, Ribston Hall in Gloucester, thanking him for sending Jeffery Farnol's novel *Peregrine's Progress*, a romantic saga which he had read twice and found entrancing, and which modern youth would find unreadable. It tells of a well-born boy of nineteen, wandering the countryside learning the tinker's trade and falling in love with Diana, a wild gypsy maiden.

Laurie and Betty's first encounter was at the White Horse in Painswick, a pub run by the Smart girls' Aunt Georgie, mother of Arthur Swain. Betty watched Laurie arrive from behind a bedroom curtain before her aunt hauled her into the sitting-room to be introduced, interrupting Laurie's rendering from *Il Trovatore*. 'Three things I noticed before tea,' Betty later wrote. 'You could talk English without murdering the grammar; you loved your music; and you were saying to yourself "Hmmm – an empty-headed little ass. Thinks of nothing but boys & dress & amusements." This made me horribly self-conscious, and I became gayer & more empty-headed.'

The friendship flourished through exchanges of books (more Farnol, and *1066 And All That*, often read aloud), theatre excursions

(*Merrie England*, *The Mikado*), Sunday walks up Robinswood Hill in Gloucester, and village hops: 'Molly and I are going to a leap year dance on the 29th. The ladies choose their partners, and everyone wears a mask until midnight. Doesn't it sound thrilling? Lady Molly hopes your elder brother will be present . . .' Jack says that he and Laurie made a non-aggression pact over girls: so Jack steered clear of Betty though he found her more beautiful than Molly. 'Was your last dance a success, with lots of pretty girls bringing you sausage rolls?' wrote Betty. 'I didn't really enjoy ours despite the topping floor and the marvellous band. Half the fellows were squiffy. I 'spect you know the type. A dress suit, a secondary school accent & no imagination.' Later she reported to Laurie: 'At last night's dance, mother heard this conversation.

1st fair damsel: Who's that young fellow playin' the fiddle?
2nd fair damsel: That be Laurie Lee.
1st fair damsel: Laurie Lee, eh. What do a do?
2nd fair damsel: 'E don't do nothin'. 'E be on the dowel.'

At first each sister propelled the other in Laurie's direction. 'Betty's the brainy member of the Smart family,' Molly wrote. 'My little big sister is a darling, isn't she?' wrote Betty. But soon Betty saw Laurie as the perfect Peregrine, 'walking through the woods with his Diana, oblivious of the world and its narrow-minded conventions, finding his poetry in the stars, his philosophy of life in the great tall trees. I want him rather badly, but he belongs to Diana, the scheming little minx. Realizing how horribly I fall short of perfection, my heart sinks. But if I met my Peregrine I should try hard to make him love me. D'you know what Peregrine means? Wanderer! Isn't it great. Cheer-ho, Betty.'

Their letters, first inspired by the fanciful Farnol ('I cannot separate our beloved Jeffery Farnol from you, heart's delight'), began to mimic D.H. Lawrence too. 'The night after I have seen you, I lie awake for hours, dreaming,' Betty wrote. 'D.H. Lawrence seems to know women uncommonly well. In *The Virgin and the Gypsy*, the chief character lies in bed and it seems to her that all her form is outlined as with molten metal. I have often felt the same way.'

Meanwhile Molly was sending frank criticisms of Laurie's poems. One was 'hackneyed', one had 'one line a mile too long', another was 'promising but a little crude. And – oh hang! It's positively morbid. You have a life to live!' But she also told him: 'Don't *ever* stop writing Laurie . . . Your lightness of touch is remarkable. I envy your colour of phrase (and I'm too conceited to envy most people).' Laurie promptly destroyed the poems she disliked, eliciting paroxysms of grief from Molly. 'Why oh why did you burn your poems? Didn't it hurt dreadfully? How can you be a fellow conspirator if you burn the evidence of your crimes?' Betty, she reported, was 'very put out' at his sending Molly his poems. 'I pointed out that you knew we always shared everything, but she said you are *her* friend, before you are mine, and stalked out of the room waving a toothbrush and towel threateningly.' What would Laurie do, Betty asked indignantly, 'if your brother were miles more beautiful than you, & wrote poetry & was altogether charming while you were merely nondescript, & some girl you knew wrote to your brother enclosing poems? Molly of course has written a poem about your poem.' She had too.

His poem was 'I dreamed of you' and fifty years later Laurie could still quote it verbatim. He told an interviewer that he had written it pushing a bike up Painswick Hill. 'I dreamed of you one April night . . . when the moon in silv'ry splendour bright . . . hung poised in a realm of clouds . . .' 'Oh, it goes on,' he said. 'I never put it on paper.'[2] But he did: and he also kept Molly's poem 'Reaction', subtitled 'On "I dreamed of you"'. ('How can I write/When through my dazzled mind/Your magic phrases dance?')

Molly was curious to know if the 'delightfully Farnolish nymph of the woods' in Laurie's poems really existed. 'Laurielee if you've lost your heart at seventeen you've done the maddest thing. I know because I did the same thing myself. So take a friend's advice and find yours quickly: it isn't pleasant to go through life without a heart.' (Molly had just ended her romance with Martin Matthias, a classics undergraduate at Balliol. She had written a poem called 'Departure' about it.) And when Laurie turned eighteen she wrote

him a birthday poem beginning: 'Others may wish you happiness/ But I, seeing you stand/As Galahad,/ Upon the brink of that great Quest . . .'

In 1933 both Molly and Laurie had poems published in the *Gloucester Citizen*: Laurie's 'Jazz', and Molly's 'Haresfield'. 'Isn't it topping?' wrote Betty. 'Please address my sister as THE Miss Smart (famous 20th century poet). I just love the people I love to be appreciated by others. Isn't life glorious? Least, it is for me.'

Clearly, Betty was a Pollyanna, but as Molly described her in 'Betty: A Sketch' (girlish laughter in her soft brown eyes, etc.), she was also wise beyond her years, kind to tramps, and 'seemed to find goodness in everything . . .' (When I met Betty, she was still finding goodness in everything at the age of eighty-two.) Laurie gave Betty the new name of 'Helen'; and she, besotted by Virgil, took to calling Laurie 'Euryalus' after the warrior of the *Aeneid*. Laurie looked him up and discovered he was slain by Volscens and beheaded. ('Silly boy, it was his *life* that mattered, & anyway, he was brave.') Seeking other mythological models, Betty reinvented Laurie as an Arthurian knight, saving damsels, and told their story as an idyll: 'As the young girl wandered through cool sacred woods . . . she dreamed of "a very parfait gentil knighte" who would offer his hand and heart. She scanned the young knights in town but they were not what she wanted. They lacked the gentle courtesy towards women as women, which the maiden knew was one of the virtues her knight must possess.

'One day, she was introduced to a young musician, whose mouth proclaimed him a poet, an idealist or a cynic. He turned out to be all three . . . The young musician was searching for a peerless creature, a Diana . . . On a cold evening, with a half-mad moon racing the stars, the young musician took his lady in his arms and told her that he loved her. The whole world was theirs. It was truly a night of magic. They loved – it was enough. Their love grew & autumn glowed with the beauty of it.'

Betty still recalls that night, 10 October 1933. Laurie kissed her and said, 'God knows I love you, Helen.' ('Bless his heart,' she says today. 'It was a fantasy. But a fantasy we wove together.')

'Laurie I'm awed,' she wrote after his declaration. 'I've dreamed for so long of your saying "I love you". It's so great a thing when one is only sixteen, that I'm rather afraid of not being good enough to deserve it . . . Golly, I'm lucky. We're going to be marvellously happy. O Laurie, a little cottage and a wireless and a grammy and books and each other. Let's go scrounging round lots of funny little shops & plan & pretend & dream. And let's go to the Cathedral. We've got to go on being companions, because that way comes understanding . . . and Laurie, when you realize that I'm an ordinary mortal after all, be generous, for always I will be, as you have named me, Helen, your Diana.'

She wove scenes of domestic bliss in a cottage with blue and white china and an inglenook, where she would darn his socks and bustle about the house, while he would dig the garden and write poetry. A blue-eyed baby boy named Keith Allen would 'warm his little pink toes on the fender, gravely watching the flames, as he listens to your tales'. There would be crazy paving, and trees to climb. 'And lavender and rosemarie, hollyhocks & lilies-of-the-valley & violets & roses, delphiniums & sweet peas, & clumps of lupins . . . I want Keith Allen to see the loveliness all around him . . . Should I send him to an elementary school? I want him to meet every class of boy & girl, but he shall never go to Oxford, even if I have sacks of money.

'This is idle fancy. But if you have any bright suggestions concerning the furnishing of my palace, send them along.' Laurie obliged with 'Low oak beams and fire dogs.' 'I should like them too,' Betty responded, 'and infinitely comfortable chairs with lots of cushions and wide arms. Long windows that stand open all day. I want trees outside, and laughter and peace within. I want cool green dresses for myself and huge ridiculous hats.'

Contemplating this scene of future domesticity from his office in Stroud, Laurie confided to Betty his black moods, the weary dissatisfaction of working at a job he regarded as futile, his desire to get away from Slad. 'My very own dear darling,' she wrote consolingly. 'I know that feeling most horribly well, I agree with you, it is hell, but it passes, & peace comes again . . . The overcoming

of cynicism rests with yourself. What you are doing now is *not* futile, and the people round you aren't futile either. Probably they all have dreams too . . . Of course I love the Slad Valley as you do. But why do you want to leave it?'

Betty listed the reasons why she admired Laurie's character: his courage in confessing that he didn't want Jack to know her (she had come to feel the same about Molly); his scorn for convention; his determination to 'go for it'; and his ability to 'take a whack and get up again'. For all her dreaminess, Betty was a girl of mature insight and sensibility. She knew that 'first love is often not last love' and that both were really 'in love with love'. Poets, she told Laurie, are 'a fickle lot' who find inspiration in one woman, and then seek another, still believing that the ideal woman exists. 'Beloved, you told me you would always love me, but you won't . . . Things I do and say will begin to irritate you beyond measure. But for my part Laurie I do love you, and on Friday I was aching for you to come and fold your arms round me and kiss me and kiss me and not stop.' And when Laurie accused her of preferring his letters to him, she said it was true: he, like her, was typically English, less self-conscious on paper. When they met, she would adopt a pose of casual flippancy, while Laurie affected a morose reserve.

Meanwhile Laurie was being advised by his older penfriend Pat, who worked as a secretary in Birmingham, studying for exams, taking elocution and English classes, writing essays on 'A wet Saturday night in the Bull Ring'. She encouraged Laurie in similar self-improvement. 'Your letter was a glorious example of English prose. Why not become an Associate of the Institute of Secretaries? You would sail through it! Why not try?' And, 'Why not enter the poetry competitions in the *Birmingham Post*? Mother won half a guinea for an essay on books for holiday reading.' She shared his appreciation of Rupert Brooke and John Drinkwater. She advised Laurie to read Somerset Maugham and the plays of John Van Druten. Her drama group were doing Shaw's *You Never Can Tell*; would he get it from the library and give his opinion?

'And now about your verse: please don't be hurt, but your short poem brought to mind Herrick's "Whenas in silks my Julia goes".

I don't like "sea" being made to rhyme with "worthily". The ending "ly" should always have the short vowel sound.' But when Laurie did have a poem published in the *Birmingham Post*, and an essay on platonic friendships, Pat (his platonic friend) was 'most awfully pleased and proud'.

Laurie plainly saw Pat, who was involved in a lesbian relationship with a girl named Phyl, as a mentor. He confided in her about his 'Helen', requesting guidance. 'I love Phyl in very much the same way as you love your girl,' Pat said, 'so perhaps I can better understand your feelings.' She marvelled that having played cricket with the boy Laurie, and sent him cigarette cards and stamps, and nursed him through 'the Edgar Wallace stage', she should now be his confidante. He could ask her anything, 'as I am one of the few people who understand you'. Helen sounded 'a delightfully winsome little creature – almost faunlike'. She hoped it would be 'a beautiful union'. But she warned him sternly against going too far. 'Laurie, because you read books, & feel a man, you mustn't think that you are an experienced man of the world. You cannot live in a world of dreams & lovely thoughts. You are kind and sensitive almost to a fault, enough to know that the physical side of love is very secondary. My dear, I wonder how old this girl is. And I wonder how much you know of all the dangers and responsibilities . . . This is your first experience of love: don't risk sullying its beauty. Did you hear about my cousin Eric, who was rushed off to a registry office? He was weak; you are not. Waiting is hard, but you must. Do you realize how advanced you are for your years?'

Laurie invited her to Slad for a weekend. Pat's mother thought this 'improper', so Annie had to write too. That weekend, Laurie and Pat talked until Laurie fell asleep in her arms. He confided that Betty's father was trying to stop her from seeing him. Laurie had had a seizure one day in the Smarts' sitting-room while playing Handel's 'Largo'; he suddenly went rigid and fell on the floor. Afterwards Betty's father asked her not to see him again, arguing that there was no future for them, and that he was only thinking of her happiness. But Betty was defiant: 'I shall go on seeing him.'

They plotted a holiday together in a caravan at the seaside. 'Doesn't it sound too utterly delicious? Waking in the morning & dashing down to a deserted beach in a bathing costume?' But the Smart parents forbade it. 'When I said,' wrote Betty, 'that it was a damned shame that we couldn't go away with you, mother replied, "Betty, we want none of that language in this house if you please." I retired crestfallen. Later however, Mother was carrying a pile of plates from the dining room to the scullery, and managed to drop one, and a well-seasoned "Bugger!" rent the air.

'The annoying part is that if I were engaged to you, no objection would have been raised. I apologize for my people. They are only worrying about what people will say. Laurie, I don't want to bother about what people will say. When I am supporting myself in comfort, and if for some reason we don't want to get married, we'll live together proudly. Then when you tire of me, I will just go away and leave you to your woods and art and poetry and your new love. We'll not be jealous, but go on remembering the happiness we have brought each other.'

In June, the month of his nineteenth birthday (1933), Laurie did go away with the sisters – along with Pat and Phyl, and Laurie's brother Tony – to camp at Stratford. They borrowed a punt from the managing director of the Daimler factory, who took a liking to them. They saw *Richard II*. They had a wind-up gramophone and played Debussy's *L'Après-Midi d'un Faune*. There was a thunderstorm, and a rainbow, and dozens of nightingales descended on the Avon and sang. Molly's poem about Laurie at Stratford began:

So I have left you there
(O Beautiful and young)
Among the willows and the dragonflies.
Your gold hair flung
From off your brow. And where
The slowly reddening sunset lies
Upon the stream, I'll find
Your soft desirous mouth . . .

'That mad magic night,' Molly wrote later. 'Remember how wet the grass was under our tennis shoes – and how shy the nightingales were at first? And how heavy the night air was with the scent of syringa – and how a fish made a sudden splash in the silence – remember? Whatever happens Laurie, whether we grow old and lose our sense of beauty – we shall have this to remember, and there's no one else I could have shared that night with as I shared it with you. I was so utterly grateful to you for not attempting to kiss me – any other man would have – bless you for that Laurie dear.

'I suppose you realize that I was hopelessly in love with you that week – shocked Laurie? Don't worry my dear. It was just Beauty-worship – of your lovely youth – midsummer madness perhaps. I left it behind me among the reeds & dragonflies. So you needn't be embarrassed when we meet. It was a marvellous week wasn't it Laurielee? And about Bet – for heaven's sake don't mention this letter to her – aren't you afraid of losing her altogether – two months is a hell of a time you know?'

Laurie had suggested a breathing space with Betty because he had now met a more exotically pretty girl with dark curly hair and a charming smile. Sophia Rogers, known as 'Sufi', had moved to Slad from Buenos Aires with her English father and Spanish mother. In one respect, Sufi influenced Laurie's life most of all, because (as he said later in life) he only went to Spain because 'a girl in Slad from Buenos Aires taught me a few words of Spanish'.[3] This sounded most unlikely, but in fact that is exactly what happened.

Ethel Rogers, landlady of a guest-house at Sheepscombe called Fortune's Well, had a brother, Alfred, who had gone out to Argentina as an accountant with the railway company Ferrocarril Central Córdoba. In Buenos Aires he met a Spanish girl, Serafina, and married her in Montevideo. They had five sons and one daughter, Sufi. In 1933, Alfred retired and brought his Argentine family to settle near their relations in Sheepscombe, buying a new bungalow named Overdale, just below Bulls Cross in Slad.

Richard, Sufi's youngest brother, now in his seventies, remembers their arrival in the valley. 'My father first met Laurie in the

Woolpack, and became friends because they both enjoyed poetry. Laurie started visiting our house and my family noticed that he had perhaps fallen in love with Sufi. I had to act as chaperon when they took walks to Laurie's mother's cottage or wanted to be alone together. I was only eleven, and just wanted to enjoy myself, but my parents insisted. Laurie was always very chummy and considerate with me. He was a joyful person, a nice chap, and very handsome. Sufi tried to teach Laurie how to speak some words in Spanish but could not make him pronounce them correctly.'

Laurie said, fifty years later, in an interview:[4] 'If only I'd known at eighteen that those strange, complicated, romantical, remote, mysterious creatures who dominated my waking and my sleeping were quite simple and uncomplex after all. Girls! . . . they sustained me in a state of anguish and torment when I was an office-boy in Stroud, new-washed as wool and wet behind the ears . . . I remember cycling thirty miles to Worcester to sit all night in the rain shriving my soul outside a girl's window with a bag of plums. The bag got wet. The plums fell out. And she married a garage man in the end.' (His diary for 18 July 1931 tells of that cycle ride. 'I saw M sitting in the garage window having a lecture on engines. This was sufficient.') But, he reflected, his naïvety was fruitful: the unattainability of girls was the source of all his juvenilia. 'And who knows, without such practice I might not have got into Pseuds' Corner in *Private Eye*.'

Betty could not sustain the two-month gap. She wrote in July to say what 'awful mutts' they had been, and arguing that they could conquer anything that stood in their way. She cited her parents' marriage. They had been married for twenty-five years, but each would be lost without the other. 'There's romance in their lives, the romance which we with our rather scornful idealistic view failed to see. We didn't see it in the lives of the country people, we didn't understand their fidelity to each other & in our ignorance we charged them with lacking the imagination to be unfaithful. It's we who are wrong Laurie.'

Laurie replicated these sentiments in old age. At eighteen, he said, 'You have this blind belief that you've discovered sex, truth,

idealism . . . you say "God – those old ones seem to have no idea how we feel!" But they have a very good idea. The old have felt it all and suffered . . .'[5]

On the second anniversary of their meeting, Laurie wrote to Betty, now studying for her School Certificate, and she replied with renewed conviction: 'We are going to come through this with our chins decidedly up. I am convinced that there never was such a love as ours, and never will be. I'm exactly the sort of woman to make you happy. In fact I'm *the* woman.

'You are in your nineteenth, I in my seventeenth year. The world is before us, demanding to be explored. My youth is dedicated like a poem, to you, full of vigour and beauty and great thoughts and tears and ringing laughter and music. I'm full to my finger-tips with life, and at present it's yours. It may not always be, but tonight my warrior Euryalus, I love you. And so goodnight.'

Molly was meanwhile lending Laurie records, recommending books, discussing Burne-Jones, whose paintings Laurie thought 'repetitive'. 'He has painted one perfect face,' Molly argued. 'Can you blame him for not experimenting with any other type? And doesn't the same thing apply to every artist? Your D.H. Lawrence (egoist that he is) tells his own story over and over again – a different name but always it's the same character.'

Early in 1934 Molly went to train as a nurse in Birmingham, and confided in Laurie. 'Oh, I shouldn't have come here – all those malformed, broken, dying bodies make me sick with horror.' She had seen gangrenous limb stumps rotting slowly from venereal disease. She longed to lean against the wet bark of trees again. She was sickened by the flowers in the wards – 'great stiff daffodils' that could not compare with the wild ones in the Newent woods. She really wanted to write, but could she make a living from it? She was a lark shut up in a cage. By April 1934 she had decided to fail her exams deliberately. She felt guilty for having cost her parents fees they could ill afford, and feared going home as the prodigal daughter. But she must leave this sordid life and or go stark mad. At the same time she was encouraging Laurie to get away himself, and not to be 'so damned humble'.

'Laurie Lee, if it isn't impertinent to ask, *why* don't you clear out of Stroud? You're simply wasting your time, and you'll never be content there. Even if you don't find happiness you'll at least be living. That's how I've felt about coming here, though I loathe and detest it.'

In May 1934, Laurie had decided: he would go to London, and told Pat. 'My very dear Laurie,' she wrote. 'And so Piping Peter is going to town? I suppose it was inevitable, and I think you're doing the best thing. You are going to see something of life outside the sphere in which you were born. It will broaden you, and make you love Slad still more.

'I have faith in your ability to do great things. If you do, I shall be proud. And if you return to Slad weary of the mad scramble, I shall understand.' He must never feel that nobody cared what became of him; she and several others cared a great deal. 'Goodbye my dear. Our friendship is one of the loveliest things in my life. Through you, and in stumblingly trying to help you, I have found such happiness . . .'

Laurie left behind other broken hearts. One Rita Louise, whom he must have invited to go away with him, wrote: 'Laurie dear, This must be the end. I have no regrets, no reproaches, and last weekend will always be wonderful to me. But I can't break away. I have no material means of doing so. Do understand. And please don't include me among your disillusionments about women. You will soon forget me. You said that I had helped you to find yourself, I hope that is true. Sincerest wishes for your success. I expect we shall meet again somewhere. Goodbye – and bless you.' (She wrote again to ask if she could come and collect her *Ulysses*. Laurie's farewell letter had 'made it almost worthwhile saying goodbye'.)

In the office of Randall & Payne, young Alan Payne, knowing how unhappy Laurie was, felt no surprise when his father sent for him and said: 'Lee has resigned and you will take over as office boy immediately.' Alan was shown the note which Laurie had left in the stamp drawer. It read: 'Dear Mr Payne, I am not suited to office work and resign from my job with your firm. Yours sincerely Laurie Lee.'

'It's a basic instinct in all of us to move from our birthplace,' Laurie said, years later. 'And most men have a yearning to wander . . .' He had to escape from 'the small tight valley closing in around one . . . the cottage walls narrowing like the arms of an iron maiden, the local girls whispering, "Marry, and settle down." '⁶

Laurie told Betty he would see her when he came back, but she replied firmly: 'When you come back, I shall not be here.' For two years he had been woven into her life. 'You stand bareheaded and young, ready to fight the whole world if necessary, you whose weapons are your pen, your pencil & the way one lock of your hair falls over your eyes . . . I'm glad I met you Laurie. You have shown me that it is possible for a man too to dream of an ideal and take joy in Nature and her myriad beauties.' Sixty-four years later Betty told me: 'It was just young love. But we did each other nothing but good.'

4 | Laurie Walks Out
1934–5

So Laurie walked out one morning in June 1934, just before his twentieth birthday. Jack and Tony were asleep when Annie waved him off from the steep cottage bank with a 'gnarled red hand'. He describes her as old and stooping; she was in fact in her mid-fifties.

He was not yet bound for Spain, merely London. He wore thick boots, and carried a small tent, a tin of treacle biscuits, and his violin in a blanket. Why did he walk? He could have cycled. The train would have cost 4s 6d. But walking out was the poetic 'I will arise and go now' route to the gypsy life, the W.H. Davies mode, the romantic troubadour's way. Laurie Lee had unwittingly begun creating his legend.

He headed towards Wiltshire, slept under the stars, and woke in the rain to find two cows breathing over him. ('The lowing herd winds softly o'er the Lee' as his friend Georgina Hammick wrote many years later.) He almost turned back, but could not face his brothers' triumph. Within a day he passed through Malmesbury and Chippenham; soon he was in Salisbury, and – taking a detour, in order to see the sea – in a week he was at Southampton.

Sleeping in a doss-house run by 'an old hag with a tooth like a tin-opener', he began busking, learning to leave just two pennies in his hat, pocketing the rest. Slow melodies ('Loch Lomond', 'The Rose of Tralee', 'Ave Maria') were the most lucrative; women were the more responsive. He moved along the coastline of Hampshire and Sussex, finding the real sea a disappointment, not what Hardy and Farnol had led him to expect: a shabby shoreline suburbia of newly built bungalows. At Bognor Regis he camped out on the sands with 'a fluid young girl of sixteen, who hugged me steadily throughout one long hot day with only a gymslip on her sea-wet body'.[1]

That is all he writes about 'Mollie' – but he kept for ever her

seven-page letter, written a few days later and addressed simply from 'The Beach'.

'Dear Laurie, You are right, it was a dream. You said midsummer madness: we were both rather in the clouds. I shall always remember how we talked about anything and everything with such ease! But afterwards I think I was a spectator, watching two strangers playing a part. Perhaps you felt that too.

'I feel that you were searching for something you couldn't find. We are both young and don't know each other at all. You said so, and you were right. I felt a perfectly sisterly interest in you, added to the excitement of finding your views on all my pet subjects & books & authors. And afterwards I felt maternal because you were so lonely & young & I was too! So it was a strange mingling of sympathies . . . We must always be friends. After all, we're both ridiculously young and this rosy halo of poetry and beauty is bound to be stripped away sometime . . . Anyone who makes a hideous mess of the country with ugly, shapeless houses makes me sick. And some of the things one sees in the muddles of politics and justice fill me with anger . . .

'You've certainly got a long way since the weekend! Chancton-bury must have been magnificent in the dark, with the sleeping town at your feet and the night breeze in the bushes, and all round you that eerie silence. Didn't you find Romans in every tree and short, dark Britons in every bush? I can't tell you how I envy you, the magic in the loveliness & the loneliness means more to me than anything, and I can find it so rarely. Yet there are you, saturated in it day and night, getting more experience, excitement of new places, and thrills of fresh beauty in a few weeks than I shall probably find for the rest of this year. Laurie, you can't think how lucky you are. And your love of music is another blessing I envy with all my heart.

'The Chilterns are at their best now, you lucky boy, some of the loveliest country in England. One can look at the wooded hills for ever and still find them more beautiful than before.

'Laurie, we may never see each other again . . . but you have courage and a strong sense of true values. I would like to keep your

friendship if you think mine worthwhile. Write to me if you care to, mon ami, when you reach London tell me how you get on. Good luck & good hunting! Yours for auld lang syne, Mollie.'

Evidently Laurie would have no trouble in finding romantic girls along the road. Mollie writes like a replica of the Molly (and the Betty) he had left behind. Or perhaps he made girls respond in this way. On he tramped. The pearl-chokered ladies of Worthing in their bath-chairs gave him, for one hour's fiddling, 38 shillings: 'more than a farm-labourer earned in a week'.

Walking over the Sussex Downs, living on dates and biscuits (an affectation, he admits; he saw himself as T.E. Lawrence 'in a desert sandstorm blowing out of the wadis of Godalming'), he met Alf, a veteran tramp in a deerstalker hat. There were nearly two million unemployed in Britain, and the highways thronged with vagrants. At night they brewed tea in billy-cans by grassy roadsides and Alf taught him about wearing layers of clothes, and how to flannel housewives and dodge police.

Via Ascot (in Ascot week), Windsor and Stoke Poges, he arrived at Beaconsfield, and beheld London. 'Cleo, my girlfriend, was somewhere out there; hoarding my letters (I hoped) and waiting.' Laurie wrote that he had met sixteen-year-old Cleo, 'the beautiful daughter of a Communist agitator', earlier that spring at the Whiteway Colony, where she lived with her family – English mother, American father – in a caravan. She had 'a husky, nutty, Anglo-American accent, huge brown eyes flecked like crumbled honey, a smooth leggy figure, lithe as an Indian pony, and we'd pretended to be in love'. In the published history of Whiteway there is no mention of such a family, but among Laurie's photographs was a snap of a pretty girl in shorts, with 'Cleo' on the back. Joy Thacker, Whiteway's historian, says one old colonist recalls a particularly beautiful girl who stayed there briefly with her parents and brother, and Jack Lee recalls 'an American girl and her brother' arriving one day when he was in Laurie's digs.

Anyway, Laurie took a tube and had an address to go to. But first he went to 3 Greville Place, St John's Wood. Fifty years later, when Laurie met John Clive, who was about to become his tenant

in Slad, he noticed Clive's London address in Greville Place and said: 'Does it have a studio in the garden?' Yes, said Clive, the studio is still there. 'That's the first place I stayed, when I arrived in London,' said Laurie. 'It belonged to a famous conductor and composer.' That studio was indeed the address, in the 1930s, of the musician Benjamin Frankel, whom Laurie had also met at Whiteway.

But sooner or later Laurie was in Putney, as he recounts. He says Cleo's bohemian family were living in a half-demolished Putney Heath house, and that Cleo's father arranged a job for him on a building site. So Laurie moved into digs above a café in the Lower Richmond Road: a room of his own at last. He quickly made friends, including a black American sailor from Missouri, an extravagant greeter ('Gouge mah eyes, shuh good to see you'), and Philip O'Connor,[2] a curly-haired aspiring poet whose verses were 'rhapsodic eruptions of surrealist fantasy'. (O'Connor later briefly resurfaced in Laurie's diary in 1958, when he ran into Laurie in Soho, and told him: 'Anyway Laurie you're better than Louis MacNeice. And I couldn't say lower than that.')

'You certainly have a bohemian group of friends,' wrote Pat in early September, '& I can understand your absorption in them. Your letter is full of the verve of youth. But what job have you got, & what are you aiming for? I suppose you're in "digs"? Tell me all about yourself & your new life.'

In her matronly way, Pat was uneasy about Laurie in London. 'I admire your courage tremendously. As you know, I've never been to London, & never had any desire to visit it. I imagine it to be a cruel, relentless beast, & I shall feel very much more at ease when you are home again.' Was he keeping hectic hours and late nights? In the town air he would catch his annual bout of 'flu. Again she urged his mind to master his body, and to resist sexual indulgence: 'Discipline of the body is essential to a happy & successful life. Think of Keats' "Beauty is truth, truth beauty. That is all ye know on earth, & all ye need to know."' She adds: 'For heaven's sake don't think I'm preaching.'

Laurie did not appear to mind Pat's homilies, because he wrote

again confiding that he could not forget Betty. Pat at once became smotheringly proprietorial about 'the boy I have watched growing through boyhood into a sensitive adolescence, & now into manhood, and who has added so much beauty to my life . . .' 'Your letter . . . made me want your head against my breast, your hands lightly touching me in the firelight. If only we could be magically transported to the kitchen at Slad . . . I know I could comfort you & help you with the many problems that have beset you.'

By day Laurie was pushing cement in a wheelbarrow, building a 'squat, unbeautiful, pretentious' block of flats on the Putney Heath site. His labouring comrades were diminutive Cockneys, old lags, con-men, drifters, the lowest of the building-site hierarchy; they pilfered, gambled, and rolled cigarettes. 'London then seemed almost 19th century, dusty, down-at-heel, secure. Wages were low but life was cheap and easy. A tot of whisky for 6d, a 9d seat in the cinema, cigarettes 20 for 11d – as a builder's labourer earning £2 5s a week I lived the life of Reilly.'[3] In the evenings he played snooker, went to Queen's Hall concerts and the Ballet Russe, and listened to jazz. He met 'stern young students and workers who held gatherings in cold back rooms. Popular Front posters hung on the walls, and there were experiments in sex, responsible, clinical and pure.'

He paints a picture of himself as a solitary, luxuriating in rootless melancholy, wandering on Putney Heath, or through the City (which reminded him of Stroud) and down the Strand. 'I walked the streets of Soho, bought foreign newspapers which I couldn't read, studied art-books at Zwemmers, smoked black Mexican cigars, and played the newfangled pin-tables in the amusement arcades.'

Pat told Laurie she had been camping with the Smart sisters, having 'really top-hole picnics', but advised him to 'cut right away from both girls'. However, he did write to Molly, and she replied ('Surely you know I've been *aching* to write to you for months?') from the Smarts' 'vulgar' new bungalow called Capri in Wellspring Road, Wotton. Betty, captain of her school, and about to read English at Exeter University, was still 'a bubbling fountain'. 'But Betty will always be the spirit of joyousness. Youth gleams from

her; her eyes sparkle and her cheeks glow.' So Betty's heart was not broken. Molly herself was fending off an amorous Cambridge undergraduate, but she assured Laurie she would not get engaged, as her brother Roy just had. Marriage ought to be abolished, she declared; if she were ever caught in that web of convention she would suffocate. Was Laurie homesick? she asked. 'I know so well that ache in your heart for Slad.'

However homesick, in October Laurie had a cheering distraction: his first poem in a national paper was published by the *Sunday Referee*, whose 'Poet's Corner' in that year also featured Dylan Thomas, David Gascoyne and Ruthven Todd. Laurie's poem won him £1. It was called 'Life', and was about grass growing and being cut down and growing again. It began:

A shower of seed falls in the earth;
and there, unnoticed by the sky, is birth.

'Life' is living landscape, said Victor B. Neuberg, editor of 'Poet's Corner'. 'This poem is sensitive to the edge of eeriness, and this is achieved with a sun-effect.'

'My dear, How proud I am!' wrote Pat. 'Go on, Laurie – I've always known you would reach up and up. When you publish your first book of poems let me be first to share your joy. Come for lunch one Sunday. Mother thinks of you stuck in a garret without enough cash to buy more than bread & tea.' She urged him to 'turn an honest half-guinea' by entering further contests. The *Weekly Post* wanted 300 words on the most interesting person you have ever met. 'Why not have a shot?' Or perhaps he could take up calligraphy for commercial gain? A boy she knew had been offered £5 a week for italic writing on Christmas cards and calendars. She sent Laurie a broad-nibbed calligraphic pen.

On the back of this letter, Laurie practised his italic script with Pat's pen. What he wrote, over and over, was the name of Sufi Rogers. Soon Sufi herself was writing to Laurie from Slad in her own beautiful copperplate hand, and her charmingly fractured English. She had met Laurie's mother in Stroud by chance, and

Annie showed her Laurie's poem in the *Sunday Referee*. Sufi told him she was taking cookery classes and would have some cakes ready for him 'when you visit us at Xmas time. My mother remember you very much, and she said, you are a very nice big friend. I have my own becylce [*sic*] and it helps me to go to the Country dances at Whiteway every Saturday and Wednesday night . . .'

The '*Lección en castellano*' she appended to her letter gave Laurie the following phrases: *No vale la pena* (it's not worth the effort), *No vale un comino* (it's not worth a cumin-seed), *Carajo* (prick: 'especial word') *No tiene inteligencia* (s/he has no intelligence), and *Bebí venga aquí* (Come here baby). (Richard Rogers, her youngest brother, says he was always called Bebí.)

'*Asomate la ventana*
paloma del alma mía
lavate la cara con agua fría
cachándote una pulmonía – Lord Byron'
(Lean out of your window, dove of my soul/wash your face in
    cold water and catch pneumonia.)

But Laurie was not yet fixed on Spain: he told Molly he might go to Italy. 'Oh yes, let's go to Italy quickly, before our hearts are cold and old. Sun on stones, and blue-blue sea,' Molly responded. 'Oh Laurielee, all the stored-up laughter in me bubbles and winks at the thought of Italy . . . I know how you felt about Heine's *Travels*; I've just been reading Munthe's novel *San Michele*, and now I shall not rest till I've seen Capri.

'And Laurie, I'm so *glad* you're coming home for Christmas! Can I meet your train? If you felt you couldn't see Betty, I'd meet your train and bring lunch; we'd get the bus to Edge Church & walk over to Haresfield Beacon – h'mm? Yes I *know* you'd want to be alone, but I'd be quiet as a mouse!'

Molly affected jealousy over Laurie's published poem. 'Don't let praise turn your head – you're dreadfully conceited and you're getting a great deal too much flattery already. But I *do* think it's damnable that I've been striving all my life to reach a spot, and in

seven lines you land there – Grrrcha! And actually I'm a much nicer person than you are! None the less, I enclose some of my heavyhearted efforts. Truthful opinions please – you can be as depressing as you like, only don't say "Stop writing".' One of them was 'A Sonnet for Laurie', beginning:

> Surely this stretch of earth will know you tread
> Your own loved ways again; will feel your feet
> Move soft amid her last-year's leaves that spread
> Brown-gold profusion through your woods . . .

So Laurie went home to his family at Christmas, but also joined Sufi's family at their bungalow deep in snow. Sufi's brother Richard, who drew a good pencil sketch of Laurie that week, says Laurie was talking then about going to Spain. Sufi's parents 'could not understand why he had the urge to travel through such an impoverished and disturbed country, making a living playing an old fiddle'. But they realized that 'he had, undeniably, a captivating personality that attracted people to him and made them spontaneously sympathetic'.

Laurie and Molly duly had their reunion at Edge church. He gave her a volume of Oscar Wilde, and their friendship altered from that day. With Betty going away, Molly felt free to offer Laurie a physical relationship (without any fussing about love) and thereafter she signed her letters exotically 'Mariquita', Spanish for 'Ladybird', an improvement on humdrum Molly. She wrote afterwards:

'My dear – I only know that the thought of the strong smooth hardness of your body against the petal-pale softness of mine set a mad orchestra ringing in my brain – so that I wanted to lift my face to the moon and shout with a mirth deeper than laughter. It was all so inevitable somehow. The idea of your going back to London seemed so absurd – I had to make you touch my lips – but I didn't know you'd send flame after flame of moonfire through me.

'Laurielee, you have given me some of the loveliest moments in my life. I shall always remember the moonlight on your mouth,

suddenly so grave. You shouldn't question gifts the gods send, you know. Desire is a flame that runs through one's body in a shower of stars . . . Goodnight, my very dear. A week – a month – a year – who knows? till then dream of me and oh! write soon! Soon! Querido mío! Mariquita.'

She began to bombard Laurie with seductive and exclamatory letters about her wild excitement and soul-shaking desire; she would soon come to him 'as a sunflower to the sun' to give him 'something more precious than all your books can give'. But the consummation must wait, because of Betty: 'She wouldn't understand that this thing has nothing to do with love. Wait until she's lost the need of your ideal in her heart Laurie, then I'll come to you, I must! just as you inevitably must claim the sweetness & comfort of my body, so I must come to you for the velvet of the bee against the satin of the snapdragon. Have you ever watched a bee in a snapdragon? isn't it the loveliest sight? Can you imagine a bee analysing his feelings?'

Ever since Laurie had gone to London, Jack too had been restless. He would walk up to the top of Swift's Hill, and wonder what he was going to do with his life. His brother seemed to have all the talents; he must find a different one. At the Erinoid factory he had risen to assistant manager, and bought his first car, a 1928 Singer, for £22. The previous year he had been given a camera for his twenty-first birthday by the family of his girlfriend Phyllis Hawke – annoyingly, Laurie proved to be a natural photographer too – and it sowed in Jack the idea of being a film director. He wrote to several directors for advice, and one, Paul Rotha, responded: Jack went to London to see him, and Rotha advised him to apply to the Regent Street Polytechnic (now the University of Westminster). They would take him for £25 a term. He went back to the factory, sold his car, got on his bike, and began to save up the fees.

That January he saw his brother off at Stroud station. As the train left, Laurie banged his head on the window, shattering the glass and cutting his head: the stationmaster had to telephone to the next stop so that they could check that he was all right. Laurie moved into new digs, rent 25s a week, at 1 Werter Road, a small Victorian

terraced house on the corner of Putney High Street. The landlady was a blonde Cockney, Mrs O'Neill ('Mrs Flynn' in *As I Walked Out*), with a meek spinster sister known as Wid, whom Laurie called 'Beth'. Mrs O'Neill was a chain-smoking Mrs Malaprop, sweeping floors in a dressing-gown each morning, transformed into a Gloria Swanson at night, while Wid hovered anxiously in the background and cooked large suppers for Laurie. As always, the women treated Laurie well, nursing him when ill and bringing him Guinness. Werter Road suited him, and became his recurrent London base for the next eight years. And when Jack eventually came to London, he too lodged at Werter Road.

Molly and Pat continued to supervise Laurie's reading, and to tell him what plays he ought to see. 'Did you see Gielgud's Hamlet? Isn't Gielgud marvellous? I admired his Richard of Bordeaux [which Gielgud directed] even more than his acting. It was even more gorgeous than the Stratford *Richard II*.' *Sweet Aloes* with Diana Wynyard had previewed in Birmingham and Pat urged him: 'Opening at Wyndhams on the 31st – go see.'

In May 1935, there was a dispute over non-union labour at the building site, and everything stopped for two weeks. A towering labourer with big fists and a square, bitter face ('prototype of the worker-hero in Soviet posters') emerged to address the men and called the comrades out on strike. This was Fred Copeman, who had already been jailed after the naval mutiny of Invergordon, Scapa Flow.[4] The next time Laurie would see him was during the Spanish Civil War, when Copeman was Commander of the British Battalion of the International Brigade at Albacete, and according to Laurie, recognized him: 'Oh, it's you – the poet from the buildings. Never thought *you'd* make it.'

The strike ended and the building work was finished at the beginning of June 1935. Laurie was feeling 'beefily strong' and fit. He was free to explore the world. 'There was a taste of peace like cream on the air. The world's frontiers were still wide open. There were rumours from China and Abyssinia, but I for one didn't heed them.' He considered France, Italy, Greece – all merely 'names with vaguely operatic flavours'. He knew no languages – except

the Argentine-Spanish phrases taught to him by Sufi. Spain it would be. He saw himself 'brown as an apostle, walking the white dust roads through the orange groves'.[5] Or perhaps he just wanted to be able to swank to girlfriends, as he admitted sixty years later.

Anyway, it was a brilliant career move. His wanderings in Spain, and his chance encounter with the Spanish Civil War, were two episodes he was able to draw on for the rest of his life.

Molly, 'restless as a flock of starlings' and now threatened by Laurie's imminent departure ('From Jack I hear rumours of Spain! They flash into my brain like splinters of coloured glass!'), announced that she was coming to London. She had dreamed of Laurie pointing to the horizon crying, 'Look – the island of Crete – the promised land – see how blue and green and gold it is. We will find it together, you and I, Mariquita!' She longed for the comfort of his 'music that sings and sighs'. So she had arranged to take the post of nursery governess to a handicapped child in a family named Whitelaw in Sutton, Surrey, where she found herself in charge of a household containing 'a tubby husband, a couple of damned incompetent maids, a high-spirited young animal of a schoolboy, three blasted pekes and an invalid child'.

Would Laurie be kind to her for these remaining weeks? 'I will come to you after tea on Thursday. Be gentle Laurie – hold me softly against the strong throb of your heart – and kiss me till I am content. Then play to me – will you?' They met several times, and for the last time on a hot summer day. They leaned on a gate in a Surrey lane under chestnut trees and Laurie said, 'God, I wish I didn't love [England] so much!' Then he took her back to his Putney room and played Debussy on his violin. 'Oh, you are wise to go away,' she wrote afterwards, 'and yet, when you go, with the light of morning in your guarded cat's eyes, you will leave chaos inside me.' It had all begun that day 'in the sitting-room of the White Horse when you were scarcely more than a gauche schoolboy and I a grown up young woman of nearly twenty one'. Now – 'Oh Laurie – Laurilee – the relentless beat of your heart! It beats into my brain, into my virgin womb, making life leap within me. All my life now, there will be the eternal thrust and

throb of your heart. So look back and remember a green Surrey lane in June and a woman who loved you with a sincerity that goes deeper than most things.'

'For the first time in my life,' as Laurie wrote in *As I Walked Out*, 'I was learning how much easier it was to leave than to stay behind and love.' On 1 July 1935, describing himself as an 'art student', grey-eyed and five foot nine, he was issued with his first passport.

A week earlier, on his twenty-first birthday, he had gone to see his father in suburban Morden. It was a dispiriting encounter. 'He handed me £8 and said, "You were due for £10, but you borrowed £2 when you were fourteen, so I've knocked that off." He told me the greatest composer in the world was Eric Coates.[6] I was a musical snob at the time and thought "He can't be my father." '[7]

Warningly, Mariquita sent a sonnet called 'Haunted!' which ended:

. . . I shall be there
Intangible and grey
To dim your dreams . . . I shall be near
To you in Silence; through all dear
Known sounds my ghost will stray,
Haunting you everywhere!

Undeterred, Laurie bought a £4 one-way boat ticket to Vigo. 'You will come back,' Mariquita persisted, 'you with your fair Saxon beauty. You are part and being of this England – and soon you will be surfeited with sun, and slim brown bodies sunning swiftly to decay – and you will long to slake your thirst in green Surrey lanes, and on the hills of Gloucestershire. You will long for the coolth of apple bloom against your lips – and voilà! you will be home. But come quickly, my dear, and don't forget or regret Mariquita. Good night and Good luck, querido.'

5 | 'Un vaso de agua'
1935–6

In July 1935 Laurie boarded a Royal Mail Line ship from Tilbury with knapsack, blanket and fiddle for the two-day crossing to Vigo. He originally had a more ambitious aim, to go from southern Spain through France to Italy and Greece, and if he had not known how to say *'Déme un vaso de agua, por favor'* he might have headed more directly for the Balkans, he said later. He knew nothing of Spain. But he was also innocent of his ignorance, and therefore untroubled by it. It was 'the most vivid time of my life, the most free, sunlit. I remember thinking, I can go where I wish, I'm so packed with time and freedom.' His first thought, stepping ashore, was how foreign it all was. The bricks and tiles were foreign. The donkeys brayed in a foreign language. But 'I felt it was for this I had come: to . . . look out on a world for which I had no words; to start at the beginning, speechless and without plan, in a place that still held no memories for me.'[1]

When he awoke after a first restless night on a green Galician hillside – snarled at by wolves, or perhaps wild dogs – he heard the shouts of women washing clothes in a stream, thumping them against the rocks, shouting and singing: almost Moorish, open-air voices that carried from hill to hill.[2] He set out aimlessly in a south-easterly direction, towards Zamora. Everything was new and strange. He discovered the blistering intensity of the Spanish sun in summer, the hallucination-inducing thirst. 'Spain is no Arcadia,' as he said in his first radio broadcast about it, in 1946. 'It is harsh, raw, bare, savage, and almost entirely devoid of prettiness.'

Nobody could describe Laurie's adventure more memorably and evocatively than he did. Nor can every detail of his vagrant life be verified after sixty years. His diaries, with their graphic observations, their aural snapshots of peasant dialogue, which enabled him to write *As I Walked Out One Midsummer Morning* (in 1968), were

stolen from a BBC car in Segovia in 1969 – a source of much later wretchedness. Did Laurie take the route he described, skirting the mountains of León and walking the valley of the Douro? Probably. His passport was stamped at La Linea on 22 September, so he reached Gibraltar after ten weeks of walking a zig-zag route: a later diary mentions setting off from Toledo for Madrid, not vice versa as in his book. John King,[3] who later retraced the journey with Laurie, by air and car, found the distances so vast that he suspected that Laurie must have hitch-hiked rather more than the two short car-rides he admits to, into Valladolid and Madrid. (And so what? he shrugged.) But the weeks Laurie spent in Toledo, and in Almuñécar, where he spent two-thirds of his Spanish year, are heavily corroborated.

Ten years later Annie recalled how anxious Laurie had made her. 'Then there was your going away,' she wrote, 'first to London, & then leaving England with your violin and a small sum of money to "journey through Spain" & I worried so often, wondering if you had enough to eat, and where you were, and where you slept. And I used to think perhaps the Spaniards were cruel and might kill you, & Jack & I were alone in the old home, for Tony was on his job travelling. That was when I started getting grey hairs. Those were cruel days to me.'

It is as true today as in 1935 that you can travel miles in parts of Spain without coming across a village. Even from an exhilarating high-speed AVE train, vast areas look unpopulated: gaping vistas of plains, hills, acres of olive groves. Even if Laurie's 'long loping stride' was covering twenty miles a day he would spend whole days in monotonous solitude. He was wearied by the bare, mile-high plain of Castilla, with 'boulders as big as churches' and air 'thin and clear as prayer'. His first night in a *posada* (a muleteers' hostel) sharing a noisy supper with carters and drovers was the first of many such stops at ancient oak doors: 'Gorged with stew and warmed to idiocy by wine, I was a stranger but felt at home.'

It is easy to see why Laurie felt at home: the villagers who so hospitably welcomed '*el rubio*', the blond young traveller, were just like the folks back in Slad, only shorter, darker, and poorer still.

'In a strange way I found it very like Gloucestershire. People seemed to be living the same kind of lives, sharing each other's dreams and passions and gossip, knifings in the back, and so on, but anyway living a coloured, red-blooded life in which they were all involved.' As he often said, the farmers, the old crones, the children, reminded him of his villagers, 'the carters, innkeepers, the dust-covered farm-boys, grandmothers and girls'. 'Here was I, a young boy, golden haired and beautiful, appearing from nowhere and bringing music which meant happiness. The whole look on their faces changed. I couldn't go wrong.

'I was just a ragged minstrel, and they received me with a kind of medieval courtesy, gave me hospitality and asked me almost Homeric questions: what's it like in your town? what's the price of bread in your city? are you married? There was gossip, wine, and a kind of pride in hospitality and generosity which one can't experience again. The corruption of tourism has destroyed that,' as he said in a broadcast in 1992. 'They loved music and the guitar, and the fact that I was carrying a violin always enlivened them. They lived hard and semi-starved lives, but if I unrolled my blanket, to stay in one of the *fondas*, and they saw my violin their faces would soften and crease, there'd be a cry of *¡Música! ¡Música!* They liked Schubert, strangely enough, especially Moment Musical, but I'd play *paso dobles* and even the old ladies would dance a few creaky steps around the patio. The violin was a passport of friendship wherever I went, and I got to learn some of the old songs which made my life more intimately shared with them.'[4]

The peasants taught him Spanish like a child, and treated him like a child, miming offers of purple wine and stews of kid and beans at trestle tables, surrounded by woodsmoke, donkeys, dogs and pigs. Often he woke up lying on a rock in the bare *mesa* 'with a circle of cloaked figures quietly watching me, like a ring of crows'. He was 'the stranger within their gates. They asked for news from the outside world. They had this inquisitiveness. Now,' he said forty years later, 'the children rushing out to greet the stranger have been replaced by hundreds of Fiats, and the country is poisoned by TV soap operas, and will never recover.' But the romantic affection

for the old Spain that began in 1935 intensified throughout his life, and resonates in every loaded phrase of *As I Walked Out One Midsummer Morning*.

In Zamora he met itinerant German musicians of his own age: Artur the violinist, Rudi the accordionist and Heinrich the flautist, from Hamburg, which prompted him to try living by his violin. 'It seemed that I'd come to the right country, poor as it was; the pennies were few, but they were generously given.' He parted from the Germans after a drunken night at a village dance, and turned towards Valladolid because its name seemed so pleasing. In a village en route he took up his violin, but collapsed with a fever in a blur of sunstroke. He was rescued – 'the first mouthful of mineral water burst in my throat like frosted stars' – and given a lift to Valladolid. In this baleful city of 'rancid shadows and scabby dogs, sweating pavements and offal-filled gutters', he acquired for half a peseta an elaborately-worded licence to play his fiddle: it looked like a Royal Charter. As in Sussex, women were more generous than men.

Thereafter he played in markets, inns, cafés and the occasional brothel. From Segovia, where he slept beneath the Roman aqueduct, he crossed the Sierra de Guadarrama and only then, he said, did he feel 'really involved in Spain'. There is no doubt, as Laurie's friend and fellow poet Ted Walker (who lives in Spain) says, that Laurie truly 'understood' Spain. 'He got the people, the topography, the richness, the attitude to life. If there's an afterlife I'd like to be part of a *tertulia* comprising Richard Ford, George Borrow, Gerald Brenan, Jan Morris, George Orwell and Laurie Lee.'

Laurie discovered Madrid – then clamorous with tram-bells, and much smaller than Madrid today – in August. The streets and bars he described are still there. In the Calle Echegaray, you can find the *tapas* bars he described: 'voluptuously' furnished, with varnished bullfight posters, and wine in stone jars, and prawns and *pajaritos* in little saucers. 'Stepping in from the torrid street, you met a band of cool air like fruit-peel pressed to your brow and entered a cloistered grotto laden with the tang of shellfish, wet tiles, and wine-soaked wood.' In Madrid he says he encountered 'a ripe young widow'. He also found a letter at the post office (filed under

E for Esquire) from Molly Smart, alias Mariquita. She had received his letter, urging her to leave her job in Surrey and join him.

'I was very surprised to get your letter – somehow I thought you wouldn't write till you were coming home – and what are years Laurie querido? Nothing but men's puny attempt to check eternity. My dear, you remind me of a gleaming dragonfly calling to a water-lily to leave her cold bed and follow the sun!' But she could not leave Sutton for the gypsy life. Betty (now at Exeter) needed her 'and though a gypsy has most things that make life worth living, she hasn't the money, which to me has become damned essential. Part of me revels in decently cooked food and daily baths. So there it is – I'm a soul in comfortable captivity. (I can see the scorn of your mouth as you read this!)

'When you return you will still be Laurie of the sensual mouth – and your surprisingly white body will be tanned to corn gold . . . I could so easily turn gypsy and follow the sun too, but mon ami remember "Vers l'oublie"? Or don't you read Ford Madox Ford? No, Laurielee, nothing is ever the same again, but one day you will come back and complete what was started on a hot July day on a Surrey hill.' From a thousand miles away, she sang her siren song about 'the grey Cotswold stone walls, the silver pillars of the beech trees, the low friendly soft drawls of Gloucestershire people – these things remain unchanged, waiting for you to come home'.

In rose-red Toledo, Spain's ancient imperial capital, forty miles south of Madrid, Laurie collapsed with a fever. Once recovered, he headed for the town's central square full of café tables, the Plaza de Zocodover. He was playing his fiddle when he spotted a family group: the father a big, expansive figure in a hat, his wife demure in white. They were the poet Roy Campbell, his wife Mary, and their younger daughter Anna. It was Laurie's first meeting with a poet, and a blessed encounter. Campbell walked tall and talked tall, as Laurie later wrote.[5] He was the antithesis of the conventional image of the poet: physically exuberant, garrulous, one who held tables in thrall with his luminous eyes and his fantastical tales; but also deeply sensitive and wildly generous. More importantly, Mary Campbell was one of the Garman girls. Laurie could never have

imagined then what a central place her family would soon occupy in his life.

Mary was the eldest of the seven Garman sisters, daughters of the late Dr Walter Chancellor Garman of Wednesbury, Staffordshire. Dr Garman, darkly aquiline, not unlike a handsome Spanish don, had ruled his family – two sons as well as seven daughters – with an autocratic, even tyrannical, hand. Their mother was Irish, the illegitimate child of Lord Grey (and half gypsy, some said). The nine 'somewhat bizarre' children[6] – Mary, Sylvia, Douglas, Kathleen, Rosalind, Helen, Mavin, Ruth and Lorna – grew up in an Elizabethan manor house, Oakeswell Hall, with a retinue of maids, gardeners, nanny and governess – until suddenly impoverished by their father's death in 1923.

In 1920, Mary and her sister Kathleen had run away from the melancholy Midlands to London. Two strikingly beautiful girls, not yet twenty, with dark hair, large slanting green eyes and wide mouths, they were instantly noticed. The sculptor Jacob Epstein gazed upon them across the Harlequin restaurant in Beak Street, Soho, sent over a note, asked Kathleen to sit for him, and fell for her forthwith. The morning after their first night together, he modelled her head, and she remained his muse for ever more – becoming mother to three of his children and (eventually) Lady Epstein. (In 1922 Epstein's wife Margaret called one day to confront Kathleen, and shot her in the shoulder; she staggered out into the arms, amazingly, of her brother Douglas, who was walking by.)

Mary, who studied at the Slade, had a similar effect on the young South African poet Roy Campbell. In 1921, aged nineteen, he was living near the sisters in Bloomsbury; one day Mary introduced herself to him in Charlotte Street. She was said to be a man-hater: but this 'only made it more of a challenge, more exciting, and more of a responsibility to capture her for myself for ever. None of my very best horses were ever easy to break in.'[7] Campbell too fell in love instantly, a 'Dantesque sensation'. He went back to Regent Square with her and stayed three days and nights. They married at Oakeswell soon after, to the dismay of the cook: 'And I always thought Miss Mary would marry a gentleman with a park!'[8]

They spent their first married Christmas with Augustus John (who called Mary 'Little Lord Fondle-roy') and his wife in Dorset, and had uproarious evenings with the gypsies and with Francis Macnamara (father of Dylan Thomas's wife Caitlin, and of Nicolette – who will enter this story later). The Campbells went to live first in South Africa, then in Sussex, where Vita Sackville-West fell in love with Mary in the Weald village post office,[9] and in 1928 took their daughters Teresa and Anna to Martigues, known as 'the Venice of Provence' because of its five canals. The Campbells arrived with £10; Vita sometimes sent them money, but Roy's aversion to all things Bloomsbury was fuelled by Vita's obsession with his wife.

In Martigues, the Campbells met Marius Jean-Baptiste Polge, a big blond handsome half-Norwegian fisherman known as Grandpère. Mary's younger sister Helen came out for a summer holiday in Martigues, fell in love with Marius, married him in 1930, and had a daughter, Katherine Francesca – who would eventually become Laurie Lee's wife. So Roy Campbell's life and Laurie's were linked via the Garman girls; but that was fifteen years later.

Roy and Mary had one day decided to leave Martigues, 'fold our tents like Arabs, and as silently steal away' – to Spain, where Roy could indulge in bullfighting under the name of Ignacio Roig. They had come to Toledo in 1935, and rented a house under the cathedral wall. Mary, a recent Catholic convert (she was a Carmelite tertiary and had abandoned makeup, cigarettes, trousers, and wine except at meals), went daily to mass and was engrossed in her new religion. Every evening before supper they would go to the Plaza de Zocodover. So here they were, in the hour of the *paseo*, when 'Laurie Lee made his début in Toledan society'.

Anna Campbell, aged nine at the time, recalls the encounter in her memoir, *Poetic Justice*: 'At that hour the whole square came to life. The girls in their best dresses strolled back and forth, receiving compliments from the youths: "*Adiós guapísima*", and so on.' Laurie startled everyone by striking up sentimental Schubert songs. Soon the general chatter drowned the sound of his violin, but the Campbells could still see him sawing away, and felt rather sorry for the

lad with his sunburnt skin. Mary asked him in French whether he was German, and he replied in Spanish that he was English. Roy bade him sit down, and soon invited him back home, to dine in a central open courtyard, after which Anna 'danced like a firefly'[10] and Laurie and Roy sat up talking till dawn, Roy reading his poems 'The Sisters' and 'Horses on the Camargue'. 'Nothing could have suited me better at that hour, and at that place and time of my life. I was young, full of wine, and in love with poetry.'

Laurie stayed for a week, exploring Toledo, seeing El Grecos, sleeping on a mattress among sheaves of Roy's unfinished poems, listening to Roy in the evenings, singing and talking. (Roy was 'drinking like a madman' at that period – four litres of wine a day.)[11] 'He'd sailed whalers, swum Hellesponts, broken horses on the Camargue, fought bulls, and caught sharks bare-handed,' Laurie heard. He had quieter daytime discussions with Mary, who reproved Laurie for his atheism: 'I wanted the excitement of doubt, the satisfaction of mortality,' he wrote, 'the freedom to make love here and now on earth. Beautiful Mary would have none of it.'

(Ten months later the Campbells had to flee from Toledo when the city was temporarily taken by the Republicans; Roy, also a Catholic convert, took the side of Franco, whom he eulogized in his poem 'Flowering Rifle'.)

Meanwhile Laurie crossed the Tagus and went on south, accompanied for a few days by a tramp – to Ciudad Real, Valdepeñas, Bailén, Córdoba, and followed the River Guadalquivir to Seville: 'Ever since childhood I'd imagined myself walking down a white dusty road through groves of orange trees to a city called Seville.' There he met a sailor who gave the first dark hint of coming trouble. 'If you want to see blood, stick around – you're going to see plenty.' On to Jerez, to Cádiz of the tall narrow lanes, to windblasted Tarifa, and to raffish Algeciras, where he stayed two weeks for threepence a night, and which he later always pronounced his favourite hideout. On 22 September 1935 he reached Gibraltar, which – as he reminisced in a BBC film in 1962 – 'crouched like a dog on the glassy sea . . . and after 500 miles of

Spanish thirst I could almost hear the rattle of tea-cups'. He walked into Gibraltar, too broke to be *persona grata*, and was allowed to spend two nights in the police cells in Irish Town. After two days of English tea he was escorted back to the frontier, to carry on walking the coast road east from San Roque to Málaga. The Costa del Sol is now an unbroken string of high-rise hotels, restaurants, discos, supermarkets – a byword in tourism for how not to develop a Mediterranean coast, almost obliterating any view of the sea. But then it was a primitive, winding road dotted with fishing villages: Estepona, San Pedro de Alcántara, Marbella, Fuengirola. 'At the time one could have bought the whole coast for a shilling.' He was in Almuñécar by the end of October 1935. And there, for the most part, he stayed.

Almuñécar (where the classical guitarist Segovia once lived) sits on the southern coast of Andalucía, subsisting since Phoenician times on its salted fish. What Laurie saw was 'a tumbling little village on an outcrop of rock in the midst of a pebbly delta, backed by a bandsaw of mountains'. It had been a Moorish stronghold, an Arab market town, and the main port of the kingdom of Granada. It fell to the Castilians in 1489 and a battered cross stands on an offshore rock celebrating the spot where the defeated caliphs sailed away when driven from Spain. But all past glories had faded by the time Laurie arrived. It was a town without distinction. He describes it as 'grey, almost gloomily Welsh. The streets were steep, roughly paved . . . and the square was like a cobbled farmyard. Part of the castle was a cemetery, part of the town hall a jail.'

It was now a poor place, 'infected with fatalism, a kind of subdued and deliberate apathy'. The inhabitants – matriarchal women and small bony men – had only two kinds of livelihood: the sugar canes ('rustling dryly in the wind') and meagre fishing. Most of the village girls were in service to richer families. The only reason Laurie decided to hole up for the winter here is that he found regular work; a Swiss, Theodor Weiss Christien ('Herr Brandt' in Laurie's book) had built a hotel on the grey strip of sand that passed for a beach – in the hope of attracting tourists, but about thirty years too soon. Herr Christien kept the Hotel Mediterráneo open while the

other hotel, the Palace, closed for winter, by offering *thés-dansants*, buffet suppers and musical concerts. He employed Laurie as odd-job man, and as violinist in the saloon at night.

Laurie shared a room in the attic with a Jewish boy named Jacobo Meyer. Jacobo was interpreter, tout, boot-boy and gigolo, knew everyone, and played a nimble accordion, so he and Laurie became the hotel band. Laurie sent his mother a typed programme, today very faded: '*Programa del concierto de violin (Don Lawrence Lee) y piano (Don Jacobo Meyer) esta noche a las 10 en el Hotel Mediterráneo.*' They played twenty pieces, including Schubert's Military March and several Spanish dances, serenades, *paso dobles* and tangos. The tune most asked for was one called 'Río Rita'.

Laurie said years later that he struck up friendships with fishermen, waiters and 'some rather grand girls, fiercely chaperoned, who came down from Granada. One, Consuelo, wrote me a little poem. She wasn't allowed to speak to me because of her strict Catholic parents but her friend would pass me notes. The poem went to the tune of La Cucaracha. "Tall compared to a poor stunted fisherman/ Blond and handsome and slim/Is a boy who has arrived/to play the violin/in the Hotel Mediterráneo/He is called Lorenzo . . ." I'd never had a poem written for me' (which was not strictly true) 'and I've adored her for ever. Her voluptuous face and huge dark eyes still haunt me. Consuelo is still one of my favourite names.'[12]

One night in November, Laurie's violin playing was heard by the only guests in the hotel, a young English couple on their honeymoon. The bride had tonsillitis and kept to her room, but heard the strains of the music while her husband sat downstairs. Twenty years later in London, Laurie met them again: they were Lionel Brett, architect, now Viscount Esher, erstwhile Rector of the Royal College of Art, and his wife Christian, famous beauty and a distinguished painter herself. The couple had met when Lionel was at Eton and they were passionate travellers. After their wedding in October 1935 they made for southern Spain, where few tourists ventured. 'It was the maddest honeymoon,' Lady Esher recalls. 'We travelled from Barcelona on buses full of chickens. We

were aiming for Gibraltar where we hoped to find some comfort in a British hotel. I had new hide luggage, which took a terrible battering as we rattled down the mountain roads. Almuñécar seemed a depressed and poverty-stricken place.' Three decades later, when *As I Walked Out* had been published, the Eshers realized that Laurie – by then a familiar fellow guest at London literary and artistic gatherings – was the boy with the violin in their honeymoon hotel.

There was brief euphoria in Almuñécar after the Socialist victory in the general election of February 1936, when censorship was lifted and a breath of freedom wafted through the Hotel Mediterráneo: the young fishermen and labourers came to dance, expressing their new liberty in blithe confidence that they were the masters now. Today, there is a small obelisk-shaped monument to Laurie Lee on the site of the hotel (demolished in 1980) and the township of Almuñécar has published a pamphlet[13] verifying Laurie's account of the town, quoting two ancient townsmen who recall Laurie and all the characters he mentions: Manolo the waiter, Felipe the chef, 'Gambas' the crippled porter, and El Gato (Francisco Gutierrez Sáez, alias Frasco El Gato), a farm labourer who joined the anarchist group FAI. They thought they had been victorious in the election, as Laurie says; but 'the news was not victory for anyone, but a declaration of war'.

That February, election month, the tireless Molly/Mariquita persisted in trying to lure Laurie home with reminders of the delights of England: 'Amigo Mío, This is not a letter – it is the silver flash of seagulls' wings on the white cliffs of Dover – it is a golden-billed blackbird bursting his little heart with ecstasy in a blossom-laden lilac bush – the first wet primrose shining from a bed of moss in an English beech wood – it is Slad, and Painswick, and Sheepscombe – and the spires of Gloucester Cathedral – it is all the June wonder of Stratford – the triumphant torchlight procession of the chestnuts of Horsepools – it is a wistful effort to regain your love for home . . . Six months! And the sun has caught you as securely as it would catch me . . . But soon it will be spring. Surely, surely then your eye will be cocked for thrushes' nests and the first March violets?'

Not a hope of that. Laurie was departing for Algeciras, where he breakfasted in the market on prawns and melons 'sweet as liquid flowers and cool as the inside of a well; when you'd finished, you could stick the wet skins on your forehead to cool your fevered brow'. On 10 March Laurie left Algeciras – possibly with a friend[14] – for Morocco. His passport shows that he was in Morocco from 11 to 14 March 1936: it was because of this passport stamp that he was detained and questioned in Albacete during the Civil War, since Franco had used Morocco as his rebel base that spring. 'I'd been in the very nest of intrigue, but knew nothing about it . . . We'd spent most of our time in the rooms of small hotels, behind shutters, smoking hash.'

That spring, Sufi Rogers was also in Spain with her family, visiting her mother's native village in Asturias. Sufi tried to contact Laurie without success. When the Civil War broke out, the Rogers family had to escape on horseback through woods and byways to the Galician seaport of La Coruña, where street fighting was in progress: they waved their British passports and thankfully boarded a Royal Mail ship back home to England.

At the end of April Molly, full of come-hither desire for sun-browned Laurie, suddenly gave up her job at Sutton. 'Lordy, if I'd thrown a bomb in their midst I couldn't have shocked them more. They tried bribery, cajolery – but the moment I started to weaken, I thought of that strange beautiful air you played to me at Putney. Anyway I have shot my bolt. And now, what? I don't know. Maybe I, too, will go abroad . . . I must do something! So answer this letter quickly Laurielee . . .

'Let me tell you of the effect your letter had on me. I dashed into my bedroom, took off my clothes and stood whitely naked as a newly peeled withy stick. Critically I examined myself in the long mirror: thick dark hair, straight sulky brow, grey eyes black-lashed, sadly plain nose, beautifully formed lips, marred by their droop. But my eyes are *alive* Laurie, wary, a little mocking – and my shoulders are most vividly alive – you brushed them into awareness with your lips, so that the bloom of them is peach-smooth to kiss; my breasts are such small eager pulsing things, I think your hands

were made to hold them amigo . . . and my heart is beating a mad tattoo of desire!'

Was her meaning clear? They must soon fulfil the promise they had made, in the long grass of Richmond. 'You may take a dozen women and I give myself to a dozen men, but that does not touch the part of you that is mine, or the part of me that is utterly yours. I wish I were rich enough to bring up a child – I think I want a child of yours more than I've ever wanted anything in my life before. Come to me soon Laurie querido . . . Mariquita.'

But that same month, Laurie had formed a friendship with a female of a very different kind. Wilma Gregory, a spirited Englishwoman aged forty-nine, had bought a house in Puerta de Granada, next to Almuñécar's church. (Today it is the site of the town's Cultural Centre.) It was another lucky encounter for Laurie. Wilma was left-wing, literary, well-connected – she dined with the Laskis, and knew the Roosevelts – and her distinctive personality (and determined temperament) fixed itself on the young poet.

Wilma (*née* Meikle) was born in 1886, youngest of six sisters. Their father, who had farmed in Swanage, died when Wilma was twelve. She gained a scholarship to Somerville, Oxford, where she fell in with Fabians, found herself 'quite good at public speaking', and went down without taking her degree to join the suffragists. In 1914 she offered her services to her heroine, Rebecca West, then living with H.G. Wells at Hunstanton in Norfolk. In 1916 Wilma published a book, *Towards a Sane Feminism*, which Rebecca reviewed with unusual respect as 'one of the few feminist books that have a style': 'neither shrill nor frenzied, but musical as a little river of wit leaping from rock to rock of solid argument'.[15] By the time Rebecca had her baby Anthony (by Wells), Wilma – who had never done housework in her life – was installed as housekeeper-companion. Wells found Wilma intensely irritating ('her presence and manner exasperates the servants') and she got in the way of their lovemaking. 'You see . . . we haven't much more than ten or twelve years more of love and nakedness and all those dear things . . . Clear Wilma out,' Wells wrote to Rebecca in 1916. 'She is an

unreal, discontented person . . . I shall be glad when she is married and off the menu.'[16]

Release came in September 1917 when Wilma married Theodore Gregory (*né* Guggenheim), a lecturer at the London School of Economics. The couple had little in common. 'I was constantly bewildered, and felt more and more lonely,' Wilma recalled, writing later to her sister. 'Well, in some ways I have always been lonely . . . but marriage I found the loneliest state of all.' In 1930 Theo Gregory became a professor in Manchester, and the couple separated amicably: 'Wilma desires to live abroad for the time being,' Theo wrote to Wilma's brother Harold, 'and . . . it is obviously better that she should do as she wishes.' So Wilma went travelling, accepting reluctantly an allowance from her husband but frequently cabling her sisters to send £10.

She had lived in Madrid and in France and then, in 1936, fleeing from wintry weather, arrived in Almuñécar. 'Inconvenient for all forms of civilization,' she told her sister Margery, 'but it has a charm, once one has accustomed oneself to the surrounding filth.' Her flat was overrun with black beetles but it was high up, out of the exhausting sound of the waves; and it had wonderful views from the roof terrace, with a date palm silhouetted against the night sky. She thought she might stay there for the rest of her days. 'One has to put up with a picnic life . . . One can buy nothing civilized in the village and Granada is 94 k away, Málaga 84 by extremely slow bus on dangerous roads which stops at all the villages to deliver the mails. But I find the village life rather fascinating and enjoy being on friendly terms with the peasants and fishermen. This is a strongly Communist region, and we live under more or less Communist regulations.' She lived 'in a manner very much below the standard the locals consider suitable for a foreigner. I hope it will disabuse them of the notion that foreigners have bottomless purses.' But she had a woman in to clean each morning, and was cast as a medicine-woman to the village children, dispensing aspirin and disinfectants, 'my ignorance of medical matters being profound'.

Wilma's niece, Rachel Aldridge, says her aunt was a difficult and prickly person. But her letters reflect a woman of enormous spirit

and occasionally of pellucid if loquacious wisdom. She said she had a French cast of mind: she liked nothing better than argument, and logical discussion of abstract concepts. She also liked to take charge. And when she met Laurie, the aimless young wanderer with poetic and musical skills, she made him her protégé and nurtured him with leech-like devotion. 'I am the entire British colony of Almuñécar in my own person,' Wilma said. 'The English boy poet claims to belong to it also, but he is only lodging in the village and will be leaving soon. I found him living as a vagrant, quite penniless & practically uneducated, with these really remarkable gifts for poetry, & art & music, handicapped by frequent though slight attacks of epilepsy or "le petit mal".'

In May, as Laurie relates, the tension in the village increased. His expedition into the hills, to take a mysterious message to a farmer about seed-potatoes (code for hand-grenades) is an unverifiable tale, but rich in *ambiente*: he waded across a river on horseback which was 'like sitting on a cupboard' and found the farmer's wife ('squatting by the stove and tossing scraps of food to the pig') serving up a pot of *migas* stew: 'a thick porridge of maize sprinkled with dried sardines, tasting of sackcloth'. For part of June, Laurie left Almuñécar with his fiddle, according to his logbook, and busked his way in Granada (staying in Calle Alhóndiga), Almería, Luja, and Murcia. The earliest account Laurie ever gave of this time was the piece he wrote in 1941 for John Lehmann's *Penguin New Writing*,[17] the pencilled draft of which is in his 1941 notebook. He describes a night of playing his fiddle with frenzied and wine-soaked passion ('I am possessed by insane happiness') in a candlelit cellar full of clapping, stomping vineyard workers who sing wild laments of desolation and death. One worker, Gregorio ('I work in the best vineyard in Andalucía, there's more wine in one grape than in the whole of Valdepeñas. But my boss Loja doesn't know or care. The man's a fool'), told Laurie of his hope for the future: 'I hear his articulation of hope, disgust and desire, now fixed in faith on the shape of a new world. He has lived the misery of the past, now he lives the paradise of the future, and behind his eyes is a naïve but steady exultation.'

On 9 July Laurie was still away, but there was a strike in Almuñé-car, and Wilma's political antennae convinced her that war was imminent, '& I'm coward enough to prefer to be as far as possible from the mustard-gas area,' she wrote to Laurie. If Laurie would give up his 'tramping', she said, it would be best to creep back to England. 'My idea would be to try to find a minute cottage or hovel with scrap of garden on the Welsh border – kitchen and bedroom & little more – where I could settle down in solitude & get things written.

'Would there be any attraction to you in the suggestion that you should live in the same village & be nominally my secretary but chiefly potter round looking after the garden, which would be good for your health, & wander off when you wanted to, & think out your "pomes"?'

He would have all her books at his disposal, and her typewriter. The only flaw, she admitted, was the smallness of her income: 'I don't cry it out to the house-tops, but it works out at a little more than thirty pounds a month & that ought to be ample. I'd want us to be communistic about it, using it jointly for our joint needs . . .' She could offer board and lodging and ten shillings a week pocket money, 'better than grinding in an office, or doing heavy work & having no leisure'. She would pay their fares. He could go home to his mother until she found a cottage; or to her sister in Bourne-mouth who 'would love to have you stay for a while'.

Almuñécar, she reported, had already had its own general strike, 'with the aim of forcing the government to own, re-equip & work the derelict sugar-factory by the Cross. If the government does not do what the village wants, the strike is to be resumed on Saturday. I am out of bread, eggs & cigarettes. Paca [the maid] left me just before the strike began. I found she was stealing my stores, including cigarettes, & cheating me wildly over marketing. Paca & her husband are threatening to *pegar* me [knock me about] . . .

'There's not the least danger of your being conscripted; there's *that* consolation in your little trouble. It would be very delightful for me to have you near me . . . I have grave doubts whether your

present open-air life is good for your health: the hardships you must have to put up with in the *posadas*, & also in the cafés, & on the road. And my fear is that Spain is going to be more & more difficult for all foreigners. If there are strikes everywhere, there will be no cafés for you to play in.'

Laurie did return to the spare room in the roof-tower of her house, but almost at once – a week after Wilma wrote her letter – on 16 July, the Spanish Civil War broke out, precipitated by the assassination on 12 July of Calvo Sotelo, minister of finance under Primo de Rivera, the political leader most in touch with the military plotters. His bullet-ridden body was found in the morgue, with signs of violent struggle. The long planned military rising then erupted. 'There were no announcements, no newspapers, just a whispering in the street and the sound of a woman weeping,' as Laurie wrote. Rumours flew in Manolo's bar – of Franco's flight to lead the rebels, of the arrival of Moorish troops, of Franco's death, of fighting in Málaga. Granada was held by the rebels.

'Throughout the afternoon nothing happened . . . Fear lay panting in the street like a dog.' That night, the war called on Almuñécar. A Republican destroyer played its searchlight over the bay. The entire town crowded on to the beach (as still happens today on the night of 15 August, after the procession of the Virgin, when fireworks fill the skies). Suddenly, there were bursting shells and the villagers ran for the hills. As it turned out, the destroyer's captain had mistaken Almuñécar for Altofaro, the rebel-held town ten miles along the coast.

After this terrifying night of shellfire Laurie had one of his fits, as he later confessed when applying to join the International Brigade. His poem 'Words Asleep' was datelined 'Andalucía 1936'.

Now I am still and spent
and lie in a whited sepulchre
breathing dead

but there will be
no lifting of the damp swathes
no return of blood
no rolling away the stone

till the cocks carve sharp
gold scars in the morning
and carry the stirring sun
and the early dust in my ears.

The citizens of Almuñécar confirm that the day after their unsuccessful attempt to take the rebel-held Altofaro, a grand piano was burned (as Laurie later described), but this took place not in front of the church, but in the Plaza Mayor. Laurie describes seeing the body of a young Falangist boy shot dead. (Such a boy was shot, named Julio Mateos.) The church was not set on fire, the villagers say, but most of the holy images were taken to the beach of San Cristobal and tossed on to a great pyre. Manuel Mateos, whose family owned the La Fabriquilla sugar refinery, denies that it was destroyed by the Communists, but they did take over the sugar production.

Wilma's sisters in England were meanwhile writing anxious letters to the Foreign Office on her behalf. On 23 July 1936 her sister Margery received a letter informing her that 'all possible steps are being taken for the protection of British subjects in Spain, although, owing to the irregularity of communication between Spain and the outside world, it is not possible at present to obtain information regarding individual British subjects'.

But on 7 August, W.H. Montague-Pollock wrote from the FO: 'I am directed by Mr Secretary Eden to inform you that Mrs Gregory was evacuated to Gibraltar on the 1st August.' A telegram confirmed this: 'ADMIRALTY REPORT MRS GREGORY EVACU-ATED TO GIBRALTAR.' Wilma – with Laurie in tow – had been taken on board HMS *Blanche*. There was no escort of shouting townspeople, says Manuel Mateos: just three or four people on the beach. The warship delivered Laurie and Wilma – 'the English

writer' in his later account – to Gibraltar. From Gibraltar they sailed to Marseilles by P&O. They disembarked at Marseilles on 7 August, took a train to Paris, and on 9 August 1936 the odd couple embarked at Dieppe for England.

6 | A Hovel with Acreage
1936–7

Laurie and Wilma arrived home in August to an England 'snoozing under old newspapers and knotted handkerchiefs'. They were met at Victoria station by Jack and his girlfriend from Stroud, Phyllis Hawke, and Laurie returned to Slad to receive 'the traditional cosseting of the prodigal'. But the homecoming soon palled.

Leaving Almuñécar had been a betrayal, he often said. He had not chosen Spain as a cause. He had stumbled on the war, simply by happening to be there. But he felt guilty about having abandoned Spain, 'already sealed off by the hypocrisies of non-intervention', and wanted to return to the friends he had made in those noisy cellars full of music and political passion who now faced, he began to realize, a catastrophe. 'I might have given up the idea if I hadn't suddenly fallen in love,' he wrote, 'but the result of that experience, which went deeper than anything I'd known before, only made my situation all the more intolerable.'

This was the version of events he wrote thirty years later in the epilogue to *As I Walked Out One Midsummer Morning* – thus casually eliding the summers of 1936 and 1937 into one. In fact it was not until August 1937 that he met the woman with whom he fell so deeply in love and who made his situation so 'intolerable'. A year passed before the *coup de foudre* struck – a year which he never later mentioned at all. He had no job and was not prepared simply to go home to Slad. Wilma took charge, and carried out the plan she had outlined to him in Spain. She found a home for them both in Padworth, a hamlet twelve miles from Reading comprising a few knots of cottages, a great house, a small church and a rectory.[1] The owner of Rosemary Cottage told Wilma that its legal description was 'a hovel with acreage'. It was tiny, primitive, and remote. No

path led there; they had to wade across a swampy common, and beyond it there was nothing but woodland.

On Wilma's allowance from her husband, she would feed and house Laurie and pay for him to enrol in the art department of Reading University as a half-time student. (All her capital had been sunk into her house at Almuñécar, which she would probably never see again. 'I would not dream of asking for compensation from the poor maltreated Spanish government,' she wrote to her sister Margery that October, 'but if Franco wins, I should make a point of sending him an enormous claim.') She had had to pay for Laurie's passage home, as well as her own, and when they reached London, she had only ten shillings in the world, '& should have had to go to a workhouse' if she had not blustered her bank manager into giving her an overdraft of £10.

'I have practically adopted Laurie, the English boy I rescued from Spain, & he is living here as my nephew,' she told Margery. 'It's pretty obvious that the village, from the rector downwards, are convinced that he is really my son: they say "your son" and then politely correct themselves & say "your nephew". However, they all appear to be sympathetic – especially the rector – & no doubt think he was a "war baby" & therefore excusable.

'He is a very nice boy to have about, most helpful & obliging, & of course I could not live alone in so isolated a cottage. On the other hand, I would not need to live in so primitive a place if I had not made myself responsible for Laurie. But I felt that someone had to do something to make sure that his gifts were not wasted, & there was nobody to do it save myself. Of his three talents, I think his poetry is the most important, but that is not a gift that can be trained, nor does it provide a livelihood; so we decided that art must be his standby.' If she lost her allowance – as she might if the new divorce bill went through, and Theo divorced her for desertion – Laurie could get a well-paid job, if trained for commerce. 'But he may turn out to be too good for that . . .'

The art department at Reading was impressed by Laurie's originality, and by his remarkable capacity as a draughtsman, Wilma

reported. 'His lines have power & clarity & are drawn with extra-ordinary swiftness & ease. His fellow students call him the English Picasso, & the masters treat him with deference & beg him not to think it necessary to conform to their methods if he prefers his own.'

It had taken Wilma weeks to find Rosemary Cottage: 'Just three rooms, all very minute, & a cupboard which serves as larder, pantry & scullery. Outdoor earth closet & woodshed; *nada más* [nothing more] . . . we cook over the open fire, & keep the door open in all weathers; otherwise the fire smokes. The windows are so tiny that it's impossible to see one's reflection in a looking-glass, so we never have a notion of how we're looking, & the place is so dark that we have lamps or candles burning all day long. It's stuffy on warm days, & bitterly cold & damp on others. There are no shops, so we depend on tradesmen's carts. I don't much like the neighbourhood: it's flat, & I hate flat country, & there are pines, & I have always disliked pines.' However, they were lucky to find anything. 'It's worse for Laurie, because he has to walk two miles to catch the bus to Reading, and the connecting buses are few.'

Wilma's days were occupied with domestic chores – 'a deplorable waste of feminine intelligence – and in this case, of masculine intelligence too, since Laurie has to do an equal share'. Cooking, pumping water, heaving logs, and the 'terrific business' of keeping the fire going consumed whole days. 'But the boy behaves as a son to me, & in spite of our loathing of the English climate & of English towns & the English countryside & English people, we stand it well enough.' Laurie found musical friends and formed a quintet. Wilma's chief amusement was a black kitten, 'suspected of witch-craft', which kept her awake by springing high in the air and dancing in circles in her bedroom at night.

Wilma mothered Laurie with relish. He was 'sketchy about meals', while she insisted on regular nourishment. 'He is liable to faint suddenly in the street or in a bus. One always has warning when an attack is threatened; he becomes very dreamy & rather stupid, as though dazed, & one just has to let him lie low for a day or two & see that he does nothing whatever.'

Unlike Laurie's briskly organized benefactress, Molly/Mariquita was in an emotional muddle. She was still recalling Stratford (the magical strains of *L'Après-midi* over the Avon, the nightingales 'pouring liquid silver from their little brown throats'), despite having become engaged to 'Roth', Eric Rothwell from Oldham, a scientist at Exeter University whom she had met at Betty's twenty-first. Laurie poured scorn on this bourgeois move, which made her indignant. 'You didn't miss me in Spain,' she accused, 'though who would miss anyone with the sun bleaching one's eyelashes?' She was full of ambivalence about Laurie, and Jack too. 'Lumme, the pain caused by this engagement seems to go on ad infinitum. I'm fond of Jack, and hate to see him hurt. Yet I know he's not in love with me . . . Oh God I'm so tired – my mind goes round in eternal circles – Ach, let's forget it.'

She had been up to Edge, to consult the trees. 'But my beloved oaks and elms turned blank unseeing faces to me. And from every bole, little devil-faces – curiously like yours – grinned and whispered "Semi-detached", "Two children, one maid and a small car!" all in your voice.'

'Laurie you're cruel! and wrong! For the first year at least (if I marry Roth) we shall be terribly poor – we shall probably live in one room and borrow shillings for the gas-meter.' She was wildly jealous of Laurie's 'hovel with acreage'. 'It so vividly fits the description "A cottage lone and still, With bowers nigh; Shadowy, my woes to still, Until I die." More than anything in the world I want a cottage – crammed with books and a good radiogram. Is the offer of housekeeper still open? I can make chips, and pancakes – If I "abscond" in the near future, may I abscond to you please?' She added a PS that he must call on her friend Alan Bartlett (ex-Jesus, Cambridge), assistant registrar at Reading. 'You've so much in common – music, drawing, literature – and your political views are identical. Sleep well upon thine eyes. Goodnight Laurielee. Mariquita.'

Laurie's taunts about Molly's engagement 'ruined' her birthday in October. She had left his letter until last, as it was so fat and promising among her flowers, books, and fluffy lingerie. But Laurie

had written with acid pen, mocking her cosy future, 'hurting me as only you can hurt. I might point out that I'm not "another man's wife". I never entered your world. You took me to the top of Box Hill and showed me your world spread beneath it – "Only," you said, "I'd have to teach you the password in order that you might enter – and I really haven't time." Then you laughed, waved your hand and sailed gaily away, leaving me wedged between two worlds – belonging to neither.'

By contrast, Laurie made Wilma's November birthday – her fiftieth – highly memorable. 'The day began,' she wrote to her sister, 'when I entered the sitting-room at 7.30 a.m. & found a huge fire already blazing & the room decorated with paper ropes & festoons & union jacks from Woolworths, & my portrait (drawn a few days previously by Laurie) placed on the mantelpiece like a sacred icon, with lighted candles on either side of it &, beneath, a marvellous Spanish effusion of congratulations & affection.'

Laurie's 'exotic foreign friends' from the university had arranged a birthday luncheon party in Reading. The students had arrived, presented Wilma with a clock, and made pretty speeches about not having thought her more than forty, '& we raced into Reading in a ramshackle, madly driven car belonging to one of them, & were very gay indeed; we almost forgot that we were in England'.

At Christmas Wilma packed Laurie off to Slad as it would be too dull in Padworth. Left 'alone with the kitten, in the immense silence of our woods & swamps', she reported to Margery that Laurie had had several of his bad turns recently. Also, he had turned rebellious. 'Towards the end of the term he refused to pay any attention to the master of the life-class – and the authorities applauded his refusal & said his originality must on no account be warped. So now he is encouraged to follow his own bent, which is incomprehensible to the non-modern art mind. Our sitting-room is hung with his productions; some of these seem to me a little nightmarish, but they are fun.'

Among the friends Laurie visited that Christmas – he did not call on Molly – were Sufi Rogers and her family. 'Our family found he had changed much,' Sufi's brother Richard recalls, 'and he

seemed to have a great compassion for the people of Spain who were loyal to the ruling government and against Franco's fascist rebel forces. So it was no surprise to us that he was determined to go back.' (Within a year most of the Rogers family returned to Argentina, where Sufi married an Argentine. In 1978 there was a family reunion in Gloucestershire for Sufi's aunt Ethel Rogers's ninetieth birthday – when Laurie presented Ethel with a teapot.)

Wilma told Margery that she too regretted not staying on in Spain to see the war through, and might return. By January the cold weather, Laurie's 'flu, and the hovel's discomfort had driven them to take digs at 80 London Road in Reading itself – 'a very dull town'. She wanted Laurie to see more of his student friends, and not to brood on the Spanish troubles. 'He has been talking of joining the International Column & though if I had a son of my own I should wish him to be among the defenders of Madrid, I think the case is quite different when a boy has a chronic malady like Laurie's and has, besides, his freakish talents for three arts.' If he went, the money she had spent on him would be wasted, she added.

In January 1937, Laurie did attempt to get away to Spain 'through the proper channels' but was turned down. He told Molly he might go back to Spain and, desolate, she launched into one of her flights: 'Laurie oh Laurielee, reading your letter this morning a cold choking fear clutched my throat. My heart broke into a million pieces, splintered in the mocking sunshine and fell among the gold crocuses. How can you resist the Spring? Doesn't your heart cry "Oh Earth, Earth beloved!" What can I say to one who travels alone, aloof and invulnerable along roads undreamed? I could say "Take me with you" but loneliness is essential to you, you would smile gently at me.

'You have been the well-loved stranger within the gates of those who love you. If you leave us, we can do nothing to delay you, save with the sorrow of our eyes, the wistfulness of our lips. Betty, Pat, Jack and I have honoured you with the hospitality of our hearts; we have given you much, but what we gave you returned a thousandfold. Always we shall be grateful to the gods for letting us

know you. Perhaps we knew you could not tarry for long with us.'

Could she come too, and work as a nurse in Spain? 'It's the only way of getting out there that I can think of. No, I am not enamoured of bloody death, and I'm even more terrified of being maimed – but Laurie I'm *dead* here, dead from the neck up! *Please* let me see you again – even if it's only to say "Buenas Noches Amigo". We can never escape each other, Lorenzo mío. For now, and always, Mariquita.'

By March she had packed her bag, walked out of her job and gone home to Gloucester where the words of his Spanish diary (which Laurie had sent her) 'beat like hailstones' on her heart. She must see him again. 'We'll take a bus up to Edge and walk over the Whitehill Valley for a picnic lunch. We'll talk and talk and view each other curiously through a haze of cigarette smoke . . . and we'll laugh, and sing old songs, and live! I need the sun so badly Laurie – my blood aches for it. I'm about to burn my boats. Where shall I go? – Arrivederci caro mío, Mariquita.'

She duly gave back to Eric Rothwell his emerald engagement ring ('please don't crow!') and her letters became increasingly intense and full of sentiments such as 'Life's so short Laurie – or is it terribly terribly long?' But she was not replacing Roth with Laurie. 'No, you never told me I was essential to you – that would have made all the difference. But Laurie, to you I have never been more than a violin obbligato, high and sweet and delicate, in tune to the throb of your heartbeat, but no more essential to you than the nightingales were essential to the flow of the Stratford river!'

By May, she had taken back her old job in Sutton, helping Mrs Whitelaw with her handicapped daughter. While Nat Gonella played 'Georgia on My Mind' on the wireless, she wrote beseeching Laurie to join her and Betty for a reunion in London, to see Shakespeare from the gallery of the Old Vic. The three met in June, and Laurie played the girls his Spanish songs. 'Laurili, Was it a vision, or a waking dream?' wrote Molly. Betty ('the spoilt baggage') had willed it to be perfect, and she always got her own way. 'Whoo! it's a crazy world in which we live Laurieli . . . I think I'm a little mad tonight.' She imagined herself in Spain, a gypsy

woman 'with dishevelled black hair, dark eyes, and a mouth red as the poppies in her hair, and brown bare feet, leaning against a great bare rock on a parched hillside singing those songs in a loud raucous voice . . .' Later, Molly went to see him in Reading, met Wilma and liked her instantly, and invited Laurie to visit her in Sutton ('I shall be alone all day . . .'), offering to pay his fare from Reading. 'Goodnight amigo. The wind will always blow you in my direction. Adiós, Mariquita.'

But the wind never did blow them together, except as good friends – because Laurie was about to fall seriously in love.

After his summer term finished at Reading, Laurie joined Wilma in July in her caravan on a site owned by her family, the Lone Pine Camp at Ferndown, near Bournemouth. There, Wilma was fighting a losing battle with rats: 'I gave them handsome meals soaked in Lysol, but the rats lapped it up and were none the worse.' She wanted her family to meet Laurie, she told her sister, 'for he's such a wise child & really amazing when one remembers – which one seldom does – his origin'. Her niece Rachel recalls the young man who shambled shyly out of her aunt's caravan that summer, looking much younger than his twenty-three years. As he later recalled, 'In my twenties I was thin, hungry, and gorgeous.'[2]

Laurie had survived his scrape with the authorities, the Vice-Chancellor telling him that 'in confidence' he agreed with him, Wilma reported. 'My impression is they are anxious not to offend Laurie . . . maybe in case he turns out to be some sort of genius. Still, I have written him a stern auntish letter, with tongue in cheek.' Wilma had also tried (she recalled later) 'to protect a succession of girls from Laurie's fascinations'. A doctor had told her that her attempts to persuade Laurie to be chaste were useless: 'all epileptics are exceedingly sensual and passionate, and it's impossible to restrain them'. At the Lone Pine Camp, Wilma introduced him to other caravanners. They were going to Cornwall, and would take Laurie with them.

It was there, on the beach at Gunwalloe on the Cornish coast, on 23 August 1937, that he met the beautiful Lorna Wishart, and was bewitched.

It was early one morning, and Laurie was alone on the sands, playing his violin, when Lorna saw him, while she was taking a walk. She stopped and said (like Miss Havisham to Pip), 'Boy, come and play for me.'

'She was married and had two young children,' Laurie wrote in *As I Walked Out*. 'She was rich and demandingly beautiful, extravagantly generous with her emotions but fanatically jealous, and one who gave more than she got in love.' She was also the sister of Mary Campbell. It seems a preposterously Dickensian coincidence that he should meet by chance a second Garman girl within two years, but there it is.

Lorna was twenty-six, the youngest and by general consent the most beautiful of all the Garman girls, born 11 January 1911. She was twelve when their father Dr Walter Garman died, at which point life at Oakeswell Hall – piano lessons before breakfast, and prayers with the maids – dramatically altered. Lorna had been at boarding school, hating it; she jumped over the tennis net with glee when she realized that the death of her father meant she must leave. The family had relied totally on Dr Garman's income. Their mother was a dreamer; it was the governess, Miss Thomas ('Tony'), who took over the practicalities, and kept the remaining children fed and clothed. They had the run of their father's well-stocked library, but the younger ones went somewhat wild.

So Lorna, unrestricted by parental rule, enjoyed exceptional freedom in her teenage years, 'roaring about Herefordshire [where her mother moved to] going to dances on the back of boys' motorbikes'.³ At fourteen she met Ernest Wishart – always known as 'Wish' – who was reading law at Cambridge with her brother Douglas (and with Salvador Allende, future president of Chile). She married Wish at sixteen, and had her first son, Michael, at seventeen, in 1928. Wish was a Communist, but a rich one: his father, Sir Sidney Wishart, Sheriff of the City of London, had extensive farming estates in Sussex. The couple first lived in Brunswick Square, sharing a Georgian house with Gerald Barry, editor of the *News Chronicle*. Wish formed a publishing company, Wishart & Co. (later the Marxist publisher Lawrence & Wishart), and

founded in 1925 the literary monthly *The Calendar of Modern Letters*, edited by the radical poet Edgell Rickword and Lorna's brother Douglas Garman.

'My mother, who was almost a child, treated me as a doll,' Lorna's son Michael wrote in his memoirs.[4] Having married so young, Lorna was ready, when she met Laurie, to catch up on the youthful fling she had missed. 'When Lorna discovered her powers,' her daughter says, 'a floodgate opened. She was wild; she was rampant.' For Laurie, a glance from the blazing blue eyes was enough, as in Browning's 'She should never have looked at me/ If she meant I should not love her.' 'We Garman girls all have these eyes,' Lorna's niece Anna Campbell told me. 'They arrest people's attention. They are very large: "*Ils dévorent sa figure*," as a French woman said of mine. They seem to drive people (not only men) slightly dotty. I know this happened with Lorna.'

Men were constantly falling head over heels in love with Lorna. The writer Llewelyn Powys, for one, was locked in adoration. She had an extraordinarily magnetic, seductive power. Molly and Betty Smart, who met her later, found her 'staggeringly beautiful and most unconventional', Betty says. (Lorna told the more homely Betty: 'I was jealous of you until I met you – and now I'm not.') 'And of course money was no problem to her, while we were all relatively poor. She gave off a flavour of strength, or concentration – like a strong whisky. It may or may not have been goodness, but it was certainly concentrated.'

'I adored my mother,' her son Michael wrote. He remembered lying in bed on a summer evening as a boy. 'My mother leans over me. Dressed for dancing in clinging sequins, which sparkle like her vast ultramarine eyes, she resembles a sophisticated mermaid. Embryonic Oedipus receives the kiss of life. After mother's departure, I bury my face into the cool pillow where the scent of Caron's Fleurs de Rocailles lingers. I listen for the familiar purr of the chocolate brown Bentley, crunching on the gravel driveway. My mother, always alone, is speeding through the darkling hawthorn heading for nightclubs which assume, in my half-asleep loneliness, vague Xanadus of Kubla Khan . . .'

Lorna had innate style: everything she did seemed to create an aura of romance. 'It was more than charm; she illuminated everything around her,' says her former daughter-in-law Anne Dunn. 'She was a transformer: if she looked at something it seemed to gain merit in one's eyes.' As a girl she had been absurdly shy. When Wish took her to restaurants, she would sit with a napkin over her head. But she learned to intimidate shopkeepers and waiters, and could at times turn almost sadistically cruel. Laurie's diary, later, describes Lorna having words with a restaurant manageress over a dish of curry. 'L's tactics are brilliant, witty, and so unexpected, so unwomanly if you like, that her opponents are invariably annihilated.'

Those who knew Lorna then describe her as 'androgynous', 'feline', 'lynx-like', 'a tiger-woman'. Later, Lucian Freud painted her in an ocelot coat, which compounded the resemblance. She was tall and lean, and moved with a graceful feline stride: she loped, she prowled, slightly round-shouldered, head down. She was athletic, physically fearless, loved walking, lived out of doors, swam in the sea in winter, had picnics on Boxing Day, rode proficiently and drove fast. Her husky voice had the rasp of gin and cigarettes. Laurie found her irresistible.

'Her small head is most unusual & really beautiful,' Laurie wrote, four years later, 'half-boyish because of her hair, half-Latin because of her eyes, strong in colour, cared for and yet with a slightly rough casual beauty about it. I feel she should be the wife of a very brilliant artist, or the slave of some old sensual Indian poet. Only such men would properly appreciate her.' A very Garman assumption: that women should be Muses and acolytes to creative men.

At first, during the Cornish holiday, Wish and Laurie got on well together. Wish, who apart from his political dedication to Communism loved trees and kept bees, was a man of integrity and considerable patience. He was determined to hold the family together, as he watched his wife falling in love with Laurie. And Lorna, ultimately, was totally dependent on Wish. Having lost her father, she needed a corner of stability in her life; Wish, nine years older, was her rock.

(Fifty years later, journalists were still trying to discover from Laurie the identity of the mysterious woman who had sent him pound notes soaked in Chanel No. 5 when he went off to the Spanish Civil War. One, William Greaves, asked Laurie in 1987, 'Who is the unnamed woman whose passionate attentions enlivened the weeks between leaving Spain and returning across the Pyrenees to rejoin the Civil War?' 'How devious of you to notice,' replied Laurie. 'I don't think I've ever been asked. It's right at the tail end of the book. What very nice salmon this is.' Had he met her since? persisted Greaves. 'That's another book,' said Laurie, 'which may be written one day.'

'For a septuagenarian with a memory as acute as it is poetic,' commented Greaves, 'Slad village school's most famous old boy has strangely uncharacteristic moments of absent-mindedness.'[5])

One evening soon after they met, Laurie confided to Lorna that he planned to go back to Spain. Perhaps he thought it would be a way of impressing her. 'Of course, I tried to persuade her that I would be doing it for her, but this wasn't true and she knew it. All the same, it was partly our entanglement that drove me, the feeling of over-indulgence and satiety brought on by too much easy and unearned pleasure . . .'

Meanwhile Wilma, knowing nothing of Laurie's new emotional entanglement, was arranging to take him to France, to study at the École des Beaux Arts in Montpellier. He claimed later, in *As I Walked Out*, that 'I worked my way down through France, heading in the direction of the Pyrenees', but in fact, Wilma took him (and paid his train fare) to Montpellier. In September 1937 – just as brother Jack was leaving Slad to attend the Regent Street Poly, and to live in Laurie's old digs in Putney – Wilma and Laurie sailed from Southampton to Le Havre, took the train to Montpellier and arrived, exhausted, at Le Collège des Écossais, a grand folly built by the botanist Sir Patrick Geddes. The barrack-like building, part Scottish baronial and part Provençal château in style, was now a hotel run by Geddes's son and daughter. It had huge libraries and salons and enormous bedrooms, and a meagre staff of housekeeper, cook and gardener. It was cheap thanks to the ill-health of the

franc. 'The garden is a desert for lack of water,' Wilma wrote to her sister. 'The only guests are a mad Russian woman doctor of psychology, a young French engineer, Laurie & myself.'

Laurie launched himself into the French language with bold insouciance. 'Twelve days ago he had not uttered a word of French in his life. He is making excellent progress, having no social timidity whatever, so that blunders do not distress him in the smallest degree. Yesterday when I came down to breakfast I found him conversing volubly with the housekeeper – making a thousand mistakes, but getting his meaning across,' Wilma reported. Old Colonel Russell, the author of *Brighter French*, was giving him a daily lesson for a risibly small sum. Laurie's violin smoothed the way for him as always. The French engineer accompanied him on the piano, while the mad Russian woman listened, 'and the rest of the day, the boy is producing with amazing rapidity more & more remarkable drawings'.

Observers versed in the effects of love will detect here, as Wilma did not, the frantic energy and glowing aura of a lover with a plan. Laurie was due to enrol at the École des Beaux Arts in October. But by then, the hotel's threadbare comforts had lost their charm, and Wilma now doubted whether Laurie would go to the art school. 'For its sake chiefly we have come to Montpellier, but now Laurie is inclined to despise all art schools, and maybe he is right. He still has a lot to learn (in my opinion) concerning the technique of oils. Alas, one can lead a student to art school, but one cannot make him paint! But the child is turning out amazingly original stuff & is perhaps best left to himself.'

In November Wilma told her sister that they were leaving Montpellier and going to Perpignan. Laurie was obsessed by Spain; Wilma felt helpless. She suspected that he might press on to the Pyrenees and try to get himself smuggled through. She had told him that he was far too late to enlist, that his 'malady' would debar him from any army, that the Spaniards did not want any more volunteers. 'But Laurie will not believe without definite proof that it is impossible for him to cross the frontier & join the International Column.

'Of course, if he were my son, and healthy, I should want him to fight for Spain.

'But the fact that he is not makes me feel, in a way, more responsible. He would almost certainly get shell-shocked, and his health depends on his being well fed and not undergoing any strain.' (Laurie had become cocksure, she said, having been persuaded by a doctor that he could control his condition by will-power.) 'He forgets that his improvement since last March is due to the care I have taken of him, & his freedom from worry. When he was living the vagrant life in Spain, ill-fed and inadequately clothed, he had many fits.'

To distract him, Wilma had typed out Laurie's poems and sent them to T.S. Eliot at Faber & Faber. Eliot replied on 9 November 1937 to Wilma in Montpellier:

> *Dear Madam,*
>
> *I have read your long and interesting letter about your young friend Laurie Lee, and sympathize with your interest and anxieties about him. It is with regret that I must say that his poems do not seem to me, so far, remarkable enough to justify our undertaking their publication. This is, however, only the opinion of one man, who often feels that excessive reading of manuscript verse may have dulled his sensibility, and I therefore advise you to make a fresh attempt elsewhere. I suggest your showing the poems to Mr Richard Church of Messrs J.M. Dent & Sons, Aldine House, Bedford Street, WC2. I shall not meanwhile mention to Mr Church the fact that I have seen these poems.*
>
> *Yours very truly, T.S. Eliot.*

But within days of their arrival in Perpignan, without telling Wilma, Laurie left their hotel and headed not for the Pyrenees but for Martigues, to meet Lorna, who had driven across France and was about to take him to the house of her sister Helen.

Wilma, restraining her anger, was perplexed: she had just spent 260 francs on Laurie's *carte d'identité* and he had left behind the warm clothing she had bought him that very day, in which to travel to England.

And it was in Martigues that Laurie first saw Helen Garman's daughter Kathy, 'a stumpy, wriggly, golden-curled little girl of five, who spoke a slurred incomprehensible French dialect'.[6] Helen, as recounted earlier, had gone out to visit her sister Mary in 1929, and had met and married Roy Campbell's friend, the handsome fisherman Marius Polge, son of a Norwegian sea-captain. Tall and blond, 'like Jean Marais only better looking',[7] Marius stood out from the small dark Mediterranean fishermen. Kathy today remembers the smell of him, the aroma of salt and heat, as he took her fishing, in a coracle across the canal, to winch the enormous nets of fish that slithered over her feet.

There is a photograph – hanging in the bathroom today at Slad – taken that week in Martigues. It shows handsome young Laurie holding little Kathy (a solemn, intelligent-looking child) on his knee, in the garden of Helen's house above the Étang de Berres, the lake whose canals link it to the Mediterranean. In the original picture, there was another figure beside Laurie: Kathy's Aunt Lorna.

'I remember the child sitting in my lap, squirming her plump body against me and looking up at me with brilliant slit eyes of squinting blue. As she licked the sugar of a bun from her fat pink lips, she studied me with intense regard. I don't know who she thought I was – this crumpled twenty-two-year-old English stranger – but it was then, she swears, she decided to marry me.'

Laurie wrote this in his 1983 book, *Two Women*, a celebration of his wife Kathy and daughter Jessy. He was actually twenty-three at the time, and of course he fails to mention that he was accompanied by the child's Aunt Lorna, with whom he was enjoying an ecstatically amorous Provençal interlude. As his diary for 23 October 1939 recalls: 'Two years ago we were in Martigues, drugged with coffee, sunlight, tobacco, pine resin, fever and l'amour . . .' Four years later he was remembering 'our uncontrollable nervous happiness on the road to Istres'. In *As I Walked Out*, he describes how his rich girlfriend 'suddenly turned up again' to give him 'a week of passionate farewell. A week of hysteria too – embracing in ruined huts, on the salt-grass at the edge of the sea, gazing out at the windswept ocean while gigantic thunderstorms wheeled slowly

round the distant mountains . . . Our love was more violent than ever . . .' Clearly it was a rapturous time, and brought on one of his fevers, which Lorna soothed.

'To be in love, of course,' wrote Laurie later in life, 'is to take on the penthouse of living, that topmost toppling tower, perpetually lit by the privileged radiance of wellbeing which sets one apart from the nether world. Born, we are mortal, dehydrated, ordinary: love is the oil that pumps one up, dilates the eyes, puts a glow on the skin, lifts us free from the weight of time, and helps us see in some other that particular kind of beauty which is the crown of our narcissism.

'. . . At best, love is simply the slipping of a hand in another's, of knowing you are where you belong at last, and of exchanging through the eyes that all-consuming regard which ignores everybody else on earth.'

Within a few days Laurie, in a display of bravado, set off alone to Ceret on the Spanish border, leaving Lorna *distraite*, Annie in a panic, and poor Wilma in Perpignan anxious, bewildered and angry.

7 | A Winter of War
   ## 1937–8

There is no more romantic, passionate and moving interlude in twentieth-century history, nor one that more engaged the emotions of writers, than the Spanish Civil War. Writers and poets were inflamed by the Spanish war as they might once have been by the French Revolution. It was never simply a struggle between Left and Right. But a people's government, intent on bringing to Spain an end to poverty and inequality, education for the masses, freedom of the press, was being challenged by an alliance of the military, the aristocracy and the Church, with Nazi Germany and Fascist Italy on their side. And they murdered poets. Federico García Lorca was one of hundreds murdered in 1936. The British government remained neutral, and for writers Spain became an irresistible cause. George Orwell, John Dos Passos, André Malraux, Stephen Spender, Arthur Koestler, Ernest Hemingway, Simone Weil, W. H. Auden and Miles Tomalin all went out to Spain, and wrote about it. Gerald Brenan was already there. Churchill's nephew Esmond Romilly, and the artist Paul Hogarth, went out at the age of eighteen. Julian Bell, who was killed in Spain, was only seventeen when he left: his aunt Virginia Woolf wrote to her sister: 'I suppose it's a fever in the blood of the younger generation which we can't possibly understand . . .'

In Britain, enlisting to fight in Spain was punishable by two years' imprisonment. Yet 2,000 British volunteers fought on Spanish soil, and 500 failed to come back. Volunteers slipped into Spain from all parts of Europe, America and Canada, most crossing the Pyrenees at night, arriving footsore and frozen, to be greeted by shouts of 'salud' and 'no pasarán'. Some were lured by the adventure. But after the horrific casualties at the battle of Jarama in 1937, new arrivals knew that death or injury was very likely.

Laurie was neither politically obsessed, nor the belligerent type.

He always said afterwards that he had gone to Spain because he felt guilty for having left; he had a debt of honour to his Spanish friends. This was probably true. But he was also making a supremely romantic gesture straight out of the medieval lays of courtly love.

Though alone, Laurie was just one of 912 volunteers who crossed into Spain in December 1937. 'Laurie slipped across the frontier to join the International Brigade last Sunday,' Wilma wrote to her sister Margery from her hotel in Perpignan on 12 December, 'but as yet there is no means of communicating with him . . .'

She admired the boy's pluck, of course, but she was furious with him. He was throwing away his chances and making the last sixteen months seem a waste of her time and money: 'He has not behaved quite fairly to me,' she said, 'for it seems now that his whole object in coming to France was to find his way to Spain.' She thought he had given up 'the Spanish scheme', and was going back to London with her, 'until', she added angrily, 'a stupid romantic woman in England, who has fallen wildly in love with him, telephoned one night.

'The woman had been telephoning from England night after night, to Montpellier while we were there, & to Perpignan after we moved here, regardless of expense in the Windsor–Simpson style. That morning, we had bought warm clothing, for England; that night he was once more determined to go to Spain. The telephone conversation that night decided things, & my own opinion is that the boy was scared stiff by the wild, romantic, preposterous situation created by her, & fled to Spain to escape it.'

(In fact, Lorna's call at the end of November had told Laurie that she was coming to the south of France and would meet him at Martigues.) In his diary for 13 December 1943, Laurie wrote: 'Six years ago, almost to the day, I crossed the frontier into Spain. What proud, muddle-headed days they were!'

As to how he had managed to get over the border, Wilma had learned that it was 'quite easy': 'One gives a guide a tip to conduct one across the frontier; at night, the guard waits until the French guards have passed, then beckons, and one slips across. At the other side one meets the Spanish guards, gives up one's passport to them

and one is sent to Barcelona if one is volunteering for military service.' Wilma's days and nights of misery, 'when I imagined that the boy might have lost his way in a blizzard, perhaps had a fall & died of exposure' had been, it seemed, 'unnecessary'.

At this point in her letter, Wilma broke off: 'the romantic lady' (Lorna) had telephoned her, to assure her that Laurie would soon be sent back, because foreign volunteers were no longer accepted by the Spanish government. But Wilma was sceptical. 'She has made such a mess of things for my poor foolish Laurie,' she added caustically to her sister, '& maybe it's my prejudice that made me dislike her voice on the telephone; I was surprised that so musical a boy had ever been attracted by her.'

Despite her anxiety, Wilma undoubtedly enjoyed the busybody role she now assumed, to get Laurie out of Spain. She wrote to Clement Attlee ('Major Attlee was kindness itself. He is all stirred up & ready to insist on your immediate return by the Spanish Government,' she wrote to Laurie) and to Harry Pollitt, head of the British Communist Party, who was going to Barcelona on a political visit just before Christmas. She badgered the Spanish consul, the police, the Left committees, and sent letters all across Spain from Barcelona to Valencia addressed to 'an English volunteer named Laurence Edward Alan Lee', with a description of him in Spanish, and the fact that he carried a violin. She got the Spanish consul to write to Indalecio Prieto, Spanish Minister of Defence, about Laurie's epilepsy. She rang Jack, asking him to go at once to Laurie's doctor in Reading to get a medical certificate saying he was unfit for military service. She wrote to Laurie at enormous length every day, sometimes twice.

She was annoyed with the boy, but 'I understand so well how irresponsible an epileptic is – volatile, as the Victorians would say, and also damned obstinate. The boy simply can't help it, and one must accept him as he is: exceedingly troublesome, not always candid, but honest, very warmhearted and very lovable.'

Wilma was right to anticipate the likelihood of fits. Laurie had already had two, as recorded in the International Brigades file written at Tarazona on 23 December 1937:

Laurence A. Lee. English. Age 23. Arrived in Albacete 15.12.37.

Father civil servant employed by British Government in their Customs and Excise Dept. His mother's address: The Slad, Stroud, Gloucestershire.

Has no fixed profession, but has worked as a clerk.

Was studying commercial art, with view to making it his proffession [*sic*]. Was studying at Reading University. Went to France on Sept 18th ostensibly to continue studies, actually to come to Spain.

His own statement:

'I stayed a while in Montpellier, and then moved to Perpignan and from Perpignan slipped through to Ceret and across the Pyrenees on Sunday 5th December.'

He did not come through the usual channels. He had tried to do so in January of this year when things were much stricter and he was turned down. He gives recommendations which seem to show that he is perfectly reliable. One of the men he knows is the present Commander of the British Battalion [i.e. Fred Copeman, strike organizer on the Putney building site, now attached to the staff of the 15th Brigade]. We have not yet been able to check this, however. His reason for avoiding normal channels is that he did not want to be turned down and did not want anybody to go to the expense of sending him out, because he could not be sure of his physical fitness for the fighting out here. He paid his own fare out, and has enough cash to pay his own fare back if necessary.

He was in Spain from July 1935 to August 1936. He was then at Almuneca [*sic*] near Motril. He says that they were then shelled occasionally and this brought on the epileptic fits from which he suffers. Because of this he was evacuated by a British destroyer in August of 1936. His sympathies however were all with the Republic and he resolved to come out as soon as he had recovered. As stated above he tried to come in January, but was turned down.

After a year without any fits, he thought he was perfectly OK and decided to come definitely and here he is.

He had two epileptic fits in Figueras, which he attributes to the increased excitement of being in Spain and of his journey over the mountains.

He seems to be a fairly good violinist and artist. At present he is assisting in the cultural work at Tarazona.

It seems clear that . . . being, generally speaking, physically weak, he will not be of any use at the front. He agrees that the added excitement would be too much for him.

On the other hand he seems a perfectly sincere comrade, who is very sympathetic to the Spanish government.

His family at home are making a great deal of trouble at him being here and are demanding his return.

It was on Christmas Day at the Hôtel Regina in Perpignan that Wilma had her first letter from Laurie, written ten days earlier. His letter cannot have mentioned anything of being imprisoned. 'All the loads in the world fell from my mind when I got your letter this morning,' Wilma wrote. 'Darling Laurie, you've no idea what a to-do we have made in our efforts to find you, and how we worried the authorities in England, France and Spain. I had nightmare days & nights imagining you lost in the Pyrenees.' She had now telegraphed Lorna and Annie; and Jack was with Annie, 'but poor Lorna has nobody and her letters are terribly unhappy . . . what can I say to console her?' Laurie told her he had reached Valencia, and was going to Albacete. 'I am very much relieved to hear that Albacete is a training centre, and that you certainly will not be sent to the front for several months yet. But if you are already in the International Brigade, I do not understand why you have not been given a regimental number.'

She urged him to return at once, reminded him that he was 'not strong enough to take part in the war' and hoped that they would discover his 'malady' before he got anywhere near the front.

'Oh Laurie, my dear, my very dear Laurie! You have no idea how much I blame myself for having brought you to France . . . I think your mother & Jack will never forgive me; only Lorna understands. I wish you were ill; then you'd be sent back & I could take you straight back to England.'

As Wilma told her sister, she entirely approved of Laurie's wish to fight fascism: she was contemptuous of young men (such as her nephews in Bournemouth) who remained in comfort at home instead of volunteering in Spain. Laurie knew she considered

physical courage the most important quality in men. He might even have found it humiliating, she conceded, to be constantly reminded by her that his 'malady' would exempt him.

'All the same, knowing that [he is] peculiarly liable to shell-shock ... I hope that he will [be discharged] before he is sent to the front.' But Laurie's doctor in Reading sent word that having him withdrawn against his will might be more damaging to his ego and his nervous system than a prolonged exposure to war. 'So I had to send telegrams and air-mail letters all over the place cancelling my demands for his return.'

Meanwhile Lorna (now considered 'sweet and brave' by Wilma) had been to see Harry Pollitt just before he left for Barcelona, '& he promised to try to find you,' Wilma told Laurie, 'to ask if you could be transferred to non-combatant work. I'd pray, if I had anything to pray to, that this may have been managed.' She might even try to intercept Pollitt at Barcelona station herself.

The news of the Republican advance at Teruel was 'magnificent', said Wilma, although the insurgents might hold out in part of the town, as they had in Toledo and Oviedo. (The battle of Teruel, the grim, walled city high on rocky bluffs, known for its hard winters, had begun on 15 December, in bitter cold, eighteen degrees below zero. A four-day blizzard left four feet of snow: men on both sides suffered frostbite, and lacked water, food and medical supplies, as trucks were stalled and planes grounded. In early January Teruel was taken, a victory widely reported and celebrated.) Perhaps, said Wilma, success in Teruel would make Conservative circles in England realize that they had backed the wrong horse in encouraging Franco. 'Oh, the harm the present British government has done & continues to do, all over the world! Ethiopia & Spain & China have all been their victims.'

The refrain of 'your loving aunt, Wilma' was 'I don't want you to be in any fighting, my very dear child.' No real aunt or mother could have fussed more over her boy. Was he getting enough to eat? Could she send him thick socks and shirts? He ought to have a good coat with a sheepskin lining. A medical certificate was waiting for him the minute he wished to be released from service.

If he had lost his violin, she would buy him another. Also a new camera, she promised. An overcoat and warm trousers would await his return to Perpignan. She had been planning a Christmas in the mountains, with skiing lessons for him. 'You are very brave & splendid, but I'd so much rather you were safe. Bless you my darling! . . . As soon as you return, we'll move on, don't you think? You see, darling, I am sure you won't be able to stand the strain much longer.'

What was Laurie doing all this time? As the contemporary documents show, he had arrived with a motley crew of International Brigade volunteers at Figueras, and had been taken to Albacete. He had arrived in Spain at a time when the 15th Brigade was acutely short of British volunteers, and the war was running against the Republic.

An undated handwritten report from Figueras says: 'I will say of the whole group of English only about 6 of them may be loyal, the rest I class as opportunists and adventurers, they may be alright but they need a lot of lecturing, particularly on morale, as they dont no [sic] what it mean's, this is the best report I can give in plain words, I hope it is satisfactory, I will add that this group was a disgrace to all the other comrade's (foreign) I wish you will report the matter to the Party in London . . .'

The report is signed 'Fraternally yours, Comrade R. Doyle'. Bob Doyle was a bold young Dubliner who had stowed away on a boat from Marseilles to get into Spain, and later in 1937 took a party of volunteers across the border from Carcassonne. Over the page he goes on: 'Also I report that Comrade Laurence Lee has on two occasions of the journey taking some kind of fits. I may add that this Comrade's conduct was excellent, that although weak he showed his willingness to comply with regulations.'

On a list compiled by the Figueras Delegation of the International Brigades of comrades sent to Albacete, dated 11 December 1937, are the names of Booth, Buckley, Corbett, Goodison, Kenna, Smith, Tompkins – and Lee, Laurence.

Another report is from Constantino Dubac,[1] also denouncing the drunken and undisciplined behaviour of Messrs Booth, Corbett,

Smith and Tighe – 'No political understanding, only adventurists going after three meals a day.' 'Undesirable.' 'Rotten, lumpen element.' 'Now at Pontones with venereal disease.' 'Deserted from Jarama.' 'Rotten, absolutely demoralized element.' His report (dated 15 December) goes on: 'Lawrence Lee [*sic*] suffers from epilepsy. He has had an attack at Figueras after one year of normalcy. His conduct is exemplary, willing to do his best for the revolution. Politically a communist. He can, I think, be used to great advantage at some base where the work is not strenuous as he seems a responsible person and trustworthy.'

Laurence Lee is listed as arriving at the Tarazona base on 16 December 1937. That morning No. 2 Company was being trained in bayonet practice, grenade-throwing and Spanish. The next day, 17 December, a handwritten report has the following entry: 'Departures: Lee to Culture by Personnel Office.'

On 28 December the Cultural Commission was instructed to send 'Comrade Lee' and others to see the doctor 'between the hours 1 and 4'.

By 1 January 1938, news of Laurie reached Wilma, still in Perpignan but now at the Hôtel de la Loge. She wrote to her nephew and niece, Richard and Eleanor Aldridge: 'As we now know Laurie had a very bad fit two days after his arrival in Valencia, his brother and I have renewed our applications to Major Attlee for his prompt return. In consequence . . . he was refused admission to the International Brigade, and is now attached to the Spanish Red Cross – or rather, to the Socorro Rojo at Albacete [the address Laurie had given Wilma in his letter: Socorro Rojo, 270 Plaza Altazona, Albacete].' Wilma's next letter to Laurie asked him: 'I see that you have not actually said that you are doing Red Cross work; you merely gave the Socorro Rojo as your address. Are you not allowed to say what it is that you are doing?' Without Laurie's reply one can only conclude that, whether or not he was actually working for the Socorro Rojo, this was where he received his letters while in Albacete.

'Albacete is on the high plateau. Laurie writes that the cold is worse

than any he has ever known; snow and sleet, fog in the morning, ice in the streets, terrific winds, and no mountains to give shelter. I had warned him of what Spanish winters can be like, but one can never really imagine such horrors until one has experienced them.

'Laurie's letters take such a long time to get here that of course he may be moved nearer the Front – or the Front may move nearer him – before the machinery for his return gets going. And this Teruel fighting must be taking masses of wounded to all the Red Cross centres. If he remains in safety, I hope he will be back here within the next week or two.'

All over Europe, it was one of the severest winters in memory. Old people in Perpignan were dying of cold, and there was ice all day long in the darker streets. Wilma hung on the news from Teruel. An American woman in Wilma's hotel, whose son-in-law had gone there, reported on 2 January that two American journalists and one British had just been killed in their car there. (The only survivor was Kim Philby, reporting the war from Franco's side for *The Times*.)

On 3 January 1938 Annie wrote to Laurie from Slad (addressed to 'Laurence Edward Alan Lee'), hugely relieved to have heard something definite from Wilma 'instead of just thinking of you wandering in sad terrible Spain, exposed to all danger. But now it will be hard enough for you with the Red Cross. I trust that you won't feel the hardships and cold too much – and that your health will be good and that you will be spared to return to us. Dear Mrs Gregory is very very good, doing all she possibly can for you my dear Son. I have been *so* worried you ought not to have gone to Spain, & cause us all this anxiety & suspense, I have cried so much and many nights I have not slept. Try, dear lad, in any way possible, to come home for we all love you. Jack is here – but Oh Laurie my darling, I wish you had been here to have some Christmas fare – music and happy times with us . . . yr ever loving mother.'

'You'll have a lot to explain to your mother, for politics seem to bewilder her,' wrote Wilma. 'In one breath she asks with horror whether you are fighting for "the Reds" and goes on to express an

equal horror at the thought that the alternative is that you are fighting for that dreadful Franco. Has she been reading the *Daily Mail* and some decent Left paper all in the same hour?'

Later in January, Molly/Mariquita resurfaced, now in a cooled-down, sober mood and living in Smethwick, writing to thank Annie for the news of Laurie. 'For my own part, I have ceased to worry about Laurie. I certainly haven't any influence over him, now, and he has set himself so resolutely against all reasonable advice that I feel he must be left to work things out alone.

'I'm quite sure that you needn't be afraid that it is Betty's impending marriage which has sent Laurie to Spain.' (Betty had become engaged to Reg Farmer, a Cambridge undergraduate whom she had met on a cycling club outing in Gloucestershire.) 'I feel sorry for Mrs Wishart,' added Molly briskly. 'I hope that for everyone's sake she won't do anything stupid. But surely she wouldn't really be likely to forsake her children for Laurie!'

Lorna had indeed left her husband and children for Laurie. She had gone to a flat at 52 Heathcroft, in Hampstead Way, Golders Green, and rang Wilma to let Laurie know her address, but still spoke of trying to get to Spain herself. She had given Jacob Epstein a letter for Laurie to take to Barcelona – but then Epstein was refused a visa. Brother Jack had been to meet Lorna, and was 'tremendously impressed' that her concern for Laurie seemed so heartfelt. 'Everybody urges me,' wrote Wilma to Laurie, 'to persuade you to leave at once & that it is very bad for you to be there; medical opinion also has swung round very definitely to this point, since the news of your illness in Valencia. If the Spanish authorities think that your health will not stand the strain, then I think, dear Laurie, that you certainly ought to come back.'

Lorna had now heard from Harry Pollitt that Laurie had been taken to the training camp: 'I guess this means you have joined the International Brigade after all,' wrote Wilma resignedly in January. She began to give up hope of his early return, and now referred to herself as 'a tiresome old aunt' whose letters were 'probably only a bother to you'. She had sent his baggage with a fruit exporter, to Covent Garden addressed care of Jack. She would give away his

wireless and his fiddle case. If she heard soon that he was coming, she would wait in Perpignan, but otherwise would move on. If he arrived after her departure, he was to take a hotel room and write to Wilma's bank for money for his fare home rather than attempt to fiddle his way through France: 'The French, never at any time generous, are especially parsimonious at the present time.'

Laurie wrote reassuringly that nobody was sent to the front after only a few weeks' training. Wilma said she might go to Barcelona or Valencia to offer herself, her typewriter and her 'notorious eloquence' in French, English and Spanish. Or she might proceed to her cousin in Athens, or to Corsica or Algeria. But she had to get away 'from this detestable clot of dullness that is Perpignan'. On 14 January, she left the town.

On the same day, Jack wrote to his brother from Werter Road, Putney: 'My dear Loll, You don't know, Loll, how glad and relieved we are to know that you're safe, and how proud we are of you to know that you succeeded in doing what you set out to do – to cross the frontier and show your sympathies towards the Spanish Government in a practical way . . .'

All the girls in Slad had been asking after Laurie, he said. 'Maybe this world of ours is a pretty hellspot to live in & you are continually searching for truth & happiness – it may not have struck you I too have similar problems – but you at least have the satisfaction of your own talent and the knowledge that you are dearly loved – yes I have met her Loll – and I most terribly envy you that. You have that anyway Laurie & I wish in that that I were you – I don't necessarily mean she – but just the "fait accompli" you have. Maybe I'm getting old, maybe I'm sometimes a bit lonely but that seems to me a thing to be carefully won & gently cherished . . . My God Laurie, I'll be getting sentimental in a moment & then what?'

He reminisced about their boyhood activities together – 'memories that have mellowed in sweetness with the passing of the few years that separate us from them'.

Was Laurie coming back? 'I must know what line to take when mother, Mrs Gregory & Mrs Wishart write to me – as they have – about you. They want you back – we all do. The question is, what

do you yourself want? Well I must say *adiós!* look after yourself old man. Yours affectionately, Jack.'

Mrs O'Neill's sister, Wid, also sent a heartfelt letter on 22 January: 'Now now, Soldier, are you happy now, back in your beloved Spain? Are you more easy & content in your mind & no more bogeys & nightmares? At least you will not be haunted by the thought that you *fiddled* while Spain burned (as you expressed it in one of your previous letters) but I hope that the physical training and the robust life will harden you & make you the man that you long to be . . .

'So – you just napped out, eh? leaving a trail of broken hearts behind – what consternation there has been. I expected anything, after that innermost, heartsick letter you sent me. (You asked me to forget it – impossible – I never can. Your ultimate action in going to Spain has proved every word.) Jack was so worried, ran hither & thither, telegrams & letters kept arriving from France, presumably from your friends & sweethearts.'

She begged him to write. 'Your friendship is more to me than the whole world . . . the friends that you have now, are I feel far above me in several ways . . . & if I can send you anything for comfort etc. . . . My thoughts will follow every step you take, I'll scan all the newspapers, & I shall be eager for news of you always. Oh Laurie, you will come back, one day, won't you? On Xmas Day we all had a glass of sherry at dinner and we raised our glasses & clinked "To Laurie" in unison – honour bright, it was so spontaneous that it made me eat my dinner up in happiness.

'My last thought every day is to whisper "God take care of Laurie all through the long night" & when I wake in the morning I ask again for care & protection of my very dearest friend. Cheers soldier, affectionately, Wid.'

By 24 January Wilma had moved on to the Hôtel Lieutand, Cassis-sur-Mer, still half-planning to make herself useful among the refugees at Almería. If she went back to England, she said, she would hurl herself into political work to overthrow the Tory government.

But at the end of January Wilma's tone underwent a complete change. Two letters from Laurie, written 1 January and 13 January, had been forwarded to her, and she suddenly began to admonish him

for what she saw as selfish fickleness. If only he had explained, weeks ago, what he was doing; 'it would have saved an infinitude of anxiety & worry to all of us'. Laurie was obviously untroubled, because Wilma now told him he 'might as well stay in Spain until the war ended'. She herself would take no further steps: 'You are evidently happy, & the risk of air-raids must just be accepted.' Perhaps he might spend the rest of his life there, and marry a Spanish girl? 'If you could manage to stay in love with the same person long enough,' she added tartly, 'to make marriage worth while.' And he ought to stay and help to reconstruct the country; it would do him good. 'A little less Laurie, a little more citizenship, seems desirable.'

She doubted if he would ever settle down to life in England, or become a serious painter. As for Lorna, Wilma had made a complete volte-face. She had assumed that Laurie had gone to Spain to run away from a volcanic situation which alarmed or exhausted him. Now she began to conclude that he was 'not big enough really to fall in love with anybody. Just bodily satisfaction, with, of course, some mental stimulation, is an immense fillip to your vanity as a male.' She taunted Laurie for preferring 'short story episodes'. 'The long novel scares you, or bores you, & is simply not your genre.'

Sounding wounded (possibly sexually jealous) and addressing him as 'dear nephew' and 'Lorenzo dear', she went on to say that she knew all men needed reassurance that their charm could make lovely young females implore him to '*se couche* upon them'. ('Yes, I hope you are revolted by your aunt's coarseness.') But she predicted that by the age of forty, Laurie would have lost his youthful, 'downy' air, and become 'a stoutish person, with eyes bleared and watery, thick greasy lips, a coarse mouth. Novelette fears of a suffragette aunt? Perhaps . . .' But this was what happened to young men who had one love affair after another: physical and mental degeneration. H.G. Wells had been a potentially great man who had dwindled, by his philandering, into 'only a brilliant journalist'.

In her view, the lack of comradeship between men and women was a prime cause of Spain's backwardness; hence the need for the sexual equality of Communism. 'Any desire to wreak vengeance on women, to make them look foolish, or to triumph over them, makes

comradeship impossible. Damn it, Laurie, you're such a kind, human, warm-hearted person really. Surely you're not going to turn into a mental sadist?' She told him how despairing Lorna's letters had been, when she imagined Laurie in danger. Lorna appeared now to be building her life on a future with Laurie ('everybody else wiped out'). 'She says she does not dare to think ahead, but she *acts* ahead, my dear. W. banished, the home in Sussex abandoned, a tiny flat in London. Very little money, I imagine.' Was Laurie committed to Lorna? And should Wilma go on writing to her as 'a sort of niece-in-law'? 'I did think that at last you had found something which would endure, & which would give you roots in life.

'Well, that's all my preaching. I don't much care if you resent it, my child. We all get preached at, from time to time.'

At Teruel, the British Battalion called into action in January had won distinction for holding up the rebel advance, but the success was short-lived. Its commander, Fred Copeman, became ill with a gangrenous appendix, and the new commander, Bill Alexander, was promoted captain on the battlefield – only to be wounded in the shoulder. The Republicans lost many men and mountains of equipment and munitions. Everyone who had been at Teruel, and lived to tell the tale, was afflicted by the horror, the cold, and the bitterness of that eventual defeat. By the middle of February, Wilma wrote from Le Revestel to her sister Margery, telling her it had suddenly become very urgent that Laurie should be withdrawn from Spain at once:

'The situation now seems to be that the Spanish authorities are perfectly willing to discharge him, and even want to be rid of him, but the boy refuses to leave, and, when brought to Barcelona to receive his discharge papers, abruptly rushes off to Madrid or Valencia without permission. In his state of health, naturally he has not been of use to them, merely a nuisance, so of course they cannot be expected to pay for his repatriation.' Wilma told her sister that she had first demanded that a British warship should be sent to Barcelona to fetch him ('a demand which, to my no small astonishment, would actually have been granted had there been a British man-of-war close

to Barcelona at that time'). She had deposited money with the British consul in Marseilles, and requested the consul in Barcelona to ask Prieto 'to be good enough to order the boy to leave Spain. My impression is that the Spanish Ministry of Defence has hesitated, hitherto, to take so drastic a step, because I have applied to so many and diverse exalted personages, in England, France and Spain, to make sure that the boy was not allowed to go to the Front; thereby I have given the Ministry of Defence an exaggerated notion of the boy's importance, and they are afraid to offend him by sending him away. This *mal entendimiento* is now, I hope, cleared up, and I am beginning to be confident that Laurie will arrive in Marseilles within the next week or so.'

She and Laurie would now go their separate ways. She would stay in France, having given all her warm clothes to the Spanish aid committee in Perpignan ('almost certainly in one of the *camions* which were bombed into fragments in Figueras'), while Laurie's clothes had gone to England. She expected to find Laurie furious with her for arranging his return. 'But I'm so fond of the child . . . In any case, he certainly could not remain in Spain, after the alarming letters I have had about him from various quarters.' It would be a relief not to have to write dozens of letters each week 'to his terrified friends in England, to say nothing of consuls, officials, M P s, *diputados*, and other socialist and communist leaders, whom I have roped into the complications created by one impulsive boy.

'If ever Laurie can be persuaded to publish anything, in any case I have given him lots of publicity, and there must be quite a big circle of readers awaiting him in three countries!'

Either on Wilma's advice or at the insistence of the Spaniards, Laurie did leave Spain. On 14 February 1938 a French visa was issued at Barcelona – '*bon pour se rendre en Angleterre avec arrêt de deux jours en France*'. He left on 19 February. '*Sale sin dinero*' (leaves without money) was stamped in his passport. Shortly afterwards the battle of Teruel, two months of horror and misery, finally came to an end on 21 February when the government forces evacuated the town.

In Laurie's travel logbook, this is his bald summary of those two months:

'Spain. Crossed frontier over Pyrenees December 1937. Figueras – Barcelona – Valencia – Albacete – Tarazona – Madrid. France. Returned via Port Bou–Paris Feb 1938.'

In later years, Laurie always spoke of the 'shadowy, deep emotional memories' of his moment of war, and he obviously suffered from great hardship there. But for many years he was far from explicit about what had happened to him in Spain. He told Allen Andrews[2] in 1961: 'I crossed the Pyrenees at Figueras in December in a blizzard and said "I've come to fight." They said, "You've got a haversack full of books, a camera and a violin – you have been landed from a submarine and you are a spy." They put me in a room before shooting me. Just by luck the chief of police talked about this prisoner with the violin to an English newspaper man who recognized my description.' This was Bill Rust – an episode he later transferred from December to February. 'So they let me live.

'I trained as a soldier, but I was mainly used in the International Brigade headquarters in Madrid during the siege, making short-wave broadcasts to Britain and America. When I came back I was conscious of having got off very lightly. There were very few survivors from the men who were with me – chaps from Oxford and the docks, Canada, France, America. I have only ever met one of them since, they went in the heavy fighting of the spring.'

A year later – 1962 – he talked to a reporter, Frank Entwisle, about those months. 'He fought in the International Brigade,' wrote Entwisle, 'but was shipped out after a bout of the recurrent pneumonia that has trailed him from his Cotswold childhood.'[3]

By March 1977 he was repeating to another reporter, Philip Oakes, the Bill Rust story: 'In Barcelona I could easily have starved to death – not out of brutality, you understand, just neglect. But after three days in the cells my name was mentioned to Bill Rust – a war correspondent who later became editor of the *Daily Worker* – and he had me bailed out within the hour. The military commander let me convalesce in his flat for a couple of days. He was frightfully decent when he realized that we were on the same side.'[4]

In *A Moment of War*, the starvation cell episode in Barcelona had expanded to three weeks (not three days) and took place after the

battle of Teruel, when Rust happened to have his drink with the chief of police, heard about Laurie, and sprang him from gaol. (Rust, a prominent Communist who had spent years in Moscow and had gone to Spain to sort out the problems within the British Battalion leadership, did not mention his rescue of Laurie in his own book, *Britons in Spain*, published in 1939 – but then at that time Laurie was still totally unknown.)

As is clear from Wilma's letters, Laurie never mentioned to her that he had been in a death cell; nor does he seem to have mentioned Bill Rust, whom she would probably have known; and never mentioned, even to close friends afterwards, anything about having killed anyone. Such are the available facts, without the aid of Laurie's contemporary diaries, stolen in 1969.

He brought home not only his diaries and a large cache of letters, but the poems he had written that winter, including the one called 'A Moment of War', published in 1940 in the fourth issue of *Horizon*:

It is night like a red rag
drawn across the eyes

the flesh is bitterly pinned
to desperate vigilance

the blood is stuttering with fear.

O praise the security of worms
in cool crumbs of soil
flatter the hidden sap
and the lost unfertilized spawn of fish!

The hands melt with weakness
into the gun's hot iron

the body melts with pity

the face is braced for wounds
the odour and the kiss of final pain.

O envy the peace of women
giving birth and love like toys
into the hands of men!

The mouth chatters with pale curses

the bowels struggle like a nest of rats

the feet wish they were grass
spaced quietly.

O Christ and Mother!

But darkness opens like a knife for you
and you are marked down by your pulsing brain

and isolated

and your breathing,

your breathing is the blast, the bullet,
and the final sky.

This poem, rightly praised for expressing so vividly what it felt like to be stricken with terror in war-torn Spain, was originally datelined (in *Horizon*) 'Montpellier, October 1937'. The poem called 'The Return' must refer to his trek across the Pyrenees in the snow – his return to Spain – and his fevered, fitful state of mind when he arrived (the Bahía de Rosas is on the coast, east of Figueras):

And the day I observed that I was a lover
I crossed the frontier to seek a wound
And fell with a fever above the Bahía de Rosas

Letting the mad snow spit in my eyes.

I put her picture against the mountain
I covered the snowdrift with her scarf
and lay with her name across my haunches
chopping the ice in a fit of love . . .

There seems little doubt that Laurie was deeply ashamed of having been sent back to England so soon. His brother Jack believes this, and Lorna refers to it in a letter in 1941. For decades, he obfuscated his experiences in the Spanish war, vaguely referring to having 'carried a gun, not a stretcher'.[5] When, finally, in 1991, he published *A Moment of War*, an old man's book written with a young man's verve and a poet's imagination, it was hailed as a minor classic of the literature of war. Fellow veterans found it fantastical. But it had taken him more than twenty years to write, and it was, he told Philip Oakes in 1977, 'an agonizing process' without his diaries. 'I can't let it go though. I have to finish the book. It's a debt I owe to dead men, to dead friends.'

Why Laurie 'could not let it go' but felt he must – at nearly eighty – unscramble his muddled memories through the haze of the 'breaks in the brain' he admitted having suffered, I shall deal with in the appropriate chapter, at the end of this book. The questions about *A Moment of War* erupted only after Laurie's death, when his version of events became a bone of contention to be chewed over by historians and poets, who took him at his word, and Spanish Civil War veterans, who did not.

But nobody would ever question the authenticity of Laurie's impressions of conditions in Spain during the Civil War – the chaos and hunger and the biting cold, the wretched suffering of that ramshackle, ill-equipped army, in which so many young men died. There was one certainty: Laurie had been there, had witnessed it and experienced it, and never referred to it without a sense of guilt and defeat.

When he got back to Victoria station, Lorna was waiting for him.

'Then I was back in her flat. In high wealthy Hampstead. She drew me in with her blue steady gaze. I remember the flowers on the piano, the white sheets on her bed, her deep mouth, and love without honour. Without honour, but at least with salvation.'

Laurie and Lorna were together for most of the rest of the year. Lorna had left Wish in Sussex, and her two little boys – Michael aged nine, Luke aged five – in the care of a nanny in St John's Wood. 'Suddenly, my mother vanished for years,' Michael Wishart later wrote, remembering his childhood. 'I was moved to a house in St John's Wood. I thought it was my fault she had gone. There followed a time of grief and anguish. Then my mother made brief reappearances. They tore open the wounds of her absence.'[6] Lorna rented a flat at 35 Mecklenburgh Square, Bloomsbury. Thereafter Laurie often referred to it as a place tinged with misery, because after a few months, in November 1938, Lorna decided to return to her husband, and sent Laurie off on his travels again: 'I took my fiddle to Italy and Greece to earn my keep, and spent the winter just before the big war in Cyprus. I didn't know anything about Cyprus. I just turned up. I'd read the name Famagusta in a poem of Flecker . . .'

Laurie later wrote of November 1938 as 'the black November . . . a day cursed with tender horror', a time of 'suffering so bitter that I wonder now how it was possible to endure it'. When Lorna sent Laurie away, she was four months pregnant.

8 | Yasmin
1938–9

Did Laurie know about Lorna's pregnancy? In the diary of his travels that winter, he mentions walking up a winding path into the little church of Lycabettos on the hill above Athens, where candles were on sale: 'I want to put a candle up for the three of us but think it would be ridiculous,' he writes. 'So I go out of the church & look again at the red sky behind the pillars of the Acropolis, and down at the cacti on the brown cliffs & then I go back, slip a coin into the box, take a candle, & lighting it from one of the others place it among them at the altar.' Presumably by 'the three of us' he meant Lorna, himself and their unborn baby.

On 16 November, the day he left, Laurie was awakened by Lorna with a taxi at the door. 'She brought me half asleep into a cold miserable fog. The flat looked grey & dull but L put the thrill of God into me. Nevertheless it seems I have to make this journey . . . two thousand miles of distraction and self-inspection.'

On the Newhaven–Dieppe ferry Laurie met a girl art student from California and they travelled to Paris together. He found Paris dull, he was miserable, his head ached. As he caught the Istanbul-bound train, he watched an Italian saying goodbye to his lover, 'stroking her face and gazing at her with tragic eyes'. Laurie left the train at Venice (in 1978, writing about Venice, Laurie said he had not been to Venice for forty years, when he had been 'a young man running from love'). He recorded his Venetian impressions on a misty day: 'The impudence of the pigeons & the way they darken the sky when the church bell rings. The blinding white grace of the ducal palace – the Church of the Salute across the water – the far off blue mists of water from the tower in San Marco – the cries of the gondoliers & their expert steering – above all the cold & the silence in the narrow canals.' He took the *Palestrina*, a comfortless Italian steamer, which moved out at midnight past

San Marco to the sea, bound for Brindisi and the Adriatic crossing to Piraeus.

Wilma, meanwhile, had been working for a women's anti-fascist movement in Paris; she was paying off her dentist's bill by instalments and reflecting wryly to her sister that she had paid 'on the nail' for Laurie's 'jaw-overhaul' the previous year. By December, she was back in London at the chilly Grosvenor Hotel: '15s 6d *per diem* for a gloomy room and an indifferent breakfast', having staggered from the train in great pain from haemorrhoids. She was still paying off a bank overdraft of £10. She remarked without rancour to her sister: 'You see I am still suffering from the eccentricities of Laurie.'

Laurie was then absorbing 'the lovely smell of resin from the pine trees, the rose coloured Bulgarian mountains . . .' as he sailed past the islands to Piraeus: 'Unintelligible signs, weird music from the cafés, girls with tambourines and cigarettes – Armenian boy who cleaned my shoes – the market – the smell of bread, of bitter roasting coffee, the piled fruit stalls, ruddy grapes, green melons, oranges with green leaves . . . the makers of musical instruments & their little shops.'

He took buses to the Byzantine monastery at Daphni, among cypresses and pines, through the dry hills to Elipsis, 'a decayed town with a ruined temple & a large cement factory'. He walked up to the Acropolis while several hundred young men in shorts practised for the Marathon. 'In the museum are many battered & incomplete statues. All the finest marbles were raped by Elgin. The Greeks can never forgive England, they talk to me reproachfully about it.' He would have tea in the English Reading Room in Athens, where he overheard 'a committee of hard women discussing hanging pictures of the royal family' and an expatriate Englishwoman complaining of having 'nothing to read but the *News Chronicle*, of all ghastly publications'. He absorbed everything: 'A smell of stale fish round the docks, the dry crusts the bakers sell for breakfast, the thick bitter coffee, the boot blacks running among the feet with their boxes & little bottles. In the gutter, witchlike crones are picking over a heap of rotting pears. They inspect each minutely & place the salvaged ones on a sheet of paper. I tap one on the

shoulder & hold out some money. She straightens her back & stares at me perplexed & amazed. Then she looks at her companion and her eyes fill with tears.'

Among painted fishing boats with curved prows, and flag-covered barges blowing their sirens for the Feast of St Nicholas, Laurie left Athens aboard the *Andros* – which pitched alarmingly as they reached the open sea. He arrived in Limassol, Cyprus, on 16 December in heavy rain, and found instant brotherhood among the young Cypriot men in cafés; they went roller-skating, played ping-pong and billiards, went to the cinema, and talked of women. 'They do nothing else. In the evening we went outside the town to sing. Singing is not permitted in the streets. Yet the harsh sounds of motor horns blow incessantly all through the early hours of the morning when the streets are deserted & keep me awake.' The streets of Famagusta were narrow and choked with camels, mules, carriages and bicycles. His poem 'Port of Famagusta', published five years later in his first slim volume, is datelined 'Cyprus, 1939'.

> With the archways full of camels
> And my ears of crying zithers
> how can I resolve the cipher
> Of your occidental heart?
> How can I against the city's
> Syrian tongue and Grecian doors
> seek a bed to reassemble
> the jigsaw of your western love?

In Famagusta he took a room with a verandah, hired a bicycle and went down on sunny mornings to swim in warm water thick with salt and sand. 'What large breasts these Greek girls have, swelling through their clothes like a storm in a sail. But perhaps it is my celibacy that gives them their size.'

On Christmas Day he went with Picton, 'a cheerful old English-man with a white beard', to the English church, and 'bellowed carols with the sun streaming through the windows. Here were gathered the crumpled sandy faces of my compatriots, and the

service echoed with the rhythmic phrase of the "virgin's womb".'

Making friends was always easy for Laurie. A tailor named Polichronos gave him Christmas lunch at his white, square house, stopping *en route* at an orange farm for a small feast of fruit including 'the nispera that I knew in Spain. And a bush with little cream coloured berries which tasted of bitter ginger. I left the farm loaded with oranges big as rugger balls.

'I am treated with amazing courtesy. Poli is newly married. His baby is three months old. We sit around the table & the women bring the food; they do not join us. There are pictures of film stars on the walls, all carefully framed, Conrad Veidt, Marion Davies, an advertisement for Craven "A", and a picture of Stevenson's Rocket. We have rice soup flavoured with cinnamon, boiled chicken with a salad of cabbage in olive oil, roast chicken & potatoes, coñac & a sweet wine. After lunch, I carry my oranges & a small cake wrapped in tissue paper which Poli's wife gave me on leaving.'

Four days into the new year he ended his celibate period by walking past Famagusta harbour, through a gateway into narrow twisting streets. 'I was looking for a whore & there were many here . . . In a house just off the square, the front door was open, the girl sitting inside was young & when she saw me she stroked her leg softly and looked out to me. I went in and we sat around a bucket of glowing charcoal. There were four girls, a plump one, a fair one, one who was nice to me but had gold teeth, and the young one who had huge eyes & was Arabian. She was silent while the others chattered. A well dressed German came in, coarse in word & gesture. We sat round the charcoal stroking the girls with our eyes yet unable to move. The' huge fat mother came in & sat with us, her legs open adding a bright touch of obscenity. The German stroked the plump girl's buttocks and smoked a cigarette. There was a knock on the half open door and a Greek came in & with hardly a word the fair girl followed him up stairs. We sat for a while longer, the fair girl came down again & fetched water. They asked me what ship I was on. Then the mother said, "You like girl – you go in room" so I stood up & they all looked at me. I pointed to the young one and said "you". She rose & went with

me. The bed was high & the girl undressed in a corner. She came with a dark smile on her face. I was so gentle I amazed myself, her skin was rough & when I touched her she shivered & her face flashed a dark smile. Afterwards I felt jubilant & warm towards her. She came with me to the door & waved as I walked up the moonlight street. The city walls were majestic & the eucalyptus trees amazingly fragile & lovely as I went back to the hotel. I felt strong & terrifically alive.'

He cycled to the ruins at Salamis: 'Broken pillars, blue & white anemones, lizards on the sunny stone. In the road were camels, and carts painted with blue spots . . . I pushed through a wilderness of trees & bushes to the sea. Peasants were ploughing a strip of land by the shore, and some were building walls of earth to keep back the sea. The soil was sandy. I went into a potter's workshop. He makes about thirty pots an hour. They sell at one piastre each. He pushes round the wheel with his bare feet. There is no legislation so far as I can see to protect either their hours of labour or their rate of pay. Even the policemen only get about £3 a month.

'In this beautiful city are so many oxen and limbless beggars . . . The girls are shuttered by neighbours' tongues, they are unable to stir or speak or let down their hair without meeting a pestilential barrier of censorious criticism. There is little love, but plenty of emotion attached to the house of a girl, her plot of land, her capital. Although the sun shines every day with a charitable benevolence, the sea is always cold & cafés are preferred to the poetical streets. The women mourn their wastage in black crêpe, hide their beauty in dark corners, and the men serenade their possessions but know nothing of their souls.' The style and flavour of this diary, with its colour and detail, suggest the kind of diaries he had kept in Spain, the ones which were later stolen. The Cyprus diary ends abruptly here.

According to his passport Laurie left Famagusta on 8 February 1939 and sailed home via Athens, Naples, Marseilles and Dieppe. He left Dieppe by night and arrived in London on 18 February 1939, exactly a year after his return from Spain.

Laurie and Lorna's child was born almost a month later on 14

March 1939 in St John's Wood. Laurie telephoned Lorna in her nursing home, and first heard his baby's cry over the phone. Almond trees were in blossom, and Laurie came and played his fiddle outside in the garden. 'I wanted a poet's child, and I got one,' Lorna was later to tell their daughter. They named her after their favourite poem, 'Yasmin', from James Elroy Flecker's verse-play *Hassan*:

> How splendid in the morning glows the lily: with what grace he
> throws
> His supplication to the rose: do roses nod the head, Yasmin? . . .
> The morning light is clear and cold: I dare not in that light
> behold
> A whiter light, a deeper gold, a glory too far shed, Yasmin.
>
> But when the deep red eye of day is level with the lone highway,
> And some to Mecca turn to pray, and I toward thy bed,
> Yasmin . . .

On Yasmin's birth certificate her name is Jasmine Margaret, but Lorna and Laurie always called her Yasmin. There was significance for them in the initial letter 'Y': it represented two conjoined Ls, for Laurie and Lorna. The details of the next few months are sketchy. Shortly after her birth, Yasmin says, she was photographed with her mother by Baron, the Jewish society photographer, whom Lorna had met in a nightclub and fearlessly rescued when he was attacked by a fascist mob. In gratitude he took the photographs.

Laurie and Lorna and the baby lived for two months at 10 Kenton Street, Bloomsbury, above a greengrocer's shop. Jack recalls this flat; he went with them for a chicken and champagne picnic (which made a change from Mrs O'Neill's Irish stew) on the banks of a stream at Chalfont St Giles. Betty Smart remembers that she and Molly were delighted about Laurie and Lorna's baby. 'No doubt I was romantic and silly, but I thought it a lovely idea.' But Lorna shortly realized that the impecunious life with Laurie and the baby would be impossible. Wish had told her that if she came home, he would bring up the child as his own – an undertaking he carried

out nobly. So Lorna returned to Sussex, and by the end of May Laurie was working as a farmhand at Upper Roundhurst Farm, Blackdown, near Haslemere in Surrey, from where he wrote to confide in Wilma about how much he missed Lorna and the baby. Wilma had spent the spring in Paris, but was back in Bournemouth living in a residential club named Sunningdale. Three marathon letters from Wilma – still affectionate, but no longer doting – are the sole record of what Laurie was doing and feeling at that time. He did not enjoy farming; the hours were long and he felt cut off. Wilma told him it was good for a poet to 'go vegetable for a while' and build up a reserve of strength for indoor endeavours. Laurie found her response 'harsh but commendably moral'.

Wilma replied at length to explain that her attitude was not moral, but economic: 'Lorna is financially dependent on her husband, cannot afford to be with you, cannot support the child without her husband's help, and did not, apparently, think of this difficulty till the child was born.

'I really do *not* set up to be a judge of other people's conduct. We all make such a mess of our lives . . . one can only try not to behave selfishly and not to damage other people . . . Our worst blunders occur when we are thinking of our own personal wants and not bothering about their place in the general scheme of things. Since I am guilty of that omission, I can't blame anybody else for being equally selfish.

'I can understand that my letter seemed to you coldly – even smugly – judicial, but I assure you I don't leave feelings out of account . . . And I certainly never supposed that it was a physical possibility for you to beget "in cold blood" as you put it. But you had plenty of leisure and isolation to *think* in cold blood, during the many months between the summer of 1937 and the summer of last year.' She blamed herself 'for having helped you to return to England, and then helped you to remain in London, and for not having made a stronger effort to persuade you to reflect a bit.

'Now that you have had plenty of opportunities of seeing what a danger there is of your being at the mercy of your emotions, wouldn't it be well to learn *not* to be at their mercy? I said that you

were less to blame than Lorna; that was because I thought she had a far stronger will than you have. Evidently she is more dependent on other people than I supposed. I had expected her to be strong and independent enough to stand by you and help you much as Frieda von Richthofen helped D.H. Lawrence.[1]

'In the circumstances, I don't see that she could do otherwise than she is doing. If she had a career, or her own family were in a position to make her independent of her husband . . . but as my old nurse used to say, "if ifs and ans were pots and pans there'd be no need for tinkers".' Lorna, she reckoned, would need a private income of £500 to £600 to maintain herself and her child. 'And Lord knows I realize how ghastly it would be for her to bring up the child in complete poverty. As things are, it is fortunate that the husband has taken to the child and is willing to bring it up with his own, and it is, of course, very generous of him.'

As for Laurie's seeing his child sometimes, that would be for the three of them, 'especially the husband', to decide. Anyway, she asked, did Laurie feel competent to share in the child's upbringing? 'In the world as it is, only the rich can arrange to have illegitimate children without inconvenience. And even for the rich, parenthood surely ought to be a responsibility rather than an enjoyment?'

He must face the hard facts, she added, and use the talents he was lucky enough to possess. 'Most men can make love and beget children; those actions are among the commonplaces of life; mere journalese, one might say. But not many can write well, and very few can write as well as you can, let alone paint. You have wasted a lot of time, and some opportunity, but you have plenty of time still – and you have one remarkable advantage: you don't mind physical discomforts. And, if you *must* be introspective, why not use that tendency in your work? Write about yourself; not necessarily about actual facts in your life, but a journal or what-not written around them . . .'

She would come to Haslemere to give him lunch one day; she was fed up with Bournemouth's suburban somnolence and filled with nostalgia for Almuñécar. 'I see that the Pope has blessed Franco and his army and told them that they were fighting for the

preservation of civilization.' She advised Laurie to ask Jack – who had now joined the GPO Film Unit – to find him a job. Or he might inquire at the Labour Exchange about building work on the army camps which were being built, as the nation was mobilizing for war. Or she would pay for an advert in the *New Statesman* offering his services. 'Don't get depressed; some more pleasant job will turn up soon.'

In July she sent another homily. She was glad he now accepted the Lorna situation. 'She is on friendly terms with her husband, has all the liberty she wants "and then some", and the kind of home she likes.'

'Sorry to be so grandmotherly about it, but there it is: you have to fit yourself into the world as it is, not as you'd like it to be, and that means not wandering about in an imaginary Arcady and making love to charming shepherdesses (who, at heart, want more solid things, such as a comfortable home and an income, and pretty clothes and a car) but doing solid work which will give, to those shepherdesses and glamour girls, a confidence in your power to look after them.'

'The question of your being a helpful counsellor to the child does not arise; you have done all that was asked of you. And my impression is that Lorna would be much more likely to make a success of her life, and have happiness with her family, if you have no further communication with her.' She reminded Laurie that 'throughout the ages, wives have "kicked over the traces" and then been taken back by their husbands, who have accepted an illegitimate child and brought it up as their own'. Wilma would find Lorna contemptible 'if she attempted to have both her husband and you'. Laurie must regard the episode as closed, and fix his mind on 'the very urgent business of growing up: getting one's values right, and putting one's emotions in their proper place (a comparatively insignificant one)'. She promised not to refer again to 'this unhappiness of yours'.

In the Garman family, nobody appears to have been exercised about who was the father of Lorna's new baby. Even if they were told, they would not have thought it exceptional. Kathleen Garman

now had three children by Epstein, who was still married to his wife; Ruth Garman had several children, by different men. And as Anna Campbell says of her parents Roy and Mary: 'Goodness, they had both led carefree lives before the Spanish influence, and were in no position to censure anyone.' Laurie's mother Annie was certainly told; she was unreproachfully prepared to bestow on Yasmin all the love she had once given to her little dead daughter Frances.

Of course Laurie did not give up Lorna, or put the episode behind him. 'Yasmin, me darlins, has two more teeth! Top ones,' he noted in the diary he began on 16 October 1939, shortly after the outbreak of war. This diary, written more honestly and sparely than anything he ever published, and kept continuously for five years, became principally an account of the love affair that brought him more happiness – and ultimately, more unhappiness – than anything he had ever known.

At the outbreak of war Laurie was back at Mrs O'Neill's in Werter Road, Putney, where the high street shop basements had become air-raid shelters, and Putney Heath had listening-posts and search-lights and walls of sandbags. Lorna was often in London, but the baby stayed in Sussex with her nanny. Epstein's daughter Kitty has a memory of standing in the hall at Marsh Farm, Sussex, with her cousin Michael Wishart, both aged about eleven, as Lorna departed for London. 'And Lorna looked at us and said, off-hand, "You are a strange pair of children, neither of you living with your mothers, your mothers always going off" and I remember thinking, in that helpless way of a child, Well we can't help it. It's you who go, not us.'

In these early days of the war, when air-raid shelters were being dug and everyone carried gas masks, Laurie drifted. He went to concerts, copied out Mozart's Violin Concerto in A. With brother Jack's musical friends, he made up a quartet. He kept a careful daily record of events, dissecting the newspapers, their leaders, their opinions (disgusted by their childish jingoism) and logging events such as the torpedoing of the *Royal Oak* at Scapa Flow, and the

Graf Spee in the South Atlantic. But mostly he just waited for Lorna.

'L came this morning with lilies and some little white flowers, their petals beautifully marked with lipstick. She brought Sibelius, a Beethoven quartet, a new flamenco & several others. We had music and the gas fire and qualities of tenderness that exists nowhere outside our bodies. And then to Pritchards for tea where she kicked me on the shin for looking at another girl.' (Lorna was intensely jealous: she tore up Laurie's photographs of a girl he met in Athens, saying, 'The Greeks have a word for it & I have a word for the Greeks.')

He would meet Lorna on Victoria station: 'Tall in her dark-blue slacks and jacket, brown-cheeked, bright-eyed, giggling like a schoolgirl as we walk arm-in-arm to look for a taxi. It is more than 2 years.' He bought Baudelaire for Lorna at Zwemmer's, and went with her to an exhibition of Epstein drawings: 'Some from *Les Fleurs du Mal* unlovely and obscene. Several fine portraits of a repulsive little boy called Jackie [Epstein's son by his model Isabel Nicholas, adopted by Mrs Epstein unknown to Kathleen Garman], some lovely nudes of a thin negress, and several variations on love & death.'

Jack brought home his new girlfriend, Elizabeth Woolf. 'J having slept with a girl at last is naturally more bound to her than he has ever been to anyone. Now . . . he has sipped the milk of paradise and hell begins for him.' In the evenings they would all sit by Mrs O'Neill's coal fire. One night they decided that Laurie's wallpaper was unacceptably drab and covered it with his drawings from Reading: 'the extravagant disconnected energies of work I produced in what seems now a totally different life'.

The first anniversary of his departure for Greece and Cyprus, 16 November, was 'a day of sackcloth & ashes, a day for anger & expostulation, a day to curse. But kinder in itself, quiet & warm, & not the blue smokey cold of last year. I would not fast or shut myself away. But I hope I may remember it for ever. *Hassan* was being broadcast and we lay dumbly together without speaking or moving. And then she went & I remained in that vast room while that nerve-wracking second half of *Hassan* continued. You're

a bloody day and you mark the end of an indescribable year.'

Soon, brother Jack did find Laurie a job at the GPO Film Unit, a reserved occupation. 'Laurie was on my conscience. He had no money, and at least I had a job,' Jack says. The unit employed the cream of the British documentary film world: Jack Holmes, Humphrey Jennings, Stewart McAllyth, Pat Jackson, Harry Watt. Jack arranged work for Laurie in the sound department under Ken Cameron, brother of the legendary reporter James. His first job was to create percussive sounds for the noise of marching feet in a GPO film about London preparing for war: 'Brian Easedale smiting a radiator with a piece of iron, whilst I tapped two wood blocks together & whistled,' his diary records. 'For dockyard noises we used drums, blew sirens, stirred water in a basin . . . It seems that 90% of sound is synthetic in films.' When Laurie went to see the trade show he disliked the film's self-congratulatory tone – 'This is how you reacted to the war and very proud you should be of your calmness, good sense & humour. But then, after all, you're British.' But the barrage balloons were beautifully filmed: 'They will always be the symbol of the first days. Great slow silver fishes, shewn shining in the sun, nosing through misty clouds, rising & falling, wrinkling lazily, and drifting dark and strange in front of the moon. Slow, obscene, yet lovely things, faintly sinister yet friendly.'

He still saw the Smart girls. Over lunch one day, Molly told him she was pregnant, and that Betty was about to marry her fiancé Reg Farmer (who became a distinguished nuclear scientist, and to whom she has now been married for sixty years).

And one day in December, Lorna rang to tell him 'the extraordinary news' that Wilma had come to live at a cottage called Morley's Croft in Lorna's village of Binsted, Sussex. Clearly Wilma was not to be discarded from Laurie's life. Twenty years later, in a letter to her sister, Wilma looked back on what she had done for Laurie. 'No doubt it was pleasant for him to have good meals and no expenses while I was taking care of him, but how boring it must have been for him to spend so much time with a dreary quinquagenarian . . .

'But the real benefit I bestowed on him was quite involuntary; by encouraging him to go to Cornwall with a Lone Pine Camp ménage, I enabled him to meet the most beautiful, aggressive and, as I thought then, most dangerous of his mistresses, and it was she who introduced him to the BBC and also to the world of literature, music and art.'

But Lorna made those introductions later. For now, Laurie had to report for work at Blackheath, where he was instructed in 'the instruments & speakers & panels and dials and switches' of the sound van. The night before he started work, Lorna came, 'in a dark-blue ribbed frock which matches her eyes & makes her all one dark sloe-blue image. We have a coal fire but our day is soon burnt out & Lord knows when I shall be able to see her again.'

The first film Laurie worked on was the story of the voyage of a cargo boat, the SS *Ionian*, from Gibraltar to Famagusta: 'lovely local music – but since the film was made [the *Ionian*] has been blown up & the film retitled "Her Last Trip".' He recorded Ralph Richardson, whom he found 'facetious but not unpleasant'. Other projects were less exciting: 'To Tooting Bec to record at a Post Office the noises of a teleprinter in action for Jack Chambers' film "How the Teleprinter works".' Laurie implacably disliked Elgar's music, which the sound unit often used for background: 'it is all as blank and similar as a spool of unused film. He has all the windyness of Gladstone, the four-square denseness of Baldwin, and the leisured ease of speaking immaculate nothings which must be one of Chamberlain's greatest gifts.'

On Christmas Eve 1939 Jack and Laurie took a packed train to icy Slad. Annie's kitchen was 'colder and more confused than ever, but irreplaceable in spite of its comfortlessness'. That evening, two frail voices began a carol outside the door. 'A voice from my feet said "Penny for the carol mister." I looked down and there was a little boy and girl hand in hand & both, it seemed, no taller than a bucket.' Laurie asked who they were. 'I be Reg Smart,' said the boy, 'and 'er's my sister. We do come from Stroud.' 'And they went stumping up the freezing bank in the moonlight like a couple of well-wrapped up dwarfs. These singers made my cup quite full.'

After having his annual Christmas fever, Laurie returned to London and Lorna, and played the records she had given him (Bach preludes and fugues), and they went through his poems together and 'primed them again'. 'At least we saw the new year in. Waking in the dark and leaving the warm, enflamed cheeks of Scheherezade is one of the most difficult things I have ever had to do.'

The winter of 1939–40 was said to be the worst for 100 years: at Putney the Thames was frozen. But Lorna brought lilies and orchids, Sibelius and Brahms and they would lie in the light of the gas fire 'evoking strong ghosts of Kenton Street'. 'Her return is like the moon, I am struck with familiar surprise and shake myself with joy. She waxes swiftly to a full, heady brilliance and then the dawn sees her face turning away, pale, and disappearing.' 'We lay still & talked and breathed warmth into each other's hair until late in the morning. I cannot think why lovers ever leave their beds . . .'

In blacked-out London, Lorna glowed: a free spirit, a scented romantic, a vision bringing flowers, music, wine, and inspiring in Laurie dozens of poems. In the evenings, when he got back from the Film Unit, he would find her in his Putney room: 'My love was waiting tonight with long slender swords of leaves and dark red roses. We played the Chopin Ballades and the Debussy Quartet. Chopin is definitely the music for desire . . .' 'L was waiting for me this evening. Again everything was forgotten, she hung her head or twisted her hair, and talking or embracing, there was little to show that I had ever flown to Greece, or Yasmin had been born.'

9 | The Green Caravan
1940–41

The danger posed by the war seemed to intensify Laurie's affair with Lorna. On fine spring days, they would escape to the Sussex countryside 'and there among the sheep we did make merry and tumbled the shadows and sunlight to brilliant effect. We averted our eyes from war flares and ignored warnings. The sun smote us . . . We pitied the sheep, we pitied all men, so lofty were we in the pride of happiness and fulfilment.' They strolled through churchyards 'doped with lassitude & mutual excitement'.

Lorna also opened doors. She sent Laurie's poems to her old friend Stephen Spender at his new magazine, *Horizon*, and he and Cyril Connolly agreed to publish three. Laurie was suspicious; were they publishing him just because he was a proletarian? Spender wrote assuring him that they simply liked his work. 'If we published poems just because they were proletarian, *Horizon* would be the size of a telephone directory.'

He added: 'Perhaps you will not mind my saying how very struck I was by your poems when Mrs Wishart sent them to me . . . more struck than by anything I have read for some time.' He found Laurie's drawings 'interesting', but preferred the poems. There was a postscript: 'I shall remember that your name is Laurie Lee and not Laurence.'

Cyril Connolly also wrote from Devon: 'If you substitute "upper class" for "working class" in your letter, it . . . might have been written by a peer fifty years ago,' he told Laurie. They were pleased to publish him because he was unknown. Besides, he pointed out, merely being working-class was 'not much of an asset from a literary point of view. A great many of the working class now write, & I do not think they write very well . . . From the *artistic* point of view your visit to Spain, and knowledge of countryside has been lucky . . . I hope this clears it up & I'm sorry for spelling your name

wrong. May I say how much I like your poems. Yrs v sincerely Cyril Connolly.'

John Lehmann, general manager of the Hogarth Press and ever alert to a new name, instantly offered to publish Laurie in his *Penguin New Writing* series. Laurie rang him – again pointing out that he was Laurie, not Laurence – and typed out three of his poems; he wrote a fourth for Spender 'as ordered' but the effort brought on a fever. He received one guinea when the fourth issue of *Horizon* was published: it carried a portrait by Lucian Freud, a review of Housman by Spender, a V.S. Pritchett short story, and the poem 'A Moment of War' by Laurie Lee. He was paid another guinea for 'Words Asleep' in *Horizon 5*.

By day Laurie was recording the sound of machine-guns and Spitfires for a film on *Ammunition*, and the voice of J.B. Priestley for *Britain at Bay*. He spent his first evening with people from Gaumont British and Movietone in a Soho pub: 'They all drink and drink – don't they ever go home?' (Laurie had not yet acquired the masculine taste for long evenings in pubs.) Each day he noted the numbers of planes shot down, and of casualties; he logged German advances and lamented the fall of Paris: 'Is there nothing we can do for France, are we so impotent after all?'

In June he took Lorna to Slad for the first time, in a train packed with young soldiers. He noticed how women, Lorna included, eyed the military with approval. 'It is bitter to be a civilian among these men.' They arrived in high summer to find the valley in extravagant bloom. 'Everywhere blossoms, orchids, moon daisies, roses, the garden a heady pool of syringa, the banks and fields vital with scent & sound. Nightingales in the woods. I lay with my face in the grass, or with my mouth to hers. Everything was the beautiful familiarity of home, she and the valley were never divided.' Laurie's poem in the next *Horizon*, later called 'Invasion Summer', reflected this sybaritic rural interlude in the midst of war:

The evening, the heather,
the unsecretive cuckoo
and butterflies in their disorder;

not a word of war as we lie,
our mouths in a hot nest
and the flowers advancing.

Does a hill defend itself,
does a river run to earth
to hide its quaint neutrality?
A boy is shot with England in his brain,
but she lies brazen yet beneath the sun,
she has no honour and she has no fear.

On a hot August afternoon when the fields were stacked with corn, Laurie went down to Arundel to see Yasmin. 'They were waiting for me, L holding Yasmin, a plump golden-haired little beauty with the "greensleeve" eyes of her mother and a chubby comfortable face, the rough lovely face of a country girl contrasting oddly with the rare fine charm of her eyes. She wonders at me at first, but toddles across the station yard desperately clutching my hand.' They went for tea. 'Yasmin crowed and chatted between us and we fed her, gazed at her, talked about her and laughed at her jokes. We watched her eating and drinking with pride . . . for a short while we enjoyed ourselves, a simple domestic trio out to tea for a treat.'

Afterwards they sat by the river 'where herons walk through rushes on dignified stilts' and Yasmin toddled up and down the path 'with furious little steps', picking up pebbles. 'She smiled at me and held her head on the side and laughed . . . She was gay and adorable, but she did not know me, which was not surprising.'

One day Laurie played truant from the studio and went down to Sussex.

'We drove out on the downs and lay among the white parachute seeds of thistles . . . I spent the night at Wilma's cottage. The mooing of heifers in Wilma's garden woke me in the morning. L came down in her scarlet frock. As we walked back up the lane towards Arundel, the all-clear sounded. Wilma left us and we lay in the wood happy but distant. The drone of planes was continuous.

About one o'clock it grew louder, more threatening, like a swarm drawing near. Suddenly the warning went again and almost immediately the ground shook beneath our bodies and the dull thump of bombs sounded in the distance. We walked out of the wood and presently saw English fighters flying back to their aerodromes in threes and singly. "The raid is over," said L. Soon the sky settled and the all clear sounded. We walked slowly down the road and entered a different part of the wood. It was hot and green and dusty. Under the leaves with a bottle of beer we lay and forgot everything but the smell of the trees and the smell of the Arun, Martigues, Kenton. The sky was buzzing with anger again but we succeeded in ignoring it, we were as detached, as otherwise intent as insects there among the broken sticks, the trailing thorn . . . And we lay together looking into one another's eyes acting our own war and peace, while our bodies listened uneasily.

'As we kissed there was a burst of machine-gun fire, loud, in the sky. It rattled across the hills like an oath. With our faces together we waited for the next, our lips were warm against each other, the machine-gun cracked again and with our lips still touching we stared into the sky in each other's pupils, incredulous but without any surprise. Then all around the ground shook, the dry leaves crackled with repeated bombs, machine-guns bred and multiplied, planes tore their harsh parabolas across the sky and the siren split them all with its tragic wail. The sky was full, cut, slashed and shattered with noise. The ground heaved with the throb of bombs. We were still kissing. "I must see this," I said so we crept through the undergrowth and I ran from tree to tree to the edge of the wood. I lay in a ditch and watched. The sky heaved and boiled. I saw planes whirling round each other like little wooden crosses tossed up by a juggler. The noise was indescribable. I lay there for some moments my heart throbbing then I ran back to L crouching under a tree. We remained there waiting and helpless, fascinated. The bombs continued to fall with horrible deliberation, so irrevocable. Everything seemed to be directly above us, everything seemed to be aimed at us, we heard the vicious tearing whines of crashing planes coming down straight to us. We were uncovered, our backs

tingled as we lay. Presently the sound of battle shifted. We walked down to the road again and looked once more down into the sky . . . The aerodrome was blazing. We sat by the roadside and the battle receded into the distance . . . We found we were sitting by the gate of the cottage hospital, and very soon the ambulances began to arrive.

'. . . Later we returned to the wood & L drinking beer from an uncorked bottle swallowed a wasp. This filled us with considerably more dread than the bombardment. She had to go and be sick, and then we felt better.'

At the end of August 1940 Laurie gave in his notice to the sound unit after nine months. He had one more job to finish, at Dover, where he was caught in another air raid. He crouched against a wall watching with awe the sheets of flames left by the crumpling balloons, and pieces of AA shell and tracer bullets striking the road a few feet away. 'Then the raiders were out to sea, and all that remained were the echoes, the gleam of excitement on our faces . . .' Next day they filmed residents whose houses had been wrecked, to a background of gunfire, dogfights and balloon strafing. He watched bombers flying in formation, fighters wheeling and circling. 'I sat in the shaking trembling van recording it . . . They were flying north towards London, they seemed invincible, & it was terrifying to watch. But as soon as they were out of range of our guns, they were broken up by fighters and they began to stream back in twos and threes, making for home.' That evening the hotel was 'bright with the chatter of facetious newspapermen picking over the heroism and unspeakable brutality of the day's events'. Brother Jack was shooting every night in the East End for a film called *London Can Take It!* and actually fell into the Thames with a camera clutched to his stomach.

On 7 September Laurie left the studios. At nightfall fire glowed over the city. 'The damage in the East End was terrific and there were 40 killed and over a thousand seriously injured. Now the vicious bloody business has started in earnest, it is a war of terror aimed at every living thing. We are bombing Berlin. Dead children

in Germany, dead children in England, terror and madness in the hearts of the survivors . . . The stench of blood and the broken limb drowns the weak voice of humanitarian reason . . .'

The next day Jack and Laurie were returning from the West End by bus when the warning went; they threw themselves to the ground on Putney Bridge. Bombs had fallen in the road next to theirs. The following night, escaping to Arundel ('Next to Slad I could be more at home here than anywhere in England – but I'm like a bloody outlaw'), Laurie was picked up by the police as a suspicious character, 'partly due I expect to my Germanic appearance. They rang up Wilma and she vouched for me.' Wilma had indeed, as she wrote to her sister Margery, been telephoned and asked if she knew a Mr Lee, whom police had found 'hanging about' outside Arundel station with no identity card. 'Only a Laurie Lee would travel in defence areas without his War Office passes.' She told them he was 'an important government sound engineer, and that if he looked queer it was because he was epileptic. He turned up brightly and stayed two nights, and cleared up my rations for last week.'

From Wilma's, Laurie went to Annie in Slad, spending his evenings among the village women whose menfolk had gone to war, playing and listening to music. Feeling like an adolescent again, as he always did in Slad, he saw two local lads, Fred Tilley and Jack Halliday, 'marching up and down dressed as policemen. You feel they are still part of Slad Players dressed for rehearsal.' He saw Molly Smart in Gloucester with her newborn son, looking 'ripe & well, lactic & quite beautiful'. He visited relations, walked up Swift's Hill, dug potatoes. ('Down among the roots & worms & stones & weeds, the damp earth takes me back to old frustration & old contentment. Ringing fork combing the soil, raking the stones, panting with the effort, thick earth sticking to one's shoes, the sounds of the village around, a dog, a cough, a greeting bright & laconic.')

Then Lorna, having just sent her son Michael ('speechless with dread and misery'[1]) off to board at Bedales, suddenly telegraphed, instructing Laurie to 'reply to Glebe House and sign yourself Alan'

– and arrived at Slad next day. Laurie sat by the kitchen fire with his mother and his mistress. 'Mother is gay for moments without thinking . . . then she will bend her old face across the candles & almost weep that we are in love and not married & together.

'L puts on her nightdress with such a soft slow twist of her body that I think of salmon & the play of rivers and the gentle gestures of smoke. I sit hunched in bed watching her silent grace, a woman, alive, adoring the hour, the closed door, my eyes & the promise of sleep. And I cannot bear to extinguish the candle.'

Proudly he walked with Lorna through Stroud. They took a bus to Hereford, and looked at a house in the hills 'wild & lost from the world'. They walked along Slad Road eating fish and chips. They took sherry up Juniper Hill among the sheep '& there we lay for a while, half sleeping under the turning wheels of the sun. Later we went down to the old stonemason's hut and hung festival leaves on the walls and rinsed our teeth with sherry . . . and her body caught glints of autumn, red nipples & long bruised leaves . . .' The afternoon was later captured in his poem, 'Juniper'. 'That evening we were slightly drunk & in love with the village & miserable that we were leaving tomorrow.'

Back in Putney, John Lehmann's letter waited with proofs of Laurie's poems for the next *Penguin New Writing*, including 'Music in a Spanish Town': 'It seems anything on Spain gets a sympathetic reception,' Laurie noticed. Shrapnel fell on Putney High Street. Laurie was amazed by the imperturbability of Londoners amid the debris of Shaftesbury Avenue and Charing Cross Road, bombed a week ago. In Zwemmer's he bought Lorca's poems and, back at Werter Road, worked on the poems he had started in Slad, until guns shook the house, 'so down into the kitchen among the women, the smells, the hideous wallpaper, and there work is impossible'.

Millions were sleeping in shelters and tube stations. In their basement Mrs O'Neill and Wid were in hysterics, quaking under the table. Laurie would go out in his tin hat, crouching against the wall, hearing the bombs screaming past and thudding into the houses. 'Five fell, shaking the ground, and I leapt into the shelter with my head throbbing like a beating drum . . . Over the next

garden, a house had disappeared, & one thought of the crawling, groaning shattered human beings buried by beams & cut with red hot flying swords; suddenly their moment, their bitter personal war, their nameless death, coming upon them with awful tongues of flame, separating them from their cup of tea, their shining shoes, their harmlessness, their sins still unresolved.

'. . . But oh, the hopeless acid in the mouth, the fear, the madness, the anger: the wrong too great for blame, too bitter for repentance, too universal to avenge.'

By October Laurie had seen a hundred raids. One night a fever came on. He lay sweating and shivering in the kitchen, hearing gunfire like maddened drums. 'The women were terrified . . . Dolly recited the whole plot of Rider Haggard's *Witch's Head* while I lay on the sofa with a handkerchief soaked in lavender water on my forehead & went gently to sleep.' Annie wrote deploring the destruction of 'that London which for years I have dreamt of exploring with your or Jack's guidance . . .' and Laurie himself had had enough. He would leave London and 'find a shack to live in' close to Lorna. On 12 October 1940 he took a bus to Pulborough in Sussex and put up at the Railway Hotel. The landlady showed him a dressing-table drawer, full of papers: Sir Arnold Bax, the composer, had asked her to look after them. 'I caught sight of a letterhead, The Dorchester Hotel: "Darling WHY can't you write –" signed "Your Jeanie" – & I thought he was an old man.' From the hotel window on market day he watched a runaway cow head down the railway line, leap into the river and swim downstream.

He rang Wilma, who told him she had heard, years ago, about 'someone who was a bit mad & owned huts & cottages near Storrington'. He set off, and found himself in 'another Whiteway'. This was the Storrington Sanctuary,[2] where one Vera Pragnall had built a cross on the hill and freed the land for settlers to claim. 'From her book,' Laurie wrote later, 'she was enthusiastic, generous & riddled with mysticism . . . also full of the most awful arty-crafty, spinning, dancing-barefooted-in-the-dew clichés . . .'

He looked at a cottage, but then spied a green caravan 'much

more to my taste', just under Chanctonbury Ring, an area shortly to be occupied by the military. Next day, Lorna's grey Bentley took them to Storrington where they walked in the woods, lay in the bracken, and in the caravan found the bed made and oil ready for the lamps – prepared for them by the wife of the landlord, Dennis Earle. 'It was delightful. We went back to Pulborough, talking of the amazement of love, fetched my bags, bought a few things & back to the caravan. How nice to light the lamp and draw the curtains.' After Lorna had gone, he found 'little love messages' scrawled inside the crockery cupboard. 'Sweet beloved, they acted on me like delayed action bombs.'

Laurie quickly settled to his gypsy life. While London raids worsened, he heard owls hooting and a distant bugle: 'I thought of that artist in Tarazona trumpeting his sharp frozen music through the cold white streets . . .' He cooked sausages, listened to his wireless, and tussled with poems, 'complicated by lack of paper'. In the morning Lorna arrived 'wild of hair & in a green tartan frock with a long line of seductible buttons down the front', bringing books, eggs, tea, sandalwood and honey. 'Bed & sherry & sunlit gloom and smooth pools of eyes in the darkness. Late afternoon crept up like a thief behind our backs. We walked round the wood & picked leaves & teased a snake. As the evening grew blue & dusky she left . . . In the oily warmth of my van this evening, to the roar of planes overhead, I practically finished my poem.'

It was paradise: enchanted forests, shifting mists, groves of silver oaks, stark Nordic pines. In the evening silence, the caravan was bathed in mist and moonlight. Mornings brought hot sun and tropical colour. He went to Worthing 'along the road which I tramped six years ago with my fiddle & a fever & the kisses of Yvonne. How ghastly that town is, what wildernesses of bungalows.' A week later he packed up his belongings at Werter Road. Another bomb fell nearby. 'Mrs O read from *D Mirror* that Hitler had reached accord with Pétain. Italy has invaded Greece . . . Spain too may be forced to become a belligerent . . .'

As autumn came, bringing storms and gales, the caravan was less cosy. 'The evening was macabre & bitter with loneliness – I began

to feel scared.' 'All day her beauty has nagged my nerves with frustration. I must get a job.' 'Tonight there is a waxing moon and lust is waxing in my loins. It makes me mad alone here.' 'Depression covered me like a raven's wings, I could not shake it off.' But Lorna would arrive and drive him to Arundel, to the pictures, or to the Black Rabbit pub to sit over a roaring fire. 'It is a paradox,' wrote Laurie, 'that the best way to preserve the thrill & intensity of love is to put as much distance as possible between myself & the beloved.'

He found congenial neighbours, Hugh de Sélincourt and his wife: Hugh 'despite his somewhat Punch mentality' was a fan of Blake, and Mrs de Sélincourt lent him Haydn records and 'played Mozart with real feeling despite her fat coarse bunchy fingers'. There was a Mrs Brook, sister-in-law of the actor Clive Brook. A Mrs Aggs held musical evenings in a cloistered house with cold stone floors. The resourceful Mabel Mallet lived in a junk-filled hut named Unto the Hills, with a sign proclaiming 'Helping Hand Studios' offering 'typewriting, needlework, portrait-painting, lyric-writing, car for hire'. Laurie bought a bicycle and went to see films in the village hall 'rather like Spanish village cinemas, hard chairs, screaming boys, cheers & claps'. Lorna would drive him to concerts at the Abbey, where he saw Lorna's aunt, 'a wild old lady of 72 with painted cheeks & charcoal eyes. Arnold Bax sitting behind us.' He walked with Wilma on the Downs. He watched people picking over the bones of a crashed bomber. He took his fiddle to be repaired in Worthing, bought Beethoven music, tried to read Havelock Ellis's *Soul of Spain* but 'I can't bear to read about Spain, its tragedy is so raw & open & seems so personally symbolic.' He learned the names of the stars, 'something I've not been able to do before'.

On most mornings Lorna would come, 'like a stroke of good fortune, showering presents on my worthless head'. She brought 'flowers, mushrooms, bananas'; 'a tambourine, shells and a pretty little chessman carved out of apple wood'; 'some good paintings & Beethoven's Spring Sonata'; '8 goose eggs and an eddying fragrance of irresistible passion'; 'a cake, rabbit and vegetables, a bit of carving,

a chunk of apple wood like the fork of a tree and a half-formed woman leaning against it, lovingly carved . . . L is very proud of the cuts and callouses on her hands, token of her labour.' She would depart at dusk, to the distant rumble of guns and planes. On frosty mornings he woke cold and desolate, 'my mind ugly and raw, clutching desperately at the precipice' until 'L came again, with a bag of sweet cakes and two bottles of wine'. He played the violin while she cooked him salmon and potatoes or corned-beef hash or steak and onions, filling the caravan with oily aromas. 'We felt secure in the warm shadows of the van. In a nightdress fragrant with sandalwood, her nakedness was transparent in purple light. We shook the storms from our hair and sank in roots of weariness. We crossed the mountain of passion, our eyes roped together, our lips firm-footed in the slopes of darkness. I was easily abandoned in the fierce languor of love.'

Annie wrote, wondering how he was faring 'all on your lone-some. Are you far from any habitation?' In November the caravan was rocked by gales, whipped by rain. But Lorna came 'looking the very acme of desire'; 'a very acolyte, dressed in all the grace and colour of a premature primavera'. 'She came bringing cakes, and the *Oxford Book of Verse*, her hair becomingly piled up on the top of her head, fixed with a large comb she said was her grandmother's. Her face was fine & lovely under the sleek ebony of her coiffure; but later, when she had posed and held her head gracefully for me, she became impatient, combing it all out and saying I couldn't get my fingers into it. Which was true, but I did like it. We played some old records (Satie, which overwhelms us with its tenderness). The storms & the tortured trees were forgotten, the afternoon became one with night . . .

'At 6 o'clock we had plates of beans & giggled, making silly jokes that do not bear repeating but we laughed with pride & joy . . . And then, with hushed voices we would speak of November 1938. But suddenly digging her fingers deep into the rice pudding she looked across the table & said, "But Laurie don't you know what suttee is?"'

'Her head is so small & fine,' he reflected, 'like a lovely diminutive

jewel. When I hold it between my hands it gives to my body a sense of unbelievable grace, my hands are beautiful with this exquisite vessel between them. I marvel at the slender form of her skull, like a rare jar decorated with vivid designs of eyes & lips, slashed with brows & shadows, dreaming & overflowing with the warm wine of hair. I cannot imagine it ever growing old. It has the strong unalterable permanence of a work of art, a piece of statuary, that could be buried for a thousand years & still startle men's eyes with its barbaric beauty. Our love is a recurrent cycle. Lying in the dark intimacy of sheets we talked of it. Later when she stood naked in the candlelight I felt amazement & humility that this stalk of flesh, this passionate totem that had so often burnt my eyes in the desolate days of my adolescence, should now really exist for me.'

They cycled up to Chanctonbury Ring. On one occasion they were woken by a shepherd who leaned over them, hands on knees, and asked, 'How d'you like it 'ere?' They affected to despair over their separate lives, but were peculiarly happy. When Laurie was offered a hut on top of the hill for 10s a week, they went to peer through its windows, but decided they preferred the green caravan.

A German bomber flew over the woods, dropping four bombs; Laurie heard the whistle of a splinter beside him, six feet from the caravan, too hot to handle. Bombs destroyed houses, burst a water main, broke the telephone wire. One night Lorna, distracted by flashes, ploughed her car through a hedge and into a ditch. She showed him two great bomb craters on each side of the road near Bury Hill: 'She missed them by seven minutes on her way home from here a fortnight ago.'

There were solitary days of 'horrible nervous terror' and lonely nights 'loud with bombs & planes & tenseness'. But he was fine as long as the sun shone and she was with him. After she left, silence fell 'like a deafening wave' and alone, Laurie faced reality. 'The caravan closed in about me and the maddening terror reappeared. Violent pains in my head & a sense of dissatisfaction in my mind. Being with her is like being at the pictures, I am in another world drugged & oblivious to the actual condition of my life. And leaving her is like walking out into the cold reality of the street, the fantasy

is over & I must examine the irritating facts of my existence.' As Britain's industrial cities were devastated, Laurie was guiltily conscious of his apparent immunity from engagement. Whole days would pass when he 'made a few drawings, did a crossword puzzle, cooked a stew, trimmed the lamps, played my fiddle, and wrote two poems, one unprintable and the other incoherent'.

His isolation did strike him forcibly. 'Buried in my van I grow ever more remote almost to madness. It is a curious situation, with men & women dead, injured, overworked, faced with all forms of danger, with Europe obsessed and strained by war, I sit in my caravan, make tea, smoke black cigarettes and play the violin. I am not boasting – I am in some way amazed that I am allowed to do it. My life is more tranquil, more lacking in incident than it has ever been. I only know that it cannot continue so. One of these days, the strain of staring at myself will become too much for me & I shall have to move back into the city of activity. When I find myself making love on sunny afternoons with the sound of battle overhead I can only think there is something marvellously right about my life – or something terribly wrong. Although I like to feel, as I have always done, that nothing but life & love is my business, I have a recurrent breath of suspicion that I have some duty to my fellow men. We shall see how long I can ignore it.'

Did anyone know he was there? In December he was asked for his tax return ('heigh ho') but not until March 1941 did the Ministry of Labour write to suggest that he train for munitions, or return to the Film Unit. But almost unwittingly he was now 'a poet'. John Lehmann constantly asked for more poems. When the next *Penguin New Writing* arrived with its note about himself under 'About the Contributors', 'I regretted the data I had given Lehmann. One can so easily be charged with exhibitionism even when one is telling the truth. I also made no allowances for the natural vanity of L & my family. Neither she or they will like it to be known that I was an errand boy, even if that was what I was in reality.' When Lorna came she was 'mildly furious'.

A seductively scented Russian pianist called Madame Alexeieff

appeared next door with two Pekes, a warm stove, and a bath. She offered fragrant China tea, 'giving me the sense of mellow contentment, and a physical luxury as if one were clothed in silk. We played *Daphnis & Chloë* & she talked of Russia with a bitter sadness. Of Chaliapin, she said: 'Yes, I suppose he was a fine singer, but he lived on the Volga & was knocked on the head when he was young, and he was only an errand boy you know.'

Foolishly Laurie mentioned the Russian lady to Lorna. In exciting her suspicions he was playing with fire, knowing that she was prone to explosions of angry jealousy. One day he found her in the caravan looking at his letters and reading through his diary. After he relates this in his diary, there are lines pencilled in Lorna's hand: 'I didn't really lend the Beethoven to be copied but was jealous of you playing it with someone else! I'm sorry if I annoyed you or got on your nerves. I love you.'

'On a germ of truth she builds up vast fantasies of infidelity & guilt. I secretly rejoice, but far from removing her suspicions I only succeed, by protestations & shiftless grinning, to appear hopelessly culpable.' She imagined he spent his time apart from her 'in the arms of revolting blondes. She threatens me with spectacular infidelities unless I mend my ways. But I have not broken them. What more can I say than that I love her? . . . Walking the black streets she said, "I feel very miserable – I feel nobody wants me." I said how silly you are when you're the centre of my life. I stood and held her in the darkness. "I don't trust you a bit," she said. Her jealousy is based partly on my poem. She takes "I cannot clear your high gold from my head" to be a reference to some blonde!'

Winter brought freezing mists and grey sleet; Laurie succumbed to one of his bronchial fevers. He sat hunched, dazed and coughing, his violin hanging from the ceiling echoing each cough and parodying it harmonically, like a musical parrot. 'The caravan sways, rocks & trembles at the slightest sound, poised so delicately on its springs that it seems to shudder even when I lay down my pen.' 'Horrible night of knotted nerves, restless mad fancies & sleeplessness.'

Back in Slad for Christmas, he found alien planes floating over

the valleys, the woods aglow under searchlights, and guns and splinters bursting over Bulls Cross: 'It is too near home; it is incredible.' He had a plum-pudding-and-crackers Christmas at Marjorie's, played games with nieces and nephews, drank port and sherry, 'visited Phyl in hospital & kissed all the struggling nurses under the mistletoe'. He chopped logs, played his fiddle, saw the new year in with Annie, and returned to find his little green caravan dark and chill. 'Poor Tom's a-cold tonight. So cold I can't settle to finish the poems I've been working on.'

When he saw Lorna again, 'burning like the bush of Moses in spite of the weather', he fell on her, 'revoking the realization of a fortnight's fantasy. I trembled & sang & stamped the cloven feet . . . hands probing into scarlet caverns, I reduced her to helplessness & took her, sick with power.' For her thirtieth birthday he bought Lorna a silver chain, and for himself a camel-haired overcoat with shoulders like yardarms. 'L came this morning and caught me all behind as my mother would say. She had just taken Yasmin to the doctor's where he removed several yards of wool from her nose . . . sad proof of a hereditary recurrence of the nose-stuffing that has made our family a thing of wonder and fear for many generations.' Plump, coy and lively, Yasmin scrambled about the caravan, blowing notes on his recorder. 'I look at her quaint, charming, homely face, her pretty squat little body and cannot yet get it into my head that she is mine.'

Annie was ailing with 'flu, the cottage's chimney smoked and there was ice underfoot, 'but I rise above it once more,' she added, hoping that Laurie had aired his bedclothes. She longed to see Yasmin ('little soul!') and Lorna, 'poor child, but I don't want her to come to this dreadful dreadful house. I love her & always shall. Did she tell you I sent a little dog to Yasmin & she loves it & carries it about. Oh Laurie darling they are cutting the trees down and I can't bear it. Soon there will be no background to our cottages. First they cut two elms one ash one sycamore then this afternoon they cut beautiful scotch pine, then a spruce. Oh dear.' Laurie was 'still with horror at the thought'.

Then Lorna came tearing up the lane 'splashing the tops of the

trees with mud', bringing snowdrops, Christmas roses, champagne. 'I can say I have never seen her looking more beautiful, champagne in her hands and her eyes. Her black sweater & black hair enclosed her face like night enfolding a star. And round her throat hung the silver chain . . . She tells me she is in love with me again, and her demonstrations do compensate for the rather disquieting knowledge that she was once, then not, in that emotional state which she now professes.

'Our difficulties are boundless. I live in a most inaccessible place, petrol is rationed, and her children are sickening for something . . . After a particularly wild shaking release she sleeps deeply, but I sleep just under the sweet surface of wakefulness. A particularly loud cry of a bird will wake me with a terrific start.'

Sometimes he bridled at being the secret lover; he could go to Binsted to visit Wilma, 'but it is forbidden country, Christ al-bloody-mighty. I skulk around the hedges like a poacher & don't begin to whistle till I'm in the bus well on my way to Worthing . . . When can I take my girl into the open?' Lorna would remind him of her marital commitments, 'fiendishly dwelling on the in-evitability of conjugal surrenders'. She told of a nightmare after which she had woken up screaming for Wish: 'How I hate that she should awaken like that.' She showed him the £50 bill for the thick silvery sealskin coat Wish had given her. 'She confesses that she wanted to impress upon me that others still thought her desirable. But I am not in need of such virulent propaganda.' She might sit quietly in the afternoons, darning his socks, but '. . . I don't know what it is to walk easily up a street with her, or to write her a frank carefree letter. I have never been able to feel "tomorrow I'll call & have tea with her" or "tonight I think I'll ring her up". I have never been able to take her & show her to a friend & say look, this is my woman: I have had none of those normal domestic gaieties of love. Always we have lived in a state of subterfuge, each second together stolen from the cannon's mouth and consumed under a canopy of uneasiness. For four years it has been like this, for four years I've dreamed about her husband. No wonder the actual state of war in which we are now living, days & nights of anxiety, of

restriction, of hand-to-mouth existence, does not seem strange to me.'

He brightened, as he always would, with the spring: 'Such a bright singing day I take on quite a different personality. I am myself in the sun, the world has glamour; when it is cold I am a corpse.' He went to London to meet his patron John Lehmann ('tall, teutonic looking and deferential') at the Café de l'Europe. Lehmann praised the richness of Laurie's latest poems and asked how Laurie had started writing poetry, and who were the influences on his young life. Laurie declined to write a 'how we live today' on life in Storrington, but agreed to write something about Spain. Annie sent his Spanish diaries so that he could begin. While in London he went to the Players' Theatre with Jack, where the master of ceremonies, Leonard Sachs, referred from the stage to 'the Masters Lee – or should it be Mister and Master Lee?'

March brought another bone-aching fever, 'throbbing in my tousled bed, sweating, arguing, groaning with thumping head, exhaustion and full of foreboding & nervous strain, aching and rather sorry for myself needing a woman & L did not come. I felt the old slow fires of temper growing inside me. But she had been ill, too . . .' He dreamed that Yasmin was hurt, and that Wish was holding her in his arms, but had handed her over to Laurie 'without a murmur, as if he understood'. On Yasmin's second birthday he sent a bracelet and a new florin, and spent the day acting an air-raid victim, lying for hours under a blanket for a first aid film. When he saw the film he thought how old he looked. Lorna told him, 'I'm longing for you to grow old – each new wrinkle on your face is a joy to me – I want you to grow old & repulsive so that no one will want to look at you.' Laurie said, 'I've nearly reached that state anyway.' He was nearly twenty-seven.

One day he met 'a dark man' in the local shop buying rice. Next day 'the negro' visited him, with a girl, to fetch Laurie and his records. He was from Kenya, Laurie learned, and had been Alexander Korda's technical adviser on *Sanders of the River*, but was 'too red' to be allowed to go home again. It was Jomo Kenyatta – later to become president of Kenya.[3] 'We had tea on the balcony

overlooking the downs, and played Ellington, flamencos and Indian records and Jomo trembled and danced in his chair and rolled his brown eyes and jerked his great bearded head back and forth. He has some fine African records. The girl, pale and English and out of touch with all this, preferred Debussy.' Later Laurie went to hear Kenyatta lecturing, in the great hall of a stately home at Little Thakeham, on African colonies: 'We heard all about the black man's burden & joined in reviling the Commonwealth.'

One terrible night in March, Lorna's 'prim, respectful' cook, Rose, was beaten to an unrecognizable pulp by a soldier. 'Wish was marvellous,' Lorna told Laurie. 'He nursed her and bathed her and held her on his knee, but Michael and I nearly passed out.' She was overcome with man-hating fury. 'Just force and lust, that's what it was, I hate the thought of men – I hate soldiers – I hate myself.' 'But as she drove away she said "Love me, love me all the time."' Laurie felt sick and appalled. 'But what can you expect of soldiers from the lives they lead, celibate, disciplined, praised out of all proportion, taught a trade of violence which they are persuaded is the most honourable that can fall to a man.'

One day the caravan's landlord, Dennis Earle, suggested that Laurie might earn his rent by gardening for ten hours a week. Laurie haggled: his rent was only seven shillings a week, and labourers earned a shilling an hour: so he would do two mornings a week, seven hours in all. He blistered his hands with digging. In the evenings he played music with the de Sélincourts or listened to jazz at Kenyatta's where they talked of Nancy Cunard and negro poetry. Annie wrote peevishly, 'If you are able to hold a pen or pencil write & say how the world's treating you. My address above. Perhaps you are very busy, poem writing or something?'

He was poem writing, but had no confidence in his latest efforts ('I have the feeling that all the others were flukes') and Lehmann found most of them 'too Dylan Thomas'. 'This was a little unfair as I don't read him.' The same week came the *New Statesman* with a warm mention of Laurie's four 'striking' poems in a review by G.W. Stonier. Laurie was also writing his first piece of prose, 'Night in Castelleja', about Spain before the Civil War, for the summer

issue of the Hogarth Press's *Folios of New Writing*, though Lorna demoralizingly declared that the subject was 'dead meat . . . Hemingway killed it'. 'I am not being modest when I say I don't think it will be any good to you,' wrote Laurie to Lehmann. 'It is just an amplified extract from my diary, nothing more.' It was the account of playing his fiddle for the stomping, politically excited vineyard workers of Andalucía in June 1936. Lehmann told him he would make some small cuts 'where I think you overdo it a little (a criticism I sometimes hear of your poetry)'.

Laurie also had a letter published in the *News Chronicle*, on 26 March 1941 (signed L.E.A. Lee of Stroud) in defence of young people toiling in factories. 'A modern war-time factory is no bed of roses, the long hours, day in, day out, tend to stifle the high spirits and craving for simple enjoyment natural to every youth. Consequently they react in violence, destruction and petty crime.'

In April he and Lorna went away for a weekend, but her car broke down 'just as we were about to spin off for a little freedom'. The car was towed away and they caught a series of buses to rainy Petersfield and found a mean little hotel with iron bedsteads, paintings of shipwrecks on the walls, and a maid named Ethel. They went to church, Lorna in a little white scarf. An usher asked if they had come for a churching. ('I wish we had been.') Back in the caravan a letter waited, offering Laurie a job as Assistant Director in what was now called the Crown Film Unit, at £5 a week. 'Rang L who is in bed with flu. She wept when I said I might go, so of course I promised her I wouldn't. (I remember once, when we were together, she wept long & bitterly when I talked of leaving her. She couldn't contemplate living without me, she cried, she made me promise never to leave her. But it didn't prevent her from leaving me.)'

John Lehmann now wanted up to fifteen poems for the third volume in the *Poets of Tomorrow* series. Four poems were ready for the next *New Writing*: 'Larch Tree', 'Juniper', 'Look into Wombs', 'End of a Season'. He wrote another 'for Lorna' and took it to her. Yasmin, bundled in red wool, was there, 'chattering like a magpie'.

'She played with me but would not kiss me. "No-o-o," she said. I watched her, having thought of her as Us, existing through Us and dependent on Us, but I suddenly knew that she was more than that, she was herself, with an independent will & spirit, and not only existed apart from us, but even sometimes looked upon me with the blank eyes of a stranger. Though unpleasantly inevitable I never foresaw this.'

Suddenly one day a plain-clothes CID man arrived and told Laurie he was breaking the law by living in the caravan. Annie wrote: 'I think it is rotten the police interfering . . . you do have adventures Laurie boy.' They packed his stuff into a barrow and wheeled it over to Dennis Earle's spare studio, built a wood fire and Lorna arranged cowslips in a saucepan on the table. 'Walking back beneath the castle to have tea we leaned over a bridge. A duck & a drake circled each other passionately. Suddenly we heard the cuckoo loud & close. It called three times from the trees above the castle. We leapt into one another's arms. We wanted to hear it for the first time together & it happened.'

London was enduring its worst raids. The Houses of Parliament had been hit, the debating chamber destroyed. Rudolf Hess landed in Scotland. Laurie watched in disgust a newsreel called *The World in Flames*, which ended with shots of London in ruins. 'The commentary reached a crescendo. "Here's to bigger & better bombs!" it shouted.' Churchill's speeches were 'hardly reassuring'. 'Nothing becomes any easier, any less complicated, any less hopeless as time goes on.' He would lie in bed reading Plato, or Martial, or *The Good Soldier Schweik* (still catching up on his untutored literary education) and listening to the crack of machine-guns and the roar of engines until his hair stood on end.

As summer came the lovers resumed their open-air lovemaking. 'We stood against the sky touching each other and she looked into my face, laughing and saying, "You are extraordinary, you are really."' This August would be the start of their fifth year.

On the flyleaf of Lorna's copy of *Folios of New Writing*, Spring 1941, Laurie wrote:

Again your lily's dazzling star
revolving in the burning springs
transfixes with its scimitar
my happy fascinated wings
and I am full content that I
should on your perfumed petals die.

There are at least thirty versions of these lines in his note-book.

'She didn't think much of my last opus . . .' he wrote. 'I affected despair at her criticism, lying on the bed with my face to the wall. She came from cooking the stew, leant over me & kissed me. "Darling," she said to comfort me, "you know I think you're marvellous. I think your poems are the most beautiful I've ever read." I laughed loud & bitterly. "I *do*," she said coaxingly, "I do really – I said so to Mavin [her brother] & he laughed too." Cold comfort.'

In June they went back to Slad. They found Annie in her garden, 'wild, wayward and uncontrolled. The back kitchen had been whitewashed & the door painted blue with a bright yellow keyhole. We thought this rather a misplaced sophistication. There were three new kittens (there are always three new kittens) making five cats in all.' Lorna and Laurie played together in frustrated harmony on Annie's horribly out-of-tune piano. Again it was hot, even in the evening, poppies and peonies blazing, syringa in bloom. 'The days following were yellow with endless sun & we were quietly indolent. In the mornings we would go to Stroud, have lunch, and return to lie naked by the lake or in the woods or the fields.' Laurie did a drawing of Lorna, sitting pensively on Juniper Hill, with her hair in plaits, the sun shining so whitely on the paper he could hardly see. They sat on walls and both drew views of the village. 'Some of her sketches aren't bad in a childish way . . . Her eye is remarkably simple, perspective is ignored, and nothing has any logical relation with anything else. Her results, therefore, are remarkably refreshing.' Laurie also photographed her, lying half

1. Laurie's father, Reg Lee

2. Laurie's mother, Annie
Emily Lee, *née* Light

3. The infant Laurie ('a frail lifeless lump'), with elder brother
Jack and sister Frances

4. Laurie aged five

5. Annie's cottage (now
Rosebank) in Slad

6. Slad School: Laurie is in the back row, second from left; in the middle row,
fourth from left, is his cousin Rosie Green, later Rosie Buckland, popularly
supposed to be *the* Rosie

7. Peace Day fancy dress parade in Slad: Laurie as John Bull, with Rosie Green as a fairy at his right

8. Laurie (back row, second from left) in Slad Wolf Cubs; brother Tony is kneeling, right front

9. A couple of swells: Jack and Laurie in their plus-fours

10. Molly Smart with Laurie, June 1932 (*Betty Farmer*)

11. Betty and Molly Smart, the girls from Gloucester, 1933 (*Betty Farmer*)

12. Cleo of Whiteway, in 1934

April 15th. 1939

13. Sufi Rogers, the girl from Buenos Aires who taught Laurie to say '*Un vaso de agua, por favor*'

14. *top left* Laurie, photographed in Southampton, having just walked out one midsummer morning: 'a pale, oleaginous shade . . . his old clothes powdered in dust'

15. *top right* Laurie in Toledo, with Mary (*née* Garman) and Roy Campbell, 1935 (*Anna Campbell Lyle*)

16. *middle right* Wilma Gregory, benefactress and self-styled 'aunt'

17. *centre* Laurie in Martigues, with six-year-old Kathy on his knee, 1937

18. *bottom left* A bronzed Laurie and his fiddle in Málaga, 1935

19. Lorna Wishart, mistress and muse

20. Laurie bound for the Spanish Civil War, 1937. This photograph is thought to be the one he used for his International Brigade identity card

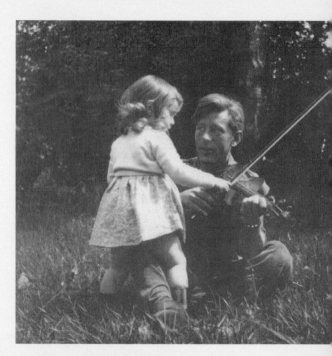

21. Laurie, his fiddle, and his
two-year-old daughter
Yasmin, Sussex, 1941
(*Yasmin David*)

22. Portrait of the poet by
Bill Brandt, Bognor, 1942
(*Bill Brandt* ©*Bill Brandt
Archives Ltd*)

23. Anthony Devas
and his wife,
Nicolette, with
their children
Emma and
Esmond and (in
the foreground)
two playmates,
April 1945 (*Devas
Family Collection*)

24. Anthony
Devas's portrait of
Laurie with two
of the Devas
children, Emma
and Esmond, and
Eileen McKinney,
1945. Eileen was
the daughter of
Ruth McKinney,
author of the *My
Sister Eileen* stories
(*Private Collection*)

naked on the grass, 'white like a new moon' sitting on the bank of the stream, doing her hair. 'She looks over her shoulder, sly & bold. It is perfectly French, reeking with wine, good food, and the flesh.'

'In all the fierce blaze of days we did little but lie among the grasses and watch the valley. Sometimes a quiet tenderness hung over us as we walked in the garden, or surrounded us like an extra fragrance as we lay close in the new summer blossoms.' At other moments 'I felt the bitterness of never completely possessing the full heart & attention of this woman . . . in the middle of a kiss her eyes open to the sky and her mind goes back to her children.'

Barrage balloons floated overhead. They lay in Brith Wood at midnight, among the badgers. Laurie waded into the pond to fetch pink and white lilies. He carried Lorna up through the nettles to the attic of the ruined cottage by the war memorial, 'hot with a sort of adolescent lust. The evening was a green and rosy gloom, creepers climbed through the broken lattices almost shutting out the light.'

On the Sunday morning in June when Germany invaded Russia Laurie went to bed with a fever '& I thought of Martigues, but the fever was neither so intense, nor did L sit gazing into my face'. On his twenty-seventh birthday they set off for London, Lorna in a chaste grey costume (such a lady, said Annie), and parted at Victoria. Annie sent a birthday parcel after him – soap, tea, sugar, cheese, butter, margarine, lard, lemonade powder, jelly, biscuits, dates, gooseberries and three roses 'all rather mixed'. 'You do know don't you that I was very pleased to have you & your dear one,' she wrote, enclosing a letter for Lorna, thanking her for 'the lovely stockings and also the "little bit of paper"'. Back at Storrington the sun was like a furnace. Laurie hoed potatoes, stripped to the waist, burnt brown, dreaming of Spain. 'L arrived in her old summer frock, scarlet, like a pimento. We lay on the bed in a stupor of heat and the red dress opened down the front and her limbs were cool and white like a sweet vegetable.' By the river at Arundel, Lorna wore a green dress which dated back to Martigues. 'She brought me four eggs, and a weasel stole two out of my bag when we were

swimming.' They lay in the reeds, and walked through banks of twisting eglantine. Herons flew above them, fighter planes came and went, waterfowl shrieked. 'I like that sound. You've no idea what it does to me,' said Lorna.

A *Spectator* review of *New Writing* declared that 'Laurie Lee's Lorcan imagery may prove baffling'. 'Apart from the Juniper poem which is personal, anyway,' wrote Laurie crossly, 'I can't see anything in the other three to baffle anyone.' But some poems of this period might indeed baffle: they present the reader with a succession of images and impressions, which only really spring to vivid sense in the context of his pastoral adventures with Lorna while battles raged overhead:

> Pondering your scented skull
> I seek its antique song of peace:
> >   desires uncovered by your tide
> >   are trembling reeds with sea-blue voices.
>
> I wind my hands around your head
> and blow the hollow flutes of love,
> >   but anger sprouts among the leaves
> >   and fields grow sharp with war.
>
> Wheat bleeds upon a wind of steel
> and ivy splits the poisoned sky,
> >   while wasps that cannot fertilize
> >   dive at the open flowers of men.
>
> Your lips are turreted with guns,
> and bullets crack across your kiss,
> >   and death slides down upon a string
> >   to rape the heart of our horizon.
>
> ('Song in August', 1940)

In mid-July 1941, the BBC wrote offering Laurie a fee of five guineas to read his poems on a programme called *Turning Over a*

New Leaf. 'I sat on the steps and trembled violently, and thought of fits and nerves sweeping the words out of my mind in front of the microphone. When I recovered I wanted to tell someone so I mentioned it casually to Steve who was building a wall. "Oh," he said, "my aunt broadcast a few weeks back." "What about?" I asked, deflated. "Sausage making," he said.'

He told Lorna, and she didn't think he could do it.

Meanwhile, not far away, Helen Garman had brought her daughter Kathy, now nine, home to England. Kathy had waved her father Marius goodbye, and he told her the war would soon be over – but she never saw him again, although Helen had bravely gone back to France to try to persuade him to leave the country too. Kathy was sent first to the Dorset village of Moreton to stay with her aunt Sylvia Garman, friend of T.E. Lawrence.[4] One day, a telegram arrived to say her father had died, of pleurisy.

She was taken to Vine Cottage, East Harting, where her grandmother Marjorie Frances Garman provided a haven for her grandchildren: Kitty and Esther, Kathleen's daughters by Epstein, and later Mary Campbell's daughters Anna and Teresa. The governess who had taught all nine Garmans – Mary Elizabeth Thomas, known as Tony, who had 'the face of a dove and the heart of a lion'[5] – was in charge of the children. Esther and Kitty were superior and unpleasant to their French cousin Kathy. 'Her name was Polge, and we called her Bulgy,' Kitty says. But in the village lived a Miss Murray, a former governess who liked to talk French and took Kathy under her wing. She called her '*mon loup*'. Helen was working for the Free French in London, so she stayed with her sister Kathleen at 272 King's Road, and both sisters would visit their children in East Harting at weekends. All the girls would sometimes call on their Aunt Lorna at Marsh Farm, where the glamour and wealth of the chatelaine dazzled them all.

That summer, Laurie decided he had had enough of isolated Storrington and decided to find rooms in Bognor, which despite mines and barbed wire was packed with cheerful holidaymakers. Deaf, drunken old landladies showed him dark, cluttered rooms. Eventually he found a furnished cottage down Market Street, near

the beach where he had once spent the day with Mollie in 1934. The rent was £1 a week. The cottage smelled of gas cookers, like Werter Road, but the wallpaper in the bedroom was the same as in Lorna's old nursery, and the homely landlady Mrs Savage proved to be another Mrs O'Neill: 'If you feel like having anyone in here all the week, don't think I shall mind.'

On 2 August he worked in the garden for the last time, collected his music from the de Sélincourts, packed his books into Mabel Mallet's car and on a clear dappled morning left the Storrington Sanctuary. 'Everything seemed sharp & lovely and I gazed about me with affection because I am leaving it. I have been lonely but not exactly unhappy here.'

Laurie's modest poetic output might have been even scantier had
he not been galvanized by John Lehmann, whose patronage was
both an inspiration and an irritation as he demanded more poems.
'I would like to go on pushing your stuff as much as possible,' he
told Laurie. '*Poets of Tomorrow* is going to press, and I shall have to
invent something if you don't let me have the goods.' 'I never felt
less like poetry but was forced to,' wrote Laurie wearily. When
Lehmann told him that his sister Rosamond liked his work, and
wanted to meet him, 'I feel almost guilty,' Laurie told his diary, 'as
if I'm cheating them all . . . it makes me uneasy that the stuff I've
produced is so slight.'

The day of his broadcasting début – 25 August 1941 – loomed.
He left anxiously for London, where Lorna swept him off to the
Café Royal with her Old Etonian painter friend David Carr,
who 'smoothly delivered light amusing stories with that languid
articulation which is the social genius of his class'. They repaired
to the Swiss pub in Old Compton Street where Dylan Thomas
was swaying at the bar: 'a young rather tubby man, straw coloured
in a pork pie hat, with a snub nose, pale eyes and a small loose
mouth. He had two females with him, both blowsy and both rather
drunk. One was talking to him in unsteady lurches and calling him
"darling" – the other was his wife. I gave him a drink & a cigarette
. . . He was bleak, dead & rather miserable, saying he had a wife &
child to keep and no job. He looked about him joylessly with wet
subterranean eyes as if the whole world was a wet Monday. I
thought him flabby and conceited . . .

'Meanwhile a dark veiled figure, thin & gaunt like a spook, had
taken a seat at our table and L called to me and introduced this
thing. A white gloved hand, cold & rubbery, reached up to me. I
saw two huge dark eyes, two thin purple lips and a dusty white

face inquiring at me from a pillar of black lace & crêpe. I thought of Kathleen. "This is the Marchesa," said L. "[Augustus] John painted her." I remembered the picture and the eyes. L introduced me as a poet. "Never live with a poet," said the thing, half in Italian – "I lived with D'Annunzio." (It was the Marchesa Luisa Casati.[1])

From another corner Roy Campbell appeared. 'Bald, trembling & smiling . . . He was delighted to see us, he said, and sat at the table, stuttering, looking from one to the other, smiling & quivering with apologies. He had been f-for F-Franco in the Spanish war and now it was like having backed the wrong horse. "I was wrong Lorna," he said. She laughed and slapped his arm. "There now Roy, after the way we used to fight, you see?" "Yes," he said hoarsely, "I admit it, I admit being wrong." He returned to his corner . . .'

Lehmann was waiting at Broadcasting House, and they went down to a hot little studio. The clock swept round to zero. Lehmann had told him to read his poems slowly and clearly, as if speaking to someone in an armchair in the same room. Laurie read 'The Larch Tree', 'The Secretive Cuckoo', 'Juniper' and 'The Armoured Valley'. Lehmann signalled to him to read more. He read 'Winter 1939–40' – 'A gentle dove the icicle is now'. Lehmann said that Laurie's poems put him in mind of the carvings of the Crusaders in old English churches. Laurie responded with his prepared lines about writing in wartime and poetry in general, and was followed by a record of T.S. Eliot reading *East Coker*. 'It was over and I felt gay.' In the foyer Lorna waited, and so did Rosamond Lehmann: 'a handsome woman with large deep eyes and silver hair, and the skull of her brother. I walked down Oxford St with her. She said that she thought my poems really beautiful – so disciplined etc. – I found myself saying how much I loathed women writers.'

At the Café Royal he bought roses for Lorna who had now joined the daughter of Eugene Goossens. Laurie had had enough of the smart places and they went to a noisy Lyons brasserie, then to a pin-table dive where Lorna had her fortune told by a gypsy. Laurie's last train had gone, and they found a hotel. 'Suddenly, my weariness left me and a great volcano of delight shook us with

joyful flames.' Next morning they bought Stravinsky's *Symphony of Psalms* at the HMV shop, and took the train back to Sussex, where they 'strutted through the streets elbowing away the crowds with our embracing and ate peanuts till we rattled'.

Laurie's broadcasting career had begun. He sent Annie a portion of his five-guinea fee.

But when Lehmann wired again asking for more poems for *Penguin New Writing 10*, 'I beat my breast in despair. I could think of nothing. I polished up four and sent them to him but I have little confidence in them . . . they don't blend as they should.'

Becoming recognized as a poet seemed to create its own momentum. Tambimuttu[2] reprinted three poems in a new Faber anthology. Kaye Webb wired from *Lilliput*: they were sending Bill Brandt down to Bognor to photograph Laurie. Annie was delighted to see his 'phiz' in *Lilliput*: 'You really are becoming famous now aren't you? I had already seen hundreds of copies, thrust in my face by all & sundry. I hope you won't get "swelled head", with all the praises you get.' On the contrary, 'I was quietly deflated by it all,' Laurie noted. 'I feel as always that the best is passed and I can never do as well again.' The day Brandt arrived, Laurie cleaned his room and lit a fire, and took Brandt and his assistant to lunch and to swim at the beach: 'I felt they were press and therefore had to be entertained.' The resulting picture – one of the most famous of Laurie – made him look 'a rugged and Olympian roué'; the other poets under the headline 'Poets of Democracy' were 'a gallery of hideous morons & gargoyles. Dylan Thomas looks sick in a pub, Day-Lewis screws horrible faces at a newspaper, MacNeice scowls like a greasy witch, Spender is flayed by an overhanging lamp.' Laurie's 'Words Asleep' was printed beneath his picture. 'I suddenly felt it was very easy to write poetry.'

But Lehmann was asking for more prose too. He suggested that Laurie might write 'some rather personal sketch or story about the Cotswolds, and your early days there' for the *Geographical Magazine*, where he was advisory editor. 'We are very anxious to have more articles about England and the English countryside . . . The Spanish diary was such a success.' Laurie duly wrote an article about the

Whitsun Treat outings of his childhood, which was greeted by the editor as 'a little work of art . . .', upon which Laurie 'sang lustily'. Lehmann pronounced it 'fresh and full of colour and amusing images' but added: 'If anything, I think it's a little too concentrated, a little too packed with imagery: if you were writing anything longer, I think you'd have to watch that. But . . . you really must go on writing prose.'

The *Geographical Magazine* wanted pictures of his cottage, the church, the squire's house, etc. Had Laurie any objection to his village being identified? A photographer was dispatched to Slad. Annie expected him on the wrong day, had left her house keys in a bag of beans at Tony's house, someone had to break in through a window, it was raining, and the photographer missed the bus and had to walk from Stroud 'and the poor boy is a cripple, did you know? What a pity it was wet & dingy & dull, and the day before was glorious.' She agonized over the fact that she had just had the kitchen painted and there was only one teapot on the mantelpiece, 'so I'm afraid you'll be disappointed about this as you don't like things to be changed'. But his article – Laurie had sent a manuscript – 'Oh my dear, I think it beautiful, your fanciful idea of a children's day of joy in lovely surroundings in beautiful weather. I laughed heartily . . . Of course I knew who you meant by the various names. Well dear Laurie will you allow me to rewrite part of it so that anyone who knew the people in S. could not be hurt in any way. NOT bald-headed Mrs Lewis, put smiling Mrs Grey, and what about "the village cripple" could it be altered? Please write by return and say I may. It's the names dear.'

But he changed nothing, and when the magazine came out with 'bald Mrs Lewis', Annie was reproachful: 'It to me marred the whole story and I cannot with pleasure show it to anyone who knows the person meant. I have taken it up to Mrs Brown and told her not to let Mrs Tilley see it or Mrs Oakey . . . I read some of the story aloud to Eileen John and Mrs Walters oh they did laugh but Eileen was disappointed that there was nothing about her as she thought she was a school sweetheart.' It was an early foretaste of Slad's reaction to *Cider with Rosie* two decades later.

While in the caravan, Laurie had gone to the cinema most weeks; in Bognor, he and Lorna went even more often. They saw *Major Barbara*, *Boom Town*, *Our Town*, *La Femme du Boulanger*, the Marx Brothers, *The 49th Parallel*, *The Maltese Falcon*, *Citizen Kane*, *Hellzapoppin'*, *Blood and Sand*, *Scarface*. Afterwards they would take home nine-penn'orth of fish and chips, or Lorna would cook 'evocative' rice dishes, 'full of onions, winkles, tomatoes and oily smells of Spain'. On a newsreel they saw what was happening in Russia: the dead laid out in heaps surrounded by weeping women. 'One felt a fever of fear & horror, one could smell the horrible humiliation of death. We were suddenly in the centre of all this foul business, & felt sick.'

Lehmann's sister Rosamond now made a determined approach to make Laurie her friend. She wrote from Diamond Cottage at Aldworth on the Berkshire Downs declaring that she and Laurie had a bond in their 'mutual dislike of women writers', and that Cecil Day-Lewis would love to meet Laurie; she would fix a date in London.

Lorna read this letter and was furious. Rosamond was a threat. She was 'an operatic goddess of a woman'[3] with a face of Dresden china beauty (or in Alan Ross's words, 'like a creamy meringue') and a sterling literary pedigree.[4] Her first novel, *Dusty Answer*, written while she was living in Newcastle married to the Methodist businessman Leslie (later Lord) Runciman, had been an overnight sensation in 1927. Her second husband, Wogan Philipps (Lord Milford), the Communist peer, failed to return to her after the Spanish Civil War. She had published three more novels, all dealing with women unhappily in love. She had two children, and told Laurie: 'I've always thought how satisfactory it would be to pull off being a good artist as well as being a successful mother...' When she befriended Laurie, she had become the lover of Cecil Day-Lewis, whom she had first met in 1936.

Bidden to Rosamond's London home in Gordon Place, Kensington, Laurie went first to see the Sickert paintings at the National Gallery, and then wandered in Bloomsbury: he went to see 10 Kenton Street, its balcony covered with flowerpots, and

Mecklenburgh Square, where he and Lorna had first lived. 'No 35 had completely disappeared, a black heap of ash and cinders with one wall left standing. Somehow I was not sorry.' He found Rosamond's house 'crowded with pictures and furniture of the decayed gentlewoman type' and Rosamond 'as tender and sentimental as her books'. When Day-Lewis arrived, he and Rosamond sat in the same chair, and Laurie told them about his caravan. Day-Lewis, who was then editing pamphlets for the Ministry of Information, was intrigued. He asked Laurie to lunch next day: they talked of Dylan Thomas and Roy Campbell. It was the start of a valued friendship.

Laurie was ten years younger than Day-Lewis and they were 'as different as two complicated men can be'[5] but they became fastly entwined. Day-Lewis was vacillating (and did for another eight years) about whether to leave his wife Mary and their sons Sean and Nicholas. Rosamond quickly latched on to Laurie as her confidant, as one of the few people who did not date from Day-Lewis's previous life. Laurie was grateful that a respected poet should take him seriously enough to show him his new sonnet sequence 'O Dreams O Destinations', and solicit his opinion.

Day-Lewis also put Laurie in touch with the composer Ben Frankel, his old Whiteway associate ('So our paths cross again aha!'), who wired to say he needed three Russian songs reworked for his new play – by the end of that week. Laurie ('Oh Lord') felt swamped and overwhelmed by this commission, and sent them off knowing they weren't right. As he feared, they weren't: 'I wish I could have pulled it off.' Jack, whose new film *The Pilot is Safe* had been favourably reviewed, arrived by car in Bognor one evening; they had fish and chips 'and boasted to one another'. But as winter approached Laurie felt flat and melancholy. Lorna calmed him, lit fires and was 'as gracefully voluptuous as of old'. She told him that when the war was over she planned to live abroad and have lots of children. Laurie said: 'Oh I didn't know anything about that.' She said: 'You're coming too – didn't you know?' He never knew how seriously to take her. He felt uneasy. 'Sometimes my brain and body seems quite sick and raw and nothing will heal it . . . The

moon is full tonight and I am empty. Up on the downs, we ate beechnuts and I said some of my poems but could hardly make myself heard for bombers. Should Yasmin go to kindergarten in the village school? asked Lorna. But what has it got to do with me? . . . After she'd gone of course I began to feel different. I was sorry I had not been more understanding, she can't help things and I know that this is the only way to live really. I am best living alone for the most part, I am irritated & sterile living continually with another person. Alone I can examine myself and cherish love, and sport with illusions.'

Laurie went back to Slad that October, found Painswick devastated by bombs, walked with aunts and cousins, visited Jack's old factory, and played Mozart and Beethoven with neighbours. 'In the kitchen the clock strikes unbelievably slowly.' He was roused by a letter from Lorna to her 'violently dearly beloved', full of fury. She had been longing to hear from him, 'vigilant at the door, pacing to the window, peering through the soapy mists for the girl who brings the letters', but his last letter 'only smelt of Slad and your affection for Slad with a burning last few lines, which felt as though they'd been thrown in as an afterthought just to keep me quiet & sound conventional.

'What's the good of you being there if you can't even think of anything to write for *Penguin 12*, you'd much better be with me or near me – at least when you were you thought of some poem for *Poets of Tomorrow*. Faithless rocket, screaming with brilliance one minute & everybody watching in awe & admiration & how many seconds later are you nothing but a forgotten piece of pinewood with shell of burnt cardboard lucky to be found in the grass by some little boy looking for mushrooms – but you might land on the thatch of my house & set fire to it, in which case it'd take more than the fire brigade to cool me down.

'It's one of those days, rare now, when I'm in a state of isolated beatitude and I can hover between here & the church in an exalted coma, smell you in Yasmin's darling curls & pray for Russia & thank who I pray to for giving me the glory of loving and being loved by you. In such a state of mind I used to go into a church at

Golders Green & pray that you'd come back from Spain & for the victory of the Spanish people & don't for a moment think that because Franco beat them that I thought how silly it was you did come back.' She had been listening to the repellent broadcasts of Lord Haw-Haw: 'He's just like the ghoulish grimace at the darkening window, the hysterical lunatic who frightens children . . . Did you hear Rachmaninov's concerto on a theme of Paganini – it was wonderful. When I gave Yasmin your kiss I showed her your letter & she said "kind Tatarty Lolly gave Yassie a koon." A koon my Lord, I crave a koon, on bended knees.'

In two days, Lorna was in Slad. They took Annie for a picnic on Painswick Beacon, and paid a courtesy visit to Juniper. But it was cold '& L twisted her hair and I thought not of Martigues but of Mecklenburgh. We were not unhappy all the time, but the orange glamour of the previous years was not there. Though the evenings at home with mother were contented.'

He arrived back in Bognor in a blizzard. The latest *Penguin New Writing* and a four-guinea cheque brought no pleasure. His old penfriend Pat wrote: 'One day, to please me, write something nice and obvious.' His house was alive with mice; he drank hot milk and crept into a damp bed 'haunted by peeling wallpaper & dismal shadows'. He was bent in the cold over a blank sheet of paper when a blue fur passed the window and 'L came in. She said the smell of the oil stove reminded her of the caravan and made her want me. I thought of Carven scent at 2 guineas a bottle and paraffin at 3d a pint. The night closed in & I again felt the need for a circle of warmth.'

With winter he was struck down with fever again. Lorna arrived with a dizzy hangover from a night out in Portsmouth. 'I curled up like an earwig while she talked to me of drinking, majors, gins, bars, hotels and all the usual Razzle clap trap.' But then she brought a chicken casserole, a pot of honey, Bach preludes. 'I played the preludes while she prepared a pungent meal and baked a cake. We lay in the twilight and I thought of the good things thrust upon me. "What a comfort it would have been," she said, "if we'd known at Mecklenburgh that in two years I'd be doing this for you." I wondered.'

They took Yasmin to a café where Lorna played Mozart on the pianola 'and Y found her tongue. A fluent dialect of her own, at times genteel and at times pure Sussex. I gave her coloured streamers on a stick which she waved vigorously scattering bits over the floor. How strong and obstinate & charming she is, her face a common supple rosy visage based, I'm afraid, on a strain quite different from L's fine skull & features.

'L was caustic & bitter about Rosamond Lehmann – as she is about almost everyone in whom I have any interest. Her jealousy is a strange rare thing & springs out of the slightest trifle. On the strength of reading one letter she contemplated not seeing me any more . . . I feel that if I was once unfaithful and she discovered it, all this fine structure we have built up would mean less than nothing to her. She would sweep it away with a curse, & loathe me for ever more. She'd take her vengeance by an immediate affair with the nearest male. Yet within the limits by which she is confined I think she would like to be, and is, my own.'

He was tormented by the thought of her husband making love to her. 'She loved me with fierce abandon as if wild to make amends. But how can she live there and withhold herself for ever – and what can I do but lament her in secret?' Occasionally they had to hide when the Wishart family were nearby ('I felt waves of fury'), and once Lorna wired to say that 'the enemy' was in Bognor and he'd better lie low. Once, he saw 'L's children running loose in the town'. He would seize a chance to see her when she was at the hairdresser in Arundel, 'smothered in pins & drinking Guinness', or in Chichester where she was giving a pint of blood: Laurie's first visit there 'since I fiddled in the street on my way to London'.

So they went on: strolling along the shore, watching bombers in the sky, shopping, having tea and scones, sitting over the fire, playing music, wandering among tombs. 'She was pliant & soft & tender, we walked encircled, with our mouths together. We thought how nice it would be to go far in a train – we said perhaps we can have a holiday among the Lakes – and felt secretly that it would be impossible. We shall have to commit ourselves for work sooner or later. We can't ignore what is happening.'

What was happening was the escalating war. The Russians had rallied in the face of the Nazi advance on Rostov 'but I keep thinking of Teruel'. After Pearl Harbor he wrote: 'Thus does the whole body of the earth succumb to this violent destructive paralysis. God knows how or when we can ever recover.' That day he was whistling Beethoven in the street when a ragged old man came up: 'May I congratulate you on what you're whistling,' he said. 'It's not often I hear that in the street.'

'And it's not often that I get it acknowledged,' said Laurie.

'This is my small life,' Laurie reflected. 'The world meanwhile is a bloody inferno ... South America seems to be the only remaining patch of earth at peace. The war stretches on over an infinity of years ahead.'

At Christmas Lorna brought Laurie books, cigarettes, exotic jigsaws and a briefcase stamped LL. 'I felt like King Solomon entertaining Sheba. My present to L was very humble – a diary.' He spent Christmas day with the Savages eating turkey, plum pudding, mince pies and real cream, 'remarkable food for the 3rd Christmas of the War'. Annie sent a book inscribed to 'Laurie Lee (the Poet)' and beads for Yasmin: 'Little Frances used to like funny little things to play with & I thought Yasmin might be a bit like her . . .'

His latest reviews for *Folios of New Writing* were encouraging. *Time & Tide* said his 'Night in Castelleja' was 'boldly & vigorously sketched; nothing in this volume surpasses it. Among comparative newcomers Mr Lee is someone to be reckoned with.' Annie wrote 'Congrats old thing!' alerting him to L.A.G. Strong's review of *Best Poems of 1941* in the *Observer*, which singled out Richard Church, Laurence Binyon and Laurie Lee as 'the only poets on whom the war has had an emotional impact'.

Inexorably Laurie was acquiring a literary reputation, without feeling that he could justify or sustain it. On New Year's Eve of 1942 he took the train for London, thick with fog, to meet Day-Lewis. At the door of the Ministry he passed Brendan Bracken, Churchill's Minister of Information. He visited 'aunt-like' John Lehmann at the Athenaeum: 'He read "Pastoral" but didn't altogether go for

it – said he couldn't get the rhythm. Again he said I must have a book – but O God! filled with what?' He went on to the *Horizon* office and met Spender, 'very tall, drooping, with a weak lisping mouth and looking like an undergraduate'. Cyril Connolly said: 'You've never sent us anything. Everything seems to go to Lehmann.' He told Laurie that John Betjeman admired his work (and when Betjeman sent his *Selected Poems* to Laurie in 1948 he signed it 'for Laurie Lee, a true poet, by John Betjeman, a lesser one'). They showed him some poems submitted in a contest to be judged by Connolly, Spender, Eliot, and Herbert Read: 'I was graciously allowed to pass judgement.' Afterwards he walked to Russell Square with Spender, who said he was tired of being never alone – 'and I said I was tired of being always alone'. In Piccadilly he ran into Alberto Cavalcanti, of the Crown Film Unit, who hoped Laurie would come back to work for them. Laurie said: 'I'm a poet now.' But he caught his bus for Victoria immensely depressed. He found Day-Lewis amiable ('I like this man; apart from his sense of solid worth he is human') but the others 'are so sharp & clever, I don't understand them & can't ever conceive of being intimate with them'. It was New Year's Eve: he was in bed, alone, when he heard the church clock strike twelve.

Rations were cut to two pints of milk and two ounces of butter a week (Dorothy sent a cake and six mince pies whose smell took him back among his sisters) and the winter weather was 'balls-aching', the air 'like thick blue ice'. Everyone in the streets looked cold, old and poor. 'The cold draws me into the warmth of a shut room, drawing girls on paper & in my mind . . . Girls in the snow are like warm fruit to be carried underground and consumed in drowsy sleep.' He made thin porridge and scratched away at thin poems, distracted by the noises of children and Canadian soldiers in the street outside. Then Lorna would waft in, scented with exotic 'Inque', making Laurie feel 'a flat spiritless oaf', and take him out for steak and kidney pie. 'We lay under warm blankets all afternoon & she was beautiful and I, empty of feeling or joy. There was a poem on the table but she read it when I wasn't looking & made no remark.' If only she'd comment, he might regain some

confidence. Withered, uneasy, he walked by the desolate icy sea after she'd gone, watching the blown snow. But on Lorna's thirty-first birthday he combed Chichester and sent her a chess set, two handkerchiefs, a little pot, a rosary, an anthology, a volume of Nat Gubbins, the *Reynolds News* columnist, and an African bangle stuffed with hair.

But he saw 'something terribly lopsided' in his way of life. He was driven 'into an arctic depression' by hearing Lorna talk about her domestic scene. 'I can get no comfort from her. I am allowed, as it were, a pair of coloured gloves and for the rest I may go naked.' In the station waiting-room at Barnham he was smitten with a nervous crisis that left him in a dazed and shivering fever for days. Mrs Savage brought him soup and he went to bed, as blizzards howled outside. For days he sat staring out of the window, 'feeling as old folk must undoubtedly feel, resentful and persecuted. All afternoon I waited in hot feverish misery for a voice or a face to comfort me.' At night he lay trembling and icy cold from sheets and pyjamas soaked in sweat. 'I groaned for the very relief it gave me to hear my groans in that horrible shivering deserted silence at four in the morning.' He saw only duplicity and hypocrisy and humbug all around. At last a wire from Lorna said she too was in bed, with bronchitis, and her son Luke also ill.

When Lorna read these diary pages, 'My, she did storm! I am amazed at the way she . . . twists [things] absolutely without scruple, and seems to forget that this life is only as she wishes it. She has what she wants when she wants it and everyone else modifies their desires to fit in with her. I don't think she realizes the privileged position she is in: she, only, is the one who can say "Today I will do this or that" while others wait . . .'

He resolved to lock up his diary. Annie's prattling letters arrived almost daily, telling him about illness and deaths in the village, and that his half-brother Reg had joined up. Rommel was driving on along the Libyan coast. Finally Laurie broke off from listening to *The Lark Ascending* and reading *Don Quixote* (he was trying to catch up on 'great obvious books') and went to the Labour Exchange seeking a job at a local aircraft engine factory ('but it's a seven-day

week and I must confess I would like to avoid that'). Anyway, there were no jobs going.

'I built up a furious fire and was preparing to go out when she walked in, bringing Christmas roses . . . the room grew hot as summer with a roaring fire. We padded the floor & lay on it, forgetting the snow. We gazed at one another through the dusky tenor of Rachmaninov's "Adagio". I felt an atmosphere of soft colours & a gentle yearning sorrow, which was not really unhappiness. I felt soothed, in tune with beauty & tenderness, and contented.' But when she left he felt bleak and lost. 'Shall I never write anything again?'

He was utterly in her thrall. This was, in poetic terms, the most productive period of his life, but it was up to Lorna to say if his poems were any good; he resisted her suggestions ('those which are successful are written without endless spadework') but needed her approval. When he showed her 'The Wild Trees', 'She read the first two verses & thumped me on the chest. She read the rest & thumped me again. "There, that shows what you can do," she said. But I often envy *her* power of writing which she doesn't seem to realize is always warm & brilliantly original. She says, "Luke much better, but has a cough like an old tree." That is typical.

'"You're a strange boy," she said. "But not strange enough," I answered. "No," she said. I suppose she sees through me all the time. Oh, she can be winning & tender, touching to a degree . . . She either exults me or deflates me. Today there were all sorts of grey undertones. Money, work & supposed girlfriends. We fought stupidly over two letters that came for me. Then waiting for the train she stressed the frightful way I am living. All very true. I am too full of the sense of my own failings to be humble. I asked her when I should see her again. She said not till I wrote & asked her to come. This infuriates me. I shall not write – that is my obstinate feeling tonight. We shall see whether she will come or not.' Seven days later he rang her, and she arrived 'in jodhpurs of all things which had a peculiar effect on me so I made 3 drawings'.

In his crisis of poetic confidence, Rosamond Lehmann reassured him that his poems were beautiful, rich and melancholy, and urged

him not to destroy anything her brother John disliked: 'He is often a sound critic, but by no means always, to my mind. What one person is?' Meanwhile brother Jack told him he ought to write film scripts, and took Laurie in a studio car to Pinewood, 'the great paint-smelling crumbling mausoleum of desolation where the Crown Film Unit are moving to'. Jack, his colleague Nora Dawson and the director Humphrey Jennings drove Laurie through devastated London. 'Seeing St Paul's looking vast and superhuman one felt active & magnificent. Jennings said: "I am not a believer in symbolism but I must say it gives me intense symbolistic pleasure to see how all those little city men got theirs and St Paul's still stood up amongst it all."' Laurie left them filming, walked back via Charing Cross Road ('price of sex books soaring') and went home to watch an eclipse of the moon.

Lorna implored him not to go to Pinewood. 'She looked at me across the table with an old look & we marvelled that Yasmin is nearly 3 & that we've known each other nearly 5 years. We returned home in a passion and the birds sang loud round the roofs, and the rain stopped & the sun came out. I hope I shall never forget her as she looked with the sun on her face as she lay in bed a few inches from me. Suddenly her dark beauty was brilliant like a precious stone, her hair sparkled in tangles of rich blue locks, and her eyes were huge and deep and full of greens & subterranean blues, and across her cheeks and her mouth pursed in pleasure at my obvious delight, moved the most lovely colours from the sky. I knew that this sudden burst of sun through the window was one of the first fires of spring . . . it seemed that all the tender & exquisite lights of heaven entered the room and were caught in her face like a crystal.'

He inscribed Lorna's copy of *Poets of Tomorrow*: 'To Lorna – "In your eyes I see/ scaffolds of love arising and the most remote heaven as familiar as bread" – Laurie March 1942.'

On Yasmin's third birthday they took her to the cinema for the first time, and shopped for a wheelbarrow, a tea-set and tractor. Laurie began to realize that 'this is no dream of a child, nothing like it, but a twisting, argumentative, obstinate, determined, frightened & winning individual. Wouldn't give me a kiss or say she

wanted to see me again. That's how she is.' He found her capricious
but good-tempered. She amused him by saying indignantly, in a
café where everyone sat in Anglo-Saxon silence, 'All the people
are asleep' and by shouting 'Bo-peeple!' Her first coherent sentences
made him ecstatic: 'I see her so seldom, her talking is like a miracle.'

Suddenly an offer came that Laurie could not refuse. Ian Dal-
rymple, head of the Crown Film Unit, proposed that he should
write scripts for him at £7 11s 6d a week, starting at once. Lorna
was appalled, but Laurie could not go on ignoring opportunities
for ever. Lorna said, 'It's like what I imagined death must be –
coming without warning, cutting short our lives.' Laurie asked his
diary: 'What *am* I going to do for this £7 a week?'

Before he joined the Unit, he and Lorna went back to Slad.
Annie cooked for them and they cleaned up the cottage and painted
chairs and a washstand. They parted desolately in Piccadilly with
'tenderness, nostalgia & regrets at this breaking up of our paradisal
existence'. He told himself: 'We have been very happy in this
backwater of compromise – we have seen each other more than
most married people find it possible to do.'

Laurie went back to lodge at Mrs O'Neill's in Putney and dropped
back into the old life there, but with a difference: he was now
invited to London's literary parties. He met Rose Macaulay, Nancy
Cunard, Louis MacNeice, Rex Warner, and of course Rosamond
Lehmann, Day-Lewis and Spender. At John Lehmann's grand new
flat in Hertford Street he drank orangeade while Lehmann 'leaned
against the wall with his lofty diplomatic smile, and dispensed
wine . . . Everyone talked loudly about the Ballet.' One night at
Lehmann's Laurie was picked up by 'a pretty young soldier', who
told Laurie he thought they had 'an affinity', produced a dark youth
with whom he said he was having an affair, and took Laurie off for
an expensive supper.

At Rosamond Lehmann's cottage for the weekend with Day-
Lewis, he was fascinated to listen to 'their throwaway conversation,
like miniature depth charges to scatter some friend in sparks. Do
they all do it?' Looking through Lehmann family albums he saw
photographs of Spender, Auden and Isherwood – 'brown smiling

Nazi-looking youths posing in Berlin attics'. While the lovers were out walking, Laurie dug Rosamond's garden. 'One feels almost guilty to be here, but they shouldn't have asked me. But we had a gay tea of smoked salmon & they are very nice to me & charming together.' Day-Lewis was 'a rock of sense, humour & easy friendliness'. Rosamond he found 'as gracious and superficial as her brother'; he took her sweetness with a pinch of salt.

When Day-Lewis had left for London, Rosamond sat sewing and confided in Laurie about her feelings for her lover. Laurie's friendship with Day-Lewis was mutually admiring: 'What an extraordinary number of things you know,' Day-Lewis told him. 'I respect you more and more.' (Day-Lewis had been guilt-stricken himself that, though a Communist, he did not volunteer in Spain.) They would play pin-tables in pubs and have Greek suppers. In Day-Lewis's Percy Street rooms they smoked cigars and talked of poets and poetry. 'We discussed the ideal way of living for writing poetry. Day-Lewis wanted a patron; I wanted to be lost in a community living an ordinary life with poetry growing out of it. But that wouldn't work, because in the community the barrier of "queerness" would spring up and the most important requirement, acceptance, would disappear.

'We both agreed in the end however that the impulse to write poetry can only really endure so long as one lives a slightly abnormal and physically unconsummate life. Marriage – i.e. happy marriage – is death to a poet.'

In this respect, Laurie's liaison with Lorna was fruitful: it was secret and forbidden, it conformed to the conventions of courtly love; it gave all his thoughts and sensations a romantic aura. As she told him herself, 'When you're away I get terrible feelings of tenderness for you – I could kiss your feet. The minute you step on the train you become a thing of extraordinary glamour.' Laurie reflected: 'What is absent is desired through a paradisal cloud of the mind; what is present may still be desired, but through a human aura of toothache, colds, worries and obvious blemishes.'

The day came when he had to start at Pinewood. He would be collaborating on a documentary, *Calling All Peoples*, with a Czech

writer, Jiri Weiss, who told him: 'When you make a documentary film it shall be za truce, za whole truce and nazing but za truce!' Their joint venture on the struggle of the oppressed nations of Europe – a subject so vast and complex that Laurie was appalled and exhausted before they began – was doomed from the start. After one day's endless talking with Weiss and the director John Monck, he was sick and longed only to go home. Day by day they worked at Weiss's home in Highgate, or in the Patisserie Valérie in Soho, and it became 'a maze . . .' 'what chaos! . . .' 'day at Highgate with Weiss arguing and fighting over mutilated script . . . I am depressed . . .' 'Had to go back to Putney with a fever . . . Mrs O'Neill weeping, Eric joining army . . . Woke in cold sweat . . .' 'Deeper and deeper into morass over film . . .' 'Monck has brilliant ideas which confuse everyone . . . endless complexities . . .' 'We are both in a wilderness & both very weary.' One day while in Highgate he walked in the cemetery: 'Ghastly place of stone needles, family vaults & broken "grecian" pillars. Bombs have fallen and thrown up grave stones. Found Karl Marx's grave, bunch of dead forget-me-nots lying upon it. I wanted to write a poem but instead argued fruitlessly all day with Jiri & Monck who get on one another's nerves.' Eventually *Calling All Peoples* was dropped. 'I am lost & undone,' wrote Laurie. 'A cold wind blows, lilac is out, and yet no birds sing.'

He had a regular salary, but he was 'practically broke thanks to all these train fares etc.' He opened his first Post Office account with five guineas from *Poets of Tomorrow* ('strikes me as very little') and 10s 6d from *Tribune* for a poem called 'Barriers'. The Budget had put twopence more on beer, 'and fags now a penny each: I can't see myself paying it'. Mrs O'Neill told him that 'tarts which cost 1s 6d, went for 4d if broken. She went into the shop and asked, got any broken tarts? No says the girl, shall I break one for you? and did.' Annie insisted he should not send her any more five bobs. 'I never want you to run yourself short & Lorna sent me some last week. Dear girl she is thoughtful, I paid a bill or two and bought some seeds for the garden etc.'

Over supper of bacon and eggs at his flat, Lehmann told Laurie

to 'start preparing for a book'. He suggested one about either Slad or Spain. He also thrust de la Mare's *Collected Poems* into Laurie's hand and asked him to review it for *Tribune* 'and God help me, I promised to'. He wrote a neat appreciation of de la Mare: 'One does not question the charm and fascination of this finely wrought verse; it has a decorative economy, a subtlety of tone which is almost Oriental', but in wartime, he added, 'the ear . . . finds it increasingly difficult to adjust itself to such delicate faery music'.

Meanwhile Laurie was himself receiving some crushing reviews for *Poets of Tomorrow*. 'The *Times Literary Supplement* suggests I have genuine feeling, limited experience and at times too melodramatic an image . . .' 'Desmond MacCarthy in the *Sunday Times* says, "These Poets of Tomorrow turn out to be very much Poets of Today with all their faults." The fault is obscurity.' MacCarthy had picked out Laurie's 'Village of Winter Carols' for failing to convey its meaning, and ended: 'The reason I go hammering at these poets is that it is painful to see so much sincerity of emotion and subtlety of observation marred by disregard of the art of communication.' Yet Mrs O'Neill's 'semi-illiterate' son Eric, who worked on the cooked meats counter at Harrods, told Laurie he had understood 'Winter Carols': 'So much for MacCarthy.'

Worse humiliation was to come. 'The review of *Poets of Tomorrow* in *Tribune* accuses me of "affectation" which is I think one of the most humiliating things that one can have said about one's poetry. Worse even than being accused of plain bad writing. Affectation, which I loathe more than anything else in others! Lorna just roared with laughter. But can I go on, after these shocking reviews? I am sure if Woolf reads them he'll not be disposed to give me my book whatever Lehmann may say.'

Cyril Connolly mentioned him favourably in the *Observer*, but the *Spectator* reviewer, Sheila Shannon, said the only influence she could detect on Laurie Lee was that of Edith Sitwell. 'However,' she ended witheringly, 'to do Mr Lee justice, I think most of his faults are attributable to a quite original lack of poetic talent.' On reading this Laurie was plunged into profound gloom. Day-Lewis told him the test of a good poet was to carry on in spite of such

reviews; but Lorna reported heartlessly that Mary Campbell had commented: 'Extraordinary how these boys get their poems published – I suppose he writes about as well as he plays the fiddle.'

Mary Campbell had been proselytizing, trying to persuade Lorna to become a Roman Catholic like her. 'Are you an atheist?' Lorna asked Laurie. 'I can't bear you to think otherwise than I do.' She seemed to Laurie to be guiltily seeking some mortification of the flesh. Lorna said, 'It makes me want to black people's shoes, or work all day at some humble job or crawl naked over the doorstep.' Laurie was sceptical of her motives: 'Catholicism is the religion of repression. It sees celibacy as a virtue. The voluptuary, tired of too much indulgence is attracted to it by a perverted pleasure in the state of wanting.'

An author inventing a voluptuary could not have improved on Lorna, with her flourishes, her gifts, her riches, her flowers. She seems rarely to have arrived in the same outfit twice. She would be swathed in furs, in tweeds, in tartans; 'in seven different blues (counting her eyes)'; 'in a scarlet corduroy suit and her hair twisted in thick plaits'; 'in a nice new divided skirt, blue, very smart'; 'in an exquisite wine-coloured coat, which makes her glow'; 'in her camel cloak which always makes her look frail & pregnant'; 'in a wide black straw hat, in the shade of which she's a dusky beauty'. In her arms she carried an ever-changing bounty: two great white magnolias; scarlet tulips; masses of lilac; Beethoven's Waldstein Sonata and books of Donne, Stendhal, Chinese poems; ravioli and bottles of red wine. And whenever they met there seemed to be some natural aid to romance – primroses, violets, cherry blossom, a cuckoo, a nightingale.

She had been discussing a break with her husband, but Laurie suspected she would carry on maintaining her congenial compromise for ever. 'L is in an unhappy state over things at home, but as I am not the alternative what can I do?' She spoke of getting a job and living on her own resources. 'She won't and she couldn't.' She would 'twist her curls, on the verge of tears, but she can't leave W because he's so dependent & she can't give me up because she's tried – what is she to do? . . . In the middle of this endless discussion

I felt very tender towards her . . .' But 'I am the great fool in all this. Obstinately waiting for a bus which went past 15 years ago.' Lorna had been married for fifteen years.

There was never any serious question of Lorna's marrying Laurie. If the subject came up Laurie made a light response: 'For five days I'd get two meals a day then for five months I'd have to cook for myself.' Yet Lorna persisted in harping on Laurie's imagined infidelities. 'I am blameless but she'll never believe it. Her smile was as hard and sharp edged as a stone. In a wave of frustration I tried to rouse her to some reaction and said "I don't think I want to see you again" and she said "All right darling."' Four days later she brought peace offerings (flowers, sherry) 'and her nightdress as a flag of truce, and every wave of tenderness was heightened by the fact that we had quarrelled & made it up'. At one moment 'she was all I love, gazing into my eyes, quick, suspicious, adoring'; at another she was 'vague and distant with a forbearing manner I'm sure she uses on her children'.

At Bognor, where Laurie was having his first bespoke suit tailored for ten guineas, fighter planes swept up and down, bombers roared back and forth, guns popped incessantly along the shore. On 1 June Laurie read about the bombing of Cologne. 'One must accept such news with terrible feelings – we are preparing a ghastly future for us all. Newspapers facetious about it: "Woe de Cologne" or "Blow de Cologne".' Jack had started on a film about submarines, and was having a submarine built at the studio. Betty Smart was now training personnel at the Hoover factory. Laurie went to see her and found her 'in a red dress with freshly washed hair streaming down. Untouchable though. She is sweet and nice, bright, modern & definitely frank about sex, but I feel rather brotherly towards her.' He had gone to see her, he admitted, 'hoping to be admired. One wishes to measure one's growth and perhaps be flattered.' A letter came from Wilma to say that her husband had been knighted 'so she is now Lady Gregory'.

He found himself explaining Henry Moore's sculptures to 'a Bond Street matron' he met on the Tube; he went to the National Gallery to see Moore's *Tube Shelter Perspective*, 'bone-grey figures

like corpses lying in rows in a long tunnel, twisted, crumbling, inhuman looking. Remarkable.' In the evenings he sometimes joined BBC and film people – Paul Rotha, MacNeice, Humphrey Jennings – at the Players' Theatre. He had been asked for another piece about Slad (on carol-singing) for the *Geographical Magazine*, and to write the commentaries for a film called *Eternal Prague* and another about Malta, to be spoken by Laurence Olivier. He helped with a film about the Battle of Britain. 'I supplied about 3 words. I almost think I shouldn't take the money – I haven't really got the brain.'

On his twenty-eighth birthday Lorna came up to London and they had Spanish omelettes at the Café Condé in Russell Square 'where we haven't been since 1938. We walked round cold blue Brunswick Square into its railless gardens where the leaves were falling & L told me of her three empty years there & how she sat under those trees carrying Michael.' After lunch they saw the film *Eternal Prague*, with Laurie's commentary spoken by Beatrix Lehmann: 'voice harsh & shocking and a disappointing lack of feeling'.

At the end of April Jack, looking 'wild and uncomfortable', suddenly announced that he had become engaged to a girl at home in Woodchester named Bim, and would marry her in three weeks' time. Annie approved: 'Jack will be happier and not so selfconscious when he is married & has a wife – someone absolutely belonging to him. He has given me money to get an outfit for the wedding.' Laurie met Bim at the studio and found her 'stocky but pleasant', but Jack 'seemed as flat as a pancake. Not much apparent love between them.'

Jack's colleague Nora – the future Mrs Jack Lee – told Laurie that Jack was not at all in love with Bim, but 'couldn't get out of it'. Laurie was horrified. 'No wonder he's miserable but why has he gone this far? And is it too late? Jack admitted that getting married was the last thing he wanted to do. I said should I speak to her on the telephone. He said wouldn't I go down and tell her? He couldn't tell her himself.'

So one June evening Laurie took the train to Cirencester, and

Bim came to meet him on her bicycle. They sat on a bank in the sunset. 'She seemed happy. I felt terrible. I told her what I'd come to tell her and she rolled over in the grass & wept. A passing lorry driver leant out of his van and said "Give it to her!" She said there was only misery ahead for her either way but she didn't care, if only he loved her. I had to tell her he didn't.'

'Meanwhile Mother writes excitedly about the wedding, the bride, the announcement in *The Times* etc.' Next day: 'Unhappy letter from Mother saying "I am quite ashamed of Jack — he ought to walk barefoot — can't you persuade him where his duty lies?" What a miserable mess it all is.'

Annie wrote again: 'Did you advise Jack or influence him in any way? because if you did you should not have done so . . . for little Bim is sweet and charming I do think she would have made a lovely wife, *not one* ever to be ashamed of . . .' Annie had met Bim in Stroud by chance ('poor darling little girl') on what would have been the wedding day, 'and she was so brave & chatty . . . Laurie you know you boys have done it on me. I wonder that you think I can stand and keep sane. I do not think Jack is like you say. I know he can be constant. But I wish the wedding had not been fixed up in a hurry, they should have waited till his film was finished . . . At the last he was rather rushed into it, and he got bewildered and worried, and now,' she concluded, maternal loyalty triumphing, 'I think it was for the best, and quite a manly thing to do.'

In the autumn of 1942 Laurie started researching a film for Jack Holmes on youth in wartime. In broiling heat 'striking the ground broadside as in Spain', he went to Paignton with Holmes by train to meet the boys of Sandridge Lodge, high above the curving estuary of the Dart, where Laurie sat in on classes, lectured on music, played his fiddle and sang 'Ilkley Moor' at a village concert, climbed trees and got up at six in the morning to do PT on the lawn with the boys.

But that night he had an epileptic fit — his first for three years. 'Can't think what brought it on unless it was getting up early & doing PT. I was out about an hour.' He went back to London

feeling low and lost. 'All my theories have collapsed – this attack was so sudden & I thought I was so well – besides it is still summer.' He was allowed to go home to Slad for a week, and Lorna went with him. They found Annie on the verge of angry tears 'because father had cut down her allowance once again, leaving only 2s of the 7s pension she was expecting & she was in a bit of a muddle over a bill for glasses'. Annie savoured later the image of Laurie and 'sweet Lorna' walking down the village street and over the fields to pick blackberries and wild flowers for the Harvest festival: it was their last visit to Slad together.

In October, youth research took Laurie to Cambridge: he sat by the Cam at the back of King's College as the undergraduates arrived for the new term. 'Cafés, tea-shops, bicycles, gowns, halls, scrubbed refectory tables & those lovely dreamlike willows over the placid river – how attractive in the blue twilight it was – how I wish I'd had some of it.'

He spent most of the autumn away in the north of England, touring youth clubs. This was another doomed project, given Laurie's instinctive sympathy with the working-class lads of Cumbria and the equally instinctive Toryism of his masters. Still, it was an education for Laurie, who had seen more of Spain than he had of England, to see living conditions in industrial Maryport and Workington: he played ping-pong and taught drawing to the boys ('incredibly black, dirty & smelly but enthusiastic'). 'What a sooty, dirty, wet weather town this is,' he wrote of Whitehaven. 'Fields of black grass, cramped children, hideous worried women, coalmines on the hills, and avalanches of molten slag pouring from the steelworks into the sea.' He stayed in a vicarage with a parlour full of aspidistras, and watched old women carrying sacks of slate coal picked off the slag heap. 'Looking down the cliff with the grey sea boiling below it was incredible to think that this was indeed the land of the proud & free to see this black bent old grandmother, dressed in sacks & rags, wheeling a pram pitifully loaded with shale through the wind & rain. I pointed out to Holmes the railway trucks packed with shining coal and said: "This is the fair distribution of the fruits of the earth with a vengeance."'

He took photographs of these sad scenes, until a policeman tore along on a bicycle to challenge him: 'Whitehaven was mobilized and the "spy" surrounded. There was much showing of papers . . . I said it was my job, so in the end he left me. And some devil made me return to the high wall and take another shot.' Some devil too made him brave the steep descent into a coal-mine, Haig Pit, in helmet and Davy lamp, transported in the suffocating, deafening din to the coal-face under the sea, where men naked to the waist heaved and shovelled. 'Oh the ingenuity of man, the remorseless, indomitable, sacrificial ingenuity. I drilled some coal & shovelled it on the belt. Who will burn it?' He took a bus across the Pennines and in Durham, 'a lovely small city after my own heart', played the Bach Double Violin Concerto with a girls' club organizer. Everywhere he travelled, as ever, his restless curiosity unearthed excellent material, and he struck up instant friendships. During dinner in Newcastle with T.D. Young, 'fat bachelor father of the city', the news came that the Americans had made landings in French North Africa, but when he changed trains at York station (in ruins) he saw the headline: 'Hitler invades Vichy France'.

Lorna welcomed him back with dinner at the Café Royal, and they chose prints at Zwemmer's (a Seurat and Van Gogh's *Beer Garden* for Lorna; Brueghel's *Winter* for Laurie). 'These intoxicating waves of affection she has for me contain a taste of bitterness because I know they do not last. The higher the wave the deeper the trough. As she stares at me in the gas light I can't help being happy but . . . there is no constancy in it. "Make me not want you so much," she says. "I can't get any peace always thinking about you – I want to be able to live in peace again." That sort of peace will not be long in coming to her, I fear . . . I can't fathom her twisted brain.'

A damp green mould covered his books and records in Bognor, so the Savages moved him into a cold spare room in their attic, with a view of back yards. 'Lorna told me she'd asked W if I might have a room in their house but he just looked at her.' Rather restrained of him, Laurie thought.

One day in early December 1942 he was dropping in his new poems to Lehmann when he ran into Kathleen Garman and her

daughter Esther in the King's Road, and she asked him home for tea. Inside number 272 was a bevy of Garmans: 'lovely Kitty now dark and very pretty; Helen, a doubled-up bright-eyed image of her mother, and graceful Kathy whom I last saw in Martigues.' Kathy had just turned eleven.

With Cecil Day-Lewis, he travelled down for another quiet weekend at Rosamond Lehmann's. Rosamond was 'more superlative than ever. "How perfectly lovely to see you" and "Of course John is *simply devoted* to you." All this is normal I suppose in many people but it is a manner I don't find easy.' Laurie chopped and sawed wood, and after dinner Rosamond and Day-Lewis sang their way through the hymn book with Laurie playing his recorder; and Rosamond read Jane Austen aloud to the two poets. What may have proved another bond of sympathy between Day-Lewis and Laurie is that Cecil too had in 1939 fathered an extra-marital child – by the wife of a neighbouring Musbury farmer who accepted Day-Lewis's son William as his own. One evening that weekend, Laurie told Day-Lewis and Rosamond that he was the father of a little girl. 'Rosamond was most curious. "Were you married then?" "No," I said. "Is the mother married?" I ignored the question. "But is the mother married?" "No," I lied, "& the baby's name is Margaret."'

11 | La Belle Dame Sans Merci
1943

Only last summer, Laurie had been living in the caravan and gardening for a shilling an hour. At the start of 1943 his Malta film, with Sir Arnold Bax's score and Laurence Olivier speaking the commentary, full of nobly phrased rolling certitudes, was being acclaimed. He dined with Eddy Sackville-West at the Savile Club and saw H.G. Wells there. 'How well they do themselves in these red plush dens. The cold table groaned with pewter weight and opulence. Salmon, hams, vast pies & salads; gulls' eggs at 1s 9d each.' He lunched at the Berkeley with John Wolfenden, headmaster of Uppingham. At John Lehmann's he met Sir Archibald Clark-Kerr, British ambassador to Moscow (who was 'very amusing about Stalin – says he likes obscene jokes'). When Laurie took Cecil Day-Lewis to dinner at the Gourmet in Lisle Street, 'How they bow to you,' said Day-Lewis. 'You must be an habitué.'

Lehmann and Sackville-West were both badgering him for new poems, and he was offered fifty guineas to write a film treatment on agriculture in wartime. 'You come to us with the highest recommendation the British Government can offer. You've got a marvellous subject,' gushed Donald McCullough, questionmaster of the *Brains Trust*, over lunch at Casa Pepe. 'I must say I'm quite black with envy.' 'So the big game starts,' wrote Laurie in his diary, 'without a fact or a thought in my head.'

He started his farming research in the areas he knew most intimately: Slad, followed by Sussex. A barley farmer drove him round the shell-damaged, bomb-cratered downs. He seized the chance for woodland walks with Lorna by moonlight: 'We sat under a yew tree among the prickly cases of horse-chestnuts. She wore a balaclava helmet which stretched her eyes & pursed up her mouth and concentrated the gaze on those features which are most beautiful.' In Dover he found the Grand Hotel, where he had

stayed in 1940, now half in ruins. Folkestone was 'like the grave'. His hotel shook at night with bombs across the straits.

At Bognor at weekends, Lorna ('looking smouldering & lovely, in her birthday bracelet') still brought flowers and cigars, but she alternated between loving declarations and threats of vengeance ('I will not share you') if he strayed. 'She will not believe. I was cold & hot & wild & cruel.' There were 'terrific explosions' out at sea.

They still spent languid mornings in London, listening to Mozart's Flute Trio, which made Lorna cry, staining the pillow black with kohl and scarlet with lipstick. They lunched at the Café Royal, and saw *Casablanca*. They went to a children's exhibition where Michael had a painting on show along with other pupils from Bedales and Dartington Hall; that night, volleys of gunfire shook Mrs O'Neill's house. 'We bombed Berlin last night so we sort of expected it. Raid lasted till 9.30 when L rang me up with love on her lips.'

At lunchtimes Laurie went to the National Gallery's concerts. One day 'the all-clear made a curious accompaniment to Beethoven's F Major Opus 139'. With Lorna and Michael he queued for the National Gallery exhibition of *French Nineteenth Century Painting*. The queue, blue-nosed in the bitter cold, stretched to St Martin-in-the-Fields; *le tout Londres* was there. Rose Macaulay muttered, 'There's a new meaning to "queuing for the pictures".' MacNeice walked by, giving Lorna a long stare. Anna, Mary Campbell's daughter, last seen in Toledo, was there, 'now 16 and a mirror of Mary'. The throng quite obscured the exhibits: 'classic Cézannes, ruddy Delacroix, misty Sisleys, putrid-coloured Lautrec nudes, soft-buttocked Courbets, Degas ironing women . . . and a soft tawny golden oh so golden "Blonde Bather" by Renoir. Dreamy blue eyes and yielding jellyfish mouth against a blue sea with cascades of apple-coloured hair falling down.'

The youth film, on which Laurie had spent so many months, was cancelled: his treatment painted a too unpleasant picture of the past and looked 'indiscreetly' at the future, he was told. 'I am very depressed. What is the use of trying to be either sincere or reasonably free from prejudice and mumbo-jumbo when one is bound to be frustrated by the official mind?'

Diligently, he pressed on with his farming research. In Cambridge, Leicestershire, Shropshire, and all over Wales, he saw how previously fallow land had become productive. He visited crumbling hill farms and became an expert on potato yields at 1,100 feet. In Oxford he stayed with sister Dorothy and her husband Leslie, who took him to the Morris Radiation factory to see women at work. Laurie was a natural reporter: he sat in on farmers' meetings, taking notes, full of curiosity, and forged new friendships. At Drayton Manor, Stratford, he visited Sir George Stapleton, a farming baronet and writer. '"Good afternoon Sir George," I said, "it's very good of you to see me." "I had no option," he said.' But within hours Stapleton was declaring, 'I've taken a liking to this fellow' and sent for Laurie's overnight bag. He sat up with Sir George – who wrote books himself – and his lady until midnight, talking of poetry and carrying on over breakfast. In Manchester he went to a Brahms and Schubert concert and met the conductor Malcolm Sargent ('charming, brilliant, very funny'). In the office of the *Warrington Guardian*, he had a birthday greeting to Yasmin set up in type.

He spent an eye-opening weekend with the eccentric artist Cedric Morris (Lucian Freud's former tutor) in Suffolk. Morris took him through pink-walled rooms hung with 'sickeningly diseased and cynical' portraits. Lorna's painter friend David Carr was there, 'drooping his grecian locks', and there was 'a shaven-headed Nazi type [who] cooked staggering meals'. Everybody seemed 'very free and easy' and used words that made Laurie blush. (Laurie was still uneasy among aesthetes. At John Lehmann's one night, he remarked, 'What a bunch of posey young weeds he does gather around him. Squinting up their eyes at pictures & bleating about the ballet. Keith Vaughan in khaki, Leslie Hurry who draws a fine line in masculine buttocks, John Craxton, Lucian Freud's friend . . . a weary gang.') Before he left, Morris warned Laurie against 'the Lehmann gang' and the corrosiveness of Rosamond's endless soul-searching.

He returned full of a 'strange uncomfortable sickness'. Lorna was in a cold fury of suspicion 'because she heard me talking to someone

on the phone'. She was so convinced of his infidelity she said she was ready to give herself to any rough old soldier: 'I felt I didn't care what happened to my body if you didn't want it any more.' 'She suggested I went & got married, but what if I did. This is a tightrope situation I cannot hope to control.'

While his own affair was plainly in trouble, he became further entangled in Day-Lewis's. Day-Lewis wanted Laurie to see his domestic scene, and invited him home in April to meet his wife and two sons at Brimclose, the Day-Lewis house in Musbury, in the Axe valley, with its panoramic views of Devon: 'Golden weather – we played games & had an easy time.' But back in London, as they firewatched one night, Day-Lewis confided that Rosamond bitterly resented his having done this. 'It is driving him crazy, juggling with the two worlds,' Laurie noted. 'He needs a bridge & said that was partly why he took me.'

Rosamond duly wrote to reproach Laurie. She had thought of him as her friend, as soon as they met, 'at the beginning of my new & happy life', and Laurie was one of the few who accepted her and Day-Lewis as a couple, 'whom I can think of as part of our shared life, with no branches back into the unshared past. The fact that he invited you to see his other life seemed to me (morbidly?!) like an attack on me. It . . . made me feel even more exposed, & at a disadvantage. I felt I should never be at ease with you again – that seeing the strength & solidarity of his other life might make you have to "take sides" in the sense of realizing that I was in a hopeless position & living in an unreal Paradise . . .' She still feared that Cecil would ultimately 'retire to the bosom of his family, & relinquish me for ever & write beautiful poetry about separation'.

One hot April day, wearing blue 'like a spirit of the sea', Lorna drove him to Myra Hess's concert at Chichester, and they lay on the grass among other couples: 'The act of kissing in public seemed to increase our pleasure. I know she is mine by the smell of her mouth, the shape of her arms, & that intangible, free flow of her soft body when she embraces me. She said, later, "I sometimes think with real pride that no one shall touch me but you till I die."' She told Laurie she had again asked Wish if Laurie could come and

live with them. 'Wish had laughed loudly: "Don't be preposterous,"
he said, "won't you ever grow up?" ' Laurie began to perceive that
Lorna was quite blind to normal logic, weirdly incapable of forming
any vision of life based on reality: 'She prefers to drift like the Lady
in a barge of fancy through fabulous & romantic cities. But how
incredibly her mind works . . . She also made the following astound-
ing proposal: that if I chose the father she would have another
daughter whom she would keep secluded for me and when grown
deliver to me in place of herself.'

Not surprisingly they quarrelled, and the quarrels were raw,
protracted and harrowing. While he noted the distant events of the
war – Gandhi 'still fasting'; seventy Junkers troop carriers shot
down in the Mediterranean; our own heavy losses when bombing
Dortmund 'almost unnoticed' – he began to ache with a pervading
hopeless misery. He was ill, not just with his usual bronchial
problems but in a torpor of nervous exhaustion. A chiropractor
named Llewellyn examined his spine and told him he displayed the
symptoms of a man suffering from shell shock. To make things
worse, Laurie was told that his agriculture film would not after all
be made; his third unmade film in succession. 'And so the long
line of damp squibs & misfits goes on.' He could write instead a
documentary book for the Ministry of Information Publications
Division, which produced books written in *Picture Post* style – *The
Battle of Britain, Bomber Command, Front Line* – that sold in millions.
It was 'the bleakest, most desultory, most negative period in my
whole life'. Jack, by contrast, was on top of the world with his
submarine film finished, and a new film lined up involving trips to
America, Africa, Newfoundland. 'And so, one by one, he is wiping
off old psychological defeats.'

The weekends with Rosamond Lehmann and Day-Lewis were
a refuge. The two men played dominoes, and shot stones with
catapults at an old tin. While Day-Lewis worked indoors, Rosamond sat beside Laurie in the sun and probed heavily about Devon.
'She also asked about L – said she had the most beautiful eyes
she had ever seen.' At dinner there were many confidences and
afterwards Rosamond played the piano, read aloud from *Invitation*

to the Waltz, and Laurie played his fiddle while Day-Lewis sang his repertoire of ballads. 'How moving in the lamplight his singing of Lord Randall is.'

In May, Laurie and Lorna were lying in a Sussex field, listening to larks and watching the planes from Ford aerodrome, when Lorna announced she was coming to London, to take a part-time job in a wartime nursery. Laurie was filled with foreboding. 'In fact I would definitely rather she didn't come. And the prospect of seeing her every night! Isn't that queer after all.' He was 'all unhappiness & nerves & bitterness'. Their affair had so long depended on clandestine trysts, any whiff of change blew like a chill wind.

On 23 May 1943 he went, 'weak with strange feelings', to meet the 5.30 train at Victoria as Lorna arrived, 'brown, nervous, with bunches of flowers'. They took a taxi to the second-floor room she had rented in Bute Street, South Kensington. She instantly made it charming, filling it with 'vases of flowers, St Teresa, a crucifix, pictures of Yasmin, pots of face cream, Rilke, Shakespeare and the Bible full of pressed flowers'. They joined Jack and Nora and Humphrey Jennings at the Arts Theatre: 'Lorna alternated as usual between a downcast-eye averted shyness with extreme teasing taunting familiarity.' She threw him the key to her room. 'At last I was the visitor. I still don't know how this will work.'

They wandered in London, had kippers in a workmen's café by Putney bus garage, visited Brompton Oratory, 'a heavy piece of municipal vulgarity', and went to see *The Count of Monte Cristo*. They took Wilma to tea at the Waldorf, and to *The Watch on the Rhine* with Anton Walbrook. One day Yasmin, who had been in hospital having her adenoids and tonsils out, was brought up to London by her nanny and they took her to the zoo. 'She's tough and plump and walks with a roll. She's very bright & charming now but has caught amazingly some of her mother's peculiarities of expression & intonations of voice. Particularly that birdlike rising exclamation "What?" when she doesn't catch what you say. On the Underground she was naturally fascinated by the escalators & magic train doors opening without hands.' She asked: 'Do mice have fires in their houses? How do they keep warm?'

One evening in June, Laurie went to dine at Eddy Sackville-West's in Chester Square, in a room hung with John Piper's pictures of Knole. There was a pile of records on the sideboard which Sackville-West – 'thin, reedy & sick-looking, curled in his armchair like a half-starved fledgeling' – presented to Laurie: 'I didn't know what to say – such richness. Denis Matthews playing Mozart, Schubert's "Death and the Maiden" quartet, Mozart's violin concerto in D played by Menuhin, and a dozen others. I was overwhelmed.' They listened to records in a room surrounded by a vivid Graham Sutherland, a Constable drawing, a Picasso stencil, two Ivon Hitchens and more John Pipers. Sackville-West had chosen four of Laurie's new poems – 'Sea Front', 'The Armoured Valley', 'Diversion' and 'The Wild Trees' – to broadcast. He asked what sort of voice Laurie wanted to read them. Laurie was momentarily nonplussed since Sackville-West spoke in 'a quaint aunt-like voice', precisely the kind of 'intellectual sissy whine' he most hated. He replied: 'Something rough – and unmetropolitan – if you know what I mean.'

Laurie left Sackville-West's at about 10.30 p.m. and went to Lorna's room. 'She had been out with Lucian Freud and had had £2 stolen which doesn't surprise me.

'A terrible cold grew upon me.'

Lucian Freud became 'a dark presence' in Laurie's diary from that moment. Freud, born in Berlin in 1922, was already, at twenty, a boy wonder of the art world, known for his remorseless, psychologically penetrating portraits. 'People who met Freud in his teens,' as Lawrence Gowing wrote of him in 1982,[1] 'recognized his force immediately; fly, perceptive, lithe, with a hint of menace.' Gowing wondered who was the woman who first appeared in a Freud drawing in 1943 'in which the mood of preoccupation, anxiety perhaps, haunting a face, similarly and sympathetically occupied the image. Two years later there were little paintings of her, cut like sculptured busts by a table edge, each with a flower, a daffodil or a tulip, under her gaze, with eyes wide-open, devouring, or else turned inward, half-closed, brooding.' This latter was *Girl with Daffodil* – in which Lorna looks decidedly cross.

Gowing asked Freud who she was. Freud answered quietly, without revealing Lorna's name, 'She was the first person who meant something to me.' Later Freud told Gowing: 'I wanted to explain that she was the first person I was really caught up with.'

Yasmin says: 'Lorna found Lucian beautiful and fascinating, and would bring him things to draw, in the same way as she had taken Laurie's poems to Stephen Spender. Lorna was a dream for any creative artist because she got them going. She was a natural Muse, a catalyst and an inspiration, and she had the same effect on both of them. She was a symbol of their imagination, of their unconscious, she was nature herself; savage, wild, romantic, and completely without guilt. She used to say she didn't know what guilt meant.'

Laurie ached and sweated and was full of nameless fears; Lorna was happy to cook for him when he was ill, but he got up and staggered home to find the women in Werter Road asking him to kill a rat; they looked on shrieking as he went at it with a brick. One evening he went out with Lorna and her brother Mavin to a Polish restaurant. As they saw Mavin off on the bus, Laurie said to him, 'Let's meet over the weekend.' 'L was furious. "I'll go with Lucian!" she shouted, and was surprised at herself.'

Struggling through his 'flu, he finished the first three chapters of the *Land at War* book and took them in to Day-Lewis. He sent Annie money and she thanked him for 'the pelf, nice pelf'. 'Dear Laurie if you have any more to spare I am really stoney . . . I was very poorly on Whit Sunday. Did not go anywhere and no one came . . . I loved to read about darling Yasmin. Her hair must look lovely, so did darling Frances's.' When friends congratulated Annie on Laurie's poems, 'there is hardly any pleasure,' wrote Laurie, 'to compare with her sentimental appreciation of my few successes.'

Lorna, by contrast, 'contaminated' his latest broadcast poems by listening with an icy smile. She had found a card from Rosamond, and over dinner with Rosamond and Day-Lewis 'L sparked at R, & she became very distant'. On his twenty-ninth birthday ('God help me') he went down to Rosamond's cottage and found himself telling her and Day-Lewis more than he wanted to about his

problems with Lorna. Rosamond was all sympathy. She thought Laurie was amazingly tolerant: 'You are the first man I've ever met who . . . furiously beset – did not counter with rudeness, indignation, self-justification, sulks, silence, plain male rage, ending in the paralysing act of getting up and going away – but just went on being gentle, affectionate and agreeable,' she wrote. 'A man in a thousand! Tell her so, if necessary.'

Two days later he called at Lorna's room and she was not there. 'Honeysuckle which she had brought from Sussex was thick in the air. I lay on the bed & slept. She did not come in till dawn.' This happened again. Now it was his turn to be filled with wild suspicions. 'Lorna went out with a fellow but came in at midnight after I was asleep.'

Land at War was a torment to write. He escaped to see Rosamond's sister Beatrix Lehmann in *Ghosts* – 'a terrible play' – and next day met Beatrix by chance at Ben Frankel's 'Hotch Potch' concert at the Albert Hall. Eddy Sackville-West took him to hear the pianist Clifford Curzon and Benjamin Britten playing the first performance of Britten's *Scottish Ballad*. One night he dined at 'one of those posh irritating restaurants' with Lorna and a girlfriend, and over several gins the two girls 'talked of gigolos and Bentleys, a world as unreal as hell. I thought the leaden heart of woman here reached the lowest depths of ignominy. I sat and watched them in a sort of arrested disgust, seeing the one as it were for the first time, and the other a creature of unbelievable folly.' He left them 'in a paralysis of anger'.

Night after night he waited for Lorna with a tight dull feeling in his chest. 'I could picture her face, stricken by that fixed slightly intoxicated smile which carries her through the jokes, the innuendoes, even the frank obscenities of whatever hangers on she has with her. I could picture her thinking perhaps for a second of me & smiling that deathly smile to herself . . . All this is so worthless, so ignoble, yet I find it very difficult to put out of my mind . . .' Should he just withdraw and let her give herself completely to that other world? Or fasten himself like a leech and guard her, receiving the cold comfort of that smile?

'Whatever I do, no more self-immolation, subjections, humili-ations. I have done enough.'

One day Lorna summoned him. At the Savoy the night before 'on some binge' she had lost her wallet with £8, her post office book, five books of clothing coupons, sundry letters and photographs. 'I'm sure she was robbed. She gets so hazy dazy after a few drinks she just doesn't notice.' Laurie found her asleep, woke her to 'a miserable drowse, lamenting she would not say what, but feeling remorseful about something. She confessed that she was unable to resist those nights. I would much rather she was in the country. I can not watch her all the time.'

This impasse went on for weeks. Lorna went her own capricious way and Laurie felt he was going mad. He would work leadenly, and pace up and down, waiting for her telephone call. Finally he would go to her room and find only the traces of her recent presence – fresh flowers in the vases, petals on the floor. One night he rang and found her at home. 'She answered in a hard cracked voice. "How are you?" "Oh very well." "When can I see you?" "Thursday perhaps." I rang off and ran for a bus. I was coiled up with anguish like the pain of poison. The bus stopped every 2 yards. She was in bed placidly reading a book. She smiled her distant smile. "Why are you doing this?" "What?" "You know very well." "But I don't." Laughter. I have never been so tortured, hopeless. I have never had less pride or cared less for pride. But still she only smiled & laughed & said "I must get some sleep." At last she says, "But what's worrying you? What d'you want to know?" (smoothing her hair with her hand). "I'll tell you anything you want to know of course" (looking at ceiling & tapping her foot). Of course she'd tell me nothing – except "Well actually I've just no feelings about you at all. I don't feel anything. I wish you'd stay the night. I don't like being here alone."

'I stayed. But her indifference, the iced friendliness of her voice!

'I never want to feel like this again. I lay thinking of the future and the bloodless torturing game it would be. Never have I loved so much and so fruitlessly, never has she so coldbloodedly let me torment myself. "I'll do what I like, go where I like, with whom

I like. See?'' There have been quarrels between us before, but not this. I have never before doubted that we should survive them. Now I do.' Lorna appeared to have become addicted to her night-clubs ('those putrid dens') and to Lucian, and told Laurie she was going to go on doing the same, so he'd better leave her alone. Work became impossible. Sleep eluded him. His whole brain, 'its order & capacity to interpret feelings & events seem to have broken down'. All he could think of was that Lorna was somewhere in London, with someone else. One night when he had waited for her all evening she turned up on the last train, 'a bit tipsy', and was very sick; he watched over her all night.

At breakfast the next day, Lorna caught sight of Rosamond's last letter and fury broke out again. As she left to catch her bus for work, she asked Laurie for the key to her room: 'I don't want to have you walking in when I've got someone there.' Laurie dumbly followed her on to her bus. 'Passing a block of flats she got off. I followed. She rang a bell and a weak-looking golden-haired boy stumbled from his bed to let us in. A friend. A kept boy of some rich man. He looked pampered & corrupt, blinking through sleepy eyes. She was glad for me to see him. I went with her to the nursery. I was dumb with pain at this new horror. I never thought I was capable of being so completely possessed by pain & misery. Deliberately, she commended me to the devil.'

That night he saw her with Lucian Freud.

'She had promised to see me at 9. I waited in her room. At 9.30 she rang through. Again at Piccadilly. It was raining hard & I knew she had no coat. I said I'd meet her at the Underground. She arrived with that dark decayed looking youth whom she has been playing with. They didn't see me. They walked slowly along the pavement hand in hand, his head inclined towards her shoulder. That moment was the worst in my life. I went cold as death. I trembled from head to foot. I walked up to them & threw her coat over her shoulder. The boy did not look at me – but slid across the road to the bus stop. L turned to me. "Where did you come from? What's the matter? You're white with fury," she laughed. I made to follow the boy. "Don't," she said. "Don't be silly." She saw me go & ran

round the corner & hid. I wanted to hit the boy hard. Instead I merely spoke a few words to him – I don't know what. He gave me a mumbling look & jumped on the bus.

'I joined L. She was sure I'd hit him. I assured her I hadn't. She held my hand which was trembling uncontrollably and I walked somehow to her room.

'I sat on the bed unable to speak. She lay down. She said her head was splitting. She said she'd been to see Cecil, they'd had a merry time talking about me. "Don't take it out of the old boy any more," he'd said to her.

'She watched my face, my trembling hands. She smiled. "Now you know how it feels," she said.

'She lay telling me bits & pieces about the evening. Her conversation with the boy. Idly she said, "The trouble is he's falling for me. It isn't fair of me I know." She said all this quite normally, either not knowing what it did to me or revelling in it. "Why did you flaunt him in front of me?" I said.

"Oh, I only wanted you to know where I was so's you shouldn't worry." Is she a child or what?'

Again he watched over her as she slept all morning. Her ability to fall asleep when with him struck him as 'almost defensive'. Both of them were in fact becoming ill. Laurie took to his bed with fever; Lorna had jaundice in Sussex. In 'blackest despair' he filled his diary with war reports: of the fierce fighting in Sicily, the bombing of Rome. 'The fire-eaters cheer in the press – they think it is a virtue, a sign of strength to be able to bomb such a place. It would have been a sign of strength if we had been able to refrain from doing so.' The battle for Catania, five days old, was raging and he felt too weak to continue his own struggle.

'I am all exposed – I seem to have no defence left. As I sit, sweating in my dressing gown, the sky is overcast & the windows rattle with an unnatural wind. Disaster overwhelms me and in spite of the deepest feelings I have for her it seems I can do nothing to prevent it. What does she feel? Cold blooded retribution, what? I feel my brain going, I have no trust. If this goes on for another week I shall have to resign my job anyway.'

186 | *Laurie Lee: The Well-loved Stranger*

In this weak and wretched state, Laurie went to see his father in Morden one Sunday, hardly in the right mood for filial affection. He waited outside St Paul's Church, where Reg played the organ.

'He came at last, driving a little car, wearing a pinched serge suit, looking shabbily parson-like, brown-skinned and old. The first time I'd been with him in nearly eight years.

'We drove through those awful stretches of Wimbledon & Morden to where he lives (ghastly place, furnished with toy dogs). And there, very bright and brittle was Mrs R – who likes to be called Auntie Topsy, whom Dad refers to as Bill or "Lady" & whom I can't bear.

'For she is hard & hideous, vain, talkative, & without the slightest vestige of humour. Her conversation is a continual assertion of herself. "I did this & that – ain't it good." Dad asks me a few questions, we converse a bit about ourselves & personal matters – she sits with her sunken eyes & thin loose mouth listening & interrupting – "That's my nephew – he's not really my nephew but I like to think he is – he rang me up. 'Hello darling' I said, I thought well I'll be nice to him & call him darling – I don't mind being nice to him even though he ain't my nephew – he likes his Auntie Tops –" Then a little boy came in from next door. "Who made your trousers?" she wheedles. "Who made them? Auntie did, didn't she? Ain't they lovely? Ain't they nice?"

'I am horrified that my father should find such a companion adequate – but he does. How limited he is. He writes hymns which are just a succession of traditional churchy chords & is proud as Punch. He plays waltzes loudly, & adores Eric Coates. The veriest echo of brother Harold, he talks continually about himself & his doings. To have been a "pukka" civil servant is the pride of his life.

'His life is finished now – and his brain is bricked up solidly by this suburban life.'

The next day Laurie went to Brompton Hospital to have his lungs X-rayed. After six hours he was told his lungs were weak, would always be subject to bronchitis and might be tubercular.

'But oh, the depression of those poor souls waiting, sick & thin, with hazy eyes & greasy feverish faces.'

When he reached Lorna's room, all her clothes had gone.

Laurie went on tormentedly wrestling with *Land at War*. He felt he was cracking up. 'Christ how can I live in this state? Or work? I wish I was a stone-breaker or something . . . This aching hopeless pain returns in sickening waves & grips me till I tremble like an ague. As night draws in it gets worse until I go to bed like a crazed thing & turn with exhaustion & think & think. But not sleep.'

Annie had no idea of the state he was in. She wrote breezily, just off to Whiteway to pick fruit, wondering who was the friend to whose son Laurie had recently stood godfather?[2] 'I hope you will hear him say his catechism now and again. It is a spiritual responsibility and I hope you'll regard it as such and be good yourself. What is it like in London now? You did not *jump* at the offer I made to come & visit you . . . Spose you did not want the old countrywoman to come up to see the smart youth of 1943, the poet etc. I'm only teasing Laurie, but I would have come if you had seemed at all eager . . . How is Lorna? and where is she? & Yasmin . . . and Jack, have you seen him? Tony came, I was glad to see *one* of my sons.'

There was a blinding heatwave and Laurie was going out of his mind. 'If I get no relief soon, I don't know what madness I shall commit.' When he finally got through to Lorna on the telephone he could only babble like an idiot. 'And she, as she did when I was working at Haslemere, apologized for being so offhand but said she couldn't help it. I wonder that she has no pity.

'The world is a grim & shrivelled place . . . I see no mercy or solicitude in her. I cannot help feeling that it is terrible that I love her, terrible that I can be neither free of it nor derive content from it. If this empty madness is all the future has to offer I would be a fool to live.'

The heatwave ended with a terrific storm. He wrote for twelve hours a day without eating; what he produced seemed 'terrible, exhausted, flat and written in a poverty-stricken vocabulary of

about 100 words. Took it to be typed by Enid and Mavis at the MOI; it looked even worse typed.'

The next day he was standing on Victoria station when Lorna crept up and kissed him. They went to Soho, to the Swiss, to Oddenino's, to the cinema, and home. Lorna challenged him: 'Why should you tell me how to live? I won't be bound down.' The fact was, he realized, he wanted total commitment, and she did not. 'Hers is the urge for irresponsible adoration. She leans to the stranger who will demand nothing, with whom she can lose herself without committing herself. But O God I want something to call my own.' She left him the next day in her brightest dress. At the studio, he was praised for his work on a film script on torpedo boats: Jack Beddington said he did not realize Laurie had such a sense of humour. 'But Lord, I am a dismal type these days. Something's gone out & closed the door & I am damp, unlit & cold.'

On her next visit, Lorna brought her son Michael with her and also her niece – 'strapping Kathy from Martigues'. Laurie went with them to an 'impossibly vulgar' film about Madame du Barry. 'Well I don't know,' said Laurie. 'The evening passed. It was pleasant being with the children.' The next day at the Redfern Gallery Lorna picked up *Sunita*, the Epstein she had bought, they lunched at the Gourmet and took Michael to a revue at the Ambassadors – 'but all this falls very flat with me nowadays. Drained empty of everything except pain.'

When he was seeing them off to their train he snapped. Lorna was 'heavy as thunder' and seemed to be clinging with suspicious tenacity to her handbag. Laurie lost control, snatched the bag; Lorna screamed with rage and they fought. Laurie collapsed, trembling. They drove in silence to the station. He was appalled by the state they had got themselves into. 'But she has no care for me any more & will not allow me to persuade her back to sanity & happiness. For myself, only I can save myself. I am alone & that I must do. I am quite unable to turn to her any more. She assured me distantly of her affection – but her words have a hollow ring. This is the depth now.'

It was a relief to spend an evening with Day-Lewis, Eddy Sackville-West and Benjamin Britten. 'For once I thought, here is a group of chaps who are talking about something I can understand', discussing poetry and 'all sorts of amiable gossip. Britten, a nice scholarly young chap with every visible sign of normality about him, is *the* composer of the day I think.' In the next few days, still intensely depressed, Laurie called on Betty Smart and her new baby. He suggested a new film to the Foreign Office but it was turned down. He discussed other scripts with Jack Holmes, brother Jack, and John Mortimer, the tall, slim Old Harrovian who was then a rather ineffectual assistant director with the Crown Film Unit. In Mortimer's memoirs he recalls Laurie as a 'small, sly Pan', piping sweet, melancholy music on his recorder in the corridors. When Mortimer took out Mavis, a 'hugely desirable' secretary, she talked endlessly of Laurie.[3]

Lorna had gone camping with the children under a harvest moon on the Downs. 'Inexpressible regret that I cannot be there. Who knows how many more moons we have?' The blisteringly hot 23 August was the sixth anniversary of his first meeting with Lorna, 'what was once referred to as "the final enchantment"' He bought her a Spanish crucifix, and some crimson gladioli, and when he arrived at her room found that she had bought some too. 'L has now an incredible number of little charms, gestures, glances, silences with which to wound me.' John Lehmann wrote to ask what day he would be bringing in his collection of poems for publication in book form. Rosamond, agitated by Laurie's silence, wanted to know the results of his X-ray, and implored him to come for the weekend: her children were longing to see him. Day-Lewis had told her that Laurie was 'under a load of trouble'.

He was sent to Weymouth on a job for a week, and on 4 September he returned by train, 'through the old lands steeped with past associations, Poole, Bournemouth, from which I left to go to Cornwall 6 years ago, travelling the same line to Southampton on my way to France, then up to Esher & the forests where we slept in midsummer. How sick the world appears. Happiness

depends on being not so much in love but in faith with a person. But to achieve that were very heaven.'

Waves of bombers crossed overhead. 'The night is like sustained thunder, like a headache, like the deep groaning of all the world. The house shakes as I write & yet I think of her all the time – O God I hope, I hope – but there she is somewhere in this city destroying me and all that ever was. I shall look at these days sometime and wonder what was the point of living them.'

On 7 September he went to see Lorna. 'She confessed much that I had suspected. This mad unpleasant youth appeals to a sort of craving she has for corruption. She doesn't know how long it will last. She would like to be free of it but can't. Meanwhile she says she loves me. Oh I can't express the absolute depths to which this has brought me . . . I pray she will get over it but I don't know, I don't know. She is tender enough towards me but devastating with her tender confessions. She goes to him when I long for her, and finds him in bed with a boy friend. She is disgusted but she still goes to see him.

'And tonight she says she is going to Cornwall with him . . .

'Can I be patient & endure. Whatever I am I still have to endure.'

Freud's biographer, William Feaver, says that Freud found Laurie's behaviour hysterical, but that all three of them tended to exaggerate the melodrama. Lucian did go with Lorna to Cornwall, where he was working on the sets for a ballet. He was as deeply affected by the free-spirited Lorna as Laurie was.

On the ensuing days, 'word by word she builds my grave, word by word she sweetens it with flowers. In the Swiss tonight she looked at me through a haze of rum & tobacco smoke over her beautiful eyes. We went home & she fell fast asleep. In the morning we made brief love. "That is your province you know," she said.'

That Saturday, 11 September, 'I was sitting on a wall when a policeman came up to me. "You're thinking about a woman. Or is that a personal question?"

"Yes," I said. "It is a personal question."

"Well, don't you worry. That's my advice. Never run after a woman or a bus. There's plenty more behind."

"Perhaps there's only one bus going the way you want to go."

"Maybe you're right," said the copper.'

On Sunday 12 September, the streets were full of autumnal thundery mists. 'I can think of nothing but this, the recurrent smell of betrayal, the pendulum of reassurance, the sickening of remembered disasters. I tremble and am full of mad arguments, bargaining with fate over the fall of a card, the flight of a bird, the frequency of lightning.

'At night in fact there was incessant lightning. I am going mad. I watched it, I shook in bed, I planned, I remembered this afternoon.

'This afternoon some music was playing. The Dohnányi Quartet. I took a razor blade to my throat. There was a dazzling burst of light, a sense of the good life calling. I put the razor down, put my head on my hands and sobbed as I have never done since I was a child.'

This was the penultimate page of his diary of that bitter summer. On the last page, he said he had been working with brother Jack, 'but if I pause for a moment a helpless, hopeless desert surges into my heart & brain & fills my whole skin with a hot burning agony.

'She rang just now while I was writing this. She has been with him, has been drinking, says everything I say is true, says if only I could convince her of the futility of what she is doing, says she loves me. But she has been with him. The image of that torments me with a strong odour of absolute wickedness & grief. I am trembling so much I can hardly hold this pen.

'But I suppose I must add that it was announced today with fanfare that Italy has surrendered unconditionally to the Allies. This means that now they will be bombed by the Germans instead of us – and the fighting will go on . . .'

Laurie was on the verge of a breakdown and Rosamond Lehmann came to his rescue. She wrote confirming a weekend at Diamond Cottage, telling him her daughter Sally had particularly asked him to bring his fiddle. She added that if Laurie wanted to get out of London altogether, he could be her lodger in Aldworth for the autumn: her son Hugo's bedsit was empty '& you would be properly

independent & needn't even sit with me in the evenings unless you choose to – and as for Mrs Wickens [her housekeeper], she'd burst with maternal love for you. There'd be a pile of wood to saw!'

She kept up the pressure: 'I *know* that being alone is the worst possible thing for you at present. You just aren't fit for it & will only sink. *And you must not sink*, for both your sakes. Try to believe – what I *know* – that your goodness and strength and truth is going to be of use to you and the world, and that a door is going to open. I love you dearly. R.'

Even Day-Lewis wrote at uncharacteristic length with heartfelt concern, asking Laurie to dine and spend the night with him, 'In fact, why not bed down there till you return to the country? . . . What I'm trying to say, in my usual bleak manner, is that I want you to call upon me, at *any* time and in *any* measure, for whatever help you want. If you will do so, it would make me feel a little less bad about my utter failure to come & see you when you were ill in July . . . This doesn't mean that I want more of your confidence than you feel able to give: but that you should look upon me as a friend who is to be relied upon, trusted, and *made use of*. Dear Laurie, for God's sake don't throw yourself away, don't sacrifice yourself, deliberately drown yourself because you believe you have failed to save another person whom you feel you ought to have saved. There is a very limited amount of goodness in the world; you are singular amongst all the people I know for the virtues I admire most – & the talents; if you allow yourself to be destroyed, you will be destroying more than you perhaps know – the sum of good will be diminished, the wicked powers unconquered. The impulse for personal expiation is a dangerous madness . . . but if expiation is what you need, you won't do it by going out into any desert, nor by allowing yourself to be destroyed, nor yet by tearing a No 14 bus to shreds. You will do it *only* by driving your cart & your plough over the bones of the dead. Take hold of the pleasant end of life again, & let it pull you out . . . R is a living evidence that there are no incurable cases. Laurie dear, we'll do everything for you that two people who love & admire you can with all their strength, sympathy & intelligence do. Cecil.'

Day-Lewis did what he could: he took Laurie to the Arsenal v. Fulham match (Arsenal won 4–3) and at each goal threw his hands in the air and howled. 'My nerves,' Laurie writes, 'were not at all good.' At the end of September, Laurie began a new notebook. He had decided to give up his old style of journal, 'written in day to day agony and weariness. The long summer is ended, it was very long, distorted with heat, fever and torment, but it is over and I can hardly remember what has happened to me. Nature is already busy suppressing those human horrors which brought me to my praying knees in a state of almost primitive abandon.

'Now I have given everything up, my job, my frenzy. Everything, that is, save a dim hope and a vague will to continue the struggle somehow.' He had given up the Crown Film Unit scriptwriting job, handing it over to John Mortimer – having first set Mortimer the test of writing a film script about Watford Junction. Inspired by *La Femme du Boulanger*, Mortimer invented a tale about a station-master's wife having an affair with a GI. In later years, Mortimer says that Laurie, rattled by his successor's tireless literary productivity, would always grumble, 'I wish I'd never sent you to Watford Junction.'

Laurie felt 'assailed by friends, eager to do things, to assuage, listen, to give me warmth. But they have come too late. For three months I had desperate need of that, but I need it no longer. Too much has been destroyed I cannot begin to estimate it. The more destructive instincts, revenge, suicide, abandon, anarchy, they have inevitably triumphed . . . It has all been too acutely a sign of the times. The potentiality for beauty, the warm gesture, happiness, trust has just been thrown away, as we have all thrown away the opportunities of this terrific century.

'All that is left to me still is that obstinate itch to work for the most painless possible peace. But it is hard when human contact is so treacherous, doubtful & faithless, when words are so false, false as the bishop's text or the slogans of nations who burn and wreck and say that it is for good.'

Lorna did not disappear, however. She invited him to the Café Royal and was 'warm and guarded. Released, at least temporarily,

from the devil. She even spoke of going to Slad, even in a negative despairing way of leaving everything and going with me to Ireland. This was like vinegar to my parched lips.' They went to Day-Lewis's place and played Beethoven. 'She anointed me with inexpressible warmth & adulation. My frozen flesh began to stir with its old workings.' Over dinner at the White Tower, Lorna told him that she could not bear it if he left London, which made him realize he should go. But 'I can never have enough'. So when she rang a few days later, he met her again, and they walked in the park under a sky 'like oily cotton waste', but Lorna threw out even more confusing signals. She told him she was too romantic, said she wanted the impossible; that London was a drug, that she could never be contented again. Laurie was 'chilled to the bone' and wished he had followed his earlier impulse and gone away. Finally on 7 October he left London for Rosamond Lehmann's. For him it was just like November 1938: 'The dismal wandering out begins again. I am alternately sadly fatalistic, & furious that this should be forced on me again.'

There were raids in London every night while he was away. 'I might have known it. Into whose keeping will it force her now? I can't go back whatever happens. I rang Putney. Wid says she has just been on the phone asking about me. She's all right then anyhow.'

Rosamond Lehmann's son-in-law, P. J. Kavanagh, says Rosamond once told him that while Laurie was staying with her that autumn, he would sit day after day typing one word over and over: 'Lorna Lorna Lorna Lorna Lorna . . .' But he managed to finish *Land at War*, a lively, amusing and original little book despite its official propaganda purpose. Day-Lewis applauded it and Rosamond congratulated herself on enabling him to get it done – 'though the fight for self-discipline and mastery over the powers of disintegration was yours alone, my poor pet'. After six weeks away, Laurie returned to London. A bomb had fallen on Putney High Street, killing many in the dance hall.

Rosamond had found those weeks 'a strange and happy interlude'. 'I have never in my life felt such perfect ease, affection, lack of friction with any member of the opposite sex. You are my brother, and I love you. You don't realize to what extent you helped to steer

me through *my* nasty crisis. Next year, if we can have the little house, things will be better. Please think *seriously* of taking a share.

'Best love darling. *Don't* be down. How I hope you'll see Lorna soon, & that all will be well. I feel it will.'

In December *Horizon* carried Laurie's new poem, 'Equinox'.

Now tilts the sun his monument,
now sags his raw unwritten stone
deep in October's diamond clay . . .

The Hogarth Press sent a contract for his first book of poems: Day-Lewis had made the selection, and jokily suggested he call it 'Laurel Leaves'. Laurie recorded three of his poems for the BBC. 'After the programme I felt very empty, there is nothing so transitory, so over and done with as a broadcast. L didn't even hear them, Jack fell asleep before they came on, our mother had 'flu.' Stephen Potter – 'tall, sandy, half bald, refreshingly normal' – asked Laurie if he'd care to have a shot at a radio script. 'I just can't believe I could ever write a radio script, any more than I could write the King's speeches.'

He thought of Lorna so constantly 'it is almost madness, writing out declarations, condemnations, appeals, in my mind often far into the night. I have written to her too of course but nothing that was in my mind to write. And from her letters I get nothing.'

The letter he drafted is tucked into his journal.

'To my love: I have no wish to criticize you. Whatever you are is my happiness and my grief, and I know that it is precisely because you are as you are – strange, lovely & unpredictable formula of woman, that I am born to love you & I would no more wish you altered than the moon.

'And I have only one desire & why should I not tell it? My desire is to be true to you, to tear from this twisted, faithless, blood-sodden world one clear immaculate image to which I can bind my heart, to which I can turn in prayer, in declaration, in all such moments of excitement and peace as are left to me in this life. It is the duty of every man to declare his faith once he has discovered it whether

in the face of cynicism, mockery or doubt. Therefore I declare that to you I will be true as long as I shall live, and that I will fight to keep that faith and will preserve it with all my strength. I will be true in heart and flesh, publicly, secretly, wherever I am, with you or if necessary alone. True I can be, and I defy the whole damned world to scorn this protestation, and it is an indescribable exultation to make it.

'It is possible you may laugh. Beloved I do not care. I have at least the comfort of my own religion. It is a good thing to have. It is a glorious & responsible thing, something to be cherished with a real & militant passion.

'In time you may fade from my eyes and become only a ghostly shadow which inhabits the books & pictures of my room, a half-remembered fragrance rising from the blankets of sleep, an idea, a theme of strange beauty which I can only repeat to myself. But whatever you become in the sly hands of imagination while you are out of my sight, to this I am devoted, to Lorna, this cherished image, & I will protect it with all the will & resolution of my heart and all the steadfastness of my body.

'If you forsake me you mortify my heart & my flesh, but you do not destroy what I cleave to. Your image is graven upon the incorruptible silence of all my days & nights, you cannot steal it from me, nor can anyone.'

Laurie was never quite the same man again. Decades later he was still dreaming of her, 'dark, brilliant, beautiful, with locks of hair woven into a dark crucifix at her throat'. Thirty years later he wrote in his notebook, 'The betrayal & desertions she was capable of making in her passion for you never warned you that she would eventually do the same to you for another. You were too young, too secure in the sovereignty of your flesh.' He was damaged; and was determined never to be rejected again. He would protect himself. He developed a carapace. It made him suspicious and pessimistic. He could disguise it, and some never guessed it, but the sweet youthful optimism had gone. He would 'never give all the heart'. He had given it once, and that was enough. He wore Lorna's signet ring until the day he died.

12 | 'No One At Home'
1944–5

The affair was 'finished, but an unconscionable time a-dying'. Lorna
still summoned Laurie to Sussex, and he could not resist going,
partly to see 'that lovely child to whom I'm more than a stranger
now'. On a wintry day with a cold wind blowing from the sea he
packed up his things from Bognor. They sat by Mrs Savage's fire
and Lorna told him: 'I can't help it. I love you – but you must just
leave me alone.' It had now been nine months since the intrusion
of Lucian Freud, but 'this paralytic sleep of winter has not been a
forgetting at all. Old wounds smart with all their hideous first pain.
I have given up any desire to struggle with this any more.'

At first Laurie kept his new address from Lorna when he moved
in with Cecil Day-Lewis and Rosamond Lehmann at 41 Hasker
Street, off Walton Street, Knightsbridge. Day-Lewis occupied the
sunlit and graceful upstairs rooms, Laurie the 'grim & grimy' basement, calling himself 'the King's Provost' – the chaperon who
prevented their liaison appearing adulterous under the old divorce
laws. (The King's Provost had been instrumental in the granting
of a decree nisi to Edward VIII's mistress, Mrs Simpson.)

Laurie's diaries in those months are punctuated with shattering
roars, clanging fire-bells, deafening explosions. 'How dull, monotonous, almost pornographic become descriptions of air raids – a
list of clichés repeated day by day by everyone,' he wrote. But his
apocalyptic tableaux of the city with the red glow of fires above,
the fear and trembling below as jagged lumps of hot shrapnel
showered down, were never dull. He seemed to feel compelled to
venture out to scenes of destruction and mayhem. One night a
factory and a furniture warehouse down the Fulham Road were
hit. Laurie made his way there, helped to fill buckets of water from
a trickling tap and climbed to a roof for an awe-inspiring view of
flames flying up fifty feet in great gusts from the now roofless

warehouse 'like a box of molten slag', and from the tobacco factory came loud explosions of buckling girders and breaking beams. By the time fire engines arrived, the buildings were gutted. 'I walked back through the streets with a soldier from Tobruk who, worried about his wife & child in Putney, had stolen leave from his barracks in Colchester and was walking to Liverpool St. He had to be back by 5 a.m.; he had left his wife hysterical & his child howling.'

Laurie's contribution to the war effort was another narration for Laurence Olivier to deliver at the Red Army celebrations in the Albert Hall, for a fee of 35 guineas. When Laurie submitted his script, Malcolm Sargent read it aloud to the braided band chiefs of the three services, pausing at the line 'his crippled eagles brood in their own blood' to smack his lips and comment with an 'apish' grin: 'Fine stuff this . . . Isn't it fun having a nice tame poet working with us.' 'The Service men laughed & looked at me uneasily. We were later discussing my introductory stanza – "Now let us rejoice" to the Hallelujah Chorus. "Dare I suggest that you write in 'let us give thanks to God'?" Sargent asked. I declined firmly, though smilingly. "I'm not so tame as all that," I said. The Service men laughed again, this time more easily.'

'I adore your narration,' Olivier told Laurie, 'but can you cut the references to Fascism. I don't like having to say them.' 'What is this squeamishness?' asked Laurie.

When the day came, 23 February 1944, Lorna came up, 'lovely in her white lambskin coat' and they shared a box at the Albert Hall with Vivien Leigh, Ralph Vaughan Williams and Sir Arnold Bax. Towering above the assembled 5,000 was an 80ft painting of a Red Army soldier, 'his face rather like Tyrone Power, a tommy gun the size of a howitzer in his hand, his boots the size of tanks'. On the stage sat the London Symphony Orchestra, the band of the Coldstream Guards, and 350 members of the Royal Choral Society. On balconies were the bands of the RAF and the Royal Marines. In the Hall were nurses, firemen, policemen, landgirls, miners with lamps on their heads. Around the stalls sat mayors in golden chains. In the boxes, ambassadors, admirals, generals and cabinet ministers; in the Royal Box, Herbert Morrison. After the National Anthem,

the lights dimmed and the spotlight beamed on Olivier. 'In absolute silence he began my prologue. He spoke it magnificently.' Vaughan Williams and Bax talked loudly through Laurie's stuff, so Lorna and Laurie talked through their music ('very English, like stale lavender water which hardly fitted the ranting histrionics of my narration') and they all glared at one other. The audience was restless – 'coughing drowned a good deal of my verse' – and Morrison's speech lasted forty minutes: 'Everyone was fed to the teeth. L & I dived out before the end, after exchanging a few words with Vivien Leigh who apologized for Olivier's performance which I praised. Cheap, pretty face she has, with the spiky selfish personality of a vixen behind it.'

That night there was another air raid. 'I wandered restlessly about, lay in the coal-hole, watched the sky. Flares, welling from the dark blue gloom overhead, seemed like huge drops of blood dropping from a wound. Tracers floated in slow arcs to meet them. Rockets rushed upwards like flocks of darting silver birds . . . The roaring noise they make as they fly upwards is terrifying; at first it melts the very marrow with alarm. But one's ears grow acute in an inferno of noise and can separate each sound & identify it: rockets climbing, various types of guns firing or their shells exploding, the sharp track of tracer guns, the hiss of incendiaries, the sound of a nightfighter from one of theirs, the wicked hum of falling shrapnel which has many sounds from a piercing whistle to a low savage beating of swan's wings.

'As I walked along Fulham rd the silence returned and was beginning to bring people from their shelters . . . When I arrived the street was a shambles, brilliantly lighted by the flare of a burst gas main. Glass lay everywhere, bricks scattered over the road. Rows of houses nearby, their fronts battered in, were full of people in their thin night-things groping around with candles.

'The all-clear went & youths from nearby shelters came whooping & shouting down the street to see the show. But the houses that had been hit were a terrifying spectacle. A few walls stood propped up with fantastic debris through which flames were savagely spreading. The cries of people trapped below in the basements,

covered as they were by piles of rubble and the fierce crackling fire made one sweat to hear them. A woman said there were ten people down there. The rescue squad arrived, firemen slowly unrolled their hoses, the crowd watched, the cries could still be heard. A neighbour on the verge of furious tears said, her face convulsed with anger, "And they call us brave! we're not brave – we've just got to bloody well put up with it, that's all!"

'Through the black smoking hole of a basement window I helped with the first casualty. I could not tell his age: his face was covered with white dust & his hair was grey. His eyes flickered sightlessly & he moaned & shivered. There was a cry for blankets but there were no blankets. We piled our coats on him and I took a handle of the stretcher & we picked our way over the glass & the bricks . . . & carried him half a mile to the nearest hospital. Women & children sat in the passages dripping with blood. Doctors were walking with torches, some, aliens, unable to make themselves understood. The windows of the ward were out. Our charge was suffering from shock, but when I took the coats off him I saw he was only a child, he was curled up as if still in the womb, dressed only in a shirt which at the back was torn to shreds & thick with dried blood. The stretcher bearer with me was stuttering hysterically. Other casualties were coming in, lying still or moaning; people walked in silently with very young children in their arms who were either asleep, or unconscious, or dead.'

He was still incensed by newspaper coverage. The day after 19 February, the heaviest raid since 1941, 'the headlines, in their infantile way, say: "London AA barrage beats raiders." To eight million people such headlines are an insult both to their intelligence and courage.'

On a visit to Oxford to see Dorothy he found his father there, 'the raids having got him down again. He has been journeying from Morden to Collier's Wood every night to sleep on the station platform.' They played music together, and quarrelled: Laurie criticized Reg's piano-playing and Reg said 'he had it on good authority that an accompanist's job was to lead'. It was the last time Laurie ever saw his father.

Living with Cecil Day-Lewis brought London literary life into his own home. One night Raymond Mortimer was there, talking 'with a loud silky Bloomsbury voice' on subjects beyond Laurie's ken: Valéry, Compton-Burnett, Stephen Tennant. 'About 10.30 a raid starts and Raymond's voice booms above the guns. Cecil grows pale & we cock our ears & mark the long trailing path of a bomb. C goes on his knees, Raymond & Rosamond spring to the corner and crouch on all fours & I am left trembling like a jelly on the sofa – and RM's voice goes on booming without a break, telling us of the exquisite Stephen Tennant caught in a raid while a green flare drops overhead. "Oh dear," he says, "this is death to one's complexion."'

Still he went down to Sussex when summoned by Lorna, to lie 'among the cold primroses & violets high in a cockpit wood above Horsham . . . A sudden peculiar little blazing up of her hot star of older days has illuminated the week . . . Regretfully, but uncomplainingly, she tells me to be careful whom I sleep with – taking it for granted that I do. Yasmin is 5 – and further away than ever. There seemed no point in sending her anything . . . each year I feel it more pointless.

'This spring has no destination – L waves frantically or dutifully from carriage windows, but we have changed trains & no longer have similar destinations.' In June it was a year since Lucian Freud's arrival in their lives. 'I am dogged by an evil shadow.'

Every letter from Annie ended with the refrain: had he seen darling Yasmin, and sweet Lorna? Laurie went to Slad for a last weekend of freedom before starting work, on 17 April 1944, with Day-Lewis in the MOI Publications Division in Room 614, Russell Square House, Bloomsbury. This was a congenial office. As well as Day-Lewis there was Nicolas Bentley, the cartoonist and publisher; and Joan Hunter Dunn (celebrated by Betjeman) to serve lunch. Laurie became the resident clown figure (later caricatured in one of Day-Lewis's crime novels as Bryan Ingle, 'purveyor of purple prose'.) At nights he firewatched with Day-Lewis and they played chess and talked into the small hours. One night when he and Day-Lewis and Rosamond went to hear a new work by Britten,

he suddenly saw Lorna. 'Uncontrollably my blood turned to sand, my mouth dried up – later I felt I had been soundly beaten all over.' When he went to play Beethoven with Ben Frankel and his girlfriend Anna, and afterwards the conversation turned to jealousy, 'I was amazed to find how much I've changed, holding fidelity a high ideal,' Laurie noted, 'which they reckon to be weakness, primitive & possessive & narrow.'

On 4 June a girl called out in the street: 'Have you heard the news?' The Normandy landings had begun. The night was full of strange sounds. 'Some infernal machine was being launched from the N. Coast of France, and coming in numbers off the South Coast of England. Papers said radio controlled, speed 240 miles per hour, & full of explosives . . .'

A few days later he was in the office when he had his first sight of a flying bomb: 'It was black and had short wings like a fighter, it was like an incredible toy; fascinated I watched it streaking towards the tower of the University. Just as it seemed it would crash into it, it hesitated, spurted flame from its tail, and fell slowly upon Tottenham Court Road. I lay by the radiator and then, after the explosion, saw a great tower of grey blue dust rise up. Slept in the ministry this evening, with Cecil. Flying bombs came in a steady stream. We got little sleep.'

Two nights later when he returned with Day-Lewis from a night in the country, they found that a bomb had come down right in the middle of Russell Square. Leaves were blown off trees and lay thick over the roads among heaps of glass. All the windows in their office had blown out and the door hung from its frame. All day they heard the sound of glass being swept up. A proof copy of Laurie's first volume of poems, *The Sun My Monument*, had been lying on Laurie's desk. The book is inscribed: 'The small cuts in the cover of this book were caused by glass splinters from flying bomb blasts in June 1944.'

Dedicated 'To Lorna', this volume forms a poetic account of his life since 1935. 'Music in a Spanish Town' is about playing his fiddle in Córdoba just before the outbreak of the Civil War; 'A Moment of War', with the dateline now 'Spanish Frontier, 1937',

and 'The Return' ('And the day I observed I was a lover/I crossed the frontier to seek a wound . . .') were brought home from the Civil War. All the poems written for *Horizon* and for John Lehmann reflect the years of Lorna's passionate embraces in the midst of war; for example, 'The Armoured Valley':

No festival of love will turn our bones
to flutes of frolic in this month of May,
but tools of hate shall make them into guns
and bore them for the piercing bullet's shout
and through their pipes drain all our blood away.

Publication day was Tuesday, 27 June 1944, the day after Laurie's thirtieth birthday. There was a bomb warning that day, and from the office window Laurie watched it 'shooting very fast through a raging hailstorm to crash near Regent's Park amidst lightning & the roar of real thunder'. He lunched with Rosamond Lehmann, and in the evening her brother John held a party at his flat: guests included William Plomer, Rose Macaulay, Eddy Sackville-West, Louis MacNeice, Henry Green, Peter Quennell, Lawrence Durrell, and of course Rosamond and Day-Lewis who took Laurie to dine at Oddenino's. Laurie's diary says: 'This might have been an excruciating anniversary [i.e. his birthday, one year since Lucian Freud took Lorna] but am too dead to feel it.

'I am a bit depressed about my book now – it seems so slight. At the party people were picking it up and putting it down as if it were a month-old *Evening Standard*.'

It was some months before he received a forthright criticism of his poems from Wilma. She told him her sister Sybil, 'a 67-year-old woman who lives in very dull surroundings', admired them: but Wilma was harder to please. 'It's the pattern or design I'm doubtful about; i.e. as to whether there is one,' she declared. 'I don't want a story, but I do want a theme, & it seems to me you lack this. Beauty of rhythm, certainly, & an amusing clash & grind & romping ugliness of words which is often exhilarating. And sometimes beauty there too. But I still ask for a theme.'

Louis Aragon's poems, she said, had themes in plenty. 'And Lorca does not lack them. Nor does C. Day-Lewis or Stephen Spender . . .' She added that having been born in 1886 she supposed her opinions were out of date. But 'I still hold that theme is to words what design is to painting. Toss your glittering words on paper, & they might as well be left in the dictionary, if they're not expressing a subject. So it seems to this ancient, now condemned to heresy by her weight of years . . .' He had plenty of emotion, she allowed, but had he yet begun to think? 'I doubt it.' For good measure she enclosed a poem by a contemporary Spanish poet she did admire (Pedro Salinas) and hailed Rosamond Lehmann's *The Ballad and the Source* as a masterpiece. She added that she had been to Binsted and seen Lorna, Michael and Yasmin, 'who were all looking very well & seemed in good spirits'.

In August 1944 Rosamond, inviting him for a weekend ('Beatrix is here. We'll have a laugh'), was obviously puzzled to find Laurie distant and secretive. She sensed that he was forging new friendships, as indeed he was. His MOI colleague Daphne Hardy – who had just ended her affair with Arthur Koestler, whose *Darkness at Noon* she had translated – ran into Laurie in Malet Street, just when she was buying his book. Laurie asked her for her address, and came to see her, rather embarrassingly, as she was already living with the designer F.H.K. (Henri) Henrion.

Then the novelist Betty Askwith, who was broadcasting a review of his poems ('You've got the real thing haven't you? The sensation of fear that comes across in "A Moment of War" is physical and terrifying') introduced Laurie to Virginia Cunard. Tall and elegant Virginia, who was doing St John Ambulance work, was one of the six Cunard sisters who were to feature almost as importantly in Laurie's life as the Garman sisters did. Virginia found Laurie charmingly naïve: 'He asked me to meet him at Piccadilly Circus: nobody had ever asked me to meet them there.' As they walked home, guns began going off and shrapnel fell. 'And he pushed me down the area steps and held a dustbin lid over my head like a modern Walter Raleigh.' She still recalls the verse he recited to her composed of the names of generals:

Hark hark, Mark Clark, the Kesselrings
It is the Eisenhower
The general Patton of events
Has made old Monty sour
His Spaatz are fitting Bradley
And he Rommels as he runs.

She was enchanted by Laurie, and fell hopelessly in love with him, but then, she says, everyone did. Her sisters Laura, Veronica, Barbara, Penelope and Grania all took to him at once. 'He had charisma. That was the word for Laurie.' The Cunards had grown up at their family home high in the Cotswolds at Notgrove, where their father, Cyril Grant Cunard, grandson of Samuel of the Cunard Line, was known as the Squire. Very soon Laurie was escaping from the flying bombs to stay in Surrey with Grania and her husband Val ffrench Blake at Nalderswood, at the gates of a house belonging to Grania's sister Barbara Charrington.

Laurie rapidly became 'like one of the family', Grania says, 'just part of all our lives'. Her husband Val, a tall and handsome officer with the 17th/21st Lancers, had been wounded in North Africa the previous year. He and Laurie formed a musical alliance, playing Brahms and Beethoven and their *pièce de résistance*, the César Franck violin sonata. Laurie also encouraged Val in his oil painting: Val was impressed by Laurie's 'sensible and instinctive judgement, quite unclouded by any fashionable dogma which he might have picked up from his artist friends'.

The artist friends had arrived in his life through a gilded couple, Nicolette and Anthony Devas, whom he met at a Chelsea party that summer. Nicolette's father was Francis Macnamara, the wild poetic Irish friend of Augustus John; her sister Caitlin was married to Dylan Thomas. Nicolette – small, stylish, shapely, fair-haired and amber-eyed – had been at the Slade where she had met the strikingly handsome Anthony Devas, now much in demand as a portrait painter. Nicolette and Anthony were house-sitting off the King's Road at 6 Markham Square (home of Georgiana and Noel Blakiston), which had a studio on the top floor, with roof garden;

the Devases made it into a bohemian but civilized gathering-place for artists, models and poets. Augustus John, Nicolette's adopted father, would frequently call. Laurie, whom she found 'a romantic-looking young man who measured up to the popular idea of a poet', immediately asked Nicolette if he might become their lodger.

Nicolette hesitated. Realizing that Laurie was on the same wavelength – 'inflections and half sentences tell a saga as fast as the wink of a cat' – she told him: 'We don't want lodgers who want to be friends.' Laurie was not discouraged. He asked again. At his third or fourth plea ('Laurie could charm the birds off the trees and argue the hind leg off a donkey') she gave in, and he was allocated a sunny attic room with a view of the trees in Markham Square.

Later, Laurie told Nicolette that her reluctance had made Markham Square all the more appealing, 'for he too wished to keep himself to himself'. He was an ideal tenant. In their house the artist's need to be left alone was respected. Laurie would hole up in his room unless Anthony Devas persuaded him to come down and join the family. In Laurie, Devas found a soulmate. Both liked snooker, tricks and pranks. Laurie's speciality was balancing a tangerine on his head, letting it fall and catching it on the point of a kitchen knife. From his attic he would shoot peas at the ankles of passers-by: one day he caught Paul Potts, a poet who lived in the basement across the square known as Poets' Kitchen, presided over by the beautiful, sad-faced Elizabeth Smart (known, after her novel, as 'Sat-Down-And-Wept').[1]

Nicolette perceived that there was a winter Laurie and a summer Laurie. In the winter he looked sickly and haggard with bags under his eyes. 'At the first ray of spring sunshine, he relaxed like a lizard . . . turned his face up to the sun and baked his skin brown . . . Sunburnt at midsummer, he deceived himself and felt robust.' His eyes lightened, he became extrovert, interested in women, and played cricket with the children. When the Devases' son Prosper was born in 1946, Laurie became his godfather. At Markham Square, Anthony Devas painted several portraits of Laurie – one, first exhibited at the Leicester Galleries in November 1945, hangs in the National Portrait Gallery today. But Laurie's face was a challenge: it

was 'like water', wrote Nicolette, 'never the same, mastered by the weather with a change of colour and texture; glass smooth, ripples, dead sulky. His weather was his moods.'

Devas, who was the local ARP warden, would hustle the family into the Anderson shelter during air raids, but Laurie remained in his bedroom playing his fiddle. During lulls in the raid they would hear the consoling strains of Mozart down the stairwell. The violin, Laurie said much later, is a solitary instrument, but it had always been his solace. 'You can stand in front of a window and play, and it absolutely destroys time, like making love. There seems to be no beginning and no end. You start in the early evening and you're still playing at midnight, and you don't know what has happened in the meantime.' He had always found it 'a deliverance from time's winged chariot'.

The war, Nicolette wrote, gave all artists a free-wheeling independence. Money was short and ambition pointless, 'so the artist got on with the job of being an artist . . . people like Anthony and Laurie, who were in a position to pursue their art during the war, never had it so good.' One day Nicolette took Laurie to see a house in Cheyne Row whose façade had fallen into the street after a landmine. The interior was open to the street, with paintings still hanging, and an eiderdown hooked on the chandelier. Walking by with her son Esmond in his pram, Nicolette heard the hooting of an owl, bringing food to its young in a nest in the corner cupboard. Laurie made this the subject of his poem 'Town Owl'.

When Rosamond Lehmann wrote, urging Laurie to 'come next weekend & gladden our hearts' and asking him to take her son Hugo out ('Just say no if it's a bore. You know how my children dote on you, but I don't want them to suck your blood'), she added: 'I did not realize you were *chez* Devas. I do hope you're happy.'

He was not exactly happy, but he had found his milieu. Chelsea was more congenial than Putney or Knightsbridge, and he found his colleagues at the MOI excellent company. In October 1944 the woman who researched the pictures for *Land at War*, Olivier Popham – later Anne Olivier Bell, editor of Virginia Woolf's diaries

– shared Laurie's small sunless office, where Laurie and Day-Lewis 'would carry on the most hilarious commentary with hoots of laughter'. 'Laurie was sometimes very poorly and subdued,' Olivier says, 'but jokes and fun were the leitmotif of our daily life.'

Lorna had now temporarily vanished from Laurie's diary, except that on 12 October he wrote: 'This morning, I considered for the first time the possibility of killing her, without rejecting it immediately.' Perhaps this is worth remembering in the context of his later poem 'My Many-Coated Man', who 'hooded by a smile, commits/his private murder in the mind'.

Instead of this drastic step, he devised another strategy. From his vantage point in Markham Square, Laurie was perfectly placed to find himself a new Garman girl. There were three of Lorna's beautiful nieces now in Kathleen Garman's house at 272 King's Road: Epstein's two daughters Esther and Kitty, and Kathy, the child Laurie had dandled on his knee in Martigues in 1937, daughter of Helen Garman and Marius Polge. The four-storey house was one of a Regency terrace later pulled down for the new Fire Station, in a parade of junk shops, cafés, art stores and greengrocers. The houses on either side stood derelict. Kathleen's house had gracious fireplaces and was stuffed with works of art: 'bronzes, drawings and gouaches by Modigliani and Epstein, amid the marvellous Benin heads and furniture which Epstein and Picasso had collected in their student days'.[2] Kathleen's Steinway piano was in the first-floor drawing-room, with its tall shuttered and balconied windows.

Laurie had already spotted Lorna's niece Kathy in the King's Road, 'nubile, arms swinging, straight and tall, her limbs clad in a tight blue frock . . . sturdily curved and comely'. She was indeed precociously shapely and long-legged, but she was only thirteen. Her less robust cousins Kitty and Esther were 'each of them a heart-stopping beauty'. The girls' upbringing, as Epstein's second family, was singular. Epstein – who continued to live at Queen's Gate with his wife and the two children he had fathered, adopted by his wife – would visit his mistress Kathleen and their three children, Kitty, Esther and Theo, twice a week. Kitty says: 'He'd come at six on Wednesdays, with a bottle of wine and flowers or

fruit, and stay an hour or two, and we'd line up and he'd look at us in a benign way. He did a drawing of me, but there was no real rapport; I once heard my brother Theo calling him "Papa" and it made me cringe with envy. On Saturdays my mother would be got up in evening dress with silver shoes and a wreath in her hair, and they'd dine at the Isola Bella in Soho, or the Ivy, and he'd come back for the night. Sometimes they'd take us with them, to things like the Ballet Russe. I remember feeling hot and teenagerish and left out and never having the right dress.'

Kitty and Esther were shy, nervous, slightly fey and other-worldly in Garman fashion. 'We cultivated being pale and interesting to the extent that we were called the Magnolia Girls. Most young men weren't glamorous enough for us. We were tremendous poseurs,' Kitty says, 'reading poetry and playing Debussy. Kathy was more down to earth.'

Within the year of 1945, Laurie took out all three Garman nieces. Esther, graceful and swan-necked at seventeen (as sculpted in clay by her father), was taken by Laurie to Yehudi Menuhin's 'spellbinding' performance in aid of Jewish relief at the Albert Hall in July 1945: Epstein had been given tickets, and passed them to Laurie. In a powdered, bejewelled gathering, Laurie noted in his diary, 'no one looked more beautiful than Esther, whose long plaits hung down like tassels of black silk'.

But there was also Kitty. When Laurie asked eighteen-year-old Kitty out, she was surprised – 'he had seemed like a romantic kindly bohemian uncle' – but flattered: he was a sophisticated older man (thirty-one) and a poet, therefore glamorous. She went back to his room at the Devases', and when Laurie made advances Kitty did not reject them. 'Partly from curiosity, and a kind of fatality. But I thought the things he said were rather corny. He put on the *Rite of Spring* and said "How does this make you feel?" It didn't make me feel at all erotic. I was embarrassed and I didn't really like it.'

But he gave her a pretty bracelet and wrote her a poem, an acrostic on her name.

'And then he rather brutally broke it off, quite sensibly, saying, "I don't think this is right." And of course my self-esteem was

bruised, and I made a painful scene, thinking I wasn't passionate enough, saying, "You can't leave me, please love me again, you can't," like any distraught and tearful girl of eighteen with her first lover. My mother went to see him, because I was so upset, and he denied it through and through.'

At some point that year, Lorna stepped in. At a party at Roy and Mary Campbell's, Lorna pointed to Kathy and said to Laurie, 'Try that one. She'll do for you. She'll be strong enough.'

Kitty says: 'Kathy was beautiful but also tough. I wasn't made of stern enough physical stuff for Laurie: he wanted a nurse. He hinted darkly at illnesses. "I can't tell you about my illnesses," he would say, "you wouldn't understand." Laurie needed a strong woman and he found this in Kathy.'

Kitty was jealous when Kathy was taken out by Laurie. She claims he sent Kathy an almost identical acrostic to hers, 'using the same words, except that mine began "Know the green wells of the sea"; and hers started "Know the blue wells of the sea" (her eyes were blue and mine were green).'

In fact Kathy's acrostic, spelling 'Kathy Polge', which she still has, dated 26 August 1945, is different:

Keep in your hair that summer golden crop
And never shall its corn-flushed harvest go
To fill death's sickle or the grave's grey mill.
Hold your heart's rose in bloom, and blossoming
Your youth, its life, shall have no need to die.
Provençal child, in whose deep eyes I drink
Outpouring wines of blue Iberia,
Live in my vision, burn its northern frost,
Grow like the sun that rises heaven high
Each year returning summer for our joy.

Kathy was in her Parson's Green School uniform when she saw Laurie leaning against the gas stove in the basement kitchen of 272 King's Road. She was then no longer living with her Aunt Kathleen, because her mother Helen had met and fallen in love with a

charming old Italian law professor, Mario Sarfatti, who had left Mussolini's Italy as a Jewish refugee. Helen and Kathy went to live with 'Sarfi' at 10 Kensington Church Walk. Laurie began to visit Kathy there and would take her to the pictures – Olivier in *Henry V*, *Jane Eyre* (which they saw three times). When Laurie wrote Kathy the acrostic, she had already decided that he was the only man for her.

Kitty took a while to get over Laurie. She left home and went to stay with a favourite Garman aunt in Herefordshire. 'I got a job in a tiresome "advanced" school. And perhaps it did me no great harm except to lower my self-esteem. I began going out with all and sundry to make up for it.'

The bizarre postscript to this brief affair is that Kitty's next serious boyfriend was her Aunt Lorna's other ex-lover, Lucian Freud. Did he too, after Lorna, go in the same pursuit as Laurie? 'Lorna, who was not usually introspective, saw what was happening,' Kitty says. 'She said "I suppose it's a way of getting closer" meaning closer to her.' Lorna appeared to accept that if they couldn't have her, both Laurie and Lucian would want one of her nieces. 'It was a confirmation of her psychological power over them,' Yasmin says. 'Also, as her nieces, they weren't threats to her.'

Kitty was naturally conscious, with both Laurie and Lucian, that she was following Lorna. 'I felt inferior to her. She was so glamorous, and rich, and we were all so poor. Also Lorna had, like my mother, great physical courage. Physical discomfort meant nothing to them, while I wasn't intrepid; I always wanted to be warm and cosseted, catching a cold on the least provocation.' She says she truly went into both affairs in complete innocence, 'naïvely assuming that because Lorna had now become a Catholic and went to mass every morning, and said she'd given her heart to God, that she had given up both Laurie and Lucian: but she hadn't inside, of course, at all, and she made me feel treacherous, which I wasn't.' So Lorna did after all feel undermined by her nieces' success with her ex-lovers.

After two years with Lucian, Kitty became his first wife, just before their daughter was born in 1948. She left him four years

later, after he painted her in one of his most famous portraits, *Girl with a White Dog*, in which Kitty gazes apprehensively ahead, wearing a yellow dressing-gown with one breast exposed and a white bull terrier lying with its head on her thigh. Kitty met the economist Wynne Godley[3] soon after, and has been married to him ever since.

Rosamond Lehmann longed for Laurie to confide in her about his new loves. She felt affronted by his secrecy and was convinced he was unhappy. 'I know you like covering your tracks, mystifying the world – but we'd got beyond that once, and trusted one another. Now I can only try to read your face and form conclusions from what you *don't* tell me – from the expression in your eyes. I don't like the feeling that you are keeping me at arm's length by interposing a cloud of your new girls & activities between us. You make me feel you no longer trust me. Perhaps it is because, last autumn . . . your misery made you go too far against what is natural to you in confidences – & now that you want to forget all that, you see me as connected with it, & want to avoid me?

'I can only *guess* that things never did come right between you & L – I can't ask . . . I waited for you to say "All is well again" or "All is over." That is all I wished to know. If I were to hear that you had found someone to love and to be happy with, I would rejoice so deeply – But I feel it isn't so. I see you . . . wrapping yourself round with crowds so as to hide yourself. Yet maybe this is only the normal effect of being a popular & also over-worked young man about town? When I knew you, really knew you, you were alone. I so admired & respected your plan for life . . .

'I don't mean that I want you to sit down & pour out the history of your new loves to me. I just want to know *who* you are now, where you are.' She signed herself: 'Your loving Rosamond.'

Having received a 'sweet' reply, and assuring him that she had not meant to be interfering, she added: 'I think you are, without perhaps deliberately meaning to be, rather a dangerous person for women! You seem to expand with such warmth & freedom towards them, it goes to their heads – it's such a rare pleasure for them to find so much subtle understanding, sensibility & attentiveness in

the male sex. They think you need them as much as they need
you. Then suddenly they discover they've come to a walled enclos-
ure with a sign: Keep Off. Keep Out. No Visitors. No Inquiries.
No One At Home. And they get upset.'

Rosamond was right: Laurie could always charm women, but
his carapace made him dangerously immune to commitment and
he was glumly conscious of hurting people. He wrote in his diary
in February 1945: 'I have been regaled all round by offered love. I
have been without heart.'

That snowy new year of 1945, Laurie had had his usual 'flu.
Annie too was ill, in the snowdrifts at Slad. She wrote listing the
deaths in the village and was sorry to have missed Laurie's broadcast
poem on Christmas Eve. 'I kept looking at the clock trying to make
up my mind to go up to Mrs Brown's but the noise of the rushing
40 m.p.h. wind deterred me.' Reg, she had heard, did not think
much of Laurie's photograph in the *Radio Times* – 'but he is always
finding fault with everything'.

Lorna's elder son, Michael Wishart, now sixteen and about to
go to the Central School of Art, did hear Laurie's poem on Christmas
Eve and wrote – decorating his letter with an exquisite Grecian
head and laurel leaves – asking Laurie to choose a picture from his
first exhibition. He chose one of magnolias, which Michael framed
for him in plain gold. He also promised to design the cover for
Laurie's next book. He said he admired 'Words Asleep' and 'I think
at night my hands are mad' ('Night') and drew a naked lady. 'I
can't say anything in a letter to you, Laurie. I shall give you a
painting which will say all I have to say. I have been painting and
am empty now. With love, Michael.' (In his autobiography Michael
wrote: 'I have always painted what I could not express better in
words.')

'Be always occupied,' Michael advised Laurie, rather endearingly,
'because I have discovered it means being happy. Boredom is
misery.' Laurie was certainly busy; he was about to take the traditional recourse of those wounded or bewildered in love. He was
going abroad, for the first time since he had left Lorna on that black
day in 1938: and again, he was going to Cyprus.

One dark, grimy day, 'when the war had been on six years and the face of everyone had a jaundiced look, dry and yellow, like bits of old leaves', Laurie walked into a pub and found Ralph 'Bunny' Keene, who told him: 'I'm going to Cyprus to make a film. Aren't I lucky?' Bunny was an Old Marlburian who owned a documentary film company called Greenpark Productions in Upper St Martin's Lane. Laurie told him he knew Cyprus from his pre-war visit. ('True, I was only there for a few weeks, but nobody knew that.') So he was signed up to tell the story of the island of Cyprus under British rule. He bought himself a safari suit and on 9 April 1945 was issued with his second passport, this time described as 5 ft 10 in and 'Government Official'.

He saw Lorna, who wrote a chatty letter ('Our little angel has chicken pox . . . I do hope you feel better, my sweet') hoping they might have lunch before he left. She referred to 'undividable you & me'. She had been listening to Rachmaninov's *Rhapsody on a Theme of Paganini*: 'Do you know the slow movement? He has a sad haunting truth in his music which never fails to give me gooseflesh . . . Did you hear the Poulenc Cantata – with Paul Éluard's poems & Laurence Olivier reading them, I thought he read badly. I think it's a mistake to put music to poems, true poems should be & are music & especially as the only sort of poem one could set to music is the lyric & that is essentially musical by itself don't you agree.' She had been planting Madonna lily bulbs. 'I adore gardening it's about as far removed from any form of neurosis as any pastime I know. I was so happy to see you again my darling let's try & meet before you go or on the day Love me Lorna.'

In a postscript she rhapsodized over his latest poems in *Penguin New Writing*, 'so new & exciting do write some more my darling & PLEASE send Tang of healing herb to *Horizon* let me know the result. Love & XXXX from us.'

She also sent him a totem she had carved herself: 'I wanted to send you a great big Chinese agate which looks like a cow's eye but it was too big for you to carry in your pocket & the whole point is to have it everywhere you go, so I'm sending you this [a

little wooden madonna] as I have the other one which makes it more of a totem because there are only 2 and you & I have them. This spring is certainly very lovely & you're right when you say about it having no heart when one's young – but now it has the richest heart never to be forgotten. I played romance for C Sibelius last night 1st time for many moons. It's so lovely darling love, have no fears – I swear I'll look after you. Y all better Love & kisses from us both. I adored the post cards send me some more for goodness sake.'

Lorna had also carved a huge wooden madonna which she placed in the grounds of a deserted eighteenth-century house near her home. She had covered her madonna with a scarlet hooded rain-cape to protect it. Michael was in the post office one day and heard a woman saying: 'Mrs Wishart's become very peculiar: she stands out for hours in the rain just staring into space.'

Laurie departed from Hurn airfield by Dakota in April. After a stopover in Cairo – 'hideous, lemon-coloured, hot, mercenary, and plagued with black kite-hawks that spun like bellicose flies over the city's rank-smelling carcass' – he took a pretty white biplane for the last lap over Sinai, Palestine, Syria, Beirut, 'where I tasted my first wartime banana', and arrived in Nicosia with a week ahead in which to prepare the script. A mad Turkish driver named Achmed, who could kill snakes, sing and 'do the stomach dance', tore 'like a ball of mercury in a frying-pan' through squat brown villages, scattering mules, goats, poultry and people. In a café one night Laurie found Nikos the handsome farmer and Vassos the villainous-looking goatherd, who became the film's main characters. 'They lived their story before the camera, arguing with a natural passion that was completely unselfconscious and childlike.' Feasting on pickled sparrows, goat's cheese, honey and rough wine, enjoying the singing and dancing, absorbing Cyprus's legends of Aphrodite, St Paul, Othello, St George, Laurie was happy. One night a man came running down the street in Nicosia, while Laurie was at a film-show, shouting out that the war was over. In his book about the experience of making the film, unthrillingly entitled *We Made a Film in Cyprus*, a beaming Laurie is photographed

basking on a bed of oranges. The easy friendship with Bunny Keene developed into a fruitful working partnership.

He arrived home, lean and brown, on 13 May 1945. Sister Marjorie had written to him in Nicosia, 'Oh to be in England, now that V-day is almost here', having climbed up the steep hill to the cricket field on 'a warm sunny evening with a strong scent of hawthorn in the air'. Laurie went home to Slad in July, and carried away armfuls of lilies.

In London Laurie now enjoyed a reputation as 'a real Don Juan'. He drifted in and out of his room at the Devases' house as he pleased. Frequently, he lodged with Virginia Cunard at 21 Raphael Street. 'The telephone never stopped ringing for Laurie,' Virginia says. 'He had more people in love with him than anyone I've ever met, and all the girls thought they were the only one.' Laurie got on especially well with Virginia's housekeeper, Bessie, a Gloucester-shire girl with a country brogue, a strong personality and a staunch view of morality; she thought Laurie a bit of a lad, but respectfully called him Mr Lee. Virginia's flat was burgled while Laurie was there, to the fury of Annie: 'So the wretches took your clothes & suitcase – I wish I could help you but I have used all my coupons – It seems to me people are doing that sort of thing all over London & getting away with it.'

Another Cunard sister, Penelope (Pen), began to invite Laurie to stay. Her husband was Brigadier Nigel Dugdale, who had been wounded in North Africa like Val ffrench Blake, and now worked in the War Office in public relations. In the summer of 1945 Laurie spent his first of many weekends at Bushton, the Dugdales' Georgian manor house near Wootton Bassett. Their elder daughter, Antonia, then aged five, recalls the excitement of Laurie's first arrival on their doorstep, delivered by her aunts Virginia and Veronica. 'He lay sleeping in the sun in the garden, and we tiptoed around because nanny said, "Mr Lee has been ill and mustn't be disturbed. He has to have his rest."'

Pen Dugdale was a natural hostess who loved filling her house with guests, and could organize things behind the scenes so that an atmosphere of ease and plenty was conjured with no apparent fuss.

'Pen was totally unsnobbish. She was a Gaitskellite Socialist; Attlee and Jim Callaghan were among her guests. She would never invite people because they were grand, only because they were interesting, so she preferred writers or painters,' says her sister Virginia. 'When someone asked "Are you one of *the* Dugdales?" Pen said, "No, I'm afraid I'm not."' She wrote doggerel verse herself ('Lord Tennyson's cry went up to the sky in the year eighteen hundred and nine; No doubt his mama and perhaps his papa said I've ne'er seen a baby so fine'). Her husband was a tireless joker, forever slipping into disguise, carrying a wig, moustache and false teeth in his pocket at all times. He kept a fairy cycle at the War Office, to ride up and down the endless corridors; he once cannoned into his boss, Sir Anthony Head, who was not amused.

As the privileged eldest, Antonia was not banished to the nursery but was allowed from the age of nine to dine downstairs and to taste the wine – her father always produced 'something special' from his cellar like a Château Latour 1934 – and to absorb the electric atmosphere. Laurie and Nigel Dugdale were engaged in a permanent battle of wits. Laurie would 'go into thought mode, brew up some *jeu-de-mot*, whereupon my father would cap it'. 'I feel like a carthorse following Pegasus in a fantastic obstacle race,' Laurie wrote to Pen. 'He flies, I lumber, you swoop.'

At Bushton were the kind of toys Laurie liked – guns and bows and arrows, and croquet. One of Dugdale's eccentricities was tying cotton around the waists of wasps, and letting them go with a cry of 'Thar she blows!' in order to locate a wasps' nest. Laurie could make coins disappear, and produce them from behind his ear; or perform with a tremendous flourish the egg trick, standing three eggs on matchboxes on three glasses of water, taking a broom and knocking the tray away, so that the three eggs fell unbroken into the glasses of water.

Antonia says her father once asked her mother, 'Penny, I think you're in love with Laurie. Are you?' and she said: 'No I'm not. I'm just enormously fond of him.' 'She was a strong person who, if she had fallen for him, would have realized it would never have worked. And so did he.'

Others who met Laurie then, including Anne Wintle, wife of Jack's colleague the film director Julian, say he was 'a charmer, relaxed, easy-going, with an eye for the women'. Yet Laurie felt he was 'in a very bad state and unable to absorb much' that July when he went to Sadler's Wells with Rosamond Lehmann to hear Britten's *Peter Grimes* ('Most exciting music, passionate, brilliant; lamentable libretto'). Rosamond was 'miserable to hear from Cecil that you have again been feeling ill . . . so many bothering troubles and complications'.

He kept such troubles from Annie, who heard only about his forays into the beau monde: 'My dearest son, most illustrious one. Glad you sat on the settee with Lady Louis and the other great ones,' she wrote. Laurie had been to the salon of Lady Sibyl Colefax to hear Cecil Day-Lewis sing. 'Room crowded with names . . . most with a mixed air of shame & contempt at being found there but unable to resist the compliment – Lady Louis Mountbatten, Sir Kenneth & Lady Clark, Eddy, Shawe-Taylor, Mrs Stephen Spender, Maurice Bowra, etc. etc. Cecil sang with great charm & effect. Lady Louis talked of negroes and the Burma Book. Leaving, we all signed our names in vellum.' 'It must have been very thrilling,' said Annie. 'I'd love to have seen you. I hope you did not step on any jade pieces littered about.' She added that 'Dirty Labour got in' at Stroud. 'Nearly all the Whiteway people are Labour.'

Laurie and Day-Lewis would also go to Long Crichel House in Dorset, where Eddy Sackville-West, Raymond Mortimer, Eardley Knollys and Desmond Shawe-Taylor conducted their literary salon. 'How did you enjoy your weekend with E. Sackville-West? Tell me what you had to eat if you can remember,' asked Annie, adding, 'He is not one of the Sheepscombe Wests is he? you descended from them on your great grandmother's side . . .'

In the midst of street parties and VJ Day celebrations Annie was cast down by having seen 'that man' (Reg), '& that as you may imagine always upsets my nerves. *He* seems all right – well, cocksure & conceited & now unafraid. Nothing to be afraid of now but – God knows what in the end will bring him low.' Reg had set off for his son Harold's in Stroud, and called at Dorothy's in Oxford

where unexpectedly he found Annie. 'He got a nasty shock to see me there I know. So it was to see him, and *not* an agreeable one . . . he had Mrs R with him in the car "Tops" she is called by the family . . .'

Rosamond and Day-Lewis had decided to found a new *Horizon*-style magazine to be called *Orion*, and commissioned Laurie to write a piece for it, about his childhood in Slad. In December 1945, Annie wrote a helpful letter of reminiscence. 'What about the beating up of the poor man who was not found till the next morning and it had been a frosty night? He eventually died of exposure. The men who did it were a heartless lot, no conscience or anything.' So Laurie began to write an article which would become, fifteen years later, a chapter of *Cider with Rosie*.

13 | 'Warm thoughts of warm nights' 1946–7

The cottage of Laurie's childhood was no longer quite so charming. 'Oh our home is abominable,' wrote Annie in December 1945, on her usual scrap of old envelope. 'It is wet and damp and cruel to live in. To dry up the walls floors & rugs it really needs central heating – so dank & no sunshine to cheer one up.' 'I went home,' Laurie's notebook says, '& found the kitchen more like a hollow in the wood than ever. Brith Wood & the old garden have completely taken possession, the walls are green, black leaves lie on the floor, ferns & twigs in every chair & rose bushes growing up through cracks in the piano. Annie lives like a squirrel, hiding away little stores of treasures, & losing them. Wrapping herself in scarves, blankets, curtains & pieces of flannel, ready to roll herself into a ball.' Jack was 'always on at' Annie, she said, to get a flat or rooms, 'as if it was as easy as writing it', and Laurie and Jack did bid for a cottage in an auction, but it went for £1,200. 'Someone with money was determined to have it,' wrote Annie. 'So we must wipe it off the slate.'

She wondered if Grania ffrench Blake, who was looking for a farm, might buy 'a nice place going at Sheepscombe called the Brooklands with buildings etc. attached, including a cottage which she might let to me'. But Grania bought a farm in Cornwall instead. Annie's dream was to live in the kind of rural retreat that would lure her boys back to stay with her. 'My dear boy Laurie,' she wrote. 'I often think of you bachelor one & wish I had a nice little home to ask you to come & stay with me for a lovely visit in beautiful summer weather – in company with all the dear ones who I loved long ago – many of them loved *me*, unworthy one as I am, so in my loneliness I recall them & their loving ways.' She urged Laurie to borrow money: 'I don't think you are stiff-necked are you?' A house would be 'for you boys and for the future, not

entirely for myself . . . You can have the bakehouse-cum-schoolroom for your own private sanctum for writing or painting or music – and how glad and happy I should be knowing you were in there, oh! please God, let it come true.' Alas, post-war prices were 'much too much for my boys. Twould be a stone around the neck.'

The ffrench Blakes' farm in Cornwall, Tokenbury, became Laurie's new rural refuge. While ffrench Blake went back to command his regiment in Italy, Laurie would go down to stay with Grania. The letters from ffrench Blake were remarkable, Laurie thought, for their 'felicity of phrase & fancy' so he always replied with an especially self-conscious flourish. 'All the clumsy knots and neuroses of London untied themselves as if by magic,' he wrote in February 1946 after a weekend shifting stones and clearing out gutters and ferreting for rabbits. 'You've got the makings of a first class dairy farm: plenty of water, fields that incline to the sun & will grow good grass, also there's a health in the air, a sweep of grandeur in the country that makes one feel superhuman . . . What lovely country for the flesh & the spirit.'

Laurie was now an authority on the wide open spaces of Britain, since he had spent a month travelling across the land: 100 miles a day along rolling roads researching for an MOI film. 'To the Brecon Beacons & Black Mountains standing huge & purple over the green valleys of the Usk,' he told ffrench Blake, 'the wild Pembroke coast with its great cliffs and bird-islands and crimson-coloured castles; snow-bitten Snowdon where the car got stuck in a pass; the Peak District and the Pennines & the Roman Wall; and the lovely Lakes, wine-dark, under snow-capped mountains sparkling in the sun like Christmas cakes.'

The resulting scenario for a propaganda film to promote the idea of National Parks was very Laurie Lee. It panned over urban streets, chimneys, power-stations, railways, the voice-over lamenting 'the crowded generations living and resting, working and dying' in cities. A girl leaned out of a town window on a summer evening, with a pot of geraniums and a bird in a hanging cage. 'Is there any country under this sky?' spoke the voice. 'There was country here

once. Green fields and free-growing flowers. They once made hay on the ground beneath that railway, snipe flew from the wild marshes drained for that power-station . . . And London – this great crust of smoke-blackened chaos – was once a small city standing alone in its fields by a country river. The land is too much lived in, too used up . . .'

But if Britain had protected areas called National Parks, it need not be a country of 'starving Sundays and nowhere to go': there would be footpaths and cycle tracks, youth hostels, and farmhouse catering; beauty spots and ancient monuments open to all. Famous voices – Clough Williams-Ellis, Professor G.M. Trevelyan, Julian Huxley and Augustus John – would speak of man's spiritual need for country life. (Ten National Parks, as mooted in 1945 by John Dower, civil servant and rambler, were set up between 1951 and 1957 in all the areas Laurie visited.)

Laurie's skill in documentary prose, or poetic reportage, was now widely recognized: the Prime Minister's secretary sent a note to say that Mr Attlee had 'particularly admired' the commentary in the Cyprus film, *Cyprus is an Island*, which was now showing in the West End. 'A slow pleasant film,' Laurie told Val ffrench Blake, 'with good music, Bunny Keene's photography & a lush pagan commentary written in those round ripe full-blooded numbers for which Lee is so notorious.' Jack's new feature film, *Children on Trial*, was also on release; Laurie went to a screening in the presence of Queen Mary, who 'sniffed heavily throughout the film, which endeared her to me'.

Laurie had also finished writing his charming little book about the making of his Cyprus film; he appeared with Keene on the wireless, on *In Town Tonight*, and gave a lecture on Cyprus to the Geographical Society before a 'grey, rustling & deaf' audience. Though disliking his own radio voice ('husky, nasal, with inton-ations of my brothers, like the dying words of an old familiar relation'), he began to be known as a natural broadcaster in 1945 after a graphic talk called 'Journey through Spain'. By a neat coincidence, in the BBC canteen after the recording he found Roy and Mary Campbell: his first sighting of Mary 'since I walked

from her house in Toledo, heading for Madrid, nearly eleven years ago. Now she is like an oldish Spanish woman, but with extraordinary facial inflexions that are Helen/Lorna.'

Laurie was now thoroughly at home in his agreeable metropolitan milieu. He saw Laurence Olivier's 'giggling yet manly performance' as Hotspur in *Henry IV*. He accompanied John Lehmann to the French embassy to meet Madame Odette Massigli.[1] Ushered in by a liveried retainer in white gloves, Laurie presented the lady with a copy of his poems (at Lehmann's whispered prompting, 'like a court plotter'), signing it with a conceit about the roses of April. '"But charmant!" she cried with her soft scented eyes.' He started collecting pictures: he bought one by the war artist Leonard Roso-man – 'a violent colourist influenced by Sutherland & Piper but with a strong individual romanticism'; and his favourite painter, Matthew Smith, now almost blind, gave him 'a head of a girl violent greens & blues & russet browns' in exchange for his poem 'To Matthew Smith':

Oil is incendiary on your moving brush;
your hands are jets
that crack the landscape's clinker and draw forth
its buried incandescence.

Through his friendship with Stephen Spender, Laurie was constantly at literary soirées. One evening he watched Spender acidly introducing three Soviet writers who discoursed interminably until 'Stephen drooped in a jelly of anger'. Another evening, in Cheyne Walk, Spender held a concert of music and poetry in memory of his brother Humphrey's wife. In the long elegant room where Whistler once painted, with snowdrops heaped on tables, they listened to Bach, Beethoven and Schubert, with Spender's wife Natasha Litvin at the piano. Spender, 'lisping . . . thunderous', read his poems; Peggy Ashcroft read 'The Lady of Shalott', a Shakespeare sonnet, and some poems by Day-Lewis:

'As Peggy read "The Album", a love poem written to Rosamond, the charge in the air made my hair stand on end. But when it was

over R leaned to me & whispered "How d'you think she reads?"

' "Pretty bad," I said.

' "I think awful, such a mechanical declamation." And as she spoke Rosamond caught Peggy's eye & two of the sweetest and falsest feminine smiles passed one to the other.'

Laurie was still snarled up in Rosamond and Day-Lewis's tangled web. In March 1946, Rosamond announced 'a miracle': Cecil had finally told his wife about her. 'She seems to have taken it calmly. She is behaving as if it never had been, which I suppose is the only way she can "carry on". She says things like: "Next year we must have a wire fence here" . . . You will appreciate the grim symbolism. It is all very painful . . . But he is absolutely *sure*, though shaken to his depths & in a state of violent crisis.'

Rosamond pronounced Laurie's article about his childhood, for their new magazine *Orion*, as 'beyond even my high superlatives' and Day-Lewis called it 'a winner', paying him twelve guineas and urging him to write a book-length memoir of his childhood: 'Now you have drawn this mutter of approbation through the clenched teeth of the Orion sourpusses, I hope you will feel encouraged to proceed with the autobiog,' he wrote, adding: 'Are you writing some poetry? I am scribbling away . . .'

Laurie's poetic muse-in-chief may have departed, but he could still find inspiration in the natural scene. 'Poems come out from time to time like rare and sickly orchids,' he told Val ffrench Blake in May 1946. These orchids, such as 'Day of These Days', would sprout on the top deck of the number 11 bus, which he took to buy his Portuguese rosé from Yates's wine bar in the Strand, as he recalled forty years later:

'It was such a wonderful morning that this poem began almost to dictate itself. As I drove through this golden light, images came of my village on an autumn day, a kind of *alegría* of atmosphere, and I began to write, "Such a morning it is when love/leans through geranium windows/and calls with a cockerel's tongue./ When red-haired girls scamper like roses/over the rain-green grass,/and the sun drips honey." And there I was hacking away, and the conductor came along and saw I was writing and didn't

even ask for my fare, which was threepence. The journey was just long enough to write my poem from beginning to end.'[2]

He escaped to the country regularly. He and Bunny Keene went to stay with the actress Ann Todd and her husband Nigel Tangye on the Welsh coast, where they watched a drowned man dragged from the sea. He went home to Slad and found his contemporaries were going grey, or bald; one of them, John Teakle, was dead. As Laurie left on Monday morning they were carrying Teakle's coffin up the steep churchyard path under a stormy sky. Another rural retreat beckoned when Rosamond Lehmann bought an Oxfordshire house, Little Wittenham Manor, with the £40,000 she had made from selling to Hollywood her novel *The Ballad and the Source*. While staying there, Laurie rang his mother, who was at Dorothy's in Oxford. Annie wrote: 'You said, "this is the first time that I've spoken to you over the telephone". Well (but keep it dark) that was the first time I'd spoken to *anyone* over the phone. Did you think I spoke distinctly?' She had just 'lost' one of her sons (Jack had married Nora, his colleague on *Children on Trial*) but she was pleased to open the *Listener* and 'I saw two poems, so I thought I wonder if one of them's by Laurie Lee & it was, & to me not too incomprehensible.'

In June, Laurie went back to Slad again and this time he took Kathy with him. She was now his 'dearest girl' as he always called her, and she plainly adored him. Wise old Annie somehow knew this was Lorna's niece: perhaps it was the eyes. 'Mother said, "I know who she is, son, what d'you think of that."' The weather was hot and steamy. 'We lay at the top of the garden, under spiked grass, upon wild strawberries. The cuckoo still sang. Down to the lake in darkness. We lay by the green-smelling reeds. I found a glow-worm which she had never seen before.'

'Everybody admired the lovely girl Katie Kathryn or Kitty & thought her very sweet,' wrote Annie. 'I think she was very nice & really such a child.'

She was still only fourteen, but looked older: 'so pretty, with a sometimes conscious childishness, yet not innocent', said Laurie's notebook. Later, in *Two Women*, Laurie described how he had

known 'this lovely girl' for years, 'steering and leading her through adolescence. Her mother seemed to have accepted my role of instructor and pathfinder and gave us unusual freedom.' And the Garman family example was of precocious amorous licence: Lorna had met her husband at fourteen and married him at sixteen. Someone sent Laurie a Valentine that year: 'No spring or summer hath such grace/As I have seen in one autumnal face.' 'Ah, time!' wrote Laurie. 'That I am loved for my white hairs.' (He was nearly thirty-two.) He would take Kathy in her school blazer for walks after school, through the bombed gardens of Kensington, 'like Carthage or Pompeii, a wilderness of wild cats and scented jasmine' or by the Thames, with the moon reflected on the water, and the distant noises of families in the thin-walled riverside prefabs. They flew Laurie's kite in Battersea Park until 'rigid & strong as a swan' it came down in a tall tree; Laurie climbed a ladder but could not dislodge it. Kathy would prattle companionably. 'Are you brave?' 'D'you like the sea?' 'Will I be taller than you?' or sometimes, 'Can't come out tonight – I've got to do 53 theorems.'

That August of 1946, when Helen Garman decided to take Kathy back to Martigues, she asked Laurie to accompany them 'as their acknowledged but ambiguous protector'.[3] They took a tin of coffee and fifty cigarettes to barter for three nights in a Paris hotel, arriving just as the peace conference was taking place. Paris was 'grey-blue, smelly, empty, expensive, sad with ennui'. Most restaurants were closed but they had beefsteak and managed to get seats on a night train to Marseilles. They stayed at a farmhouse just outside Martigues on the Istres road, because Kathy's 'huge, waddling grandmother' ('with swollen mouth, legacy of a bottle-fight in Marseilles, greasy black dress and big boots') was living with her lover in a one-room shack. Laurie and Kathy walked among pines, bathed in the still green lake 'like the rippling skin of a snake', ate bouillabaisse with their fingers, watched the fishermen winching in their catches and the American soldiers behaving like conquering troops. On 21 August, the anniversary of the Liberation, there was a seven-course feast. Seeing the welcome Kathy received from the Provençal villagers, who exclaimed at her beauty, enveloped her in their

embrace and wailed about her *pauvre père*, Laurie said he first 'truly noticed [Kathy's] clear gold beauty, and the depth of her eyes . . . She had no guile or suspicion of treachery.' It was her trust in him that would win him, once he came round to realizing how much he ought to value it.

Laurie was reaching a peak of professional creativity when he took part in Cyril Connolly's *Horizon* symposium in September 1946 on 'The Cost of Letters', which asked writers how much they needed to live on, and what they considered a suitable second occupation. (John Betjeman said he would be 'a stationmaster on a small country branch line'; Connolly himself replied 'a rich wife'.)

Laurie wrote: 'The commodity most necessary to the writer is not money at all, but time . . . long avenues of it stretching far away before him, free from congestion, side-tracks or concealed entrances.' He did not recommend second jobs: 'A he-man's job as a woodcutter or crane-driver, with a couple of hours' writing in the evenings? Romantic fallacy! The body's exhaustion is also the mind's. A State job, then – Ministry propagandist or BBC hack? No; they fritter and stale like nobody's business.' ('It will be a black and evil day that lures me into an office again,' he had written to Val ffrench Blake that year.) As for a State pension for writers, Laurie declared that hardship and near-starvation were no bad thing for young scribes: 'Let younger writers first serve this apprenticeship, and show something for it . . .'

Laurie said he wanted 'to avoid the dissipation of regular work for others' but welcomed 'the rewards of scattered commissions . . . I like writing for a waiting audience.' He had no shortage of commissions. Uys Krige, editor of *Vandag*, the liberal South African monthly, asked him to 'open windows on Europe' with essays (at three guineas per 1,000 words) on Spender, Day-Lewis, MacNeice, Dylan Thomas; or an essay on Spain, or on the artistic documentary film: 'That would be a piece of cake for you.' But Laurie, self-confessed 'worst read poet of my generation', was too busy writing a BBC talk called 'Free Trade in Poetry', on how the Spanish war had inspired British poets: 'Shelley, Browning and others fed lustily upon the sun and flowers of the Mediterranean. But . . . they were

inspired mainly by its classical nostalgia, its static past; never by its present agony or possible future. Those native poets of ours who wrote of the Spanish War were, I think, the first to see Europe alive.' Annie listened to his talk at the house of a neighbour, Mrs Warner, who had been moved to tears: 'as she said, I remember him as a little boy running about with his scooter having games with Jack'.

Laurie had now also written – despite his earlier misgivings about his ability to do so – his first radio play in blank verse. It was a small masterpiece. *The Voyage of Magellan*, produced by Rayner Heppenstall for the Third Programme in October 1946 with Frederick Valk and Bernard Miles, was a reconstruction of Magellan's first journey round the world to the 'spice islands' in 1519. In his introductory note Laurie remarked that man's first circumnavigation was 'as revolutionary to the human mind, perhaps, as anything that has ever happened to it' and he wrote like a man inspired. He seemed to have dredged from his seafaring Lee ancestry a folk-memory of ship's rations, salt-meat and scurvy, and borrowed the narrative device of Coleridge's *Ancient Mariner*, having a surviving sailor tell the tale to a blind beggar. In rich, evocative language – 'heightened towards poetry . . . aiming first to capture the eye' – he brought to colourful life the clamour of sixteenth-century Seville, the reckless courage and daring of the voyage to Tierra del Fuego, the mutinous fury of the sailors, the violent death of their captain.

> We did not love Magellan, – but he was a captain.
> Beggar, we were all blind at the dawn of that journey,
> but with his black-eyes he led us – five ships,
> five creaking worlds in a green universe of ocean.

In its evocative power the play is closer to Browning's dramatic monologues than to his own poems. It was later published by John Lehmann with drawings by Edward Burra, and is now almost forgotten, but it remains easily one of the best things Laurie ever wrote.

Magellan was regarded as a landmark in radio drama (the *New Statesman* ranked it with Sartre's *Huis Clos*), yet a decade was to pass before Laurie wrote another. A note in his diary suggests that

he felt radio plays were a dying art. He and Rayner Heppenstall had talked over coffee of 'the last sweet days of blind radio. Literature will go out of radio when television comes in.' Also, Laurie had little confidence in his own creativity. In Day-Lewis's new detective novel *Minute for Murder* (under his pen-name Nicholas Blake), which was set in an office based on the MOI, there was a character named Ingle, caption writer, purveyor of purple prose and office joker: 'I have all the creative writer's equipment, except creativeness,' Ingle says. 'Curiosity, exuberance, spiritual stamina . . . But I can't invent. So I write flaming captions.'

All Laurie's curiosity, exuberance and stamina were deployed that autumn when Bunny Keene invited him to accompany him to India for two months, to write two films for the Tea Board: one on the tea planters and pickers, one on local customs. Nobody remains less than overwhelmed by a first trip to India, and Laurie duly returned with a notebook so crammed with stories and impressions he could have written a book – as one of his colleagues, the future novelist Emma Smith (then aged twenty-two, and on her first trip outside England), did, making India on the eve of independence the background to her second novel, *The Far Cry*.

Keene, Emma, Laurie and two cameramen, George and Teddy, embarked on 5 October 1946 on the SS *Andes* for the voyage to Bombay, which took two weeks. 'Laurie chases all the girls one after the other,' Emma's diary noted on the voyage out, 'talks to them, lies on the deck, plays deck-tennis, and deserts them for another.' (He was, however, writing to Kathy, and when there was a shipboard sweepstake, he bet on a horse called Kathy, which lost.) A fellow passenger named Vivien was going out to marry an Army officer she barely knew; 'V fears India and her marriage,' wrote Laurie. 'She lies in my arms and says I shall drive her mad.' When they disembarked, 'Vivien spots her John – a weak-looking officer with whiskers. She is in tears.' Laurie was also in demand to play his fiddle on board for singsongs, concerts and dances: 'kissing of hands and the girls in raptures,' observed Emma. He had a running contest of puns with the cameraman George ('I asked the Captain this morning if he'd washed his Andes . . .')

On the night *The Voyage of Magellan* was broadcast, Laurie was in the straits of Gibraltar, huddled over the ship's crackling radio: Laurie pronounced the production 'hammy' and coolly abandoned the attempt to listen. He would rather stand on deck and watch the lights of Tarifa and Cape Trafalgar, Ceuta and Tangier. When they eventually arrived in Bombay's teeming streets, they saw shrunken children with legs 'like rusty knitting-needles', horses 'thin as latchkeys', 'a boy without eyes led by his brother', endless bargaining and begging ('Memsahib, memsahib, baksheesh') and encountered the searing heat that felt like being hit on the head with a flat-iron — as Emma's vivid diary records. They travelled 1,200 miles by train to Calcutta and chose a bearer named Babu, 'bright & crafty as a mongoose', to go with them to Assam. Both Laurie and Emma were repelled, in those dying days of the Raj, by the English colonials' arrogant assumption of superiority, and horrified by the Indians' unquestioning cringing servility. When they played tennis at the Burra-sahib's bungalow in Nazira, there were twelve uniformed ball-boys, and everywhere teams of turbaned servants handing round tea and sweetmeats, while empty-headed tea-planters' wives appeared to do nothing at all. They were all caricatures of what they had been led to expect. 'I have not met a man yet who could talk of anything but sport,' Laurie wrote in his diary. 'I have not met one either with a sense of humour or a sense of the ridiculous. Irony is invariably taken seriously, one must be always on guard.' Emma was more scathing: 'The awful creatures at Dibrughar, ordering whisky after whisky in the middle of the day, lolling at the bar in their shorts and boasting to each other of past drinking bouts — looking so silly, their lives just one string of parties and polo and rubbish.'

Laurie told Val ffrench Blake (an old India hand) that India was more astonishing and even more beautiful than he'd expected; Calcutta on the eve of partition was 'chaotic & in the grip of panic: no buses or taxis, stabbing in the streets [on the night of 27 October seventeen people were killed and ten injured with knife wounds], Bren guns & sten guns, & the station knee-deep in refugees from southern Bengal'. With Hallam Tennyson and his wife they watched

the Kali Puja celebrations, with fireworks and music and singing, little oil lamps in tiny boats sent floating down the Ganges, and ritual sacrifice of young goats.

He heard from Lorna, and from Annie. Annie wrote: 'I do not want to go to India ever. I do not like your description of it at all. I would rather be in England, especially now seeing the lovely changing leaves on the beech trees.' He wrote sweet letters to Kathy: 'Calcutta is a tough place. We got no milk yesterday morning because the milkman had been murdered. There is stabbing every day, so I carry the knife I bought in Marseilles . . . Keep warm,' he told her, 'by thinking of warm things, warm thoughts of warm nights among the jasmine bushes.'

Their journey north to Assam was held up when the rail track was washed away by a flood, but after the heat and violence of Calcutta, Nazira seemed idyllic. They occupied a handsome white bungalow on a bend in the river. Laurie rhapsodized over the misty green Naga hills, the light cool sun, exotic flowers, falcons and eagles, beautiful children riding buffaloes through the paddy fields, brilliant butterflies, and constellations of fireflies at night. At the gold-topped temples of Sibsagar he was struck by the grace of girls in draped white saris and long thick plaits. He watched vultures fighting over a dead calf, and in the luxuriant jungle 'caught a whiff of something rank like goat – it is jackal'. Everything was photogenic, from water hyacinths to cow dung in the yard. They began filming by bringing down some Nagas (a sturdy people: 'no shrinking or servility' about them, noted Emma) and reconstructing a forest fire and a flood. Laurie went pigeon shooting every morning, ate bananas by the dozen, and one evening, when there was a circus, he got the fire-eater to teach him the trick of eating fire.

He noted 'the grace of even the poorest peasant women', their 'pathetic contentment – their powers of waiting. And the poverty of production, tiny cows with spindly calves, trickles of milk, mothers with withered wrinkled babies, hens laying minute eggs, land producing 2 to 3 poor harvests a year. Prodigal but poverty-stricken fertility.'

While Keene and the others went on filming, Laurie returned

to Calcutta, wandering the streets and markets with their 'multitudes of coloured visions – girls with their garlanded hair & flowing mists & silks', struck by 'tragic children in rags & the smell of ghastly cooking, some hideous mess that fills me with a strange atavistic sorrow & fear'. The English, striding through the Taj hotel, were 'painful to look at, such disasters of form, feature . . . and their skin – is it lack of sun, too much carbolic, or what. The wearing of shorts by all ages incongruous.'

Everyone he met warned him of the coming bloodshed after partition. Mr Wadia of Indian PEN told him: 'Pakistan biologically, ethnologically, economically impossible.' On 11 December 1946 Laurie steamed out of Bombay for the homeward voyage, suddenly lonely: 'I feel sure it is partly my fault; I have grown sour, empty of poetry, & given to vile humours. It would not be so bad if the crowd weren't so lifeless, or if there was some privacy. We move at a crawl through the tropic sea.' The hours hung heavily, filled with 'morning baths & changing for dinner – things I have never done regularly before'.

But at the ship's carol service he played his violin, learnt a new carol (Christina Rossetti's 'In the Bleak Mid-Winter'), won game after game of deck tennis, and stopped off at Mombasa where the East Africans looked to him much happier than the demoralized and fearful Indians. From the still Red Sea they crossed the Suez Canal into the teeth of a gale, pitching violently, green faces all round while Laurie played picquet. He dressed as a pirate on New Year's Eve and was dancing with a 'Nell Gwynne' from Arundel when 1947 dawned. On 3 January he beheld the 'haunted' coast of Spain. With borrowed fieldglasses, he scanned the distant barren foothills. 'All day I watched that violent landscape – the setting of the sun, superb and symphonic.' He could see Almuñécar and the pass through the snow-streaked sierras to Granada. 'It is 11 years since I last looked there. What a longing I have to return.'

He arrived home on 7 January 1947 to find 100 letters and £100 in cheques at Markham Square. Just as he was unpacking, 'comes lovely K, her corn hair stooked on top of her head, her blue eyes swimming. I showed her my treasures, gave her her presents, shoes

[he had taken with him an outline of Kathy's size five foot, which is still tucked into his India diary] and turquoise jewellery, & we were happy.' The next day they went to watch 'dark, sweet' Anna Campbell, now twenty and dancing with the Anglo-Polish Ballet, rehearsing in a dim basement. 'Lovely to watch these slender girls leaping in a brisk Russian dance. The director walks up & down, puffing a cigarette & inventing steps with a twirl of his hand.' That day, a telegram arrived from Annie: 'Ring Dorothy re dad's cremation tomorrow.' Reg had become ill while cranking up his old Morris, and died peacefully in bed on the day Laurie arrived home.

Jack drove Laurie to Streatham crematorium. All the men of the family attended: the three brothers, including Tony, the youngest, 'ageing, hollow-cheeked'; half-brothers Reggie, now 'old', and Harold, 'nearly bald, pale in his factory mackintosh', and the sisters' husbands Leslie, Harold and 'dear Maurice, overcome & weeping copiously from his one eye'. A few days later everyone gathered at Stroud for the reading of Reg's will – a solemn assembly in Harold's front room, relieved by a scream when the floor cracked and the sofa beneath Dorothy and Harold sank into the floorboards. Reg had left five pounds to 'Mrs R', the rest of his estate to be divided equally among his eight children. Annie was glad: 'I feel that dad has acted in a very good & fair way. As Marjorie says it is right, you are *all* his children.' Jack remembers inheriting £180.

Annie was overcome with forgiveness and remorse. 'Laurie how I wish you & Jack had seen him more often & I feel somehow that it was my fault. I hope you do not feel it was – because I grieve about him passing on before I ever could be reconciled to him, or to hear him speak kindly to me for I always loved him.' She was glad Laurie had mentioned his father generously in his *Orion* story: 'I only wish *he* had lived to read it, poor old boy.'

After Reg's death, Annie declined. Any hope she had harboured of his return was now finally dashed. Mothering had been the purpose of her life, and at sixty-eight she had no one to mother. Her boys discussed what was to be done with her, that day in Stroud. They paid the outstanding quarter's rent on the cottage,

but Annie would never live there again. She wrote from Oxford:

'Laurie you do not really think I ought to go back to Slad & live in that old cottage do you? You do not condemn me to that – because I cannot face it. I mean – with silken hangings and Persian carpets; if I were only 37 as I was when we went up there first, when I was strong and had you all round to help me, how different it would be. But one cannot go back, and as you know I never had a husband, at any rate only for short periods, to support me. If I had known what I know now, and realized how strong I was in many ways, I might have kept him. But what did he leave me to do? Think, only think, what I did do . . . It is a great miracle you have all done so splendidly.'

They decided that Annie should be looked after; the cottage was cleared ('. . . I do hope you didn't burn ANYTHING as amongst newspapers and letters there were little personal things precious to me and I do not want them lost . . .') and she moved into Steanbridge House, the former squire's house which now took in the infirm, from where she wrote happily that she was 'living the life of a lady – in bed, warm & comfortable & being waited on, not a dream but true . . .' Her room had a view of the lake, and for the first time she had an electric fire and electric lights, walnut furniture, and pictures of a Highland burn, a Madonna and Child, and a sunset. 'But dear Laurie I feel an imposture, a fraud as I could do some housework at home if I were better able to stand and the house were really warm. Dear Laurie bless you dear boy – you have been so kind to me and I shall remember it as long as I live, if I never tell you again.'

It was Annie, still in touch with Lorna, who sent news of Yasmin. For her eighth birthday she had been given a Shetland pony. 'She said, I wonder what I have got for my birthday and the pony neighed outside the door. The little girl is going to join the Catholic church. Lorna says she is now a Roman Catholic and wants me to be, but I don't know. Jack is very busy with his new film [*The Woman in the Hall*] Ursula Jeans is his leading lady . . . Where are you and what are you doing?' Laurie, too busy to write, was having a highly sociable time: attending parties at John Lehmann's, going

to the opera (at the first night of *Carmen*, in a jewelled *galère* he saw Queen Mary, 'her hair full of diamonds', Mrs Winston Churchill, Sir Alan (A.P.) Herbert) and dining at the Garrick with Henry Irving's grandson, Laurence. He was also writing another play.

It is true to say that the entire prose output of Laurie Lee's life had already been commissioned by 1947. John Lehmann had long ago proposed a book on his childhood, following the 'Whitsun Treat' article. And in March 1947 Cecil Day-Lewis offered an instant advance from Chatto & Windus, the publisher for whom he was now working, as he did for the rest of his life, for the story of Laurie's Spanish wanderings. He even suggested a clause in the contract to say he need not deliver the manuscript for three years, 'if you want to get the autobiography written for John first'. If Laurie had gone ahead as commissioned, and had included the Civil War in his Spanish memoirs for Day-Lewis, he could have completed his lifetime's opus by 1950. But he was quite exhausted: 'Illness has returned to me with my evil London,' he wrote in May. 'My poor old Laurie,' said Annie. 'Please do not do too much and get yourself knocked up. Oh dear what a careless mother, no good to any of her children.'

The new play in blank verse was *Peasants' Priest*, which had been commissioned for the Canterbury Festival that summer. Laurie went down to Canterbury to see it after taking a week off in Paris in May with Bunny Keene. He had used the story of Wat Tyler's Peasants' Revolt over the poll tax of 1381, when the preacher John Balle led his rebels in the march on London to storm the Tower. Echoing Eliot's *Murder in the Cathedral*, Laurie's play opened with a prologue by a chorus of a figure in a tragic yellow mask, and another in a comic green mask:

YELLOW MASK:
It was yesterday, it was today,
a black winter and a red summer;
a blackened death, a crimson birth;
it was today, and yesterday . . .

Dramatically and tautly, it relates the story of the murder of the Archbishop of Canterbury through characters named Barfoot, Flint and Skelp, and ends with John Balle – 'lean as a stave, rough as a wolf, and brilliant of eye' – being led away to his execution. As in *Magellan*, Laurie displays extraordinary imaginative gifts, a flair for rhetoric, a remarkable grasp of the idiom of the medieval mystery play, and an intuitive skill in incorporating political and religious themes: hypocrisy, redemption, the plight of the common man. As Balle is led away he says:

> The end is not far off. What have we won?
> Like foxes creeping from our holes, we've proved
> the sun is up, that angels walk the grass,
> and there's still heaven to be won on earth
> when we've the trick of love to win it.
> So with that lesson learnt, let's back to darkness,
> to hide in holes till faith shall let us out.

Day-Lewis seemed to think Laurie was in a slough of despond after finishing the play. He wrote that summer, hoping Laurie was 'pulling out of the pit, & taking up the pen again', because a dispute had arisen over who was publishing him. Over dinner, Eric Gillett of Longmans had mentioned to Day-Lewis that he was publishing Laurie's Cyprus book, his Canterbury play and his Spanish travel book. '"Just a moment, Gillett," I said coldly. "I am publishing the Spanish travel book."

'What am I to tell Mr Chatto & Mr Windus about this?' Day-Lewis asked Laurie. 'Longman also thought you were going to give them your autobiography.' Leonard Woolf himself then wrote formally from the Hogarth Press, which was part of Chatto & Windus and which had published Laurie's book of poems: 'Dear Mr Lee . . . I hope you won't mind my drawing your attention to the fact that according to the agreement we have the right to consider publication of your next work.' 'If you do not want to become a bone, with angry publishers snarling over you,' warned Day-Lewis, 'you had better retire swiftly to your Italian villa.'

The Italian villa was the house where Kathy had gone to stay, on Lake Garda at Torri del Benaco, owned by Helen Garman's companion Sarfatti. Later that year Helen married seventy-year-old 'Sarfi', and so Kathy acquired a charming, steady and rock-like Italian stepfather who 'looked rather like Edward VII', Kathy says, 'with a lovely twinkle in his eye'. Her stepbrother Walter was born in May 1948.

'Ask Kathy to write me a little letter . . .' Annie chivvied, as she did constantly from then on, longing for letters and visits. 'Dearest Laurie Let me know just a few words how you are Love from yr loving mother . . .' (She enclosed a blank page for him to fill in: 'Dearest Mother . . . (space) . . . From loving Laurie.') 'Try to write a few lines to this person soon if you have time . . . it has been perfect Whitsun Treat weather but no Whitsun treat, gone are those days. Oh dear I get very bad asthma you know I pray God to take it away. I haven't seen any one of my children since last Sunday when Jack & Nora came also Tony & Ruby [Tony's wife]. Marjorie & Diana also came but they never stay long. Have you seen sweet Lorna & Yasmin lately? I hope so. I wonder if I'll ever see her again and I wonder if I'll ever see Yasmin. Is anything wrong dear Laurie that I do not hear from you . . .'

Nothing was wrong, but Laurie was suddenly flung into the Rosamond Lehmann–Cecil Day-Lewis maelstrom which was now in real crisis. Day-Lewis wrote – 'This is an S.O.S.' – from Devon urging Laurie to come down. 'The hideous, destined thing has happened. I've had to write & tell Rosamond we must part; God knows if it's the right decision . . . And it has just about finished me. So do come if you can (wire to Colyton 126 telling me what train to meet). But I shall perfectly understand, Laurie dear, if you don't feel up to it. Love Cecil.'

Laurie went. It transpired that Day-Lewis had finally told his wife Mary that he was leaving her for Rosamond, but when she drove him to his train she wept so heart-rendingly that in the station-yard he had said, 'Turn round and we'll go back.' So Rosamond was to be jettisoned instead, and Day-Lewis was in despair.

But Laurie had a violent toothache – it was an abscess – which provided a diversion as Day-Lewis and Mary had to drive him round to find a dentist. 'That eased the situation, and I provided a kind of catalyst. I think in a way that saved it, though not for ever.'[4] The upshot of Laurie's visit was that he and Day-Lewis decided to take a holiday abroad together.

Before going away with Cecil, Laurie got Virginia Cunard to drive him down to see Annie: 'It was like a dream,' Annie wrote, 'and yes dear old Chubby you did look so *well* I can rest content . . . What a blessing for you that you have so many good kind friends to rally round you . . .

'But you must never think that you are alone or isolated . . . this old mother loves you and thinks a lot of you since the days when you were a tiny one, then a dear little boy, so loving & often naughty, then a headstrong youth, out at your musical-dancing affairs till the small hours, earning a wee pittance to start your little "hoard" & coming home to lie in bed reading. Till I went in your room and took the book out of your hand & blew out the candle. Remember those days Laurie? However, that is long past and you came home safe after many adventures with Mrs G. & still things went on happening and still do . . . I like your lovely friend Virginia . . . I wish she were here to take me a nice little run up the Steanbridge Lane to Elcombe, along the top of the valley . . .'

Laurie and Day-Lewis's fortnight in Denmark in July 1947 was the first time Day-Lewis had been abroad, apart from a pre-war weekend in Paris. Day-Lewis told Laurie not to worry about how his health would stand up to it; in fact he rather hoped Laurie would need looking after: 'nursing brings out all my usually-repressed maternal & power instincts'. They sailed to Esbjerg, stayed at the Hotel Cosmopolite in Copenhagen, went to Elsinore and to the Tivoli gardens, and came home in high spirits. When Day-Lewis's next collection of poems came out (1948) it was dedicated to Laurie Lee.

Rosamond was grateful for Laurie's letter about the trip, which gave her 'a far more vivid picture than all Cecil's letters put together. He has never been a good letter writer . . . his little missives . . .

say nothing, mean nothing.' She was still desperately impatient for commitment from Day-Lewis. 'I am sick, *sick* of hearing him say "I can't face" – or "daren't risk" – etc. etc. I am sick of hearing him talk of his "roots" – as if roots were always healthy, as if they didn't often bind & strangle –

'Is he very frightened of Mary? I think he is . . . And he can't bear failure in anything – and now he feels he must simply go to earth & write poetry about it . . . Oh Laurie . . . I do understand what he feels about her & the boys – I understand almost everything really . . .'

Laurie, who was by then staying at the ffrench Blake farm in Cornwall, appears not to have been exasperated by Rosamond's egocentricity, even when she wrote of the 'enigma' of what bound Day-Lewis to his wife: 'They are like two wheels of a bicycle propelling the stark frame of their life together . . . What a pity, for her sake, she isn't a widow.' After this heartless sentiment Rosamond added that her heart was wrung to hear that Laurie felt 'incapable of writing'; 'I'd give my eyes to be some help.'

But Laurie had his own resources. Rosamond's agitated histrionics contrast strikingly with Laurie's happy and loving letter to Kathy that same month from Cornwall where, far from languishing with writer's block, he was enthusiastically sickling and scything and chopping down trees. Writing in the late summer twilight in his attic room, he was longing to see Kathy again and to dance with her 'before I get gout'. 'Grow, grow, my golden girl, grow & be strong & cook a nice apple pie, & change your thick hair as the sky changes in all its variety, and learn to chase cobwebs & miseries, & look at me with your blue eyes that say swim with me through the dark waters of night, then it will be all right.'

A month later Laurie accompanied Kathy, her mother and Sarfi on yet another holiday – at a farm near Aberystwyth. Kathy remembers rushing across a Welsh field shouting, 'I've passed my school certificate!' The extra significance of this milestone might be explained by a quotation from Kathy in Laurie's diary earlier that year: 'Wait till I've passed my school certificate.'

14 | Kathy Come Home
    1948–9

'Charm is the ultimate weapon, the supreme seduction, against which there are few defences. If you've got it, you need almost nothing else, neither money, looks, nor pedigree,' wrote Laurie, in his perceptive analysis of charm in 1978. He was a supreme practitioner of the art of effortless attraction: men, women and children fell under his spell, and part of his appeal was his boyishness. He had a little-boy-lost look. The families Laurie collected – or the families who collected him, inviting him to their country houses and on their holidays – fell into a definable pattern. The father was clever and amusing (and frequently Etonian), the mother lively and beautiful, the children agreeable. Laurie always sang for his supper with his stories and his music, his enthusiasm for food and fondness for competitive games and pranks; and he wrote rapturous thank you letters. 'I always feel frightfully well after a day or two among your mole-hilled mountains,' he wrote to the ffrench Blakes in January 1949.

He invariably brought some new toy, like the exploding matchbox he took to Beatrix Lehmann's one weekend, which gave people an electric shock whenever they struck a match. Alan Ross recalls Laurie infuriating John Lehmann by letting loose a clockwork creature under the feet of Elizabeth Bowen, the Sitwells and other grandee guests. Such foolery captivated children: the Devases' three, the Dugdales' three, the ffrench Blakes' two, and Rosamond's children Sally and Hugo Philipps. Sean Day-Lewis says that unlike most of his parents' guests, who engaged in impenetrable literary or political discussions, 'Laurie Lee alone was able to become a boy again, initiating games, making bows and arrows, giving out intimations of mischief.'[1] When Anthony Devas painted Laurie surrounded by children, Annie wrote: '*What* a very jolly picture. You look a very happy "uncle" – you remind me of my old

grandfather, Uncle Tom, and even my mother. This is all to praise you, for they were all kind and loved children.'

Emma Devas (Lady Monson) remembers her parents saying, 'Laurie can't go on for ever being Peter Pan.' In the summer of 1948 they invited him along on their holiday at Deal in Kent, where they were staying with Norman Hepple, and Laurie took Kathy ('a Wilson Steer child in a blue dress wading thigh-deep in the waves'), renting rooms in a house next door to Nat Gubbins, the *Reynolds News* columnist. Rodrigo Moynihan was there too, with his wife Elinor Bellingham Smith and son John. For the Devases, these seaside holidays were the apogee of family life. This was the first of an almost unbroken series of six blithe summers with the Devas family.

Laurie had begun 1948 in hospital, having a painful sinus operation. He wrote to Val ffrench Blake from his bed at St Thomas's, saying that the BBC had commissioned a new poem for Epiphany, and one for Easter. 'Lee is earning an unaccountable reputation as a bard possessing the private ear of the Christian Muse,' Laurie wrote, 'in spite of the fact that the poems seem to come down pretty heavily on the side of the pagan deities.' He was out in time to hear Roy Fuller giving a constructively critical analysis of his poetry on the Third Programme.

Laurie's second collection of poems, *The Bloom of Candles*, had been published at the end of 1947. Dedicated to Annie, it included one, 'First Love', inspired by Kathy in Martigues ('her heart revealed by the wash of summer/sprung from her childhood's shallow stream'). John Lehmann had the book printed in New Zealand because of the British paper shortage, and shipped home with a meat cargo 'ponging of mutton fat', Laurie said. It was only twelve pages and twelve poems long. 'No more vivid use is being made of English today,' said G.W. Stonier in the *New Statesman*.

Roy Fuller took a broader view. 'This poet's interest has never been the contemporary world,' he said in his radio programme. 'The distinction of his poetry has resided in an innocent lyricism, a sharp eye, a striking use of colourful and strong words. In almost every poem there is a word or image which gives that pleasurable

shock without which lyric poetry can never rise above the third rate. And once or twice, in "Bird" and "First Love" for instance, Mr Lee shows signs that he can give his poetry the more complicated organization which alone will enable him to bridge the deadly chasm which yawns for all poets round their thirtieth year.'

But the danger, as he saw it, was that Laurie's colourful and strong words might not be adequately supported by the content of the poems. He quoted from 'Summer Rain':

Where in the valley the summer rain
Moves crazed and chill through the crooked trees
The briars bleed green, and the far fox-banks
Their sharp cries tangle in sobbing shades.

'This, I think, is sound and fury. For rain to be crazed, for briars to bleed and cry, for shades to sob, there must be a very dramatic and very plausible situation. But, in this poem, Mr Lee does not present it. There is rather too much whipping-up of language in the whole book . . . One is asked to give a larger response than the poet's emotion deserves.' Sometimes, he said, Laurie descended to the mock-pastoral. Fuller singled out 'the cheeks of girls are as baked-bread to the mouth': there was 'something half-baked' about it. 'I would like Mr Lee to dare much more – dare to be complicated, dare to write of other things than nature, dare to use more verse forms, more rhyme – dare, perhaps, to write about the world as it impinges on us in 1948.'

It was fair comment, Laurie conceded, writing to Fuller the next day from Virginia Cunard's flat. 'In fact it made me laugh . . . I especially liked your "half-baked" crack, though if you were here I'd ask you to come out into the back yard and repeat it.'

However, Laurie 'disagreed profoundly' with Fuller's challenge to him to write differently. 'You dare me to eschew nature,' Laurie declared. 'I shall dare to be more natural. You dare me to be more complicated but I shall dare to achieve simplicity. I have no desire to cater for a brief unhappy fashion of intellectual confusion; I would walk out of this jungle of entanglements altogether, & I

believe that others, instead of moaning in the marshes, should do so too.' Laurie had rehearsed this ringing apologia in his notebook before writing his letter.

A jocular rivalry between the two poets had begun in 1944 when Cecil Day-Lewis had reviewed Fuller's *A Lost Season* along with Laurie's *The Sun My Monument* in *Time & Tide*, and had preferred his friend Laurie's work. Then a fan letter to Laurie had arrived, misaddressed, *chez* Fuller. 'My cup is full,' he wrote to Fuller. 'The normal pleasure which any fan mail brings is heady enough; how much more intoxicating is it when it has been read by one's dearest rival.'

Cecil Day-Lewis now urgently wanted Laurie to get on with writing about Spain, and allowed him to share his office in William IV Street. But the days would be frittered in conversation and games of chess, and nothing emerged from Laurie except more poems: it was when he walked home across Trafalgar Square in the twilight that he would see 'great shoals of starlings' and imagine the square under water: the starlings were like mussel shells, and the submerged city image developed into his poem 'Sunken Evening'.

Kathy, who spent much of her time looking after her baby brother Walter, had by now fixed on Laurie as the man she would marry, but Laurie still saw himself as the uncommitted bachelor. 'I was a known bachelor, and had always turned my face from such engagements. Sometimes I used to dream that I was, in fact, married and I'd wake up with a violent start. I needed the company of men, but I required isolation even more.'[2] When Annie wrote Kathy a fond letter in November 1948, wanting to know all about the baby brother, she also asked: 'Have you seen Laurie lately? for he has been to Paris and I don't think he is back yet.' Laurie had indeed gone to Paris, for a fortnight, taking Jennifer Gault, eighteen-year-old daughter of a cousin of the Cunard sisters. Jennifer's mother had sent her daughter to Laurie to be cheered up after a break-up with a boyfriend, perhaps not realizing that Laurie clearly was, like Dickens, extremely partial to girls of seventeen or so. He had kissed Jennifer among the wheatsheaves at her parents' house, and the

Paris interlude – while her mother was away – was Jennifer's first visit there.

They stayed at the Hôtel d'Alsace, where Oscar Wilde had died, and went to the Louvre and the Deux Magots. Jennifer knew there was no long-term future in the affair. 'But Laurie was a wonderful influence in my life,' she says. 'He opened my eyes to all sorts of things. He had great charm, and was very secretive. Well, he had to be.' Her liaison with Laurie continued sporadically for several years; and when she became Mrs Hunter-Blair, they remained friendly, Laurie becoming a godfather (again) to her son Tom.

Annie was now feeling very isolated, in a nursing home run by Nurse Critchley at Painswick. No woman was less suited to life on her own. 'It seems such a long time from morning to night, alone, no one pops their head round the door and says Hello, let alone come inside to have a chat, so I'm a dull old stick . . . Marjorie is coming on Sunday, but there is the rest of the day and tomorrow and Saturday to get through.'

But the loneliness of Annie's declining years was greatly relieved by the generosity of the Cunard sisters. Virginia and Pen had already invited her to come with Laurie to Bushton Manor in the late summer of 1947, and she went again for the next two Christmases. She had been dubious about going – 'should I be an intruder in the magic circle?' she asked – but they loved having her. Virginia and Laurie collected her from Painswick and drove her to Bushton. They stopped at a garage which said 'No Naked Lights'; 'Mother,' said Laurie, 'you'd better put on some clothes,' which Annie thought hilarious. They gave her a room with a four-poster bed, and she was enveloped in the warm bosom of a family again, with 'music & singing & the games & the crib'. She was at Bushton for the new baby Sam Dugdale's christening. Laurie sent a telegram: 'Three cheers for young Sam/Three cheers for his Mam/With love and good wishes/From Larry the Lamb.' 'Isn't he a ridiculous old thing?' wrote Annie to Kathy. 'But Laurie was always like that.'

In the new year of 1949 Laurie arranged for Annie to have a longed-for visit to London – staying with Virginia Cunard at Raphael Street, in the care of the sainted Bessie. It was another

fulfilment of her dreams. She yearned to see pictures ('I don't mean films I mean paintings') so they took her to the Royal Academy and to the Rossetti Studios, where music was played and Cecil Day-Lewis sang and Rosamond brought flowers. 'I liked so much Cecil Day-Lewis's singing and his looks. I've never met people so good and kind before. Bessie was an angel to me. I have been overwhelmed with kindness.' But she swung between appreciation and maternal reproach. After a birthday telegram from Laurie in February she wrote: 'I was so glad you had not forgotten me, I know you have been very busy and active in the social world with your friends, Cecil Day-Lewis etc. so I will not bother you, but nonetheless I'd like to have a letter.' The dependable Bessie – 'I wish I had a daughter like her' – loyally kept her informed of Laurie's activities: 'Bessie says you have been enjoying yourself with parties and going to the theatre . . . Well dear boy good for you and may your happy times continue . . . No one has come this afternoon, now it is five o'clock I wish one of my sons would walk in and sit by me in my room and talk . . .' In fact he had been busy moving house. The Devas family had just moved along the King's Road into 12 Carlyle Square, and Laurie naturally went with them.

In May, Annie sent Laurie £1 as he told her he was off to Paris. This time he was taking Kathy, and they were going on to Italy. Her mother Helen had been suffering from shattering migraines, the early signs of what was later discovered to be a brain tumour, which eventually robbed her of most of her sight. Sarfi's brother in Florence knew of a surgeon in Milan, and Sarfi took Helen there. At first, Kathy's cousin Esther went with them to help with baby Walter, but Esther missed her lover Mark Joffé and his young son Roland (now the film director), whose mother had run off when Roland was a baby. So Esther came home, and Helen summoned Kathy to Florence, in the care of Laurie.

In Florence they met up with Laurie's friends Daphne Hardy, his former colleague from the MOI, and her husband Henri Henrion. Kathy went off to see a friend in Siena, and Laurie in a rash moment of bravado followed her on foot through Chianti country. 'The heat was terrific & I was carrying about 30 kilos on

my back,' he told Val ffrench Blake. 'But I did the 70-odd kilometres in two days and terrorized the local peasants on the way with my wild blond looks & Nordic tongue. They took me for a German; old women & children fled into the bushes at the sight.' He had tramped through wheatfields full of poppies, slept under olive trees and honeysuckle hedges 'when the moon rose to a bedlam of frogs, crickets, cuckoos, dogs & nightingales'.

He had watched the sun slip into the Arno from San Miniato, slept in the monastery of Fiesole, picked syringa from the gardens of the Roman theatre among pillars and Etruscan tombs. He had been entertained at vast, echoing, rose-clustered villas. He was 'stuffed with impressions like a jar of olives', Laurie told ffrench Blake, in 'a maze of classical landscapes & a kaleidoscope of gorgeous glowing frescoes'. The Henrions had driven him to San Gimignano, not yet tourist-infested, 'a place that makes the hair stand on end . . . on a hill surrounded by wild oak woods, & creaking with medieval secrets, nothing can have changed here for 600 years. Thirteen great stone towers clashing their bells & fresh memories of Dante at every step. It is quiet & still in the spicy yellow sun, & people sit in groups as though sleeping in a dream of the past. There is no tourist sense here at all . . . Nothing has stirred me so much.'

Kathy and her friend Charissina, daughter of the philosopher Leone Vivante, Sarfi's fellow internee, were sitting outside a café in the semi-circular Campo in Siena when suddenly Laurie appeared, bronzed and fit, his back scarred from the weight of his pack. Siena was 'an exquisite city, just my size and colour', Laurie wrote. He had seen the 'violently exciting' sculpture of Donatello, the 'sombre, human, exquisite' paintings of Duccio. 'These, & the Botticellis in Florence are what I came to see, I feel.' He played his pipe in cafés, and went on to Assisi, Perugia, and back to Florence.

Kathy, in her seventeenth year, thought that after his romantic gesture in walking so many miles to see her, Laurie would ask her to marry him then; but he didn't. She was installed instead in her Uncle Gualtiero and Aunt Eloisa's great oak-panelled apartment in Florence, and stayed there for another eight months. She learned to speak Italian, joined the university club and took up dressmaking.

'She didn't write,' Laurie records, 'though she sent me some smoked cheese for Christmas.'

Lorna still kept in touch: she sent Laurie a postcard that July, from Lourdes. (Lorna's mother died that year, and Yasmin had been seriously ill with appendicitis.) 'I quite see why little Bernardette fell out with the humans, both from having too much flesh & too little vision,' she wrote. 'I am going to the waters for you tomorrow July 2nd.' It is signed with a cross. This card was tucked into Laurie's India Diary, at the page where he noted that he was reading *The Song of Bernardette*, finding it 'curiously moving – inspired & eerie – passages of her vision brought tears to my eyes'.

Laurie enjoyed a wildly sociable bachelor summer – his last summer of singledom – not just at Bushton ('sun, flowers, games, sweet company and the quiet indulgence of the senses') but at less familiar country houses: he baffled Annie by mentioning names she had come across only in newspapers. 'You say you were in the swimming pool of the Whitney Straights who are they? I seem to have heard about them in a former life are they Americans? you mention Roosevelt's little granddaughter in the same breath and Lady Winchilsea – who is she?' And on 21 July 1949 he went back to the seaside, to Tenby in Pembrokeshire, with the Devas family.

They were invited by Geraldine Lawrence, who had commissioned Anthony Devas to paint her nieces. Geraldine was a spinster of independent means, the daughter of a wealthy pit-owning family. She was a woman of presence and character, a pillar of the community, a JP, a rather terrifying figure to the children ('The Ogre of Lexden Terrace' in a caption in the Devases' 'Holiday Book'), but also an accomplished artist herself. She loved having artists to stay, and would lend them the house next to her own, facing the sea. Little Rock House was a tall white bow-fronted Regency house with green-shuttered windows. Geraldine would provide a full larder and a bottle of gin on arrival. 'She was the hostess everyone dreams of,' the artist John Ward says.

Steep cliff steps led down to the sandy beach with its rock-pools. Every day guests took paintboxes and picnics on to the beach and competed to find the biggest prawns. These were cooked in a pan

of sea-water, and eaten for lunch with hot bread from the nearby baker. At the house – crammed with books and paintings – the children were encouraged to make apple-pie beds, causing shrieks of rage. In the evenings everyone gathered at Geraldine's after supper for entertainment: one of the 'payments' she expected was a singsong round the piano, and costumed charades.

Geraldine was a passionate traveller, forever off to Paris or to the racing at Chantilly. But most of all she loved southern Spain and its fiestas, bullfights and *romerías*. So when she met Laurie they fell upon one another with reminiscences of Andalucía. Over many years, every letter she wrote Laurie arrived in a vividly hand-painted envelope, with a watercolour of a bullfight, or of the brawny straw-hatted and tough-booted peasant women in the fields between Seville and Jerez, with 'tough forearms and leathery faces, like tortoises'.

The Devas Holiday Book is a priceless record of the Tenby summers. Everyone contributed; even the au pairs wrote poems ('Le chanson de Tenby') in charming franglais. Artistic endeavour was not only encouraged but obligatory. Nicolette and Anthony's guests had to join in painting beach scenes and sea-shells and wild flowers, sketching one another and writing limericks, as well as snorkelling, harpooning and competing for the biggest catches of fish. Emma Devas, now Lady Monson, says that underlying the fun and games in her family was a strictly professional anti-dilettante attitude. 'My father would insist on punctuality and proper dress. None of his children was allowed to behave like my mother's family, the wild Macnamaras.'

After this sybaritic summer even Laurie had to admit defeat when invited to Cornwall again by the ffrench Blakes in August. 'There's nothing I should like better than a trip to the Tokenbury tin mines but alas . . . I can't possibly go off on the loose again for some time. I have been burning the summer at both ends; a month in Italy, a month in Pembrokeshire and so little work done I blush to think of it.'

In fact he was collapsing with pneumonia, and spent two months convalescing at Dorothy's in Oxford, reading quantities of novels

Laurie records the day's bounty in the Devas family Holiday Book
(*Devas Family Collection*)

in which (as he told Pen Dugdale) 'practically all the characters contract pneumonia & most of them die of it'. His doctor was 'the one who saw John Masefield through a bout of pneumonia back in the spring when we were all so busy choosing a new Poet Laureate. He is dying for me to get better as he wants me to teach him how to blow fire from his mouth, and he approaching 60, too.'

Annie wrote recommending George du Maurier's novel *Trilby*. Cecil Day-Lewis sent commiserations from 'Wystan, Stephen, Edwin Muir, everyone in Venice' where they were attending a PEN conference, with 'interminable, egotistic, bawling, exhibitionistic, abstract, sententious speeches'.

'This started as a weekend and nearly finished as a dead end,' Laurie told Pen Dugdale in October. 'It was high, sweltering summer when I was driven to bed & now it's autumn . . . I wanted to write when I was up and about again, but I am still only half up & half about. And yet the fascinating thing is that these weeks of bed, of contemplation laced with fever & lightheadedness seem to have changed the whole course of my life. I wonder if it is really so.' (It was so. He had begun to think of marrying.)

By November Annie, now scarcely able to get out of bed with rheumatism, heard from Bessie that Laurie was better and 'back at your London Haunts'. She had heard that he had been 'judging poetry, & going to the prizegiving at the Central Hall Westminster, seeing Princess Margaret. I'd have loved to have a peep at the proceedings . . .' She had heard too that he had been enjoying music ('you and Col ffrench Blake are like children with rows of icecream in front of you, except you have cantatas') and Guy Fawkes night with children. Did he recall being frightened by a banger Uncle Sid brought back from abroad as a child? His Uncle Fred, her youngest brother, had just retired in Perth, she told him, with his boss's encomium: 'All who knew Mr Light spoke of him as a gentleman: he was one of nature's aristocrats.' 'Isn't that splendid dear Laurie but all your uncles had good manners and a way with them, that's where you got it.'

Annie's letters in these months, her last year of life, read sadly,

but they reflect her loving nature, her motherly nostalgia. Pen had been to visit her ('so kind of her to come & see the old person') and had posted off Laurie's Christmas gloves for her: 'better not have red gloves,' Annie told him, 'as I am afraid Chelsea is a hotbed of Communism.' She longed to see Jack's 'dear old smile', but he was away in Germany, making *The Wooden Horse* with Anthony Steel.

'Oh how I long to get out. I suffer so much in the mornings. I look at the clock, and when 12 comes there is dinner but *never* anything like the lunch you described that Bessie cooked for you – and you polished off the lot though kindly leaving the dish.

'Dear L if they knew you in the old "school treat" days – when you used to go along & dispose of an incredible number of cups of tea I believe once it was 22 and lots of buns & bread & butter etc. Did they think I wonder that you were starved at home? Dear Mrs Frank Brown Mr Tilley's mother used to sit at the top of the table where they pour the tea and smile benevolently at you. Did you and your brothers enjoy those far-off teas dear? And the entry in the Parish magazine: "Miss Eileen Brown at the piano and young Laurie Lee played selections on his violin." I always thought of Young Lochinvar come out of the West. It is nearly six and I thought someone might come up but no one has . . . Where are you going to spend Christmas Laurie? Have you made any plans? I have not really. No shopping nor made my Christmas puddings nor any mince pies.

'I feel sometimes the things that have happened to you aren't real. But you are the son who has led a life of contrasts – such contrasts – A book of your life would be very varied, interesting & lovely, because many people love you & many more would if they could know you & see you & hear you talk and hear you play.'

In December she told him that she had again been invited to Bushton for Christmas 1949. 'Isn't it sweet and kind of them . . . I can't help crying a bit when people are like that, for I am terribly lonely here & so often cold. Wish I was in that lovely four-poster at Bushton. In *Picture Post* there are lovely pictures of children

Christmas shopping. Oh to put the years back & to get to town with some money & to take you three little boys up to Barkers or some other nice shop & do some lovely shopping, but what useless wishing.'

If Laurie was concerned about his mother, he was also thinking seriously about his own future. He had done precious little productive writing that year. In July, HM Inspector of Taxes had written asking him what income he had apart from Casual Literary Earnings, which had been £120 in the last year. In his book *Two Women*, published in 1983, Laurie related that during that autumn of 1949, 'intimations of a sterile death moved upon me. I also missed the presence of that acquiescent and radiant girl who seemed to care for no other company but mine.' He decided to telegraph to Kathy's mother and ask her to come home. She told him to send the money for Kathy's fare, which he did.

Early in 1950, an equally momentous decision was taken by his friend Cecil Day-Lewis. He finally left his wife Mary – not for Rosamond Lehmann, but for the actress Jill Balcon. As Rosamond put it, bitterly, in a letter to Laurie, 'he transferred his overnight zip bag from my bedroom to Miss Balcon's'. (The couple had fallen in love after an exchange of fan letters and a dinner with Epstein, who was sculpting Jill's head.) Laurie said, in much later retrospect, he was not entirely surprised. 'Rosamond's pressure on Cecil to marry her had been emotionally wearing. I did not see how he could get out of that dilemma. He was tugged between these two loves. He couldn't decide who to desert. The only solution was to take a third and not choose either of them: to betray both.'[3] Rosamond was in utter despair. 'We shared ten years of what I thought the deepest and most permanent commitment. He broke our mutual vows, and laid waste my life, and also his wife's.' And at just the time when she needed him most, Laurie was himself distracted by mid-life decisiveness. At thirty-five he was about to shake off the Peter Pan image: take a proper job, move into a flat of his own – and get married to Kathy.

15 | The Festival Jester
1950–54

'I feel like a murderer; but for Jill I could do murder & one can't say more than that,' wrote Cecil Day-Lewis to Laurie. Rosamond was suicidal, and he himself was 'flying through a very low cloud indeed', although 'absolutely committed to, and in love with, Jill'. He had promised Rosamond 'because she thinks I am off my head' that he would not see Jill Balcon for three months. Would Laurie take her out to lunch? 'It would be your Good Deed for the Day ... You always seem to be helping me out of crises, & I hardly ever ditto you.'

He added: 'I do hope your reunion & plans go well.'

The reunion was with Kathy, at Victoria station. Laurie had last seen her in Siena, 'a shapely, tight-limbed, flat-bellied young beauty' but after eight months of spaghetti and idleness she seemed 'more radiant than ever, but twice the size'.[1] Laurie led her straight to the scales, saying, 'If you're over twelve stone, I won't marry you.' She was eleven stone twelve pounds. Laurie was still living in his attic at Carlyle Square, but they took a flat together at 37 Collingham Place SW5, up five flights in a West Indian house with 'trains under the windows and the smell of steaks in passage ways'. (Laurie claimed he carried Kathy over the threshold but collapsed after one flight and she carried him up the rest: 'She's a very strong girl.')

Though 'beset by fevers' Laurie had found a salaried job, the last he ever had. He became chief caption-writer for the Festival of Britain, the jamboree to mark the end of post-war austerity set up on twenty-seven acres of bombsites on the South Bank. With the Skylon, the Dome of Discovery, the Guinness Clock, the *Reclining Figure* by Henry Moore and Epstein's *Youth Advancing*, it would epitomize new artistic ideas, modern standards of design. The fastidious Roy Fuller thought the whole concept 'self-consciously bright and bragging and English'.[2] Looking back twenty-five years

later, Sir Misha Black said that the Festival's only influence on popular taste was to release 'a flood of the worst kind of modern architecture the country had ever seen, and from which we have been suffering ever since'.[3] But for Laurie it seemed then 'a kind of Xanadu'. And his contribution to the Festival was 'the quirkiest and most timeless'.

On Tuesday 17 May 1950, without even noting it in his diary, Laurie married Kathy at Kensington Register Office. Cecil Day-Lewis and Jill Balcon were the only witnesses. Jill remembers that Laurie was sucking a peppermint and Kathy, clutching a tiny spray of lily-of-the-valley, looked like a Renoir: 'She had a down-to-earth kindness, an unvarnished quality, with skin like a peach.' She also looked 'so young we thought we'd be accessories to a felony' (she was eighteen, and had a special licence signed by Sarfi; Laurie was twice her age, a month away from thirty-six). Kathy's eyes had a shine, Laurie later said, that he only ever saw again when she won a steam-iron on stage at the Walham Green Empire.[4] After the wedding the quartet fell into the Prince of Wales pub among some dustmen and a newspaper-seller. A barnacled bottle of champagne was produced; the dustmen raised their glasses and said: 'Here's to a long life with plenty of trimmings.' On leaving, Day-Lewis and Jill looked into the estate agents Marsh & Parsons, spotted 73a Bedford Gardens for rent, and took it as their first joint home.

They lunched at Elytis in Soho, and Laurie went back to work at the Festival office, at 2 Savoy Court, in the afternoon while Kathy went to the fishmonger and asked for a nice piece of sole for supper 'because I've just got married'. Laurie sent a telegram to his sister Marjorie: 'Have married Kathy. Let the family know.' Jack's wife Nora says he simply told her, 'I've decided to make myself responsible for Kathy,' which struck her as a curious way of announcing one's marriage.

'Yes,' he wrote to Val ffrench Blake, 'I went & got married. It was sudden, like falling down a man-hole, but my seat on the coals is quite comfortable. No one knew about it save Day-Lewis who was raised from his bed to be witness. But I was charmed by your letter, it made me laugh both ha and he.'

Col. ffrench Blake had sent him a spoof army charge sheet, which Laurie filled in:

Name: Lee. Occupation: Poet and/or Peasant.

Brief Description of Residence: Flat in Negro Quarter of Earls Court . . .

Lee pleads Guilty to all items indicated on charge sheet.

Future movements: Earls Court to Festival of Britain, Festival of Britain to Earls Court – till further notice.

Tokens of esteem etc: Gratefully accepted.

(The ffrench Blakes sent a charming table.)

'Delighted to hear you're getting married,' wrote Dr Alan McGlashan, the doctor who had attended Laurie the previous year. 'Madly curious to know W H O.' There was general astonishment that Laurie should marry at all, since (as one friend said) he had for so long enjoyed the comfortable patronage of 'grand ladies who gave him lodgings'. Most of his friends had never even met Kathy; but once they did, they were captivated. She was so young and sparklingly beautiful, and completely under Laurie's spell. It was her idea to marry, both later said. Laurie had told her: 'I warn you, it's going to be very difficult. I may not be able to be the person you want me to be. I may do things that hurt you. I may not give you enough love.' But she had 'a certainty' about it. She felt 'a sense of dedication'. She says after all, she did come from a very strange family. The Garman girls were sexually magnetic and Muse-like in their devotion to artistic men. 'I told him, "I want to look after you." I said I had enough love for both of us. I knew it was a challenge, I knew about the true love he'd had before. But I was protected by a kind of confidence, almost arrogance. I felt sure of my ground, quite powerful and invulnerable. Partly because I was an outsider. I didn't feel threatened by the other women, at all.' It is indicative of Kathy's trust in Laurie that she allowed him to put an apple on her head and aim darts at it through a blowpipe.

On the day they married, Kathy says, Laurie wrote a letter to the tax people 'saying he couldn't afford to buy his wife a broom'.

But within days he was sending a donation of £2 10s to Bernard Miles towards his Mermaid Theatre – 'at least equal to £222 10s from a rich Philistine!' said Miles, requesting names of others who might subscribe: 'e.g. address of Jacquetta Hawkes?' Mrs Hawkes, the archaeologist, later Mrs J.B. Priestley, was enthusiastically checking Laurie's Festival captions, having been struck by Laurie's poetry and also by his name: 'as improbably euphonious as mine is angular'. (Laurie always said he was lucky in his memorable, alliterative name, which was widely assumed to be invented.)

A fortnight after their wedding Laurie took Kathy to Bushton. Antonia Dugdale, who had proposed to Laurie at the age of six, and had been accepted, was expecting to hate 'the woman who had stolen my man'. 'But five minutes later I was in love with her too. She had such beautiful eyes, a lovely complexion and corn-coloured hair.' During that weekend, Laurie told Kathy about his epilepsy. 'I wasn't scared,' she says. 'I was very strong; I was always able to hold him tight when it happened.'

Laurie was at his most fulsome writing to Pen Dugdale afterwards: 'still drowsy with the honeyed richness of my weekend, still fatted with cream and flushed with strawberry ices, still tinkling with the music of your piping laugh & sweet-voiced flute . . . Bushton endures in the flowers we carried away, in the lilac's purple sunlight & the lilies' cream-green shade . . .

'Dear friend, we did enjoy ourselves. You could tell that by the faint frenzy in my eye . . . But then Bushton is as full of pleasures as an egg is of meat . . . thank you for all your bounty; for your eternal readiness to sport & play, for that lovely room & luscious bed, for your gorgeous meals, your ever-delightful company & your complete domination of the weather.'

'*To think I don't even know her!*' cried Rosamond Lehmann of his bride, writing from 'a sort of Rest Home' where she was trying to recover from 'the most cruelly dealt, the most utterly unexpected blow of my life'. She reminded Laurie that he had been 'most deeply knit into what [Day-Lewis] has torn up and destroyed' and she could not bear the thought of his carrying on 'seeing C'. Laurie gently told her he could not be a judge of Day-Lewis's behaviour.

Rosamond replied that although it would be a 'big hurdle' for her to see Laurie, she wanted her children Hugo and Sally not to lose him: 'They are so devoted to you, & have gone on asking me, poor things, how you felt about it.' Rosamond's affections were restored when Laurie took out her daughter, 'my heavenly Sal', who 'came home starry-eyed from her blissful day with you. Oh, I am so *glad* she has got you back.'

Annie, meanwhile, was fading. In her last letters she still hankered after her old cottage, and her mislaid belongings, including Laurie's published stories: 'Your stories are *you* and I loved them for that. No one ever finds them for me. So I can't help feeling sad. Yes,' she added, 'I saw that Aly Khan & Rita Hayworth's baby was called Yasmin. I had a card from Lorna: she does not forget me ever. Have you seen her lately?'

Annie died, aged seventy-one, on 30 August 1950, and was buried in Slad at the top of the churchyard, near her four-year-old daughter. Laurie placed a poem inside her coffin, and a photograph of Yasmin. Her gravestone 'In memory of Annie Emily Lee (née Light)' reads: 'She loved the world and all things in it.' Laurie's diary for this time is blank. But about thirteen years later – in his Mexico notebook – he recorded one of his long, disturbing 'dreams of truth & the dead'.

'Mother. Dorothy telling me she is dying. Go on, I say. Aching with emotion. Family gathers. I won't go with them – walk off, remembering her alive.

'Overhearing them say Good riddance – he'd spoil the party. Party, I cry.

'I hear them telling truths of me. "He's no longer of the family." It's true.'

A spirit of gaiety prevailed at the Festival of Britain offices; and Laurie, in tweeds and pipe, was its resident jester. 'The small Festival Press Office rang to the twanging guitar and rubicund voice of Laurie Lee singing a rumty-tumty Gloucestershire calypso . . . Beer was flowing, of course . . .'[5] He was surrounded by old friends:

Hugh Casson, Alan Ross, Lionel Birch, John Piper, Stephen Potter, Henri Henrion and Daphne Hardy. Laurie's small team furnished 'tens of thousands of descriptive words . . . brilliantly written and edited', as Misha Black said, but 'only a fraction were ever read'. Still, it was an opportunity for florid and orotund phrasemaking.

Facing the main entrance, on stone, were these words:

Land is the blanket of Man's birth;
His launching-ground to the stars.

A geological history of Britain for the Land and People pavilion was narrated in Laurie's richest prose. 'Britain's crust, like a cloth, has been dipped in the ocean, soaked, rinsed, and hung up in folds to dry. At one time it was part of Europe . . . And from the rising seas, when the ice-caps melted, Britain emerged an island.' Limestone was formed from 'skeletons crusting the sea floor'. Birmingham was once 'an inferno of blown sand'. 'The Lincoln marshes crawled with crocodiles . . . the Kentish Weald rose and fell like a breathing island.'

The text eulogized British craftsmen, British freedom, British justice, parliamentary democracy. The English Tongue, it proclaimed, 'writes sonnets, talks shop, sings music-hall, and speaks volumes. Once the dialect of a handful of islanders, it is now the mother-tongue of 250 millions.' 'The English Bible . . . put the Divine Word into common speech and inspired the native genius for language.' In the Lion & Unicorn pavilion, which celebrated the Briton's characteristics of strength and individuality, choice texts were emblazoned: 'In the Beginning was the Word, and the Word was with God, and the Word was God.' 'We are such stuff As dreams are made on, and our little life Is rounded with a sleep.' 'The English man of letters is a giant gorged with words. With the English Dictionary in one hand, he has written three million books with the other.'

And so on, in what Desmond Fitzgerald (in the *World Review*) designated 'Festival English': a didactic, Arnoldian style of prose, reminiscent of Georgian poetry and William Morris wallpaper,

prating retrospectively of a 'forever England' of greenwoods and larks arising, mixed with 'documentary or *Picture Post* English, suitable for conveying information that might be a bit "above" the reader' – in short, exactly the kind of stuff 'turned out by poets, often good ones, who are driven by circumstance to work in the BBC and in government propaganda departments'.[6]

It was Nigel Dugdale who suggested that a corner of the Lion & Unicorn pavilion should reflect the eccentric side of the British character. Laurie's 'fantastic cast of mind'[7] made him the ideal 'Curator of Eccentrics'. He launched an appeal in the *Times* letters column in November 1950 for 'curious, unusual or ingenious objects of eccentric conception'. The press loved the idea of the eccentrics of England rallying to the call of 'Mr Laurie Lee, the poet', for something rich and strange. The publicity, Laurie reported later, 'was benign and well-wishing'. 'Imagine,' he said thirty years on, 'eighteen months of one's life spent convening eccentrics.'

Laurie's office became a museum of crackpot oddities. 'He sauntered into my office one day with a violin and mandolin made from used matchsticks, and gave a spirited performance of a Telemann concerto.'[8] Someone offered a brilliantly engineered machine, 20 feet square, with the sole object of blowing out matches. There was a staircase with weighted steps to give the feeling of going upstairs when going down; a deflatable rubber bus for going under low bridges; a brick mousetrap maze scattered with pepper in which the mouse bashed its brains out with sneezing: 'But you cannot have six months of mouse massacre,' said Laurie, 'just for the fun of the thing.'

Early in 1951 these objects were selected for the showcase:

The Cuthill Smoke-Grinding Machine
A Roundabout of Eggshells
Davoren's Self-Wiping Motor-Cyclist's Goggles
A Nose-Guard for Drinking Tea
A Tea-Set of Fishbones
A Mandolin Made of 10,000 Matchsticks
The Archives of the British Snail-Watching Society[9]

A life-size Emmet-built replica of Lewis Carroll's White Knight presided, standing alongside a screen showing cartoons by Tenniel, Lear, Pont. An extra device – the 'Morale Raiser' invented by Lt Col. Nigel Dugdale – was strapped to the back of the White Knight, who was looking gloomy. An electrically-driven velvet-gloved hand patted him on the back and said, 'You're a wonderful fellow . . . you're so attractive', etc. The King, it was reported, visiting the Exhibition in the pouring rain when it opened in May 1951, seemed nonplussed by Eccentrics' Corner.

In 1951 Kathy and Laurie moved from their Earls Court flat over the railway to 49 Elm Park Gardens, a tall brick Victorian house 'the colour of sulphurous kippers', run by Chelsea Housing Improvement Society, which provided homes for impoverished artists. Emma Smith's husband, Richard Stewart-Jones, a Chelsea councillor, told Laurie and Kathy (to Emma's disapproval) to take paintbrushes and canvas along, to secure the flat. The border of Chelsea and Fulham was still essentially a working-class area, and the square had an almost Mediterranean evening life – doorsteps spilling with families, children running in and out of the gardens. Number 49, a former ambassadorial residence, was divided into five flats. Other residents included the painter Jane Lloyd, her husband the artist Jeff Hoare, and the handsome sculptor Elisabeth Frink, brigadier's daughter, with her fine strong bony profile and helmet of hair. Her flat was a shambles, 'the muddled aftermath of endless parties'.[10] But her studio was 'a white, quiet place, littered for action', with 'a scribble of notes and images, and the various bits of homely junk, plaster, wire, old newspapers and firewood, which she uses to build up her figures', as Laurie said on television nine years later. The Lees first occupied the ground level, and later moved up to the top two floors: rooms with high ceilings, tall windows and fine plasterwork.

In the spring of 1951 Rosamond Lehmann wrote from Golden-eye, Ian Fleming's house in Jamaica, where she was enjoying Noël Coward's 'enchanting astringent affectionate society'. By May, Rosamond and Laurie were reunited, with cuckoos and nightingales

in attendance, 'a moment of such pure happiness', said Rosamond, 'that it has given me back my life'. At her son Hugo's wedding that autumn, Rosamond finally met Kathy ('so sweet') and Laurie played the piano. That evening Laurie, Rosamond, her daughter Sally and Willy Mostyn-Owen went to see *Caesar and Cleopatra*. Kathy was sure to understand, Rosamond said: and of course she did. She knew from the start she had to share her husband with a wide circle, and must slot into his busy social life, or stay at home while he was out with old friends.

Anyway Kathy soon had a job which kept her occupied in the evenings. Nigel Dugdale owned a glamorous French restaurant named Père Auguste (later Villa Villa) in Gerrard Street, for which he wrote droll ads in the personal columns of *The Times*. Pen had decorated it in dark red striped wallpaper with gold cherub wall-lights and a vaulted ceiling, and Nigel rightly envisaged that the nineteen-year-old blonde Kathy would make an alluring barmaid in black stockings and pinafore. She earned £3 10s a week plus tips. It was an amusing place where Dugdale would hold court, inventing puddings like Shusha Baskusha, a concoction of meringues and exotic fruits, borne in aloft with four lighted sparklers stuck into the meringue peaks.

During the Festival summer of 1951, Dugdale went on television to publicize Eccentrics' Corner as 'Major Oswald Murgatroyd M.O.W. (Master of Wasp Hunting)', the character he had invented in *Time & Tide*. Laurie took all his friends' children – Dugdales, Devases, ffrench Blakes, Philippses – to the Skylon and the Big Dipper, which he loved. A set of plates, printed with Laurie's five lyric couplets on the seasons of the year, were on display:

'Four seasons square the rounded year,
And all in Nature's glass appear.'
'With leaf-green eyes, and lips half-curled,
Spring leads a white lamb through the world.'
'Butter the hedgerow with cream-fat roses:
Gorged with his garlands, the Summer dozes.'
'Ancestral Autumn, with hands of brass,

Shakes the last apple on the grass.'
'The Wintry crow creaks home to hide
And frost locks up the countryside.'

One afternoon in April Celia Kirwan (later Goodman) was looking into a delicatessen window in the King's Road when Laurie approached her: he had mistaken her for her twin sister Mamaine, who was married to Arthur Koestler, and whom Laurie had accompanied home the night before from a dinner at the Henrions'. Celia and Mamaine, *nées* Paget, had been unusually cultured débutantes. Celia was a pianist, and she and Laurie soon discovered that they were on the same musical wavelength. They began meeting often to play music at the house of Celia's friend Ralph Jarvis, a cultivated and musical banker. So Doddington, the Jarvises' Elizabethan (and some said haunted) manor house in Lincolnshire, became yet another of Laurie's weekend refuges, and throughout his life his affection for Celia was unfaltering.

For that summer's official 'Festival Holiday', Laurie and Kathy went back to Geraldine Lawrence's house at Tenby with the Devases and other artists, John Ward and Norman Hepple and their wives. The 200-mile journey from Chelsea to South Wales took two days in the Devases' car, with an overnight stay at the Imperial Hotel, Hereford, and long enough stops *en route* to paint watercolours. Laurie took charge of logging the weather, the mileage, and prawning records, noting each day's tally in his italic hand. Every excursion and mishap became an event in the Holiday Book: 'Michael's cow-pat'; 'the crash'; 'Esmond's bad foot'; 'Tragedy' (Anthony accidentally shot dead a seagull with his airgun). John Ward and his wife were drawn swooning at the beauty of Little Rock House; Ward also drew Geraldine, breakfasting in her swan-shaped bed, among her Dufys. Laurie drew everyone going in to bathe, and wrote a poem in heroic couplets called 'Pembroke Evening', ending –

For years to come we shall recall this scene
When tongues nostalgic speak of Geraldine.

GOING TO BATHE

Laurie's Holiday Book drawing of hosts and guests going down to bathe at Tenby (*Devas Family Collection*)

Laurie was in his element at Tenby. 'He adored good company; it stimulated him,' John Ward says. 'He had none of that grim Cézanne lack of communication fashionable when I was a student.' On the last day of the holiday Laurie got up at 6 a.m., at low tide, and wrote 'I LOVE GERALDINE' across the sand, which she would see when she got up at 7 a.m. to feed her pet seagull, Lucifer. She was ecstatic.

In August Laurie and Kathy went off in the Henrions' car to Martigues, in 'a desperate attempt to get some sun out of this mouldy summer', he told Val ffrench Blake, 'and for six days we sat & watched the Mistral blowing up the sea while I drank absinthe & grog & shivered, and then we got involved with a forest fire which burnt out 150 acres of hill scrub & pine trees & warmed me up for the first time this year'. They joined the Jarvises for a further two weeks in France, but were back in time to hear Laurie's talk on the Home Service, 'An Obstinate Exile' (produced by Gilbert

Phelps, an old university friend of Betty Smart's husband), about his reluctance to live in London. London might be the greatest show on earth, Laurie said, but it wouldn't impress the villagers at home. Its flowers had no scent, its mushrooms no taste. 'Fancy having to buy flowers anyway. I can never get used to it. We used to chuck them like rubbish at the neighbour.' 'But why oh why,' Emma Smith wrote, 'don't you write that book about your child-hood you started years ago?' (He had read aloud to her the first chapter, the *Orion* article, in 1947.) 'It's a crime not to, and if you don't do it soon you never will.'

But Laurie's procrastinating years had begun. He had already had almost all the experiences he was ever to use as a writer, but had yet to sit down and write them. There was a 'prolonged uncertainty' about his health, as Rosamond Lehmann anxiously put it. By September he was 'deep in the hands of the medicos', he told Val ffrench Blake. A series of chest X-ray appointments at hospitals in London and Romford would delay their arrival in Cornwall until mid-October for 'sun-lit days and full-moon nights punctuated by regular doses of cream & honey'. Afterwards, he wrote: 'We have both returned to this shrunk-shank place as sleek as fatted calves . . . I am showing my blisters around with a terrific swank as if they were war wounds, and all the poets, with their milk-white paws, are especially jealous.'

Laurie was obliged to start planning a book in earnest when John Lehmann wrote to say that the Society of Authors' Travelling Scholarships Committee had unanimously nominated him to be awarded £200, 'and the only condition is that you spend it abroad . . . Just immediate banishment, & nothing more severe.' Lehmann hoped that the journey would produce 'a flood of poems – and prose galore'. Laurie decided to take Kathy to Andalucía, and to write the book which became *A Rose for Winter*.

Before leaving, he made a schools broadcast on Madrid. 'Madrid first came into being when King Philip II stubbed his finger into a map and said: "I want a new capital, and I want it there – right in the middle of Spain" . . . And that is exactly what he got.' He vividly described from memory a day in Madrid's life: the boot-

blacks shining shoes as bright as chestnut conkers; the market with live chickens, and great flat loaves of bread like cushions; the cafés, the donkeys, the boys singing for pennies; the din everywhere; the deserted siesta hour, the bullfights, the flamenco dancers, the evening *paseo*.

After a glamorous appearance at the Chelsea Arts Club Hallowe'en Ball, Laurie and Kathy sailed from Tilbury for Gibraltar. They stayed in Algeciras, in Seville, in Écija with its towers, in Córdoba, and spent three snowy weeks in Granada (including a week under the blankets when Laurie had a bad fever, and lay close to death until he heard voices gathered round his bedside saying what a beautiful widow Kathy would make). In Granada, too, Laurie heard that he had been appointed MBE for services to the Festival of Britain. He had cards printed which came out as 'Laurie Lee Mbe' – 'that well-known East African grocer'.

Laurie's Spain had not yet changed much since the 1930s, but 'how hard the baked ground of the olive groves looked', he noted. 'Ground to which my body used to cling in a very drunken rapture of sleep.' He enjoyed being Svengali, introducing Kathy to everything, constantly testing her powers of observation: 'Turn around,' he would say, so that she had her back to the bar. 'Now tell me what's behind the bar.' 'He knew I would just say, "a few bottles",' she says. 'But he took in everything.' Kathy's golden-haired olive-skinned glow was complimented everywhere, and the chambermaids taught her how to respond. 'When men call after you, you can giggle if you are unmarried, but if married, never.'

In January they reached Almuñécar, 'sheltered, hot & sunny', Laurie told Val ffrench Blake, 'with fruit blossom in the fields, and oranges & bananas ripening'. They stayed at the Hotel Mediterráneo, where 'I am still remembered, though the golden boys of my youth are now pouch-eyed & fat, with strings of children & invisible wives. In their faces I see my own condition.'

Wherever Laurie went, he made friends. He could not enter a bar without talking to people, hearing their life stories, sitting up till 2 a.m. He practised his guitar every day, learning new songs from the carolling chambermaids. 'Cathy speaks Spanish much better than I,

though she started from scratch 6 weeks ago. She dances the Sevillana & is a great success.' As a Provençal child she had watched Spanish dancers and gypsies; she danced flamenco, Sevillanas, Malagueñas and Sabateados to the manner born. In Córdoba they were told: 'But you're Lorenzo and Catalina! There's a song about you.' This song – *'El sol se llama Lorenzo y la luna Catalina. Cuando se acuesta Lorenzo, La luna se levanta Catalina'* (The sun is called Lorenzo and the moon Catalina. When Lorenzo goes to bed, the moon Catalina rises) – became Kathy and Laurie's party piece.

Suddenly they were summoned by telegram to North Africa, where brother Jack was making a film melodrama called *South of Algiers* with Eric Portman, Wanda Hendrix and Van Heflin ('a piece of old hokum', Jack says now, 'quite fun, but cliché stuff') and he needed Laurie's help with the script. 'We were lying watching the sun & moon drift over the classical blue sea, watching the fishermen each dawn raking the still waters for their tiny catches of scarlet fish, listening at night to the guitars and the girls singing, and not expecting to stir until it was time to take the boat from Gibraltar, when suddenly all the cacophony of the high-pressure film world broke upon us,' wrote Laurie to Pen Dugdale, 'and in less than no time . . . we were in Africa among the ghostly Moors.'

It was a long train journey through unexpectedly lush green fields, 'with white-robed Arab women walking through the grass like spirits' and 'brown camels mincing through the wheat' to the sophisticated city of Algiers, 'a town of which I have always dreamed'. He added: 'Warmest thanks to Nigel for injecting us with financial salvation,' as Dugdale had sent money for their extra journey. Laurie arrived 'shaking with fever' at Bou-Saada, went to bed for two days, waking to see 'Jack's pink face peeping round the door'.

The film set amused him vastly. 'What vain & florid ghosts these actors be! Oh they are continual entertainment, sitting all day in the lounge of the hotel, beetroot-coloured with makeup, sticking each other with sly verbal pins, quarrelling with poor Jack, wheedling me to write them extra scenes. But I had to come – I couldn't resist the challenge – it was such a drama.'

Desert life was all new to Laurie, the landscape of naked rock and sandstorms, the snow-tipped blue mountains, and the wild unseen voice of the muezzin calling the faithful to prayer at dawn and at noon. Bou-Saada (the city of happiness) was full of gaunt bearded men with faces like mountain goats, 'and the women are so heavily veiled that they look like bundles of washing with just one dark eye peeping out'. When King George VI died in February they observed the two minutes' silence out in the desert. 'We had eight Arab soldiers dressed as bandits for the film. At 2 o'clock they formed in a line and fired their rifles into the air and stood rigidly to attention. We were among great bare hills, and as we all stood silent the echo of the guns went roaring and rolling all round the mountains . . .'

They arrived back at Tilbury in March, Laurie with 'several kinds of fevers, including flu, folly & procrastination'. Rosamond Lehmann welcomed them with 'inexpressible joy' from her new flat in Eaton Square: her daughter Sally had just won a scholarship to Oxford. Kathy set about making a flamenco dress, with sixty yards of white flouncing and as many yards of Woolworth's lace. She was performing at the Albert Hall ('Olé!' cried Laurie) where she danced a magnificent solo. Laurie was suffused with pride: 'I am always fascinated by technique and efficiency – even in games like billiards,' he had told Val ffrench Blake once, after Val had taken him to see the passing-out parades at Sandhurst. When Kathy mastered flamenco he boasted of her faultless precision.

Laurie's mysterious illness persisted. After a musical weekend at Doddington, Celia Kirwan recommended a chest specialist she knew: 'I have seen three specialists in the last ten years,' Laurie replied, 'and the only thing they were all agreed on was that it was not a physical trouble . . .' In July they went again to Tenby with the Devases; but Laurie had been told he must have a lung removed (hence his later references to himself as 'Wun Lung Lee, the famous Chinese poet'.) Before his operation they went to Bushton, and on 16 September 1952, with the Devases, they were at the Farnborough air display, where they witnessed the terrible disaster of that year when a prototype de Havilland DH 110 jet fighter

plummeted into the spectators, killing twenty-six. The Lees and the Devases were near enough to feel debris falling all around them, and Rodrigo Moynihan, who was also there, wrote to his son praising Laurie's bravery as he sheltered six-year-old Prosper.

Laurie described the disaster to Val ffrench Blake. 'We were in the line of flight and the cockpit fell in front of us while the engines passed over our heads and hit the crowd behind us. From the moment he [John Derry] began his dive 8 miles up till the shock waves exploded and the aircraft fell to pieces a kind of smooth pattern of almost classical tragedy seemed to emerge; the triumph of breaking through the barrier; the clap of thunder which followed the aircraft, and cheers, and death. Perhaps the greatest moment was when [Neville] Duke took off while they were still carrying away the bodies and climbed to eight miles & did the whole thing again.'

After his operation, Laurie went to recuperate in Cornwall where 'the air and the life were plenty big medicine'. Typically, he became even more competitive with only one lung, and even gave 'holding his breath under water' as a hobby.

Over Christmas he wrote his first account of crossing the Pyrenees into the Spanish Civil War as 'A True Tale of a Spanish Adventure' for another BBC schools programme. 'Some years ago, when I was a young man . . . a cruel Civil War broke out among the peoples of Spain. All war is terrible, but a civil war – which is a sort of murderous family struggle on a large scale – is probably the worst kind of all . . . When I heard the news of this war it made me very sad, because I had a lot of friends out there, and more than anything else in the world I wanted to try to help them.

'All the sea-coasts were guarded by ships, and the frontiers by soldiers . . . and the northern part of Spain is joined on to France by a great wall of snow-covered mountains called the Pyrenees, which are just like battlements, only thousands of feet high . . .'

Months later, an astonishingly detailed letter arrived, to say how popular his talk had been. A BBC education officer had heard it in a school class, and sent a 1,500-word report detailing the children's reactions – their intense concentration, their laughter and

enthusiasm for 'one of the most exciting stories they had ever heard'. 'We were not quite sure why the frontier guard should fire on sight at anybody. If it was a civil war, surely the traveller might be coming to fight for their side. They were quite clear, incidentally, what civil war implied.' A useful secondary career, recycling experiences as talks, had begun: the following September he did another Schools broadcast, on 'Village Life in Cyprus'.

That April of 1953, Laurie took Rosamond Lehmann's golden, glowing daughter Sally to Paris for a week. Rosamond seems to have trusted him (despite his susceptibility to girls of that age, which she surely knew about) to be an honourable and avuncular companion to her eighteen-year-old daughter. 'They had a marvellous time,' says P.J. Kavanagh, the poet and writer, whom Sally later married. 'Laurie was hailed everywhere, the two Roberts, Colquhoun and MacBryde,[11] sitting outside Le Dôme, calling out "If ever I saw blessing in the air" . . . as Sally and Laurie passed.' It was soon after this interlude that Sally captured the heart of Kavanagh, a fellow Oxford undergraduate who had himself spent a year in Spain; and through Sally, P.J. Kavanagh and Laurie became lifelong friends.

On the wet and cold day of the Coronation, 2 June 1953, Laurie and Kathy were at Doddington Manor in Lincolnshire *chez* the Jarvises. The villagers watched three television sets mounted in the church. 'Silence & smell of mackintoshes,' noted Laurie. 'Children's tea in granary then grownups tea of ham & tongue salad. Anthony Jarvis [Ralph's son] planted a tree by the school. Then I played fiddle for children's maypole dance in stable. Judged fancy dress dance. At midnight I lighted bonfire [Laurie had cut down a dead holly tree for it that morning] – good blaze.'

Next day they watched the Queen drive along the Fulham Road in an open car in a white hat: 'pretty tired face beautifully made up'. A relentless series of summer drinks, dinner and garden parties and receptions ensued, with music and singing. They went to the Derby and drank champagne; to Lord's with Hugo Philipps; and at Bushton and other country houses they enjoyed the novelty of watching the Test Match on television. Kathy danced at El Patio, and at the Festival Gardens. Laurie dressed in Field Marshal's uniform

to stand in for Viscount Alanbrooke for an Anthony Devas portrait.

Some were mystified by their weekend disappearances: where did they go? Laurie had no money, no car: Kathy still rode a pushbike. But Laurie and Kathy, now a double act, were constantly invited. 'There was something wild about Kathy – that Celtic look,' people say. Her beauty 'took the breath away'. 'I was quite pretty and not unintelligent,' Kathy says. 'I suppose we made a good couple.' 'With you two I always feel it is the hosts who should give thanks to you,' as Bryan Guinness, later Lord Moyne, wrote, 'as you bring so much of – happiness yes but it is *not* the word I want – blessedness is the word, in the sense of the Baraka – an Arabian conception of Blessedness which my friend John Hamilton of Egypt (who so much wants to meet you) found in the Sudan. Anyway you have it . . . & leave it behind you like John Aubrey's spirit that disappeared with a melodious twang – but we wish you would not disappear.'

Guinness, a poet himself, had met them at the Dugdales'. He was so taken with *The Bloom of Candles* – 'It is a long time since I have been so much stirred by new poems' – that he invited them to stay. So Biddesden in Hampshire, one of the most beautiful houses in England, with Arab horses and peacocks in its park, became yet another weekend refuge for Laurie and Kathy.

They were back in Tenby that summer: every episode of the journey in the Devases' car was noted by Laurie: the Oxford by-pass café ('This café is dangerous. Pork pies poisonous'); Laurie falling in the Thames, Prosper saving Laurie; the picnic in a hayfield on the Wye; the shooting of air-guns at bottles and mushrooms; the puncture five miles from Tenby. Once again there were intense prawning competitions (Laurie got 105 prawns on 14 July) and the usual jolly mishaps, sketched or painted: a burning motorbike drawn by Esmond Devas; Kathy's parting present of two chickens, drawn by Laurie, one called Catalina, one called Lorenzo; Anthony with two lobsters; 'A Wet Day' – people sitting in armchairs indoors, children drawing on the floor; an old lady and dog terrified by one of Laurie's fireworks.

Laurie's old patrons were still demanding new work from him:

Stephen Spender launched his magazine *Encounter* with contri-
butions by Day-Lewis, Auden, the Sitwells, and unpublished letters
by Yeats, but 'It would be lovely to have something of yours . . .
We pay £10 for 1,000 words & corresponding rates for verse.' John
Lehmann wanted Laurie's 'wonderful visual freshness and sparkle'
for the *London Magazine*. With Rex Warner and Christopher Hassall, Laurie was editing the PEN anthology of 1954. They sent out
letters to established poets, soliciting material. Clearly Laurie (in
bed, ill) had objected to the standard of the results, and told Hassall,
'I do not see why we are bound to accept inferior work as a result
of these personal invitations.' 'But think,' asked Hassall. 'Would
you send back a poem to de la Mare which you yourself had
solicited?'

That year de la Mare, aged eighty, was awarded the William
Foyle Poetry Prize *in absentia*. 'Three poets told me they are making
less than £100 a year from poetry,' said the *Daily Express* diarist,
reporting the event; Laurie was one of them. He certainly could
not have existed by poetry alone; but poems, as he was discovering,
are endlessly recyclable through anthologies and poetry readings.

Laurie always said his poems were written for the voice: 'They
are not intellectual poems, they are sensual. They celebrate sound
and colour and smell and light.' Adrian Mitchell, then an undergraduate at Christ Church, invited Laurie to read his poems to the
Oxford Poetry Society, along with Anne Ridler. Mrs Ridler told
Laurie that her pleasure in his poems had been intensified by hearing
his reading 'as a light is doubled in a mirror'. 'I have always envied
music its temporal advantage – its easier transport, so to speak,
making its heaven here & now & hailing us all into it. But poetry
well read aloud can do that: yours makes the visible world exist –
"the round world is filled with exultation" as the Whitsun sentences
express it, "& that which containeth all things hath knowledge of
the voice".'

At Bushton, after-dinner singsongs ('On Top of Old Smokey',
'The Streets of Laredo', 'Ae fond kiss, and then we sever', 'Ye
banks and braes o' bonny Doon', 'Barbara Allen') were always *de
rigueur*. Laurie would sing 'It Takes a Worried Man' with variations:

'It takes a married man to sing a married song . . . I'm married now, but I won't be married long' and 'It takes a curried lamb, to sing a curried song . . .' In the early 1950s these impromptu performances developed into organized concerts, called the Barnstormers, in the village hall. Val ffrench Blake dressed up with side-whiskers and a high collar at the piano. All the relations (Charringtons, ffrench Blakes, and Hanbury-Tracys) took part, even Sam Dugdale aged three in Chinese pyjamas with Teresa aged five at the piano. Five Cunard sisters dressed up in 1920s Charleston dresses and beads and performed the Beverley Sisters' song 'Sisters'. Antonia Dugdale danced a ballet solo; Veldes Charrington (now Lady Raison) played the violin; Kathy danced flamenco and Laurie played his guitar. Kathy, Laurie and Antonia played recorders in a trio.

Laurie could make spaghetti grow through the cracks in the dining-room table. He could eat fire. He would lead the children Pied Piperishly to the shooting ranges at the Wootton Bassett fair. 'When they discovered helium balloons,' Antonia recalls, 'Laurie's idea was to weigh down a balloon so that it would travel along level with us. So he tied his keys to the balloon, and we walked along with the keys alongside us, until suddenly a current of warm air lifted it up – and we all leapt up, but it floated out of reach and it was goodbye Laurie's keys.'

Some of Laurie's friends wondered, what on earth did he do all day? His appointments diaries were full with lunches, dinners and music recitals. You could draw a line from Chelsea through Pimlico to Belgravia and Mayfair: that was the London in which Laurie's friends lived. Also, it took time every day to keep his account of cash received and spent (he had learned professional book-keeping at evening classes in Stroud) and of letters written and received. He recorded his weight each day. He checked his thermometer and recorded the highest and lowest daily temperatures, in a book labelled 'Hot/Cold', with complicated graphs. Like many writers, he gazed out of the window a lot. He watched over his window-boxes ('2 November – Four geraniums still blooming') and the trees in Elm Park Gardens: 'leaves falling steadily'.

But he was also writing *A Rose for Winter*. He wrote the opening

25. Laurie, Crown Film
Unit scriptwriter, 1944

26. Jack Lee, film director

27. Laurie working
hard on his film in
Cyprus, 1945

29. Rosamond
Lehmann

28. C. Day-Lewis
and Laurie

30. Laurie and seventeen-year-old Kathy on holiday in Deal, 1948 (*Devas Family Collection*)

31. Annie Lee at the christening of Jack's son Johnny, 1949 (*Nora Lee*)

33. Kathy and Laurie on the road near Martigues, 1951

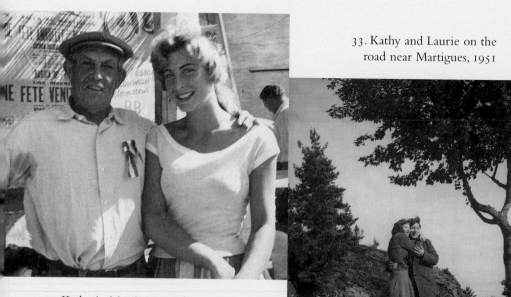
32. Kathy in Martigues, with an old fisherman friend of her father's, 1951

34. Kathy, photographed by
Laurie, late 1950s

35. Laurie on guitar, Kathy
practising her flamenco in
the bungalow in the
Vatch, 1959

36. Laurie, Curator of
Eccentrics for the Festival
of Britain, 1951 (*Larry
Burrows/Life Magazine–
Time Inc./Katz Pictures*)

37. T. S. (Tom) Matthews
with Kathy in Spain

38. Major Nigel Dugdale with his wife, Pen, and five-year-old daughter Antonia at Bushton Manor (*Antonia Young*)

39. Virginia Cunard and her sister Pen Dugdale, with Smokie (*Antonia Young*)

40. Elizabeth Jane Howard and Kathy at Lake Maggiore

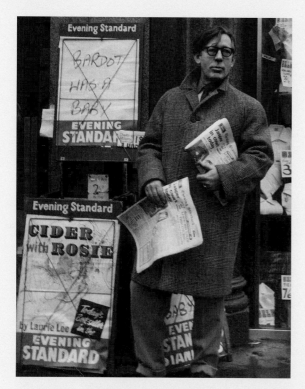

41. The best-seller: Laurie with *Evening Standard* placards for *Cider with Rosie*, 1960 (© *Mark Gerson*)

42. Antonia Dugdale, photographed by Laurie, Paris, 1961 (*Antonia Young*)

43. The yokel of Slad: Laurie with old yoke and pails, 1961
(*Topix Collection/Scotsman Publications Ltd*)

44. Yasmin aged twenty-two, photographed by Laurie on the
wall of Rose Cottage, 1961

chapter ('We had come to the southern city of Algeciras . . .') as a radio talk for the Third Programme, but suddenly he had no publisher for the book. John Lehmann had been booted out of his own company by Purnell, his majority shareholder: 'I was sacked like an office boy,' he told Laurie. But other publishers came to the rescue. On 11 October 1954 Laurie signed the contract for *A Rose for Winter* (originally 'A Rose for Twopence') with the Hogarth Press, who would pay £75 on signature, £75 on publication. Then André Deutsch, who lived just off the Fulham Road, was introduced to Laurie by Nicolas Bentley. 'Like most people I fell in love with Laurie,' Deutsch says. 'It was instant love from me to him. Because of his personality, his attractiveness, his mind.' Deutsch agreed to publish Laurie's next collection of poems, if he could manage to make the number up to twenty.

That summer Laurie had taken his fifth holiday with the Devases, again to Geraldine Lawrence's at Tenby, Laurie catching more prawns than anyone, and drawing en route a swollen, goggle-eyed rabbit, staggering across the road, dying of myxomatosis. Back from Tenby, Laurie made two trips abroad in August and September. With two of the Cunard sisters, Virginia and Veronica, he and Kathy motored to Chartres, Orléans, Pau, then briefly to Spain again. At Christmas he was back at Bushton with the entire Cunard clan. 'You are the spirit of Christmas both,' he wrote to Pen and Nigel, 'and a Christmas without Bushton doesn't seem a Christmas at all . . .' Antonia remembers that Laurie kissed her under the mistletoe that year. She was fourteen – which (as he told one close woman friend) was his favourite age.

16 | 'Write about your own life'
1955–8

'Now he has the right life for him; knows all the bright young writers and the foremost painters, hears all the literary scandals, is given free tickets for the best concerts and, every year, finds benevolent friends who enable him to spend a few weeks in Spain or some other foreign country.' Thus Wilma Gregory, in a letter to her sister, summarized – accurately – the life Laurie was leading by 1958. Not yet famous, still earning little, Laurie did have the professional esteem of fellow poets, and plenty of 'benevolent friends' providing a full social life and, long before packaged foreign travel, prolonged summers in Mediterranean villas.

In the mid-1950s anyone distinguished in the arts – writers, actors, poets and musicians – knew everyone else. At the Apollo Society's evenings of poetry and music Laurie would read with Spender, MacNeice, Day-Lewis and Jill Balcon, Marius Goring, Peggy Ashcroft. His diaries remark the beauty of Natasha Litvin (Mrs Spender) as she played Liszt, Dadie Rylands's reading voice 'like sunwarmed terracotta'; Irene Worth's 'actressy listening pose, which almost drowns the performers'. At one Apollo evening he met the young guitarist Julian Bream, and he and Laurie hit it off at once 'through the Iberian connection' as Bream puts it, and of course the guitar, which Laurie played 'intuitively'. Laurie liked Bream's way of referring to his art ('the old gut-plucking lark' . . . 'Dowland job – on the old plonk box') and the fact that he could play C.P.E. Bach, Sor, and Villa-Lobos beautifully even when apparently drunk. Bream lived near Laurie at 20 Bolton Gardens and they drank at the same local, Finch's in the Fulham Road (and later at the Queen's Elm, following the charismatic publican Sean Treacy, an ex-pilot from Galway), and both had a passion for fireworks. The effect when Laurie tied two rockets together at Bream's 1957 Guy Fawkes night party has never been forgotten.

As a poet Laurie reached a pinnacle with *My Many-Coated Man*, his third and last volume of new work, published by Deutsch on 8 May 1955. He dedicated it 'to W. G.' – despite Wilma's harsh reaction to *The Sun My Monument* in 1944 – 'out of affection and gratitude,' he told her, 'for all you did for me.' It contained half a dozen of his best loved and most anthologized poems: 'Town Owl', 'Twelfth Night', 'Boy in Ice', 'Apples', and the sinister 'My Many-Coated Man' itself.

'Laurie Lee is one of my favourite poets,' wrote Cyril Connolly in the *Sunday Times*. 'He has not a great deal to say, but a most delicious way of saying it.' He linked Laurie with Blake, Clare and Lorca: 'He never tries to be a philosopher . . . but is content to portray changing moods and weathers in simple lyrical form, relying on a sharp eye and an exquisite ear.' He said Laurie invited comparison with Dylan Thomas, 'but the one is a Van Gogh, the other a Samuel Palmer, a maker of ravishing verbal woodcuts'.

One critic found 'a curious emotional nullity' in this post-war, post-Lorna collection but it became the first Poetry Book Society choice; Vita Sackville-West praised it and so did Bryan Guinness ('every page has the shining, thrifty concentration of a jewel; every phrase tells & burns its way into the imagination to set it on fire'). Atticus in the *Sunday Times* admired Laurie's bohemian credentials: 'Mr Lee, unlike most of our poets, has never been bureaucratized. He has never taught, never lectured, never taken political orders, never worked (or almost never) in an office – never sold out, in a word, for respectability.' 'I don't know quite how I exist,' Laurie told Atticus. 'It's a miracle really.'

In the spring of 1955, while brother Jack was in Indonesia directing *A Town Like Alice* with Virginia McKenna and Peter Finch, Laurie was in Spain with Bunny Keene planning a film – 'drank much in many bars, seen good dancing & heard some good music,' he wrote to Pen Dugdale from Madrid, 'but the film is very heavy going, with many difficulties.' They took a train through fields of caves – still inhabited – and reached Cuenca for the procession of the Virgen de la Luz. In Cuenca, the charming medieval town perched on an outcrop of rock east of Madrid,

Laurie is still fondly remembered by Alejandro, former patron of El Sotanillo bar, as 'Lorenzo', a '*desgarbado*' (slovenly) figure who would spend hours in his bar, singing and playing the guitar and chasing girls with live crabs. 'Cuenca I loved, and next to Cuenca Alejandro of El Sotanillo,' wrote Laurie to his fellow poet Ted Walker, who visited Cuenca in the 1970s. 'Ask him what he did with the ten shilling note I signed & which he nailed to the tavern wall. I always mean to return & get it back.' (It's still there.)

From Valencia, Barcelona and Gerona, Laurie joined Kathy, the stage designer Jocelyn Herbert and her husband Anthony Lousada in Provence. On the publication day of *A Rose for Winter*, dedicated 'to Cathy & the Benefactor' – Laurie by then had changed Kathy's name to Cathy, which he preferred, although she has since reverted to her original initial – they were still away in Martigues. And perhaps it was as well to be out of the way. The *Spectator* reviewer was Kingsley Amis at his most acidly xenophobic. Amis deplored 'Mr Lee's vulgar and sensational little book' along with all writers who lyricized 'abroad' and gave the impression that 'the other fellow's grass is greener'. He saw Laurie's poeticism as an indecent degeneration from the more elaborate and unfashionable graces of prose. He declared the book 'a string of failed poems – failed not very good poems too'.

As for Laurie's impression of the Spaniards, 'so far as this can be debarnacled from rhetoric, generalization and rhapsody', Laurie seemed to interpret 'their instability or hooliganism as gaiety, their coxcombry or self-pity as unselfconsciousness'.

The critic John Davenport sprang to Laurie's defence the following week: 'Spain is hard and unsentimental. Mr Lee does not sentimentalize it. He respects the rock-like integrity individual Spaniards have retained.' He added: 'Is it an impertinence to hope that [Amis] may gain some tolerance from his coming experience of furrin parts?' (Amis had just won a Somerset Maugham Award and must spend the £500 on travel abroad.) Robert Conquest weighed in, supporting Amis in 'the important task of giving hell to "poetic" prose'. Amis then responded, writing to the *Spectator* from Portugal to say 'I'm not being grumpy about furrin parts, only

about people being silly about them.' Privately he told Conquest he was all for escapism, 'but people should . . . not try to inflate their pleasure-etc trips into a spiritual pilgrimage AND THEN COME AND TELL ME ABOUT IT in a travel-book . . . Lee's book was notable as much for bloody stupid *ideas* as for crappy style, and these ideas are shared by other craps (Davenport & his "rock-like integrity" etc.). I really do mind the ideas more than the style, bloodiest as the latter undeniably is.'[1]

Laurie was never going to be one of Amis's gang. So it is interesting, with the advantage of biographical foreknowledge, to mention at this point that a few months later, Elizabeth Jane Howard – who was eventually to be the second Mrs Kingsley Amis – was having a romantic holiday in Spain with Laurie Lee.

Throughout that summer, Laurie's literary friends rallied. Rose Macaulay ('Goodness, what a book!') found *A Rose for Winter* 'funny and delicious. How unerringly you alight on the right words that sing & clang & shine, & set the scene to music! the smells & the flavour & the dusty tang which is Spain' and 'Oh Manolo, I shd like to meet him!' Elizabeth Jennings was 'appalled by Amis's ludicrous lack of intelligence and taste' and Emma Smith found it 'absolute heaven . . . As for Kingsley Amis and his dastardly stuff I would like to wring his neck, except poor man I feel sorry for him . . . all his own writings must have seemed so mingy murky dingy in comparison, he was just EATEN UP with envy.' Alan Ross was quietly complimentary in the *London Magazine*. Laurie's father-in-law Sarfi wrote from Italy to say that Hemingway (whose *The Sun Also Rises* he had just read aloud to Helen) 'is nowhere beside you as a writer'. Even Wilma, in hospital in Aylesbury having two toes chopped off, confessed to enjoying it. After a lengthy discourse on Liberia (she had a Liberian nurse), she wished she too could revisit Almuñécar, 'especially because I, unlike you, was on friendly terms with the small farms, cottages, villas, well away from the *pueblo* . . . Salud to your Kati. She sounds a person.'

Laurie was too busy holidaying to record any of this. He went to Guernsey with the Devas family, replicating Tenby with added sunshine, shooting fish underwater and executing some good

drawings including a portrait of himself looking pleased with a net full of mullet. And after a weekend with the Dugdales at Bushton, he set off on 4 September 1955 for Spain with Elizabeth Jane Howard.

At thirty-two Jane was a celebrated beauty with her intense dark eyes and hair drawn tautly back from her high-cheekboned face. Trained as an actress, she had married the naturalist Peter Scott at nineteen, had a daughter, and bolted; she had modelled and worked in publishing before her first novel, *The Beautiful Visit*, won the John Llewellyn Rhys Prize in 1950. She had met Laurie through Cecil Day-Lewis and found him 'instantly companionable'; he made her laugh and she loved his mobile expressive face. That summer, Jane was unhappy after her affair with Arthur Koestler ended. 'Laurie suggested I go with him to Guernsey, but the Devases couldn't have us, so he said never mind, we'll do something else, just the two of us.' Jane had never been to Spain before. They had an exhausting all-night train journey from Paris (with nothing to eat or drink for twenty-four hours) via Toulouse, Carcassonne and Perpignan. 'And at Gerona station there was a crowd of people we knew, like Rodrigo Moynihan and Elinor Bellingham Smith. Our holiday wasn't a secret and it didn't matter. It was a very happy time.'

'Yes, we were lovers,' Jane says, 'but it wasn't meant to have a future. We have always been loving friends. Always.' They stayed in cheap *pensiones*, explored villages by local buses, visited a guitar-maker to order a guitar for Julian Bream, saw a bullfight and went on to Estartit on the coast. 'A troupe of children would follow Laurie everywhere. They were enchanted by him.'

Laurie had not read Jane's novel. 'We were sitting on a rock one day, when he said, "Someone who looks like you can't be any good at writing," and I pushed him off the rock into the sea. The bravest thing I ever did with Laurie.' She signed her next novel, 'For Laurie, admiration, gratitude and love from Isabel.' Laurie had renamed her 'Isabel' because in Spain, 'Jane' is unpronounceable. 'Sometimes he called me "A Typical Kurd" – a reference to travel books which have a picture of a peasant in a blanket squinting into the sun and the caption "A Typical Kurd".'

She knew about Laurie's epilepsy, and thinks they warded off an imminent attack while there. 'I think all poets suffer from chronic anxiety, and they are not much good if they don't,' Jane says, 'and Laurie was very highly strung. In order to be sure that he would be protected, he would threaten to be ill, or suggest that he was getting ill, to make sure there would be someone around.' On the way back they stayed overnight in Orléans and in Paris.

Kathy's acceptance of Laurie's trip abroad with Elizabeth Jane Howard may seem surprising but Kathy says it did not seem at all remarkable, at that time; anyway she accepted it. Laurie remained very affectionate towards Jane throughout his life. Twenty years later he was writing to her and remembering Gerona: 'your long, exhausted, exquisite shape, face down, sleeping in your stifling room after the two days' train trip from London . . . your face half lit over the table at the beach with the dark sea behind you, the unexpected euphoria around us, the game of love that kept on refusing to believe it was a game. Panic, protection, most of all freedom, happiness, and always your extraordinary beauty.'

Laurie's visit to Bushton that August turned out to be the last of its era. On 6 September, while Laurie was with Jane Howard in Spain, Nigel Dugdale died in a terrible accident. He was swimming with his daughters Teresa and Antonia at Weymouth, where the diving board, anchored in the sea bed, had dug itself a crater. He dived in – unfortunately with his hands behind his back – hit his head on the sandbank, and broke his neck. When his daughters dragged him out he was already dead. He was forty-eight; his son Sam was only six. Fifteen-year-old Antonia had to attend the inquest and was asked whether her father might have intended suicide: the notion was absurd.

Laurie wrote the obituary in *The Times*: 'Nigel Dugdale, professional soldier, sportsman, humanist, bon vivant and wit, was one of the rarest and most unclassifiable spirits of his age . . . one of the great English eccentrics,' he said. 'His kindness and humour, and his agile, practical imagination were never at rest . . . With a toy, or a trick, or a turn of phrase, he could melt the most brass-bound of conferences or restore the spirits of the shyest child.

'He was also a poet – a poet of words, ideas, appetites and friendship . . . One sees him now, bright-eyed, brimming over with feast and holiday, moving among his guests and anointing them all with his cherished wines and rare good spirits. We were all his guests, and the party is now over.' That Christmas, the first without Nigel, Pen and the children were joined once more by Laurie and Kathy.

Having hardly been in London during the summer, Laurie still recorded a 'Letter from Britain' talk for the BBC World Service about the prolonged heatwave he had missed: 'London's usual summer is sweet and piercing short, as temporary as young love. But this year has been unbelievable, historic, something to write poems about . . .' A month later he broadcast another letter about Guy Fawkes night, by which time he had left London again for a wintry visit to Warsaw to celebrate the centenary of a Polish poet named Mickiewicz. Laurie had never heard of Mickiewicz, but five English poets had been invited, and only Laurie could go. He was curious to experience life behind the Iron Curtain, and the trip made excellent *Encounter* fodder. Typically, while breakfasting on pork and eggs, Laurie spied Graham Greene at another table. Greene received him with 'detached warmth, as though it were the Savile Club', and asked rather testily, 'Shouldn't you all be at meetings or something by now?'

The following spring, Laurie took Kathy back to Andalucía. The weather was dire. Laurie filled two notebooks, observing 'the snob habit of wearing sun-glasses – in a people who have been able to look at the sun since Creation . . .' and commenting on 'the fat young wives producing those exquisite classic-faced children, so quick of smiles, of wit, of grace, for what? to become fat, worn young wives – what are these beautiful children for?'

But the best word-picture of Laurie and Kathy in Spain is given by Geraldine Lawrence in an illustrated letter to Nicolette Devas. That May of 1956 Geraldine was at the Hotel Reina Cristina in Algeciras, where her sketches were on show at the hotel. She found Laurie and Kathy, who had been lashed by rain and wind for four weeks, 'poor dears', on the quayside. They were waiting for 'The

Girls', Virginia Cunard and Pen Dugdale, to arrive on holiday.

'You know, Nicolette, I had so longed to come across Laurie & Cathy in Spain and I can't tell you how delightful it was . . . Laurie knows Spain better than I do, yet he has such delicacy of enjoyment, and of sharing his pleasure; he never for one moment lets it be thought that he knows it all better than anyone else.' Off they all drove – Geraldine with the Stewarts and the Campbells from Gibraltar, and the Lees and Cunard sisters in a rackety hired car.

The destination was Almorrhama, where there was a *fête champêtre* or *romería* on the first Sunday in May. 'And it all went like a dream,' reported Geraldine. 'Laurie and Cathy practically stopped the fair. It is a delicious scene – cork woods, swings in the trees, booths with lemonade, hot shrimps, olives, where we sat down to our chicken and salad picnic . . . We suddenly heard a pipe playing and along came Laurie . . . He was enjoying it all so: the warmth, the sun, and the arcadian little fête was just what he loves.

'Joan Stewart said: "Everyone in Gibraltar wants to know what Cathy is like." I said, "Well she's very beautiful and very artless too: I mean she takes her own beauty quite coolly, she doesn't play up to it, but if you walk along with her all the Spanish men are sighing and moaning like the flowers of the forest . . ." Then a most wonderful thing happened. A *huge* moving crowd slowly came over to us, about 100, with Cathy dancing and Laurie playing & everyone enraptured: they surged around us, everyone yelling Olés and encores.

'From then on, those two really *were* the *Romería*. News spread among the people who had come over from Gibraltar . . . As we drove away people put their heads into the car and said, "I say, is Laurie Lee the writer here, because Lady Mary Walker does so want to meet him, and so do the Brinton-Lees."[2] I said, "Well look here, d'you see that green dress with white spots in the crowd, that's Laurie Lee's wife and he's behind with the wicker wine bottle." "Oh thanks frightfully," they said and scurried away. They really had everyone *longing* to know them . . . John Hastings said afterwards, "You know Geraldine, I'd always heard so much of

Laurie Lee and I don't think I have ever met anyone whose charm so held one under a spell.'"

On another evening they all went into the hills to see cave paintings, and their guides took them back to their little *cortijo* and out came the sherry and brandy and guitars, and everyone sang in the lamplight, and a young mother with babe in arms played castanets. 'This is how life should be lived, isn't it?' said Laurie happily. Later they were in the sailors' quarter of Algeciras, 'where a hideously ugly man sang deep flamenco and Cathy brought down the house by dancing wonderfully – she flings her whole self into it: she has got the static, still-footed part of the Spanish dances now, and of course her beauty, her hair in a plait & the fact that she was English sent all their temperatures up.

'The hideous man rose and bellowed out a song to her, from the depths: "Ah, if I had a woman!" he yelled – "a woman, such a woman as you, I would not walk in the streets in the sunlight, nor under the stars – I would live deep, deep down in a c-a-a-ave and you would be my sun and my stars and the air I breathe." Cathy listened, her eyes modestly cast down, while all the men wrung Laurie's hand & told him what a man he was having this pearl, this woman without compare, as his wife.'

Kathy, who had been taking flamenco lessons with a Swiss woman in St John's Wood, says this was the time in her life which she and Laurie 'really shared'. Laurie was proud of his lovely young Provençal wife. 'He was very particular about doing things to a certain standard. So he was pleased with me. And in one way it was wonderful. In another way it was exhausting. We were always on the move or among people. If he had a dark day, and had to lie low, I would go out on my own, past the war-wounded and out of work men who spent all day leaning on the wall, and they would shout "*Guapa!*" The hotel maids teased me if I got upset. They told me: "Remember we are far superior to them. Walk with your head held high! Be proud!"'

In September they flew to Nice to join the house-party of Audrey and Jeremy Harris, who had a villa with cantilevered pool at Cap Ferrat, and were keen on boules and charades. Laurie harpooned

himself in the ribs while snorkelling, but they took a few days in Martigues, and returned briefly before Laurie flew off yet again on a journalists' trip to Greece, sailing around the Aegean on the *Semiramis* as a guest of the Greek government.

Between travels, Laurie was writing the script for *Journey into Spring*, a now classic half-hour documentary film which Bunny Keene directed for the British Transport Commission. It was shot around Gilbert White's Hampshire village of Selborne, with Laurie's words ('This is England, hanging on the lip of spring . . .') spoken by Stephen Murray, and music by Edward Williams. Edgar Anstey, who had commissioned it, said Laurie's commentary was better than they had ever imagined: could he suggest a fee of 100 guineas instead of the seventy-five earlier proposed? The film was nominated for a Hollywood Academy Award in 1957. But when Laurie went to see it he commented, 'Many sloppy bits in the writing I must say.'

They were back at Bushton for Christmas 1956, made memorable by Laurie's carrying in the pudding, flaming with brandy, and dropping it. There were bits of pudding all over the floor with flames dotted about. 'Everything went with a bang,' wrote Laurie to Pen, 'including the pudding. Laurie's not so handy/With puddings fired with brandy/For flaming puddings floor him/O come let us abhor him.'

The Lees seemed to be at every party, as their friends recall, such was their popularity, and nobody minded that they never gave parties themselves. In jest, Laurie would say, 'We don't return hospitality, because that might look as if you didn't like it.' But he increasingly did mind being unable to reciprocate the luxurious offerings of weekends where everything was arranged with lavish style and grace by unseen hands. 'I can't have anybody here,' he would say, and by 1960 he was noting, 'There is a natural level of squalor in this flat, little sense of comfort, no visual imagination . . . Curious feeling of no food in the place too.' Their more sensitive friends perceived that there must be a darker side to Laurie's sunny personality, that he must be difficult to live with, being so often ill, and unquestionably self-centred. 'Don't discover anything

about self except black now,' reads an enigmatic diary entry for 18 January 1957. Kathy seemed meanwhile a warm, blithe spirit, who supplied without complaint whatever he needed, and centred her life around him.

Their social round was punctuated by the occasional funeral. 'The last year one of continual tragedies,' Laurie noted in 1958. 'What drives these young men to suicide?' He listed the artist John Minton, who killed himself at forty, and four others. 'Rosamond writes of the doom of them & asks "any idea why". I think it is the unbearable plurality of experience which bombards us now, too much expected from the artist, no safe leisure of sensation, too many people; impossibility of finding in the flood any substantial moral or immoral rafts to cling to: breakdown, breakdown.'

In March 1957 Laurie discovered he needed glasses, though still able to observe how many buds were unfolding on the sycamores in the square, or to note 'Comet visible after sunset NW horizon.' Did the eye test bring intimations of mortality, of 'I grow old, I grow old . . .'? That month, an English teacher, Neville Smart, who had first been struck by Laurie's poetry in *The Bloom of Candles*, invited Laurie to come to Kingsbury County School in north-west London, to address the sixth form about poetry. Laurie courteously replied:

> Dear Mr Smart,
> Thank you very much for your letter & for your flattering suggestion. I simply couldn't do it though. I feel I've no right to lecture anyone about poetry, particularly the young. You can teach them far more than I can.
> Roberta was a remarkable girl & I congratulate you upon her. She had a strong & original style of writing, but there wasn't much I could tell her. She lectured me, rather. I think she'll do well.
> Forgive me for not being more helpful, but this isn't the first time I've had to find excuses.
> Yours sincerely, Laurie Lee
> PS I sent Roberta a copy of 'The Bloom of Candles'. She wrote to say she didn't think much of it.

Roberta Green, the girl mentioned, had written several highly accomplished poems in the school magazine at Willesden Grammar, Mr Smart's previous school. In the fourth form, she had written 'Warning to Prospective Lovers':

Like a bee
She softly purrs with honeyed words,
Fluttering gossamer wings;
And like a bee
She stings.

Now a psychotherapist, and a grandmother, living in Fulham, she recalls that when she sent Laurie her poems, he invited her out to dinner: a tense occasion, as her strict Jewish grandmother insisted on coming too, fearing that Laurie might carry Roberta off to the white slave trade. What the incident reveals is that Laurie, aged forty-three, was willing to make a blind dinner date with a seventeen-year-old schoolgirl poet.

That summer Laurie made another foray into reportage. He went to Cannes in May to cover the film festival for *Encounter*, and proved himself an adept practitioner of the reporter's craft. On the first evening he was refused entry to a screening because he had no dinner jacket. He wrote to Jean Cocteau, President of the Festival: 'I am an English poet . . . Last night I was thrown out of the evening show because I was not wearing "smoking". I came to Cannes to study the films, not to take part in a dress show. May I, in admiration to your president, supreme poet, imagist of my youth, & as one who would not care much for the dictatorship of clothes, protest against this petty law?'

Cocteau replied: *'Mon cher Laurie Lee: Faites comme moi. Venez voir les films à 7 heures – ainsi j'évite le smoking et je me couche le soir. De toute manière je joins une feuille de passe-bien . . . Salut fraternel de Jean Cocteau.'* The girl at the Hôtel de Paris desk translated this for Laurie, and said, 'Is very good that – you must keep it.' 'Is very good & I will keep it,' wrote Laurie in his notebook.

He also kept the *feuille de passe-bien* on Carlton Hotel writing

paper: *'Monsieur Laurie Lee est venu à Cannes sans son smoking – mais avec son coeur. Vous serez très aimables de le recevoir comme il le mérite. Jean Cocteau.'* Laurie tried flaunting this the next evening: superiors were sent for, tongues clicked, and he was told, 'Well, monsieur, you must wait even so till the lights go down.'

His notebook absorbed everything: the Cannes palms and pines, the white-gloved gendarmes, cormorants plummeting into the sea, the scent of 'sun-sickened' lilies, the price of white wine, the posing starlets, the prowling men, the atmosphere of big money and the power of the photographers, the evening sun that gave everyone a halo. He congratulated Maria Schell 'on the miracle of the eternal summer in your smile'. 'She embraced me & said, have a ham sandwich.' One morning 'in this city of sensuality and materialism', he suddenly heard the Archduke Trio in a deserted bar. 'It was ten in the morning,' says his notebook. 'The tears streamed down my cheeks. 10 days of solitary confinement in this paradise suddenly unexpectedly broken by the notes of Beethoven so clean & spirit-borne. If they did this to me in prison – and this I believe they do – I would break down & betray all & everyone. I know my weakness.'

He also had one of his dreams of Lorna.

'Dream: Slad. It was green light of country summer dawn. I was restless on the big kitchen bed. My young wife was busily talking in her sleep. Somewhere above a creak of boards, a presence. Then, horror, from the bedroom above, footsteps descended the wooden stairs to the kitchen. Who could it be. The stair-door opened. It was she, beautifully dressed, horrifying white. She took off clothes & lay on my side – the incomparable body. C asleep now with her lips open. Breakfast – half-naked – she looks winningly at me, asks me to spend the day with her – then Lewis Eyers[3] begins to fit a chain across the kitchen window. Why should he choose this morning? The sun shines. Village servants bring coffee & join us. I know I can't escape or be alone with her.'

He wrote his Cannes article for *Encounter* at speed – despite distractions including the Test Match, an eclipse of the moon, and a glittering Savile Club dinner for Robert Frost. His report was

perceptive and sharp, with a running joke about Eddie Constantine and Eva Bartok. It brought praise from Rosamond Lehmann ('Laurie how like an angel you do write. You are a veritable Lorelei: more Lorelei-like than angelic, full of the most seductive guiles and wiles . . .') and from Cecil Day-Lewis: 'I read all about you & the starlets, bless their little cruppers & fetlocks.'

In July Laurie and Kathy embarked on a month-long Grand Tour of France, Italy, Switzerland, Lichtenstein and Austria. The trip was organized by Tom [T.S.] Matthews, former editor of *Time* magazine under Henry Luce (until they quarrelled). Born in 1901, Matthews was an American aristocrat, trim, stylish, witty; educated at Princeton and at New College, Oxford, the son of an Episcopalian bishop and an heiress, Miss Procter of Procter & Gamble. He had four grown-up sons, and now lived in Chester Square with his second wife, Martha Gellhorn, former wife of Ernest Hemingway. Matthews, meticulous and disciplined and from a background as different from Laurie's as could be, became one of his most valued friends.

Matthews drove them across Europe to Portofino where he had rented Il Castelletto, a glorious villa high up the steep hill, with a flower-decked terrace overlooking the bay, where they sat at sun-down or in the moonlight among fireflies. There were spectacular storms and blazing hot days, visits to Ann Queensberry in Rapallo, and on the feast of St Peter, brilliant fireworks. Matthews, who was a poet as well as a journalist and author, wrote every morning, finishing his book on press barons, 'an excellent job, taut as a bowstring, shafted with arrows and most winningly aimed', Laurie told him, and noted his example: 'If it hadn't been for you I don't suppose I would have done any work at all. But I've got two poems and a finished radio script, thanks to you . . .' Laurie was appreciative of his 'first deep taste of Italy' since his walk through Tuscany in 1949, and as Matthews was not a sun lover, it was 'self-sacrificing' of him to arrange such weather, 'an act of the purple over-flowing heart'.

The day he got home, Laurie heard that his brother Tony – of

whom he had been particularly fond, calling him the visionary of
the family – had died on 2 July, of cerebral meningitis, leaving a
widow, Ruby, and a young daughter, Anthea. He was forty-one.
At Stroud hospital, where cousin Marion Light was matron, Jack
had found Tony in a darkened room, blind and dying. It was almost
ordained, Jack says. 'Tony was a sweet boy and he never had a
chance.'

Almost without pause, Laurie was away for the rest of the summer.
Kathy went to Martigues, while Laurie drove with the Devases to
Tenby once more, recording and sketching the more hilarious
moments. After judging the Guinness Poetry Prize, Laurie flew off
to Greece in September again as 'a fancy guest of the Greek
government with other writers of several nations', he wrote to
Tom Matthews from Athens. 'I don't know why they do this.'
They cruised the Aegean on SS *Philippos*, and had a few days on
Hydra. 'Back from Greece thank God,' says his diary.

'If all the year were playing holidays, to sport would seem as
tedious as to work,' as Prince Hal said. Laurie was understandably
conscious of being too busy playing to get any writing done. When
he wrote to Roy Fuller (a close second for the Guinness prize)
looking forward to Fuller's *Collected Poems*, he added: 'I could
collect *my* lot on an ash tray. A bit envious I am.' Fuller dedicated
the volume to Laurie. 'I never cut your throat much in the past,'
said Laurie, 'but you've certainly become my favourite poet now.'
('No, we've avoided knifing each other too lethally over the past
dozen years,' replied Fuller, 'which is more than I can say about
any other living poet.') Their friendly rivalry continued and when
a second fan letter to Laurie was misdirected to Fuller's Dulwich
flat, Fuller sent it on with a note: 'TO L.LEE – WARNING.
My flat must no longer be used as an accommodation address for
what is doubtless an amatory or subversive correspondence. Your
rival, R. Fuller.'

By the end of 1957 Laurie had become 'rather sick' at his own
lack of output compared to that of writer friends: 'It makes me
want to kick the wall,' he told Matthews, who had finished another
book of poems. 'Do you write them at night, or in the can, or

walking home drunk through the streets?' All Laurie had written lately was an introduction to Epstein's work, praising his massive and controversial *Ecce Homo*:[4] 'Squat, square, the totem of our crimes, he stands before us in a pitiless, blinding light. No chisel was ever less compromising than Epstein's in this work. Ten thousand churchfuls of sentimentalized Christs are denied forever by this raw and savage figure.'

It was now almost ten years since the Hogarth Press had commissioned *Cider with Rosie*. What galvanized Laurie finally into writing it was editorial director Norah Smallwood's offer to pay him 'to give up all other work and get on with it'. Laurie told her he just needed enough to pay the rent, and named what seemed to her the astonishingly small sum of £500. So in November 1957 he marked his determination by resuming his journal-keeping habit (a reliable sign of self-discipline) on the day the second Russian satellite was launched, carrying 'Little Lemon', a Samoyed dog, spinning around the world fourteen times a day. Laurie was riveted by all things astronomical, especially space travel; five months later he was rushing home from seeing the Marlon Brando film *Sayonara* to catch Sputnik II. 'Stood on roof in bitterly cold wind, grit flying in eye, determined not to miss it until a bright star glided silently south-east, passed almost overhead, quite fast, purposeful, with its dog in it, heading for final extinction in the atmosphere. It was extraordinarily moving.' He did not share the Canine Defence League's fury about the dog, which had died in space on 10 November.

Laurie did not renounce socializing, however. He was still at endless parties among 'a snowflake crowd – the Tynans, Felicity Hoare, people who say "I met you years ago at such a place" and I not able to remember them or it'. His journal featured a cast of gossip-column characters: 'delicious fat old Russian Moura Budberg'; Gerard Hoffnung; Edgar Lustgarten at Woodrow Wyatt's; Enid Starkie ('admired Cathy in obsessed lesbian way "like my niece – brainless girl – beautiful eyes"'); Ram Gopal ('May I call you Mr Laurie?'); Olga Davenport ('frenetic intellectual hunger, all conversation reverts to who was in love with her – names,

names, I died with exhaustion'). 'Dr Bronowski talks to C for an hour, she then asks his name. Daphne Hardy says to Dr B: "The nicest thing about television is that one can see one's friends without having to talk to them."'

The gossip was of Caitlin Thomas 'in Rome & almost in the madhouse'; George Weidenfeld 'divorcing his wife, ex-Mrs Cyril Connolly, and naming Mr Cyril Connolly' and strange new fashions: 'the new sack dresses behind whose shapelessness men can imagine their ideal figure'. Anthony Devas was painting the Queen, 'stiffly encased in a dress the colour and texture of half-eaten trifle'. (During sittings 'HM discusses bosoms of film stars which she deplores'.) The banker Michael Behrens took him often to the opera. He heard W.R. Rodgers speaking about Yeats: 'Said Yeats thought poetry should be able to be shouted across the street to a friend (I said: "AND PEACE COMES DROPPING SLOW!") and that he couldn't write with anyone else in the room, "even" a child. (Me neither.)'

He spent several long evenings talking till 2 a.m. with his favourite painter, Sir Matthew Smith, in his Chelsea Cloisters flat, reverently recording the old man's reminiscences. Laurie had first met Smith in the Strand years before with Lorna. 'Remembered your name,' said Smith. 'Beautiful – "Laurie Lee". I thought of the Rhine.'

Smith was a modest, unassuming man. 'You know it was Churchill got me my knighthood,' he told Laurie. 'Never met him. I never met anyone. Too shy or proud or something. Could have met Derain, could have met Matisse, Picasso – all those. Never did. My fault. Too negative . . . But I was in a room with Churchill once. I went up to him & said, "May I shake your hand, sir?" A young man said, "Sir Matthew Smith, sir." Churchill said, "I know, I know, I know, I know!" I think he was cross with me. Being too negative.'

Exuberant with creativity, Laurie wrote his longest ever letter to Rosamond Lehmann's daughter Sally, who had married P.J. Kavanagh and sailed with him to Djakarta where Kavanagh was lecturing for the British Council. Laurie advised Sally to keep journals, and Kavanagh to 'put on his Willie Maugham face and

plan a wicked book. I feel sure you could not have done a better thing than to take this place in your twenties stride . . . what you see won't be seen again.'

He told them about the Guinness prize-giving. ('Never, since Warsaw, have I seen Poetry so richly sponsored. Uniformed foot-men, chandeliers as big as haystacks, gallons of Black Velvet, endless champagne, hundreds of sparkling brimming glasses with a poet's nose in each.') He told them about Enid Starkie 'biting & bibulous . . . gripping my hands and weeping over long-lost friends'.[5] 'Plump Socialist Naomi Mitchison was also present. She straps down her bosom in order to present a united front.'

Laurie soon began to parody 'Jennifer's Diary' in his account of the social whirl. 'Then there was a big nuptial dance for Colin Crewe and Sally Churchill, at the Swedish Embassy with a brilliant array of Burke's stranded gentry . . . Colin was a shy & charming groom & stood with Sally to receive us. They stayed with us till dawn . . . one old lady said to me, "I should have thought they would have left by now. If I were that gel I would wish to fly with my lover, not hang about hyar." Caroline Jarvis staggering prettily in her cups . . . Crumbling Stilton-Milton [Shulman] . . . Willie Mostyn-O, with his pink marble shining face . . . John Spencer Churchill, Randolph my son, Auntie Eden, villainous John Roth-enstein, Lady Hambleden, Lady Dufferin & Ava, Lady Djalan-of-Java, Lady Oranmore & Browne, and Judy Montagu-of-Course. A good negro band, some close dancing, and a lot of sick young girls running for the cloakrooms. Oh, my friends . . . you've no idea how Gomorrah begorrah we are.

'. . . I have to report a serious development in the character of Cathy. Heretofore only mildly moved & bemused by an evening's drinking, she has suddenly grown wildly vocal in a most dramatic way, shouting dogma & theories and beating the table & putting the fear of God into one and all. Not Cathy but Caitlin she's growing to be. She's a strong girl too, as you know. Heaven help us all, I say.'

He was, he added casually, 'on chapter 3 of a book I'm supposed to be doing for Hogarth'. As he later said, he spent that winter

'almost permanently cloistered in my snug, paraffin-reeking, sooty-windowed garret seven days a week' and he had felt strangely happy, scribbling softly away with his 4B pencils on the back of old BBC scripts. (Laurie did not believe in buying writing paper; stationery, he felt, should be something you came by.) He would be moved to tears and to laughter while writing, his childhood days returned with such immediacy. It all came back 'in pavilions of sound, and pavilions of colour'. He told Wilma he had 'moods of staring at white paper', but she told him he was lucky in not having his mind cramped by classical models – a barbed Wilma-ish reference to his lack of formal literary education: 'Whatever you write is bound to be original, entirely yourself.' Laurie claimed he was not tempted to go out much. In fact *Cider with Rosie* was slotted in between many parties and bouts of 'flu (temperature 102 degrees), and seeing Mr What win the Grand National, and counting daffodils, and recording the temperature, and hearing the Hepple children being looked after by Kathy downstairs: 'As Cathy tries to keep them subdued her shushes are much louder than their noise.' By the time he finished his first draft he was broke, he said: 'I took my fiddle out into the streets and made £4 15s one afternoon in Willesden.' Luckily Jasper Gilbey of Gilbey's magazine, the *Compleat Imbiber*, rescued him by paying him for two poems, 20 guineas' worth of gin and crates of wine at trade prices. Laurie advised Alan Ross and P.J. Kavanagh to try this: he drew a chart showing each poem producing one crate of drink, each crate producing two more poems, and so on exponentially.

The new Guinness prize entries were coming in, he told Kavanagh, 'including two excellent poems by Ted Hughes & Roy Fuller. Hughes was new to me . . . Uncle John [Lehmann] has taken him up.' Lehmann was in financial straits at the *London Magazine*. Laurie was not surprised: in his view the magazine had a repellent format and a heavy pedagogic solemnity. 'John's forewords sound like a brisk rapping of canes in cold morning classrooms: "Enough of that fooling boys! To the task! To the task!" In fact what is wanted is a little *more* fooling, more iconoclasm,

more wit, more irreverence, more warmth. Even the outsider boys read like prigs & pets.'

Wilma, now seventy and living in a cottage near Aylesbury, was also writing 'a weirdish, probably idiotic book' which might be 'a ponderous bore' or 'perhaps remarkable, its style almost distinguished & certainly amusing'. She had been diddled by a gardener to whom she had lent £40, 'a very bad egg, & I am a weak old fool to pity & help him. Well, there! I'm a muddler, & always was.' Laurie sent a cheque to help out. 'Do you feel rather sick about politics nowadays?' she asked him. 'Nothing one reads about Gaitskell, Left or Right, seems to add any reality to him. As for the Conservative leaders, what could be duller?' Laurie had just made a rare political foray himself, to the Ban the Bomb rally on Good Friday 1958 in Trafalgar Square, hearing Philip Toynbee and Canon Collins (both 'woolly but passionate') and Michael Foot. Laurie marched with the demonstrators as far as Marble Arch 'among the beards & pony tails, duffles & slacks, horn-rimmed specs, the uniform *New Statesman*/Third Programme minority, with whom I am clearly identified', but asked, 'Why Aldermaston? Like marching to protest to an arrow-maker's hut – why not to the homes of statesmen & generals?'

Further financial salvation arrived from another Society of Authors travel award. Laurie tried to discover the identity of the benefactor who donated the money by writing a letter. 'I am female,' she replied anonymously, 'over sixty, belonging to the Protestant north rather than the Latin south, and I write too, hence I prefer, so as to be on equal terms with my colleagues, not having name around as to these travelling allowances. I do hope that you will use the money to get away, forget your worries and enjoy yourself. Best wishes.'

So Laurie and Kathy went off on 23 April 1958 to the island of Ibiza. Today the notorious nadir of package holiday venues, it was then a quiet backwater. From Palma they took a six-hour slow boat 'full of beatniks and Germans' and arrived just in time; an airfield and 'lunchbox villas' were sprouting, and a year later it was

tourist-packed. But in 1958 there was still 'an unearthly silence, bad roads, empty beaches, very little traffic', he wrote to Tom Matthews, and the islanders were 'proud & distinctive'.

They took a small furnished house (an ugly concrete box) with a roof terrace, for a guinea a week, just outside the walled medieval village of Santa Eulalia and five minutes from the beach. Nearby was a freshwater pool surrounded by oleanders where nightingales sang. He told Matthews that it was '65 degrees, landscape flowery but not ostentatious; many resident painters and their women, all very bearded and serious'. It was not Ischia or Capri, but there were friendly natives working in the fields looking like Bible figures, and the local absinthe, called *palo*, was four pesetas a glass. Matthews arrived with his close friend the artist Cathleen Mann, the former Marchioness of Queensberry, bringing tea, coffee, alcohol and cigarettes. Every morning both Laurie and Matthews stayed in their shuttered rooms with white wine kept cool in buckets of water. In the afternoons they swam, and in the evenings they drank under the trees. There was nothing to do but work, drink and swim. Laurie did not even shave, until a man in a bar said, 'I encounter your beard very ugly,' and turned out to be the local barber, who shaved him forthwith.[6]

Matthews too was writing a book (*Name and Address*), about his childhood, his over-protective mother, and his irascible Trollopian father; his book was eventually reviewed in tandem with Laurie's in America. 'I could have stayed in that shabby village for months,' Laurie later told him. 'Its rhythm suited me and I found a wax-like calm about it . . . I think about it as a place of serenity.' After Matthews had gone, Laurie reported stormy skies and strong winds making doors bang like paper bags. 'A nervous young American painter has complained, showing us two ruined canvases where his brush slipped on hearing Cathy leave the house or enter it. I think he will soon leave, as no woman ever shut a door in her life except strategically.'

Laurie had walked up a distant fir-covered hill and sent Matthews this triolet:

Lee climbed up that hill;
We all knew he could do it.
So steep it could kill
Yet he climbed up that hill;
There's a cairn for him still
On the top, marked: 'Rest! Poet.'
Lee climbed up that hill:
We all knew he could do it.

On 11 June ('4,600 pesetas left') Laurie and Kathy took the night boat to Barcelona, and a bus to Calella on the Costa Brava, to meet Virginia Cunard. From Gerona on Midsummer Day he wrote a nostalgic card to Elizabeth Jane Howard – 'to Isabel the dark and the beautiful' – before they travelled on to Figueras, Marseilles and Martigues. They were away for nearly three months.

At Easter, Rosamond Lehmann had written of her anxiety about her daughter Sally 'in that beastly Djakarta'; she had sold her Utrillo in order to pay for a visit there later in the year. But first she was off to the US on Good Friday. 'God speed and Good Flyday,' Laurie had replied breezily. When Laurie got home from Ibiza on 1 July, for the third time in three years he returned from abroad to learn of a premature death: on 22 June, the golden Sally had died suddenly in Java, of polio, at the age of twenty-four. Laurie could never bear to talk about it, her husband P.J. Kavanagh says. Kavanagh himself later translated his grief into the haunting memoir *The Perfect Stranger*; Rosamond wrote *The Swan in the Evening*, in which she said that Laurie was 'one of the most passionately resentful of all those who loved and mourned her'. Laurie certainly never forgot Sally. Whenever he described a particularly appealing golden-haired girl in his diary he would say 'like Sally'.

By August, he was paring down his third draft of *Cider with Rosie*: 'I don't know which relations to drop,' he told Tom Matthews. 'I can't see the wood for the Lees.' From New York Matthews sent a new-fangled transparency viewer, so Laurie's Ibiza pictures – of Kathy in the river-pool, and the sun going down behind a glass of Campari and ice – looked quite stunning. Cathleen Mann organized

a viewing-party, at which 'Vyvyan Holland (O Wilde's strange son) went into a trance at the three-dimensional effects of it,' Laurie told Tom. 'It is the envy of one and all.'

Kathy went off to Italy while Laurie carried on writing, between excursions to the Oval, to a PEN party for James Thurber, to dine with Peggy Ashcroft and Julian Bream, and to a weekend at Bushton. He spent a musical weekend at the Cedars, Crondall, Hampshire, the home of the former Celia Kirwan, who had now become Mrs Arthur Goodman. Their house, Laurie decided, was the one he most coveted of all his friends' country places. The Cedars was in the heart of a village, 'like a ripe stone in a peach' and 'only two steps from the off-licence and three pubs, and 5 minutes from the boggy beech-wooded countryside. I don't really like living two miles across beet fields, or perched in a windy park. When I make the break with London,' he added, 'and I hope it will be soon, it's just the sort of place I'd wish for myself.'

He also made a tour of the Western Highlands with the Henrions, visited Bryan Guinness in Dublin to thrash out the Guinness poems ('I drank 23 Guinnesses the first day and rode round the wet city in a horse and trap'), went back again to Dublin with MacNeice in August, and wrote to Barbara Castle about the Cyprus problem. It is a wonder that he ever finished the book. 'There is really nothing to stop me now, except self-hatred, and I don't feel passionate about that,' he told Tom Matthews. 'I keep your image in my mind as a more disciplined example than my own and pan the typewriter like a fruit machine, praying for lucky combination and prizes. But all is chance in this game. "Nevil Shute till you see the whites of his eyes," I say . . .'

Finally on 28 October he could record: 'Finished Typed Draft of Book Cider.'

Leonard Woolf wrote him a sharp little note saying he did not really care much for this kind of book, and did not encourage the writing of childhood memories. 'But I think in your case we will publish it,' he ended grudgingly. The letter was 'dictated by Leonard Woolf and signed in his absence'.

Elizabeth Jane Howard, now Mrs Jim Douglas-Henry, gave

Laurie over dinner the manuscript of her own next novel, *The Sea Change*, and he responded: 'Dear Artist Isabel. To read these pages after my own is like watching a dolphin swim . . . You have nothing to fear but your brains. It was lovely seeing you (a blue-green dream) last night, and dear old shaggy Jim . . . Forgive the grease stains on the file. I caught a late bus from Piccadilly, and a girl on it gave me a doughnut.'

With his book at last finished, the mood of Laurie's notebook, in which he often noted jokes, became more than usually jocular (there was an evening of Scottish songs and Brecht's songs at the Arts Theatre: 'A braw Brecht nicht,' wrote Laurie) and full of dreams. Sometimes he would wake himself up laughing at the puns he thought of in his dreams: 'Talking to a Dr Blow about illegitimate children, then saying "Bye, Blow."' Sometimes he dreamt up a Spanish proverb – 'It is best to have a rich grandmother, but next to lean on the elbow of a friend' – or a line from a poem in Spanish – *'Quiero verde, verde quieto'* ('I long for green, quiet green'). On 18 November 1958, after meeting the young writer Jeremy Sandford, who knew Yasmin (now aged nineteen), he had a dream about his daughter.

'It was arranged for me to go to see her & they were both in riding kit. She was not very beautiful but had a fresh bright face & blue clear eyes. She was very friendly & chatty. She had a slight pock mark on her nose (like mine) & an injured middle finger, slightly twisted, owing to some childhood accident. She gossiped. "My father makes a hobby of Opel cars," she said. "He doesn't, you know," I murmured, sotto voce. Her mother laughed knowingly with me.'

In 1958, the new arts magazine *Motif* appeared, featuring Lis Frink, with an introduction by Laurie that expressed the earthiness and eroticism of her sculpture: 'It is spontaneous as an ejaculation of lava, a round of images shot into the air by the convulsions of buried truths.' Frink's *Man*, *Bull*, *Horse* and *Bird* sculptures and drawings were invariably 'male, solitary, attacking or at bay'. 'In her helmeted men and warrior birds we see the postures of eternal conflicts. Eyes roll in the dark, a forest of darkness, the forest of

gods and demons. Wings spread in challenge, claws strike, the beak-mouths scream. Jagged as shrapnel, these forms are both wounds and weapons; they bristle with terror or stretch in long crows of triumph. The drawings are like glacial writings on rock, or the panic scratched by the nails of a dying man. Together they are the shades of our violent past – as well as the masks of our present selves.'

Laurie saw Frink as the embodiment of primitive woman, 'a hoarder of myths, a familiar of spirits, a courage-giver, a buckler-on of swords'. 'Her iconography is brutal, uncompromising, virile and sharp as knives.' She was 'possessed of an archaic beauty and gold-bronze finish as though she herself were self-created, or was some oracular Delphic presence . . .'

Laurie's words, as Frink's biographer Stephen Gardiner commented, 'read like a love letter to her art'.

At the end of a madly sociable week in November (musical soirées, poetry readings, a ball), Laurie was knocked down by a lorry. He was just saying to himself the lines of the psalm, 'Like as the hart desireth the waterbrooks', when he stepped off the pavement and 'I was hit & spun round twice & rolled in the road & got up all in one smooth movement. Nobody moved or approached me, or asked about injuries. They just stood staring in fishy groups. I staggered to the pavement feeling sick & exhilarated. My trouser was split from thigh to ankle. I had missed death closely. It should cure me of absentmindedness. Had a stiff brandy with Jill & Norman [Hepple].'

Another night in December, Laurie was in Soho with the Cockney writer Frank Norman, learning all about rhyming slang and porn shops, when they ran into Philip O'Connor, Laurie's 'Verlaine', whom he hadn't seen since Putney in 1935 'when we were young men congratulating each other on our genius'. 'He said he'd been in the madhouse. He put his arm on mine & said, "Well anyway Laurie you're better than Louis MacNeice. And I couldn't say lower than that could I? Goodbye, man, bless you."'

The year ended with yet another premature death on 21 December. Laurie and Kathy had been out seeing Orson Welles's

Othello film with 'the Lambton girls'. When they got home, 'Emma Devas was there & from her face I knew her father had died.' Anthony had begun a portrait of his twelve-year-old son Prosper that morning, and the two had then walked in Hyde Park. It was Prosper who found his father slumped in his chair; 'But he died in an instant,' noted Laurie, '& it was better at home.' Devas was forty-seven. Christmas Eve 1958 found Laurie at Putney cemetery, bearing the coffin with Norman Hepple, Noel Blakiston, Humphrey Brook and Emma's husband, Lord Monson.

From the funeral Laurie and Kathy went on to Bushton where, minutes after they arrived, the real candles on the tree were lit, and the whole tree and its cotton-wool snow went up in flames with a great whumph. Everyone stood transfixed with horror, but in seconds Laurie had opened the french windows and pushed the flaming tree outside, where it fell into the snow with the sound of glass balls shattering in smithereens.

That Christmas Laurie wrote another acrostic for Kathy:

Could I in verse iambic
Appraise your gentle aura
Then would I in one sonnet
Hoard all your beauty's wealth.
Yet such neat-rhyming trickery

Could only freeze in aspic
All your live warmth and *alma*
These lines are yours – and yet,
Heart of my married hearth,
You make a wilder poetry.

17 | Back to Slad
1959

'Dear Mr Lee:

I am a factual person who dislikes mystery but I am also in a predicament about giving my name, so I must ask you not to speak of it. You see, I write books myself and I don't want myself as author to be mixed up with the travel award.'

Thus Winifred Bryher, historical novelist, succumbed to Laurie's second inquiry in January 1959 and wrote from her Bauhaus home above Lake Geneva, revealing that she was the mysterious benefactress who gave money to the Society of Authors to enable writers to go abroad. Winifred Bryher[1] was the pen-name of Winifred Ellerman, aged sixty-four, lifelong companion of Hilda Doolittle (the writer H.D.). Winifred's father had left a fortune from newspapers and shipping, and since money gave her complete independence, she wanted other writers to share it. In the 1920s she bought Edith Sitwell a house, and gave James Joyce a monthly allowance in Paris. 'I think you respond to the sun and the Latin south,' she told Laurie, 'so I am enclosing a cheque to help you to return to Spain or wherever you would like to go.' She herself preferred the icy wastes of Greenland: 'Mountains as high as the Alps, icebergs of fantastic shapes, gay, laughing Greenlanders. I don't know why the North always calls me. It is something against which there is no struggling. Have a good time in the south.'

Cider with Rosie was now in production for publication in the summer of 1959, and Norah Smallwood of the Hogarth Press expected it to have a modest success and sell perhaps 800 copies. She asked John Ward, then a *Vogue* artist, if he might do 'a few illustrations for Laurie Lee's autobiography'. Ward knew Laurie from Tenby, and they had played cricket together in Putney. He says: 'I went to see Mrs Smallwood in her eyrie, where I once heard her saying on the telephone: "Mr Jones, what I don't know

about photolithography can be written on the side of a black-
currant." Leonard Woolf sat there like an old prune. Norah told
me that if they broke the bank they could pay me £175. I had a
wife and four and a half children to support, and a mortgage of
£11 a month. But I had an instinct for commissions that were
worth doing.'

Ward too was a countryman, from Herefordshire. 'I grew up in
those cottages. I knew the Sunday school treats, the wild flowers,
the kitchen ranges, the pitchers of milk, the flagstones on the floor.'
He asked Canterbury art school for a student to be his model, and
met eighteen-year-old Pamela Kay, later an accomplished artist,
who posed as Annie, Crabby, Granny Trill: 'One feels such gratitude
towards anyone who can catch a character and hold a pose.' His
Cotswold-dwelling sister lay on the carpet as the drowned Miss
Flynn. For the Uncles he drew men from his army days. He used
his own son William for Laurie the sick boy.

Ward and Laurie – who was just back from a trip to Tangier for
Queen magazine – sat in the garden of the Chelsea Arts Club,
looking through his sketches. Laurie had jotted down a few points
of detail about the dim cottage interior, its pools of lamplight and
deep evening shadows, the need for more litter on Annie's bedside
table: books, vases, flowers, candles. 'Mother looks absolutely right
in the servant sketches. She was perhaps heavier later in body and
face. Wilder hair. The old granny making wine should be more
shrivelled, bent, half witchlike. The little girl's face is lovely, but
body not perhaps childish enough. The drowned girl would be
mostly concealed by water reeds, though her face – staring, and
haunting, and masses of floating hair, could be seen. I do like these
though . . . I think they're splendid.'

Laurie told Wilma he originally thought drawings unnecessary
'when the writer has taken pains to create a scene in the readers'
mind . . . But John Ward knows the country, has an eye for wild
flowers, and his impressions of me as a child are remarkably like.'

That spring, Kathy went into hospital to have the ovarian cyst
removed which had prevented her from conceiving after nine years
of marriage. Their childless state had been as mystifying to them as it

was to their pitying friends. Each had collected several godchildren, Laurie's latest being Emma Smith's daughter, Lucy Rose Stewart-Jones: 'Collecting godchildren is so clearly your vocation,' Emma wrote, adding that Laurie need not send presents: 'the thing is for you to fly kites or stand on your head or take her to the zoo or teach her to sing.'

In Kathy's absence Laurie wrote his account of Ibiza for *Encounter*, 'which bears no relation to our visit', he told Tom Matthews. 'Forgive it.' John Lehmann was 'more than a little sorry' that *Encounter*, 'rather than your old friends on the *London Magazine*' were publishing an extract from *Cider with Rosie*. Was this not 'the book which I managed to rescue for you from the debris of J.L. Ltd?' he asked. Laurie felt chastised, and apologized, whereupon Lehmann assured him that his letter had been tongue-in-cheek. 'I hereby declare that I am interested in *everything* you write, whether prose or poetry.'

The warm reception for *Encounter*'s extract (the 'Grannies' chapter) gave a hint of the success that was to come, making 'all my wintry labours and dark hours at the desk . . . justified', he wrote to Wilma. Wilma had written admiring the Grannies and said she'd half thought she might be one of them. 'My mental image of you is anything but Granny,' replied Laurie. Kathy emerged from hospital with a pretty little scar, and was invited to spend three months on a Greek island, looking after Lucy, daughter of Barbara, the former Lady Rothschild, from her marriage to the classical scholar Rex Warner. Barbara (who was also sister to Peggy Ashcroft's husband, Jeremy Hutchinson QC) was now married to the painter Ghika, and their beautiful house on Hydra was to be filled with house-guests for the summer. Laurie was to stay behind in England for the summer publication of *Cider with Rosie*. But the book's publication was delayed for four months, by a printers' and bookbinders' strike. 'I haven't really faced what I shall do while Cathy's away,' Laurie told Celia Goodman. 'I've been offered a furnished hut near Stroud and may live there till September.' This was Woodside Bungalow, a cottage down in the corner of Slad called the Vatch.

On the day Kathy left, Laurie went off to Barcelona with Julian Bream, introducing him to Caracoles restaurant where you could get a plate of eponymous snails and a glass of wine for eleven-pence. Laurie took his fiddle, Bream his guitar. 'Laurie saw the dramatic potential of the situation,' Bream says. 'He knew the Spaniards thought nobody outside Spain could play the guitar. So we would pretend we were just a couple of fellows with instruments, and we'd start to play, and Laurie loved to observe the expressions on people's faces.' It happened just as planned. 'J crouched on his stool & played some Albéniz,' Laurie wrote in his diary, '& the bar was reduced to a whisper, & the gypsy guitarists from the cabarets fell on their knees & clutched his ankles in agonies of pleasure. Even the fat old patron cynic Caracoles himself came to listen, astonished, & crying out afterwards, "And of all things, an Englishman!"'

On the rainy first of July, Nicolette Devas delivered Laurie to Woodside Bungalow, and they went over to the local pub, the Star, and talked to an old man serving drinks. The next day the same old man was carried out in his coffin. 'Talk about omens,' noted Laurie gloomily. On his first weekend he went to a lunch party at Peggy Phillips-Birt's dove-covered cottage nearby. Peggy, preparing the salmon mousse, suddenly said 'Bloody cat!' and handed Laurie a dying dove, torn at the throat. 'Had to kill it. Talk about omens,' noted Laurie again.

It was an extraordinary summer. He at once discovered how much (and how little) life had changed in his old village. In the butcher's he was saluted by old familiar schoolboy faces, now grown fat and bald. But the place itself had not changed at all: 'the smell of herbs, distant sound of crowing cocks, dogs, owls, children's voices, train whistles, heavy smell of jasmine in twilight – even with my eyes closed I know I am here. A bird calls and that bird means Slad. Have birds dialects too? Why not? they are parochial breeders.' The conversations in the Star were noteworthy: 'Got a rabbit the other day. Big 'un. An' would you believe it. 'Ad a wire round his neck I'd lost two months afore. Buried right in 'is fur. Don' know 'ow 'e lived I'm sure.' . . . 'Wuss thing I ever seed –

rabbit in a net with 'is eyes gone, pecked out, still alive . . .' 'Very few young 'uns know 'ow to trap a rabbit now . . .'

He rode to Stroud on his ten-shilling bicycle and, as of old, had a puncture. He walked with his sister Marjorie and niece Anthea across Rodborough Common to hunt for bee orchids and found five. 'Very rare. Now rarer.' There were days of thunderstorms when he needed his snakepit boots; then blinding heat and heavy July greenness. The sun was alluringly brilliant over Swift's Hill in the mornings. There were chattering magpies, butterflies, snails bright as liquorice. He dined at Steanbridge House, now a guest-house owned by Mrs Collier and her daughter Gwyneth. He had never been inside the great house in Squire Jones's day; it was now 'sad, bare & empty, the gardens a wilderness'. He liked to say, in letters: 'I live near a wood called Madding Grove, far from the Budding Crowd.'

He wrote to Kathy in Hydra, 'Dearest girl . . .' offering advice about looking after the sometimes fractious child. 'I think you are doing wonders with little Lucy, but changes of personality only happen in the films . . . You mustn't blame yourself ever. Treat a bad day of Lucy like a bad day of weather, which will pass. Be at all times your own serene sweet self, your firm and placid Nanny Powell [the Dugdales' nanny] *alter ego*.' He told her he had washed his socks at last. The villagers kept him supplied with their home-grown vegetables. His thermometer recorded a variation of 20–30 degrees in a single day . . . 'It's sexy weather, the sort of weather for my long languors in attics. However I'm not tempted too much by provocative shapes from my window. The only shapes I can see are beaky magpies . . .'

To Kathleen Garman, now Lady Epstein, he sent condolences on the death of her husband. Epstein's last years had been stricken with tragedy: Theo, his son by Kathleen, had died in his twenties, and their daughter Esther had committed suicide over Mark Joffé, leaving young Roland Joffé's upbringing to be taken over by Lady Epstein. '[Epstein] was the greatest of them,' wrote Laurie, 'a mountain among scratching moles. I think of you & feel the loss of him but join in gratitude for the riches he left us.'

★

One August afternoon Laurie was sitting out on the steps in the heat, when he heard the sound of a galloping horse and a cry from the seventeen-acre field above him. He found a girl lying face down in the grass, blue-jeaned leg twisted, face bleeding, shirt torn. It was Gwyneth Collier, who had been thrown and dragged by her horse. She had been on her way to ask Laurie to play his guitar at a barbecue. Laurie propped her unconscious head in his arms: he was quite alone and nobody ever passed by, so he shaded her with branches, ran down and stopped a car, and an ambulance was summoned. She had a suspected skull fracture and a broken femur. 'I felt tender but awful. The smell of her blood stayed on my clothes.' Five days later she was still semi-conscious, but ate a peach. 'Miss Willa Gibbs, American writer of historical novels, who lent the horse, has got rid of it through guilt.' The local paper told the story of how 'no less a person than Laurie Lee, the poet and writer'[2] had gone to Gwyneth's aid. (And twenty-five years later Gwyneth, now Mrs Jeffries, met Laurie in Gloucester at a book-signing, and told him he had saved her life.)

'The summer has been the kind I have always remembered,' Laurie told the paper, 'a gold sun each morning and slow hot days, of people panting and saying, "Hot enough for 'ee?"' He'd dislocated a thumb playing cricket for Sheepscombe, got blown across the room by an exploding stove, and sliced a finger with a potato knife. He wrote to Kathy about the finger, now bandaged. 'Lord, how it bled. Who would have thought the old man had so much blood in him? (*Macbeth*, Act II, scene ii.) It was like a murder: blood all over the floor, the walls, and quite a bit on the ceiling.' He told her he was living on sausages, that the local cider was very strong, there were thirty-eight pubs in Stroud, and 'some beautiful girls in Stroud paper shop'. 'I was looking last night at some coloured pictures of you. Yum yum. That is all my news. Signed in blood, Your redhanded L.'

Most Friday nights he took the train to Bushton Manor, for 'warm green jasmine-scented evenings of iced gin & music among the croquet hoops'. He told Pen Dugdale that he loved Bushton best of all places 'next to this valley'. 'Don't think that any detail is ever overlooked or is not deeply cherished.'

He was quite solitary, he told everyone, in his 'Woodside Monastery'. But he was covering his tracks. One August night it was 'hot & lavender hazy, and a moon past the full rose red' when Pen's eldest daughter, Antonia, now a lithe nineteen-year-old Royal Ballet student dancer with 'dusky Alexandrian face and gold earrings', came to visit him. She had loved Laurie since the age of six, and the conviction that she was in love with him had not waned. Laurie had observed her springing about 'like a sleek young cheetah' while at Bushton, and now she came 'bouncing on her heels with frank young wanting'. Laurie knew very well how romantic those green valley slopes on summer nights could be. He had sent her a proof of *Cider with Rosie*. 'Please guard my book,' he wrote, 'I'll guard you.' 'She came a hundred miles, carrying three bottles of wine, helpless with love . . .' The late summer brought continuous baking hot golden days. Sometimes Antonia would visit in the afternoons, or they arranged to meet in London. Their relationship was to continue intermittently for ten years.

Julian Bream came down to stay before departing on an American tour. From the States he wrote Laurie long, confiding letters full of woes about problem guitars, the whistle on his strings, the audiences who would listen enraptured to the opening G minor chord of the Lachrimae Pavan, but would then repair to the bar to play 'heathenish neurotic synthetic juke boxes, blaring at full blast'. Among 'well-dressed, cheese-smiling individuals' he felt like Moses in the wilderness. 'I'd give every dollar I've earned to be back in Caracoles and with the gitanas at this moment. Or back with you in the Queen's Elm . . .' His new Mönch guitar was 'no bloody good. Sounds like a lot of rusty tin tacks being shoved around in an old baked-bean tin.' Would Laurie write a letter in Spanish to Ignacio Fleta in Barcelona 'to work the old magic & produce a real box for me'? (Laurie in fact got his Spanish doctor, Dr Martinez in Chelsea, to write the letter with noble Spanish flourishes about '*luz, alma y vida*'. Laurie went with Bream to pick up the guitar. But it didn't suit him after all.)

One August day, Norah Smallwood wrote to say that *Cider with*

Rosie was to be the Book Society choice for November. Laurie was incredulous. 'What a true proper place for this to happen – in the village and among the people . . .' He told Tom Matthews his book was 'a fluke. Self-pleasing, disjointed and quite old hat.' But he was beginning to think he might cover his advance. He also began to realize his own appeal as a native rustic son of Gloucestershire. One day at the end of August he took a bus to Stratford-on-Avon, to read his poems at Hall's Croft, as part of the Shakespeare Festival. The enchanted reaction of a local reporter – 'He captivated our hearts, and sent us away as though Puck himself had poured an unction on our eyes' – suggested the kind of reception he might expect in his home territory. 'Laurie Lee is a shy, slow-speaking, modest man. His voice is born and bred of the country. It breathes the scent of summer hay, the wind, the autumn moon and the soft voices of the woodland . . . It is good to know that such men as Laurie Lee still spread the gospel of the country to the world.'[3] After his reading Laurie dined with Shakespearian scholars ('an historic barn full of wagging beards') and on the way home stopped at Gloucester to visit Gwyneth Collier in hospital. He took her three roses, three peaches and a goldfish in a bowl.

From his sister-in-law Nora came a letter to say that Jack wanted to divorce her and marry another. Jack had first met Isabel Kidman in 1956 while he was in Adelaide working on *Robbery Under Arms* with Peter Finch. Isabel, wealthy, married with two young children, grand-daughter of the legendary Sir Sidney Kidman, 'The Cattle King' of South Australia, had opened the door to Jack and for her, it was love at first sight. Now she had come to London. Laurie wrote in sympathy to Nora, and in the light of his own new situation it is interesting that he expressed such anger with Jack, and with Jack's proposed way of dealing with a 'cliché situation'. 'Sometimes, somewhere, there's always another woman, but civilized people have always been able to cope with that one. It's not new love but a projection of the old one, and doesn't count a damn compared with a marriage. But here they go, asking for divorces, and thinking that happiness can be founded on the ruin of two families, as though that kind of happiness was one of the Rights of Man and that such

a solution is somehow frank and honest. I wonder when we'll learn that it's the children who have the rights and always have had, if parenthood makes any sense, and that nothing counts against their claims, and how one can contemplate solving a temporary or personal problem at the cost of incalculable permanent damage to two families . . . strikes me as absolutely crazy.' It was to be another three years before Jack did leave Nora for Isabel.

Laurie was back in London, in the Queen's Elm, when he saw the headline 'Cathleen Mann found dead in bed'. He should have dined with her and Tom Matthews the week before. Sleeping pills were found. 'It was impossible to expect this,' he wrote to Matthews, 'with her bright voice and that active face and her aura of life and vitality . . . What I didn't know was that she was ill and expecting to grow worse. In a way it is welcome relief to know that it wasn't plain unhappiness . . . she didn't wish to be ill or wasted, and who can say that she hadn't the right? We must die, and if one knows one must die after a great deal of suffering, why then not die before it? In any case I shall remember Cathleen as she was, all life & sparkle and dotty rainbow dresses dispensing cheer with either hand.'

Matthews, in St Louis, was distraught. 'I have lost my chance of convincing her that I loved her and didn't take her lightly . . . Oh I wish she hadn't Laurie, I wish she hadn't . . . Do you suppose that if you and Cathy and she and I had gone off somewhere together again . . . ? I'm glad we had Portofino and Ibiza . . . For God's sake let us survivors not make the same mistake of omission among ourselves, and fail to let each other know that we are here, to be counted on, to be spoken to, when necessary, from the heart.'

Laurie agreed. 'I don't know why it is that we remain so little aware of a friend's troubles – unless they actually scream for help, which they seldom do. The most unlikely of them are on the brink of hell, and we don't know it until it's too late. But you are absolutely right, we should take no chances, the least we can do is cherish and reassure.'

Laurie was with Antonia at Elm Park Gardens on a warm Sep-

tember night when the nine o'clock news announced that the Russian rocket Lunik II was nearing the moon at two miles a second and would hit the moon in twenty-one minutes. 'I made two omelettes, and the moon was out of the window, buttery golden & half full, like an omelette turned over. With a minute to go we turned off the lights, sat in the window, and watched the sky with field glasses – the moon waiting, clear & dusty . . .

'I counted 60 – the moon never changed – did I expect dust or disintegration? "Another minute," I said, "to allow for speed of light" – the wireless was linked with a Jodrell Bank telescope, & we held our hands, hearing the last bleeps of the rocket as it raced to the moon's white skin. Behind the rocket's signals were the gravel sounds of space & the raw Midlands accents of Prof Lovell's assistants. Then the signals ended abruptly. The rocket had struck.'

The next night Laurie met Kathy, home from Hydra, at Cromwell Road air terminal. She was deeply bronzed and wore a pink dress and her hair was 'quite gold, & fine gold hair on legs & arms'. They had a quiet reunion, drinking brandy till one in the morning. His notebook says: 'It's nice to be accompanied, but marriage is a kind of schizophrenia. I can only concentrate when alone . . .' This was true: Laurie increasingly saw himself as someone who preferred to be solitary, but with creature comforts attended to when he wanted them. It was not long before Kathy knew about Antonia. Because Antonia was such a close friend of both of them, and such was the generosity of Kathy's love for Laurie, she accepted this development: she had been away on Hydra for four months after all, and says she was pleased, for Laurie's sake, that he was being looked after while she was having 'a marvellous time'. No wonder their friends still speak of Laurie's good fortune in finding Kathy. Nobody else, they felt, could have stayed married to Laurie. And nobody was ever to know how she felt in her heart about it.

A few days after Kathy's return, they were at the funeral of Sir Matthew Smith. Laurie had gone with Cathleen Mann the previous year to visit him in hospital ('v yellow, old, like Chinese poet') when he grasped their green grapes in wonder: 'Aren't they

beautiful – beautiful – the shape of them – feel how heavy they are.' The mourners were 'like a scrapbook of old photographs. In front the wide white halo of Augustus John shining bright as Matthew's chrysanthemums. The gaunt South American Indian cheekbones of Lady E[pstein] – and little Kitty a gypsy beside her. The great absences of Epstein & Cathleen Mann. After the service we all spilled out on to the pavement, no one exchanging a word. (Inheritance of Matthew's passion for secrecy & keeping his friends apart?) Exotic John hobbled out & stuck a black-tarred boater on his head. He was buried at noon. There was also an eclipse of the sun.'

Two weeks later he heard that 'dear Matthew' had left him £350 in his will, 'to Laurie Lee (poet) . . .' He had also left him a portrait of the glamorous and fascinating Ann Elwell.[4] 'And I didn't see him for a year, and it's impossible to thank him.' When the cheque arrived the following March (by which time he was starting to earn money, from *Cider with Rosie*), Laurie bought a plot of land in Slad – near the war memorial, the site of the derelict cottage where Joseph and Hannah Brown had lived, the old couple in *Cider with Rosie* whose removal to the workhouse was one of the book's most moving episodes. It was also the cottage where he had taken Lorna on their golden afternoons. In fact, Laurie sold the plot some years later, without ever building on it – but Smith's money planted the seed of the return to Slad that was vital to the next stage of the Laurie Lee legend.

The day after the Tories won the October 1959 election, 'Election over & lost,' Laurie noted, 'we came back to Slad as the clouds gathered. Fields bare, scorched brown like India.' He brought Kathy back to Woodside Bungalow to introduce her to Slad life. With her, or alone, he walked for hours – from the Camp along Calfway, down Catswood Lane, through Fletcher's Farm, along the fields to Jones's pond, savouring everything. 'Found wild hops growing up the lane by the Rifleman. Last blackberries. A badger flat in hedge like a rug, run over, decayed, but with his fine head. Many paths grown over now – rabbits & children gone. Full moon at dusk, large, orange, hunter's.' In grey rain, with trees dripping, and

rainbows of oil on the roads, and cows still and steaming, 'the place looks as it ought to look'.

He filled pages of notes from bar-room conversations, with their snatches of country lore. Why trap badgers? he asked Fred Green. 'It's for the skin an' the fat, Laurie. Worth a lot that is, the skin. They makes shaving brushes wi' the 'airs, the bristles, Laurie. An' they 'as this fat just unner the skin, shift anything that will Laurie. Catch 'em in the morning, boil 'em in a copper for the fat.' He heard hilarious stories. 'Once when Fred Green drunk, they tied a foal to his bike. "Drat you, get away, stop followin' I."' In local brogue, people said 'you' for emphasis at the end of sentences. 'He got more money than I you.' 'Then 'e made a mistake you.'

Early in November Laurie's radio play *I Call Me Adam* (his last, as it turned out) was broadcast on the Third Programme. It was the story of Fletcher Christian and John Adam, the *Bounty* mutineers, setting up a new society, 'a patch of Eden' with eighteen Tahitian men and women, on the uninhabited South Sea island of Pitcairn. 'One or two good moments,' Laurie noted. 'C & I did our best to keep awake.' He thought Wilfred Babbage, as Christian, 'stiff and awful, stuffy officer type, clipped, engendering no pity'. But it was a superb play. Like *Magellan*, it is hauntingly atmospheric to read: evoking the heat and fertility of the tiny island, the labour of building, the gradual souring of ideals, the growing argument, rebellion, violence, death. Laurie had an extraordinary instinct for drama and an ear for dialogue. Strangely, there is no reference in his diaries to either the research or the writing. The play was never published and (in common with *Peasants' Priest*) it was not listed by Laurie among his works in *Who's Who*. It was eclipsed, like everything else, by *Cider with Rosie*, which immediately afterwards took over his life and made him seriously famous.

This happened almost overnight, when he was forty-five. So the account he then gave of his previous life was the one that stuck. Laurie Lee was launched as a memoirist of a rural childhood, with 'lively blue eyes and a Gloucestershire burr', a fellow of modest desires ('All I want from life is £10 a week and no questions asked') but possessing a colourful past. His legend, as issued that month in

publicity handouts, was repeated endlessly ever after: 'At twenty he ran away from home to make his fortune, went to Spain with £2 in his pocket, because someone had told him how to ask for a glass of water, and travelled from Vigo to the South playing the violin . . . He later went back to fight in the Civil War – "when it wasn't yet fashionable to oppose dictators" . . . After being nearly shot as a spy, he fought for the anti-Franco forces and broadcast from besieged Madrid' . . . 'On the Marseilles waterfront he met Cathy, the barefoot girl who danced to his guitar and later became his wife. "I fell in love with him at the age of nine," she confessed. "But of course we had to wait."' So the muddled half-facts took root.

On publication day ('Same day as Lolita,' he noted glumly) Laurie was in bed with a cold. 'A week of silence for me.' His publisher Norah Smallwood had written to every bookseller saying if this book didn't sell she'd eat her hat. Laurie noted in his diary that he had £445 in the bank, £210 in the post office and £50 in premium bonds.

From his sick-bed, feeling 'woozy', he sent a copy to Wilma, 'my best and severest critic': 'I can't hope that you will altogether approve' (but she did). He told Tom Matthews that he felt low: 'The reviews so far have been rather flat.' The first was Isobel Quigly's in the *Guardian* and she inclined to the Amis view. 'Laurie Lee's prose is of the kind that has turned "poetic" into a dirty word. Lush, strained, top-heavy, and quite painfully unsuited to most of the functions of prose, it alternates between half-embarrassing felicity and overblown, over-flavoured selfconsciousness.'

But then came Harold Nicolson in the *Observer*, who pronounced it 'a first-rate work of art'. H.E. Bates called it 'a prose poem that flashes and works like a prism'. Margaret Lane in the *Daily Telegraph* said, 'Writing about one's childhood can be a snare' but Laurie had managed to take the reader 'straight into humble hedgerow, cottage and village' without falling into the sentimental heresy that country childhood and poverty were paradise. And perhaps most influentially, J.B. Priestley, in *Reynolds News*, declared: 'I have only one

complaint against Laurie Lee – he does not offer us enough of his work . . . he produces so little that we are in danger of forgetting how good he is.

'Often he trembles on the very edge of affectation and overwriting . . . But always . . . he dances out of danger, and coins phrase after phrase with which to delight us.'

Elizabeth Jane Howard, one of the first to appreciate the book ('I'd rather please you than anyone,' he told her), asked to interview Laurie for her television programme *The Bookman*. 'No one I like talking to better,' said Laurie. 'You make me feel easy always . . . let's meet in a bar, on delicious expenses.' In the Teddington studio on a foggy day in November, they recorded the interview and he recited his poem 'Apples', but forgot the words and had to be prompted by Jane, who knew it by heart. Afterwards he sent her the poem with only the first word of each line, the rest a series of blanks: 'Love to Jane, who filled the gaps with her eyes.' Alan Ross sent a note: 'You'll be a filmstar yet, you old T V charmer.'

'One pleasure, come what may,' wrote Laurie in his notebook, 'is lying in bed with a beautiful young girl and hearing The Critics say nice things about one on the wireless.' 'Aren't these every man's dreams of paradise?' he asked his journal. 'What have I done to deserve them?'

One night, the doorbell in Elm Park Gardens rang at 2.30 a.m. 'Drunk young Irishman barges upstairs. "I wanted to see the man who wrote the most beautiful poem of the 20th century," he says. "You look like a farmer, not a poet. What are we going to do about your appearance?" He then deliciously misquoted "April Rise" – "where did you get the words, the words?" Drunk, coherent, dotty, unshaven, young. Thought we'd be stuck with him all night. He just as suddenly left us.'

Day after day came auguries of success. Foyle's Book Society ordered 100,000 copies. Siriol Hugh-Jones gave him a rapturous review on radio: 'This astonishing, entrancing, shining and sparkling and glittering book . . .' Peggy Ashcroft, visited in her dressing-room at the Royal Court, said, 'Why don't you write a play about it, & I'll play the part of your mother?' He met James MacGibbon

in the Queen's Elm to discuss getting an agent. Christopher Fry wrote a fan letter. So did Mrs Mary Wilson, wife of Harold. It was Book of the Year for Harold Nicolson, Kathleen Nott, and, in the *Sunday Times*, Dilys Powell, despite the fact that she usually found childhood reminiscences 'a thundering bore'. Laurie was cautious and bemused. 'It is selling about 250 a day. I wonder for how long?' He told Wilma: 'It is a very light & local book and I find its present success a freak of coincidence for which I thank good fortune & don't pretend to understand.' He always attributed his freakish success to having written his own dustjacket notes ('sure to become a classic') and to the printers' strike and the lack of competition: 'At Christmas there was little else on the shelves. It was either me, or James Pope-Hennessy's *Queen Mary*, or bath salts.' (In fact it was a highly competitive bestseller list that winter – including Jessica Mitford, Lady Diana Cooper, Nevil Shute, C.P. Snow and Nabokov's *Lolita*.)

The question of how true was his picture of his childhood village soon erupted in literal-minded local papers. Several set out to investigate Laurie's story of the 'forty-year-old unsolved crime' – the braggart who boasted in the pub one night of the riches he had made in New Zealand, and was found next morning frozen to death, having been beaten and thrown over a wall. Annie, back in 1945, had reminded Laurie of the story – which is perfectly plausible anyway. The *Cheltenham Chronicle* found the villagers of Slad still closed in a web of silence. But some remembered what had happened 'and some even said they knew who did it'. Charlie Green, now eighty-four, remembered the victim as 'Albert Burt, a wood turner from Small's Mills at Pitchcombe. The money was his army gratuity.' The *Stroud News* declared: 'It was exactly as Laurie Lee said' and even named one of the culprits.

Anyway, who cared? In one single day, 15 December, *Cider with Rosie* sold 1,600 copies and shops ran out of supplies. Three days later, suddenly cavalier about money, Laurie took Kathy to Paris for a weekend at the Hôtel Voltaire. (After one lavishly expensive dinner they reverted to the old favourite, Le Chop Danton, opposite L'Odéon.) And on New Year's Eve Laurie took a party to the

Chelsea Arts Ball: Nicolette and Esmond Devas, Norah Smallwood, Janey Ironside, Norman and Jill Hepple, Tom Matthews and his wife Martha Gellhorn. It sounds hellish: everyone packed in 'like potted brawn'; a cold supper distributed, of '1 polythene-wrapped baby chicken, 1 tomato, 1 roll, 1 sheet lettuce' and 'glasses ritually smashed & trodden on floor. Many scant-dressed girls.' Laurie apologized to Tom Matthews afterwards; it was not the civilized scene to which he was accustomed.

Cider with Rosie had a brief preface: 'The book is a recollection of early boyhood, and some of the facts may be distorted by time.' A getout clause. But it did not save Laurie from a libel action. A man in a mackintosh arrived one morning at Elm Park Gardens. Kathy answered the door and was told, 'Madam, I have to give you this.' It was a writ from Bentleys, the Stroud Piano Company of Woodchester, which objected to the line on page 272: 'There was a fire at the piano works almost every year, it seemed to be a way of balancing the books.' Bentleys had been making pianos in the area for fifty-four years, although Laurie had no idea of their existence.

'Ending 1959 with the book heading the lists of Christmas bestsellers,' noted Laurie, 'then we run out of stock and get slapped with a libel.' They went to Bushton, but 'Christmas ruined,' says Laurie's notebook. 'Books withdrawn from all Glos libraries & shops. None in London anyway. Christmas & the book is poisoned.'

Laurie was at top table at the Foyle's 'To Greet the Sixties' lunch
in January 1960, and the new decade boded well. *Cider with Rosie*
was on top of the bestseller list, and was serialized everywhere. As
sales neared 100,000 Pat Kernon, his accountant, gave advice on
surtax. Publishers and magazines clamoured with contracts. Very
soon, a small ad in *The Times* offered 'Furnished cottage and 5 acres
woodland high on remote Cotswold hill overlooking "Cider With
Rosie" valley.' Rosie even became a *Times* Crossword clue: '28
Across: With her, cider.'

But there were clouds in Laurie's blue sky, and not just because
of the libel writ. 'I stopped walking on air and started wading
through protests. A chill wind blew from the west . . .'[1] Writing
about one's family is always a minefield, and Laurie's Aunt Alice
and cousin Frances were deeply upset by his tales of Uncle Sid and
his fake 'suicides'. When the *Evening Standard* billboards advertised
'Uncle Sid' for part three of its serialization, Laurie 'telephoned
and stopped it'. The *Standard* rang next day: 'Uncle Sid slipped out
in Birmingham.' Laurie rang his cousin Frances and wrote 'Hope
it's alright' in his diary.

It was not all right, and he had to draft craven letters: 'Dear
Frances, What can I say? What I wrote was written purely out of
pride & affection for a remarkable man who was also my favourite
uncle. Don't you realize that your father has always been a great
legend in the district, admired & respected by all . . . and that he
was the hero of my boyhood? The last thing I wished to do was
to hurt any of you. I have always loved your family. I may not
have shown it, & you may not believe it, but it is true.

'Your letter has made me almost sick with unhappiness. I cannot
bear . . . to have unwittingly been the cause of your anger. I only

hope that you will live to learn that my affection and loyalty has never wavered for you all, & never will. Laurie.'

He wrote another to his aunt ('Please read this') saying he was 'desperately unhappy, grieved to the uttermost', and 'dear Auntie I could weep'. He implored Jack to go and set things right. 'I walked into the lion's den,' Jack says. 'It took all day, but I relished the battle. Frances kept saying "How could he!" I had to say, you must understand that Laurie loves you. And eventually they made peace. Laurie had done the same kind of thing for me, over the girl I was supposed to marry.'

Then there was the libel. When the writ arrived, Laurie's first instinct was to go down to the piano factory and apologize. His publishers urged him to do nothing: their solicitors would handle it. But the resulting apology and disclaimer (describing *Cider* as 'a novel') appeared in Hogarth's name only, not Laurie's. 'The piano works, infuriated by what seemed a deliberate withdrawal on my part, went for me with a personal writ demanding heavy damages,' as Laurie recounted it. Laurie's diary says: 'Piano works now after *my* blood.' They were asking £5,000. 'This is literary success,' noted Laurie drily. The case was not to be heard in the High Court until July, with the payment of damages by Laurie and Hogarth.

But in other respects 1960 was an *annus mirabilis*. The writer Margaret Lane, the Countess of Huntingdon, who had reviewed *Cider* so warmly, held a glamorous dance at her house in Roehampton. Lady Selina Hastings, the elder daughter of the house, wearing her first off-the-shoulder black dress, told Laurie she had loved *Cider with Rosie*. 'And he spent the entire evening with me. He was so seductive. He said "I'm no good with all these sophisticated people. I'd much rather be with you." I fell completely in love with him. We danced, and sat in the garden, and he held my hand and said, "May I kiss you?" and kissed me very gently, and then asked me how old I was; I said fifteen, which I wasn't until March. It was my first kiss. He wrote to my mother afterwards, "Selina took wonderfully good care of me and I have some crushed gold baubles in my pocket as a memento."' (She didn't see him

again for thirty-five years, when he had a book launch at the Arts Club in Dover Street. Laurie was at the top of the stairs, leaning on his stick, almost blind. She went up to him and said, 'Laurie,' and he said at once, 'Is that Selina?')

But at the ball, all eyes were on Kathy, dancing in her shimmering grey-green gown. Laurie's wife was in her prime at twenty-eight, a decided asset. She was declared to be among London's most beautiful women and was frequently painted and sculpted.[2] At the Dorchester for the presentation of the Foyle's Poetry Prize to Robert Graves, Laurie sat next to Dame Sybil Thorndike and wore a piratical patch over one eye. On his souvenir programme he wrote to Kathy, 'I can see with only half an eye that you're the best girl in the room.' Mrs Laurie Lee was described by the *Guardian* next day as 'the Alexandrian type' of beauty.

But to a Spanish journalist, Rafael Pineda, Señora Lee was 'a woman with exquisite Saxon beauty, reminiscent of the sublime models of the painter Bainsborough [sic]'. Pineda interviewed Laurie for *El Nacional* about '*Un Vaso de Sidra con Rosie*' and addressed Laurie throughout in the formal Spanish style as '*Poeta*'. 'Poet, permit me to congratulate you on your extremely beautiful wife,' he began, whereupon 'Cathy, in a pose of classic serenity, vibrated delicately.'

'Poet, what is the dominant note in modern English poetry?' Laurie replied that it was neo-puritanism; young poets were frightened of language '*genuino e incandescente*'. Amis and Wain – '*Los Jóvenes Furiosos*' (angry young men) – suffered from a British disease: fear of sentiment, of saying what they felt. 'They resort to satire or obstruct their language with an esotericism which says nothing.' Amis, he said, disliked writers who wrote about abroad: 'but then Homer would never have written about Troy'. Asked to define linguistic puritanism, Laurie replied: 'The fear of using words whose temperature exceeds 35 degrees Fahrenheit.'

That spring, *Cider with Rosie* was launched in America as *The Edge of Day*. Laurie had not wanted the title changed, but his publishers (Morrow) assured him, 'There is no sale of cider in the States. The closest thing to your cider is applejack, and that has a rather low standing in the minds of American drinkers.' Then D.C.

Jarvis's *Folk Medicine* (an American book) came out, advocating cider-and-honey as a panacea, and *The Times* reviewed it under the headline 'Cider with Jarvis'. Laurie sent off this review to Morrow. They replied that Jarvis's remedy was 'not cider at all but cider vinegar, a very different thing'.

Anyway the American reception was ecstatic. Even Dorothy Parker found it 'an entirely delightful experience'. 'Charm is a word that it is as well to keep away from, if possible, and so is beauty, but I think both are needed in speaking of *The Edge of Day*. This is not to say that parts of it are not exceedingly funny . . .' Elizabeth Janeway warned: 'Read straight through, it is almost too warm and glowing and may provoke those inclined to skepticism to go looking for an old copy of Stella Gibbons's *Cold Comfort Farm*.' Tom Matthews, whose own childhood book *Name and Address* was also out, wrote in the *New York Times*: 'Laurie Lee has done it. Blessed be his name.'

Laurie was keeping notes on the effects of success. No longer did people respond, when introduced to 'Laurie Lee, the poet' by asking him if he'd ever known Dylan Thomas. Writer friends would say: 'Ah, rich now, eh?' 'as if I got away with the slate club funds'. His family, he recorded, were 'kindly but cold. I had blown the gaffe on early family poverty – as though the neighbours never knew.' (It must be galling for his family, he conceded, 'after spending 35 years building up a background of affluence' to know that people were reading about how poor they once were.)

'Some villagers look away when they see me, others (that weren't mentioned) slap me on back and offer me a drink. All swear my story is false. All have different version. One old man who clipped my ear not so long ago now calls me "Sir". Always wanted to go back. Hope to buy cottage. [He'd been offered '2 cottages for £1,500' in Slad.] Never had so many free meals. Writing energy goes into answering letters.' This was certainly true: he was getting more than twenty letters a day.

'Are you enjoying your celebrity, or does it leave you no time for your work?' wrote Wilma perceptively, from a hospital bed in Devon, having had her appendix removed. 'Very diffidently, I

venture to suggest that you might find it worthwhile, before long, to write about your months with the International Brigade.' It was three decades before he took Wilma's advice. But meanwhile, the *Evening Standard* asked Laurie to reminisce about his teenage years, so he related – for the first time in print – a brief résumé of his wanderings in Spain and his unwitting arrival at 'the heart of the 30s tragedy'. 'The Spanish Civil War found me trapped in a village on the coast near Málaga. Through the dust of battle came a neat British destroyer to take off its nationals. Tattered tramp though I was, bearing no more than a fiddle, I was piped aboard to a salute of officers.'

Wilma, by now living in London – within a mile of Laurie, in Redcliffe Gardens – read this tale in the *Standard* with indignation. There was no mention of her vital part in his story. She wrote to him denying that they were piped aboard the destroyer, and questioning his version of his adventures. Laurie replied the following day: 'My dear Wilma: You do pack a wallop I must say. You are right of course, yet quite wrong. There was nothing in that article that was untrue, but there were important omissions which I had to make, including yourself. A short newspaper piece was no place to bring in everything. You must wait till I write a book about it . . .'

The eventual book, *As I Walked Out One Midsummer Morning*, made no mention whatever of Wilma; in the episode of his evacuation from Almuñécar ('and all for a couple of tramps') he said he was accompanied by 'an English writer', anonymous and genderless. But by the time he published that, Wilma was dead.

Freedom to travel, Laurie had said, was what *Cider*'s success brought. Laurie and Kathy seemed to enjoy this freedom already, but in the summer of 1960 they broke even their own travelling records. They went to Portofino again, returned to Martigues and to Andalucía, and in the autumn made their first trip to the United States. But first, at Easter, they were invited to Wolfsgarten, a sixteenth-century hunting lodge near Darmstadt on the Rhine, with peacocks and golden pheasants, and wild boar in the forests.

Celia Goodman had introduced Laurie to her friend Peg, *née* Margaret Campbell Geddes, now Princess Peg, wife of Prince Ludwig of Hesse.[3] The Hesses combined good works and arts patronage with lavish hospitality on a truly royal scale at their several castles. Despite a horrendous start to their marriage – an air crash had wiped out almost all Prince Ludwig's family who were en route for England to attend his wedding in 1937 – 'Lu' and Peg were a singularly joyful and devoted couple. Laurie and Kathy took the Trans-Europe Express to find a chauffeur in grey waiting at Frankfurt. 'Mad Royal Easter,' Laurie's notebook says. 'Bach Passion & Mozart Seraglio in Darmstadt. Breakfast with Prince of Hanover, lunch with Princess Metternich (& meal at their great palace on Rhine), tea with Bismarcks – all related to Queen Victoria & Tsarina of Russia. My bedroom huge with tapestries, covered bath, Van Dycks. Silver oddments, matches, engraved L for Ludwig.' It was the first of many visits. 'Lupeg', as the couple styled themselves, were very smitten with Mr and Mrs Lee.

Laurie came home with a fever. But hardly had they returned from Germany when they set off for six weeks in Italy, France and Spain. The first stop was Portofino again with Tom Matthews and Martha Gellhorn. Laurie and Tom flew to Milan, writing silly quatrains en route:

The country poet in the air
Should question what he's doing there.
He thinks he's Godot, even God,
His feet are clay, or maybe clod.

and:

Flying over white Mont Blanc
One is British, one is Yank;
Both are wrapped in one wool blanket
And still airborne – God be thank it!

and last thoughts:

Let the cloud be my shroud
But please bury me in Stroud.

They met Kathy, who had been to Lake Garda, and again porters hauled their bags up the steep climb to Il Castelletto on a hot thundery night. Matthews, disciplined as ever, worked each morning, but was sick and low-spirited. Laurie spent many wakeful nights, 'disturbed by T walking the terrace'. He and Kathy would escape into Santa Margharita, 'much cheaper than Portofino'. After dinner one night, Martha Gellhorn wanted to go dancing but 'T already rather far gone'. Matthews fell heavily on the uphill trek home by torchlight. Laurie accompanied him to a doctor in Genoa, who put him on the wagon. The Mistral came roaring in, 'a smooth metal-grey porridge of cloud'. Then it was Laurie's turn to be ill, with a fever. He was disenchanted with Portofino: 'Something entirely characterless about this town, it's like living in A Present from Polperro – the deadness of people who have always lived only for tourists.'

Things cheered up with the arrival of Julian Bream. (Laurie liked introducing Bream to friends: he also took him to Bushton that year where the young Dugdales performed for him. 'He's a very easy going chap, but being a professional isn't at all easy to please,' Laurie told Pen. 'But I know how moved & touched he was by Teresa's and Sam's playing. As for Antonia's dancing, I doubt whether the like of it has often been seen in Wiltshire.')

After Portofino's annual million-lire firework display Laurie and Kathy were driven by Julian Bream through Provence to Martigues. Then they took trains and buses to Barcelona, Valencia and Albacete, hitched a lift to Jaén and eventually reached Málaga. While in Málaga they took a bus up to Churriana where the writer Gerald Brenan, 'Don Geraldo', the doyen of British exiles in Spain,[4] held court. 'Brenan like a mandarin, facially reminiscent of Henry Miller,' noted Laurie. 'Bought house in 1953 for £1,200 – frankly finds it cheaper – wife charming slow-spoken Southern American bit like Auntie K [Kathleen Epstein].' Under a broad nispera tree, *gambas al pil-pil* were served in a garden blazing with blue jacaranda and

scarlet catalpa. A coterie of the 'Gargoyle Set' from the Soho drinking club were there, including Henrietta Moraes, who had lived with Michael Wishart, modelled for Lucian Freud and was a painter herself ('no talent really but GB encourages with all conviction of old man lusting for young girl'). Everyone prattled of parties in Marbella and Torremolinos, 'all threatening to go to Rocío – ugh,' wrote Laurie. It was a foretaste of what was beginning to destroy his beloved Andalucian coast. Torremolinos was already 'like Peacehaven, based on the cheap peseta'.

They next got off the bus at Estepona and finally reached Algeciras ('this town still my favourite'), where their old waiter friend Manolo served plates of snails and *callos* (tripe), and they went with Geraldine Lawrence to a bullfight: at the kill the matador 'stared at bull as though at angry father in family crisis'. During the evening *paseo*, in the little white streets near the brothels, children sang and danced for them: 'erotic pushing of hips, perfect foot stamps, serene proud smile, arms up; what freedom, confidence these children have – slapped down only for bad manners to strangers'. They saw Francis Bacon, 'seedy and sinister', in a bar with a friend.

Laurie was not well and the June heat was fierce. 'I haven't written a word,' he wrote to Tom Matthews from Gibraltar. 'I wish I had your discipline.' Gerald Brenan sympathized: 'One doesn't write well in this country. The mind goes to pieces. One just indulges one's sadness and one's euphoria and one's bent for frivolity.'

The Stewarts of Gibraltar[5] had long urged Laurie to come to the Romería del Rocío before tourists ruined it. A new easy road had just opened. 'Original *rocieros* like us, who drove through rivers to get there and slept on the ground, feel aggrieved,' wrote John Stewart. His wife added: 'How many times have we and Geraldine said, as we broke into our second gallon of *vino*, "If only Laurie and Cathy were here . . . We're tired of taking deadbeats there, ineffectual gapers. We even took Gerald Brenan who was chasing after a piece of Torremolinos tail and must have seen quite a unique view of Rocío through her languid thighs. What about all that lovely lolly that must be pouring in from your golden book? Take a handful and come. Our *coche* awaits . . . *Cariñosamente* Joan.'

The *Gibraltar Chronicle* reported that the writer Laurie Lee had visited the police station in Irish Town. 'Twenty five years ago a very young and tattered Laurie Lee arrived with a fiddle, three pesetas and two very sore feet. He had not sufficient funds to enter Gibraltar, but he was given a bed for a few nights in a cell.' Out to the dusty plains they drove next day, with Geraldine and the Stewarts and the Searles[6] pitching their tents near Puerto Santa María, and talking under eucalyptus trees over demijohns of red wine until they realized that it was no longer sunset but sunrise. Mrs Searle (dark) and Kathy (blonde) made a striking pair, dancing Sevillanas for the crowds. But in the middle of all the excitement Laurie had an epileptic fit. 'I said, "I think there's something wrong with Laurie,"' John Searle recalls. 'Everyone was clapping, it was very noisy. Spanish dancing and clicking can have a psychological effect on people. Luckily Dr Toomey was with us.'

'I thought you were so *tough* the way you sweated out that fever. I am quite sure there is some curious troubling spirit unleashed in that place,' said Geraldine later. She wrote from the quay at Algeciras to tell Laurie, now back in England, that Kathy had left for Italy 'looking like a goddess carved in amber'. Manolo, bringing shrimps, had asked after Laurie 'and I told him that you *tuvo calentura* [had a fever] at the Romería. He said I was to tell you *se les echaban mucho de menos y que se allieve.* [They missed him and wished him better.] *Que se allieve bien, Lorenzo, Geraldina.*'

Laurie had missed the Royal Academy summer exhibition which included a group portrait, *Concert at the Chelsea Arts Club 1960*, by Paul Wyeth – with a fur-hatted Laurie playing his recorder. He had also missed the BBC arts programme *Monitor* on the sculpture of Lis Frink, featuring Laurie's commentary and an interview with her in the Queen's Elm. Her *Bird Men* (one of which Laurie had bought for £100) were 'the most personal and unsettling apparitions Frink has given us', he said. 'They might have been bred for Edgar Allan Poe. They are no springtime choristers, they are augurs of death. If they sang they would spit out splinters of iron.' That summer Laurie also took part in a programme on Epstein.

By then he was back in Slad at his bungalow in the Vatch, playing

music with old friends including Arthur Swain at Painswick, basking on Swift's Hill on midsummer day among moon daisies, purple orchids, thistle and vetch. Blackbirds and pigeons were loud in the mornings. He was filmed in his old haunts for a BBC programme produced by Monica Sims, who recalls that Laurie knew exactly where wild strawberries could be found, and stood on Painswick Beacon, saying, 'This is where Charles I walked up the hill to hold his parliament in Painswick, and looked down on the Cromwellian troops in the valley.' He umpired cricket. He picked 'enough mushrooms for a week of breakfasts'. As the local author he opened the first of many village fêtes at Woodchester: Kathy was presented with a bouquet, and Laurie made a speech, to prolonged applause, about the lost rural world, deploring the commercialization of everything: 'We are a starved society living in the midst of plenty; our possessions are many, our satisfactions few.' He also 'sold £30 worth of autographed *Ciders*, and won five bottles of beer & one Gordon's gin', he told Tom Matthews. 'I was the golden boy. They began to treat me with sardonic pride. I spent much of the summer weighing marrows and tasting cakes. I was briefly the valley's favourite son.' On his forty-sixth birthday he was presented with no fewer than three old cider horns.

This return-of-the-native act in Slad was an astute move in creating the Laurie Lee legend. As he said, 'Every branch of every tree, every curve of every field, and every twist of every hedgerow is the mythology of my life.' In retrospect he thought it took courage to go back: he had left Slad as 'a turnip-faced grinning oaf', and instead of coming home on his knees, begging for church bread,[7] 'I returned a bag-eyed poet who had written a book about them all, and broken taboos.' He had revealed local legends. 'This upset them in the way that tribal Blacks can be upset by somebody taking their photographs. They think their souls are being damaged or stolen. They are still wary of me. They put a finger to their lips when I come into the Woolpack and say "Careful what you say, he'll put you in a book."' Nevertheless, what they said in the pub filled enough notebooks to furnish another *Cider* volume, if he'd wanted. 'Old Wally Bishop now in pub every night. His brother

had just drowned in a water tank. Late brother kept him in order. Gets deranged on one drink; is now deranged daily . . .' 'Met old Bill Tuck (84) in his green Elcombe corner. Once a quarryman and stonemason. Did the stonework of Uplands church, the drywall at Bulls Cross.' 'Beautiful young village girls in short stiff-petticoated bell-like frocks, piercingly light & graceful, with their bare legs glimpsed in the high grass.' He struck up a close drinking companionship with Frank Mansell, who worked for the telephone company but also wrote poetry, 'as Cotswold as a dry-stone wall'.

Though Laurie was writing no new poetry now – his output to date was sixty-seven poems – he was still known as a poet who had written a book, rather than (as later) a prose writer who had formerly written poems. In June, a Pocket Poets edition of Laurie Lee was published in a Vista Books series priced at 2s 6d that included Rupert Brooke, Edward Thomas and Gerard Manley Hopkins. Laurie wrote a foreword to say that he 'scarcely recognized' his early verses but was 'not yet prepared to disown' them. He ordered two dozen copies. He had dedicated this little book 'To Y'.

The libel case was eventually heard in the High Court on 19 July. Helenus Milmo QC declared that the piano factory fire was an imaginary episode; Laurie recognized that he had written something untrue and damaging. He was to pay 'substantial' damages of £5,000, a cost shared between himself and Hogarth. He told Wilma that the libel had 'clouded much of my pleasure in the book's reception & also I feel polluted it in some way – dragging into court a book never intended to attack anyone . . . The paragraph was merely a jaunty little fantasy which mentioned pianos because I like them . . . I didn't even know this firm existed any more.' None of the publishers' lawyers had spotted the danger. 'Do you wonder I'm cross?' Wilma assured him that 'Your wonderful book has NOT been polluted by that wretched libel case; nothing can tarnish its beauty nor shake its lasting value.'

The lasting value of first editions, of course, was increased by the libel. In later editions, piano factory became 'boiler factory', chords became 'booms', and the sentence 'It seemed to be a way of balancing the books' vanished altogether. (Years later when Val

Hennessy told Laurie she had an edition with the libel in it, Laurie 'grabbed it from me and I almost had to fight him to get it back'.)

But argument persisted over the principle of using fictional stories in biography. 'If we know that one episode in the book is untrue, can we have any confidence in other episodes?' one R. Rowland Hill asked in *John O'London's Weekly*, whose editor defended Laurie: 'An autobiography is "recollection in tranquillity". It need not be true in the sense that a legal document is true.' Laurie added his 'nine pennyworth': 'My book was classified as "an autobiography" ... but ... it was an attempt to give the *feel* of my early years, of a countryside & people.' Hence his short preface: 'The book is a recollection of early boyhood, and some of the facts may be distorted by time.'

'Memory can be more real than events,' he wrote in a notebook. 'Details may differ but the shape, the feeling remains. If all my friends who shared that life wrote their recollections I think not one version would agree with another.' And in his later essay on 'Writing Autobiography' he confronted the question again: 'If dates are wrong, can the book still be true? If facts err, can feelings be false? ... In writing autobiography, especially one that looks back at childhood, the only truth is what you remember.'

Another piece of Laurie mythology was developing too: of leading two separate lives, in town and country. The village had the stories, but London's social life was vital to him; and he could work there, better than in Slad. He began to see his Gloucestershire valley as 'like a novel in which you're present throughout the year, a kind of unfolding of a long tale, in which you're conscious of everything that's happening through lives, deaths, childhoods, and so on. I find London a kind of anthology, almost a bedside book of snippets of life and gossip. It's a snippet world, London.'

Often, when he went to London, Antonia would meet him at Paddington station, ready to drive him to poetry readings or literary luncheons. She was happy to be there just when he needed her, she says. She could not have married him, or seen him more than once a week or fortnight. 'The strain of pleasing him was so great, it could never be relaxing: one was always trying to get it right;

but you felt wonderful if you did.' And he was appreciative. Laurie knew how lucky he was.

Kathy says theirs was a marriage 'against the odds' but she always believed she had done the right thing; and continued to send Laurie sentimental Victorian Valentine cards ('How do I love thee? Let me count the ways . . .') signed 'Madame Lee'. She had, after all, both an inborn Garman family attitude, like her aunts Kathleen and Mary (beautiful wife serving the needs of a genius husband), and a Mediterranean acceptance of a woman's place. Life with Laurie still offered plenty of amusement. Kathy won the shipboard quiz when they sailed from Southampton on the *Mauretania* for New York in August 1960.

Laurie was at first dismayed by the 'chaste silences' of life on a great liner, and was cheered by the Irish influx in Cork Bay: 'boys in blue serge suits, just like the boys in Stroud – violins and accordions playing & the older boys drinking and singing – certainly liven up the old place'. American reporters found Laurie 'a highly unorthodox character'. He arrived with his violin, a guitar ('picked up in a poker game', they were told) and his recorder. His first stops in New York were Fulton's Fish Market ('my wife's a fisherman's daughter') and the top of the Empire State 'but he can't stand heights'. The *Herald Tribune*'s Maurice Dolbier was sceptical: 'A poet with a dazzling imagination and a lively sense of humor could make difficulties for any interviewer soberly intent on separating fact from fancy.' Had Laurie really seen President Tito on Fifth Avenue? Was it true that Congo tribesmen are crazy about Guinness? (Maybe.) He was 'a poet who writes an occasional lyric for the gin people, paid in kind, to sidestep the tax man'. He praised American writers, reeling off the names of Salinger, Faulkner, Hemingway, McCullers, Capote, McCarthy for their vitality of language. 'By comparison now, English is pretty cold cabbage.' (But when asked by Elizabeth Jane Howard, for *Queen* magazine, 'Which three living writers do you think will have the most impact on society?' Laurie said he couldn't answer 'because I'm not much of a reading man'.) *Newsweek* recounted his 'peripatetic 46 years as a bandleader, poet, wandering minstrel, scenario writer, and

volunteer in the International Brigade in Spain' and asked if he would go on with autobiography. Laurie replied that the Spanish Civil War had been 'done to death'.

They jetted home in time for the presentation of the W.H. Smith award to Laurie. This was worth £1,000 – more than he had earned in a lifetime of poetry writing. In the Lincoln Room at the Savoy, in front of television cameras, he received the cheque from Peggy Ashcroft's elegantly gloved hands. (Afterwards, 'Cheque went round pub, kissed, creased, covered with lipstick, had to be ironed.') He said he would use the money 'to buy freedom and confidence and time . . .' He thanked his publishers, 'whoever they are' (still disgruntled about the libel), and said, 'Little did I think when Rosie first led me under the hay wagon . . . that she was leading me to these glorious halls, and to this illustrious company . . .' On stage was a cart of apples, and at the end of the evening he let off an indoor firework that showered streams of coloured paper over an audience that included Leonard Woolf, Yehudi Menuhin and Ian Fleming.

He told Celia Goodman, 'I have a strong suspicion that when the judges [C.V. Wedgwood, William Plomer and Harold Nicolson] sat over the dinner table staring at the short list, one of them said, "Oh let's give it to Lee, it'll help pay off his debts." I know how the lightest straw can affect a decision of this kind.' (But twenty-five years later Dame Veronica Wedgwood declared that literary worth was the sole criterion to her 'austere literary mind' and she had absolutely no doubts about the book's quality: it had a magical freshness, every page was written with affection, and it was 'so enormously alive; you can hear the voices'.[8]) In interviews, Laurie played the rustic: 'I'm a peasant by nature and upbringing. I'm not going to go mad and spend it on wild women and fast cars.'

The following day he was writing in the *Evening Standard* about how success had changed his life. It was 'mixed grit and honey'. Some friends avoid you, he said; total strangers invite you, letters arrive demanding advice. You can go to France for the weekend, or to America. 'Then this beautiful cheque, £1,000 and no questions asked . . . Few poets, save the dead, make a living today. Free time to a writer is like canvas to a painter. Apart from poetry I've written

only two books of prose – scarcely sufficient to prop up a piano. But without some form of patronage to buy me the time, I doubt that I could have written either.' Would he write a sequel to *Cider*? 'I'm too scared as yet to try.'

Laurie was on an unimagined pinnacle of fame. At a party in November he met T.S. Eliot, whose attitude to publicity was the antithesis of Laurie's; in St Louis, he told Laurie, *Life* magazine had made his life a misery by following him wherever he went. *Cider with Rosie* was parodied in *Punch* ('Raindrops glittered on the whitethroat-happy hedge in shifting opalescent arabesques and the leaves were a filigree of chrysoprase against the washed Aegean-blue of the over-arching sky . . .') 'Laurie Lee' became an answer on *Round Britain Quiz*: 'Who was paid £1,000 to buy freedom, confidence & time?' They guessed it.

But nothing that year could compare with what happened to Laurie at the end of November. It was his habit to call at the Queen's Elm on the way home. In Sean Treacy's pub, famous for 'the best conversation in Chelsea', he could always find friends, have a game of snooker, play his fiddle or recorder, and stay after hours. 'Dropped in at Queen's. Drink till 2 a.m. That's a pub,' as he noted one night in October.

On 28 November 1960, while Kathy was visiting her mother in Italy, Laurie was playing his violin in a quartet at a friend's house in Old Church Street. This is how he described the evening in his notebook. 'Left at 8. Looked for Satellite Echo in frosty sky. Called at Queen's Elm. Sean there, James Cameron, wife & daughter. Showed me a write-up in *Harpers*. Fetched out fiddle. Played two quick reels. Bar not very full. Caught sight in mid-reel of rosy-cheek girl, watching me, curled mouth, shy sly smile, loose dark hair, fringe. But the eyes blue & red mouth. I felt an astonishing shaft go through me. Not thinking I felt it, I knew. In a moment the girl had gone through the door. I had to follow her & called. She turned, smiling faintly. "What's your name?" I said. "Why?" "Well, I'm sure I've met you before." (Corn.) Still smiling: "You have, once. My name's Yasmin."

'21 years old. So like Johnny Lee [Jack's son]. Working for a flower shop, lodging Notting Hill. She stood looking at me. Smiling. I still had my violin in my hand. "Stay here. Don't go away. Promise you won't go away." "I promise." I dumped the violin. Came back. She was waiting.

'Off into the cold night. She chattering. Amused, quick, young, old, nervous, shy, excited. Meal at New Assam. Drink. Walking. Me shivering with pleasure. Holding arms. She talking. Mother's inflections. How she'd planned to do it. Nearly lost her nerve. Saw thing in *Harpers*. Made up her mind. Knew there was something. Had suspected for years. Asked her mother right out. "What d'you think?" said she. Back home. So natural. Lay on the bed till 3 a.m. Me half asleep. Happy. She still chattering, chattering, filling up 20 years . . .

'Morning. Coffee at Lyons. Which she likes. As her mother & I did. Smiling with I swear love. Promising to see me again. Soon. The greatest occasion of my life? Simply was. But will she? . . .'

Two days passed. He began to think he'd been a fool to let her go. She might write and say, 'I'm sorry. I was crazy. Goodbye.' He was changing to go out at 6 p.m. when she rang. 'It was all right. "Don't worry," she said. We talked on and on. We should both have been somewhere. "What have we been doing all these 20 years?" she said. She hadn't eaten much since Monday. Could I meet her midday Friday? It didn't matter what we did, or where we went, did it? We ought to see a lot of each other . . .'

'London suddenly seems to make sense,' he noted. 'At parties, not caring, smiling to self.'

Yasmin says that in her teens she had had a growing feeling, in her heart, that Wish was not her father. After Frensham Heights School she had gone to Worthing College of Art – where Laurie had watched her one day, he later confessed, coming out of college. When she bought the little Pocket Poets edition of Laurie's verse, and saw the dedication 'To Y', 'It was just too odd. I thought, this means something.'

'I really didn't think, when I went to see him, that anything would develop between us. I didn't know that he would be so

quick, and would recognize me at once. It was hilarious in the Indian restaurant. He just glowed. And he introduced me to poppadums.'

Later Yasmin went for a walk with Wish, wondering how to broach the subject of Laurie, 'and he was very sweet, and broached it himself'. He said he had always thought that Yasmin should have been told when younger, but had been advised that it would complicate an already dramatically charged family. The differences between Wish, the committed Communist, and Lorna, the Catholic convert, had been exacerbated by extreme passion on both sides. 'Both of them were fanatical. So their politics and religion had polarized them.' But Wish had been a totally loving and accepting father to Yasmin. She remembers long walks with him, when he searched for flints and arrowheads.

'But I was Lorna's child. "I wanted a poet's child, and I got one," my mother told me. And I thought, "This is all very romantic and beautiful but what about me as me?" I wasn't free of all that until I married.'

How did Lorna react when Yasmin went to find Laurie? 'I think it threw her rather and made her feel insecure. She was quite possessive: her things were her things, and I was *her* daughter. She didn't show any great joy, I must admit,' Yasmin says. 'She was having her tonsils out at the time. But after she'd had time to process it she was pleased, for me. Then it became very normal and civilized.'

Laurie and Yasmin began going on outings, just walking round London; they sent Lorna a postcard of Nelson's column. 'What I loved about Laurie immediately was his capacity for enjoyment. My family were lovely but they did not have that sense of freedom that he had.' He took Yasmin to the point on Battersea Bridge where he had thrown Lorna's letters into the Thames and watched them come bobbing back on the tide. They went to Westminster Abbey, and to Brighton.

'Darling Yasmin: I loved our day by the sea,' he wrote. 'I told Cathy last night and of course she doesn't mind & was very moved by it all, and you must meet soon.' As Yasmin's cousin, Kathy knew, of course, that Laurie was Yasmin's father. Laurie, elated,

confided in Pen Dugdale: she was flattered to be singled out for his confidence.

That which was lost was found. All Laurie's atavistic feelings were released. He even told Yasmin about the carapace he had been enclosed in since 1944. 'I adored seeing you . . . Thank you dear love for your red-sealed letter & all you said in it. It is meat & drink, red wine & beef, to have these thoughts from you. I, too, have a shell, though it's not as pretty as yours, and I've been in it for years. But we don't need shells any more in fact, unless it gets stormy & then we'll share one together.

'I'm glad we wandered into the Abbey . . . the vanity of the rich dead, who want to be remembered, is rather touching, like the poor who scratch their names beneath the rich men's tombs. But most of us want it really, and I wanted it through you, and never thought I had it till now, and that's better than any old Abbey.'

He sent her his childhood pictures, and one of himself playing the fiddle in the pub, 'a memento of you know what – that wonderful miraculous chancy Chelsea night which I shall treasure until I die. Sometimes, waking in the night, or in moments of panic during the day, my mind used to fill with moments of past horrors. Now it fills with that occasion, and the sheer happiness of it, the unbelievableness of it, is like salvation floating ashore in a bottle.'

19 | Rose Cottage
1961

'Don't desert me whatever you do,' Laurie wrote to Yasmin. 'You are the one spark in my shadowy life.' Shadowy feelings did lurk behind Laurie's conviviality, as some suspected: disappointment, guilt, old torments of Lorna's rejection, his failure to have a child with Kathy. Now he was rejuvenated: Lorna had left him, but Yasmin had come back. Yasmin's letters were wax-sealed with a 'Y', 'but I think you should get some red wax,' he told her. 'The silver, though elegant, looks like something raked out of the Aga on a grey morning.' He kept her letters 'in a little pile, like banknotes . . . Every so often I grow panicky & take them from the drawer expecting to find dust. But there they are, plump & warm, and I stare & can't believe it.' (He sent 'oblique love to mum'.)

Yasmin showered him with Christmas presents, just as her mother had – 'candles & purses of gold, a bagatelle table, and a musical box'. He told her: 'You are my Christmas angel, but don't disappear from me . . . I love you.' He wanted to seize the 'perhaps little' time they had left. But he was, as usual, going away. Princess Peg had invited Laurie and Kathy back to Wolfsgarten for 'a genuine old world German Weihnachten Christmas'. With Julian Bream and his guitar they left for Dover, Laurie writing to Yasmin as they raced through Kent, 'where all the black leafless bushes stand in rows of Ys'.

On Christmas Eve at Wolfsgarten there was 'a banquet of Princes (Hanover, Bismarck, Metternichs & Hesses)' but Laurie stayed in bed with a fever. 'Then in the middle of the night,' as he told Yasmin, 'the castle burnt down. Drunken firemen were called from their Christmas parties, and we were forced to flee into the snow carrying the princess's jewels.'

It was true. Julian Bream was sleeping in the guest wing, where he woke up to hear '*Feuer!*' (He was, he says, later held responsible

'in a most friendly way' for starting the fire by his smoking.)
'Underneath us was the most elegant ballroom, with priceless
pictures and books and furniture. So we all set about evacuating
the treasures.' Prince Ludwig gave Bream an overcoat that had
belonged to Edward VII. The rain poured down as they wrenched
down Venetian mirrors, paintings and busts of European royals.
Laurie, shivering with fever, made notes: 'Fabergé, present from
Tsarina – flames & sparks blowing across house – Lu changing suits,
getting posher as fire grew worse. Firemen drinking schnapps –
Cathy extricating herself from drunken fireman's clutches.' Bream
remembers: 'There was a cabinet full of ancient coins, and I said
to Laurie "Take one end"; but he was so weak all the coins fell to
one side and spilled on to the floor. And Laurie said: "Heads it's
mine."'

'Lupeg' were wonderfully insouciant. Prince Ludwig watched
the blazing roof and said he never did like those bloody windows
anyway. Princess Peg said she'd had nightmares about fire for twenty
years and was almost relieved now it had happened. Everyone joked
over breakfast next day about the 'housewarming'.

'I'm getting worried about Christmas,' wrote Laurie to Pen
Dugdale. It had all started when he dropped the flaming Christmas
pudding at Bushton. Two years ago the tree had caught fire. 'Last
year was the libel threat over the Piano Works fire. And now the
burning schloss. Next year, if I live, I shall spend the festival in a
cold bath wearing an asbestos suit.'

He told Yasmin about sitting down at a table for fourteen with
a whole side of venison, 'with chocolate cakes the size of cartwheels,
& Rhine wines as delicate as summer air which even you could
drink with innocence . . . Darling, I have thought of you every
day, and dreamt about you, and sent you messages by mental pigeon
post . . . I simply adore you.' Yasmin realized how lucky she was.
A few years earlier, he might have found her as awkward as any
father finds a teenage daughter. They had missed the difficult stage.

Sometimes, Yasmin says, he would say ruefully, 'If only you'd
come and look after me.' 'And I'd think, "But you're being looked
after by Kathy," and I'd be quite cross. All his own insecurities

came out in his immediate relationships. You became an asset or a disadvantage according to how you performed with his friends. But I realized it came from his own ridiculous feelings of inadequacy.'

'It strikes me that since I found you/you found me, I've been away most of the time & I don't want to go away so much again,' Laurie wrote, but in January he was off to the Caribbean to write for *Mademoiselle*. 'Think of me, & wish me back.' The letters he sent Yasmin reflect an exuberant mood, akin to that of a man newly in love. He wrote to her from Port of Spain, 'the right place for a fever – with hot & cold Caribbean winds blowing & hot rum to drink'. He was surrounded by 'hot scarlet flowers, ibis, humming birds, green coconuts & tree oysters . . . forests like Rousseau's, snakes, and dark faces peeping out'. Pierre, his driver, recommended fried scorpions, which he said tasted like shrimps. He loved the shop signs, 'De Rite Shoe Shop'; 'Sincere Company Limited'; 'Mr Chin-a-Fat, manager'; and an Indian restaurant playing Greek bouzouki music and advertising Paella Valenciana.

For ten days he travelled through Caribbean paradises, not yet familiar to tourists – Barbados, Antigua, Martinique, Guadeloupe. He had another fever at the Blairgowrie Hotel at Montego Bay, occupying a luxurious bungalow in a tropical garden above a bay full of mangrove islands 'like salads floating on the water'. The birds made noises like sewing machines or clock springs running down. Gaunt buzzards wheeled overhead. 'The people are most elegant walkers, and the country folk with dark smokey faces remind me of Auntie Kathleen. They have long thin arms and large expressive hands.

'I don't really know who I am here. I am a nameless homeless observer,' he wrote from his verandah at sundown, with a glass of rum and a penny Jamaican cigar 'which I think must be made of sugar cane'. The piece he wrote was loaded with evocative imagery.

Yasmin, still shy, introverted and unsocialized, was thrown in at the deep end of Laurie's London social life; he sometimes took her to parties, and she remembers Peregrine Worsthorne being 'very sweet' to her one night. He also took his niece Anthea, now aged fifteen, to whom he had been a good uncle ever since his brother

Tony's death; she put up her hair for the farewell to John Hay Whitney, the US ambassador. Laurie's diary was full of gatherings that spring: a jeans & sweater ball; a dinner in Hamilton Terrace ('Told to be casual: everyone in dinner jackets'), and soirées where he met L.P. Hartley, Sir Herbert Read, Eugene Ionesco, Henry Green. He sat on a Brains Trust panel with Monica Dickens and John Braine. At Ronald Searle and Kaye Webb's he met Michael Redgrave ('Laurie! how are you? We last met sixteen years ago with Beatrix Lehmann'). James Mason, who was playing Humbert Humbert in *Lolita*, was 'a large, solid friendly man, collects Victorian bun pennies' and Robert Graves's entire family were at Diana Cooper's: 'Four huge pies and a bit of singing – John Julius interminable; Iris Tree with Aztec face, metal white hair in splinters over forehead; Graves sang a lot – a curious self-absorption which mars him.'

In March Laurie took Kathy and Anthea to Boulogne for a weekend at the Hôtel Bayel. (He wanted to show Anthea a real French restaurant, just as he had promised to take her to everything she wanted to see in London: Madame Tussaud's, and pavement artists, and the ballet and a recording of *Juke Box Jury*.) Three weeks later, he took Yasmin on a similar trip – to Calais and Boulogne. On the way back they ran into Yehudi Menuhin. Menuhin's wife Diana approached Laurie on Calais station. 'Clever darling,' said the maestro. 'She always recognizes people.' They lunched together on the train: 'Yehudi eating raw carrots. Mild, generous, wise, yellow slanting eyes. She garrulous, talking of him as "the Fiddler".' Nigel Tangye was on board too, with two girls – which reminded Laurie of 1948, when Tangye had spotted him crossing the channel with Jennifer Gault and her friend Cynthia, who had also been visiting a lover in Paris. At Dover, the official looked at Laurie's passport, snapped it shut, returned it briskly. 'Thank you Mr Lee. And thank you for *Cider with Rosie*.'

Laurie, as always fascinated by the moon and the sun (he watched a total eclipse on television: 'Moving moment when moon slips over sun's face, a corona blazed forth, then great glare as sun rim

emerges again'), was naturally excited about the first man in space, Yuri Gagarin; he noted the 'pity & jeers for America whose carefully bred astronauts were sleeping, their courage ready, but not their equipment'. So in May, when Laurie and Kathy were sailing back from America on the *Queen Mary*, Laurie was especially pleased that during the Captain's cocktail party the telephone rang. 'Captain answered it. Turned to Anglo-American guests and said, "The Americans have put their man in space & got him back safely." Cheers all round.'

Laurie had achieved a notable esteem in the United States: a school textbook on 'Advanced Composition' included the 'schooldays' extract from *Cider*, with questions such as 'What were the specific deficiencies of the village school and its program? What advantages, if any, did this schooling provide for Laurie Lee?' As he told Tom Matthews, the book was subtitled: 'Shakespeare, Queen Victoria, Laurie Lee, Samuel Johnson'. 'What would my old mother think?'

Home from America, Kathy took charge of the search for a cottage in Slad. Only one was perfect: stone-built, oak-beamed seventeenth-century Rose Cottage, just behind the Woolpack, facing west across the valley, with the only flat garden in the village. But it had just been sold to the manager of the Bon Marché in Gloucester. Kathy met him at Bulls Cross in the rain and pleaded tearfully with him. Four days later, he wrote to say they could have Rose Cottage, adding, 'I liked that picture of you in the *Tatler*.' The photograph, of Kathy in her glamorous black velvet gown, was taken on the *Queen Mary*, and this clearly impressed him.

Rose Cottage had been lived in by the Fern family since 1860. The previous owner was Mabel Fern, who had married the postman Harry Vick. Laurie remembered seeing old Mrs Vick among her roses when he was a boy, and Jack remembers pinching twopenny bars of chocolate from her shop. She was a lay preacher, and when she went away to the seaside to end her days, she left everything behind: cupboards of hand-sewn linen and corsets, the Fern family bible, texts such as 'The Lord Will Provide', and a shed full of rusty worm-eaten spades.

'I've bought my cottage at last,' Laurie told Tom Matthews: 'It

is in the heart of the village, six stumbling paces from the pub, door to door.' He was euphoric. He planted morning glory in his London window-boxes. He held a drinks party for brother Jack. He took Yasmin to the Test Match, 'best summer day so far', and to an Apollo Society poetry reading (with Julian Bream and Peggy Ashcroft) where he was surrounded by his womenfolk: Kathy, Yasmin, Antonia and Anthea. (Antonia remarked, quite unwittingly, on the resemblance between Anthea and Yasmin.) When filmed in the Queen's Elm leaning against the bar, glass in hand, for a television programme called *To Stay Alive*, he twinkled merrily: 'I'm concerned in the celebration of living. I'm not concerned about the consolation prize of the hereafter. I like this world. I haven't yet heard of a better.' At the unveiling of a Lis Frink at the Carlton Towers he saw a PEN colleague who said, pompously, he was there 'to celebrate the marriage between industry and art'. 'Friend of the bride or bridegroom?' asked Laurie. Augustus John was there, his suit covered with cigarette ash, drinking Beaujolais from the bottle, flirting with Kathy. 'I said as we parted, "That's my wife you were flirting with." He roared and said, "I withdraw nothing."'

Life was good. Every weekend they were away: at Doddington with the Jarvises, at Culham Court, Henley, with the Behrenses, and Amersham with the Canfields: playing croquet, watching cricket, lunching with Lord and Lady Hambleden and Lady Diana Cooper. 'Large picture of London river. I thought Canaletto. Said to Lady Diana, "Is that Canaletto?" She said, "No, the Tower Bridge of course."'

But was he writing? 'Can't be very busy,' he wrote in his diary that October, 'just seen spider's web stretched from window to pencil on desk.' When he allowed a journalist, Allen Andrews of *Harper's*, to see inside his flat, Andrews described Laurie's workroom as 'more a temple of ritual evasion'. 'I do all sorts of things in the morning rather than write,' Laurie told him. 'I note down the temperature and the barometer reading. I count the buds and record the blooms on the geraniums. I count all the money in my pocket and examine the dates. I separate bun pennies into one pile, Jubilee

Victorian into another, Edwards into another. I put all my sixpences into a beer mug and at intervals buy travellers' cheques.

'And then I stare at the wall on which I have fixed a chart of the daily temperatures over the past three years. It is partly a mechanism but it is, too, a confirmation of order. There, spread out on the wall, I see the year grow unsteadily to a peak from January and then come down again. A seismograph of the year. It keeps me in touch with the force of the sun and the cycle of time. I like to see it in front of me.'

He did read 500 poems for the Cheltenham Poetry Prize, and reeled from 'so much bad Eliot'. He submitted one poem, 'Bird in a Square', when the *TLS* in July ran poems from twenty-one living poets (Larkin, MacNeice, Ted Hughes, etc.), and an editorial singled out Laurie's poem as 'the least gimmicky and pretentious'. He made a record of his poetry with Christopher Logue on the flipside (and wrote a poem addressed 'To the Man on the Other Side'); the reviews unanimously praised Laurie's warm voice and beautiful poems, while poor Logue's work had 'a certain nastiness' and 'crosspatch whimsicality, effectively emphasized by his rather needling tones'.

To Elizabeth Jane Howard's question in *Queen* magazine, what did he expect to achieve in the sixties? Laurie said he was 'not obsessed by output, but would be content with one book and four or five poems'. His royalties enabled him to turn down work he didn't want to do. 'I don't want a car,' he told Allen Andrews. 'We are too cluttered up with possessions. You can carry a whole universe in your head and be unable to move for the debts on your washing machines and stereos. I've lived on a very low standard of living until now. I'm free of that particular tension which says you've got to live up to £1,000 a year or £1,500 or £10,000. I have my fiddle hanging on the wall like a sword of Zorro, knowing that I can take it out, go out into the street and earn myself a slice of bread.

'I have a wife whom I hang on the wall, next to my fiddle. She's completely untrained in what women should demand because she has a Mediterranean background. As the daughter of a fisherman

Cathy is used to seeing a husband when he comes home, being sometimes glad but never surprised.' Laurie struck Andrews as 'a three-dimensional personality: recessed and warm'. They went to the Queen's Elm and to Finch's while Laurie told him the story of his life, including the tale of Cleo and the Putney building site, and the war in Spain. 'In my middle forties, I think I'm lucky to be alive. I've had bad illnesses, I've been washed out to sea in a canoe, I went through the war and I was in a condemned cell in Spain. I shouldn't be here.'

Music and painting were as important to him as writing, he said. He was 'surprised' to find himself a literary figure. 'I suspect it has more to do with sales than sagacity.' His next book — 'half noise, half silence, half light, half darkness' — would take him another seven years.

That summer of 1961, Laurie and Kathy were on everyone's guest lists. They had invitations to stay at four villas and a schloss. They joined the Behrenses at St Jean Cap Ferrat, the Hepples at Lake Garda, Peggy Ashcroft and Jeremy Hutchinson at the Villa Abati, Malcesine. They were driven by the Hesses' chauffeur through the Tyrolean passes to Schloss Tarasp Graubundenwild, in romantic mountain country. Laurie wrote Yasmin an account of their adventures. 'In Malcesine we saw two men fighting with knives, in Trento we saw a car crash into a ditch, in Bolzano we found that Cathy's passport had been left behind at the hotel near Milan, so we all had to wait a night while the hotel posted it on. But nobody minded because we discovered Bolzano.

'Our castle is fantastic: right on top of a rock, 9th century, built by the Hapsburgs. We eat in the armoury, where the stairs are cut out of the walls & my bedroom hangs over the cliff & if I throw a cigarette out of the window it falls 2,000 feet. The head of the bed where my pillow is has only a board between me & oblivion . . . there is an eagle's nest clearly visible across the valley.'

From Tarasp they were chauffeured to St Moritz and took buses and trains to Lake Maggiore, to stay with the Harrises at the Villa Capanna. They got back 'brown as Bisto' and on 8 September 1961 Pen Dugdale came over to Slad, to see their new cottage on a

perfect day which they referred to as 'the opening of the Rose'.

On 13 September they moved in, with nine bags, guitar and violin, and Laurie bought a large new notebook. 'Heavy dank smell of mothballs, matting rotting on floor,' he wrote on day one, 'but place full of domestic treasures.' They went through drawers, finding linen and lace, nine bibles, and a cross-stitch sampler embroidered with the words 'God First'. (Kathy embroidered another sampler for Laurie saying 'Me Next'.) From his study overlooking Swift's Hill he could see where stones had been quarried out of the hill to build the village, and Fletcher's farm where he went haymaking as a boy. Laurie felt he had 'dropped anchor' at last.

Of his first night in the old lady's black iron bedstead with brass knobs and heavy flock mattress, Laurie noted: 'Roll into hollow, sleep well.' From his bed he could watch the moon going down into the trees. The garden was a wilderness of weeds ('self-seeded spinach like elephant grass, onions tall as street lamps, monstrous cabbages apparently shot through with shrapnel, all knotted into a Bolivian hell') but the unpruned roses were blooming. He bought billhook, pruning knife, gloves, whetstone, oil, rust-remover, paintstripper, woodworm-killer. 'Built bonfires, burnt canes, weeds, old lady's bonnets, gaiters, rags, old lino and mats. Neighbours brought broad beans, carrots etc. and peered over wall: "Doin' a bit of diggin' then?"' Kathy did more than her share of the digging. They had no running water, no telephone, no gas, and escaped to Culham for civilized weekends.

The walled garden was virgin territory, profuse and disordered, and 'I was as virgin as the garden.' The front of the cottage had small mullioned windows and one ancient climber that had 'withered to a cat-like claw'. Laurie began by burning all the vegetables ('the village coughed for days') and dug the whole thing over except for a box hedge. Up came 'bushels of broken clay pipes, china dolls' legs, teapots, knucklebones, coins and cutlery, pots and pans, silver shoebuckles'.

They planted clambering 'Albertine' roses, white clematis, honeysuckle and wisteria, trailing willow, white lilac, cherry and

peach trees against the wall, sunflowers and hollyhocks – ritually pouring wine over the roots with each planting. They raised the borders and terraced them with dry stone walls, and screened the rhubarb patch with a larch trellis of 'Sander's White' roses. Laurie was photographed pruning his roses, pipe in mouth, drawing water from his spring which old Mr Tuck, the stonemason from Elcombe, said had never dried up in the last hundred years.

In the Woolpack for a Saturday night singsong, Charlie Foxwell from Painswick brought them 'a boiling of black kidneys'. 'Black kidneys are local potatoes, dark purple skin, rare and sacred, grown from handed-down seed, kept for special eating Christmas Day & Boxing Day. No seed sold. I remember them as a child.'

Outside Stroud Town Hall there was now a push-button map with an arrow pointing out of town 'To Slad Valley'. 'No other villages shown.' Soon he was noting, 'First tourists arrived wanting books signed.' They put his picture up in the pub. Laurie was gazing down the slope to Annie's old cottage one day when Mr Nipper, the Slad odd-job man, sidled up. 'I could a bought that place for £600 a few years back. If I'd known you were going to cover yourself with glory I'd a bought it & put in a tea-garden.'

He had opened a floodgate of reminiscence. Wherever he went, villagers stopped him. Harry Bartlett cornered him in the Star and told him all about the eight mills there had once been in the Slad Valley. He was given an old leaflet advertising 'auction of 4 Slad cottages (1883)'. One was the cottage of George Brown ('or Topper Brown we called him'), which went for £30 then. This was the derelict site bought by Laurie with the Matthew Smith money. 'The fourth cottage is the one I've now bought. Says "pleasant dwelling house with good walled garden, brewhouse & piggery (opposite school)". Harry B says brewhouse meant wash-house with copper. "Brewhuss we still calls 'em."' Someone else told him that labourers used to wear yarks (yorks) tied round legs, to keep trousers from rubbing against knees. 'Labourers in yarks,' wrote Laurie, 'leaning on their farks.'

Laurie was truly happy to be home. His hands were stained with dandelion juice. He watched the full harvest moon rise over Swift's

Hill at 8.50 p.m. on 28 September. 'Fine warm still day of absolute peace. Spent it preparing lawn in garden (using drawer for soil carrier). Walk through valley golden and still. A thrush, after rain, drinking from an apple leaf.' He went to see Painswick Clipping on a brilliant clear day. 'Three hundred children circle church hand in hand, sing medieval hymn "Daily, daily" then during chorus, skip up to church wall and back. Little girls with chaplets of flowers in their hair, some carrying baskets embroidered with flowers. Moving ceremony, older than Christian. Bishop of Gloucester gives address, children file through church & are each given a bun. I add a sixpence to each.'

Peggy Ashcroft, who was in Zeffirelli's *Othello* and rehearsing *The Cherry Orchard*, motored over from Stratford. Yasmin came for a weekend, 'loving the place with a quiet sense of possession'. He finished levelling the ground and scattered 6lb of grass seed. 'The following dawn,' he reported to Yasmin, 'the birds were all out there tucking in.' He rigged up a washing line, zigzagging across the lawn with table napkins attached, with the line through his bedroom window so he could pull on it and frighten the birds without leaving his bed. By 12 October the grass was two inches high.

He told Celia Goodman with pride that his cottage was central like hers, with bus-stop, church, pub, post office and telephone box all just a few steps up the bank. He had been fiddling hard, but longed to play with 'the only live person who brings me pleasure'. He bought a tape recorder ('It may seem one of the more vulgar gadgets of these affluent times, but really I do not care') and they made a double track of her piano and his violin. 'It's like being back with you . . . your piano sounds a dream. The shorter Mozart are particularly good though I'm a bit shaky on the Brahms & the Franck.'

Wilma wrote to say that her autobiography, doomed from the outset by its title *Reluctant Feet*, to which she had devoted 'the best of my brain & most of my health', had been turned down by a literary agent. Laurie soothed her – 'one agency's opinion isn't the word of God' – and said if she sent it to Chatto or André Deutsch he would write a letter to accompany it.

He and Kathy went up to London when invited to dine with Princess Alexandra at John Julius Norwich's. The Princess ('plumpish, rather shy, beautiful hazy eyes') sat by Laurie and told him she was 'hungry for the natural life, for spaces like Islay, genuinely disliking London. Said she'd really like to marry a farmer & keep chickens . . . Talked of Julian Bream & his wonderful face. Asked about Spain. Said in 5 years, when she was free of her duties (Princess Anne then taking over), could we all go to Spain together, over the old tracks. (Had read both my books & knew of my "dying" in Granada.)'

Because he was up in London again for the W.H. Smith award to Nadine Gordimer, he managed to miss Yasmin when she called at Slad twice, on an urgent mission. She had come to tell him she had fallen in love with a handsome young psychologist called Julian David.

'Darling, I'm terribly pleased at what you tell me, yes I'm sure I am,' he wrote, unconvincingly, 'and why shouldn't it happen to you – of all people it should, and all the better because it doesn't happen easily. I knew that when it happened, you would be taken completely by it, & that you would be shaken to your marrow. I don't care who he is if you can feel this for him, and I pray that it will prove to be true.'

He was having 'a small fever' he added, and 'I'm jealous, but I want you to be in love & I don't really think I shall lose you.'

Two weeks later she told him they were going to marry. Laurie was intrigued by the casualness of her tone, 'but I know you're like me, the bigger the news the more deadpan one's voice in telling it. You're not the sort to be swept away by nothing, thank goodness.

'What a year it has been for you, November to November; two new men in your life . . . but then what a year it's been for all of us . . . I've felt the most utter contentment at hearing the news, because it puts part of the world in order, and after a period of waiting, some of it dark, you've emerged into the proper daylight which was ready for you . . .

'I'm proud & glad. I thought I'd be jealous, even physically

jealous, and I'm that too, I'm glad to say. But at least it shows who I love.'

In November Kathy went to Italy to see her mother, and Laurie resumed his metropolitan winter life where, at a Foyle's literary luncheon for Bertrand Russell, among a leftish *galère* including Lord Attlee and Michael Foot, he was 'the tweedy poet' (*Londoner's Diary*). Yasmin stayed with him at the flat, buying things for her December wedding. He took part in a BBC *Perspectives* programme on solitude. Chad Varah, founder of the Samaritans, spoke on loneliness; Laurie spoke of his yearning for solitude – 'the right atmosphere for work'. In fact, Laurie had plenty of solitude, but was not writing, and not at ease about his life. The ecstasy brought on by the reunion with Yasmin had been short-lived; he was having 'terrible nightmares (no, not so terrible, but nightmares)' involving strange men, floating shadows; a man 'making up to Cathy & I seize beer bottle to strike him. Sees the expression on my face & runs in panic. He doesn't know I haven't strength to lift the bottle let alone hit him.'

On the way to their honeymoon, the newlyweds Yasmin and Julian called at Slad and took champagne. And on 17 December 1961, with Kathy away and Yasmin gone, Laurie met Antonia in Paris for a weekend. They went to the Grand Guignol, and returned at midnight to the Hôtel Cardinale to find a police barrier across the Rue L'Échaude, and the fire brigade in attendance. A plastic bomb had exploded in the club opposite, blowing in the front door and windows of their hotel. They had missed it by half an hour. And Antonia had of course not told her mother where she was. It was a narrow squeak. The year of 1961, having started with a fire, had ended with a bomb.

20 | Laurie the Magician
1962–3

'I had a name, before I published *Cider with Rosie*,' Laurie said, looking back in old age, 'and then there was a great displacement of loyalties. When *Cider with Rosie* came out, I think it was considered to be rather a letdown. It sold too much, and I wasn't asked to their literary parties any more . . . It changed the orbit of my friendships. You don't sell five million unless you're suspect as a writer, I'm afraid. I should have been more inscrutable, dear boy. I couldn't be inscrutable.'[1]

When *Faber Modern Poets* was published in 1960, Laurie had been included in the fraternity of Forties poets, alongside Eliot, Graves, Dylan Thomas. Now, he might be seated with Spender at a luncheon, but he felt he was at a remove. When he went with Elizabeth Jane Howard to a Mansion House banquet in June 1962 – 'Yeomen of Guard, madrigal singers' – he found himself the only one in a dinner jacket among 'other white-tied plump decorated poets C Day L, Spender, Auden. I suddenly ashamed,' he confided to his diary.

In the new year of 1962, Kathy was suddenly called back to Italy where her dear old stepfather Sarfi was dying at eighty-four. She was away for two months. Laurie had bronchitis, and was feeling he 'might never smile again'. But when Celia Goodman asked how he was getting on without Kathy, he confessed he could not complain: 'I've been free to curl up with hot drinks and sleep & read & read (in active life I read so little) and sleep.' A Fortnum's hamper of delicacies had arrived from Princess Peg: 'Chicken breasts & Pâté; tinned Wild Boar & Pheasant – a regular Hesse of Pottage.'

He noted privately: 'Chaos in my workroom. Floor stained with tobacco. Knocked oil-stove over. Floor covered in paraffin. Like living in army tank. Electric fire spits, dead bar comes on, glows red, spits & goes out again. Work with dressing-gown over cold

thighs.' But 'girl comes every afternoon, preparing tasty teas'.

'Why so fortunate,' he asked himself. 'Seen off on train by quiet devoted woman [his next-door neighbour] who had driven me to station. Packed luncheon of chicken, ham, peach, pear, grapes. Arrived Paddington to be met by beautiful girl who gives me a glass of Guinness & drives me home.

'Also out in evening with handsome woman [Elizabeth Jane Howard] & return to find girl, cool as a stick of chicory, curled in bed, waiting. And I nearly 50. Shall I one day think of this luxury with tears of age & longing? Yes.'

Yasmin wrote from her honeymoon at her brother Michael's house in the south of France, and Laurie sent love to the couple, 'but as far as Julian is concerned, mixed with the right amount of jealousy'. The following month he wrote to Yasmin on her twenty-third birthday. 'Twenty-three years since I heard your first cry on the telephone. (The same age as I was when I met your mother.)

'I've been reading some more old dreams I had about you in a 1952 diary. Haunting they are, but very final – as though you were the ghost of some departed. They were very sad, but it's a pleasure to read them now.' (In one of the dreams, in his 1952 Dreams notebook, he is sitting 'with the golden child . . . "When shall I see you again," she said earnestly. "Or does seeing me make you unhappy?" I held her hand. I was too full of emotion to speak. But what I was saying inside me was "No, there is nothing in the world more than to see you. And nothing that gives me greater joy."' In another dream, 'the young daughter is kicked by a horse and dies. Terrible inexorable remorse, now there is no one. To the mother, despair, then wild hope: she cannot just die & disappear like this. There must be something else left of her, in the garden? Yes says the mother. At the bottom of the garden I see two young bushes growing: they are her.')

He was still feverish in March – Dr Martinez puffed up the stairs, played Laurie's guitar and prescribed penicillin and lime juice – when Kathy came home with 'barmaid-bright blonde hair', and they returned to Slad for the summer: seven degrees of frost and

'the countryside is crouching like a whipped dog', he told Celia Goodman.

Frank Entwisle, a feature writer from the *Evening Standard*, came down to do an interview for a series on 'Heartwarmers' and described Laurie as 'a well-fed Michael Foot' (annotated by Laurie: 'Just a well-fed Michael Foot-warmer'). Over dinner, Entwisle told Laurie that his eyes had pricked with tears when he read *Cider with Rosie* and he thought the book would still be read 100 years hence. They talked of the Spanish Civil War, and Laurie was almost honest about his homecoming: 'He fought in the International Brigade,' wrote Entwisle, 'but was shipped out after a bout of the recurrent pneumonia that has trailed him from his Cotswold childhood.' Pneumonia was a socially acceptable cover for epilepsy.

Every few weeks he was off to perform at another evening of Poetry and Jazz, organized by the young publisher Jeremy Robson, in town halls and theatres and student unions, in Cardiff and Coventry and Cheltenham. Poetry readings, until then regarded as snoringly boring, had become the height of early 1960s cool. *The Times* ran a leader on the resurgence of the spoken word via poetry readings, San Francisco style. Robson's core team was Laurie, Dannie Abse, Christopher Logue, Adrian Mitchell and – top of the bill, drawing the crowds – Spike Milligan the clown-poet: 'jumpy, light, funny,' noted Laurie, 'yet offstage green-eyed & deadly serious.' Spike won over every audience: 'I was going to begin by reading one of Shakespeare's sonnets,' he would say, 'but then I thought, why should I? He never reads any of mine.' He used an epitaph which he would rewrite to suit any locality:

Here lies the grave of Mary Charlotte
Who was born a virgin and died a harlot.
She remained a virgin till her 17th year
A remarkable thing in Gloucestershire.

Discarding pages like confetti, Spike would end with a sad poem he had written during the war: 'Young are our dead, like babies they lie . . .' Logue and Mitchell, in jeans, injected tough contemporary

realities. 'This is Hanratty week,' Logue began, in the week James Hanratty was hanged. Then Laurie 'in an elderly brown suit with bandy trousers' came on with his pastoral brogue, his unassuming manner. 'I'm a bit drunk,' he told the cheering undergraduates packed into Oxford Town Hall. 'I got on the wrong train and arrived too early. I've been sitting in the public library drinking gin out of an inkwell.' Everywhere, queues formed; they turned 500 away at Hampstead. The following month at the Festival Hall, Robson added Ted Hughes, Stevie Smith and Vernon Scannell, and 3,000 people came. Laurie would tell the same stories: 'A small boy came up to me and said, "Are you Mr Lee?" "Yes." "Did you write a poem called 'Apples'?" "Yes." (Pause.) "My teacher made me learn it." (Longer pause.) We spent a moment of scowling intimacy together.' Then Laurie would say, 'I don't think I'll read "Apples",' and would tear up a sheet of paper, scattering it on the stage. 'I'll read instead a poem called "Day of These Days".' And he would tell how he wrote that on the top of a London bus.

Audiences were charmed by Laurie, as much for his engaging personality as for the poems themselves. At the end he brandished his forty-eight-page Pocket Poets volume: 'My life's work,' he would say. 'You can have it for two-and-six.' Spike Milligan fondly remembers Laurie as 'the most open-hearted man I knew'. 'Laurie was always fun to be with,' Dannie Abse recalled, 'though on one occasion while on tour he somehow secretly deposited some girl's navy knickers in my luggage – almost causing me trouble when I returned home to my wife.'[2]

Vernon Scannell once appeared with Laurie on Harlech Television in Bristol. They were met by a young producer whose first words were, 'Let's go along to wardrobe straight away.' 'Wardrobe?' Laurie said. The young man replied, 'Well, let's face it, you don't *look* like poets, do you?' 'What have you in mind? Bardic robes?' asked Scannell. The young man said he thought leather jackets and jeans. 'Laurie, who was wearing a baggy tweed suit and, with his long undisciplined hair, looked decidedly poetic but in a style of a bygone time, said firmly, "I've looked like a yard and a half of old

knitting for many years now, and I've no intention of changing." '
They went on as they were.

When Celia Goodman asked Laurie whether he was writing any
new poems, he told her: 'Poetry has become like a room in my
life where I know I can be happy, whenever I wish to retire there,
but I keep the door locked & don't go in much.'

Country life was his refuge. 'I'm a minute landowner now in
my old Glos village,' he told Val ffrench Blake proudly. Nine bean
rows could he build there. He rolled the new lawn each night with
a beer barrel and fought off the rioting rhubarb. The garden was
his 'pillared temple'. It had 'a kind of beauty that is sometimes
difficult to share – like showing the neighbours one's holiday snaps'.
The real pleasure of gardening was a solitary one: 'going out before
breakfast to examine each plant for minute advances; the flattery
of bees visiting one's sown flower; the bird nesting in one's planted
tree; and the hours bent down, working over the garden's face,
close up.' A mistle-thrush had nested in a roof gutter; she sat
anxiously while the builders began noisily replacing the gutter. But
they lifted the old section with nest and put it carefully back again.
'Country people do this,' noted Laurie. 'Bill Washburn, farmer,
hasn't been able to use his tractor for a week: bird nesting in
axle.'

A cottage garden needs seven years, he knew, but already that
summer Rose Cottage was 'half-embowered in tangled creepers',
wisteria and passion-flower. Snowdrops, violets, crocuses and tulips
were followed by rampant colonies of pansies, petunias, violas,
snapdragons, sweet williams. Nasturtiums erupted in every crevice.
He preferred 'vigorous and native anarchy' to setting things in rows
at graduated heights, and he wanted no hot-house exotics. 'Such
a simple obsession may be the refuge of one's years, the desire to
keep a finger in time, to play a minor god, or even to come to
terms with death. I only know that small as my garden is I again
have a living root, that even for me something can come to
perfection; that I still have a place on earth.'[3]

He had a formula letter for friends. 'Ours is a rumplestiltskin
cottage with roses like crumpled Kleenex.' He would describe

himself as 'very deep in my valley, lost in a pleasant green-seeded haze'. 'Whatever the weather turns out to be, there always seems to be a kind of amnesty in the morning when the sunlight is so radiant on the fields you feel you could eat them.' Elizabeth Jane Howard came and pronounced the cottage 'quite perfect – although I do see that you are prey to relations & neighbours'. Laurie looked fifteen years younger, she said, so the life suited him. When Nicolette Devas came over with the sculptor Lynn Chadwick, Laurie killed an adder with a stone. 'An hour later we saw him, head crushed, tail still waving.' In June he took Alan Ross, who was cricket correspondent of the *Observer* as well as editor of the *London Magazine*, to a match at Sheepscombe, the steepest cricket pitch in the land, where the bowler has to run uphill and is invisible to the batsman until he crests the rise.

'Taking your advice,' he told Pen Dugdale, 'I went to a local stoneyard and bargained for that carved stone urn, hand made, quite old & I was prepared to pay £10–£14. But I got it for £5.' Filled with geraniums it was 'a Lucifer of the morning, catching the early sun'. Pen invited him to open her summer fête at Bushton, and after a mild protest ('I'm sure you could do better. How about Jack de Manio, Virginia's friend?') he did it beautifully. Pen had not yet found out about Laurie and her daughter; when she did, she felt bitterly betrayed and refused to see Laurie for many years, even though Kathy herself wrote to Pen that year telling her she should not worry, because nobody was being hurt, and she and Antonia would remain good friends. She said each relationship had its own place, and no one had the right to own someone entirely. 'I'm lucky,' she wrote, 'that I have so much love in me I find it easy to forgive, and as a result we have all had moments of sunshine and mutual concern one for the other.'

Whenever Laurie succumbed to another fever, a microphone in the trees relayed birdsong to his sickbed. Summer brought 'hot gingerbread days; haymaking on hills opposite: Fletcher's, Webb's, Teakle's, leaving hay standing in gaunt megalithic blocks instead of the voluptuous breasted haycock . . . Oh the golden fields.

Aztec pheasants walking royally & unafraid thro' stubble near Whiteway.'

While the builders were in, he took a room during the day over a pub in Stroud, with 'a view of the brewery and a nice whiff of hops', let to him on the understanding that he drink two bottles of beer a day ('At the moment I'm well ahead with my rent,' he told Val ffrench Blake). Every day he caught the nine o'clock bus into Stroud, and the 4.30 bus back up the valley 'to tea & garden sunshine'. 'Today we took tea to Teakle's field above the school-house. Golden country, curving fields, heavy woods, no bungalows or motor cars. At dusk, went with spade to common & sliced off tump of wild thyme for garden.'

In the Woolpack (which had a new sign, described by Laurie as 'a brown depressed carthorse carrying what looks like bulging armchair cushions'), Laurie steeped himself in bucolic life, his ear ever cocked for the local patterns of speech. Each snatch of dialogue told a story, funny or sad.

'Frank Green came in. Paddy said: "Did you hear your father had passed on Frank?" "No. No bugger told I." He picked up drink. "Well – cheers." But he looked thoughtful for a bit. "Marvellous old man though," we said. "85, 86, still gardening, to the end." "Well, he never did a bloody stroke for I."'

'Ernie Cook ranting on about giving up drink: "I'm giving up the bloody stuff you. Ain't touchin' it no more. It drives I round the bend. No good to yer 'ealth or yer pocket. I've got to the bottom of this drinkin' racket. All these bloody brewers make millions but they ain't goin' to make any more out of I."'

'Met Ernie Vick in the lane. Was postman for 20 years. Got to know nature by getting up at four in the morning, having the world to himself. Used to sit on wall listening to nightingale before dawn on way to work.' 'They buried Charlie Green this morning. Said to be the best poacher in Gloucestershire. Sat with dog in Star every night.' 'Long talk with Norman Vick who left his gardening to tell me about well on my bit of land, deepest in the valley. Showed me photo of Slad cricket team 1925. Sunny faced young

boys, some only 15 or 16. Memory enlarges the men remembered, hence myths of giants.'

'Lewis Eyers in his gaiters and cap: Last of the true Slad line. His kind never seen again.'

'Wally Bishop ("'ere, I want to tell 'e summat") found dead this morning in his Elcombe kitchen, his head in a bucket of water. Two years ago remembered his gaiety in the Star, enjoying late release (nearly 70) from farming. Brother found drowned in water trough on farm. Wally sold everything, went on merry spree . . . Became quiet and sad. Was seen yesterday walking past Woolpack, head down, with dog.'

Every time he met a villager in the lane or the pub, they would reminisce: 'Frank Green: "You was always hurrying up the road, with your head down reading *Comic Cuts*".' 'Harry Bartlett: "Remember hunt meeting at Slad? Fox went down to Jones's pond, took head off a swan, & then got away."'

That summer Elizabeth Jane Howard was artistic director of the Cheltenham Festival. She flung her energy into it (being paid £300 for eight months' work), inviting Kingsley Amis to discuss sex and censorship in literature with Carson McCullers, Romain Gary and Joseph Heller, and putting Laurie on a panel to discuss autobiography.[4] The panel talked of writing to 'capture a vanished world', and argued about how truthful an autobiographer could be. Not very, said Elspeth Huxley: most people cheated wildly, they had to protect the living, and memory was never reliable. It was, in fact, all something of a fraud. Laurie was candid about why he had written *Cider with Rosie*: his publishers had given him a sum of money and told him to get on with it. In his notebook he wrote: 'See no point to these things.'

The Festival ended with an auction (Laurie sold the manuscript of 'April Rise' for £8, 'Apples' for £9; Day-Lewis sold one of his detective novels for £80) and a cabaret. Laurie sat on the edge of the stage and played his guitar and sang Spanish songs and was 'entrancing', says Judy Campbell, who performed 'A Nightingale Sang in Berkeley Square', the song written for her in 1940. As a finale Jane had spent £100 on fireworks: some members of the

Committee harrumphed that they had 'had enough of that sort of thing in 1940, *personally*', but Laurie told her it was a dazzling display, 'some of the best I've seen in this country, partly due to the exquisite setting, which lit up those great park trees . . . There hasn't been a more imaginative lit fest ever. You are a bit of a treasure in my life.'

Jane told him: 'I think I've got to change my life rather a lot . . .' (She was about to bolt again, leaving her second husband and eloping to Spain with Kingsley Amis.) One day in London, Laurie told her, he had noticed a girl in the street, 'a baked-bread girl I thought I'd love to know, and looked harder and it was Nicola' – Jane's daughter, aged eighteen – 'I never thought she was like you but she is now, about the hair and eyes, perhaps that's what got me.'

That summer, Kathy had gone to Lake Garda for two months to be the helpful daughter to her widowed mother, now almost blind and needing a companion to read to her, and someone to help Walter with his school work. Aunt Kathleen Epstein was there too, and little Roland Joffé. Kathy reported to Laurie: 'Roland Joffé is so interested in living. And Walter his usual appreciative self . . . Six o'clock in the morning, bells are ringing across the wind. I'm just longing to have you safe and sound again in our gentle cottage. Always your adoring Mrs Lee.'

While she was away, Laurie would find the London flat 'lightly touched by willing hand'. He also went to Nice for two weeks at Cap Ferrat, and was driven from there to Spain, where in September he met up with Monica Sims to make a film for her BBC television series *Let's Imagine*, in which she took writers back to their favourite places. Laurie was to retrace his 1935 steps through Andalucía to the strains of a plangently haunting guitar. 'I walked knee-deep in the heat,' he recalled, in his commentary, 'alone in that space of dusty skies and horizons . . .' They filmed in Vejer de la Frontera, a village he'd once walked through, hungry and blistered, on the way to Cádiz. They filmed Moorish villages, the white bulls of the Andalucian savannah, the donkeys and muleteers and swineherds and *vaqueros*. They filmed in Tarifa where Atlantic and

Mediterranean meet, and in the market, the quayside and the narrow streets of Algeciras.

Monica found Laurie a delight to work with: patient, generous and inspiring. 'Talking to small children he made their faces light up, alive and eager.' Their cameramen, known as Don Quixote and Sancho Panza, were unaccustomed to random outside broadcasts and to Spanish heat. 'And they expected hot three-course meals every day. But Laurie managed to rustle up plates of sardines on dusty roads, and knew exactly where to get the best sherry in Jerez. The whole expedition ran on brandy and sherry, starting at breakfast.'

When they flew home Kathy met them at Gloucester Road. It was touching, Monica Sims says, to see their reunion. Laurie's diary says: 'Two days London, exhaustion, indulgence, and retribution.' Back in Slad, they found the neglected garden choked with weeds, the last roses dying, the cottage damp, the village at its wettest. 'Gale all night, house shook.' Laurie's friend Frank Mansell had been arrested on his birthday for driving when drunk. A local spinster, 'Miss Godsell's companion', had drowned herself in the Avon.

Kathy's warm exuberance, despite Laurie's independent life, was remarkable. She wrote to Tom Matthews full of girlish enthusiasm for his new book of poems 'which fascinated me in every way. You wouldn't believe it but I'm quite a good judge.' She told Celia Goodman that Laurie's life was too hectic, with the Cheltenham festival and BBC television work, for them to get away; and 'he keeps rushing back and forth to London'. (Once, he was spotted by a neighbour: 'Col Brooking turned head surprised to see girl run into my arms on Paddington station.')

Kathy, now aged thirty-one, spent a lot of time that year, as Laurie records, 'just gazing at the ground or out across the valley. Someone who felt locked out: a wistful fugitive wondering where and to whom she most truly belonged.'[5] But when visited by journalists, Laurie and Kathy in their cottage presented an idyllic image to the world. 'Down the slope, beyond a grey stone pub, I saw a little cottage,' a typical interview that year began. 'The hillside

opened out behind me . . . The tiny windows were shiny, dark and secret . . . But from the interior of the cottage I now heard the sound of a violin playing . . .'

Inside, Laurie was in corduroys, khaki army surplus shirt and baggy tweed coat 'which combined to give an effect of rustic grace. His light blue eyes in his bronzed gentle face looked out at me with a type of whimsical domesticity, in which there was a touch of wildness . . . While Laurie works at his poetry, Kathy makes wine from nettles and elderseed and other country recipes . . .'[6]

It was a pretty picture. Kathy did indeed make wine: elderflower, beetroot, carrot and damson. Laurie was writing not poetry but one of his best-known essays – on 'Autobiography' – commissioned by the *New York Times Book Review*, in which he said, 'The urge to write may also be the fear of death – particularly with autobiography – the need to leave messages for those who come after, saying, "I was here; I saw it too."' He was also bedridden in October 1962, 'waiting for inflammable flash-up of world' as President Kennedy declared his blockade of Cuba.

A visit to Celia Goodman at the Cedars was restorative for both: 'I am refreshed & in love with music again,' Laurie wrote afterwards. The surroundings (Celia's music room, in the Queen Anne part of her house, overlooking the garden) 'make it sound richer and shinier. In London it sounds damp & displeased.' Laurie had brought Celia's children a kaleidoscope and Kathy was 'beautiful and splendid and sweet,' said Celia, 'to do all that singing, and all that nannying too.' 'I enjoyed my weekend so much coming out of the quietness and silence of one's own company,' Kathy wrote, 'not that I'm a complete hermit but only that people like yourself are not around, people with sympathy and understanding . . .'

After New Year's Eve at the opera with Mike Behrens (Sam Wanamaker's production of *La Forza del Destino*), Laurie felt 'cold and low'. The long hard winter of 1963 brought the worst blizzards since 1881. Sheep were buried in snowdrifts, easy prey for foxes. Kathy departed for Italy in a winter gale. Laurie took to his bed with 'flu, and thoughts of death. Not long before, the irrepressible Geraldine Lawrence had died of cancer. Laurie had been to visit

her a few days before her death. 'She was a shrunken corpse, skin of dried pink paper, but she had ordered champagne for us. She said "Do you know I feel better today?" It was goodbye.'

He was in bed with a fever. 'Lay 36 hours alone. Jack visited. Girl came to take over.' A telephone call reminded him that it was Bunny Keene's funeral that day. His old friend, with whom he had been to Cyprus and India, had died of a coronary. 'Kind old Bunny, ex-Marlborough, gentle, talented, frightened, handsome: His wife Jane, beautiful, sad, in her late 30s died 2 months ago. I feel bad about being so unfriendly the last years. Should have gone to his funeral Chiswick today, but for this fever. This is how we'll all go. A pause between mouthfuls.'

Norah Smallwood of the Hogarth Press tentatively asked, 'Can you not spare time to come and tell us how Opus 2 is getting on?' It was not getting on at all. But despite the snow, he turned out to Poetry and Jazz evenings in freezing theatres. Then he escaped to the sun. He was off to Mexico for *Mademoiselle*, producing a classic 'Mexico, land of contrasts' essay – 'sky-scrapers of glass and mudbaked hovels, colonial churches and Hilton hotels, Parisian boulevards and open-drain back streets, blond Americans and obsidian Aztecs'. His Edwardian hotel had brass cuspidors, potted palm-trees and bell-boys; outside were Indians selling stuffed *tamales*. He had been warned to watch out for altitude sickness and beware the spiced food, but he had never felt better. 'I walked on my toes, the altitude cleared my head, food was various and delicious, and after three quick tequilas I felt I possessed the secrets of the world . . .'

He recovered his old knack of finding quirky behaviour ('a man in a doorway eating fried eggs from his hat') and was excited by Diego Rivera's *History of Mexico* murals on the palace of Cortés. In the evenings he wandered the streets, bars and nightclubs. A driver took him on a 600-mile round trip through Guadalajara, to the temple of Tula, the holy city of the Toltecs; and to Querétaro where he watched a boy digging opals out of lumps of quartz and throwing them into a bucket of water where they sprang alive like instant fire. In the market a group of Indians 'appeared to be eating

the heads of wolves'. He was enraptured by the colonial architecture, its colour and grace and Gothic detail; and by young men in tasselled hats, donkeys in embroidered harnesses; girls with waist-long hair in red skirts and black stockings.

At noon one day he came upon San Juan de los Lagos, where 60,000 pilgrims assembled for the feast of the Virgin. 'The sight was staggering, like a mass gathering of Biblical tribes. A thousand white tents, flapping in the hot, dry wind, covered the hillside round the little town, filling the woods and canyons. A roar of life rose above the encampments, a mixture of music, laughter and cries; smoke from a thousand fires filled the sunny air; magnificent horsemen rode among the tent poles . . . I sat in the square and hired a wandering orchestra to play for me. For about 3s 6d I got a heart-rending song accompanied by four fiddles, three guitars and a trumpet.'

Back from Mexico he spent twelve manic days at his desk, writing the article from 10 a.m. to 11.30 p.m. 'Y pregnant,' his diary noted, 'but fearing she might lose it. She lost one last autumn.' Innately superstitious, and inspired by the possibility that he might be a grandfather before he and Kathy produced their own child, he had brought back a corn-doll fertility aid from Mexico.

'On the first night of my return,' he wrote in *Two Women*, 'when Cathy was asleep, I slipped a box of Mexican corn-dolls under her bed. I reckoned we needed the help of any gods we could gather.'

While away, Laurie had missed the drama of brother Jack finally leaving his wife Nora for Isabel Kidman. The last film Jack had made in Britain was *Circle of Deception* (1960), starring Bradford Dillman and Suzy Parker, since when his career had been rather in the doldrums. A newspaper had referred to him – at forty-eight – as 'the veteran film director' and he felt it was time to go. He left Nora at their house in Chalfont St Giles. 'I deserted her and my sons in the middle of the night, and drove to London through snowdrifts.' So Jack went to make a new life in Australia. When Laurie got home, he received Nora's letter ('One turned to Laurie, feeling that he was wise, and that he knew the human heart,' she

says) and told her he was 'entirely behind you and the boys' and that 'you will always have my love'.

That February Laurie was interviewed in the Queen's Elm by Sally Vincent, an unusually keen-eyed journalist, for the *Daily Mail*. She was too perceptive to buy the usual flannel. This must be the only interview with Laurie which did not recycle, or even mention, Slad, *Cider*, or Spain. Laurie was determined not to give much away, but the result was an insightful portrait.

He looked, she said, like a lugubrious goblin, with his 'lanky, folded face and long pointed ears'. 'When he puts his glasses on you miss half the folds, his face broadens and he looks like a jolly nice chap. Around the rims of the lenses are traces of ink. He tells me they are plain lenses, and that sometimes he inks them over. The fact that when he does this – if he does it at all, for he is seven-eighths fantasy – he cannot see at all seems not to have occurred to him. This is the depth of Laurie Lee's self-protection. He leaves himself as defenceless as a child who goes wide-eyed and pink when it tells stories.

'But somehow finding him out makes you the loser, he keeps his secrets all the same. If you ask him how old he is he says his mother doesn't know which year it was. Then there's his home. You can't go there. His best kept secret of all is his wife. All the newspapers describe her as Laurie Lee's beautiful wife. He describes her as an enormous woman with enormous blue eyes and enormous sandy hair.' Clearly it was best just to go along with him.

She asked him exactly what he did all day, and he told her about taking the temperature and counting the buds on his geraniums. 'Laurie Lee and his wife have no children,' Sally wrote. 'He says he doesn't want to see pocket editions of himself running about all over the place. "Horrible that would be," he says. "They repeat your own weaknesses and you take it out on them because you're too idle to take it out on yourself. Nothing's more irritating than your own faults and that's why they're the ones you always complain about in other people. You never see people so hot and bothered as when they've got somebody else's sins to take their minds off their own . . . when they're discussing capital punishment or how

to persecute someone. Those Tory floggers . . . Inversion and evasion gone mad, that's what they are."

'His glance rests on somebody's rather idiotic-looking dog. "Having pet animals is evasion," he declares. "People who love animals are only making substitutes for the more difficult business of loving people. I don't like dogs. They seem to take on the worst aspects of human beings. The drooping tail, the self-consciousness, the guilt . . . I like wild dogs though. I like animals when they're left alone. I like foxes and stoats and squirrels. I respect birds."'

He told her he hadn't had a job for fifteen years, and reiterated the pitfalls of too many possessions. 'I'm free,' he said. 'But anyone can be free, you know; anyone can live alone and not be told what to do.' 'Sometimes you have to take Laurie Lee with salt,' Sally Vincent concluded. 'Only don't get it on his tail.'

Ironically, in view of Laurie's stated thoughts on having children, Kathy was already pregnant.

He describes in *Two Women* what a puzzle it was that ripe, golden Kathy, 'boxed up in sterile London', was inexplicably childless after twelve years of marriage. He tells how he brought her back to Slad and, by some magic, one morning found her perched on the kitchen window-sill. 'She looked at me transfigured, her eyes full of confusion and triumph. "Oh, Lol!" she said. "Would you believe it? . . . I'm pregnant."'

That day, 5 March 1963, the *Daily Express* had published a poem commissioned from Laurie about 'Spring'. Laurie's mood was hardly spring-like: he was beset by dramatic nightmares full of guilt and retribution. One recurring dream, described at vivid length in his diary, involved his seduction of a headmaster's wife in the garden of a great public school – while the headmaster played Chopin through an open window – concluding with Laurie's being expelled in front of the entire school, and given a packed lunch for his train journey which turned out to contain 'plaited snakes'.

Still, the poem called 'Spring' duly appeared. On a copy of the *Evening Standard* he had scribbled tentative lines. 'Snow on the boots, Spring in the blood, Light in the treetops, Ice in the roots. March with its toe-nails . . . Scratches the roots . . . Ice on the

eyelids – But don't sleep now, But sleep no more – in the cellar –
& Spring is at the door.' What appeared was this:

> Spring in the bloodstream, snow on the boots;
> March with its toenails stirs the roots.
> Gold in the mountains the gods look south:
> Dreams of wet honey unfreeze the mouth.
> Ice on the eyelid, but sleep no more –
> Death's in the cellar, but life at the door.

Tucked into the drafts of this poem are these pencilled lines:
'"One day, when you're a grandfather" they used to say, and
laugh.

'Now that I am a grandfather, they laugh again, and push my
wheelchair with cool-gloved hand.'

He had just heard that Yasmin's pregnancy too was confirmed:
he was to be a grandfather in September.

They went down to grey and stormy Slad. Kathy had lost some
blood and Dr Brayshaw came through gales from Painswick. It was
a warning, he said. She was not to do any heavy work, and they
were to prepare for the worst. 'Decision will be made for us I
think.' Laurie wrote asking Tom Matthews to send Kathy a bundle
of beauty magazines: she had been 'overdoing things'. Laurie himself
was in Upper Wimpole Street seeing a doctor about his throat, ears
and nose. He had a week in bed but had to rouse himself to make
an ITV film called *Boy Meets Girl*, about rural courtship. They
filmed in Sheepscombe and he was interviewed by Dan Farson
('square, pink, soft face, remote bored eyes') at Forester's Inn. The
cameramen did shots of Anthea and a boyfriend running down
Swift's Hill in cold afternoon sun, and there were long convivial
evenings with the film crew.

Commiserating with Tom Matthews about the end of his ten-
year marriage to Martha Gellhorn, Laurie told him about Kathy's
pregnancy, to Kathy's annoyance: 'We had been keeping it quiet
just out of superstition, I wanted to feel safe & sure first,' she wrote
to Matthews. 'It is a little miracle, isn't it. I still can't believe it

though at last I'm beginning to change shape. I've been making gallons of home made wine. Laurie can't stop drinking it and it has no after effect, but keeps him happy while he's on it, this is most pleasing and satisfactory to me.'

Everyone joined in the astonishment about the 'Blooming Burgeoning Floribunda Lees', as Jeremy Hutchinson put it. 'It is so wonderful I can hardly write about it,' wrote Peggy Ashcroft. Impending fatherhood galvanized Laurie into selling poems. The University of Kentucky at Lexington regretted they could offer no fee for a manuscript: 'We have several hundred manuscripts of contemporary poets and we have paid nothing for any of them.' But dozens of anthologies were reprinting 'April Rise', or 'Christmas Landscape', and the royalties (a guinea here, four guineas there) mounted up. For *Mademoiselle* he went twice to Holland: 'like no other place on earth, a gift from the sea'.

On 20 April he and Kathy heard the first cuckoo, and he was writing to Yasmin that night at 11 p.m. when Kathy called out, 'Ah, he's moved.' 'Baby first moved,' Laurie noted in his diary. Outside in the drainpipe, five mistle-thrush chicks sat 'like 5 fat dowagers trapped in a rubber dinghy'. Kathy too, at five months, grew 'rather large'. Laurie took a series of loving photographs of her with a pigeon that came and roosted under the kitchen table; Kathy wept when it left. Then a jackdaw came and took over; quite tame, following her everywhere, seemingly guarding her. (The photographs Laurie took of pregnant Kathy and her feathered friends are among the most touching in *Two Women*.)

In September Yasmin stayed in P.J. Kavanagh's flat off Sloane Square while waiting for her baby; Lorna went up to see her for the day, and so did Laurie, so the two met again at last, the first time for at least thirteen years. 'Suddenly all was normal between them,' Yasmin says, 'as their daughter was having her first baby.'

On 19 September Laurie wrote to Yasmin, sympathizing with her waiting days, 'but the rarest orchids are always the most trouble to grow'. At one end of Avenue Road, St John's Wood, was the nursing home where his grandchild would be born, and at the other, 400 yards away, the Hampstead Theatre which was showing

James Roose-Evans's stage version of *Cider with Rosie*: 'but your production won't suffer any comparisons,' Laurie wrote to Yasmin, 'being first-hand flesh & blood. Anyway I'm glad of the continuity, because there hasn't been much of it in the past.'

Eleven days later, on 30 September 1963, Laurie was in bed with a fever when he heard Kathy groaning. 'Three weeks early. I thought of country girls who complain of colic then find a baby lying in straw at their feet . . . Lay by her & noticed that the bed was wet . . . Went to the Atwoods' 7 15 a.m.' Joan Atwood, their neighbour, drove Kathy to hospital with her little blue bag and book. During the morning, Mrs Atwood shouted to Laurie: he was wanted on the telephone. 'It's about your daughter.' You mean my wife? 'No,' they said, 'your daughter.' It was Lorna, ringing from Yasmin's room in London, to tell him that Yasmin had just had a daughter, 7lb 2oz. 'A daughter, a grand daughter,' wrote Laurie in his notebook. 'I could hear it crying. So Cathy's was bound to be a son.'

For a few hours more he tried to work, then rang Kathy's hospital at 4 p.m. 'Nurse says there's a message – tell your sister in law not to come to tea tomorrow.' Then Marion, Laurie's cousin, the hospital matron, came on the phone: 'She said, "You got a daughter." Silence. "You dropped dead or something? I said you got a daughter. 7lb 2oz."'

In his diary he wrote: 'Monday Sept 30, 1963, two girls, daughter & granddaughter.'

Yasmin concluded that this amazing coincidence was the work of Laurie the great magician.

He spent the evening at the hospital: Kathy was 'quickly blooming in her separate room'. They had champagne and the baby was brought in. 'She was wrinkled & purple, her head bruised darkly from the birth, skinny, with an old woman's hands & tiny bent legs. She curled back her lips to wail & I saw Cathy's mouth.' Marion handed her, howling, to Laurie. 'I kissed her forehead & she lay still. The first flattery.'

Next day he sent Tom Matthews a card: 'A daughter born yesterday, 7lb. All well but me.' Kathy, awash with flowers and telegrams, wrote forty-eight letters. The vicar called, and Kathy

told him that she hardly ever went to church, but her daughter would bring her back. 'When he left I burst into tears . . . I saw the most remarkable sunset I had ever seen,' Kathy wrote to Laurie, 'the trees dripping pink and gold and the extraordinary blue of the sky. I brought three young mums-to-be to have a look, to have a nice effect on their babies. The girls in the main ward are a real bunch of gasworks toughies, but they are funny, and fun to visit.'

A photograph appeared in the *Stroud News*, showing Kathy with hair in plaits and sleeping baby. As Laurie walked about the town everyone smiled and stopped to talk; a policeman made rocking gestures with his arms. 'A famous baby. All say she looks like me.' The Registrar of Births had just read *Cider with Rosie*.

She was registered as Jesse Frances. Among the old photographs in Rose Cottage was one of Jesse Frederick Fern, a handsome young man who had been killed in the First World War and who is commemorated in Slad church. Kathy decided that the baby, male or female, would be Jesse. (Later, Laurie decided that he preferred 'Jessy'.) When mother and daughter came home, Laurie had removed the gate, made a cane archway with nasturtiums and sunflowers, hung kites and flags and nailed Jessy's birth certificate on the door. The birth was announced on *Woman's Hour*, where Laurie was interviewed. He went to see *Cider with Rosie* at Hampstead, but could not visit Yasmin and her baby Esther down the road, because Wish was there. He went next day: Yasmin looked 'beautiful'.

Laurie wrote petitioning the six godparents: Elizabeth Jane Howard ('I have always felt that if it was a girl she should have you. It would enrich her so much and you could teach her all your womanly magic'); Tom Matthews, whose lifelong grumble had been his burden of sons; Michael Behrens, who had said that if they ever had a girl he wanted to be godfather; Peggy Ashcroft; Laurie's cousin Frances; and Antonia Dugdale.

So Jessy became an integral element in the Laurie Lee mythology. 'I'd been away from this valley for twenty years, when suddenly she appeared and was born here, as I was. My return here was a mysterious act of fate,' he said twenty years later. 'The special magic, the mystery which still haunts me, is that having come back –

whether it was the angle of the light, the slope of the fields, something – but suddenly there was Jessy . . . a late miracle born to my roots. It was almost as though my return to Slad was not only to revisit my childhood, but also to find Jessy.'⁷

For Jessy, being born in his village was indeed an inextricable link with her father. He would wrap her in a blanket and take her into the garden under a full moon, and hold her aloft to be bathed in moonlight. He would feed her to the sound of the slow movement of Schubert's Trio in the hope that she would always associate music with pleasure. 'Laurie is so sweet with her,' Kathy reported to Celia Goodman. 'I always thought he would be much more detached. He feeds her with music when she cries – lovely trios, duets, quartets, I do hope she'll be musical.

'Oh Celia I keep thinking I'm dreaming it all, like those dreams one has which seem more of reality than of dream quality . . . I do hope I don't wake up out of this one. I never realized one could feel so satisfied and happy – I think the joy is enhanced by Laurie's own joy. I think finally he is going to be able to recapture joy again even if it's only for a short while.'

They exuded this joy to everyone. Peggy Ashcroft wrote that her day at Rose Cottage with the threesome was 'one of the most golden I ever remember – every minute of it – from entering under triumphal arch, the first sight of the pram, the first glimpse of Jesse, every glorious minute of the tale of labour, the croquet match & the picking of the blackberries and through it all Cathy shining like all the mother goddesses that have ever been'. Congratulations and blessings flowed in, from Monica Dickens, from Lady Diana Cooper, from Elizabeth Jennings who said, 'I'm so glad that my priest in Rome's prayers helped to bring you a child.' Jessy was baptized on All Souls' Day and lay in Laurie's arms in Aunt Alice's christening robe while he recited his 'Poem for Jessy's Christening'.

Sweet Jessy, late, but no less wanted,
Here in my arms now lie undaunted;
Much of my life has gone before you,
But what I've left of love is for you.

Welcome, dear child, come now to charm me,
Your little furnace heart to warm me.
Pray that the next few years shall find us
Gathered as close as blood can bind us.

For all your half-blind puppy features
I find you fairest of all creatures,
And see your mother's beauties rise
Already in your dawn-blue eyes.

Unknown as yet, still dim, you are
In my dark sky the freshest star;
A lanterned bush with light inside thee
Set in my desert world to guide me.

Grow then, young tree, and recreate
The spent leaves of my laureate
And I will be thy root, my queen,
And thou my crown of evergreen.

Their first Christmas with the baby was different from any they had known. Kathy's mother came from Italy to see her granddaughter. 'I haven't seen my mother-in-law for 15 years,' Laurie told Celia Goodman. 'We don't quarrel, but just observe a policy of withdrawal.' His withdrawal was so total that Kathy sent him away altogether. 'TERRIBLE CHRISTMAS ON MY OWN,' says his diary.

'The birth of my child,' Laurie later wrote, 'meant a farewell to the child bride who bore her.'

21 | Jessy
1964–6

Seasonal affective disorder, or SAD, might have been invented to describe Laurie's wintry malaise. 'Monotonous now, these winters,' groaned Laurie, in bed with another fever in January 1964. 'Comes so quickly & then I can do nothing . . . Winter is becoming a write-off. I can't go out or see anyone – have to cancel dinners – people doubt the reason. But worst of all, the depressions and helplessness.'

That winter, Jessy was a consolation. 'Likes me to sing to her, especially off key; entranced & rocks her head. That leaning forward, close-up look of studious curiosity I love: eyes round with fascination, mouth moves as I speak, trying to follow sounds. Laughed aloud several times. Can hold & shake a rattle.'

Every chuckle, each wriggling attempt at crawling, was logged in Laurie's notebook, day by day. He was entranced, besotted, transfixed. Like many middle-aged fathers, Laurie was in danger of being a baby bore: 'How they ensnare one at this age, the silken nets they loop around you,' he noted. Even his most indulgent friends found his doting accounts of his baby's progress a bit trying. Jessy's first word was 'Dadda', he told them: 'what else?'

He compared notes with Yasmin, signing himself 'Grand L', about the weight, first teeth and sleeping habits of Jessy and Essie (Esther). He pinned photos of Yasmin as a baby on his study wall 'and can't tell whether it's Y, E or J'. Jessy 'has a delightful old man's face – tiny white button nose like Cyril Connolly, & small twinkling eyes'. At Easter, the two six-month-olds met. Laurie compared Essie's bright-blue shining eyes ('fixed, intelligent, but of an unvarying light, like an electric bulb') with the livelier light in Jessy's which 'flickers around smiles and emotions like a live flame in a wind'.

Proudly he took Jessy in her Moses basket to luncheon at Lady

Diana Cooper's in Little Venice, with Peter Quennell and his wife Spider, and Kitty and her husband Wynne Godley. In the long dining-room hung with de Lazslo portraits, Rex Whistler murals and a *trompe l'œil* from Chantilly, Lady Diana, 'in fur coat before blazing fire', exclaimed at Jessy's complexion, and at Kathy's beauty.

They had become a trio. 'It was absolutely lovely having the Lees here,' Celia Goodman reported to Princess Peg. 'His adorable daughter is full of laughter and smiles and very sociable. Cathy was looking wonderful, thinner and even more beautiful. Laurie also seemed well in spite of so much illness this winter. He adores his baby as well he may.'

That weekend, Celia read from the *Iliad* in Greek, and they compared Chapman's translation, which Laurie preferred, to Pope's 'exhausting jig': 'I am sure his bright epigrammatic style is wrong.' One evening, Laurie announced that the US satellite Echo II might be seen at 5.50 p.m., and they all went out into the clear frosty night 'and sure enough a small light appeared in the sky in the south-west, and passed over the garden, disappearing beyond the cedar tree'.

Jessy was indeed a most charming child, with a 'fat-lipped' smile, a Beethoven brow and a mop of golden curls, recorded by Laurie's adoring camera. She laughed if he sneezed or whistled, slept by day in a pram in the square surrounded by builders' electric drills, woke each night and demanded entertainment. To Yasmin Laurie confessed that he would really rather she stayed like that for ever: 'I don't want J ever to crawl or talk, but just to look up from the floor & smile when I come in, like she does now, & lie kicking to be picked up & carried round the garden.'

'Face changes like a beauty,' he wrote in his notebook. 'Washed-out, pinched, screwed-up eyes, vacant. Then glowing, quick, coy, watching conversations head left, head right, like a tennis match. Sometimes soft, almost melting tenderness in her eyes, meeting mine. When I kiss her belly or toes, she lies back, eyes half-closed, fat fond smile on face, or eyes close altogether in carnal bliss.'

They got back to Slad 'just in time for the winter' at the end of March, to a cottage 'damp and cold as the grave'. There were

blizzards, frost, hail. 'The only one who thrives is Jessy,' he told Tom Matthews, 'who is pink-cheeked as a baby seal.' Jessy was handed around the pub to cries of acclaim. Two village children, Hazel and Margaret, brought trinkets and posies, made coronets of daisies, and covered Laurie with parsley-blossom as he lay in the garden 'till I looked like a snowdrift'. They danced on the lawn, made biscuits cut into hearts and stars, crayoned a large picture captioned 'A House of Love to the Three Who Live in Rose Cottage'. 'They are too good to be true,' said Laurie.

The mood was infectious. 'J is increasingly delicious,' he told Celia Goodman. 'She crawled yesterday for the first time – in fact she sprang like a lemur across the floor on her knuckles and toes, after a biscuit.' When he first played his guitar for her she splayed her fingers like a pianist. ('Clearly notices music.') He enclosed a snap of Jessy with guitar, at kitchen table: 'See the absorption and the delicacy of the fingering.' On Mayday morning as the cuckoo called, he took her out to pick cowslips and gillyflowers. It was 'a celestial May, weeks of heat and shimmering white blossom – white clematis, azalea, lilac, peony, and Jessy in her white lace & sun-bonnet', as he told Celia.

He even wrote a new poem, 'Night Speech', having at first resisted the Arts Council's £30 commission for the Stratford festival. The poem had to incorporate lines from Shakespeare: Laurie chose 'The bright day is done,/And we are for the dark . . .' from *Antony and Cleopatra*. He joined in a Society of Authors discussion (chairman: Roy Fuller) about how to sell more poetry books. Laurie, of course, was unabashed about selling his wares at readings. At Lewisham library he 'slightly shocked the librarian' by producing a briefcase full of books for sale. 'Sold all of them. For this talk I was paid only £20 less than the hired killer who shot down gangster in local Catford club the other night.' That July Simon Phipps, Bishop of Coventry, read 'Day of These Days' in Coventry Cathedral to the accompaniment of Bach, and told him 'the effect was magical and immensely touching'. Several composers began setting Laurie's poems to music: Samuel Barber and Sir Lennox Berkeley both chose to use his 'Twelfth Night'. Sir Lennox, a

Gloucestershire man, was commissioned by the Stroud Festival, and after months of intensive work, trying 'to keep the feeling of absolute freshness that all your poetry has . . . the very thing that I like most about it', his *Signs in the Dark* was performed by the Hirsch Chamber Players and the Stroud Festival Choir in October 1967. Laurie sent him bound copies of the poems, in his own hand.

But most of his work now was radio talks and magazine commissions. Though Laurie always found writing laborious he was an accomplished hack who could turn out nostalgic sentiment about anything: the magic of water, for instance. 'I discovered water at the age of four, at the mouth of our cottage pump . . . A magic plaything with a brilliant life of its own . . . like liquid sky . . . Fire is masculine, blundering, crude; water is feminine and far more subtle . . . Water is all things to me, and most of them good.' For an *Evening Standard* series, he wrote about 'The Street Where I Live', describing Elm Park Gardens as 'a kind of buffer-state between Chelsea and Fulham, a layer cake, a Chinese box, with its curious eruptions of communal life on Guy Fawkes Night when the whole square is ablaze' (and when Laurie would light Roman candles and Catherine wheels held in his teeth). He wrote a poetic tribute to Churchill's funeral ('A cold east wind blows over the roof of Westminster . . .'). For *Mademoiselle* he went to Clare, Galway, Connemara, Kerry, Cork and Dublin. By going away for ten days he missed Jessy's first tottering steps: 'hardly recognized the blonde curly sun-burnt heavyweight standing in play-pen on lawn' when he came home. 'I never want to leave her.'

The summer of 1964 was a time of high contentment, when Laurie one day used the heading 'A Happy Day' in his diary. For weeks on end, the sky was cloudless, the garden still. They would breakfast in the garden before Laurie went off to Stroud. Kathy and Jessy would meet him from the bus home, and they would walk with a flask of tea, to the long high grass of Bulls Cross or Swift's Hill, or take a bus to Dursley. 'C & J waiting at bus stop with kite, picnic . . .' 'J in papoose, down Teakle's field, over bridge, up 3 Webb's fields to Swift's Hill, J happy in her bag on shoulder drumming my head.' Jessy claimed to remember the

sensation of freedom of those rides on Laurie's back, the long views over Stroud to the Severn.

'The wind blows through the grass & Jess slaps her fat legs & shouts among the harebells.' 'Put J in carrier whistling, singing, shouting & took her to Juniper & got blackberries.' 'J sitting happily on rug, chattering. Cathy happy too, serving strong tea from thermos.' '7 in evening, sun still on our side but gone from the village. We walk slowly down into the shadows, J rosy, ready for bed.'

For once, summer in the south of France held no allure; Laurie went without Kathy, and told his diary 'only wanting home & the garden & the bright faces & the children'.

'Jessy was always so jolly at six in the morning,' he remembered later, 'beaming a smile like the sun rising. And I'd lay her on a shawl, and we'd go round the garden, and listen to the peonies and poppies opening; they make a stretching, squeaky noise. I heard them with her, I hadn't heard them before. And she'd lick the roses. I call that the supreme act of sensuality: to lean over and lick the dew off, which I've always wanted to do.'[1]

The fascination with Jessy was total. 'J discovered echo' . . . 'J found way up stairs, puffing, groaning "oh dear", using her knees like a mountaineer' . . . 'J fell down stairs, but without real hurt, falling like a fat plump pillow slowly from stair to stair' . . . 'Tonight very gay, in my arms, dancing round & turning her head like a ballroom beauty as we turn & spin – would not let me stop – looking with mad gaiety out of the corner of her eyes to see that mum was watching.'

He did have moments of 'sudden panic in all this pleasure to think of death, & death for all, & for the world, nothing to be left of this'. But the fruit of this paternal bliss was to be that apogee of sentiment, *The Firstborn*, which he wrote first for the *Evening Standard*. By the time she was being photographed blowing out her first birthday candle, Jessy was famous. Laurie was much interviewed about fatherhood: 'When A Poet Becomes a Father at 50' ('A late only child is specially vulnerable to indulgence') and wrote an article called 'What I Would Like to Give My Child'. The picture, in dozens of interviews, was roseate. 'Laurie Lee unhooks a Spanish

guitar from the wall to sing flamenco to his small daughter, Jessy: "I said I'd never have children till I could see them being bathed in a tin bath in front of a Cotswold cottage fire just the way I was."' He was photographed walking out, pipe in mouth, Jessy strapped to his back. 'With a shepherd's crook in his hand he walks for miles through the woods of his childhood on a perfect October day.' 'Sunshine slanted through the leaves bringing a golden glow to the little white-washed cottage in the heart of the Cotswolds.' Kathy was 'lovely, auburn-haired . . .' The contented baby chuckled. They still had no telephone, television, washing machine or refrigerator. The impression was of three lives locked in serene simplicity.

Three days before Laurie's fiftieth birthday, Princess Peg sent a note headed 'BAD NEWS': Celia Goodman's husband Arthur had been found shot dead that morning, his dog Guy beside him. 'Celia calm but broken utterly.' The safety catch on Goodman's gun was faulty; perhaps, the coroner concluded, he had sat down to smoke a cigarette, propping his gun against a tree, and the dog had jumped up suddenly, releasing the trigger. He was not yet fifty, their children only seven and eight. Celia had been on her way home from Aldeburgh on the fateful day. For the fourth time in eight years, Laurie wrote a 'good' letter to a young widow after an 'utterly wasteful and tragic' death.

'This is a bitter loss,' he wrote. 'I remember last March, going to the woods with Arthur. He was a happy child . . . The gun was a sort of talismanic wand by which he was granted his intimacy with that particular world, the trees and red sky and the birds . . . There is no comfort in it . . . Except that it was where he liked to be and not in the squalor of a road crash or hospital (or old age) and that one feels that he was happy at that moment, expecting to see you tomorrow.'

This year, instead of enjoying their usual Guy Fawkes night in the square of Elm Park Gardens, Laurie lit the bonfire at Sheepscombe's village firework display, with Jessy on his back, rockets whizzing over the valley and the whiff of gunpowder. But in mid-November they went back to London ('J running shouting through pigeons to see the Trafalgar Square fountains') and Kathy took Jessy to Italy,

returning 'looking beautiful as a queen in her furs', in time for the launch of *The Firstborn*.

Illustrated with Laurie's own photographs of mother and baby, this charming little book ('She was born in the autumn and was a late fall in my life . . .') was received with much rapture. 'A proud-dad confection I'm afraid,' he wrote to Celia. 'I will have to watch it.' Even the hardest heart melts at the idea of the newborn. One letter typically said: 'But Laurie, I wouldn't have believed that even you could have done it. Anything new about anything so old; anything beautiful, even, about anything so private.'

But when he wrote, 'I have got a daughter, whose life is already separate from mine, whose will already follows its own directions, and who has quickly corrected my woolly preconceptions of her by being something remorselessly different,' he surely wrote with hindsight, having watched, twenty years ago, Yasmin's transformation into a self-willed toddler.

The question is, did Laurie not hesitate to call his book so blatantly *The Firstborn*? Yasmin, her primogeniture thus denied, was understanding. 'He did send me the book, with a note saying he had me in mind too when he was writing it. I could understand it: if you have a baby at twenty-five, and it's stolen by fairies in the night, and you think you'll never have another, and then you do have one at fifty, it must seem like a gift from the gods. I had been kidnapped, and now at last he had his own baby who would not be taken away.

'I might have felt differently if my mother had lived with Laurie and I'd known him on a personal basis as Jessy did. I think Laurie had an extremely conventional idea of honour and propriety. He was married now, and this was *their* firstborn. His relationship with my mother was something quite other. Also, he was incorrigibly a dark horse, a man of privacy and intrigue, who loved having a secret.'

When they returned to Slad for the summer (the cottage damp again, and also smelling of dog, a relic of their winter tenants), Laurie discovered, as he had with Yasmin, that a mobile toddler was a different proposition from a cradle-bound infant: 'Jessy aged 18 months trampled on the crocuses.' 'Tough, aggressive, independent,

restless, domineering now . . . J very belligerent, strong rebellious. Hits out at me if anything goes wrong. At her gayest, most playful & charming just before going to bed. But sleeps badly. And when wakes, howls.' But then, on May Day, he heard the first cuckoo with her. And she knew sixty words; he listed them all from Daddy to Baccy. And when she said 'Ark at rain', 'Chickens sleeping' and 'Daddy, moon!' it was a miracle. Like Ted Hughes's small daughter Frieda[2] she was moon-crazed: 'Woke her night of full moon, and she leapt in my arms, wouldn't sleep again for hours. Morning ran into garden: "Moon gone." ' She seemed to have 'a natural whimsy' but also compassion ('Poor cows in the mist'). She loved poly-syllables like *'fantastic hippopotamus'*. Her voice was distinctively husky and raucous: in church one day the kneeling congregation were praying in silence when Jessy yelled, 'Wake up, Jesus!'

She was to go to Laurie's old village school in Slad, now reduced to only nine pupils and threatened with closure. Laurie – 'I am pressed to agitate against it. Have been cast by newspapers as defending my old school' – dutifully wrote to local papers pointing out that the village without a school would become 'nothing but a bus stop in children's lives'. In June he went to see Anthony Crosland, then Education Secretary, about it, to no avail.

He went again for a fortnight to the Behrenses' villa at Cap d'Antibes without the family and returned at the end of June on an evening of 'buttery sunlight' to find Kathy and Jessy both in pink, the child with a rose in her hair, waiting at the edge of the beechwood as he came up in the bus. Jessy ran at him like a golden bull with 'fat wet orchid kisses'. Rose Cottage garden was 'full to the brim with roses, like the hold of some mossy-green barge laden with petals for some scent-making port in Arabia'. He had trained wild briars among the climbers 'like a revolt among the peasants'. Madame Albertine had clambered right over the roof; the foxgloves were seven feet high.

Yasmin was now pregnant with her second child; Laurie hoped she would have a boy. 'I'm in the centre of a hushed dynastic pause,' he said, and when on 8 July 1965 Yasmin's son Gabriel was born, he was atavistically delighted.

Laurie knew he must write another book soon. The royalties from *Cider* cushioned him from real need, and he was always in demand to make nostalgic little television films about 'my village' ('So I'm up to my neck in local colour: damp green at present,' he told Tom Matthews), but otherwise he was getting only two-guinea reprint fees for anthologies or five guineas for a poetry reading. Matthews tried to arrange for Laurie a creative writing fellowship at an American university, Brandeis or Princeton; but Laurie baulked at this: 'Part of my nature is a phobia of being turned down – which is why I seldom ring up even close friends to suggest myself, but am delighted when they invite me.' Eventually he told Matthews to desist: he did not want to go away. 'I would have loved this once, but I think it is too late now. What with my commitment here, life with Jessy etc. and a growing middle-aged fondness for home, I can't really envisage going off for a prolonged sojourn abroad.'

Laurie said 1965 was the quietest summer he could remember, 'almost entirely without news from outside'. Kathy's half-brother Walter Sarfatti and Roland Joffé came to stay. One night they went up to Painswick Beacon at 9 p.m. to see the chain of torches lit across the land launching Operation Neptune, the project to save Britain's coastline. 'Line of dark figures on ridge at dusk. Jonathan Blow, lord of the manor, with 18-month-old son on shoulder, lit beacon. Another glowed on Robinswood Hill. Soon could count eight . . .' Jessy rode in a pony and trap with Laurie when he opened a church fête at Sudgrove House, the home of the show-jumper Pat Smythe, at Miserden. They went down to Yasmin's farm in Devon, where Laurie lay on bales of hay while daughter and granddaughter played the old game of removing his glasses.

When Yasmin had a solo show of paintings in Worthing that summer, Laurie bought one 'which I would have wanted whoever had painted it – the honeysuckle & rose, which is you, me, my mother, and summer, full of light and perfectly delineated . . . a window into the summer world'. While there, he saw Lorna, to whom he now referred always as 'Mum'. 'I had a lovely day with Mum,' he told Yasmin. They had driven about Sussex talking

non-stop and ended up in Bognor having fish and chips for old times' sake. 'Our first day together for perhaps ten years, thanks to you.'

'The relationship had been resolved and normalized by time,' Yasmin says. 'Laurie still made jokes about the power she had over him; but the jokes were a way of exorcizing her enormous and absolute power. There was bound to be a strong dynamic at work psychologically between them, given the degree of infatuated passion there had been.'

Kathy struck a blow for freedom that summer by taking secret driving lessons whenever Laurie was away. On 23 September she passed her test and told him she had a surprise. (He thought she was going to say she was pregnant again.) He bought a little Morris Traveller, plus a new red notebook in which to log every mile, noting (for a few months) the time of departure from Slad and arrival in London, the stops at filling-stations and the mileage on the clock.

Elizabeth Jane Howard, now Mrs Kingsley Amis, gave them dinner in the jungly conservatory of their dilapidated Maida Vale house. Jane says she would never have done so if she had known about Amis's *Spectator* review ten years before; 'But Laurie's kind of writing would never appeal to Kingsley.' She had never told Amis about herself and Laurie. 'He wasn't very interested in my past. Just as well: let it lie, really.' The two men later met often on judging panels and in the Garrick bar. But Laurie never forgot. In 1981 he said: 'Every weekend at Paddington I make sure my stuff is in front of Kingsley Amis on the station bookstall.'[2]

Jane's new novel, *After Julius*, was in Laurie's view 'supercharged, well written and also very funny. Every page is what is known in photographic printing as superform doubleweight lustre. Of course I have a following interest in the ghost of Dan.' (Dan is a fascinating character with several attributes of a younger Laurie: an impecunious poet with a rustic accent, a long white scar on his chest and a predilection for well-bred girls, party tricks and fireworks.)

In London Laurie continued to work in a mysterious way. The new year of 1966 found him at home in bed with a seasonal chill

and Tom's annual gift crate of Perequita wine. He always let the flat while in Slad (Nell Dunn was one tenant) but now they often had lodgers, even when there themselves: Rebecca John, granddaughter of Augustus, stayed there while preparing her portfolio for the Central School. Her father, the First Sea Lord, Caspar John, had a Cotswold cottage at Needlehole, where Laurie had once enthralled Rebecca during a walk, explaining every stone and hedgerow. 'I was in awe of Laurie, and lapped up all the jewels on offer.' And Kathy, who had once danced flamenco in a circular skirt at her parents' house, seemed to her a goddess. In Elm Park Gardens, however, Rebecca would observe Kathy forever running upstairs from the kitchen with trays, waiting on Laurie in his study. To Kathy, this was her unquestioned destiny. But Rebecca was made uneasy by it. Laurie seemed distant, Kathy lonely. 'I had never seen anything like it. My mother never danced round my father.'

Josceline Dimbleby too remembers a summer weekend at the Astors' house, Bruern, when Laurie played his recorder and Josceline, who had just left the Guildhall School of Music, sang Scarlatti arias. Laurie was 'instantly friendly and extremely flirtatious. I was very embarrassed that his wife was there with the baby, and kept wondering what she must think.'

In the pub, Antonia says, Laurie was incorrigible: 'He'd see a pretty girl, gaze into her eyes and say, "You do know, don't you, that your eyes are enough to make any man kill himself for love?" and the girl would melt before such flattery.' The public Laurie was easy-going and full of mischief. He also seemed to slot neatly into an artistic peer-group, one whose signature appeared with those of Hockney, E.M. Forster, Elisabeth Lutyens and others, on a letter to *The Times* that April: 'We 54 voted Labour and do not support US policies in Vietnam nor British endorsement of these.'

Privately, however, he was often deeply depressed. '4 April 1966: A week in bed, most of it alone. Terrible vacant timeless time. Sleeping shivering, watching television. Bitterly cold weather too.' Wintry SAD had taken hold, complicated by his double life, about which he had pangs of guilt, reflected in dreams such as the

nightmare he had about Pen Dugdale finding out about the relationship with Antonia. He was also convinced that his old friends were disappearing. He told Celia Goodman: 'A rather burdensome winter with too much fever had left me with that particular desolation which you too must know from time to time, only I'm sure you fight it better. Worse still, all the friends I ever knew seemed to have gone from my life – I don't know where, or why. I felt very chilled and joyless . . . I was particularly heartened to get a message from you, and to know that a friend survived.'

Laurie returned to Slad that spring to play the celebrity, judging bonnets at the Stroud Licensed Victuallers' dance. 'Weak & depressed as illness makes me, & squalid as cottage is, these returns sometimes full of anti-London charm. Tea by fire, small children crawling around, Martin [Lomberg, a neighbour's child], shining red-faced climbing on one knee & jealous Jess climbing on other. Damp death-trap that this place is, it is hard to resist such moments, threadbare as they may be against the cheerless reality of the place.'

His notebook recorded: 'I am so cold all the time. And weak. Feeling pains in my chest. A little weeding brings me out into a sweat. Still not recovered after 3 weeks chill. Fifth bout this winter.' Lewis Eyers told him 'there'll be a white one tomorrow' and there was: snow in April. 'Fierce blizzard. Went to Stroud to buy rug. All shops closed at 9.15. Everyone ill in Slad. And me. Sick bouts of fever; very low, all doors closing; drink, music, love, friends – hope I will not grow too cold to love Jessy.'

Within a week, working its usual magic, spring arrived and Laurie was out taping birdsong, taking Jessy into the garden before breakfast to look for spider-houses in the dewy grass. The temperature rose, flowers erupted, they went for picnics in the Colne Valley and at Arlington Horseshoe and on the 'most perfect May Day I can remember' they were having Bloody Marys and lunch in the garden at Combe with Tom Matthews and his new wife Pamela. 'The sun & the village are working their usual consolations,' he told Celia, '& I have been busy building stone walls and have lost several pounds and gained some patience and played a tape of the Mozart which I had not for months.'

He had just bought Beech Cottage, down the lane, to renovate and rent out furnished, and Kathy drove about buying secondhand furniture for it. They took Jessy to the Mediterranean, to the Behrenses on the Côte d'Azur, 'where life was so splendid it was almost without sensation', he told Yasmin, '& there was nothing to do except eat, drink & wallow in the warm sea; Jessy turned a nice pale toast colour . . .'

He was thinking of going abroad for the whole of the next winter, but instead of escaping to the sun he was suddenly taken into St Stephen's Hospital, with gallstones and a hernia – which he told Kathy not to mention to anyone. He was in a ward 'full of tough cheerful young motor cyclists with broken limbs' but 'not a very good patient', he admitted, 'imagining the worst & watching the great black wall roll up around me. Mainly I suppose I resent losing contact with Jessy. This is the first time for a week I've been able to hold a pen or write a word without boiling over like a kettle.' He was there all through Christmas 1966, which was 'a bit of a blur', he told Roy Fuller. On 10 January Kathy left for Slad, 'and I am being taken over by friends'.

It seems extraordinary that ten years elapsed between Laurie's
first and second volumes of autobiography. Even for a slow and
painstaking writer, this looks like excessive care. As the decade
progressed, Laurie was distracted. His persons from Porlock
were commissions from magazines; recurrent and persistent
depressions; and that old obstacle, the pram in the hall. Jessy aged
three, although 'winning & voluptuously loving', cramped Laurie's
former social style. He explained to Tom Matthews that he and
Kathy were 'so domestically disorganized' that seeing friends for
dinner was impossible. Weekends too were out, Kathy told Celia
Goodman, because of Jessy's 'terrible energy' in the early mornings:
'Once we were staying away and she woke at 3.15 and never went
to sleep again. She was perfectly all right the next day – but I
wasn't.'

Laurie at least could still escape occasionally; after a trip to Cyprus
in July 1967 he told Tom Matthews he was 'back from the arms
of Aphrodite into the more bouncing ones of Jessy'. For once, that
summer, he was commissioned to write something that was not an
exotic travelogue: the American magazine *Redbook* sent him to
Aberfan, the Welsh village where 116 children had been buried
under a toppling tip of coal-waste one year before. So he had a real
story to cover. John Summers, who was there for the *Telegraph*
magazine, says the Aberfan families told him how much they liked
Laurie – 'and they were ready to tear the skin off most journalists
who hung round there'. Summers decided that Laurie was the kind
of person you wanted to do something for. It was he who found
an old Leica camera for Laurie, for £17 10s, and he who introduced
Laurie to the blue Japanese Pentel pens with which he wrote letters
for the rest of his life.

The Aberfan piece could hardly fail to be moving, but Laurie

brought to it his instinctive sympathy with small village lives, in 'a huddle of anonymous terraced houses of uniform ugliness unrelieved except for chapel and pub'. There was no need to inflate his prose. His quotations from the parents who had lost their children, some of whom he met in the graveyard, had sympathy and immediacy. The children who survived, he noted, were lavished with expensive toys and treats. 'Unhappily the bereaved can't help feeling their loss twice bitter when faced by these rewards of survival. "Isn't it enough that they lived?" they often ask. The presence of the children who were spared adds to the tragic problem. Aberfan, it is said, suffered from two disasters – first the landslide, then an avalanche of money.'

Rosamond Lehmann suddenly resurfaced that year, seeking Laurie's help with the title for her 1967 book about her dead daughter, taken from a song that ended 'with one star awake, As the swan in the evening moves over the lake'. In *The Swan in the Evening*, Rosamond mentioned that Laurie shared her belief that a fragrance of flowers, 'an unearthly aromatic sweetness', filled her flat when (she was convinced) her daughter's spirit was present. But as Laurie privately said, 'Of course I didn't witness anything – but I couldn't hurt her feelings, poor woman.' In fact he was appalled by her self-delusion. 'She took me into the flat one day and said, "There, Sally's been again. She knows those are my favourite flowers. You can smell it, can't you?" It was self-deception on such a moving scale. She was getting love messages and flowers every day from a medium, and was convinced that they were genuine. Anyone who had a touch of awareness would know that Sally didn't write like that, didn't think like that.'

When Jock Gallagher from the BBC went down to Slad in the autumn of 1967 to suggest a radio programme about rural England, he found Laurie 'cool, almost to the point of hostility. Almost unaware of my presence.' Jock tried quoting from his article on autobiography in the *New York Times*: 'For me it is a celebration of living and an attempt to hoard its sensations.' 'Hmmn,' said Laurie. 'It's rather good isn't it.' But he remained stubborn, and Jock rose to leave, until Laurie asked: 'Haven't you got any more

flattery then? You could always try money.' The programme they made together was the first of many.

When Laurie congratulated Cecil Day-Lewis on succeeding John Masefield to the Poet Laureateship in January 1968 he was, inevitably, in bed with 'flu. But what chiefly preoccupied him that winter was finally finishing *As I Walked Out One Midsummer Morning*. At last.

For the tale of his Spanish adventure he drew heavily on his precious diaries: how else could he have recreated so vividly, in his mid-fifties, the feeling of being carefree and twenty, 'fat with time', without responsibilities and with the world on his side. 'I haven't a good memory,' he said. 'Without the diaries I couldn't have written the book. With them, the physical sensations all return. Wham! It's like playing a tape.' And he was also free to excise totally the rather important presence of Wilma from his story, since she had died in 1963.

To refresh his memory of *tiempos perdidos* he took Kathy and Jessy back to Gibraltar, Algeciras, Ceuta and Almuñécar in March 1968. He had been longing to take Jessy to Spain. 'Cathy was greeted with rough cries by many old friends,' he told Celia Goodman, 'and Jessy punished with kisses from policemen at which she shouts "Here! You! stop it!"' She also, his notebook records, flung her chubby arms quite indiscriminately round 'an old gypsy witch, an elderly waiter, an Arab woman and a bus driver'.

Laurie went back again to Spain the following month, via the ferry to Santander, this time with Antonia who drove him about in a hired car, and by the end of April he had finished the book. 'I consider it absolutely valueless,' he told Celia. 'Indeed I doubt that I will show it to anyone. Yet I feel wonderfully relaxed now that it is done.' As well he might: Laurie had succeeded in capturing, for generations of readers, a flavour of Spain which – whatever Kingsley Amis might think, and no matter that several other writers, V.S. Pritchett for instance, had walked across those sierras and stayed at *ventas* and *posadas* before him – is still recognizable and true today.

Laurie told Celia he had been reading about the Hesse family. 'What a sombre thread of doom seems to run through so much of it . . . One can't help admiring the way Peg and Lu have maintained their spirit when one considers how life has insulted them with more than their share of tragedy,' Laurie wrote. But within weeks, Prince Ludwig was dead, at fifty-nine. On the day of the funeral, despite 'utter utter misery', Princess Peg was writing to Laurie about 'the fun we four had together, the adventures, the laughs, the red wine (or white for that matter!); burning castles; songs and Easter eggs. I suppose I will carry on somehow . . . but the centre of my heart is empty & will always remain so.'

Laurie went to Wolfsgarten for the memorial service, but collapsed on his return, 'and for two weeks have had to keep to my room with drawn blinds & under some rather heavy sedation,' he told Celia. 'From the middle of June I passed through an unexplained trough . . . It hasn't been too good with me since Christmas, but the last bout was the worst and it steals away much of the pleasure of life. Part of the pain was to hear Jess calling to me from the summer garden & to be quite unable to go out to join her. Also reading, writing & even music were denied me for days . . .

'One consolation: the book I was so uncertain about has been surprisingly well received by the publisher's readers. I still think they are over-praising it, but I have been comforted by what they said.' His publisher was to be André Deutsch: not, after all, Chatto & Windus, who had been waiting for this book ('Opus 2') for nearly ten years. Deutsch explains that it was after a W.H. Smith prizegiving at the Savoy, while Deutsch was driving Laurie home, that Laurie suddenly offered him the manuscript of his Spanish book, if he wanted it. 'Are you kidding?' said the incredulous Deutsch. ('I nearly drove up Nelson's Column.') It turned out that Laurie had been irritated, at the party, to be asked by Ian Parsons of Chatto, 'How's life in Slough?' This was to Laurie an unforgivable error: so Deutsch got the prize, and told *Smith's Trade News* that the new book was 'simply a masterpiece'. Norah Smallwood was extremely distressed, but Laurie assured Deutsch that he had 'cleared' his move with Chatto. The title, it had to be explained,

was a traditional opening to old ballads, a way of saying 'once upon a time', but it was constantly mangled (the Day-Lewises called it 'As I Walked Out One Somerset Maugham').

Jessy had started at Slad school, 'going off down the lane with a bow-legged swagger'. She was only there for a couple of terms before the school was closed; Laurie then somehow arranged for her to attend Painswick Primary in summer, and a school in Park Walk, Chelsea, in the winter. ('I don't think it did much for my education,' Jessy says.) These constant migrations, soon complicated by a hamster, a goldfish and a bright blue budgerigar named Cherry, a present from Peggy Ashcroft on Jessy's fourth birthday, also had the effect of making Jessy think she had no family apart from her parents and Jack's two boys, Johnny and Howard. (At Johnny's wedding in 1969, the precocious six-year-old Jessy said to the bride: 'And are you going to sleep with Johnny in that bed?') 'I had a life dictated by Laurie,' Jessy says, 'and as far as Laurie could see, there was no need for me to acknowledge the local relations he had around Slad. The three of us had this different life, travelling up and down to London. So I grew up thinking I had no family, when in fact, counting both sides, I had eighty-seven cousins.'

Jessy's godfather Tom Matthews and his vivacious third wife Pamela, the Anglo-Irish, horse-loving widow of Colonel V. Poliakoff ('Popski'),[1] had now bought beautiful Cavendish Hall, Suffolk, which had been Pam's childhood home. 'Cavendish sounds rather eighteenth-century pastoral,' said Laurie. It was indeed, and it opened up another sumptuous country refuge for the Lees, with horses for Jessy to ride. They found Tom 'trimly set like Virgil in his Palladian villa'. 'What a touch Pam has, and what an eye,' wrote Laurie, 'and what vigour to get things done as she wants them in this frustrating against-the-wind world.' He sympathized with Pam's difficulties in getting a good Spanish couple. 'One of the saddest things to have happened to Europe in the last six years is the corruption of that people, and the rapidity of it. Tourism, industrial expansion – I thought they'd be the last to go. Well, they've gone – right over the top.'

By September 1968, despite having overcome the hurdle of

finishing the book, Laurie was in a mysterious state of nervous depression, and in November, in an attempt to 'get himself sorted out' says Kathy, he spent a week in the National Hospital for Neurology and Neurosurgery in Queen Square, Bloomsbury. His diary on 13 November records that he was being injected with Valium and was 'woken 10 times'. He was still not well in January when Princess Peg heard about his illness.

Peg, after her first Christmas without Lu, was staying in the palace of Drottningholm with her friend the King of Sweden, aged eighty-six. His old palace was 'a living cosy museum, vast but warm, and every clock ticks, and there are flowers in vases . . . The king and I walk through snow-covered parks and watch the full moon come up at 15.30 hrs.' Clearly Peg thought it would be good for Laurie (and herself) to be reminded of people who bore up well in the face of real tragedy. 'The king has lost two much loved wives & his eldest son was killed in an air crash so he knows. And can give tips on how to carry on – not become a sad bore – or egocentric, & how true it is "laugh & the world laughs with you" etc. Anyway I'm full of good intentions but sometimes suffer from battle fatigue . . .

'I was depressed & worried to hear you have been ill again – & sincerely hope the "rainbow pill" treatment is really making you feel better at last.'

Alas, the rainbow pill was no match for winter SAD. 'Winter seems always to be a time of heavy groans for me, and I don't spare my friends the sound of it, which by now is something I should have learnt to do,' he confessed to Celia Goodman.

'The last year has been a bad one in every sense, public & private, I hardly travel at all now, & for the last 6 months have found it increasingly difficult to write even letters. I've no doubt that this is a phase, but it loses more time than is tolerable & wastes more friends than I can afford. This is not so much a letter as a wave through a dark window. With love, Laurie.'

For some years Laurie had been encouraging Antonia to find a husband, and that year she told him she had met someone she wanted to marry. So the convenient arrangement of being looked after in London and chauffeured on foreign trips would come

to an end. Antonia's wedding to Nicholas Young was to be in September, on the publication day of *As I Walked Out One Midsummer Morning*.

Laurie did manage, in the spring of 1969, to write a spirited foreword to a new edition of Roy Campbell's memoirs, *Light on a Dark Horse*. Campbell had died twelve years before, in 1957. His wife Mary was at the wheel on a lonely road south of Lisbon when a tyre burst; Campbell was killed and she was badly injured. Laurie's foreword was a warm tribute to 'a romantic idealist', the only poet he had ever met who was not faintly disappointing to meet. 'Roy Campbell was . . . perhaps one of our last pre-technocratic, big action poets who, like D'Annunzio and Byron, were not only the writers of exquisite lyrics but whose poetry was part of a physical engagement with life . . .' he wrote. There was something fantastic about Campbell's stories of derring-do, Laurie said, but 'Personally, I much preferred his style to the English passion for understatement, which is only boasting stood on its head.' The publisher Guido Waldman told him he had hit just the right note, and sent 50 guineas. Laurie also wrote a fulsome foreword to a book of poems by his Slad Valley friend Frank Mansell: 'The poet's voice reverberates with the resonance of the Cotswold Highlands, with all the smooth-wrapped hardness of moss-dressed stone . . .' Thanking Laurie, Frank said: 'What we are really doing is creating legend, leaving a landmark, a sarsen stone to show we passed this way.'

The spring migration to Slad in 1969 once more coincided with snow, sleet, hail and gales. 'They say it's always like this when the Lees come back to Slad,' Laurie told Tom Matthews. But he had one more excursion to the sun. He flew to Gibraltar and was driven to Ronda, where he produced a poem called 'Gitano y Gitanas',[2] datelined 'Ronda, Spring 1969'. Laurie's diary is very blank for the rest of that summer. He undertook his usual poetry readings, and judged the Young Writer of the Year for the *Telegraph*. Tom Matthews arrived in his Jensen in July to cheer Laurie with a week's laddish jaunt up to Hereford, Ludlow and into Wales. They called on Emma Smith in her Welsh cottage, and Emma recalls Matthews lying in a stupor on her lawn.

388 | *Laurie Lee: The Well-loved Stranger*

The prospects for Laurie's new book were certainly propitious. Four extracts in the *New Yorker* would pay a total of $20,000. For this he had to endure the editor William Shawn's queries over the punctuation which spattered each galley-sheet: 'Every comma is questioned. They cut out all my jokes (perhaps rightly) and also each and every one of the few references to sex there were . . . You feel as if Nanny were giving you a wash and brush up so you'd be ready to go down to the drawing room.' André Deutsch, after an unforgettable sales conference at which Laurie played his violin and Deutsch carried on a very loud business negotiation on the telephone during Laurie's recital, printed an initial run of 50,000 copies.

Meanwhile *Cider with Rosie* sales were boosted by its becoming that summer a set text for O-level English Literature pupils, who were asked questions such as: What did Laurie Lee mean by saying 'Nothing happened at all except summer'? What did they under-stand by 'the grass scaffolding the sky'? Had Laurie succeeded in recapturing the presence of his mother? The first coaches full of teenagers began to arrive in Slad as teachers took their pupils to see Laurie's old family cottage – just as Laurie was trying to assume a new public image in order to relive, at fifty-five, his wandering minstrel youth. He told Sally Beauman (now a successful novelist, but then a young *Telegraph* feature-writer of twenty-three) that he was sick of being written about as a country bumpkin. 'Writers come down to Slad and they get bemused with elderberry wine . . .'

What she saw instead was a metropolitan figure in his Chelsea eyrie 'in his Alabama planter's suit and Bermuda tan' – although the photograph showed him setting out for a picnic on Swift's Hill, with Jessy and Kathy in her Jackie Kennedy shades and headscarf, carrying a hamper.

'No one ever comes in here,' Laurie told Sally Beauman, allowing her a glimpse of his Chelsea study overflowing with papers, old yellowing news-sheets, boxes full of letters, books and manuscripts piled on shelves, spilling from cupboards, covering table and floor. 'I used to mock my mother,' Laurie said, 'because she never threw anything away. "Ooh our mother, she's terrible." Now I find I'm

just like her.' But Sally found the living-room 'a beautiful jumble: jugs of flowers, sheets of music, a guitar, photographs, books, plump sofa and chairs, a screen hung with brass rubbings and on the walls, paintings of blue girls by Laurie Lee'. He told her: 'I always wanted to be a painter. Best of all after music I liked to draw. But I also like to feel wanted, and nobody ever said to me, we'd like some more of your paintings.' Otherwise he'd be an artist now, 'earning lots of money, surrounded by beautiful girls'.

They lunched at the Chelsea Arts Club, 'heavy with leather and portraits of stags and maids serving Brown Windsor and cabbage in the dining room . . . reminiscent of a small Cambridge college, or Bloomsbury'. In the garden with its fountain and benches in little arbours, Laurie ordered barley wine and told Sally she must not over-emphasize 'the Gloucestershire angle'. (But he never completely sloughed off the hayseed image; and when it suited him he was perfectly prepared, later, to be visited by journalists in Slad.)

He did not look forward to going back to Spain without a companion, but the BBC took him there in August to make a film to promote his book. This brought about 'the Spanish disaster'. In Segovia the BBC car was broken into, and his priceless 1935–7 diaries were stolen. It was the bitterest of ironies that this should happen just when he was publishing a passionately pro-Spain book which has inspired countless readers to travel there. 'A nightmare,' he said later. 'Nothing could be worse for a writer.' Not only had he lost for ever his record of his Spanish Civil War days – on which his promised third volume would so depend – but he had lost his faith in the Spanish people. 'The one thing I thought I knew about Spain was how honest it was – you could leave anything anywhere.' He was driven from Segovia by Michael Astor's son Jamie and his then girlfriend Marina Warner – who were travelling around Avila and Seville on a working holiday – and got back to torrential thunderstorms in Madrid.

'What a nasty thing to have happen to you, and in a country you feel so special about,' wrote Tom Matthews, to whom Laurie had dedicated the new book. Matthews suspected that the theft must have been General Franco's secret police at work. To Laurie

it was not just 'nasty'; it was 'the end of a 30-year love affair'. It was the unhappy result of travelling in cars stuffed with expensive cameras, he added. 'The police thought it rather a joke – but I lost some things that can't be replaced, including a photograph of Kathy on the roof of Santa Eulalia which I always carried in my diary.'

He had kept those diaries safely since 1938. 'I was in despair,' he remembered, twenty years later, when struggling to write his Spanish Civil War book from memory. 'And the anxiety hasn't lessened. I feel myself imprisoned in the need to complete the trilogy.'

As I Walked Out One Midsummer Morning was bound to be a Christmas bestseller. But on publication day Laurie was 'shaky', taking his knockout pills when not on show on the publicity circuit. He was also buying Littlecourt, the house next door to Rose Cottage, having borrowed money from Deutsch on the strength of expected sales. About these he was mulishly determined to be disappointed. But Cecil Day-Lewis, who could not come to the launch at the Chelsea Arts Club – 'I avoid publishers' parties like the Black Death. Also, I am recovering from a coronary' – told him the new volume was every bit as effective as *Cider*. 'The early days of the Spanish war you do marvellously.' Edward Blishen called it a gem. S.J. Perelman had sent 'a deep comradely bow'. The *TLS* said it was 'a work of art, the finer for appearing artless'. All reviewers were tantalized by the last paragraph about the rich lady who had abandoned her husband and children for him. His final sentence, 'I was back in Spain, with a winter of war before me,' had left them 'clamouring for more'.

E.S. Turner unwittingly pinpointed Laurie's dependence on diaries in his review in the *Listener*. '*Who's Who* tells us that Laurie Lee "travelled Mediterranean 1935–39",' he began. 'Now we begin to see what heavy gold of tales untold is concealed beneath that bleak phrase . . . This is a bonanza of a book. I suppose those who complained that *Cider with Rosie* was over-lush and full of overblown self-consciousness and an impossible feat of memory to boot, will look askance . . . It is too much, they will cry. How did he have time to notice, and how could he remember, that the dog which

savagely bit him had "eyes like yellow gas"? How could [he] . . . remember all the phantasmagoria of heatstroke? How could any writer in search of copy be so fortunate as to find his inn shared by four circus dwarfs sleeping in one bed? These are things I am content to let others worry about.' And of course all this telling detail came straight from the diaries, packed with the sensations that would otherwise elude anyone's memory.

'I hope you're pleased by the public reception. I daren't mention your name now or people will think I'm name-dropping. What is it like to be famous again?' asked Michael Astor, adding that he was counting on Laurie to come for Christmas: 'A nice long one. No strangers.'

Laurie was indeed famous again, but he felt quite raw, he told Celia Goodman, with 'that inevitable sense of emptiness one gets when one launches something'. He was suffering 'mental cramp and the slow-downs'. Having been briefly revived by a weekend at the Hampshire house of the enterprising Farnham bookseller and former Grenadier Guards officer Charles Hammick, he wrote Hammick a gloomy letter afterwards, about his doubts that the book would sell. Hammick had to tell him his fears were groundless. The book was selling well in Farnham.

Hammick quoted Auden: 'Just as a good man forgets his deed the moment he has done it . . . if a writer thinks about his past work at all, he is more likely to remember its faults than its virtues.' Further, 'He needs approval of his work by others . . . but he can only be reassured by those whose judgement he respects.' 'This last is very true,' said Hammick. 'When you have forgotten the immediate impact (or lack of it, in your mind) of sales figures, and the critics . . . then the opinion of those whom you respect will come to roost, and this, other than your own conviction, is the only test that counts . . .'

Laurie was consoled and apologetic. 'It was pretty sloppy of me to have written so boringly to you, grousing & grumbling, especially after the euphoria I got from Farnham. I suppose I was depressed by having let one book go out into the world before feeling deeply committed to another. It is a time of emptiness & silence. Also, of

course, I am having a pretty regular recurrence of this silly illness which means I am only able to write about two and a half days a week – and that time completely taken up with business letters.'

This was so; his letters book from that time is little else but bills, taxes, rates, solicitors. And in December he had five days in bed with a temperature of 103. 'Life at half-cock,' says his notebook, 'slowly stifled by an implacable & relentless stupidity . . . Friendship offered, not rejected so much as left to decay through inertia. At home, have nothing to offer my friends but flustered chaos.'

So ended the 1960s. From his slough of despond, Laurie managed to write a light-hearted introduction to *A Flook's Eye View of the Sixties*, a book celebrating the twenty-first anniversary of Wally Fawkes and George Melly's cartoon character Flook. 'Flook himself, like most of us, is a self-indulgent opportunist,' Laurie wrote. 'He is the kind of being I would really quite like to be – modest, gregarious, quick of wit and mind.'

Life would be heaven, Laurie told Hammick, 'if I felt I need never write another word – just communicate with my friends through brain waves'. Once again it was to Celia Goodman that he confided the details of his malaise. 'My trouble is mostly concerned with the *physical* act of writing, and it is obviously one of those dotty things that one can't explain but that one hopes will pass eventually. The result of it – and I suppose of other influences – is that I am compelled to lose one or two days every week or two to a deep drug treatment which lays me out completely. It has been going on now for about 18 months. The loss of time is the worst thing – and of opportunity to write to one's friends, or to explain why one couldn't.'

23 | Dear Mr Lee . . .
1970—74

As I Walked Out One Midsummer Morning was at the top of the bestseller list, with Elizabeth Longford's *Wellington* and Kenneth Clark's *Civilisation*, but a lingering despondency – along with heavy 'flu – hung over Laurie at the start of the new decade. Like any Peter Pan Laurie disliked ageing: 'I have to face up to the old face now,' he told Tom Matthews. 'Every day seems to encompass the whole of life. I wake in the morning feeling young, quick, full of hope; in the evenings I am a tottering old man.' He feared he had written his last book. 'He has enough material for another book in his head. But anything over 500 words will make him ill for days,' Celia Goodman wrote to Princess Peg. 'About three days a week he is under deep sedation . . . He feels everything is his last chance to do things. Kathy looks wonderful, but the strain must be very great.'

On good days Laurie could still be sociable: for the Flook book he had lunch in the Dorchester with assembled cartoonists, comedians and Diana Dors;[1] and he could write cheeringly to others. Elizabeth Jennings ('sick – in mind and body') thanked him for a letter of 'intuitive poetic understanding', and he wrote cheeringly to Tom Matthews, who was in the London Clinic with a duodenal ulcer.

He also began writing skittish and effervescent letters to Georgina Hammick, wife of Charles the Farnham bookseller. She was thirty, the mother of two small children, and a published poet before becoming an admired writer of short stories and novels. Like Nicolette Devas she saw at once that there were two Lauries. 'In public he was all bonhomie. In private he could be sharp, and often a hugely gloomy, Eeyore person with an innate disbelief in the possibility of promised pleasure. He expected disappointment.' She and Laurie liked the same jokes, knew the same poems, and could finish one another's lines, catching instantly a reference to William

Blake or to the more obscure seventeenth-century poet and satirist George Wither. So began an intimate penfriendship based on a punning literary one-upmanship that neither could enjoy at home. Even when 'the very act of writing scrambles the brains' or feeling 'slow-headed today – yesterday was drug day', Laurie could always sparkle for Georgie.

'What a fun-pun person you are,' he wrote. 'Sharp's the word – so sharp indeed you put me on my metal and I'll cut you in the street one of these days . . .' 'Your letter was brilliant & I promise never to compete with your mind again . . .' 'You do find the most alpha-plus quotations. Admirable girl, & so good for me. One of the reasons I took to poetry is that I could never remember anybody else's. You can do both. Unfair.'

He called her jokey names: 'Dear Miss Understanding' or 'Gorgeous Georgie Goolagong' (he was very keen on the tennis player Evonne). Laurie ended that letter with 'Too Goolagong hangs the light in this valley lamenting' (playing on the line from his poem, 'Summer Rain'). Georgina tried to discuss contemporary poetry with him – 'I had deep enthusiasms myself' – but found he was not interested in the work of new poets. He asked her for Ted Hughes's *Crow*, but never spoke of the poems. (To Siriol Hugh-Jones in 1960, he had said of Ted Hughes: 'I can understand you falling for a younger poet – it had to happen – but I was an expert on badgers when he was still mewling and puking in a buzzard's nest.') 'As for Dylan T,' he wrote to Georgina, 'I can understand but don't want to know. Even more than most writers I demand single-minded devotion or nothing. If my works her neck don't crick, what care I whence comes her kick?' – a reference to George Wither's

> If she be not so to me
> What care I how kind she be?[2]

Their allusive, in-jokey, self-referring correspondence could only properly be understood by the two participants. He felt free to tease Georgina. 'But as for teasing Cathy, she doesn't always get it, so

we will indulge in that at our yellow Pekin peril . . .' 'What would you like for your birthday Georgie dear; a casket of your favourite ambiguities, evasions, riddles, recoils, retreats, & tiny beautifully-executed sideways leaps – or a tiger lily burning bright, claws safely sheathed and out of sight?'

Much of their banter was based on Georgina's feminist stance: anathema to Laurie, who saw women principally as nurturing creatures. She challenged him: why did he always keep his women-folk at home? Weren't women more than slaves in kitchen and playthings in bed? He wrote back to 'Darling Georgie Simone' (as in de Beauvoir): 'Listen to me . . . it is possible to have an equal relationship with a girl, one whose mind is a delight, with whom one plays intellectual tennis with pleasure (and no sulks), and to see her in the kitchen, cooking one's dinner; AND, at times, to see her as an object apart, thank God, to be dressed up, undressed, adored, caressed, and put to bed like a doll. End of message . . .'

To Georgina he confided about sexual fantasies: 'They can be kinky, quirky, pre-Raphaelite, Genghis Khan-can, sadistic, maso-chistic, set in ivory towers or cellars, but one should never be ashamed of them any more than of one's sleeping dreams. It's true that few lovers ever get the chance to act out their fantasies together – and I think it's probably better that way, because fantasies are generally too fragile to take the weight of our physical presences in them.' But he had, he added, once 'magically' had such a chance.

He hinted at his reluctance to declare love. 'Haven't you ever said in an idle silence, "Say you love me," and not wished for a word more than just that? Love's deepest satisfaction, security, comes from that whispered "Tell me, tell me again . . ." But what do you tell? Symbolic, secretive, endearing, incendiary phrases . . . But NEVER all your heart – or from me she doth depart.' (A reference to Blake's 'Never seek to tell thy love'.) 'How I know this to be true, don't you? and how one wishes it not to be true. The bliss of not needing to hold back anything. In the hooded cowled whispers of the dark close night one should be . . . able to receive & gather in all love's echoes & messages. Without hindrance or doubt.'

This intense correspondence continued for two years, even when Laurie could not write to anyone else: 'Silence, you must always know,' he told Celia Goodman, 'does not mean forgetfulness . . .' But in the end he and Georgina were 'bound to fall out', she says. 'When he called me "thickness" or "Dead loss" it was for not reading between the lines. He wanted sole devotion. He said, "You can always find time if you want to," but it's just not true. You have other obligations. But he couldn't see that. It was difficult to please him for any length of time. He was always suspicious, trying to set traps for you. You walked a tightrope.'

She also made the error of questioning the second line of one of his most anthologized poems, 'Apples':

Behold the apples' rounded worlds:
juice-green of July rain . . .

'"You have to say JOO-ly," I told him. "Why didn't you go for August? That would sound better, and it's more true of August anyway, and you wouldn't have that ugly emphasis on the wrong syllable." He shook his head in sorrow and disappointment, that I had the temerity. He considered it a huge impertinence, which I daresay it was. I had crossed some invisible line.'

She enjoyed, for a while, their intimate sparring. It was a chaste affair in words, a verbal flirtation. He was fatherly, and sometimes ticked her off like a father. He assured her she was 'loved, cherished in mind & matter, looked forward to, relished deeply in recollection'. 'But I was also nervous of him at one level,' she says. 'His tricks and games were tests, you weren't meant to win. He would catch you out for not reading his last letter properly. "Oh you don't read my letters I can tell."'

On one occasion, Laurie arrived unexpectedly at Georgina's house. It was awkward. She had to attend her son's sports day. She put him up in the spare room, which was unsatisfactory – 'the mattress was not feather-filled' – and there wasn't time to cook the kind of stew he liked. He became ill: he broke out in such a terrifying cold sweat she thought he might die. She rang Kathy,

who said that if Laurie took his pill and went to bed for the rest of the day, it would be safe to leave him. In the evening she drove him back to Slad. During the two-hour journey he told her that nobody had ever got over seeing him ill, citing Rosamond Lehmann as one who hadn't. Reassurances made no difference: he would not be comforted. But what remained in Georgina's mind of this 'frightening' visit was the homecoming at Rose Cottage: 'all the lights blazing, a delicious supper ready, the table laid, jugs of roses and lilies everywhere, Cathy calmly in charge. And Laurie's undisguised pleasure and relief at being home and safe.'

'He was funny, kind, generous and good with small children,' Georgina says. 'He also had a dark and cruel and unforgiving side. He liked bright women, but still demanded that mothering, that womb-like embracing, at home.' When Georgina's first book of short stories, *People for Lunch*, came out, Laurie said: 'I gather you've written a rather good book,' but did not read it.

Every year followed a pattern now: a long chill and fevered winter, a spring 'the cruellest since the birth of Prufrock' redeemed by sunshine in May. He told Celia Goodman in May 1970 that he had found 'a temporary balance of serenity after the see-saw of doctors, drugs, dumps & doubts. After the sticks & thorns of April, the garden is suddenly gloriously, almost vulgarly, blowsy; and I stay in it from morning till dusk. My two girls are blooming – Cathy forking the garden in a muscular fury of self-expression. I am not writing much yet (everything has been out of focus for so long). Music is still my consolation. Oh, that you lived in the neighbouring parish.'

He was now in need of a new companion for his foreign trips. In July, Laurie asked Elizabeth Jane Howard to come with him to Spain to help him research for a book. 'There was something in the papers about my wanting an assistant/companion, and feminine, and intelligent, and I have had over 50 replies, but how could they compare with you? . . . please write and say yes. Love Laurie.'

'Strictly business,' he added, 'strictly pleasure.'

One of the young women who came to see him at the Queen's Elm about the assistant job was the writer Miranda Seymour, then

twenty-one, who decided instantly that it was a job she did not after all want. Laurie was 'older than I expected; and I was slightly unnerved by the kind of companionship he might require'.

Jane could not go. But Laurie was 'profoundly nourished' by her reply, 'because I need such words from you and no doubt always will. It was crazy of me to have thought you might have been briefly free to go with me in July, and perhaps tactless to have written to suggest it, but not crazy to have wished it possible.

'I had a reasonably good time in Spain,' Laurie added, 'and my companion was young, attractive, dull, witless, and at first inclined to be aggressive, and had to be slapped down hard, good and early, after which she drove me round quite well.

'I would like to see you very much, almost more than anyone else, as I need what you have for me and it don't grow on trees . . . I love you. L.'

Her god-daughter Jessy, he said, was now 'a husky, loving, strapping Cathy type . . . She is a good reader but a poor writer which is OK by me as we could do with some readers in this family.' With Kathy and Jessy he had spent part of the summer with Lis Frink (one of whose *Horse and Rider* sculptures he had just bought for £50) at her farmhouse in the Cévennes. In the autumn he took his two girls to New York, staying at the Chelsea Hotel where Georgina Hammick, calling herself Queen Bee, wrote him a pun-filled announcement of the birth of her daughter Rose. 'Dear Glory Bee [Laurie Lee] Will your honey suckle Rose? We are giving her that name in the hope that she might be A Rose for Winter (she's undoubtedly the Last Rose of Summer) . . .'

They stayed with Tom Matthews's son Paul (whose new baby Joshua Lee Matthews became another of Laurie's godsons) and Laurie had Algonquin lunches with the *New Yorker*, *Playboy* and Frances Koltun from *Mademoiselle*, who told him, 'I shall forever count my talks with you among the best hours of my life.' But on the return flight he caught a BOAC virus which became pneumonia: an opportunity for more punstering postcards from 'Wun Lung Lee' to Georgina: 'It was Old Monia who drove me to the new-curled World, where I picked up NEW Monia, who

sent my temperature blushing up into the chill-turned hundreds. But then I like a change of girl from time to time. I suppose it's the nympho-monia in me.' By November he told Tom Matthews he was improving thanks to 'those modern Wonder Drugs which fortify the resistance of the body by lowering that of the spirit'.

They were with the Astors for Christmas at Bruern again, but Laurie went out in the snow and came down with another chest infection. Princess Peg wrote cheerily from Wolfsgarten, where Rostropovich was staying with her: 'Are the ups long enough for travel & work – enjoyment & a laugh or two? Or has that devil "ill-health" got you by the heels & nose as well?' Michael Behrens sent a verse from Portugal:

Far from the winding lea
On Algarve's fractured shore
La douceur de la vie
Makes us miss Laurie more.

But even the sickest person could be soothed by being on Roy Plomley's ineffably bland *Desert Island Discs*. Music, Laurie told Plomley in January 1971, gave him the deepest sense of enchantment. His eight chosen records were: Duke Ellington's 'Stevedore Stomp' – 'the first jazz record I ever bought'; 'Seguidillas', a pre-Spanish Civil War recording of guitar with La Niña de los Peines ('the true Spanish voice'); the Spanish carol 'Belén', sung by Victoria de los Angeles; Julian Bream playing Dowland's 'Lachrimae Antiquae'; a Chopin Nocturne played by Artur Rubinstein; George Harrison's 'Isn't It a Pity'; the slow movement of Beethoven's String Quartet Op. 132 ('this would be almost as important as food to me') and finally Menuhin playing a Bach Chaconne. His chosen luxury was 'an inexhaustible supply of yeast and sugar in order to make wine or beer'. Plomley was the least probing of interrogators. 'Your Spanish War experiences presumably will be Volume Three?' Laurie: 'Yes.'

To the question of how well he would face loneliness, Laurie replied: 'Pretty well I think. Even in the crowded world of today

I've often chosen it. It isn't that I don't like people, I'm very gregarious, but I like to be able to withdraw from people . . . I only seem to operate for myself best when I'm entirely alone.' It was Tom Matthews who insisted on putting up Laurie's name for Garrick Club membership that year. Laurie of course felt like Groucho Marx about it: 'What kind of club can it be that wants me in it?' But Matthews told him: 'On your page it *might* be possible to squeeze another signature in, but it would take a very fine nib. In short, you're so popular you'll be a shoo-in.'

Just as Laurie was hoping to play down his countryman image, the village was invaded by film cameras for the BBC's televised *Cider with Rosie*, with script by Hugh Whitemore. Luckily Slad still looked much as it had half a century ago, once they disguised telegraph poles as trees, and removed bollards and aerials, and the new porch from Laurie's old childhood cottage. The designer Eileen Diss recreated the school in the now disused old building. Hundreds piled into Stroud Subscription Rooms to become extras at £5 a day, and a search began for the perfect Rosie. Annie was played by Rosemary Leach who, having grown up in Diddlebury, Shropshire, where she was the schoolmaster's daughter, found Slad 'just like coming home'. They re-enacted the Treaty of Versailles holiday of 1919, with a six-year-old Whiteway boy playing boy Laurie in John Bull outfit; Chalford Silver Band led the procession through the village to Steanbridge House.[3]

Laurie sat in Rose Cottage garden 'out of the way like a hedge-hog'. He feared that Claude Whatham, the director, might over-romanticize with lyrical camera-work, 'floating through cornfields with Vaseline smeared across the lenses'. To interviewers he stressed that Slad wasn't unique, and that 'what I was writing about was not myself but a way of life, in which poverty, epidemics, filth, malnutrition, and early death were as important a part as beauty and days filled with sun'.[4] He was quietly metamorphosing, at fifty-seven, into the crusty veteran who tells the world it is not what it was. 'We have lost the sense of wondering and discovery. Life is impoverished now and TV imprisons one. It steals your time and diminishes your imagination. Every night you have a

45. Kathy and Laurie at Rose Cottage with Jessy, the Firstborn, 1964

46. Laurie with his daughter and grand-daughter, 1964. Left to right: Julian
David, baby Esther, Yasmin, Kathy with Jessy on her lap, and Laurie –
father and grandfather

47. Laurie with Jessy and
guitar, outside Rose Cottage
(*John Summers*)

48. Laurie, Kathy and Jessy,
Christmas 1964 (© *Express
Newspapers*)

49. Troubadours: Laurie with Jeremy Robson, Vernon Scannell and Dannie Abse, at a 1960s Poetry & Jazz evening (*Jeremy Robson Collection*)

50. Georgina Hammick (*Georgina Hammick*)

51. The Queen's Elm, on the corner of the Fulham Road and Old Church Street

52. The Queen's Elm denizens, 1976: (left to right) Lord Valentine Thynne, Jak the cartoonist, Peter Owen, Laurie, Kerry Hamilton, Marshall Pugh, Jan Kenny (Mrs Sean Treacy), Sean Treacy, Elisabeth Frink, Babs Craig, Bill Travers, Virginia McKenna, Dr Geoffrey Dove and the artist Bill Thomson

59. Wine, women and song: Laurie in the garden of the Chelsea Arts Club, 1977
(© *Bryan Wharton*)

60. The churchyard at Slad, Laurie's final resting place

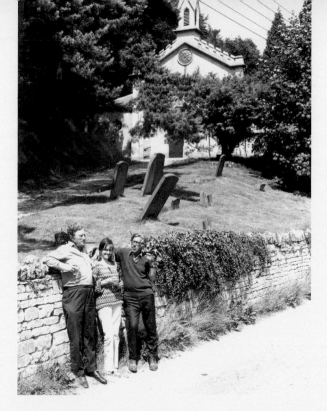

57. Laurie with fellow poet Frank Mansell and friend in front of the Slad churchyard, 1970s

58. Laurie, saviour of the Sheepscombe Cricket Club, aged eighty

55. Jessy aged seventeen, 'the one compelling interest in my life', photographed by Laurie, 1980 – from *Two Women*

56. Jessy ('I rely on Dad being around a lot') with Laurie in Santander, 1996

53. Julian Bream (and guitar) listening as Laurie recites at Bream's local church in Dorset, late 1970s

54. Laurie (watched by Kathy and the landlady, Nolie Covington) signs a book for a fan in the Woolpack: 'There aren't many pubs where you can sell your books' (The Citizen, *Gloucester*)

ration of horror. Pakistan and Vietnam, massacres, famine and children weeping. But the viewers' compassion is no longer engaged.'

As for Spain, 'What people go for is not to discover the world and foreign ways but to be guaranteed familiar food and sunshine . . .'

The paperback of *As I Walked Out One Midsummer Morning* was just out, and Georgina told him the jacket was terrible. Laurie angrily agreed: 'Authors are not shown their book jackets for some extraordinary reason. I was appalled. Didn't I tell you – or didn't you listen? Shoals of protest letters from me to Deutsch and Penguins. "What's this middle-aged Skid Row alcoholic doing crumpled up in the ditch of a phoney Harrods plastic Englishe hedgerow?" I ask them. "The book is about youth, adventure, discovery and 80% about Spain." Too late, they'd already printed 90,000 copies. They promise a new jacket for the next edition and an artist, thirtyish, very professional, is sent to Slad to talk about it.

'I suggest a young man, preferably uncrumpled and light-footed, walking through a vast empty and torrid Spanish landscape. I got the result last week: it shows an old man, wearing Chinese hat and crumpled Maoist peasant jacket and trousers, tottering shoulders-drooping down an anonymous road. The artist wrote, saying, "I know you didn't wear a hat, but I would like to keep it as it would save me the trouble of drawing the back of your head."'

Laurie concealed from the world his lowering illnesses ('jittery afternoon', 'off day', 'sleep morning'). He would never write about his miseries, he told Georgina: 'I can write poems about love, about wanting, almost never about loss. A bad limitation perhaps, where my poetry is concerned. Due to some flaw – of pride? Vanity perhaps? More than that – I believe that nothing can be called back, except ghosts.

'My mother wasted most of her life on hope. I have no hope. I turn away from the sepulchre instead of haunting it. Also fortunately – though bad for art – I have learnt to endure, dumbly. To me it's loss of face to be seen to be suffering. I'm a melancholic man who likes to be thought merry . . .'

Summer had been 'a washout', he told Tom Matthews, but 'our

spreading Jess-nut tree', now aged seven, had completed her first literary commission, a piece about her parents for *Vogue*:

'My mummy is clever and makes lots and lots of wine and drinks it and she also digs hard in the garden. My daddy is more clever than mummy. He doesn't dig in the garden. He writes books and looks after us all. My mummy has long fair hair, blue eyes, pink cheeks and drives the car. I love her. Daddy has a light brown face, silver hair. Today he doesn't go under the sea any more, but he drinks wisky and plays the violin and guitar. He's often ill or lazy. I wouldn't choose any other mummy or daddy. They shout a lot and mummy's got a very loud voice and dad's got a very soft voice and they shout at me and each other . . .'

'The years are like a sieve,' wrote Laurie to Celia Goodman, 'whose meshes grow wider & wider, through which one's most valued friends drop out of sight for ever . . . But you are the fine diamond which seems to have escaped the general fallout, to my comfort.'

In November 1971 he went back to Copenhagen, alone. 'I am moving (without surprise or protest) into the area of Departures,' he told Georgina Hammick. 'In fact, tomorrow has a curious unreality about it. There is no reason to be going where I am going. Nor any reason not to. It's like leaving the tent pitched in the howling Antarctic. By going, one leaves more room in the tent and exchanges an overheated claustrophobia for the calm solitude of cold. A tiny rehearsal for death, in fact (without being melodramatic) . . . My black joke for the day: If you shot a Czech with a rubber bullet, would he bounce?' He took the ferry from Harwich ('dopey all afternoon . . . 3 Bacardis, 4 beers') and sent a postcard on arrival: 'The city is cold grey and Sunday. I do wish you were here. (There is an island called Lolland.) Everybody is drunk and I wish I was. For breakfast I had Porn on the Køb.'

That winter the *Telegraph* magazine sent him to fly on Concorde. Laurie, who kept a vigilant record of every air crash, noting all flight details and numbers of dead, had always been both fascinated and awed by flight, ever since his first flight in 1933 when he was piloted by Sir Alan Cobham in 'an old Imperial Airways liner'

round Gloucester. Now it was arranged for him to fly in the cockpit of Concorde from the Cotswold test-base near Fairford to the north of Spain and back. It took just 105 minutes – a journey that had taken 'two years of foot-slogging and scheming in my youth'. He concluded: 'True, for the first time I had travelled faster than sound. I had even reached Mach 2.07 without pain. But emotionally, in fact, I'd been nowhere, seen nothing. We might as well have been circling over cloud above Cheltenham.'[5]

While Kathy and Jessy stayed with Helen in Italy that winter, Laurie had 'a peaceful solitary Christmas' when words of praise were showered on the televised *Cider with Rosie*. It was found to be enchanting, lyrical, evocative, authentic, masterly. Some found it too reticent about poverty and bleak winters and Annie's feckless improvidence; Mary Holland pointed out that Laurie had been wryly aware of writing from middle age, so that even hunger was sentimentally remembered. 'Take away this saving self-knowledge and he can come very close to Patience Strong . . .' But as a final moving touch Laurie himself was filmed in the lane, turning his head to watch the child he had been walk by. And Hugh Whitemore got the Writers' Guild award for his script.

Laurie now wrote only on commission. He wrote about Berkeley Castle's history for the *Telegraph* magazine; he went to Hong Kong ('full of Lees', he reported) in March 1972, and in May to Beirut – still a prosperous, cosmopolitan pleasure-ground then – maintaining in print at least his exuberance and lively curiosity. In London, he was at every literary gathering: the Authors of the Year party, the launch of a new bookshop. 'There was Laurie Lee,' wrote Jilly Cooper (a neighbour in Bisley) after the Royal Academy summer exhibition party, 'looking gloomy, as if he didn't want to drink cider with anyone.' He protested, and Jilly sent a mollifying note: 'Dear Laurie, I only said you looked gloomy because in real life you look so lovely. We must have lunch . . .' (As Jilly once wrote, '"We must have lunch sometime" is London for "Goodbye".')

He was constantly asked to judge things: poems by the young for the *Daily Mail*, poems by inmates of H.M. prisons for the Arthur Koestler award; the Whitbread award with Elizabeth Jane Howard

and James Pope-Hennessy. He read an Anglo-Saxon poem at a Queen Elizabeth Hall concert of electronic synthesizer music. At the Stratford poetry festival in July, he gave his 'familiar and warmly captivating busking act as poet-entertainer'.

While he was away in Beirut, Cecil Day-Lewis died at Lemmons, the Hertfordshire home of Kingsley Amis and Elizabeth Jane Howard, and was buried at Stinsford in Dorset a few feet from Hardy's grave. Laurie wrote to Rosamond Lehmann:

'Darling Rosamond, Your letter moved me very much. I am garrulous about everything except the loves which touch me closely (as you well know) & this one I will discuss with no one. I have not been quite persona grata for many years in that direction – except for his vague but distant goodwill. You are right about the awful mask, but I don't think it covered a "degeneracy of spirit" but rather guilt & unhappiness, which of course he would never admit to anyone . . . He kept up a good front, but he was always aware of the destruction he had caused to himself & others; & I think secretly he was always haunted by the Smiler & the Knife – the Smiler was for his friends, but the Knife was self-inflicted & he carried it deeply.

'We both have our conjoined memories at this moment . . . A lot of rot is being publicly spoken & written about him but I am having nothing to do with these final rituals. I know how I remember him, and I think that you & I, standing in our separate silent wings, are of course closer to the truth than those temporarily on stage. Love as always, Laurie.'

At Day-Lewis's memorial service on 25 October 1972 at St Martin-in-the-Fields, he sat in a side pew. 'Widow in white. Air of theatrical first night – last entrance K.A. & Dark Lady of the sonnets [Amis and Elizabeth Jane Howard] – large black hat, black coat, black glasses. Fauré's Requiem. Music going on too long. Jill [Balcon] led out to receive on steps.' He left by a side door. When Sean Day-Lewis approached Laurie for help with his father's biography, Laurie replied, 'I don't feel I can talk about him, even to you . . . What remains is either vague or too difficult, although he was the man I liked most among my friends, and was the kindest to me.'

Laurie had made a decision that summer of 1972: 'I haven't said much about it but I don't mean to live in Slad any more,' he told P.J. Kavanagh, 'except perhaps for a brief summer visit. I've had a good ten years there & now I think it's best to leave & keep it preserved in my mind before it rots before my eyes.' Perversely, in the same letter Laurie tried to persuade the Kavanaghs, now living nearby, to buy Snows Farm in Slad. 'I'd buy if I could. Believe it or not, I haven't got the money, only a mortgage . . . But I'd like to think you were all up there.' He advertised Rose Cottage for rent at £10 a week in the *Sunday Times,* and had a deluge of responses. Not long before, he had bought (for £400) the Sheeps-combe village cricket ground, where his uncles, grandfather and great-grandfather had all played, to prevent development and pre-serve it in perpetuity. 'Sheepscombe is my ancestral village. It is one of the real classic cricket grounds with one of the best views in Gloucestershire.'

But he had decided that creative artists can only work in cities. 'Gloucestershire has never produced an artist of great stature because it is too satisfying a place to live.' He also felt he was drowning in *Cider with Rosie*: following the television film, the play was now being performed in every local rep, college and school. A horse called *Cider with Rosie* won at Newmarket at 100–6. Richard Covington, landlord of the Woolpack, had concocted a 'Cider with Rosie' cocktail for the trippers. Laurie felt 'completely bound by country matters': opening a flower show, attending a fork luncheon with local gentry, presenting the Jack Weston challenge cup at the Sheepscombe Cricket Club.

'In several ways the summer has been a nightmare,' he told Tom Matthews, 'but we won't go into that.' Back in London that autumn he grew a beard, self-consciously realizing that it made him look older. He appeared in it at an anti-Franco deputation to protest against Spain joining the Common Market, organized by Wogan Philipps (Lord Milford), who told him he looked 'very imposing & handsome, magnificent in the fur coat, the envy of all in the deputation'.

Inside he was feeling far from enviable. 'I can think of warmth

& need of my old friends, but I can't write or do anything about it,' he told Celia Goodman in February 1973. 'I have come to a stop & the head no longer controls the hand.' Alarmed, Princess Peg wrote from Tarasp, urging Laurie to join her and Benjamin Britten in the peace and snow: 'good & bad days shared'. Celia reported to Peg: 'Laurie, after four months in the flat, has just gone off to Tunisia. Cathy sounds absolutely at the end of her tether. He just gets iller and iller: as she puts it, it is a slow relentless doom.

'So it is knockout drugs, depression from having taken them, drink to kill the depression, and then back to square A again. Cathy wants to get out and do something to use her mind and get away from household chores, for she has no help with them. But as she says she is untrained, though in my view a great asset . . . Oh what an awful life for both of them, and it has been going on for so long – almost for ever, so it seems to Cathy.'

Kathy wrote to Celia:

'The subject of Laurie is so complex and difficult . . . We really are at a loss as to what to do for him – my whole life revolves around the problem. It's so difficult to explain to either doctor or friends how this clever lucid & witty man is privately plunged in a war against despair – loss of hope & frustration. In a strange way it is the strength of his will that makes doctors shrug their shoulders. I think they would try to help more if he was reduced to a gibbering idiot – when it's too late of course. It's such a shame that no one in the medical profession cares enough to take that extra trouble over a man like Laurie.

'They don't seem to realize that his difficulty with them is part of the symptoms of his illness and they get hurt and moody when they feel he isn't listening to them and start to label him with words like paranoia. They don't seem to realize that perhaps he does know his own situation better than they do, that by listening to him they could be learning more about a disease that people know very little about. Epilepsy allied to a simple ordinary mind is difficult enough but in conjunction with such a sharpness of focus as L's has, is more difficult. It's not even a cure that Laurie needs as such, but a man with deep understanding & insight with sympathy & humility.

Such a man would keep his head and hand steady as he writes, better than any drugs – so I feel. It's really a matter of touring the world as in a fairy story to find the right person . . . Or self-cure which Laurie is trying to do against many odds.

'. . . I keep my end up by being a little vague about everything which of course is the last thing I should do but actually it does keep a certain amount of cheerfulness going – J is good at this and L can drink his way into it. There are moments in all this when I hear music in his room and there's a moment of light and I can't tell you what it means – we all relax, it's true balm – but so short-lived – often it's a tape of the old days with you and Laurie playing – but how rare and rarer these moments are. Dear Celia we must get him to write again – after all this is really what it's all about – he does have something to give – why should he be wasted. He did write a poem, the first in years, the other day – again another moment of sudden happiness. Laurie says people get so bored by illness, but a few rare friends (like you) have the right spirit. After all dear Celia with all the fights and struggles you've had I know you understand.'

The poem Laurie had written was a moving sixtieth birthday tribute to Princess Peg, when all her friends, including the Prince of Wales, clubbed together to buy her a new Steinway grand. It ended:

> May you, at will, savour that deathless gift –
> Owed to so rare as you –
> Nightly to draw the furred walls of peace
> Round your day's limbs, to slip again
> Into your chosen house,
> Where we, your friends, shall play back to you our love,
> And he himself slide into his chair beside you.

Laurie affected to be wryly amused in 1973 when Philip Larkin's *Oxford Book of Twentieth-Century English Verse*, 'which was criticized in the press for having too many poets from the 1940s onwards in it', excluded him completely – and yet Laurie was a guest of honour

at the Foyle's luncheon to launch the book, sitting a few feet from Larkin. After the speeches the actress Margaret Rawlings stood up and declared, 'I would like to applaud a poet not in the anthology – Laurie Lee'; and Ralph Richardson declaimed 'Hear, hear.' John Lehmann wrote the next day to say that if Miss Rawlings had not mentioned it, he might have done so himself: 'A scandal.' But the damage was done; Laurie never forgave Larkin, or got over the slight.

He made a trip to Tangier and Marrakesh for *Mademoiselle*. 'I reckon I spent two months on that job,' he told Tom Matthews. 'Not worth it.' His notebook vividly reflects a depressed state of mind. He walked in cold rain in cobbled streets, noting poverty, 'smell of boiling seafood', people with small eyes. He was losing his sense of taste: 'most expensive meal I've ever had & couldn't taste a thing'. In the market they sold gaudy plastic toys and shrieking fretwork plates; occasionally a tribeswoman looking like a Murillo in a candlelit tent stall sold rock salt or sandalwood: 'Everything else sham.'

He was tired and sick, 'legs aching & shaking', kept awake at night by storms and quarrels in the streets. 'Used to land in Tangier straight off boat into town. Now half mile walk along quay. All new & hideous concrete. Nothing gets easier or cosier. Rough crossing – most people sick – Algeciras unrecognizable. A kind of Detroit of skyscrapers.'

Tangier's sandy beach was somehow obscene: 'No girls, only solitary furtive figures, elderly Anglo Saxons, or leathercoated pimps, or djellabahed louts trying to sell wallets & themselves. Robed figure (brown) lying on sand like Henry Moore. Some Arab boys startlingly dressed by elder Ang Sax boyfriends I suspect – one about 13 beautiful in brown cap, brown sweater, fawn woollen Norfolk trousers & long brown boots; another striding long-legged in crushed raspberry from head to toe.'

He had a 'crisis' on the beach: 'Had to run for it & draw shutters. At 2 a.m. people were stamping on the floor overhead – it was murder – switched on wireless – BBC just audible. (In Algeciras now, no music or singing. Only TV voices & commercials.)

'In front of my pavement café someone borrowed penknife to slit the throat of a chicken (holding him down with foot on neck). Haven't heard a single intellectual remark made in this city, either by inhabitants or tourists – money, work, hotel, how much you gimme, hello Charlie, good car, football, & talk goes on non stop.

'There's no fun in my face now either.'

Foreign ways no longer charmed him. Why did men stand about or sit in cafés all day, talking and whistling, while women scurried about, loaded, anxious, carrying food, 'keeping things going'?

How come, when he tried to summon the barman, 'suddenly eleven inert men ordered whiskies'? 'Difference of eating & drinking at bar & at table,' he noted. 'At bar you can pay & go at will, joke with barman. At table you are trapped in a ritual, brought unrecognizable & cold food, wine one hasn't ordered, then waiter disappears; when after 2 hours boredom you wish to get the bill it is like a savage sentence which you must pay to achieve liberty.'

He felt 'pitiless even to cripples – how bitter I am become by my old age. Losing my temper when men in small shops don't understand one of 3 languages but only frown; I shout. In bar near hotel, nodded & smiled to Arab with fez – he tipped it on front of his head – was this insult? smell of cats. Whores yawning in café at 8 p.m. All's fair in love & whore.'

On his last day he went shopping ('Bracelet £1 – too much'; 'Bargained for birdcage – didn't buy it') and panicked when he thought he had missed his ferry ('was I stuck for another week?') On the homeward voyage 'drank whiskies all afternoon with Capt Renshaw – he bachelor with 2 room flat in Hove, furniture covered with plastic wrappings, seldom there – "very lonely".'

Tom Matthews took him to the Garrick to be introduced as a new member. 'Sorry I left so abruptly,' Laurie apologized afterwards, 'but I suddenly felt ill and didn't want to be burdensome (probably too much good drink).' In March 1973 their old friend Ralph Jarvis had died. When Laurie rang Celia Goodman about it, it was 'the only time Laurie has ever telephoned me', she said. They met at Jarvis's memorial service in May, repairing afterwards to Fortnums

for tea. 'Laurie has grown a beard . . . It is greyish, but of course it doesn't alter his personality at all,' Celia told Princess Peg. 'He seemed very sad and dejected though.' Jessy, at nearly ten, was always dashing off to play with friends, or rushing at him in high spirits when he felt awful. 'I tried to din it into him that if she didn't dash off with her friends that would be something to worry about. But he feels that Jess is his "last love" and he can't help setting too much store by her, so he is sure to be hurt, for how can a child realize that? It would be asking it to be grown up, a contradiction in terms.' Laurie wrote afterwards to apologize for burdening Celia with boorish conversation ('and on such a day too'.) 'One should never bother one's friends about such things.'

Yet that same month, Iain Morley, head of English at a Brent comprehensive, took two coachloads of fifth-formers, studying *Cider with Rosie* for O-level, to Slad, and when they went into the Woolpack they found themselves, to their amazement, talking to a warm and friendly and receptive Laurie Lee. 'He even offered to send me his signature for all those who had not got it, and wrote a special letter to a girl called Jacky who had been ill and missed the trip. We were all very struck by his affability and kindness.' The trip from Brent was repeated every summer for the next four years.

(Iain Morley took early retirement in late 1988, disgusted with education in the London borough of Brent, then in the grip of the 'loony Left'. He was therefore pleased to win £4 in a *Spectator* competition shortly afterwards for the following clerihew:

The world of 'Cider with Rosie'
Is traditional, touching, even cosy –
Thus causing discontent
To educationalists in Brent.)

When schoolchildren first 'swarmed' through Slad, in 1969, Laurie said he wished they would stay away: they could never see the village as he had known it as a boy. 'I sat playing in the middle

of the road. These children come and see cars whizzing through at 60 m.p.h. They expect a remote little village full of eccentrics, bullies and daffies. They read about me as a scabby little boy. They find a grey old man.' But a girl wrote to say she had visited Slad that June in 1969 before her English exam, 'and I was not in the least disappointed. What I saw was a stage-set worthy of a play. For us the outing acted as a sort of tranquillizer. I thought it was very quiet there, and I will never forget it because you have passed on the magic through your book.' The Gloucestershire poet U.A. Fanthorpe, former English mistress at Cheltenham Ladies' College, wrote a poem called 'Dear Mr Lee'[6] which probably expresses best the fond feelings children everywhere began to have for the author of *Cider with Rosie*.

Laurie was, as the Irish say, 'a street angel, home divil' – sweet to outsiders and children, but sometimes monstrously irritable with his own family. The indifferent way he treated Kathy was observed with dismay by many friends. He criticized her cooking, and seemed to berate her for not being a different kind of person. (Once he even told her, in front of guests, to go and change her dress.) Yasmin remembers his need to be quiet. 'He had a very highly tuned nervous system, and if anyone clattered plates, it would spark him off and he would lash out.' Much contrition was called for. After a splendid Cavendish weekend, 'I'm afraid I got as high as a tree'd kite at the finish,' he apologized to Tom, 'but I hope I'll be forgiven.' Laurie was not visibly drunk; but he did drink without regard to the pills he was taking every day. In his 1971 diary he lists these:

Ethosuximide 250 mg (clear brown capsule) 1 a day;
Epanutin capsules 100 mg 3 a day
Phenobarb. 30 mg 3 a day
Valium (yellow) 5 mg 3 a day
Tofranil 25 mg 3 a day
Mogadon large white 2 a night
Sod. amylo. 200 mg when required; Mysoline when required.

From 1973 Laurie's doctor in Painswick was Jim Hoyland, who describes Laurie as 'a law unto himself' medically. 'He had his own battery of idiosyncratic drugs and ignored new developments in the treatment of epilepsy, preferring to stick to what suited him.' What Dr Hoyland enjoyed about Laurie's visits was talking about poetry.

'All epileptics are shy about epilepsy,' says Dr Hoyland, who himself became epileptic in his sixties, possibly (like Laurie) as a result of a blow on the head in youth. 'There is a stigma: people are afraid that you might pass out and start frothing at the mouth.' It happened very rarely, but it explains a great deal about Laurie's secretiveness, that he was constantly aware of the possibility of, and often trying to ward off, a blackout. To Philip Oakes, on a train journey down to Slad, he confided his constant, terrifying apprehension about being suddenly afflicted by an attack. He was 'pursued by caravanserais of demons'.

The televising of *Cider* had brought a letter from brother Jack (who had once bought a film option on *Cider* himself for £100) in Sydney, urging Laurie to come out and visit him, suggesting that he approach BOAC to pay his fare – 'after all you're pretty famous now'. The visit was finally arranged for November 1973, when Kathy and Jessy went off to Italy for Christmas. As Celia Goodman told Princess Peg (who was in London to attend Princess Anne's wedding), 'By a series of separations they will probably get over this present sticky patch.'

It was Jack and Laurie's first reunion for ten years. But something came between them afterwards. They met only once again, in Slad a year later, but after that Laurie did not speak to Jack for the rest of his life. Jack bitterly regretted the rift. What happened? Their close boyhood companionship, as Jack says, had been irrevocably damaged by their separation at school. And Annie would chide Laurie for scorning Jack ('he did all he could for you when you were lost in Spain & afterwards, & I never hear you speak a good word for him and it hurts me Laurie it does'). But they had long outgrown childhood grievances. Both had done well in different fields, and before his last flight to New York, Laurie had told Jack

that if they came down in the sea, Jack could have one of their cottages. And they had some good times in Sydney.

'It was his drinking period, of course,' Jack says. 'He would start on beer at eight in the morning, and when the pubs opened at ten he'd say he was going to the post office, and would be missing all day, in what he referred to as the stews of Sydney.' That Christmas, Jack drove Laurie 850 miles to Adelaide. Laurie wore a heavy overcoat in the car though it was terribly hot. 'Laurie, that coat of yours pongs,' said Jack. Then Laurie announced he was going to take a pill, which knocked him out for the entire drive. Jack, annoyed, parked the car deliberately in the sun when he stopped for a beer.

It may be, Jack thinks, that Laurie heard later that his brother had told this story, and never forgave him 'because he was one for taking offence'. Julian Bream, who got to know Jack on his Australian tours, thinks Jack and Laurie in fact shared traits and were so alike they were bound to irritate one another. And Kathy believes that the rift was caused by a dispute over pictures. When Laurie started collecting art, he asked Jack and Nora to keep his Paul Klee, Leonard Rosoman and Henry Moore paintings in their flat at Denham. Later these all went to Rose Cottage. When Laurie told Jack he needed cash and was going to sell the Henry Moore, Jack bought it from him for £100, and left it with Nora when he departed for Australia. Nora eventually sold it, with Jack's approval, when their son Howard was going to Cambridge. This may have rankled with Laurie. Nobody can be sure what made Laurie suddenly cut Jack out of his life after 1975. The Australian trip ended amicably enough.

Once in Adelaide, Laurie was a great hit with Jack's sister-in-law Anne Kidman and her family, entertaining them on the violin, recorder and kazoo. Anne drove Laurie round the pubs ('he did love pubs', she says) and he gave Anne's son Will, then aged ten, a tiny silver gun which could shoot a bullet through a pile of newspapers. ('He told me it would kill a man if you shot him in the temple,' Will says.) 'Yes, everybody loved him,' Jack says. 'But then Laurie was a great charmer, certainly one of the most charming

men I've ever met.' An interview in the *Australian* that Christmas was perceptive about Laurie ('a middle-sized, middle-aged man with thick greyish-blond hair, rather noticeably small hands and feet and a soft clear voice'). 'Despite his wit, his tendency to self-parody and to bouts of teddy-bear humour,' Elizabeth Riddell wrote, 'he says he is, and I believe him, a melancholy and solitary man.'

In January 1974 the two brothers, along with Humphrey Fisher, son of the Archbishop of Canterbury, went to the Test match against New Zealand. Instead of watching from the members' pavilion they stood on 'the Hill', which Laurie had wanted to see ever since bicycling to see Gloucestershire playing the Australians as a lad. The spectators were pot-bellied, stripped to the waist, and each had an ice-box of beer. New Zealand were batting when the trouble began. Laurie and Jack were caught in crossfire between cheering New Zealand fans below, and jeering Australians above, hurling cans and bottles at one another. Laurie was struck on the head by a bottle and large drops of blood fell on his Somerset Maugham tropical suiting. Next day he made the front pages of both the Sydney and Melbourne *Herald*s. 'I bled like a slaughtered calf,' he told them, but 'I fell into the soft arms of some young student nurses, who held my wound closed with their long scented fingers until the bandages arrived.'

A bronzed Laurie arrived home to Kathy in a pair of stripy blue convict's trousers and went straight to bed: 'Fever. stomach. cold. Woozy all day. Big pill evening.' Two weeks later he was 'still coughing and seismatic sneezing' followed by 'Drinking. Drunk. Hangover.' His trio of books in a gift set had been among the top five sellers at Christmas, as André Deutsch told him over lunch at the Gay Hussar. Laurie bought himself a youthful denim suit at Austin Reed, but in many respects the year of his sixtieth birthday looked like being one he might prefer to forget. Or so the diary evidence indicates.

'24 Feb. Drinking heavily. Fell down at station. Broke glasses.' Next day: 'Bed stomach cold fever.' 3 March: 'DC 10 Turkish airline crash in Paris all 347 killed, over 200 Brit. worst ever.

CAUGHT CHILL.' By 31 March, which was a 'perfect day' (i.e. sunny) his alcohol tally was a neat '6 beers 6 whiskies 6 sherries'. Neither of his daughters could please him. 'J abominable. Rude. Restaurant J bad manners.' Even Yasmin was now 'scatty'. But in this sour catalogue, he still inserted the occasional joke: 'I say I say. Lord Elgin's lost his marbles. Oh how a museum.' And

> I'm dancing with wool in my eyes
> For the girl in my arms is a ewe.

Tom Matthews, who had just published his book on T.S. Eliot, took Laurie to dine at the Garrick. 'A cloud of benign unknowing seemed to settle on me during the latter part of the evening,' Laurie later apologized; had they really ended up dancing down Piccadilly at 1 a.m.? Matthews nobly took charge of Laurie's sixtieth birthday celebration, inviting Laurie and Kathy to the Commem Ball at his Alma Mater, New College Oxford, on 25 June – 'a glimpse of golden youth in my green old age,' wrote Laurie afterwards. 'It was worth waiting for my jubilee to sup the sweets of New College Oxon and prance with its beautiful people. You eased me across the San Andreas fault of my decade, and made it a night to remember. Thank you, friend, for all the trouble you took . . . For Cathy it was of course a more natural bliss in which she bloomed. I don't think she's been inside the mysteries of college quarters before . . . never could a man have passed into his silver years in such excellent style & company.'

On his actual birthday, he got through '1 bot. whisky altogether'. Through the rest of that year, a jagged line could be drawn, with whisky rescuing him from 'subdued panic'. 'Bad day in bed. Pill' would be followed by 'all day recovering'. He bought krugerrands and garden furniture. A hit-and-run driver knocked down the Rose Cottage garage wall. There were many nights in 'the Elms' when he records being 'very drunk' followed by 'hangover'. And days when he 'kept going on drink all day'. Life was full of tax forms and tribulations, and rain came in through the roof. Douglas Chisholm, the Chelsea barber who since 1972 had been cutting Laurie's

luxuriant hair (about which he was rather vain: it made him look rather artistic), tried to warn him, as a friend, that he'd be an alcoholic if he carried on like this. He drank too much at the Spanish Embassy on election night in October 1974 – it was also the 'anniversary of Spain's discovery of America' – when Labour scraped its majority of three.

Towards the year's end, however, he managed to carry off a social occasion that might daunt anyone. One Saturday that November, they were staying with Jim Rose – who was now chairman of Penguin Books, and a long-time friend and fellow music-lover – and his wife Pam in Sussex when the Roses' neighbours, Lord and Lady Rupert Nevill, invited them all to dinner, saying 'Rupert's boss and his wife are coming' – i.e. the Queen and Prince Philip. Laurie was seated by the Queen. Pam Rose recalls: 'A lady called Lulu de Waldner had brought some pâté de foie gras "for la reine d'Angleterre" which was handed round. When Laurie said, "Oh I thought it was kipper paste from Tunbridge Wells," Her Majesty was very amused and put on a Gloucestershire accent to talk to him.' After dinner Laurie, Kathy and Prince Philip sat on a sofa together, with much laughter. Prince Philip complimented Kathy on her blue eyes, and later he and Laurie exchanged books. Laurie sent his trio of bestsellers. In return, Prince Philip's volume of *Selected Speeches* arrived, inscribed 'for Laurie Lee: some of my embarrassingly large old stock. Philip'.

24 | I Can't Stay Long
1975–9

After five fallow years, André Deutsch suggested that Laurie should publish a collection of his travel pieces and essays. Recycling journalism – or as Laurie put it, clearing the 'barnacled chaos' of his room – is the traditional refuge of unproductive authors: *I Can't Stay Long* was 'self-indulgent', Laurie admitted to Elizabeth Jane Howard, 'and perhaps a mistake, but who cares'. 'It has its *longueurs*,' he told P. J. Kavanagh, 'though I can't be ashamed of it altogether.' Rereading his essays – on 'Charm', 'Love', etc. – he was struck by the 'confident enthusiasm and unabashed celebration of the obvious'. Most of the places he had visited with such exuberance were now ineradicably changed by war, prosperity and tourism. But it was a useful and illuminating repository of Laurie's observations over three decades. He bet André Deutsch £25 that the book would never sell 5,000. Deutsch knew better. Eventually, a brown envelope arrived at Deutsch's house in Fulham containing twenty-five pound notes.

Laurie's mid-1970s pocket diaries are much possessed by money, drink and death. As inflation took hold, he noted the soaring price of everything from cassettes to train fares. His Chelsea rent increased to £560 a year. He still owed £4,500 to Deutsch, though this was soon repaid. Jessy started at Queen's Gate School at £275 a term, and Laurie reckoned he was left with £78 a week to live on. Quotidian irritants such as tax returns, residents' parking fees, a rail strike, a rates revaluation and a tax appeal jostled with grim entries about deaths. Two of his half-sisters, Dorothy and Phyllis, died in 1975. Jim Donleavy, the Queen's Elm barman, 'died (heart)'. So did Aristotle Onassis, Lord Montgomery, King Faisal, Sir Arthur Bliss, Sir Carol Reed, William Hardcastle, all noted. Benjamin Britten died (heart) at sixty-three. Frank Mansell's mother died, and Mrs Twining of Slad (ninety) whom he had once taught the violin. The Behrenses' son lost his wife in a riding accident. Claude

Whatham, director of *Cider with Rosie*, lost his son ('motorbike'). Often, such deaths were the only entries in the diary.

He still recorded each blooming daffodil, the daily weather, the state of the moon, his own weight. But he was also making a daily tally of what he drank. 'Champagne wine 2 large whiskies.' 'Champ. 4 beers, red & white wine.' On 5 April 1975 he got 'v. drunk' when Frank Mansell won on the Grand National. Retiring to bed with hangovers, fevers and taking pills was a continual refrain. Increasingly he felt he was losing all sense of taste. During dinner with the Roses one night, 'Tasted 1st course – then legs went cold. Fever coming on?' 'No taste this week. Brain slipping.' He marked with an 'X' days when he took his knockout pill. 'Pill 8.30/4.0 Out evening pub. Mistake.' And so on. He used to say, 'I write on wine'; now it was plain that what he did on wine was not write, but perform.

The diaries' pocket-sized impression is of a life of anxiety and irritants, but to the outside world, Laurie Lee remained an amiable sprite. Interviewers found him 'relaxed, courteous and good-humoured'. The *Guardian* man who went down to Slad in 1977 had a good day out: they shot at Sainsbury's beer bottles with a .22 rifle in the garden – Laurie now had a gun licence – and Laurie played his violin, took him to the Woolpack and down to the pond where, he said, he'd once brought 'a debby girl' and photographed her in the nude: 'These long-legged girls are built for walking through grass.' And those who met Laurie in pubs in the 1970s saw the bar-room charmer who gathered around him an adoring coterie. He lunched at the Garrick with Tom Matthews, Hugh Casson, the High Court judge Billy Hughes, John Betjeman. But he was drinking recklessly. On one Dublin spree with Matthews, he arrived in the city at 2.30 p.m. when the pubs were closed. 'Perhaps I should eat,' said Laurie to the taxi driver. 'You would not be doing a better thing,' the cabbie replied. Afterwards Laurie thanked Matthews for 'leading me out into the paths of light & Kildare Street. You were in splendid form; it was I who cracked in the end. I can't write more now because I still have the Molly Malone fever (103 degrees). But I wouldn't have missed our jaunt nor will

I forget it.' Two weeks later he told Matthews that 'the travellers' cheques I lost in Dublin were found in a Nighttown Bar near the Liffey and handed in to the authorities intact. God bless Ireland.'

In London he had another nocturnal scrape. On 19 February 1975 he was on his way to Maunkberry's, the Jermyn Street club, in the early hours, when three thugs demanded money in Piccadilly underground; he said he had brandished a pair of secateurs at them from the pocket of his fur-collared coat. But his diary says they got his Barclaycard.

They were in 'damp, cold' Rose Cottage in the snowy spring of 1975, during the building work on Littlecourt, the much bigger house next door. Laurie wished he could just hibernate until the day when 'heard cuckoo, saw full moon rise with Jess, perfect day, cut grass'. Littlecourt is not traditionally pretty, but it is a secret house, wood-clad, backing on to the lane behind the Woolpack, with a wide, steep south-facing garden and terrace overlooking an incomparable panorama of Swift's Hill. Laurie installed a big picture window to capture the whole valley, knowing this to be a vulgar excrescence on a period house, but masking it with climbing 'Albertine' roses and clematis. It was the view that made the house, and this was 'one of my great refreshments' for the rest of his life. He knew exactly where the sun came up over the trees in the morning, and the moon over the hill at night. He could leave the Woolpack as the sun went down, and be home (eighteen paces) before shadows fell.

In the heatwave of June 1975, dairymaid dresses in ruffled cheese-cloth were in style, and words from *Cider with Rosie* were used as fashion captions in *Vogue*. Courage off-licences offered *Cider with Rosie* paperbacks with three packs of beer. Daimler used the *Cider with Rosie* passage about the Squire's Daimler in its ads. Laurie simmered in Slad as the temperature climbed to 90, and told Tom Matthews they lay 'panting like dogs in the heat', with occasional forays to 'Weston-super-Nightmare' and local horse shows with Jessy. On their silver wedding that May, Laurie and Kathy dined out with friends at the Country Elephant in Painswick. Laurie was commandeered by the local press ('Laurie Lee in Fight to Save

Valley') to lead a petition against a Bovis Homes development of 700 houses in the Slad valley: the first of many. Visitors came (including brother Jack and his wife, for the last time), but Laurie was either bedevilled by whisky ('Eastcombe W.I. V drunk') or saved by it: 'Crisis morning averted by whisky.'

Alan Ross found his old friend Laurie was now 'happiest in the pub, surrounded by cronies, people sitting at his feet, listening to the sage talking'. The *Telegraph* magazine suggested he might as well write a piece about his favourite pub, the Queen's Elm, which now stands sadly empty on its corner of the Fulham Road. 'The Elms', as he called it, was more like a club than a pub, a byword for camaraderie, centred on the ebullient personality of the Irish landlord Sean Treacy who, in Laurie's words, kept the clientele 'in a perpetual state of good spirits'. Moreover, Treacy would protect Laurie when he wanted to be alone; and like the Woolpack landlord, was willing to sell Laurie's books behind the bar.

'It's not the comfort, it's not the service, it's the people,' Laurie's 'Elms' notes began. 'Oliver Reed, Michael Craig, Bill Travers, Ronald Fraser, Sean Connery, Eric Sykes, John Tavener, Lucian Freud, Bobby Birch, Donald McCann, Reg Bosanquet. Cartoonists Gerald Scarfe, Frank Dickens, Jak. Artists Bill Thomson, Lis Frink, Nicola Bayley. Peeresses, Olympic swimmers, diminutive Corsican crooks, Turkish pearl divers, Jet Harris Cliff Richard's guitarist, Ava Gardner, bare-midriff models, students, Irish, Russians, Basques. Photographers. Cops. Robbers. Lone drinkers. Writers. Poets. Golfers. Psychiatrists. Barristers. Judges. Drifters. Dentists & doctors. Bank managers. The Vicar of Chelsea. 6 o'clock empty. 7 o'clock accountants & solitary boozers, & a warm wave of erotic air . . .'

What Laurie loved about 'the Elms' was its honest squalor. Behind its handsome Victorian art nouveau doors, it was 'a stage set surrounded by bottles. Scene of love affairs, suicides, changing of partners, where tears & blood might flow . . . I suppose one of these days Sean will retire, and someone will wash the dried blood off the walls and sweep the grey tears of disappointment off the floor and jazz it up, which will be sad.' On the walls were Treacy's collection of pipes (later sold at Christie's) and framed cartoons by

the *Evening Standard* cartoonist Jak, himself a legendary drinker – a Judo black belt and high-spending ladies' man. Treacy published his own bar-room anecdotes in *A Smell of Broken Glass* – in which Laurie features as busker, billiards champion and darts-player who aimed his darts through a two-foot blow-pipe. Once, Laurie had burst through the door of the pub in a djellabah, brandishing an Arab flintlock rifle which he pointed at Sliwo Isaac, the Babylonian Christian barman from Baghdad, and cried, 'I've come to take you back.'

The barmaid was Mavis Cheek (not yet a well-known novelist), a remarkable blue-eyed black-haired beauty. Treacy would place the most popular drinks on the bottom shelves so that Mavis in her mini had to do a lot of bending over. Having just split up from her husband, Mavis found Laurie a sympathetic listener on his stool at the bar. But he was never alone for long. Girls flocked. He and Bryan Wharton, the nattily-dressed *Sunday Times* photographer, were usually surrounded by pretty girls, and each thought the other was the lure. They talked of doing a book together, about sea-ports: what larks they could have in Marseilles, Algeciras, Famagusta . . . Laurie accused Wharton of dressing too flamboyantly to be a photographer, and bet him a bottle of whisky he couldn't take his picture without Laurie realizing it; he lost the bet, since Laurie was distracted by Wharton's then girlfriend, a beautiful Yugoslav, while Wharton snapped away. Laurie was 'an old flatterer and a flirt', Wharton says, 'but never predatory'.

Laurie's charm in action was something to witness. Jill Balcon saw him at a BBC luncheon, holding a table of women producers spellbound. 'It was rather enthralling to watch. People who are good at being flirtatious always know they are.' Mavis Nicholson wore a fetching lavender frock 'to look Cider with Rosieish' when she interviewed Laurie in 1975 for her Thames television programme *Good Afternoon*, and Laurie, in white safari jacket ('my Ernest Hemingway look'), gave her a lot of flirtatious sidelong eye contact and made teasing claims such as 'I'm not a women's libber by any means; I like chasing women up trees and tying them to the topmost branches.' Mavis took to Laurie and brought her

teenage son Steve to meet him. 'Laurie said to Steve: "Do you like books?" and Steve said "No." Laurie said, "Ah well, it's up to you. Here's £1 and you don't have to spend it on a book."'

On the programme he told Mavis: 'I know what you're going to say – I haven't written much, have I?' He said it took him half a day to write a letter to the gas company. Writing was 'sheer agony'. But he always needed his old diaries: 'I re-read them and they are startling and staggering. They bring back an avalanche of feeling and emotion that would have been lost and forgotten if I hadn't written it down.'

When *I Can't Stay Long* was launched, Laurie spoke at an *Evening Standard* luncheon with Dame Margot Fonteyn, and did the usual book-signings, but was certain the book was 'dying the death'. J.B. Priestley admired the essay on 'Charm'. 'It seems a long time since we drank rum together in our room in that old hotel in Mexico City,' Priestley wrote. 'I am now old and grumpy and try to keep away from London.'

Melvyn Bragg invited Laurie on his television programme, *Read All About It*. 'He took some persuading,' Bragg recalls. They spent a long evening in the Queen's Elm, during which Bragg told Laurie he had grown up helping out in his dad's pub in Wigton. Laurie told Bragg he would come on his programme if Bragg passed a test: to take, and remember, an order from everyone in the Queen's Elm. 'We had drunk an immense amount, and I had to concentrate like mad, and all these hardened drinkers tried to put me off my stroke,' Bragg says. But he managed it, and Laurie duly came to the studio to record the programme, still grumbling that he didn't want to, didn't like this sort of thing, and was 'unpredictable'. And so he was. After the rehearsal, Laurie locked himself in his dressing-room (with bottle of whisky) and would not come out. They recorded the programme with a panel of three instead of the usual four.

Laurie had dedicated his book 'to Pen and Virginia with love'. He wrote to ask if they would mind, and they said they'd be thrilled. So the falling-out with Pen Dugdale – which had lasted since she had discovered the liaison with Antonia in 1962 – was now ended.

Pen herself had remarried, and with Antonia now a mother herself, the rift was healed. 'Pen and Virginia,' he told Elizabeth Jane Howard, as she had inquired, 'are venerable sisters I've known for ages, long before I met you, and who were good to me in my golden days, and I wanted to offer them something, though I hadn't seen them for years.' He told Jane he would dedicate a book to 'Isabel' too, 'before I die. It is overdue and most certainly one of my life's imperatives. Gerona,' he added, 'is always with me. I have never ever talked about it, let alone tried to write it, yet the most vivid impressions remain . . . Dearest Isabel, I have been out of touch with almost everything. I have missed you.' She sent him 'unaltered love'.

He took Kathy and Jessy to Tangier one Christmas, to New York for another: 'madness really', he told Tom Matthews, who suggested that they stay at the Royalton (today the height of glitz): 'It's old-fashioned and there's nothing fancy about it.' They returned each January to Laurie's wintry fevers and hangovers. It was Kathy, endlessly tolerant, who wrote to Celia Goodman thanking her for a 'beautiful' letter, which moved Laurie so much he had shown it to her, 'which is unusual'. She told Celia how important her loyalty and affection were, 'from someone who understands the meaning of creative work and thinking . . . I sometimes feel that Laurie is very much alone. I know the truth about the stress in his life . . . especially as he has been so hurt by the establishment critics. The *Scotsman* reviewer described Laurie as a man of not very much feeling. I could wring his neck.'

In fact, the criticism of *I Can't Stay Long* was mild, apart from that of Eve Auchincloss in the *Washington Post*, who accused Laurie of 'slack and wanton verbiage': 'His language is swollen, hectic, off-target (briars bleed, skies ache).' But even she had to admire the gritty, self-mocking journalism of 'A Wake in Warsaw', 'Ibiza High Fifties', the Cannes film festival piece, and the down-to-earth reportage of Aberfan.

Thanks to beer, whisky, Cinzano, wine and fevers lasting for days at a stretch, Laurie was having a 'difficult and chaotic time', he told the *Telegraph*, putting off delivery of his Queen's Elm piece.

He had also agreed to write a piece for *Vogue* on 'My Day'. In his notebook, 'Whose day?' he asked himself. 'How many left – with age, tumbling faster down a slope into a dark slot marked "Don't Remember." "Lost." '

In the account of his days in the flat (where he spent most of his time now alone, leaving Kathy in Slad), he described being brutally torn from dreams each morning by a 6 a.m. jet-plane landing at Heathrow. How come two dozen Dutch businessmen, 'briefcases snapped on tiny ambitions', had this godlike power to murder Londoners' sleep? At 7 a.m. he switched on Radio 3 – 'the most civilized way to wake' – hoping for Telemann or Scarlatti; Schumann was 'indigestible as beef at this hour of the day'. He slept in a room 'walled-in by books, unframed pictures, packets of other people's poems, antique glasses, oil-lamps, crucifixes of straw and wood, spools of recording tape, bits of sculpture and jars full of swizzle sticks'. His clothes were scattered, some suits lying undisturbed for months. His 'locked cell', his workroom, was even more disorganized and squalid, with 'a leaking roof, four kinds of peeling wallpaper, a sagging bookcase, cardboard boxes full of wine and papers, first editions signed by friends long dead . . . defeated poems, old manuscripts . . . the rusty medallions of once bright lecheries and loves'. Cupboard drawers 'fluttered with letters exhaling the heated breath of girls whom marriage has now chastely cooled or plumped into Titian matrons. Little in this loaded room is ever thrown away. There are no visitors. I am its lone curator.'

He reflected: 'I remember the days when I could carry all I owned in my two hands. I decide I really must get this stuff sorted out. I know I never will.' (And he never did.)

In the shaving mirror he now saw the shade of his father, 'whose relationship I denied as a boy, and whose mirrored ghost returns each day at this time to haunt me'. He had lunch with a TV researcher, a beautiful young girl, but she spoilt things by asking, 'Has anyone ever told you you look like Angus Wilson?' (His notebook said: 'Danny Kaye yes, even Alec Guinness – but never Dame Angus, whom God preserve.')

He recorded drinking for five hours at a stretch at the Garrick

with Pat Kernon, Willis Hall and Jeff Hoare. His weight went up to fourteen stone. He wrote with some fellow-feeling when he reviewed Dylan Thomas's biography by Paul Ferris. Laurie was 'close enough to Dylan not to be dazzled, or to judge him', he said. Only the Severn had divided them in childhood. They both published their first poems in the same *Sunday Referee* column, both came to London in the 1930s, and Laurie had lodged across the street from Dylan in the house of his wife's sister in Chelsea. 'Has too much been made of him? Perhaps it has,' said Laurie. 'Most of his best work was written by the time he was 30' and 'although he was a star poet and performer on both sides of the Atlantic . . . yet for much of his later years he was also vulnerable, sick, self-disgusted, lonely, unhappy and mortally frightened'.[1]

Despite the woes and muddles of Laurie's life, Jessy recalls their country weekends in those years – at Cavendish, Biddesden, Culham, Bruern, among families with children and horses and rows of wellies – as the best times of her childhood. At Biddesden, where a grey Arab stallion called Zebedee would canter over to greet visitors, and hot Ribena was served in the mornings, she was 'the happiest child'. Bryan Guinness, Lord Moyne, looked forward to the Lees' visits with 'rejoicing' and organized country tasks like chopping logs and pulling up nettles. After one weekend there in March 1976, when Laurie's nose had been lacerated by the branch of a Biddesden tree, there followed a 'BLACK WEEK': a chaotic time when Laurie lost his passport and travellers' cheques, and abandoned a planned trip to Australia.

The summer of 1976 was again memorably hot: a summer of parched lawns and Mediterranean evenings. The cows were motionless, the garden full of butterflies, and at Slad Laurie sat out at midnight under the stars ('Moonlight like honey'). He loved such extremes of weather, 'the smell of sun-burned leaves and the droning sound of insects' wings, and animals hiding under trees and nothing moving except the stream'. When the rain finally came, it leaked into his bedroom. He went to the West Country Writers' Lunch, and a dinner for the twenty-fifth anniversary of the Festival of Britain, and several poetry readings, when he was 'a

proper old ham', says Ted Walker, his fellow poet, 'with his alarm clock'. This Laurie would place ostentatiously on the table, in case the readers overran their allotted time.

Ted Walker – whose bond with Laurie was chiefly Spain, where Ted now lives – found Laurie in the street during the Stroud Festival on 9 October 1976. 'Laurie was trailing along miserably through a lightly falling drizzle, holding a nice cut-glass tankard with a wan drop of beer in it. "I'm a favourite son of Stroud," he said. "*Un hijo preferido*. They've given me this thing today. Got my name on it, look. I hate cut glass. But I don't know what to do with it, there's nowhere I can put it down. Someone'll find it and seek me out."' He took Walker to 'a roughish bar'. 'After a few pints Laurie said, "We'll be expected at dear old Christopher Fry's reading, won't we? Half past seven kick-off."' (A week earlier all three had performed at Chichester.)

Laurie led the way, still clutching his tankard, to the packed Subscription Rooms. Walker and Laurie stood at the back, where Fry recognized them and gave a half wave. While Fry was reading from *A Phoenix Too Frequent*, Laurie whispered, 'Follow me.' They went into the foyer, negotiated an imposing staircase with red plush carpet, a landing, another corridor with coconut matting, then another with old worn boards. 'At the end we reached a door behind which one knew there would be mops and canisters of Vim and galvanized buckets, and a chipped sink and tea-making equipment for ladies in floral wrap-around housecoats. In we went. "This," said Laurie, "is where I wrote a good deal of *As I Walked Out One Midsummer Morning*."'

There was 'a state of confusion on the domestic front', Laurie told Tom Matthews. Matthews was a lifeline, 'a rock in the ocean', offering weekends, theatre visits, dinner at New College, a trip to Dublin. But Laurie was constantly writing apologetic letters. After Dublin: 'Dear Tom, You were both much more generous and patient than I deserved and I can't think why you put up with me.' After an aborted weekend: 'Dear Tom, Sunday was a disaster. I'm so sorry. I hadn't been ill for months then it had to happen just then. This sort of disappointment and deprivation of looked-forward to

treats goes back to my childhood.' After inviting Laurie and Kathy to a dinner at Brooks's for Hugh Cudlipp in January 1977: 'Dear Tom, It may sound unbelievable to organized people but Cathy & I have not been out to dinner together for a long time. I am not particularly proud of this but then we are a most disorganized & rather out-of-touch family. I have been trying to get some bookshelves built for 13 months – 4 carpenters have come & looked & disappeared without trace.' (But Laurie did get to the Cudlipp dinner, a memorable evening. 'My Lord Cudlipp in his cups grew positively cuddly.')

This was the Queen's Jubilee Year, and Laurie found himself together with Kingsley Amis on the judging panel to find a jubilee poem better than Betjeman's, for the *Daily Mail*. Over bottles of Glenlivet on the floor of Amis's house in Flask Walk, Hampstead, they sorted out the entries. Laurie was struck by 'the drowsy evensong drone of the church harmonium' in many poems, and the way the amateur poets saw the Queen as a vulnerable wife and mother who had suffered. 'She has sometimes a look of pain on her face and yet she always carries on with the job. I think people have responded to that,' Laurie said. Kingsley Amis wasn't having any of that. 'Nobody said about George V or VI how tedious it must be to launch a battleship,' he snorted.

Cider with Rosie's continuing success, as Laurie eventually admitted, was what stopped him from needing to bother to write other things. By May 1977 the hardback was in its thirteenth impression and it had sold a million in paperback; Penguin celebrated this in some style, giving him a gold fountain pen and a miniature Lis Frink eagle, and a party at the Chelsea Arts Club on a glorious summer day. 'I really bought this place on the blood of the village,' he told a reporter, of Rose Cottage, 'though that may be too harsh a thing to say, because what I wrote was a book of love.' The Hogarth Press reissued *The Firstborn* in paperback. There was a Decca triple album of Laurie's readings. *I Can't Stay Long* was a paperback bestseller and when Laurie read extracts on *A Book at Bedtime*, in January 1979, Jill Balcon wrote thanking him for 'spellbinding evocations'. Her son Daniel Day-Lewis (now twenty-

one and at drama school, 'very like Cecil – gloriously funny & handsome') had 'practically wept, as I did . . . I felt you were talking to me. You are so deeply associated with Cecil in my mind & heart & therefore with the most central part of my life & its happiest days.'

Poetry had left him for ever. 'You need the passion,' he told one reporter. 'You have to write for someone.' Instead, he would turn out a nostalgic piece for *Reader's Digest* on 'A Village Christmas',[2] or a personal reminiscence about love – a subject on which he was assumed to be an expert. In the article he wrote for St Valentine's Day in 1979[3] Laurie came closest to describing the two distinctly different female types he had long regarded as his ideal. One was the Rosie type – gold-haired, with petalled curls: 'The recurrence of this healthy, romping, innocently carnal little blonde has been with me like perpetual summer.' The other was the type he had first discerned as a boy in the publican's daughter: 'something sinuous, slant-eyed, oriental or celtic, with hair black as slate or the oils of Oman. You did not play lightly with this smoked night-figure. The involvement was graver, more deeply entangled, and her reincarnation over the years has ever in some ways been witchlike, announced by a pricking of the thumbs, a fatal chill of excitement.'

From what crevice of the mind, he wondered, did 'the dark one rise, that she should so incessantly command my senses?' He had met the dark one since, 'in flashing glimpses or in longer possessions, under different names and in different places, in India, Spain, Cornwall, London. Looking back, I see this recurring image as one of the preservatives of love, a succession of occupations by a spirit unique to herself and to which all one's passions belong.

'I don't say that this way happiness lies (believing mere happiness to be one of life's shallower experiences).

'This hovering visitation need not always be a physical presence. It can be a quality of mind, a way of regarding the world.

'But for me, trapped all my days in my double helix, slowly spiralling between sunlight and shades, the stronger and most compelling has always been the dark one, her panther tread, voice full of musky secrets, her limbs uncoiling on beds of moonlight.'

This is the closest Laurie came, in print, to confessing to the hold Lorna – or the spirit and essence of Lorna, or Lorna's physical and spiritual type – had over him. And the mention of 'Cornwall' is the only public reference to the place where she first cast her seductive enchantment.

In the same year Laurie firmly turned down the *Telegraph* magazine when they asked him to write a serious analysis of how post-Franco political changes had affected Spanish life, arts, mores and religion. But he would, of course, go to Venice for them, to write about Harry's Bar. Forty years earlier he had arrived in 'a melancholy city cloaked in November mists, with signs at canal corners saying *Andante* and *Grave*'. It took him the best part of a day to find Harry's Bar, which 'looked like a small country bank'. On the bar were plump white sandwiches 'moist and cool as the breast of nuns'. After a few dry Martinis, 'keen and crisp as arctic crevices', he sampled Bellinis, Tiepolos and Giorgiones. He got on famously with Arrigo Cipriani, whose father Giuseppe had founded Harry's Bar. Cipriani gave him some short stories and said he had always wanted to be a writer himself.

Jessy was now entering her teenage years. This bolshy stage is commonplace and a pain for all parents – but it must be said that Laurie was not good at facing it. His diary reflects many exasperated scenes – 'J hopeless. J hopelessly rude. Filthy language from J.' 'Jessy in a hate you all mood and a fury of ill-temper.' 'J roughens daily.' 'Cathy screaming about her hairstyle.' 'Much makeup & exhausting dancing alone in room. Mother and daughter at each other's throats.' Sometimes he feared Jessy might leave home altogether. But then, a father who was out in the pub or lying in a darkened room for much of the time was hardly helpful to mother or daughter. And Laurie's epilepsy, he insisted, had to be kept from Jessy at all costs. 'Carefully planned to conceal illness from J,' says his diary on 22 March 1976. 'Took pill after she left for school – forced self to get up, shave & dress before her return.'

Keeping Jessy happy, keeping her protected, and keeping her at home became a major preoccupation. When she was born, he had

(rashly) written: 'I don't want to educate my daughter at a level above her parents, so that she'll be . . . an uneasy aristocrat fed by parent serfs. I want to try to keep her classless. Her childhood is too precious to hand her over to the boarding school factories . . .

'I've no mind to pack her off to some boarding school, to lose sight of her for months at a time, only to get her back stiff as a hockey post.' But in 1977 they moved her out of her London school, Queen's Gate, to board at the highly academic, strictly regimented Cheltenham Ladies' College.

Laurie thought he was protecting her from London temptations. Kathy says it was 'to separate her from these two adults going on all around her'. Jessy says she was furious: 'I'd been closeted in the triangle of the family. And now my parents had sent me away.' Her father wanted to protect her from any influence that was not his, she says, by keeping her away from friends. 'But he would also ask me, why aren't you making any friends? So I got confusing messages.'

When Jessy's blue budgerigar, now aged ten, fell off his perch while sitting next to Laurie in the big window, he was put in the deep freeze, occasionally brought out to show guests, whereupon Laurie would say, 'That's where I'll end up one day.' In the same year, 1977, Laurie bought Jessy a new pet: a horse called the Red Baron, known as Red. 'The horse was a major love affair,' Jessy says. She was an unconventional and intrepid bareback rider. The following June Laurie bought more livestock: a pair of Store Cattle at £269 each. They got warble fly disease and it was Kathy who had to run round the field to anoint their backs with something that smelt like Jeyes Fluid.

Jessy was 'not at all what I had planned', Laurie wrote, in May 1978, in an update on *The Firstborn* which the *Daily Mail* commissioned. In the photograph she was a sultry milkmaid with long curls in an embroidered dress, surrounded by flowers. 'She is fourteen now and as tall as I am . . .' (She was five foot ten and as shapely as her mother had been at that age.)

The 'tiny bruised plum' he had eulogized in babyhood had become 'a rich round peach centred with an immoveable diamond

stone'. Almost nothing that he had wished or expected had happened between them – but then, he had foolishly wished her to
grow up into 'a wisp of Colette-style sensitivity'. This was, he now
admitted, 'a doddering dad's vulgar fantasy'. He had pictured her
'inquiring grave-eyed and listening to my god-like illuminations,
seeking my presence above all others, comforting me in the evening
with chords of Chopin and perhaps waking me in the morning
with a light kiss or a flower.

'She has taught me to know better. As she has grown up, I too
have had to grow up, and learn to bury away my wistful images of
her.'

In retrospect, his words in *The Firstborn* had been astonishingly
prophetic. 'A late, only child is particularly vulnerable,' he had
written, 'a target for attention she might be happier without, or
liable to be cast into roles that have little to do with her nature in
order to cut out some parental fantasy.' Jessy was already rather
irritated by the 'Laurie Lee's daughter' tag. She hadn't even read
Cider with Rosie.

And what, meanwhile, had become of the next book, the book
Laurie 'cared about most', about 'the real Spain of the Civil War'
which he had promised would be out in time for the fortieth
anniversary of the war in 1976? (In 1977 he was 'half way through';
in 1978, he was saying it would be 'ready next year, with luck'.)
In fact he was to carry the unfinished manuscript around in his
battered briefcase for nearly fifteen years. One day in 1977 Philip
Oakes, an old friend and sometime poet from Yates's wine bar days
in the 1950s, who was now on the *Sunday Times*, interviewed him
in some depth about it. Laurie told him he was writing one page
per morning (in the usual soft lead pencil on the backs of radio
scripts). 'His problem is that he has no notes on the period,' said
Oakes, relating the story of the theft of Laurie's diaries in 1969, and
the despair this caused. Laurie felt 'imprisoned in the need to
complete the trilogy. I've got to write the book before I'm free to
write anything else.'

'It's a winter story, a lonely story, a story of muddle and brutality
and heroism,' he said. 'I was thrown into jail several times.' He

told Oakes he had been 'in it for real. I mean that I carried a gun, not a stretcher. I felt that an atrocious crime was being committed against my friends and it was being ignored by France and Britain and America. I still believe that Franco was one of the great monsters of the twentieth century, a man who turned his country over to the fascists for bayonet practice. But at the time, I didn't fit my feelings into any dialectic. Nor do I now. I didn't know any of the other English writers who were over there: not Orwell, not Spender, not John Cornford. I wasn't aware that they existed. They were intellectuals and I'd only just come from a Gloucestershire village. I was barely hatched.'

He also told Oakes about the five scented one-pound notes, sent to him by 'a girlfriend' as a Christmas present in December 1937. 'The government men sniffed the envelope and said they'd look after it for me. Months later when I left Spain I asked what about my cash? and the officer in charge looked me in the eye and said "Comrade, you are going home. Do you really need the money?" And I stared at the floor in shame and said, "Of course not," and the notes still heady with Chanel no. 5 went back into the drawer.'

Considering what was eventually to happen after he wrote *A Moment of War*, it is interesting that in this same month Laurie wrote to Bill Alexander, veteran Commander of the British Battalion of the International Brigade at Teruel, to ask him for names of survivors of the Civil War from the winter of 1937/8, and Alexander replied with a list of the names and addresses of twelve of them, all still living then: including Frank West, carpenter, who had been at Tarazona, and was taken prisoner in Aragon; Miles Tomalin, the writer (and father of Nicholas), who had been in Barcelona; Patience Edney, a nurse in a front-line casualty station; Bob Doyle, Irish seaman, and Bob Walker, Scots Guards engineer, from the British Battalion; and of course Alexander himself. He was sure 'they would all be pleased to answer any questions or talk over their experiences. I could suggest other names – people with different experiences – if it would be at all helpful.'

In Laurie's notebook that year, too, is a list of historical facts and queries about the Spanish Civil War – with page references to

Hugh Thomas's massive and definitive history of the war.[4] Laurie was, at sixty-three, plainly trying to sort out the historical facts from his own increasingly vague and muddled memories.

He told Oakes it was an agonizing process. 'I have vivid mental pictures of places, weather, faces, fear and other sensations. But they're all without reference and in no special order. Trying to assemble them in a book is like attempting to piece together a love letter which has been scattered by a cyclone. Going about it I feel I am scraping at my sinews with a rusty knife. I can't let it go though. I have to finish the book. It was a long ride to the graveyard for so many of my generation. It's their story, as well as my own, that I have to tell. It's a debt I owe to dead men, to dead friends.' Oakes says today that he felt at the time 'a tremor of doubt' about what Laurie – who did not strike him as a fighting man – told him. The story of the scented pound notes (which was of course quite true and typically Lorna) sounded like fantasy. 'But I was so fond of him,' he says, 'I just couldn't say, "Oh, come on, Laurie."'

25 | Two Women
1980–83

'You come through an anonymous black door from the street, and there is this bar, a restaurant and beautiful gardens. I can come here and eat or take a nap and no one will bother me. I am behind walls that only a few people can enter, and most of the time, I am alone.'

The Chelsea Arts Club in Old Church Street was Laurie's home from home, his hideaway, equidistant from his flat and from the Queen's Elm pub. The club was founded in 1890 in the King's Road, when hundreds of artists had their ateliers and workshops in that quarter, as a gathering place which, by agreement, was to be 'bohemian in character'. In 1901 it moved into two old cottages (with a billiard room) at 143 and 145 Old Church Street, which runs between the Fulham Road and the King's Road. Its shabby country house interior fitted Laurie like a glove – more so than the Garrick – and it was only 180 paces ('I am a great counter') from his flat. In the year he joined, 1949, other new members included Edward Ardizzone, Rodrigo Moynihan, John Minton, Henry Lamb, Henry Moore, Ronald Searle, Ruskin Spear, John Ward and Carel Weight. In the Chelsea Arts Club Laurie was a fixture, at home among writers and painters all looking vaguely like minor figures in literary memoirs, hovering around the snooker table where Laurie had once played with Sir Alexander Fleming. On one wall of the dining-room is Paul Wyeth's 1960 painting *Concert at the Chelsea Arts Club*, with Laurie playing his recorder; by the 1990s Laurie was the only one in the picture still alive. Today, the club's ladies' bar is the Laurie Lee bar, a quiet donnish study with red walls covered with drawings, Indian rugs, red velvet curtains, piano, smoky fire and a very good bust of Laurie by Lynn Bamber. People would enter here like disciples and kneel at his feet to talk.

In 1980 Laurie moved across the square and rented the top-floor flat at 40 Elm Park Gardens, which he bought the following year:

'an excellent investment' according to his accountant Pat Kernon. It was his den: a small sitting-room with green velvet armchair, television, videos, hundreds of books, and a Lis Frink sculpture. On the walls were his violin, crucifixes, a corn dolly, a Victorian pub mirror emblazoned 'Fine beers and famous lagers', paintings by friends and by Yasmin. In the corridor, a desk piled with papers. On the wall, Laurie had pencilled (in 1987) the point where the last of the evening sunlight came through the kitchen window in winter: Nov 21, 3.35 p.m.; Nov 30, 3.30 p.m.; Dec 15: 3 p.m., etc.

No money was spent on unnecessary decorating. There was an old-fashioned bathroom, and in the bedroom an imperial bedstead left by a previous occupant and a wide mahogany cheval mirror. The small back bedroom was where Laurie wrote. Rarely, a visiting journalist would be allowed a peep at 'a room of unspeakable chaos'.

The flat was his fortress against the outside world. He told people it was 'full of locked rooms containing rejected manuscripts and other men's mad wives'. 'I have no housekeeper, no cleaning woman, no mistress, no visitors,' he would say. He also claimed never to answer the telephone (though his number was in *Who's Who*) and that his doorbell did not work: 'Bells of any nature, door bells, telephone bells, fill me with the greatest alarm. It is either bad news or someone saying, "You don't know me but . . ."' His passion for privacy struck journalists as wilfully obdurate. Arranging to meet him was complicated. 'He makes arrangements about arrangements about arrangements,' said Angela Levin of the *Mail on Sunday*.

The public Laurie, as he approached seventy, could have lived out the rest of his life on his past glory. He became a Freeman of the City of London in 1982. He was constantly anthologized. He was still a fixture at Foyle's lunches (e.g. for Angus Wilson, when he sat between Baroness Falkender and Cate Haste, Mrs Melvyn Bragg; or for Sir Roy Strong, who sent him a postcard of himself, thanking him for having encouraged him to write). Artists would follow his footsteps across Spain (by car) and exhibit their paintings. At any given moment, half a dozen local rep theatres would be

performing *Cider with Rosie*, in either the original James Roose-Evans or the later Nick Darke adaptations. Amateur players would descend on Slad to visit Laurie's old home, where Wally and Ruby Marwood got used to being invaded, and on the Woolpack, where they often found Laurie: he would be photographed with his arm around the girl playing Rosie, gallantly telling her she was just like the real Rosie only prettier. One January, when Tom Matthews sent his annual crate of Perequita wine ('Glug', said Laurie gratefully), he invited Laurie to come and see *Cider with Rosie* at Colchester. 'I've seen it three times,' replied Laurie, '& there must be better ways to meet.'

Poetry readings sometimes felt like 'a dry run for my memorial service' (as he told P.J. Kavanagh, fellow poet-performer and conspirator in wrangles over fees). But audiences were never disappointed by Laurie's wheezy, gentle-voiced performances. ('In his voice you hear poetry, the dryness of rustling leaves, his tones belong to the earth,' wrote Michael Watkins in *The Times*.) The charm was indeed seductive. Even Geoffrey Grigson ('a formidable literary bruiser' in Kavanagh's words) was charmed by Laurie, Kavanagh says. 'He could still sometimes slough off the self-exploitative character he had created for himself.' When he met Princess Michael at a party, she too was captivated and invited him to lunch at nearby Nether Lypiatt.

His predilection for whisky was accepted and forgiven; it added to the air of mischief. When Mavis Cheek from the Queen's Elm, now chairman of the Writers' Circle, asked Laurie to judge their short story competition in October 1981, he refused to perform the adjudication in public, but agreed to be filmed at his flat, discussing each of the short-listed twenty stories, halting the filming every so often to slip out to the kitchen for a swig of whisky. 'By the time we finished he was pretty pie-eyed,' Mavis says. 'But his judgement was good, and he gave a sober adjudication.' (Afterwards, driving down the Fulham Road, Mavis and her crew were stopped by police, who searched the boot. 'But when we said, "We've been filming Laurie Lee," the miracle was, the police had heard of Laurie and let us go.')

A few months later, when Laurie was among the publishers' choice of the '20 Best of British' writers, some of them (including V.S. Pritchett, Anthony Burgess, and Rosamond Lehmann) assembled for a photograph at Lord Snowdon's studio. Reporting the shoot for the *Sunday Times* magazine, Ian Jack noted that John Betjeman was 'tirelessly congenial despite 90 minutes posing in the same position', while Laurie Lee 'was helped to even greater congeniality by the whisky concealed in his briefcase (which Beryl Bainbridge was pleased to share)'.

This was all very well, but what about that dog-eared manuscript still entitled *A Winter of War*? Jock Gallagher, his BBC friend, was allowed glimpses of it and so was André Deutsch, but Laurie would not let it go. He fobbed them off with excuses about rewriting and insisted he would type it himself. Then one day Gallagher happened to see some of Laurie's photographs – stunningly romantic pictures of Kathy and Jessy posing in leafy rural places – and decided to galvanize Laurie by suggesting he publish the photographs in book form. In August 1981, Laurie signed the contract with Deutsch (£4,000 on signing, the same again on delivery and on publication) for a book called *Two Women* – 'the two women who have occupied most of my late adult life, enclosing it in a double embrace, like bookends' – without mentioning a word about it to either his wife or his daughter.

The state of his relationship with his two women requires scrutiny here. In May 1980 the *Sun*, which had just run a series, 'The Tortured Teens', on teenagers from hell, asked Laurie to write about Jessy, now going on seventeen. He produced another lyrical essay on a girl in adolescence, a headstrong, ebullient creature, a 'billowing extrovert' who swept through their lives 'as though the windows had just blown in'. 'Beautiful, without a doubt, with a round corn-gold head and a complexion as rare as her mother's. She has all the vitality of a sunburst, huge passions, a voice of Viking command and bubbling South Sea enthusiasms.'

He said Jessy regarded books as 'chiefly for throwing', and conversation for interruption and argument. 'I don't think I've ever sat down with her in a state of quietness, relaxed, just knowing her

to be there. Even when she's asleep the experience fills her room with a nautical flapping of sheets in a storm, with tossings and heavings.' She liked Hammer horror films, the Beatles, the Osmonds, *Starsky and Hutch*, Mike Oldfield, David Bowie, and 'the honest to God animalism of Police'. (He originally wrote, and excised: 'Love is the tonsils & torso of the many-splendoured Sting.')

'She hates to be alone, yet has a paradoxical independence. She treats her horse and her friends with the same rough-handed affection . . . She is very funny, thank God, and as quick as anyone could wish. But for all her gaiety she can plunge into blank despair, and withdraw to some close-shuttered cell to ask the walls the truth of herself . . .'

'My daughter, I must confess, is a self-indulgence,' he added, waxing introspective, 'and the one compelling interest in my life . . . the most exciting thing that has ever happened to me. I believe her forces have kept me alive.' He admitted to having spoilt her, and burdened her with expectations, both 'natural blunders'. 'But she has taught me more about women than I have ever learnt in a lifetime of devoted interest in the subject. Perhaps because I have had to order, placate, reassure and understand this one more intensely than any other.'

Watching her dancing, alone, he felt 'all the sad enchantment of seeing something about to take wing . . . she would be risen and away and gone from me at last, leaving the dropped dolls, the circling goldfish, the empty hamster cage and the horse in the field with its turned, raised head'.

'My love for her,' he declared, 'is the unchosen, unquestioned fact of my existence, something that neither moods, exasperation nor even occasional flashes of dislike can alter. It is a love of pride and compassion, an urge to protect and guide, something for which I must suffer, forgive, stand waiting in the rain, ask no questions, or even kill. (This feeling I know will last out my life.)'

In fact, Laurie's frequent exasperation with his womenfolk had begun to create a sense of dread at home. Both Jessy and Kathy felt intense relief when he left for London: 'The sense of relaxation, of release, was fantastic.' At the same time he ensured that they felt

totally dependent on him. Whenever he was interviewed he made a point of mentioning his pride 'that with my little pencil I can feed and clothe these two great glowing engines of health'. He could make Kathy, his child bride, now forty-nine, feel foolish and incompetent, correcting her like a disobedient child; hence the scatty air she sometimes displayed. Her habitual demeanour became one of apology as she tried to smooth things over. 'All the demands on her, all the waiting at his command,' Jessy says, 'meant she couldn't act for herself, and everything she did was wrong. I would talk to Dad about this, and he would attempt to kiss her in front of me, but it wasn't convincing. And yet I know he loved her, and there was no other woman on the planet who would have given her entire self to him as she did.

'He was always immersed in his own thoughts, his brain ticking over, so whenever there was a fracas, the most annoying thing about it to him was that his train of thought had been broken.' People noticed that by this time, Kathy and Jessy were like two teenage sisters; both referred to Laurie as 'Daddy' and sometimes Kathy felt like the younger sister. 'He had these two children, my mother and me,' Jessy says. 'He always saw us as children, hence our dependence. And he was a great father to us both. His moods weren't reliable, but his love was never questioned.' Kathy recalls that one night in 1977, in front of visitors including the publicity director of Penguin, Jacqui Graham, Laurie threw his dinner on the floor and walked out into the garden – and Kathy found herself relieved 'that at last he'd shown other people the intensity of his rages'. A neighbour, meeting Kathy for the first time, found her 'unbelievably self-effacing'. 'I was born to be an artist's wife,' she told him, 'or at least bred to be.'

Jessy says: 'I had the impression I was too big a girl for him. He was always saying how beautiful I was, and taking photographs of me, but I felt instinctively that I wasn't his type, I was far too noisy and just too big. He would say, "I'm so proud of you," but I never really believed him. I got so used to the fact that I wasn't up to the mark, and blind truths would come flying out.' She was very conscious of his having imagined 'a dreamy waif, a delicate flower'

of a daughter, and of his disappointment as she blossomed into 'a rousing and awakening reality'. 'Nobody could have fulfilled the expectation of *The Firstborn*. What a thing to live up to! And I was the sole focus of attention, and the solace of both sides in the parental battle.'

Yasmin – who, so far as Jessy knew, was just a cousin of her mother's who sent especially thoughtful birthday presents – observed from a distance her half-sister growing up and felt it was 'very hard for darling Jess'. Yasmin, by now mother of three teenagers, and married to a psychologist, could see that Jessy was suffocated by parental neuroses. 'Obviously she had lovely times, but she also suffered a great deal before she was able to blossom.' And Kathy too was, in Yasmin's view, subjected to Laurie's idea of wifeliness. 'He wanted her to sit in the country making wine and picking flowers – to give him a sense of domestic stability: but what about Kathy? She was really a Trilby to his Svengali.'

So here was Laurie, planning to publish his exquisite photographs – he always had an artist's touch with the camera, as with the pencil – of these two lovely creatures about whom he felt so ambivalent, and keeping it all a secret. When André Deutsch went with Diana Athill to Laurie's flat to see the transparencies, they were astonished. The photographs were beautifully composed, loving, romantic, mostly set in country gardens. The most striking was of Kathy lying back magnificently naked in the grass. 'Are you sure Kathy wants this published?' Deutsch asked, astonished. Laurie replied that not only did she want it, she 'would be upset if he left it out'.

But Kathy knew nothing about any of this. And before Laurie submitted his text, two unforeseen upheavals took place that rocked the foundations of the domestic triangle dominated by Laurie. First, Kathy fell in love, in her fiftieth year, with a young film-maker who came to the village to see Laurie. And he fell in love with her. After years of Laurie's prolonged absences, paternalistic putdowns and humiliations, Kathy enjoyed the novel experience of being truly adored and cherished. Laurie saw what was happening. The lovers even took a holiday in France, and Laurie knew all about it. Kathy glowed, and seemed rejuvenated; it was a passionate affair.

But it was a short-lived interlude. Kathy was adamant that she would never, ever leave Laurie; and within months the problem was resolved, in the unhappiest possible way: her lover took his own life. Kathy's grief was agonizing and she says she could not have coped at that time without Laurie's support. He was all kindness, understanding and tender sympathy. 'The three of us were so enmeshed,' she says, 'that whatever tragedy happened to any of us, the other two understood.' But Laurie never spoke of what had happened to anyone (though Georgina Hammick, in whom Kathy had confided, wrote offering help and solace). He fell into a silent, melancholy state, 'living in a sealed capsule, seeing no one', he told P.J. Kavanagh.

Kathy's therapy was to fling herself into church matters ('my holy days', she calls those years) by becoming intensely involved in the Churches' National Nuclear Freeze campaign. She wrote endless letters to clergymen and bishops asking how they felt about the fallacy of the nuclear deterrent, and the government's betrayal of the teachings of Christ in allowing the manufacture of destructive weapons in the name of peace. A year after her lover's death, she went to the East Anglian coast (where he had lived) with Tom and Pam Matthews, to walk along the seashore. But by then she was reconciled to her loss, and whole-heartedly consumed by her anti-nuclear campaigning.

Meanwhile Jessy, who had left Cheltenham Ladies' College (which she had always detested) one year into her A-level course, was determined to leave home. Laurie rented her a rather grim bedsit in Cheltenham 'to keep me near him'. She was singing with a rock band called Beat About the Bush – she has a remarkable singing voice – and the rock scene led inevitably to experiments with drugs. In London, when she was at Queen's Gate and friends were taking uppers and downers, she had managed not to be tempted. In more sedate Cheltenham she succumbed. 'I only had to look at a magic mushroom and I was flying away with the fairies.' In October 1982 she 'just flipped'.

Laurie said later it was 'more a crisis of identity than anything else'. She says: 'I stopped sleeping, stopped eating, became hyper-

manic, close to the edge. I was so thin and bony I couldn't get into the bath without putting a towel in first. I was questioning God and the devil and Mary and Jesus. Dad couldn't face it. He couldn't cope with the fact that I was bonkers. And when the psychiatrist said to Dad, "This is a lot more to do with you than it's to do with drugs," Daddy was furious and walked out of the room. My parents tried to blame drugs and my friends. Both were in deep denial when the psychiatrist told them they had to take some responsibility.'

She came home from Cheltenham, and it was Kathy who had to cope. Laurie, meanwhile, stayed in London, writing the words for his *Two Women* book, recalling how he had fallen for the schoolgirl Kathy, and expanding on *The Firstborn* and his later essays about Jessy. He was pondering on death, too, and wrote to Mark Le Fanu of the Society of Authors that November for advice about his will. Pat Kernon, assessing Laurie's capital worth to be £125,000, advised him and Kathy to leave in their wills a trust for Jessy's benefit in property and other assets, exempt from gift tax.

Despite his assiduous account-keeping Laurie found his tax and VAT returns extremely trying. He drafted a letter to Pat Kernon about having mislaid various counterfoils – £55 from the BBC for repeats of poems, £69 for an Arts Council talk, the receipt for a £12 desk lamp, etc. 'I am beginning to worry a bit about my life,' Laurie told Kernon. 'I am growing old, trying to finish my last book – probably the last book I shall ever write – but I don't seem free to get down to it.

'Every day for the last six weeks I have been searching through counterfoils, bank statements, vouchers, bits & pieces of paper for our VAT returns, and struggling to do my tax returns. But I am beginning to wonder whether I am a writer, an apprentice book-keeper or a messenger boy. All I know is that figures curdle my mind and make me literally ill. (In this I take after my mother: see *Cider with Rosie* page 135, para 2, lines 8 & 9.) All I can say is "Help!" – but there does not seem much of it around.'

Laurie stayed in London during Christmas of 1982. On 16 February 1983 he delivered his secret book to his agent, Pat Kavanagh. She thought it 'beautifully written and very affecting'. 'I

suspected that it was an almost impossible task fraught with booby-traps, but you have avoided all the dangers so completely . . . It is just wonderful.'

By May, Jessy seemed to be recovered, and moved into a new flat in Cheltenham, from where she wrote to her parents: 'I've got the Bowie tickets (hooray),' adding, 'I've got no money and no food unfortunately.' Laurie's *Selected Poems* came out, dedicated to Jessy. He wrote to André Deutsch, of his poems: 'I realize there are quite a few instances of juvenile excesses here.' In a brief foreword he explained that most of the fifty-two poems spanned a single decade, i.e. 1940–50. 'They were written by someone I once was and is so distant to me now I can scarcely recognize him any more. They speak for a time and a feeling which of course has gone from me, but for which I still have close affection and kinship.' He gave a copy to Kathy, signed 'with unselected love from the old man'.

And in October 1983 'that difficult book' (as André Deutsch still calls it) was published. *Two Women* was warmly reviewed, for its lyrical text and its pictures. But Kathy was shocked and angry – with Laurie and with Deutsch. Newspapers reprinted some of the photographs – including the one of her naked in the grass. What would the milkman think, and the man at the garage? Everyone assured her she looked beautiful – and even she had to admit, her body was beautiful – but she made Laurie promise that any later editions would not carry that photograph.

In interviews, Laurie kept saying he was 'uncertain' about how the book would be received. He told one journalist that he had never, in thirty years of marriage, said 'I love you' or 'Darling' to his wife. 'Darling is the phoniest word, mostly used in acts of betrayal or anger,' he said. He had done this book 'as a trophy of my love for Cathy and Jessy. I do hope they see that.'[1]

Two Women was an odd work for one so secretive, wrote Henry Porter of the *Sunday Times*. 'He is notorious among his friends for his secretiveness, and clearly enjoys constructing little mysteries round his life. This may date to his bachelor days when he maintained a number of affairs at the same time.' In fact Porter's interview was

444 | *Laurie Lee: The Well-loved Stranger*

almost aborted. They met one Monday morning at the Great Western Hotel on Paddington station, planning to take the train to Stroud together. Instead, they fell into the bar and into an intimate conversation – about women, love, and lust – that lasted until six in the evening. Porter fell completely for Laurie's charm: so much so that he later made Laurie godfather to one of his daughters (reporting to Laurie that at four she was 'bossy, flirtatious, imaginative and very bad. God knows what she is going to be like at seventeen').

But at the end of that day Porter's notebook was blank. He told Laurie: 'I'm in desperate trouble, I've got no interview.' So Laurie suggested they meet again the next day in the Queen's Elm.

The resulting interview began: 'As Laurie Lee passed a girl on the way out of the bar, he pretended to get his foot caught under her partner's chair. The young man rose in confusion to free the trapped foot. Lee ignored him, gazed with wonderful charm at his girlfriend and apologized for disturbing them. She smiled beautifully, and he departed through the door murmuring "pale . . . slim . . . wild creature".

'Later Laurie explained: "At my age you become invisible. One is no longer in the market and young girls simply look through you . . . So you see, I've had to develop one or two techniques for being noticed."' Laurie was 'full of a wistful remembrance of his youth', Porter recalls. To prove his invisibility he and Porter – who is a tall, handsome fellow – walked together up the Fulham Road to Brompton Cross, and sure enough, the girls looked at Henry and ignored Laurie. 'You see?' said Laurie. (He was sixty-nine.)

But Angela Levin found him 'still handsome' anyway, 'with thick white hair and blue eyes flecked with yellow like glass marbles'. He was wearing a hearing aid, which he claimed to have dropped into the wash basin that morning. '"So," he said with a sly grin, "I'll only be able to hear you if you sit very close to me."'

He was 'lovable' but somewhat exasperating, in Angela Levin's view, 'a professional eccentric' living alone in a Chelsea garret. He told her: 'I have always been a devoted family man, but I am also a loner. I cannot write unless I am alone. I am like a fisherman.

My family often don't hear from me for a few days, but they know I will be back again on the next high tide. I think you should leave anyone you care for regularly, but make sure you go back before it is too late. It is always lovely to be with them again. But I am also very glad to get back to my little cell.' He also said that if Kathy 'made trouble' about the nude photo, he had an answer ready: 'Her aunt was married to the sculptor Jacob Epstein and *she* is nude in public areas all over London.'[2]

In publication month, October, Laurie had arranged that he and Kathy were safely away in the skies, flying to Malaysia by Singapore Airlines to write a travel piece for the *Telegraph* magazine's series on 'Dream Holidays', for a fee of £600. Kathy, exhausted by the emotional crises of the past year, badly needed a dream holiday. After much pre-travel fussing about cholera and typhoid injections and malaria tablets, they were to have three nights at Raffles Hotel in Singapore, then depart by car (Kathy driving) for Malacca, spend a night in Kuala Lumpur and three days in Penang 'generally relaxing by the sea'. In the event it was not very relaxing.

On 22 October 1983 – one year to the day since her first crisis – Jessy 'flipped' for the second time. Kathy and Laurie had just arrived at the Kuala Lumpur Hilton. It was their neighbour Margaret Pollock, who had been asked in advance by an anxious Kathy to look after Jessy, who had to go to the rescue.

Margaret is one of those dependable, rock-steady women to whom anyone would entrust a wayward daughter. Laurie had come across Peter and Margaret Pollock when they first moved from Manhattan to Knapp House in Slad, with their children and horses, in 1978. Peter was a jovial Viennese refugee, vice-president of an American engineering corporation which had relocated to Cheltenham. Margaret, a trained electrical engineer herself, sang and played the piano and the Pollocks had become like family, Kathy says, 'because we had become very isolated then'. Margaret was appointed one of the three trustees of Laurie's will. Since Jessy appeared to be on the brink of another crisis, Kathy had asked Margaret to be available. When Margaret took her into her home, Jessy was having paranoid hallucinations. Her psychiatrist quickly

moved her to a nursing-home outside Gloucester, where she was given hypnosis ('when all my childhood stuff came out') and was knocked out for a few days. She was to stay in the home for two months. When he got back, not surprisingly, Laurie was slow to get round to writing his jolly piece about Penang. He went to see Jessy and they walked in the garden of the nursing-home, having long confessional conversations, during which Laurie found a ring that Jessy had lost, placed it on her finger and told her: 'We're wedded forever.' Looking back, Jessy says she was so used to the bizarreness of her life, 'even going mad did not seem strange'. It was after she came home that her relationship with her father found a new footing, based on a shared 'paganism' and affinity with the natural world.

That autumn, while Jessy was still in hospital, Laurie went round dutifully signing copies of *Two Women* in bookshops but he told friends that he had written the book because he had felt that the edifice of his family was crumbling. Tom Matthews, P. J. Kavanagh, Celia Goodman, Pat Kernon and John Arlott all wrote full of concern about Jessy, but praising his book: 'You crafty old craftsman, you've done it again! The book's a beauty – what they'll call a classic one of these days,' wrote Matthews. 'Perhaps you don't enjoy much actual living, but you MUST be happy about this. I think you can sink back on those laurels now, if you really feel like snoozing. I'm proud to have known you.'

'It took me two years to plan it, and to keep the secret,' replied Laurie. 'But all the time I was preparing and writing what I thought was a tribute to "the Two" I realized it was also a farewell. I am more convinced now that this was so, as I see most of it breaking up before my eyes. But it's no time for snoozing or resting on poisoned laurels, old friend. We know there's still more to be done.'

He told P.J. Kavanagh that the 'family and I are having rather a rough time'. 'You were generous and vivid about *Two Women* – but I think your remarks referring to poets' detachment, though true of most, alas are not so true of me. I am unsleepingly concerned, particularly now, when I see what I feared slowly happening and what I most care for crumbling before my eyes. Yes, the 2 women

were flattered by the book (it *had* been kept secret) but C was distressed & embarrassed by the nude, and if there is a reprint I am having it replaced.'

Two years later Laurie told Mary Blume of the *Herald Tribune* that he saw Kathy and Jessy 'receding, pushing away from me . . . It is often the most loving people who are finally the most alone . . .' Tom Matthews sent this piece to Kathy, who said she had reprimanded Laurie for saying such a thing. 'It's extremely untrue, but he often speaks of moving away from us,' Kathy told Matthews, 'God forbid just yet. In fact he has two women quite incapable of moving away from him . . . It's more than likely we'll all go off together. All of us.'

And six years later, talking again to Mavis Nicholson on television in 1989, when Mavis expressed horror that he should have ever done such a book secretly, Laurie again explained that it had been meant as a gift of love. 'But writing it was a major masculine blunder. On the other hand, I was feeling old and I thought it might be the last message. The last pages of that book were a secret farewell to them. ['A love lives by slowly moving towards its end and is sharpened by the snakebite of farewell in it.']'

'I'd never really told them how much I loved them,' he told Mavis. 'But of course once I'd declared it, they knew where they stood, and became very casual and cool. Never tell a woman just how much you love her. Blake wrote a poem, "Never seek to tell thy love", about this –

I told my love, I told my love,
I told her all my heart,
Trembling, cold, in ghastly fears.
Ah! she did depart!

'And I realized that, love as deeply and as fondly as you may . . . it's as well if you're canny, not to declare yourself too much.'

26 | 'An old poet rambling on'
   1984–6

The annual Royal Academy dinner is a grand occasion, held in glittering surroundings, attended by 350 of the great and good. It was Sir Hugh Casson's idea to invite Laurie to give the address on behalf of the guests at the dinner on 18 May 1984.

Laurie did not care for making speeches. But he had always been fascinated by artists, and often said he really wanted to be a painter. So he agreed. After-dinner speaking is always a cruel test of endurance, obliging the speaker to choose between spending the dinner in nervous sobriety or reckless conviviality. Laurie veered towards the latter, and this was a particularly daunting occasion. He was sitting next to Princess Diana and was absolutely captivated by her. The first speakers were the Prince of Wales and the Rt Hon. William Waldegrave. Sir Hugh thanked them and told a joke with a punchline in three languages by way of introducing Laurie Lee, 'a friend of many of us here tonight'. He had first met Laurie in his Festival of Britain office, 'when he was busy with a machine for grinding smoke, and playing Bach on a violin made of spent matchsticks'. Despite his distaste for public speaking, he said, Laurie had been persuaded to reply on behalf of the guests, and to propose a toast to the Royal Academy.

Members then rose to drink to the guests. Laurie too rose, and was told, 'No, Laurie, we're drinking to *you*.' So he then got up with a nervous 'Can I get up now?'

'I'm amazed and astonished to be standing here tonight,' he said. 'It is a dazzling dislocation of my normal way of life.' It was as if he had been sailing in his little coracle on an immense ocean, and had suddenly been dragged up into a vast and glittering vessel, hauled to the captain's table and bidden to sing before being thrown back to the fishes.

Could they have got the wrong Laurie Lee? He knew of at least

four Laurie Lees. 'One is a racehorse. One is a professor of stained glass, one runs a boutique in Lambeth, and the other is a Battersea bricklayer who spends his weekends doing a drag queen act in Campden Hill pubs.' He had been asked to speak for seven minutes, in rhyming couplets if he wished. 'Do you know what seven minutes of rhyming couplets cost these days? Only Clive James would do it at the price.' He then took out his famous clock, with a great rustling and some delay as he searched for it. A sound of loud ticking accompanied the rest of the speech – which went on a great deal longer than seven minutes: more like twenty-seven. His friend Hugh, he said, had told him he must come 'and I will see you get all the drinks you want in the world . . .'

He then made several references to Sir Hugh's small size: 'a light footed Ariel, a Puck, who had once written to *The Times* signing "We, the undersized" . . .'

'But bless us,' he said, and began his speech proper. And there was, at its heart, an excellent speech, with an apposite theme: the difference between the writer's life and the painter's. Writers never put on great binges for themselves like this one, he said. Writers are hermits and painters are brotherhoods, he wanted to say. But he got them the wrong way round – at which point his concentration left him completely.

'I've been rehearsing this for several days,' he said, several times. 'I've blasted all the mercury in the mirror. Where was I? Oh yes. When I first came to London I wished to be a painter. I thought how marvellous to be a writer. Imagine the painter with a studio the size of Leighton House, surrounded by nude, long-legged models, drinking iced hock at ten o'clock in the morning, ripping off a brilliant canvas, to be sold for 2,000 guineas to a cringing dealer and off they go to the Café Royal in champagne and slippers for the rest of the day.

'Imagine the writer – hunched in his little attic, a glass of flat beer at his elbow. They don't give him half-clad beauties lying on the rug to sort out his verbal confusion. No, this is one of the perks of the painter. "Where are you going Fiona?" "I'm posing for Sir Ruffan Tumble R A." "Starkers again?" "Yes mummy." "Oh,

super." No writer or novelist would get away with it! So imagine the writer in his attic. Two years of writing his novel, two years of slow compassionate isolation . . . then you send it off to a publisher, and he sends you a post-dated cheque, rather small, and says he doesn't think it's as good as your last one . . .

'This is a problem. Where was I? I've been rehearsing this for four weeks. Where was I? Was I talking about Hugh? You must forgive me. I was not . . .'

By this time there were murmurs in the hall. Laurie carried on, with much rustling and riffling through papers as he tried to find his place. 'I'm not asking for sympathy but I think the difference is one of arrested movement and restless . . . somewhere along. Can I go home now? Where was I?' A few rambling minutes later (about writers having to clamber through acres of boredom before lighting on a moment of truth, whereas painters can create a moment of truth in an instant) there followed a good half-minute of total silence during which Prince Charles rose from his seat to assist him, because Laurie swayed and appeared to be about to fall over.

'Could I go home now?

'I've got to read it. Do you know I thought I could get away with it but I can't. Where am I? Painters are brotherhoods and . . . never lay on binges like this. When I first came to London I wanted to be a painter. And I used to cling to the edges of painters' lives because I thought they had a better time of it. Imagine painters . . . they have a studio the size of Leighton House . . . Have I said this before?' (Silence, then murmurs, then a 'Yes you did!') 'Yes I did. Now come on. Right. The fundamental difference is . . . God I wish I hadn't done this. It's him that did this. I've never made a speech before . . .

'Seurat. The bathers are held in a unique stillness of light.

'I'll never be asked again. Now stop that! They're trapped. No I've forgotten. I'll not waste my . . . They're caught in a moment of thrall and they're there for ever. Now will you listen to me because this is important. Keats. I'm talking about the differences of painters and writers. One has the quality of holding the moment and a writer can't hold the moment because he has to move . . .

Keats seemed to sense this when he was looking at the frieze on the Grecian urn. "Thou still unravish'd bride of quietness, Thou foster child of silence and slow time . . . Bold lover, never canst thou kiss . . . yet do not grieve; Forever wilt thou love, and she be fair . . ." This time of stillness is something I envy. I envy the artist his physical freedom, his gregarious friendship, his appetite and love of life. I have never met a dyspectic . . . dyspectic? dyspeptic artist in my life. They stand up and attack canvases. Picasso, Miró, Braque, Augustus John, Henry Moore, most of them seem to live to a ripe old age . . .

'I had a little Hockney, nothing would it bear, But 192 per cent increase in value every year . . .'

There was prolonged and relieved applause.

But up spake Laurie again. 'I was sitting outside my village pub the other day . . .' and he proceeded to tell his stock story about the two schoolgirls asking him where Laurie Lee is buried. He ended with a toast to the Royal Academy, and a hope that no politician would ever try to crop its extravagant glories . . . 'as I stumble towards the end of my . . . this is a mess, a real mess'. (More applause.)

Lord Hailsham, the Lord Chancellor, proffered the use of his chauffeured car to get Laurie home, and poor Laurie, whose misery can only be imagined (since there are no diaries for these years), sent him a book in gratitude. Afterwards, some were more sympathetic than others; the reactions reflecting the character of the beholders. Melvyn Bragg remarked to Lord Rees-Mogg: 'Well, William, we were there.' In Anthony Powell's account in his published *Journals*, he describes Laurie's speech as 'an absolute fiasco, appalling meaningless ramblings'. The much kindlier John Ward says: 'Public speaking was not really Laurie's thing. Especially not at the RA, one of the more exacting audiences.' And kindliest of all, Prince Charles wrote the next day from Highgrove a letter of warm praise and sympathy. He had surmised that Laurie would far rather have been somewhere else altogether, but assured him that he had 'made my wife & I laugh a great deal & I loved the way you created some memorable phrases and apposite alliterations!

Please, please can you send me a copy of your speech, as I would *love* to read it in a quiet moment.'

Lord Hailsham wrote too. 'Dear Laurie Lee: I am glad you got home all right. I have just been reading yr book with much pleasure. I was delighted to meet you, & perhaps to be of service with my official car. Yrs sincerely, Hailsham.'

The writer Angela Lambert recalls that when she was due to give an after-dinner speech in the late 1980s, and Laurie was seated next to her, he put a hand over her glass and said: 'If you are going to speak you must not drink.'

A few weeks later, Laurie celebrated his seventieth birthday. 'Good God! he's not seventy surely?' said Jessy, when a reporter rang her. 'He doesn't like people to know his age.' There was a jolly lunch at the Garrick with his two women and a dozen good friends including Jill Balcon, Sean Treacy, André Deutsch and Jock Gallagher.

Jock Gallagher and André Deutsch had now waited fifteen years for volume three. 'The assumption that Laurie was lazy and non-productive was a nice disguise and he slipped into it very comfortably,' Gallagher says. 'But he genuinely was rewriting it, over and over, in longhand.' When alone in his garret, he would rearrange each word 'and caress them' as he put it, until they were right. A paragraph might take him a day. Gallagher offered a word processor, gave him a tape recorder; but all Laurie recorded was the sound of birdsong, and nocturnal wildlife rustling in the under-growth.

'He knew this would be his last book, and there was a morbid fear of giving it up because that would be the end of Laurie Lee. He liked being the centre of attention, and while everyone was waiting for the next book he was at his happiest; once he'd handed it over there would be nothing more to write. He would be a former writer, and that he dreaded more than death.'

In February of 1984 there had arrived a welcome diversion from the book, in the big, handsome, bear-like person of John King, who directed films for the BBC. King had been 'banjaxed' by *As I Walked Out One Midsummer Morning*. 'I realized I was listening in

my head and dreaming the dream. It's not travel writing: it's poetry.' Now he was going to film it, with no screenplay, no stars, no wardrobe, no dressers, no props, no on-site catering ('Why feed people as well as pay them?') and a skeletal crew. All he would need was a young man to play Laurie, and all Spain for the location. Alan Yentob of BBC-2 gave him £45,000, with which to make two fifty-minute programmes. First, King persuaded Laurie to come with him to Spain and revisit the route he had walked. By car of course. They flew to Santiago in April 1984, drove to Vigo, and began the recce, driving hundreds of miles to Madrid and then Andalucía. Laurie always carried a ginger beer bottle of 'medicine', i.e. whisky. 'I saw at once that nobody could have walked his walk, and done all he said he did, in the time allotted,' King said. 'But so what.'

They would use Laurie's own voice reading his story, and Julian Bream's guitar music. King found an actor who looked reasonably like the young Laurie, John Wild, and all the other dramatis personae would be Spaniards picked up en route. Finding locations was easy: all the bars were full of old men talking and drinking much as they had fifty years before. 'Much of Spain is still untouched,' King told me, 'once you get away from the tourists. We didn't need a designer going round saying, "Please take down your aerials." Poverty precludes change, and in the process preserves beauty.' In any case, what Laurie's book had evoked was atmosphere, and sense of place. 'He remembered the girl whose skin smelled of olives. And we found a girl who was just like that. So it all came to life.'

Laurie was jaundiced about the whole shoestring expedition. 'I can't go anywhere abroad on my own any more,' he told his accountant. 'I went to Spain, unsupported, to research for a possible TV approach to *As I Walked Out*. It was hell. There I was – no agent, no publisher, no family, no assistant, no girlfriend – carrying my bag alone through the rain to get to the Underground to Heathrow, and I thought why am I doing this at my age? I must be crazy. Never again, say I.'

In November it was a quarter of a century since *Cider with Rosie*. In a two-part celebration called *Vintage Cider*, on Radio 4, Kathy

told Marjorie Lofthouse: 'We've lived for ever on this one book really. And this is a cottage in his village, and everything happens in this room, and I run around it in a chaotic way, just like his mother, so it mirrors his own childhood cottage in a way.' Asked if Laurie was a romantic, Kathy said he was: he always went out on the terrace for the first glimpse of the full moon rising. She would take him cocoa and blankets as he sat there. She added: 'He can be dreadful, but he's my loved one, and we put up with it all, and somehow it's worth it. He's very funny, and very loving, though he can be a damn nuisance sometimes.' Laurie, though he did a hilarious imitation of the Finnish translation of *Cider with Rosie* (wondering what on earth they could make of Slad in faraway Finland), had 'an air of anxiety about him, despite his success', said Miss Lofthouse. He told her: 'I've done rather well out of that book. I don't think writers should ever do too well out of one book. They should always be lashed by hunger. Sometimes I'm a bit ashamed I must admit.'

Still, the evergreen popularity of *Cider with Rosie* ensured an unflagging interest in Laurie himself, and at frequent intervals he was in the corner of his pub or his club, telling again the story about the schoolgirls coming up to him outside the Woolpack and asking where Laurie Lee is buried. (He had two versions of his reply. The polite one was, 'Laurie Lee is usually buried with his nose in a pint of beer, if you'd care to join me in the public bar,' and the saucy one was 'Oo arr, come up the wood, girls, and I'll show you where Laurie Lee wants to be buried.') He told every interviewer that he saw his wife and daughter no more than once a week. For a magazine he described his Sundays. Kathy would make him a large cooked breakfast, and he would potter in his room among the piles of papers, 'which I just move about a bit' followed by pottering in the garden, 'clipping this and that and restoring Acts of God or the ravages of animals'.

When Kathy returned from church to make lunch, he would say, 'It's time to go and find out what time the trains are running' – a ruse to go with Frank Mansell to the Imperial Hotel in the railyard at Stroud, then back to Slad and a quick one at the Woolpack.

At 1.30 p.m. Jessy would arrive with a bird-like toot on her car horn and come striding down the path and knock him over. This was the high spot of his Sunday 'in the words of a foolish, fond old man'. After lunch he and Jessy would walk through the old beech wood, drink at the spring, visit Jessy's horse the Red Baron ('he looks at us with elegant aristocratic disdain') and touch a certain post in the road. The touching of this post was a ritual, 'a magic gesture; we leave our symbol there'. Then there would be tea on the lawn in summer, or by the fire in winter. 'Then I go back to what I came for really: the farewell from Stroud railway station.' Jessy would kiss him as the train moved out and say, 'Got a fiver, Dad?' And off he would go with his Walkman plugged to his ear. 'Up the valley towards Sapperton tunnel I get that feeling, I'm back alone now! I love being with my loved ones, but what bliss it is to be alone.' And so back to the Queen's Elm, and home, to settle down 'with my books and the quietness'.

He told Mary Blume in the *Herald Tribune* in 1985 that he was 'gregarious, but with a pronounced defensive attachment'. 'In his own words he is often shy and extremely devious, with spurts of self-advertisement.' He wore the 'secret contented smile of a man who all his life has been cosseted and adored by women' and summed up his life as 'enduring and trying not to be knocked down by cars'. James Fallon of *Woman's Wear Daily* found him 'disarming with his air of befuddlement, absent-mindedness and apparent fear of almost everything, but underneath it all is a hustler's astuteness about the world: he will stop people in the street and tell them that if they buy one of his books he will sign it on the spot. Laurie Lee is an industry unto himself.'

Laurie regretted that his face lacked 'the mature, masculine dignity a writer's face should have'. 'I've got a pendulous, asexual face that quickly settles into that of a female dog-breeder . . .' He always now wore a pale suit and a cravat or his Garrick tie, confounding the fixed idea people had of him as a bumpkin – 'straw in hair, cidrous in speech, inane grin on face. I should be living in a hollow tree curing rabbit skins, not in a flat in Fulham, popping out every now and then with a wise country saw.' Laurie

was content to let others play that game. Back in Slad, Jim Fern, who had been in his brother Tony's year at school, was now offering *Cider with Rosie* days out, guided walks around the valley with a lunch stop at the Woolpack. Laurie was perfectly happy for 'Little Jim' (who is six feet tall, of soldierly bearing and today still extremely fit at eighty-odd) to entertain the tourists who flocked to Slad. And when the *Daily Mail* revealed that the real Rosie had been found, now aged seventy and living in a semi in the Cheltenham suburbs, Laurie made no demur. Rosie Green was the fairy at Laurie's elbow in the John Bull photograph of 1919: dressed by sister Marjorie in an angel's outfit with cardboard wings and a wand with a star. In *Cider with Rosie* she recognized herself as 'Poppy Green', who had 'a polished pumpkin face'. ('I loved her. She was like a portable sweet shop.') She was actually Laurie's cousin, and had married the village policeman, Tom Buckland. When she was an extra in the televised version of the book, Laurie had signed her copy 'To you know who, with long ago love from you know who.'

But as Laurie explained dozens of times, 'Rosie' was just a composite. 'There were six or seven girls in the village school she could have been – Doreen, Bertha, Betty, Clarice, Edna, Maureen, Poppy, and Rosie. When it came to thinking of a title for the book I had to make a choice. Cider with Edna? Cider with Doreen? It could have been any of those girls, but Rosie sounded right.' Women would come up to him in Woolworths and say 'I was Rosie, wasn't I Laurie.' They were all Rosie. And it might not even have been Laurie who rolled under the haywagon with her. 'I was a watcher,' he often said. 'Observing everything. I sprawled in the long grass and saw what was going on.' The title was 'a bit of a cheat. It intrigued people, although there was very little cider, and come to think of it, not much Rosie.'

By now Kathy was working almost full-time for the Nuclear Freeze Campaign, 'busy bullying bishops', as Laurie called it. In 1985 she garnered the support of the new vicar in Slad for a Hiroshima Vigil (forty years on) and was dashing round the diocese with posters. 'I

never imagined that I would be sitting at a large round table in the hall of the Church House of Gloucester Cathedral watched by five or six bishops in their robes,' she told Tom Matthews. When the non-proliferation agreement was signed, Kathy wrote to Matthews: 'I see at last Gorbachev has agreed with me – three years ago I said that we should have an International Law preventing the using of nuclear power for war or weapons. I go a bit further than him.' 'My wife has left me for a Synod,' wrote Laurie to Matthews in February 1987. 'Her ambition now reaches the Heavens.'

He was proud that his wife was now a churchwarden. 'She winds the clock, she lights the fires in the mornings, she puts out the hymnbooks, she tells the vicar what to say in his sermon.' He himself seldom ventured inside the church 'because it's too cold and though I want to be buried in its graveyard I don't want to expose myself to an early death'.

In March 1985 one of the cornerstones of his London routine was no more, when Sean Treacy died. 'He was an orchestrator of people,' Laurie said in his funeral address. 'When he was not in the pub it seemed empty. I went in there last night and the lights had gone out. There is no replacement for Sean.' He carried on using the pub until it shut down – it became, briefly, a wine-bar named Mwah-Mwah – but increasingly he was a Chelsea Arts man, famous for carrying always a Waterstone's tote-bag containing bottles of Ruddles ale and his own pewter tankard. Tom Matthews fretted that he could not get Laurie to have lunch with him any more. 'There's still so much to say and so little time to say it in . . .' wrote Matthews. 'Friends should meet sometimes.' But Laurie told him, 'I haven't had lunch with a friend – except by chance – for several years now. It must be the way I live.' However, after they met briefly at Robert Graves's memorial service in January 1986, Laurie wrote affrontedly: 'Dear Tom, I am not so deaf that I am unaware of someone turning his back on me. I went along to the Garrick, and had some drinks with Billy Hughes, who seemed quite glad to see me. Next time I find you walking alone in Piccadilly, I'll trample your coat-tails.' The following year Matthews wrote, knowing Laurie hated to be pinned down, that he would be in the Athenaeum

having lunch on 11 February and Laurie could choose whether to show up or not.

Brian Patten, one of the younger poets at the Chelsea Arts Club, wondered why Laurie so seldom ate in the club. In his diary for 2 March 1985, Patten wrote: 'Laurie came into the Arts Club clutching a copy of the Penguin paperback of his selected poems. He flashes the cover. "A handsome youth," he says of the photo of himself on the jacket . . . He takes a can out of the large heavy duty plastic bag he's carrying. "I'm going to put this tin of soup in the oven and heat it," he says when he joins us in the Whistler bar. "When it's heated it will burst open and I can scrape the soup from the oven door."'

A rumour was spread by Jeffrey Bernard, the notoriously unwell *Spectator* 'Low Life' columnist, that at some grand luncheon he had seen Laurie take lamb cutlets from the table and put them in his pocket. Laurie said this was not quite true. He did take cutlets home to re-heat for his supper, but he put them into a carrier bag, not his pocket. He said: 'I don't like eating in public and I don't like waste.' Val Hennessy, a good friend of Laurie's from the Chelsea Arts, said the reason he did not like eating in public, 'poor darling', was that his false teeth made it impossible to chew things without dropping bits on his white suits. 'So he really preferred to take things home for later.' She interviewed 'the old rascal' for *The Times*, in 1986 when John King's film was about to be televised, and referred to Laurie's reputation for being 'partial to the hard stuff'. He'd been on the Terry Wogan chat show, he told her, and had taken his recorder along, to surprise Wogan with an Irish air, whereupon 'the twinkle in Wogan's eye turned to ice'.

So what was Laurie writing these days, asked Val. 'Cheques,' he replied, gazing evasively out of the window. 'Gas bills, VAT returns. I spend a lot of time answering letters from people wanting their poems published ("So, Susan, you have left me/Then") and from students doing dissertations on *Cider with Rosie*. My serious objection to being on the syllabus is the daft exam questions they set. But I won't say more on that topic in case they take me off the syllabus and my royalties dry up and I'll be poverty stricken.'

Eliciting no response to her next question, Val asked if he was slightly deaf. 'One never says one's deaf, you know, as one never says one's an alcoholic. My GP recently asked me what I'd drunk that day and I replied, "Two beers and a short," which is alcoholic code, as all GPs know, for fifteen beers and half a bottle of whisky.'

She tried again, about work in progress. 'That's the question I always shy away from,' he replied, topping up their glasses. 'Furthermore, I don't even think of myself as a writer now. More an interpreter of something which I think of as being magically unique, that is this world and this life which, in spite of shadows and occasional pain, has been a perpetual excitement and joy. The fact of being alive is a miracle, no matter how shabby some of the details of my life may be.' But there was a book coming: 'It's a book of defeat, pain and disaster. About a winter when the anti-Franco side were in retreat, Franco was winning and our side had no arms. I'm also writing my Deathbed Confessions, but that's all I'm prepared to say. No one wants to hear an old poet rambling on about his next book.'

'Sans teeth, sans eyes, sans taste, sans everything.' Laurie often quoted this line, from Shakespeare's *As You Like It*, after 1987, as his eyesight, hearing, appetite, sense of smell and taste all faded. More than most people, he had lived by his senses – his writing was almost entirely founded on sensual experiences – and lamented their loss. 'What I regret is not being able to smell the flowers, or wet grass when it has been raining; and not having the keen edge of appetite of a child. That's all gone,' he said in 1989. Cataracts and an eye condition called split iris made it hard even to read. Words would break up and stagger out of line, and his legible, elegant handwriting began to decline.

Of course, he claimed there were certain sights he could still appreciate: landscapes, and girls' legs. (At the Chelsea Arts, it was remarked that if a pretty girl in a short skirt was around, Laurie certainly knew about it. Sarah Such of Penguin once got up from the table with a flash of thigh; and Laurie, his white stick beside him, said: 'I think that was what we used to call "a glimpse of stocking".') But he was generally constrained. 'My movements are blocked every way,' he told P.J. Kavanagh. 'If I could just jump into a car at my whim all would be easy, but as you know I need to wait on a driver, even to get to Stroud.' Parties were no fun: 'Once more than a certain number are gathered together in one place I can neither hear nor speak,' he wrote after a big gathering at Jilly and Leo Cooper's. He was liable to panic and leave early: 'I talk too much, & hear myself doing it, and the more I talk the sillier I become.'

Others saw him differently. 'He loved talking. He soothed people, stroked them with words, his voice marinaded in cider,' Henry Porter says. 'But he also listened very attentively.' He had the gift of making the people he talked to feel better about themselves, P.J.

Kavanagh said: 'You came away with a spring in your step.' Brian
Patten noted in his diary: 'Sometimes in ordinary conversation
Laurie's language would take flight. He could paint vivid portraits
with words and recall incidents in rich detail. It was a wonderful
facility of his, speaking with the same lyric intensity as he wrote.'
When Patten mentioned to him that he'd been to Deyá, Robert
Graves's village in Majorca, Laurie closed his eyes and recited from
memory Graves's poem 'Lost Love'.

> His eyes are quickened so with grief,
> He can watch a grass or leaf
> Every instant grow; he can
> Clearly through a flint wall see,
> Or watch the startled spirit flee
> From the throat of a dead man.
> Across two counties he can hear
> And catch your words before you speak . . .
> This man is quickened so with grief,
> He wanders god-like, or like thief
> Inside and out, below, above,
> Without relief seeking lost love.

(Laurie recited this poem at a commemoration of Graves at the
Imperial War Museum in April 1988.) 'In the richness of Graves's
early lyric I see his own intense lyricism,' Patten wrote. 'It dawns
on me he's exactly the same age as Dylan Thomas would be, had
he still been around.'

And yet there were also days when people would stop to talk to
Laurie as he sat writing outside the Rose (another Fulham Road
pub) and he wouldn't even look up, Henry Porter says. 'He just
wasn't to be disturbed.' A neighbour recalled: 'He used his loss of
sight and hearing as a clever way of avoiding people. If cornered
in the Woolpack, he could be charm itself, if fans had come from
Canada or Australia to see him. But he could also be incredibly
elusive. You could call him and he just wouldn't hear you. He
could walk right past you in the lane, looking the other way. Or

he would suddenly say, "I'm off," and go off on some secret mission.'

In 1987 Val Hennessy noted in her diary that Laurie (aged seventy-three) was furious to find himself referred to in a paper as 'eighty-year-old Laurie Lee'. He wrote to the editor saying, 'This is an outrage. You have ruined my love life. Everyone knows I'm only 59. Kindly print an apology or send me four bottles of best malt whisky in lieu' – and he was amused to receive four bottles including one separately wrapped with the brand-name 'Old Grandad'.

Brian Patten's diary noted, in the same month: 'Laurie's looking ill and doddery, his face red and rather forlorn. He sits down by the fire with his bottles of Ruddles, taken from his bag. He's worried now about being alone and his growing deafness bothers him, though he doesn't want to use the hearing aid he has with him. He takes it out of his pocket to show me as if it's a small toy he's found and is not quite sure what to make of. He's been given a prescription for medicine but refuses to take it (or so he says – I'm seldom sure how much of what Laurie says is touched with poetic licence). Later I walk him from the club and see him home, four or five minutes to the door, because he really doesn't look too well. He says he has left a piece of paper with a number on it, weighted down by a stone, outside the door of his flat, in case of emergencies. When I got back to the club I phoned Val H and let her know about his health, so she can phone him in the morning and check up on him.'

Nobody could have imagined that Laurie had another ten years to live.

'Sometimes I sit back and think, Damn it, what a bore, the Laurie Lee's daughter business.' In the late 1980s Jessy, after a secretarial spell at the BBC in Birmingham, took a job managing an adventure playground for children with special needs at Seven Springs, near Cheltenham.

Being Laurie Lee's daughter was something of a special need in itself. In January 1986 a two-page spread had appeared in the *Daily*

Mail about Jessy's problems – 'the tortured life of a girl placed on a public pedestal by her father' – describing her wayward youth on the Cheltenham pop scene, her wild parties and drug-taking ('I have nearly been round the bend from taking naughty things. But it's all because I was brought up in a cocoon by Mummy and Daddy. Although I adore them, I had to escape'). Laurie was 'devastated' by this article, and rang André Deutsch, who put him in touch with the libel lawyer Lord Goodman; an out-of-court settlement was reached. Within months, Laurie and Jessy were engaged in a damage-limitation exercise, being photographed by the *Sunday Times* magazine in a loving father-and-daughter pose for a 'Relative Values' interview (in which two members of a family give their separate versions of their relationship with one another). Laurie again described Jessy's 'punitive charm' and their shared rituals, their mutual intuition: he could see through her and she through him. Sometimes, for instance, they had the same dream on the same night. Jessy would dream that she was a child again, in Brith Wood. 'I'm on a string, flying like a kite, with Dad holding on to the string. He's totally in control, but he's not going to let me go and fly off into oblivion. It's a wonderful experience. And he has the same dream, where he's holding on to the string. That's how close we are . . . It's a total love affair, my relationship with Dad.'

Of course, Laurie admitted, there had been troubles. 'As part of the special cruelty of the times into which Jessy was born, she's been exposed like all her contemporaries to the threat of the drug-pusher – at school gate and club and wherever the young get together. Then about three years ago she had a breakdown – more a crisis of identity than anything else – from which she's made a valiant recovery.' He said he was anxious for her, and admitted reacting 'in the age-old atavistic way of a father when suitors come for his daughter's hand – I'm jealous'. (Jessy says he was always reluctant to let her meet boyfriends in the Woolpack, even when she had to say, 'Dad, I'm thirty-three.') 'While I wish to give her her freedom, I care very much what she does.' He was guilty of putting too much pressure on her to be what she was not, he

confessed, and he demanded the expression of love, 'which is perhaps unreasonable'.

He was conscious of the fact that most girls of her age had 'some sort of bounding dad, called Ian, who's about 38 and always playing golf or squash', but Jessy said she never thought of him as old. 'Dad has this remarkable ability to understand everyone's life, whoever he's with: myself, my friends, Mum, her friends, his contemporaries.

'Though I've felt overwhelmed by him and under certain pressures, Dad's always provided me with the right mix of freedom and security . . . I remember once, he caught me smoking in a pub in London. He walked up and said, "Oh, Jess" – he doesn't smoke – "can I have a drag on your cigarette, please?" I gave it to him and he just walked away with it. He then bought us a round of drinks . . .

'And I rely on Dad being around a lot. I know that he may take a long walk one day, but he'll still always be around. And I'll feel protected.'

It was in the same year, Jessy thinks, that Laurie made his confession to her about Yasmin being her half-sister. She had always supposed Yasmin to be just an unusually kind and generous cousin 'who always sent me birthday cards, and some lovely earrings in opal, my birthstone'.

Laurie had been agonizing for years over how to tell Jessy. She found among his papers, when he died, several drafts of the letters he'd tried to write; one of the letters was tucked into his will. But eventually he asked her to come out to supper, and said there was something he had to tell her. 'I thought at first he was going to say I wasn't his daughter. And then I thought, he's going to say I've got brothers and sisters. He was so upset. I think he couldn't bear it any longer, and it was causing pain, particularly for Yasmin. It was like watching a small child in such pain I could hardly bear it.'

She took it very well. 'I said I just wished I'd known earlier, because I would love to have had a sister. I wouldn't have felt so lonely. Dad forbade Yasmin to have much to do with us really. Well, forbade is a rather strong word, but I think it was the case – from absolute terror that I might not forgive him. But it was misplaced, that fear. And sad for him, that he had to live with it

for so long, when it would all have been all right.' Afterwards Jessy went off with a girlfriend and 'I got very drunk and became very upset all night. But I didn't let him see that.' It may be significant that Ernest Wishart had lately died, and that Yasmin had gone away with her family to live in South Africa, where she remained until 1994.

Tom Matthews (still writing, with another new book out) reminded Laurie that if he lived through January he would be eighty-eight; and Laurie too was not faring badly, considering the shaky health he had enjoyed all his life. In November 1987 he spoke to Graham Bridgstock of the *Evening Standard* for a column called 'Me and My Health'. He had been told he had the blood pressure of a five-year-old: 'I was astonished. I thought I was at death's door.' He had given up smoking twenty years ago and said alcohol had taken its place. He catalogued his ailments from childhood onwards, including a thrombosis in his leg, and described his periodic with-drawals into a darkened room. 'I still get this recurrent pneumonia when the lungs are full of pulsating barbed wire and the temperature goes up. I hide away like an animal in the long grass. The only cure is to lie still and wait for it to pass. Sometimes it takes a couple of days, sometimes two weeks.'

But he did not mention losing a lung, and nor did he utter the taboo word, epilepsy. (Jessy still had not been told about his epilepsy. She did not find out until she noticed that the drugs taken by epileptic children in her care were the same as her father's pills.) Kathy says: 'He didn't want to show weakness of any kind. And he had a great fear of loss of control.' But he did say he was 'prone to scrambling of the brains'. 'My theory is that a strong healthy man isn't likely to be creative. It is illness and pain that encourage him to live another life. But it does make you turn your attention to the reality of having to leave this world one day and if I ask myself if I'm reconciled, the answer is, I'm not.

'I love this world and all its trivialities, the little domestic details, the postbox on the corner, the wet gutters, the leaves, the buses, the sunset.'

Laurie was increasingly called upon to preserve such things. He was enlisted in the campaign to save Stroud's bus station, to plant a tree to complete a new hedgerow in Stroud, for the international Peace Forest, and to front a 'Keep Eastington Rural' demo, protesting against Gloucestershire County Council's plans for 1,000 new homes. He released masses of coloured balloons, declaring: 'May they land with a soft caress on the heads of the blessed and with great lumps of bird-dirt on the heads of the developers.'

He had a compliments slip printed saying, 'Mr L Lee thanks you for your recent letter, but regrets that owing to illness, he is unable to send an adequate reply.' But he was conscientious about replying to most of the hundreds of letters he received. Many people just wanted to thank him 'for sharing your life'; others wanted to say he had inspired them to write: 'I find I write my diary for the reasons you describe in "Writing Autobiography"'; 'At 17 I feel there is a world outside waiting for me and in old age I want to be able to say, "I have lived." Thank you for inspiration.' People wrote to tell him that *The Firstborn* had been read at the christening of a baby, or at a child's funeral; others sent poems, paintings or their autobiographies, hoping he would find them a publisher. They asked him to address their literary societies, or to make a film about the modernization of Spain. (Two months before he died he was dictating a letter: 'Dear X, Too late now I'm afraid. Immobilized by bad health. Spain out of reach for filming. Alas. Best wishes, and all success in your endeavours.') Teachers requested items for auctions, or his presence at school authors' weeks. Among his letters there was a long questionnaire from a schoolchild which he diligently answered:

'Do you believe in God?' 'Not in God, but in gods.'

'Do you think you've been corrupt [*sic*] by the consuming society?' 'No. I have very few possessions, and I live in austere surroundings. Material riches deaden the appreciation of life. I was never so alive as when I was poor.'

'Do you like writing?'

'It is my only life, but I both hate and love it; it exhilarates, exhausts, frustrates, and in the end, with luck, rewards.

'I would like to have been a painter, a painter without a message except the sensual celebration of flowers & women: Renoir, Degas, Matisse – but Renoir supremely.'

'You travelled quite a lot. Why? By curiosity?' And so on.

A 'mature student of humanities and social sciences' said she hoped he did not mind her writting [*sic*] but was she right to 'enliken' the passage 'Into Spain' to the birth of a baby? A boy asked, baldly, 'How do you approach your writing? what preparation do you do if any? what advice could you give a young writer who wishes to broaden his horizons?' Laurie dictated his reply to Kathy: 'I feel sure you'll cross many horizons. You ask for advice but I wouldn't be so patronizing as to offer you any. I'm sure you'll understand.' A young 'poet' said: 'I endeavour to highlight & illuminate people's "sense of wonder" in my work which may be surpressed [*sic*] by the speed of todays rat race living.' He enclosed some greetings card doggerel.

Laurie appeared accessible to people. A letter addressed merely to 'Laurie Lee, Slad' would reach him. And he gave off an aura of geniality, unlike other notoriously irascible and reclusive authors. People confided to him their love affairs, their long-distant school-days, their aspirations in life. They asked for signatures and advice. What was he writing next? Where did his anecdotes come from? Could he explain this poem? A Stroud vicar had met a young man in Valladolid who was following the Laurie Lee route. A lady of forty-three ('I have a lively personality and smile a lot') wanted to work for him, in return for accommodation. A young Canadian whose grandfather kept the Fountain Inn on the Slad road said Laurie's books had given him 'a fulcrum upon which to face adversity in my own life'. A Mrs Crockett apologized for having tried to buy him a drink in the Woolpack. 'All I wanted to do was say thank you – not buy your time . . . I do realize now that many people must do the same thing and it must be difficult for you to have a drink in your own local without someone like me destroying your peace. Accept my apologies.' Others wrote boldly in advance that they would be in the pub, carrying his book: 'Do hope to see you,' said one who added: 'I'm big and "bonny" and brunette.'

Perhaps he did not mind all the attention. Val Hennessy says: 'He loved getting letters. He was a lonely old sod really. He used to send me a book of first class stamps and say please send me a letter.'

It could be said that Laurie hardly needed to write that promised last book, or anything more at all. Like J.D. Salinger and *The Catcher in the Rye*, he had written a 'modern classic' a quarter of a century ago which had entered the canon and conferred immortality;[1] he could survive on just being Laurie Lee. He might, if asked, turn out a couplet, as he did on St Valentine's Day for *The Times* in 1987 –

In you, today, I hear the first note of spring,
Feel the earth's turning towards the sun –

– but anthologists constantly reprinted his old poems, or chapters from *Cider with Rosie*, whenever they wanted nostalgic pieces on country childhoods. New devotees discovered him all the time. In 1986 David Blunkett, not yet in parliament but leader of Sheffield City Council, wrote to say that a friend had read *Cider with Rosie* on tape for him. As a blind person he had found Laurie's word-picture of childhood and Slad life 'unequalled'. 'I was able to feel and experience the things you described in a way which brought them alive.' He said most of his reading was to do with his work; the contrast between that and the feeling of affinity with nature and warmth of community in *Cider with Rosie* was 'stark'. If Laurie was not overtroubled with visitors, might he come and call? He did call, had a glass of cider with Laurie in the Woolpack, and five years later recorded a *Down Your Way* radio programme featuring Slad. As he said at Laurie's memorial service – by which time Blunkett had become Education Secretary in Tony Blair's cabinet – Laurie's description of his schooldays was 'not exactly New Labour' but his village school had 'hammered home the golden rules', which is what Blunkett's department was advocating today. He particularly responded to the story of Joseph and Hannah Brown, their sad ending in the workhouse, 'and the kind, killing authority that arranged it'.

Though never in Salinger's league in his quest for privacy, Laurie had become choosy about whom he wanted to see. He complained when an estate agent advertised a cottage as being 'next to Laurie Lee', and when his new tenants at Rose Cottage took over in 1987, they sensed that Laurie was reluctant to let it in case he was stuck with uncongenial neighbours. But John Clive, a film-maker, was not remotely awed by being next door to Laurie Lee, and had not even read Laurie's books – 'which is probably why we got it. After the fifth glass of whisky at the Arts Club Laurie seemed to think we'd be all right.' On their first day at the cottage, as the Clives' curly-haired daughter Florence toddled down the lawn, Kathy remarked that the Clives were a threesome, just like the Lees twenty-five years before. (Also, by an amazing coincidence, the Clives lived in the St John's Wood house which Ben Frankel had once occupied, where Laurie had stayed when he first came to London.) Despite Laurie's reluctance to get involved with new people, they became friends. One Easter Laurie arrived on their doorstep playing the violin, and he and John's wife Michelle Newell – an actress – would recite poems by heart together. 'He was extraordinarily generous to us,' Clive says. 'I had to put the rent up after six years because it seemed so low.'

In ten years there, Clive says he never saw Laurie doing anything at all. 'Whenever I happened upon him he was usually staring at the valley – either from the terrace or through the plate glass window. He seemed to listen continuously to Radio 4 and references to it would pepper his conversation. "I Can't Stay Long" is just what he would say, until he remembered he could trust us and sat down for a while.

'I got the impression that he was slightly ashamed of himself for no longer being a poet. There was a tinge of sadness there.'

As I Walked Out One Midsummer Morning, the John King film, was shown on BBC-2 in 1987, and was acclaimed for being authentic, true to Laurie's own words – helped by Laurie's voice on the soundtrack – ravishingly photographed by John Williams and 'excluding anything that might shatter the illusion that the Spain we see is exactly what Lee saw as he made his long walk 50

years ago'.[2] In the *Radio Times*, Laurie said the south of Spain was now 'a concrete cliff of filing cabinets for tourists. It's one of the worst things that could have happened, next to a nuclear war.' But in the film, one saw only the timeless and unchanging side of Spain, El Greco's house in Toledo, the *posadas* and the *bodegas* and the olive groves and the endless dusty roads across the plains. In Segovia cathedral John Wild (the actor playing Laurie) was bathed in the glow of its stained-glass windows. (Virginia Cunard, now Barrington, wrote to Laurie: 'Poor Mr Wild, he was good looking enough and as my mother would have said, "a nice young man for a tea party" but that old Laurie Lee magic was missing.')

An English artist named Michael Still, who with his wife Helga runs an artists' retreat in an old *castillo* high up a crumbling trackway in the hills behind Almuñécar, realized that the Castillo of the film must be Almuñécar, and got in touch with John King, suggesting that he should now follow up his film with another, of *A Rose for Winter*. This was the beginning of Laurie's renewed association with the little town he had lived in with Wilma in 1936. Still's good friend, the enterprising mayor of Almuñécar, a doctor named Juan Carlos Benavides Yanguas, wrote to Laurie in August 1987 to say that the town was filled with excitement, having seen John King's first film of Laurie's Spanish journey, to realize that 'Castillo' was Almuñécar. They could not imagine a more sensitive description of the difficult life of Almuñequeros in 1936 as that in Laurie's book. 'Almuñécar is now an open and hospitable city,' he said, and the city wished to reward Laurie with its '*máximo galardón*' (the greatest acknowledgement), an Aguacate de Oro, a golden avocado, so that Laurie's name would be 'forever linked to the heart of our people'.

So King made a second evocative film, this time with a budget of £54,000. He found Cordelia Roche, an actress uncannily similar to the young Kathy – so like her that Kathy shed tears when she watched it. As before, King took a minimal crew, and although the Hotel Mediterráneo had been pulled down in 1981, with Still's help they found suitable locations, and local Spaniards to play the maid Paca, the Murillo-like gypsy beauty and the young beggar girl

from Tarifa. The people of Almuñécar were far from camera-shy. Laurie had written that they possessed 'a natural resistance to civilization's more superficial seductions' and King found they had not changed, despite modernization and tourism. 'Once, we were filming in a bar, but the owner was not exactly right. Just as the camera was rolling, in through the door came a man pushing a trolley of gas canisters, whistling. I asked if he would mind playing the barman. He put down his canisters, took off his overalls – and I didn't have to direct him, he *was* the barman. He could slice ham. He could shout orders to the real owner, who cowered in the kitchen. Acted as though he owned the place. Both Cordelia and John got slightly pickled, because this guy kept bringing out sherries – "Try this, it's the finest of them all" . . .'

The fey waiter Manolo, who wrote Laurie a new poem every day, described by Laurie as 'carved as though for a cathedral niche', was played by a young goatherd; King spotted him walking down a mountain road, and shouted 'He is Manolo!' In two minutes they had him abandoning his goats and into a waiter's jacket. (Among Laurie's papers in Slad are the poems Manolo wrote out for him, in exquisite copperplate script.) When *A Rose for Winter* was shown on BBC-2, it was as highly praised as its predecessor.

Before long the mayor of Almuñécar put up a monument to Laurie, '*el gran escritor*'. Val Hennessy wanted to take Laurie there, and report on it for the *Mail on Sunday*. But he told her he panicked in crowds, and the thought of flying filled him with dread. 'You'll bring me home in a box,' he told her. 'And if you do, make sure you don't leave my duty-frees behind.' Anyway, he heard there were delays at Gatwick, because of Spanish air traffic control disputes. 'Stranded passengers have been offered yoga classes, Catholic masses, and entertainment by clowns. Such things would drive me mad. Can't we go to Bournemouth instead? I wish I'd been given the freedom of the city of Bournemouth.' While Laurie prevaricated, and cynical Chelsea Arts friends suspected that the monument was a figment of the Gran Escritor's imagination, Val flew out to Spain and among Almuñécar's 'construction cranes, concrete apartment blocks, tacky souvenir shops and topless sunbathers' found the

monument to Laurie Lee – 'thrusting skyward on the seafront by a *supermercado* and the La Roca apartment block'.[3]

The monument is, to be frank, a small but phallic obelisk in the style of the traditional Spanish dovecote. Its plaque says:

El pueblo de Almuñécar en reconocimiento al gran escritor Laurie Lee que vivió en nuestra ciudad en los años 1935–36 y 1951–52 y la inmortalizó bajo al seudónimo de 'Castillo' en sus obras Cuando Partí Una Mañana de Verano y Una Rosa para el Invierno
Almuñécar a 21 abril 1988

Val reported back to Laurie. He peered 'through smeared bi-focals' at her snaps of his monument. 'Ho-ho-ho. It would be extremely indelicate of me to say what it resembles, good gracious,' said Laurie, ordering a double scotch. He was still dubious about going there, said his doctor wasn't happy about him flying, and suggested they go to a Spanish restaurant in London instead. 'We can do the snaps with me sitting in front of a bullfight poster rattling some castanets. Your editor will never know.' So that's what they did: they had *paella* at Mesón Don Felipe near Waterloo station, where Paco twanged a guitar and a flamenco dancer named Caroline twirled and stomped, with Laurie muttering, 'I bet T.S. Eliot wouldn't have done this. Ted Hughes wouldn't either.'

(For Laurie as for Philip Larkin, who asked himself ironically 'Wonder what Ted Hughes is doing?', Hughes represented a monumental iron-willed selfhood, and imperviousness to the world's intrusions, compared with their uncertainty and vulnerability.)

Meanwhile a ceremonial presentation of Laurie's golden avocado was arranged at the Casa de la Cultura (right opposite Wilma's former house) in Almuñécar. Kathy went in Laurie's place, and read an impressive speech in Spanish. A dozen journalists were flown out to see a press preview of *A Rose for Winter* at the Stills' beautiful *castillo* with its serpentine pool. In the ensuing five years, Laurie and Kathy went several times to stay there. The first time Michael Still drove them up the winding mountainous tracks, Laurie became very excited – 'Look Cathy: this is just how it was'

– because although only a mile inland from the town of Almuñécar, there is no electricity or gas up there, or water supplies except springs. Laurie even did some local radio and television interviews in proficient Spanish. He asked Michael Still to be at his side as translator, but proved not to need him. He also fell in love, Still says, with the attractive blonde Helga, Still's sculptor wife, and would thereafter telephone them twice a week, often just when they were showing guests the film of *A Rose for Winter*.

In 1988 the Gloucestershire musician and singer Johnny Coppin set some of Laurie's poems to music, and asked Laurie to read others, standing at the window of his cottage, for a CD called *Edge of Day: A Seasonal Anthology in Words and Music*. Interviewed about this for Radio 4 by Christopher Cook, Laurie said he liked the 'radiant simplicity' of Coppin's settings and that he was pleased to have some of his own almost forgotten poems revived. 'Two or three of my poems crop up on the BBC for *Poetry Please*, and I think in the BBC there must be a file which says "Christmas, Spring, Summer, Autumn", and they go to that file every year, and always pick one . . . But these might have been forgotten if he hadn't given them this gloss, this resonance.' (They included 'Invasion Summer', 'Milkmaid', 'First Love', 'Thistle', 'Landscape', and 'Asleep We Are Divided', as well as the more familiar 'April Rise', 'Day of These Days' and 'Field of Autumn'.)

In a long conversation with Cook, Laurie reminisced about playing his violin with Celia Goodman, and said he had not played since his E-string broke during the great storm of October 1987. He told Cook about his twice-yearly trysts with the setting sun on Haresfield Beacon. Haresfield is a jutting bowsprit of land on a 1,000-foot-high Cotswold ridge with a dramatic view of the Severn plain and a sheer drop practically all round. 'It was an Iron Age fort, strategically so unique that it must have been where the local tribes took refuge when the wild Welsh came over the river and tried to attack their flocks and chicken and women. I go up there to see the sunset on the longest day, the 21st of June, and on the shortest day, the 21st of December.

'I'm fascinated by the movement of the sun in relation to our valleys. It sinks behind May Hill on the longest day, and then it moves slowly back to behind Berkeley nuclear power station, out of sheer shame I think. You can just see the edges of Bristol and the great curving horseshoe bend of the Severn, and then Gloucester, and Cheltenham, and the Malvern Hills which are like something from India or Malaya.' On the shortest day he would be there by two o'clock, and on the longest day at about quarter to eleven at night. They would take a celebratory basket of chicken and wine. 'It's a magical experience, but of course it's mixed with melancholy because that is your longest day. From then on, we're for the dark.'

Once, he could look across that plain and see nothing between himself and Welsh villages of the Black Mountains and the Brecon Beacons. 'But now the M5 runs across it . . . hundreds of cars going backwards and forwards, pouring money into the Ayatollah's coffers . . .'

In April 1989, Laurie, Kathy and Jessy took a ferry to Santander, and Jessy drove her parents across Spain to Almuñécar, via Toledo and Jaén – 'Daddy in the back with his whisky, Mum and me with gin and Martini, having one for the road as Dad would say. John Martyn on the stereo and we were all friends together.' It was a happy interlude. Then, immediately after they got back, Jessy re-encountered a handsome young man she had previously met at a ball (when he was dressed as Rudolph Valentino), and they decided to get married. His name was Damian James. He worked for an oil company, and was tall, presentable, gentle and strong. But neither Laurie nor Kathy was convinced that the engagement was a good idea. As she drove to Slad to see her parents Jessy recalls feeling an extraordinary sensation, 'like grief'. 'In my head I could hear Dad's voice saying NO! But he said: "This is your decision, and I will support your decision."'

A letter from Jessy to her father in October 1989 reflects their attempts to sort out their differences amicably. 'Darling Dad, It was so lovely to see you on Sunday. Thank you for such a lovely day – and venison in unison! I hope your toothy-pegs are still in place – I wait for the day when they fly across the room!!

'I felt much better after talking to you . . . Things are good on the whole, but there are a lot of challenges for us both – I am wanting and willing to change up to a point, but it has to be mutual, as you know. Anyway I really hope things work out the way they should as we do love each other very much and feel a deep protection. 80% good – not too bad eh?!'

In June 1989, Mavis Nicholson invited Laurie back for one of her *Mavis Catches Up With* . . . series (revisiting former interviewees) on a hot summer day in the garden of the Chelsea Arts Club. Laurie, in white linen suit, greeted Mavis with outstretched arms, and they walked arm-in-arm across the grass, Laurie reflecting that it was fourteen years since they last met, since when 'my life has been a desert of disappointed expectations' (i.e. not seeing Mavis).

Mavis at once pointed out that since 1975 Laurie had published only one other book, *Two Women*, his 'secret farewell' to Kathy and Jessy. She asked whether he dwelt on the imminence of death. Laurie replied: 'Prospero says, "Every third thought shall be my grave" and round about a certain age, you become very conscious of the ending of a splendid life, in which I've been blessed by all kinds of luck and devotion.' But the interview then took a very determined and penetrating tack.

'You have not been a prolific writer, Laurie,' said Mavis. 'I'm a very slow writer,' he said. 'I could have gone on writing *Cider with Rosie* 2, and 3, but I didn't want to write ten books on the same subject like that vet, that James Herriot.'

'It made you a lot of money . . .'

'It came in one hand, and went out the other . . . taxes . . .'

'And you were a club man and a hearty drinker.'

'When I published that book, beer was a shilling a pint. When it won the W.H. Smith prize I went down to the Star, our local pub, and said, "Drinks on me for the next 20 minutes," and all my chums came in and it cost me about fifteen shillings. So all my money didn't go on drink. It couldn't. I know you're upbraiding me but I'm not a drunkard. I am a heavy drinker, which is a very different thing.'

'But heavy drinkers do isolate themselves from people,' Mavis said.

'I do live an isolated life,' said Laurie. 'Although I do depend immensely on my friends and couldn't exist without them, I like to know that I can withdraw to a private cave if necessary. It is not generally known that I never drink after nine o'clock in the evening. And I don't go round beating up people. It doesn't affect me that way. I don't go round roistering and shouting and quarrelling. I fall over the furniture and then go off to sleep. I'm a very pacific drinker really. But I won't deny the accusation that I am a heavy drinker. I suppose I drink till I drop, but not every night.

'Drinking to me is a defence against panic, fear, and if I can do without it I will.

'Panic and fear is a visitation I've had most of my life. A fear of not being able to control the next day. A lot of people depend on me, and to be a writer you've got to depend on a clarity of mind. If any of those dependencies are in jeopardy, my defence is a few Scotches.'

'But do you never feel that the feeling of panic is brought on by the Scotch? Doesn't that make you drink more, rather than alleviate it? I mean, it's addictive, we know that . . .'

'Yes, it is addictive, but it's also in place of prayer. I do pray, but I'm not so convinced of the power of prayer now, as I am convinced of the power of malt whisky. I find that one answers more directly and more positively than the other. The answer to a prayer seems to get held up in the post sometimes, but if I have a bottle of malt in my pocket, I know that the answer will be immediate.'

'Does it cause trouble in your life? It can.'

'I don't think so, to be honest. "To be honest" that's a politician's phrase. My daughter says, you can get more out of him when he's drunk than when he's sober. So I think she's a realist. She's never been appalled at that particular habit of mine. My wife's accepted it, apart from breaking the furniture. Not that I break up the furniture, but I fall over the charming side-tables occasionally.'

'Do you drink to oblivion? People who drink to oblivion say

they do it so they don't have to think, they don't have to lie awake dreading the next day.'

'I'm very aware of that oblivion. I'm not seeking it, I'm just seeking reassurance. And pacification of the state I might be in.'

Laurie, who had been sweetly courteous throughout in the face of Mavis's persistent questions, wrote aggrievedly to the producer John Tagholm afterwards. Mavis rang to apologize, and spoke to Kathy, who said, 'What a wonderful interview you did. At last he's admitted something he's never admitted before.'

Laurie began the new decade by having several weeks in bed with pneumonia. 'Both Liz Taylor and I pulled through,' he said later, though he had been seriously ill, and Kathy told Tom Matthews in April that they could not plan a trip to New College Oxford this year as they did not yet know how Laurie's new drugs would work. 'But while we live in this very twilight existence . . . you know me, Faith Hope and a certain amount of Charity govern my life so one does keep relatively cheerful.'

In May 1990, forty years after her parents' wedding, on a gloriously sunny day, Jessy was married to Damian James in the church at Slad, thus becoming (for a few years at least) officially named Jesse James. Canon Brassell of Gloucester Cathedral officiated and Kathy, as sacristan, prepared the vessels for communion. Kathy described the scene to Tom Matthews: 'Bride and matron of honour sipping sherry and dancing in the sunshine in vivid silk kimonos, Laurie sitting in a quiet corner hoping he wouldn't pass out before the trip up the aisle, and Mrs Lee ironing the silken train . . . It all went extremely smoothly after my months of worrying – not a hitch & no panic and beautiful weather – so there we are, 'Tis Done.' Laurie had a photograph taken just before going into church, 'the last time alone with my daughter and not somebody else's *wife*'. The honeymoon, arranged by Laurie through Michael Still, was in the hills above Almuñécar.

By the following year, Laurie was 'reduced to a state of almost total blindness', as he told Kate Figes, literary editor of *Cosmopolitan*, who had asked him to review for her. 'I cannot read Braille & don't

much like Talking Books. I'd quite fancy however being comforted by the voices of Edna O'Brien, Jilly Cooper or Elizabeth Jane Howard reading one of their latest novels, to me personally of course if possible.' That summer Jock Gallagher, who was organizing a literary festival near his home at Bewdley, arranged a recording of *With Great Pleasure*, the Radio 4 programme, in a local church. Laurie would choose his favourite poetry and prose; Jill Balcon and Martin Jarvis (Laurie's chosen voices) were to read. But no material arrived, and at the last minute the actors were told that Laurie had backed out; he was ill. (Laurie's first excuse, says Gallagher, was that – like the vagrant in Pinter's play *The Caretaker* – he had no decent shoes.)

Gallagher appealed to Stephen Fry to step in, and Fry's choice of poems and prose arrived by fax from his parents' home in Norfolk. 'And there was much too much,' Jill Balcon says, 'and no time to do the kind of preparation I like to do, no time to rehearse, and the tickets had been sold out on Laurie's name.' Then Gallagher heard, on the day of the performance, that Laurie was coming after all. Jill came downstairs in the pub where they were staying – 'the sort of pub that stank of beer' – and heard the familiar voice, and there was Laurie in the bar.

The recording went ahead, with Stephen Fry introducing his poems, Jarvis and Jill Balcon reading, requiring a number of retakes. 'Martin Jarvis was wonderful,' Jill says, 'he could do things on the hoof, and said, "I quite like living with danger," but I thought to myself, I don't. I stand or fall by my professionalism, and that night I fell.' Meanwhile Gallagher went searching for Laurie, found him in a pub, and told him he jolly well had to make an appearance. 'No,' said Laurie, 'people don't want to see me at this time of night. You had a good evening with your friend Stephen.' Gallagher said: 'Laurie, these people have been waiting for three hours to see YOU. You're going on stage now. I'm going to tell them you're here.' So it was that at about 11 p.m. Laurie appeared at the back of the church hall, doddered up the aisle amid cheers, and 'charmed his way out of it by praising us to the audience', Jill says. He put his arms round both actors, proceeded to do some readings from

Cider with Rosie, which Gallagher had in his pocket, and received thunderous applause.

Few people now had any confidence in Laurie's ever producing that final book. It was a race against time anyway; he was almost too blind to write. 'In the last year I was only able to write a page a week, I couldn't dictate it; it was much too private and too painful to dictate to anyone, and in any case that is not my way of writing.' But in the summer of 1990 the *Sunday Times* announced that Laurie had completed his final volume. 'No one, not even his agent Pat Kavanagh, has yet seen the manuscript of *Window on the War* but after eight years' toil [actually more like twenty] Lee regards it as a true large-scale offering. It can be purchased, he says, by any publisher offering a six-figure sum: "It's not going for a couple of crates of malt whisky."'

To the writers and poets of England, Scotland, Ireland and Wales:

The equivocal attitude, the Ivory Tower, the paradoxical, the ironic detachment, will no longer do.

Are you for, or against, the legal government and the people of Republican Spain? Are you for or against Franco and Fascism? For it is impossible any longer to take no side. Writers and poets . . . we wish the world to know what you, who are amongst the most sensitive instruments of a nation, feel.

That was the loaded challenge of the *Left Review* symposium, *Authors Take Sides on the Spanish Civil War*, published in 1937. The signatories included Auden, Spender, Pablo Neruda, Tristan Tzara and Louis Aragon. Most respondents – 127 – were unequivocally on the side of the Republic. Sixteen were neutral and only five against, including Evelyn Waugh who said if he'd been a Spaniard he'd be fighting for Franco. Eliot sat on the fence, as did Pound, Wells, and Vita Sackville-West. Orwell said the whole exercise was 'bloody rot' but he almost lost his life fighting in Spain. Sean O'Faolain responded with contempt: 'Don't be a lot of saps. If X and Y want to cut each other's throats, why on earth must people "have to choose between them"? If you want to know, I do think Fascism is lousy. So is your Communism, only more so . . . But there are other ideas in the world besides either of them, thank God.'

Few conflicts in this century, after the Great War, have so gripped the artistic or romantic conscience as did the Spanish Civil War. Poets 'exploded like bombs' about it, as Auden said in his poem 'Spain'. Even those who did not go out there felt impelled to write about it: C. Day-Lewis, card-carrying Communist, wrote 'The Volunteer':

Tell them in England, if they ask
What brought us to these wars,
To this plateau beneath the night's
Grave manifold of stars –

It was not fraud or foolishness,
Glory, revenge, or pay:
We came because our open eyes
Could see no other way.

By 1990 Laurie was possibly the only writer who had been to Spain during the war but had never told the tale – although he had started it in *As I Walked Out One Midsummer Morning*. He had read (and dismissed) Hemingway; he possessed the books of Orwell and of Koestler, who had been held in solitary confinement for three months in Seville. The words 'long-awaited' had been fixed for years now to the words 'third volume in Laurie Lee's autobiographical trilogy'. His story was now a matter of very distant recall, as he said. But he felt he had to tell it. 'I shall never be free. The only way I could have paid the debt which I felt so strongly to those people was to have given my life, and I didn't. Afterwards I always felt guilty. Guilty to have survived.' Thousands of volunteers had died during the conflict. So he 'scoured the attics of [his] mind' to uncover the events of fifty years before. It was 'a debt of dishonour – to the friends I left behind in Spain'. With such emotional declarations, Laurie justified the time it had taken to fulfil his own moral imperative.

Tony Lacey, publishing director of Penguin, became Laurie's chief publishing contact after 1988. Lunch with Laurie Lee, he discovered, meant a bibulous afternoon at the Chelsea Arts Club: champagne, wine with lunch, Armagnac afterwards. 'And if you asked for a pint of bitter he would generously bring you a whisky chaser as well.' Though the paperback *Cider with Rosie* had never been out of print for nearly thirty years, Laurie constantly sought reassurance: 'I suppose you'll be letting it go then,' he would say glumly, as if

Penguin would ever drop one of their perennial bestsellers. He also referred often to the book still to come. But sometimes he would say he wasn't sure he wanted it published at all. Lacey began to suspect it might all be a tease.

Then came the night in late 1990 when, as they parted outside the club, Laurie said: 'Do you want to publish this book or not?' Lacey replied: 'Of course.' Laurie asked: 'How much is it worth?' A difficult question, sight unseen. 'I said, "Well, let's say £50,000." He said, "OK, you're on." We shook hands in the middle of the road, and a car came along and started hooting, and Laurie tapped the car with his stick and said, "I'm a ratepayer here, I've lived here for years" . . .'

Lacey remembers waking up the next morning and thinking, 'God, what have I done?' 'Then I thought the book might not really exist, in which case the money didn't matter; but anyway, I consoled myself that any book by Laurie Lee was bound to be OK.' (Another publisher had already offered Laurie £20,000, sight unseen.)

A week later the manuscript arrived, entitled *A Winter of War*, with a note from Laurie's agent: 'I gather you and Laurie have already done a deal . . .' Lacey read it over the weekend with 'intense relief'. 'It was brilliant, spare, harsh, a masterpiece.' But Laurie insisted that he had to show it to his 'literary advisers' and took it away. Literary advisers? He had asked P.J. Kavanagh to recommend someone at the *Spectator* who might give an opinion. Kavanagh suggested Christopher Howse, jovial and bearded Catholic intellectual who knew a thing or two about history. Howse met Laurie at the 'French Pub', the York Minster in Soho, where neither could hear the other speak, so when Laurie mentioned a payment for the reading task – Howse would have done it for nothing – he had to say 'What?' several times, as if forcing up the price. Laurie led him outside to the pavement with an air of embarrassed conspiracy and offered £150.

Howse was asked specifically to say whether Laurie's book ought to be published. He said yes it should, and corrected a few literals. He was not asked to say whether it rang true: 'It seemed to me

about as true as *As I Walked Out . . .*' he says. 'The most striking incident was his sleeping on the altar when billeted in a church, an act to which he gave inauspicious significance.' ('I threw down my bags, stretched myself along [the altar] and lit a cigarette. With this idiot impulse of brash bravado, I believe I stained the rest of my life.') After Howse had written his report, Laurie sent him another £50 – in gratitude, or from a wish not to appear mean. They never met again, although in 1996 Howse tried to get Laurie together with the writer Peter Kemp, who as a young Cambridge graduate had fought on Franco's side at the battle of Teruel – but in vain.

Laurie's editor on the book was Mary Omond, who fell in love with Laurie 'like everyone else'. She was struck by his courtesy and old-world graciousness, his air of vulnerability. She had the feeling his manuscript had been typed a long time before. Their editing sessions took place in June 1991 upstairs in the Chelsea Arts Club, Laurie bringing his Ruddles. 'For Mary, who put me in order,' he dedicated her copy of the book. He was, she says, extremely concerned about accuracy, and because he was nearly blind, she wrote out the proof-readers' queries on foolscap paper in huge black infant-school print. 'I sat at the table drowsing through my girl's extravagant letters and inhaling their heady unforgivable magic.' Might he mean 'unforgettable'? Laurie wrote: 'N O. Unforgivable magic. How could she rouse me to such intensity when I was so far away?'

As Laurie's story unfolds in the short, 190-page book, it goes like this: He crossed the Pyrenees ill-shod and alone in December 1937 and said: 'I've come to join you.' Far from being welcomed, he met suspicion, was accused of being a spy, and imprisoned in a pitch-dark and freezing hole in the ground for a fortnight. His fellow prisoner 'Dino', a Spanish deserter, was eventually taken out and, in Laurie's hearing, shot dead, leaving Laurie holding his cap. He was then taken to a camp for newly arrived volunteers at Figueras barracks, among Cockney, Scots and Welsh volunteers; in the town he was seduced by a sensuous Andalucian girl of fifteen

or sixteen named Eulalia. Transferred ten days later to Brigade HQ at Albacete, seeing an air raid over Valencia en route, he was once again interrogated as a spy and only narrowly escaped the firing squad, a young boy being provided to 'comfort' him on the eve of his execution. Moved to Tarazona de la Mancha for training, Laurie was reunited with Eulalia (whom he now knew to be a murderer) and posted to 'special duties' with a sinister Stalinist hit-squad whose job was to track down and liquidate traitors to the cause. He was then summoned to Madrid to make a propaganda broadcast to America from the besieged city, playing his fiddle into the microphone in the midst of a Fascist artillery barrage. Eventually he got caught up on the fringes of the dreadful battle of Teruel in January 1938. Five miles from the front, with a gaggle of Spaniards, he was under bombardment and shellfire; in a confused confrontation he killed a man ('I remember his shocked, angry eyes') and 'began to have hallucinations and breaks in the brain'. He was found and driven back to Tarazona, received orders for his reluctant repatriation, and was handed back his girlfriend's letters, but not the Chanel-scented pound notes. On his way home he was arrested in Barcelona as a deserter and spy and again imprisoned in a cell for three weeks, until the war correspondent Bill Rust, later editor of the *Daily Worker*, persuaded the authorities to release him, and took him to his apartment. Finally Laurie was sent home, to be met at Victoria by his girl with 'her blue steady gaze . . . her deep mouth, and love without honour. Without honour, but at least with salvation.'

A Winter of War was a great title. But shortly before publication, Laurie asked if he could change it. 'It's too grand a claim,' he told Lacey. 'I wasn't there all that long.' So it became *A Moment of War*.

Nobody ever knew exactly how long – or how short – Laurie's time in war-ravaged Spain had been. In fact it was nine weeks. In the book it seems like four or five months. Wilma – the only person with a clear idea of what actually happened to Laurie in those months, though never mentioned in the book, of course – was long dead. More than half a century had elapsed between the events

of the winter of 1937–8 and the book's publication in October 1991. Laurie's first piece of prose about Spain, written for John Lehmann in 1941, when he still had his diaries and it was fresh in his memory, was about pre-war Spain. The earliest published references to Laurie's war had been in 1959, when *Cider with Rosie* came out and press stories revealed that Laurie had been a strolling troubadour for thirteen months in Spain, and a year later 'went back to fight with the International Brigade and was arrested as a spy. Then he was invalided to Britain.'

The following year Laurie told Frank Entwisle that he had been 'shipped home after a bout of pneumonia'. In succeeding years, he began to say he had been shot at, or condemned to death while in Spain.

In 1969 came the catastrophic theft of his Spanish diaries. It was then that he began drinking more than he ever had before, which is not generally recommended as an aid to memory. By the time he spoke at length to Philip Oakes about the Spanish war, in 1977, he said that piecing together the facts was 'like retrieving the pages of a love letter that had been scattered by a cyclone'. He told Oakes it had not been easy to join the International Brigade. 'No one wanted to have anything to do with me. There was no organization. By the winter of 1937 the war was virtually lost. There was a final flicker of euphoria when it seemed that the Republic stood a chance. But it was a forlorn hope, and the long slide downhill began to a bloody death. What was so awful was that we were killing our own people out of mistrust. The International Brigade was falling apart. There were spies everywhere. If a man fell under suspicion we couldn't afford the risk of assuming him to be innocent. He might belong to a counter faction. So he was killed. We shot each other with apologies.' When Laurie told Oakes these yarns, as related earlier, he had written to the former battalion commander Bill Alexander for a list of civil war survivors, and was taking notes from Hugh Thomas's *The Spanish Civil War*. So he had done some research.

All writers mope and chafe when their writing nerve goes, and with it all conviction and confidence. The sense of expectation

about that next book must have been daunting for Laurie, though the creative impasse was masked by his habitual secrecy. By January 1984 the *Gloucester Citizen* reported that Laurie, who had 'left readers in the dark' ever since *As I Walked Out* ('What happened after the Spanish Civil War – was he hurt? did he kill? how did it all end?') had now finished a pencilled draft of the next volume. Later that year, in *Vintage Cider* on Radio 4, he said that *A Winter of War* was now ready for publication: 'I was arrested several times,' he said. 'Carrying violin and camera and books and letters and mementoes, pictures of my girlfriends, they couldn't believe that I'd just come over the Canigou peak. I could have been shot. How could they afford the risk of trusting me? I still don't know why they didn't shoot me. I never believed they would. I had absolute faith in my good fortune and that I think saved me. It's not a happy story. It was a time of winter, and defeat, and hunger, and despair.'

Bryan Wharton – who had been to several battlefronts as a photographer – says Laurie never claimed to have been involved in fighting. He did tell him he was riven with guilt about having unwittingly led a young man to his death (presumably in Tarazona, with the hit-squad). In 1986 when the Imperial War Museum asked Laurie to take part in a sixth-form conference on the Spanish Civil War, with Stephen Spender, Laurie declined.

Jock Gallagher, to whom Laurie often talked about the work in progress, says he never claimed to have joined the International Brigade. He said he was 'with the Brigade', as in 'travelling with'. 'He never communicated any heroic feelings about his time there. It was a cold, wet, alien experience. He felt lost, watching other people suffer, feeling he was bad news to his friends, the cause of others' suffering. He said, "It's a book nobody will like." He was haunted by his experiences, seeing savagery for the first time, the death of romantic young people.' Gallagher thinks he used the unfinished book 'half as an excuse for not doing other things. He was frightened of writing it. He had had to dredge very deep.' Gallagher was so relieved that the book finally emerged, he didn't question a word.

Laurie's publishers gave a celebratory lunch at the Ivy, with much to celebrate. Every newspaper featured the blown-up mug-shot of Laurie's innocent, dreamy-eyed young face, legibly stamped 'Commissariat', on his identity card. The book was serialized in the *Observer*, met a chorus of rapturous and enthusiastic praise, and went straight into the bestseller lists. Across the Atlantic critics were equally impressed. It was declared that the seventy-seven-year-old author had written a more profound, more intense, darker and less sentimental work than his previous books. The Oxford don Valentine Cunningham gave it the kind of credence, in the *Times Literary Supplement*, that would vouchsafe its respectability. In a review headed 'On the Road to Teruel', he said Laurie's account was 'momentous, extraordinary, compelling, stunning, mesmerizing'. Laurie's sense of smell predominated, hence the 'fabulously scented inductions to be invoked in that magically wide-eyed, synaesthetic prose'. And of all the testimonies to that icy war in the high sierras, 'nobody has, I think, succeeded so well as Laurie Lee in dramatizing the wintry horrors – personal, political, military, geographical – when Spain's potential for sourness, sickness and rot took over completely'. What impressed Cunningham above all was Laurie's truthfulness: '. . . what Spain did for Laurie Lee was to bring home the importance of, and to enable, truthful words, truthful art, in the face of the liars, rhetoricians, and propagandists'. John Sweeney in the *Literary Review* also found it 'an honest book' and a 'great, heart-stopping narrative'. Edward Blishen in the *Guardian* called it 'a story that aches with unforgotten cold and trembles with unforgotten terror'.

The *Times* reviewer was more moderate: it was really 'a series of postcard observations from the periphery of the war' with 'a rough chronology': its coincidences 'strained credulity'. But the writing was full of rich cameos, poetic cadences, potent images, lyric intensity. In the *London Magazine*, Jeremy Lewis was sceptical about the 'phenomenal memory' that could recall whole conversations fifty years on, and said some would find his story 'at times, verging on the fantastic'. Laurie's old friend Val Hennessy, who reviewed it lovingly in the *Mail*, was also 'extremely suspicious

about the luscious sixteen-year-old Eulalia (tight black dress and long Spanish-Indian eyes) whose slim body almost bare to the waist is eagerly meeting the young Lee's "with the quick twist of a snake" on page 36. She strikes me as the seductive fantasy of a canny old rogue, particularly when she miraculously crops up again 400 miles away running her mouth across his chest and emitting an unforgettable fragrance of "fresh mushrooms and trampled thyme, woodsmoke and burning orange".'

The *Morning Star* reviewer naturally concentrated on the rescue of Laurie from the Barcelona death cell, 'at the end of his few months in Spain as an International Brigader', by its late editor Bill Rust (who had died in 1948). Rust had heard of Laurie's incarceration, vouched for his authenticity and arranged his release. 'It is tempting to speculate,' commented the reviewer laconically, 'given Bill Rust's own recollections of the Spanish Civil War, what he would make of these confessions of a disappointed idealist.'

A Moment of War is indeed a marvellous piece of writing. The early paragraph about crossing the border into Spain is a foretaste of the telling detail within: 'At my back was the tang of Gauloises and slumberous sauces, scented fish and opulent farmlands; before me, still ghostly, was all I remembered – the whiff of rags and woodsmoke, the salt of dried fish, sour wine and sickness, stone and thorn, old horses and rotting leather.'

And there are dozens of key moments in the narrative which have the convincing ring of truth.

On the lack of weapons: 'Few of us yet knew that we had come to a war of antique muskets and jamming machine-guns, to be led by brave but bewildered amateurs . . .'

On the 'almost wolf-like hunger' felt by the starving volunteers, fed on acorn coffee and thin donkey soup: 'I'd been hungry before . . . I remember as a boy being so in love with bread and butter and the cloudy meat of a new-boiled egg that I could hardly wait to go to sleep at night so that morning breakfast could come again. So it seemed now, that long moment of delayed consummation, as we sat round the table while the sisters fussed and quarrelled by

the stove and carried us at last the stew in a great earthen dish.'

On the dawn awakening by the sound of a bugle: 'a sound pure and cold, slender as an icicle, coming from the winter dark outside . . . the crystal range of the notes stroking the dawn's silence and raising one up like a spirit'.

On the discovery of courage under bombardment: 'I was surprised at my detachment and lack of fear. I may even have felt some queer satisfaction. It was something I learned about myself that night which I have never quite understood.'

On the wondrous arrival of gifts from home: 'On Christmas Day I tasted, with almost erotic excitement, a twopenny bar of Cadbury's Milk Chocolate, and smoked a shilling packet of Players. I was affected as much by the piercing familiarity of their flavours as by the homely reassurance of their wrappings.'

On the contrast between Madrid in 1935, and the besieged city of 1938: 'Now there was emptiness and silence . . . I went to seek out my old landlord and his wife, and found them freezing in the kitchen trying to heat some water over a smouldering brazier of oily rags . . . This was not the towering man I'd known . . . who once, when I was playing the violin in the courtyard, struck a chiming clock with a brandy bottle for daring to interrupt.'

And on the mixed terror and self-loathing of having killed a man: 'Was this then what I had come for and all my journey had meant – to smudge out the life of an unknown young man in a blur of panic which in no way could affect victory or defeat?'

Laurie had dedicated his book 'To the defeated'. This factor possibly protected him, at that time, from the public divulgence of private disaffection voiced by several veterans of the International Brigade, who privately circulated their objections to the book and their doubts about its authenticity.

In November 1991 Bill Alexander, the commander at Teruel, sent his old comrades a detailed critique of *A Moment of War*, and so did another veteran, John Dunlop, who had been in the front line during some of the heaviest fighting.[1]

Alexander, who had admired Laurie's earlier works, appreciated Laurie's support for the Republican cause, and his dedication 'To

the defeated'. But as autobiography this book was 'a fantasy', he claimed. He could confirm that Bill Rust had got Laurie released from prison, because Rust had told him so; Rust had arranged a medical examination, and Laurie 'was found to have epilepsy', said Alexander, 'and sent back to Britain. He never joined the British Battalion and the I.B.'

The story of Laurie's movements and the dates in December 1937 'do not add up', wrote Alexander: 'Two imprisonments, then a ten-day stay in Figueras, then Albacete, then Tarazona when "a few days after his arrival" he went to a meeting where Harry Pollitt spoke. This was Christmas Eve, 24 December 1937.' Laurie's description of life in Tarazona was quite unlike the experience of others at the time. 'The Commander was Major Alan Johnson (ex West Point, USA) a stickler for organization and discipline . . .' Laurie's stories of amorous encounters with Eulalia, claimed Alexander, were uncannily like a story told by Arthur Landis in his history *The Abraham Lincoln Brigade*, published in 1967.

'Why should Laurie Lee, unknown, inexperienced and untrained, have been selected for the mysterious, unexplained special duties?' Both Alexander and Dunlop were convinced that only Communist Party members of proven character, courage and dependability were recruited to the SIM (Servicio de Investigación Militar). 'Much of LL's story,' Alexander concluded, 'must be classified as fiction and fantasy and not a true picture of his own real experience.'

On the other hand, he allowed that in contrast to the 'muck and fantasy' of the bitter anti-Republican writings of Orwell and Jason Gurney, Laurie's book did contain 'some positive points'.

But the veterans found themselves wondering why Laurie had waited so long to publish his book – until the possibility of verification had faded? – and why Laurie had never associated with other International Brigaders, when so many others had kept up the comradeship forged in Spain. 'On his return LL avoided contact and discussion with other I.B.ers,' declared Alexander, citing Wogan Philipps and his wife Tamara, the former Mrs Bill Rust, with whom Laurie had been 'reluctant to talk about Spain'.

And, of course, both took exception to Laurie's descriptions of British Brigaders as 'ex-convicts, alcoholics, wizened miners, dockers, noisy politicians, dreaming undergraduates, motivated by failure, poverty, debt, the law, betrayal by wives or lovers'. Slanders, said Alexander. 'He does not attempt to explain how these men, deprived of weapons by the Tory government, were able to stop the professional armies of three dictators for nearly three years.'

Well, the diehard old International Brigaders never liked anyone hinting that they were disorganized, woefully ill-equipped, or anything but splendid and dedicated fellows. It was a war of chaos and confusions, criminal deceptions and cruel delusions. And Laurie, presumably, knew nothing of these behind-the-scenes rumblings among International Brigade veterans. But he did ask Mary Omond to make a couple of changes before his book was republished in paperback. He had mixed up the names of Largo Caballero, the prime minister, and Azaña, the president. He had also referred prematurely to the Ebro. 'Ebro must have been a mistake when transcribing notes,' he told Mary. 'I do so apologize for the mess.' No doubts about the facts were raised, publicly, in Laurie's lifetime; so he was able to enjoy a resurgence of popularity.

He seemed somewhat subdued when Cal McCrystal arrived at the Chelsea Arts Club to interview him for the *Independent on Sunday*. They met in Laurie's corner, the Laurie Lee bar, Laurie wearing his Garrick tie, a cream linen jacket and a mushroom waistcoat. 'Laurie Lee cannot see well enough to read *A Moment of War*, the final book in his trilogy,' McCrystal's sympathetic piece began. On the table lay a mess of books, a magnifying glass, flickering candles and empty bottles. He was sipping hot whisky; his eyes were 'rheumy and benevolent behind thick bi-focals'.

'Reading the book,' said McCrystal, 'all one's senses are arrested by the dying Republic as though one were there, right now, with the young blond Briton from the Cotswolds: the "reek of burnt dust" as the bombs fell, the taste of bean soup, the snowy silence "broken by a goat-bell or the chirp of a bird".' The book was 'a remarkable feat of memory'. Laurie explained how he was able to recapture an experience, and replay it in his mind: 'I have carried

the recollection of Dino's forage cap over the years. It never left me.'

But McCrystal feared that 'my questions do not stimulate him, for he lapses into long silences, re-emerging with apologies for his mind being elsewhere. In Spain, perhaps? No. He's distracted, he says, by a domestic upheaval currently afflicting one of the club barmaids.' McCrystal said he detected 'a degree of nonchalance, if not fatalism', in the book. 'You are absolutely right,' said Laurie. 'I had a feeling that life had been given me, and all its chances and its glories and its miseries were part of the deal. I didn't for a moment question or complain about any of the experiences I had.'

They were interrupted by Dr Geoffrey Dove, 'a GP who shadows Laurie protectively on his drinking expeditions'. Dr Dove, Laurie's London doctor and a long-term fellow habitué of the old Queen's Elm and the Chelsea Arts, brought another hot whisky, handed Laurie a four-pack of Ruddles County Ale and told McCrystal not to tire the author.

Bryan Wharton came along with a pile of his photographs; Laurie peered at 'a former female acquaintance with very long legs'. 'He is silent again, and I wonder what he is thinking about . . . And when I beg him to inscribe my copy, there are several moments of uncertainty before he uncaps his felt-tip and, his face almost against the page, writes: "For Cal in memory of a warm though speechless encounter."' Afterwards Laurie apologized for having wasted McCrystal's time.

But six months later, when the paperback edition was published, Laurie aged seventy-eight was positively bushy-tailed with renewed success. Once more, on 2 July 1992 in a Radio 3 interlude, he told Chris Eldon Lee of the 'terrible, bloody period in my life' when he was 'almost executed by [his] own side . . . It was quite a freakish coincidence that I escaped.'

'I still wonder if my book was powerful enough,' he said. 'I think it follows the truth of that monstrous winter in as much detail as I could recall, considering the time that has elapsed. *As I Walked Out One Midsummer Morning* was a story of freedom, happiness, sunlight, but *A Moment of War* was the sun behind the cloud, defeat,

disaster, cruelty and horror. But it was a book I had to write, out of a debt I owed to my friends. It's not a book of heroism, but it is a book in which I tell a truth which is larger than my own particular experience. I not only experienced a certain amount of the suspicion and cruelty and brutality and hopelessness of war, but if I hadn't gone and revisited and written that book, I would have lived a life of undischarged responsibility.'

At the Penguin party for the paperback, at the Arts Club in Dover Street, a reporter asked him would he be writing any more? 'I really don't know. Anything I write now might seem rather irrelevant after my storming days of youth.' He racked his brains. 'I could of course write about love . . . Failed love, rejected love, all sorts of love.' He twiddled with his hearing aid which he said was tuned to the sports coverage on the radio. 'I keep hearing this voice saying "Extra time",' he said. 'It's very encouraging.'

During his radio interview of July 1992, Laurie had intimated that he might yet write another book, covering the last fifty-five years, 'because I think to break off my life aged twenty-three is a bit peremptory don't you think?

'Since I came back from Spain I've lived and loved, gained love and lost love, and married a most beautiful lady and have a most beautiful daughter, and I've been blessed with their companionship, and with the good fortune of being back in my valley, and knowing that I am where I belong, in this close embrace.'

29 | The Old Man of the Woolpack
1992–7

'The longer I live here, the more devoted I am to this place but the less I hear from old friends. It is like floating up-river in a boat which used to be crammed with the noise of children, but one by one they disappear and eventually you are left alone sitting at the front of the boat slowly going out to sea.' In Laurie's last five years, aged seventy-seven to eighty-two, journalists could always rely on him for a well-honed wistful or nostalgic sentiment. They liked to portray him as the Old Man outside the Woolpack, 'watching the shades and shadows and the seasons change', in the valley which had become as synonymous with Laurie Lee as Haworth is with the Brontës – a local monument and tourist attraction, ready to reminisce about the days when the carrier's cart would take you in to Stroud for twopence. In fact, there was a great deal more life in the old dog yet.

At a previous Cheltenham Festival, Laurie told his audience in 1992, a newspaper report said that Laurie Lee was in his 'twilight years' and probably would not be seen in this world again. 'Reading that certainly kept me going,' said Laurie, to much laughter. Keep going he did. He was energized by his late burst of success with the completed trilogy, now among the paperback bestsellers. He was back at literary events in London such as the *Sunday Express* book prize luncheon. Among the judges was Clare Francis, the yachtswoman turned novelist. 'I was sitting opposite this benign white-haired figure,' she recalls. 'He smiled at me in a friendly way, and when I whispered, "Who's that chap?" and was told it was Laurie Lee I almost fell off my chair. I thought he never came to London. I grew up on his books. I went to sit beside him and found him totally un-English, in the sense that not only did he love conversation and people, but he liked women and set up an immediate easy intimacy which is very, very rare. He made you feel like

a co-conspirator. So I knew he would be a friend.' Thereafter they met every year when the *Express* prize or the Hatchard's Authors of the Year party rolled round, 'and we'd pick up where we left off'.

'It was a joy to be with him. He would describe a sight remembered from Spain, fresh in the telling, and one was entranced. He missed very little. He was a true Romantic, in the old-fashioned sense. I understood why he went off alone with his violin, because I was the same.' Clement Freud offered to cook dinner for them both. 'I'd love this beyond the dreams of gluttony,' Laurie wrote, 'but my jaw remains clamped against such temptations. I am forced to survive on low tides of whisky and plankton.' (He had a growth inside his mouth, which proved benign, but it meant he couldn't eat.) 'One day we may at last join Clement for foie gras and trumpets.'

Mavis Cheek, the blue-eyed barmaid from the Queen's Elm, was now a successful novelist, and she too would gravitate to the side of Laurie's armchair at the Chelsea Arts, for a joint moan about publishers. She loved Laurie because he listened. 'He wasn't a chap for blokey talk. Men don't want to talk about sunsets. He had good male friends, but he was a woman's man. He adored women in an old-fashioned and wholesome way. He would wax lyrical about my eyes. He played at being flirtatious, slightly laughing at himself. He did kiss me once, but not offensively, not black and blue like some of the men up there.' She felt he was much more at home in London than playing the bumpkin in Slad. 'He knew in his heart,' she says, 'that *Cider with Rosie* had been the ruination of him.'

His Chelsea Arts Club friends now saw to it that he never walked home alone. Sometimes his neighbour, the tall and glamorous Jill, Duchess of Hamilton, would accompany him; but usually it was his hairdresser Doug Chisholm, or the painter Don Grant. ('Unless there was a pretty girl around,' says Doug, 'and then you'd be dropped.') He recalls Laurie stopping on the pavement to turn round three times and make a bow when he saw the new moon – 'and he could barely stand up'. Philip Oakes remembers him looking

frail and stooping, 'as if cowering from a fierce blast – a bit like Richard Goolden playing Moley in *Wind in the Willows*'. Vera the barmaid would serve him a 'Laurie Special' – baked potato with tuna or chicken. He adored the pretty Katie Paltenghi, who managed the club, and she regarded him as 'a second dad', a soul-mate, someone to confide in – especially when she found, at thirty-three, that she had breast cancer (from which she recovered). 'Laurie was just always there,' she says. 'Thank God for Laurie.' He was reluctant to see people anywhere else. His accountant Pat Kernon had to tell him firmly: 'The Chelsea Arts Club is absolutely delightful, but it is not easy to explain the niceties of bond investment there.'

Down in Slad he was equally a fixture. The good-natured landlord of the Woolpack, David Tarratt, allowed Laurie to summon him on a mobile phone, so he would sit outside the pub with his vade-mecum, a dark red Waterstone's PVC bag containing his personal pewter mug, and would give two rings when he wanted another light ale. This impressed all the interviewers who came down to listen to his wisdom. The interviewers he most enjoyed were young and pretty. Mary Killen arrived from the *Telegraph* to talk about his lifelong obsession with light, the sun and the moon. 'I often go and sit in the garden wrapped up in blankets and say – "The moon will rise over *there* tonight, behind that tree or hillock, at the appointed time," ' he told her. 'Confirming this never fails to restore my feeling of the slow revolving almanac of the year.

'A kind of primeval reverence surrounds the orbit of the moon. Before a full moon rises, there is a quietness in the valley, almost an anticipation. When it slowly lifts its light above the horizon's edge, all the farm dogs begin to bark. It may sound rather precious, but the motions of sun and moon are a constant reassurance of my place in the valley and I feel lucky to have found a fixed point in order to see all this.'

Laurie's status as a school syllabus author was cemented when in January 1993 the Schools Examination and Assessment Council published an anthology of texts which all children aged fourteen should study. It inevitably caused a fuss: no two people ever agree

on such a selection. This one included Laurie alongside Shakespeare, Chaucer, Dylan Thomas, Dr Johnson, Wordsworth, Keats, John Clare, Browning, Dickens's *David Copperfield*, Wilde's *The Importance of Being Earnest*, and poems by Derek Walcott and A.S.J. Tessimond. Doris Lessing was included, but not Jane Austen or George Eliot. The novelist A.N. Wilson said the Education Secretary should publicly burn 'this rag-bag of mutilated texts'.[1] A *Times Educational Supplement* columnist called it 'a gruel-thin literary diet masquerading as a feast' and discerned an underlying political desire to present to children 'the dishonest vision of a world which is simpler and safer. Just as all recent educational policy has looked back to some mythical golden age – basic skills, the security of learned facts – so this anthology represents a simplistic pick-and-mix approach to literature . . . Thus *David Copperfield* and *Cider with Rosie* are the two texts which every pupil in the country can now be guaranteed to read, whatever their background.' Daniel Johnson in *The Times* detected that the Cambridge don Dr John Marenbon, SEAC's English committee chairman, had selected for the anthology a common theme – 'the relationship between youth and age, children and parents . . .' Johnson concluded approvingly that these texts were mostly 'teachable'. He was right. Teachers of all levels and types of pupil have always found *Cider with Rosie* to be a book that guarantees an affectionate response, one of recognition and familiarity, no matter how distant from Laurie's is the background of the contemporary city-dwelling child.

Laurie, one of the few living authors selected, took no part in these arguments. He was putting on a cap and gown to receive his only honorary degree – along with Dr Sheila Cassidy, who was tortured in Chile – from the Cheltenham and Gloucester College of Higher Education. Two days later Laurie wrote with Pooterish courtesy to the *Stroud News* thanking them for mentioning his honour, but regretting that the photograph captioned 'Laurie Lee' was in fact the former Bishop of Gloucester.

In June 1994, Laurie was eighty. He told everyone his mother might have muddled the exact date; all she said was that 'I know it was Thursday because it was early closing.' Secret celebrations

were planned by Kathy and Susan Sandon of Penguin. On the hot sunny Saturday of 18 June, Penguin held a buffet lunch in the garden of the Chelsea Arts Club, and presented Laurie with a new stereo and a huge violin-shaped birthday cake. Among the guests were Elizabeth Jane Howard, Julian Bream, André Deutsch, the Cunard sisters Virginia and Pen, Antonia Young, Jim and Pam Rose, and the Eshers (the honeymoon couple from the Hotel Mediterráneo in 1935). Celia Goodman gave him a Schubert CD, Georgina Hammick gave him a pen. Sir Hugh Casson, Tony Lacey and Dr Geoffrey Dove made speeches; Laurie made a mischievously barbed one. John Martyn the singer happened to be staying in the club, and played an impromptu 'Johnny B. Goode'. For many Chelsea Arts Club members it was the first time they had met Kathy and Jessy: Laurie did not usually allow them to venture inside.

The Slad party was held in the garden of Down Court, home of Mrs Anne Mills, once used for the interior shots of Laurie's childhood home in the BBC's *Cider with Rosie*. The Woolpack cricket team took on Sheepscombe, and Laurie handed over the keys to the new pavilion for which he had paid, and gave the entire village a glass of beer. A ploughman's supper was served. There were fireworks and music from madrigal singers, and Laurie was toasted by Brian Jones, also eighty, whose uncle had been the Squire Jones of his childhood. Laurie raised his white stick aloft and invited everyone to his ninetieth.

He was actually rather ill that summer – though he looked hale and durable in his panama hat in the elegiac television film David Parker made for HTV of Laurie in his haunts in the valley. After a spell in hospital, he was told he absolutely should not fly, so he at once booked a flight to Málaga. With Kathy and Jessy he went back to the Stills' *castillo* at Almuñécar. He returned bronzed and invigorated, and dictated a letter to Kay Dunbar agreeing to speak at a 'Ways with Words' literary luncheon in Bath the following spring: 'I'm ghastly old and to your fellow revellers would appear like Banquo's ghost. On the other hand you mention that the immortal Frances Partridge might be with you, so I feel I could

hide behind her extra years and spirit.' There was a handwritten postscript: 'I used to play violin duets with Frances Partridge. She was more tuneful than I.' His talk was a triumph, says Kay Dunbar: everyone was moved by his warmth and humour. Laurie told his audience he still had a couple of books in him, if he could get hold of a magnifying typewriter: 'The trilogy stopped when I was twenty-three. I have such areas of life to cover: confessions, celebrations, marriage, infidelity, children.' Children? He had never publicly acknowledged 'children' before. Or infidelity.

He also told Clare Alexander of Penguin that he would produce another book – possibly based on his wartime diaries. She went to some trouble to acquire for him a magnifying typewriter; but he just could not write like that, with keyboard and screen. And he was too blind now to write by hand.

He still sometimes played a Bach sonata on his violin, but no longer attempted Paganini's 'Devil's Trill'. He preferred to listen to chamber music ('I don't want lots of hullabaloo'). Operatic voices gave him a sense of anxiety ('I don't like raised voices: they suggest domestic discord') and he never played what he called 'great gusts of roast-beef music – Elgar – blaring me out of the room'. He remained devoted to Schubert: 'a rare genius whose innocent yearning for affection was expressed in music as pure as spring water . . . a source of deep consolation to me'. When Classic FM asked for his choice of records in 1994, this was his list: 'Mozart's "Serenade" (tea shop trio); Suppé's "Poet & Peasant Overture" (light orchestra); Elgar's Violin Concerto (original Menuhin recording); Chaliapin (frag. *Boris Godunov*); Schubert's Trio No. 1 in B flat, D898 (slow movt) by Casals, Thibaud & Cortot; Bach's Double Violin Concerto (last mvt) Oistrakh father & son if poss; Mozart's String Quartet in D minor; "Recuerdos de la Alhambra" played by Julian Bream; and Mozart's Violin & Piano sonata frag. Allegro played by Laurie Lee with the pianist Denis Matthews.' (Laurie had played duets with the late Denis Matthews at the home of Jim and Pam Rose.)

On Radio 4, Kenneth Branagh was to be heard reading *As I Walked Out One Midsummer Morning* in a woefully inadequate voice – 'too

high and dry for such a lustrous text', said Gillian Reynolds in the *Telegraph*. 'The words came out as though he were peering at those great glowing descriptions through some dusty shop window.' The artist Don Grant, who painted the Princess of Wales and the Duchess of York naked under their Ascot hats, wrote to Laurie: 'What has that luvvie Branagh done to your book? Its beauty still shines through, like a handsome woman's face behind a veil, but why could you not have read it yourself?' Later that year Isis, the Oxford audiotape company which had recorded Laurie's incomparable voice reading the first two books in his trilogy, re-released them and Laurie signed 2,000 covers for the boxed sets.

As an octogenarian he was more than ever the favourite son of his valley. He opened a supermarket in Stroud on the site of the Ritz cinema of his boyhood, spurning a bouquet of flowers ('too Jilly Cooperish') in favour of a bottle of Jack Daniels. He joined Jilly and Joanna Trollope in campaigning to save Stroud Library, which had been his 'university'. He cut the ribbon at Hoyland House, a smart new NHS surgery at Painswick, describing himself as one of Dr Jim Hoyland's most indestructible patients: 'I think I first went to him when my voice broke. He's kept me going ever since.' He opened Painswick's annual Victorian street fair, where villagers wore period costume, arriving in a horse-drawn carriage in his panama hat and cream linen suit. Having an oft-stated aversion to the *New English Bible* (he was enraged that 'Arise, and take up thy bed and walk' should become 'Get up! pick up your mat and go home'), he was enlisted in the Tyndale quincentenary celebrations in Wotton under Edge. 'I stole many good things from Tyndale,' said Laurie.

He received a rapturous reception in the packed Stroud Subscription Rooms on a cold, wet Monday night in March 1995 when he spoke against plans to build ninety houses in the valley, now an Area of Outstanding Natural Beauty. Wrapped in a tartan blanket and stifling a hacking cough, with a temperature of 100 degrees, he apologized for speaking first but 'I am the oldest man here.'

The Slad valley, he said, was 'the green lung that feeds with refreshing air the town of Stroud. If we permit this to go ahead

without resistance, it will be a self-inflicted wound that not even time will heal. The word "development" is just a euphemism for ravagement and exploitation . . . The valley, with its landscape of tangled woods and sprawling fields, should be left to rabbits, badgers and old codgers like me.' Laurie had now 'fixed the valley, through his books, as part of our living archaeology', as Professor Peter Wilson of the Vatch wrote to the local paper. 'To destroy it now would be an act of monstrous environmental barbarism and economic folly.'

The *Daily Mail* asked him to write a piece about his campaign, and Val Hennessy agreed to write it for him, producing a credible parody of Laurie ('It was in these meadows where I breathed the first faint musks of sex and where Rosie Burdock shared her cider with me during hay-making, on a motionless day of summer . . .') and when it appeared, by-lined Laurie Lee, he told her they were paying him twice what she'd have got, 'and a number of my old chums and my publisher have phoned to say, "You're writing better than ever, Laurie."' This was possibly his last stand, he told John Ezard of the *Guardian*. 'But I don't want to spread the idea that I have possessive rights here. I have no wish to deny anyone a place to live in.'

But why stop at Stroud? In the new year of 1995, Laurie sent a plea for world peace to the *Stroud Journal*: 'May the Serbs, and the Croats, the Protestants and Catholics, the Israelis and Palestinians, the Scots and the English, Labour and Conservatives and disenchanted lovers everywhere shake hands and embrace and agree with each other at last.'

One day in April 1995 Laurie sat – shining white hair, bow tie, cherubic pink face – in the window of the crowded drawing-room of Lord and Lady Monson's Kensington house on their fortieth wedding anniversary. People queued to pay court to Laurie and he held forth. Emma Devas, Lady Monson, had asked him if he would like to say a few words; Laurie demurred, and she had been told he might not be up to it. So she turned to Leighton Thomson, the gentle and scholarly vicar of Chelsea Old Church, who had married

the Monsons (and had buried Emma's father Anthony Devas, and prepared Jessy for confirmation) and asked if he would kindly propose a toast. Five minutes later the vicar rose to speak – and so did Laurie. Laurie reminisced fondly about Emma's childhood, her roller-skating round Markham Square, and selling her paintings for sixpence from the doorstep. Leighton Thomson says he rather gave up in the face of such oratory ('Who needs a toast when there is magic like that?'). Lady Monson says: 'I have a photograph of me and Ivan in fits of laughter, with Leighton on one side and Laurie holding forth on the other. And nobody could get either of them to stop.'

Two months later Laurie's old wizardry seemed to be at work again. On 26 June 1995, his eighty-first birthday, Yasmin's daughter Esther had a son, William, Laurie's first great-grandson. 'It was the cream on the cake,' says Yasmin. Laurie sent William a gold watch.

As one who could spend a whole morning composing a letter of thanks, Laurie was now extremely busy. Christopher Fry, another literary monument (approaching ninety), who had once given Laurie a pipe 'so light it feels as if the tobacco is suspended in air', wrote a poem for Laurie for his eighty-first birthday at the West Country Writers' Association lunch in Torquay. Laurie was 'dumb-founded'; Fry's verses were 'so warm, artful and unexpected (I love the singing rhymes, & the brilliance of "gowp at" & "cowpat" . . .) Dear friend, you have been kinder to me than I can find thanks for, or the merit to deserve it.' A hotel in Cheltenham named its honeymoon suite 'the *Cider with Rosie* suite': 'Perhaps the bridal mattress could be stuffed with the finest hay,' Laurie suggested, 'with a jar of sweet cider by the bedside.' He presented them with a watercolour entitled 'Laurie Lee's Cottage' to hang on the wall.

He was now a grand-old-man literary survivor and relished the role. He said he had reached the stage of 'immaculate degeneration'. He presented the Society of Authors prizes in the great hall of King's College London. He was at Olympia for Penguin Books' sixtieth birthday party in March 1995. At the Foyle's luncheon in July, Spike Milligan didn't show up so Laurie was placed next to Claire Rayner. 'She thinks I'm Spike Milligan,' he told the *Times*

diarist, 'and has been laughing at my jokes very encouragingly.' Seamus Heaney, recently winner of the Nobel Prize for Literature, said at the Cheltenham Festival that the first time he had attended nearly thirty years ago he was runner-up in its poetry competition. 'I sat next to Laurie Lee, and that was a big high for me at the time.' When Laurie shared the Cheltenham stage with Andrew Motion, future Poet Laureate, there was no mistaking which of them was the star turn.

At the May 1995 Hay-on-Wye Literary Festival, he made a slow shuffling entry on to the stage, hand held aloft in a salute of thanks for the tumultuous welcome, 'a triumphal procession of one'. Bulmer's Cider were sponsoring his appearance. 'Bulmer's have been a great consolation to writers over the years,' he said in his countryman tones. As one reporter remarked, 'he has the gift of old-fashioned eloquence, schooled as he was on the Prayer Book and the King James Bible'. To the stock tale of the schoolgirls in Slad he had now added another, of how he used his white stick to ask for help in crossing the road from beautiful young women. 'I grip them,' he said, 'holding on with great craftiness . . . It is . . . elbows and things that I cling to. And then, when we are safely over, I say: Thank you very much, young man, you've been most helpful.' After his performance, the queue for his book signing was the longest in the festival. Bulmer's later gave a reception for him. He sipped Symond's Old Hazy with a Bulmer's employee called Rosie, and told her she was prettier than the original.

Jessy, who was now working with homeless families in Cromwell Street, Gloucester (later infamous as the scene of the Fred and Rose West murders), came home to live at Rose Cottage, her marriage having foundered. All three mourned when Jessy's horse the Red Baron died on Twelfth Night 1996. By this time Laurie had outlived several of his older friends. Princess Peg of Hesse still kept in touch as she whizzed between Aldeburgh and Salzburg. But in 1995 Pen Dugdale (now Loveday) died, having sold Bushton ten years before, and Tom Matthews died that year too, at ninety-four. Laurie wrote a tribute for the New College magazine, declaring that when Tom settled in England he brought with him a rare piece of America,

civilized urbanity and humour. 'Tom Matthews was a poet and a shepherd of poets . . . He loved words, their power and beauty . . . We remember Tom as a handsome paternal figure, generous, hospitable, catholic in his curiosities, who when sitting among his guests at dinner, would be as likely to break into a Mississippi Ragtime as to quote freely from Plutarch or Pound.' Laurie and Kathy went to Oxford for the opening of a new library, the McGregor/Matthews room at New College.[2]

'Laurie Lee is a literary legend,' declared the *Gloucestershire Echo*, as if people might not have noticed, in January 1996. 'The poet and storyteller who made the landscape of his childhood come alive is this county's most famous son.' He deserved a knighthood, they decided, as a just reward for his genius, and for 'continuing to fight to this very day to preserve some vestige of a bygone age that he so richly celebrated'. Henry Porter took up the cause in the *Telegraph*: 'He has given at least as much pleasure as Sir Kingsley Amis or Sir Victor Pritchett.' And what did Laurie think? 'Well, he did have the artist's ego,' said Tony Lacey.

But honoured or not, Laurie had, by his final year, achieved all the immortality an author could wish for. His name was invoked whenever Spain was mentioned, or rural life, or childhood, or Christmas. 'A Laurie Lee style childhood' was shorthand, however misguidedly, for a carefree idyll. In March 1996 an evening of Laurie's poetry and prose was organized at Cheltenham Ladies' College. Brian Patten sent a poem in which he imagined a grand-daughter of Rosie having to study Laurie's work at school. It began

> She's sitting in the back row of the class
> Warm and lank and dreaming . . .

and ended

> English literature demands
> That his verses be stripped bare
> Though I imagine Laurie would
> Rather do the same to her.

'It wasn't exactly respectable, but Laurie was delighted with it,' Patten says. 'He said the concert had been a bit like the kind you put on after someone's dead.' In May he was at the Chelsea Flower Show, in the green latticed tent of Jill, Duchess of Hamilton for her Flora for Fauna project (promoting plants that encourage butterflies): 'I have checked the various herbs in my garden,' Laurie wrote to her, 'and added buddleia and mignonette and look forward to floating waves of Peacock and Tortoiseshell which, launched by you, may even yet salvage our summer.'

On 28 June 1996 Michael Wishart died, of cancer, aged sixty-eight. At his funeral his mother Lorna, now eighty-five, prowled about with her familiar feline stride, stricken at losing her favourite son and soulmate, but still strong and unsentimental. Laurie sent a touching card, and he and Lorna planned to meet again, says Yasmin, but they never did. That summer Laurie went into hospital, and on the same day, a month after Michael's funeral, Lorna drove out in her car to go to mass and was hit by another car, breaking her collar-bone. She has never fully recovered from that accident.

Laurie, increasingly blind, had begun dictating all his letters to Kathy about seven years before. ('I am getting an aged aunt to type this for me . . .' he wrote wickedly to Val Hennessy. 'Yours through a glass darkly, but with the brightest love.') He also got Kathy to note down any odd thoughts he wanted to record. These had an increasingly valedictory tone:

'I've had a long bright life but now I feel the dark doors closing.'

'He left this life with a light laugh. All my best friends are dead, and some are not even my friends.'

'I don't know whether I owe more to women than they to me.'

'John Arlott, poet, whose voice painted the air with summer.'

'I'm still a going concern, but a little concerned about going.'

'Golden wedding conversation: "I'm proud of you." "I'm tired of you too."'

'Caught in my valley, the great doors closing on me

'The thread of light grows greener, the birds' cry sharper, as they prepare for spring.

'My room still cluttered with starts and endings will at length be sorted, and I hope forgiven.'

In summer 1996 Laurie collapsed, and was taken to the Royal Gloucester Hospital by Kathy. There was fluid on his lung and he was told he should be admitted straight away. Laurie refused, and was allowed to go home as long as he came back that evening. 'It was the one time I cried,' Kathy says, 'because it suddenly came to me that he might be dying.' At home, Laurie issued orders about various pieces of writing left lying around his room. After two weeks in hospital, he came home much better. (He rang me, sounding chipper, on 17 October 1996, promising to arrange a lunch at the Chelsea Arts one day soon, to discuss this book.) That autumn, he was frail, but still well enough to come to London.

Antonia, now a widow, and having begun a new career as a sculptor, bought a Georgian house on the river, at Hammersmith Terrace, and invited Laurie for lunch in the garden. 'I felt he blessed this garden,' she says. 'It was important to me that he'd seen it and approved of it.' The pretty grandmother clock that Laurie found for her when she first had a house of her own stands in the hall; and a bust of Laurie, sculpted by Antonia, looks out from a corner of her drawing-room towards the garden and the river. 'I'm passionate about the view of the river, and I wanted him to see it.'

In November 1996, the Imperial War Museum held a sixtieth anniversary celebration for veterans of the International Brigades. Laurie clung on, to the end, to his Spanish Civil War veteran status. A 1995 Radio 4 programme, *The Art of Travel*, had featured Laurie telling again the story of how, during the Civil War, he had spread his coat on an altar and slept on it and how the desecration still haunted him. Listeners and critics were moved by this confession. That year, the Spanish parliament granted Spanish citizenship to all those who had fought in the International Brigades. (Juan Negrín, the Republic's prime minister, had long ago promised this in return for their courage, and now that Franco was dead the promise could be fulfilled.) Fewer than 500 veterans were still alive, eighty-two of them in Britain. It was reported that Bill Alexander welcomed

the news on behalf of the Britons who fought in Spain, 'including Laurie Lee, the author'. Laurie went to the Imperial War Museum, mingling with veterans who were all (including Laurie) wearing their medals. He re-encountered Martha Gellhorn, who had been a reporter in the Civil War, and had a long chat with the Spanish ambassador, proudly showing him his ancient passport with its stamp '*sale sin dinero*' from February 1938.

Early in January 1997 Laurie signed, in a shaky hand, his last contract: a £1,000 advance on the Robson Books edition of *The Firstborn*, which was to be published in May. Laurie signed book-plates, and wrote to Jeremy Robson: 'Mother and daughter doing well and much pleased by being born again.' In March, his agent wrote to say he would soon be receiving his £35,000 tranche of Penguin's five-year renewal licence covering the paperbacks of *Cider with Rosie* and *A Rose for Winter*.

On 16 February 1997 Laurie went into hospital for tests. 'The signs upon me do not presage bright news,' he wrote to his doctor, Roddy Jaques. Bowel cancer was diagnosed, and an operation arranged. Laurie began dictating many letters. He wrote to Clare Francis about her wish to become a member of the Chelsea Arts Club, 'which I'm sure no one could deny you . . . but I'm going into hospital this weekend and will therefore be unable to become one of your loyal lobbyists. Also as an honorary member of the Club I'm officially denied a vote. But I do hope that when I rise from my bed and return to London, I shall find you there, adorning the bar or the spring flowers in the garden.'

On 12 March Laurie wrote to Antonia, whose exhibition of her sculptures was to take place in April, before she had started her head of Laurie: 'I'm so very sorry not to be able to come to your grand multi-talented show. I had been looking forward to this, and to having my breath taken away with admiration, but unfortunately, I'm going into hospital. I know that your exquisitely fashioned heads will be a great success (even though one is missing). I'll be thinking of you. Love, Laurie.'

He wrote to his investment manager checking on the valuation of his funds. 'The various dividends continue to arrive,' he said,

'though spaced out like Marathon runners . . .' He even dictated a letter to an actress playing the part of his mother in *Cider with Rosie*: 'Dear Mum, I'm so glad to hear that you've agreed to carry the Lee banner to the outside world, and with it all the colour and wild dignity of the original. I send my warmest love to you – and to Rosie lying in the long summer grasses. I will be thinking of you on the night of the opening, and may my loyal spirit accompany all of you always.'

In his interview with Mavis Nicholson, eight years before, he had told her how he would sit and watch the landscape from his window, finding it more precious now than he had in childhood: 'a grand kind of extravaganza with no beginning and no end. Everything is ordered, the graveyard beyond me has a quiet sense of expectancy, it's waiting for me, and that will be my second home, and I will be back in my roots. I acknowledge that with a feeling of gratitude because I know where I am, I know where my beginning was, and I know that will be my end, and I am quite ready for it when it happens.'

On his way into the Royal Gloucester Hospital for the last operation, he told Kathy and Jessy what he wanted engraved on his tombstone: 'He lies in the valley he loved.'

Kathy and Jessy understood Laurie's insistence on coming home from hospital to die. 'I have a terror of medical authority,' he had said in 1987. 'I think, please don't let me fall into their hands. Let me be born at home, stay at home, die at home.' He told Jessy, 'Promise me that I'm not going back in there,' and she assured him he would never go far from her again, ever. 'I said, "We'll do it by magic," and we brought him home on 1 May 1997, the day the Labour government was elected. He was *compos mentis* enough to be elated about that, and we drank a toast "to Labour, Love and Laurie" . . .' They moved his bed downstairs, so that he could see his view of his valley, in the sunny sitting-room. Antonia sent flowers, and Kathy wrote to her: 'L was so pleased. In spite of all his vagueness he kept telling me to move them here, no, move them there, no, have them against the white table and so on.'

During Laurie's last days in May, Kathy kept a constant vigil,

and Jessy was there all day; with the help of Dr Jaques and two district nurses, Teresa Creton and Gay Seguro, they managed. His retired GP, Dr Jim Hoyland, called. Dr Geoffrey Dove too arrived from the Chelsea Arts Club. 'Geoffrey was with us on the last day. He saved all our lives,' Kathy says. As Laurie's mind began to falter, Jessy would get him to recite his poems with her. 'I managed to recite "April Rise" by heart to him. "If ever I saw blessing in the air . . ." and "Slow moves the acid breath of noon . . ."'

The last days passed with the aid of Mr Kipling's baby treacle sponges, and morphine when necessary. They made sure Laurie was in no pain. The day before he died, he called out to Kathy. 'Cathy, come here.' 'Yes, Lol?' 'I've got a secret,' he said. She said, 'Yes?' Jessy was listening. Both waited. But Laurie said nothing more.

There was a baby alarm in the kitchen, so they could hear his every breath. Kathy says she knew beforehand when he was going to die. 'And even though he was unconscious, he still called out "Mum" and she held on to his hands,' Jessy says. 'Suddenly there was this tiny little moan, it was like a wailing song. Oh, oh! We thought he had enough morphine in him to knock out anyone. It sounded like a tormented soul from purgatory: I've had nightmares that he might have been trying to say something. I had a very strange two hours with him before he died; I grieved with him. I could feel him going, in my solar plexus. I sent him away on his journey with Schubert's Quintet in C. It was our music, his and mine. I played it three times, and by then I wanted him to die, to go and be free from earthly torment. In so many ways he was tormented, all his life; such a tormented man.'

Kathy was pleased that she had preserved 'Laurie's fantasy' of his two women; that he was able to die with just his two women around him, 'enclosing him in a double embrace, like bookends', and nobody else. 'At least he was able to have entirely what he wanted at the very end. He could hear our voices. And we were both able to say goodbye. At the moment of death, he looked so young, and sun-tanned, he smelt lovely and he looked lovely.' Kathy went in to spend the last five minutes with him, while Jessy

listened from the kitchen. 'I heard Mum say, "It's all right. Go now. We'll be together soon," and she raised her hand above his head and gently drew it along the length of his body – as if to help him on his way.'

It was Tuesday, 13 May 1997. 'It was so magical, powerful and poignant, the actual moment he died,' Jessy says. 'Everything went golden, an extraordinary light filled the house. And there was a brilliant rainbow right across the valley, so astonishing that many people in the valley photographed it – such a strange phenomenon, in black sky. A transcending moment. And it was so quiet that he was instantly gone and away.

'I looked at my watch and it was 9.25 and all of a sudden I heard his last breath and I had a feeling of such strength – his strength perhaps. And we went into the garden and danced, and then picked masses of white tea roses, Dad's favourite – and sprinkled their petals on him. We had this extraordinary sensation rushing up through our feet and we just had to dance.'

The funeral in Slad on Tuesday, 20 May 1997 was a village and family-only affair. Brother Jack came home from Australia. Jessy carried a spray of lily-of-the-valley, as Kathy had on her wedding day. In light summer rain, his coffin was borne up the path opposite the Woolpack to the churchyard. Laurie had insisted that he should not be buried in the new graveyard above the church; he must be in the lower churchyard. He had said: 'I came back here because starting as a scruffy little scab-kneed boy, and going round the world, in many countries, I've never found a place which has such intimate significance for me. The trees, the very slope of the valleys are so intensely special to me. I want to be buried between the pub and the church, so that I can balance the secular and the spiritual, and my long sleep will be punctuated by rowdy Saturday nights in the Woolpack, and Sunday morning worship in the church. It would give me a feeling of continuity.' His poem 'April Rise' was read in the church:

If ever I saw blessing in the air
I see it now in this still early day
Where lemon-green the vaporous morning drips
Wet sunlight on the powder of my eye.

Laurie's obituaries eulogized him as a national treasure and a local landmark – a writer rooted in a particular place, like Hardy in Dorset, and the Brontës in Haworth. When Laurie had greeted his readers in Slad, it was 'as if Dickens had shown tourists round his blacking factory'.[1] The obituarists hymned his 'voluptuous, enamelled style', his skilful way of treading 'the slippery path between myth and memoir'.[2] They allowed him to retain his secrets: 'I am a person of concealment. No one has ever managed to get through.'[3] Some pointed out that Laurie's output was slender. But Jane Mack, who had made a study of Laurie's work, argued in the *Guardian* that his range and scope were wider than was generally supposed: the poetry alone 'ranged from Lorca-inspired surrealism to war poetry in the spirit of Wilfred Owen', there were three verse plays, several film scripts, and 'even in his MOI report, *Land at War*, his style shines through ... Who but Laurie Lee could make an official document read like prose poetry?'[4]

He was 'A Many-Coated Man', which was the title borrowed for Laurie's memorial service at St James's, Piccadilly, in October 1997. His BBC friend Jock Gallagher gathered a dozen men who had known Laurie in his several coats: as poet, musician, traveller, clubman, countryman. Laurie's army greatcoat cloaked him in secretiveness, Gallagher said: he imagined Laurie 'looking down on us with childlike delight at the difficulty we have in pinning him down'. Fellow poets Christopher Fry, Brian Patten and Roger McGough read their own poems for Laurie. P.J. Kavanagh read Laurie's poem 'The Pollard Beech'. McGough said that when his own late-born first daughter arrived, in his early fifties, Laurie told him to enjoy it: 'Before you know where you are she'll be asking you for money.'

John Mortimer recalled Laurie sending him off on his bicycle

from Pinewood Studios to Watford Junction – the beginning of his writing career. Richard Ryan, then Irish ambassador in Madrid, recounted having told Laurie, in their last conversation, of a recent visit to Segovia. Cunning gypsy women had stolen his wife's handbag. 'Dear boy,' Laurie said, 'don't be boring. Don't tell me about handbags. Tell me about their eyes, their teeth, their hair.' David Blunkett, Education Secretary, recalled his glass of cider with Laurie in the Woolpack. After the service, there was a wake at the packed Chelsea Arts Club. The sculptor Lynn Bamber's head of Laurie was on display for the first time. It toppled over, luckily unharmed, on the billiard table.

But Laurie did not rest in peace. On 31 December 1997, in the *Spectator*, an article by Simon Courtauld ('A Not Very Franco Account') commemorated the battle of Teruel sixty years before. Courtauld had spoken to Bill Alexander, who repeated all his old doubts about *A Moment of War*. Courtauld himself added that Laurie's dates in the book did not make sense. Reporters rang Kathy, who was 'angry and upset' that Laurie's account should be questioned now that he could no longer answer for himself.

To several journalists – and to me, in the very week I had embarked on writing this book – Bill Alexander said he was sorry that Laurie had not made *A Moment of War* a novel. He admired Laurie's writing and was always grateful that he dedicated his book 'To the defeated'. But he felt he must now put the record straight since a recent book, *Britain and the Spanish Civil War*, by Tom Buchanan, had cited Laurie's account as fact, and it might now be read by history students. (In fact, Buchanan's use of Laurie's material was not all that misleading. He commended Laurie's book for its 'sense of tragedy and futility'. In his chapter on 'Intellectuals', he related Laurie's dispiriting journey to Albacete, adding, 'Lee's war did not last long: after taking part in the desperate fighting at Teruel he suffered a temporary breakdown and was sent home.')

The reaction of most writers was summed up by the novelist Allan Massie, who declared that it was naïve to expect a poet's version of events to be historically accurate. He cited other authors

– Waugh, Ford Madox Ford, Orwell – whose impressionistic, imaginative memoirs contained novelistic episodes. 'Hemingway's *A Moveable Feast* is full of invention or, if you prefer, packed with lies. Yet this book gives a keener sense of what it felt like to be young in Paris than any reconstruction by a scrupulous historian could provide.'[5]

Laurie's old friends were not terribly shaken by the fuss. 'After all, *A Moment of War* does not pretend to be a heroic book,' Jim Rose said. 'It is the story of lamentable failure . . . It is an unvaunting book.' Michael Still likened the book to an abstract painting: 'Writers represent their own truth as painters do; they select, adapt and transmute, based on an original truth, but taking artistic licence.' The poet Vernon Scannell, a gallant soldier himself, pointed out that Laurie's previous books had been 'full of the fanciful exaggerations common to the genre'. Scannell suspected that for romantic Laurie, whose Ministry work in the last war had been useful but scarcely heroic, 'the imagined drama of bloodshed, heroism and sacrifice possessed a powerful fascination'.[6] It didn't matter whether his experiences were factually true.

'I don't care two hoots, myself,' his fellow poet Ted Walker agreed. 'A good tale is a good tale. What does an artist ever do but select? I don't suppose what Laurie and Rosie did under that cart was exactly as described – but so what? It's Truth we're after, not boring old quotidian lower-case truth.'[7] Writers' autobiographies – and their letters – are choreographed performances, often embellished. In 1927 V.S. Pritchett set out to write a book, *Marching Spain*, about walking across Spain. He slept in *ventas* on stone floors with peasant families, and 'once shared a pigsty with very clean piglets'. Nobody ever dreamed of accusing Pritchett of being dishonest, but as he revealed in 1970, he had been 'purposely silent about knowing Spain already [he had actually been living in Spain for some time as a foreign correspondent] because I wanted to preserve an instantaneous impression'.

'It comes as no surprise to me that some old tankie would crawl out of the woodwork to smear an author's name, after he's safely dead, of course,' wrote a *Guardian* reader in Manchester.[8] He

argued, as did the writer Michael Eaude, that the objectors were all lifelong committed Communists, who 'have been disseminating disinformation about the Spanish civil war since 1936' and would always view with disfavour Laurie's less partisan view of the political commissariat.

Meanwhile Dr Barry McLoughlin, an Irish historian based in Vienna, who had been researching in Moscow's Comintern archive, had examined the files of the International Brigades. He had seen documents relating to Laurie's early days in war-torn Spain. In these[9] (quoted in Chapter 7 of this book) Laurie was singled out from the volunteers by Bob Doyle for his excellent conduct despite his illness. In the report by the American officer Constantino Dubac on a group transferred from Figueras to Albacete, Laurie was described as 'willing to do his best for the revolution' and recommended for an unstrenuous post at a base camp, as he seemed 'a responsible person and trustworthy'. Here was clear evidence that Laurie had indeed joined the International Brigades in December 1937, before he 'fell with a fever below the Bahía de Rosas', as his poem 'The Return' put it, 'letting the mad snow spit in my eyes'.

McLoughlin paid further visits to the Comintern archives during 1998 and furnished me with many documents. He identified Laurie's comrades, and his likely interrogators, including the American 'Sam', who was probably Tony de Maio, a sinister US officer who worked for Servicio de Investigación Militar, Spanish military intelligence. (Later de Maio was accused by ex-volunteers of being involved in the shooting of Americans in Spain.) Laurie was certainly transferred from Tarazona to the Cultural Commission, where his musical gifts may well have been put to good use. But his activities during the first five weeks of 1938 remain unverifiable. During the Teruel conflict, in which the British participated from 31 December to 3 February, all the volunteers who had arrived with Laurie were still being trained at Tarazona.

Some of his adventures are chronologically impossible; some seem far-fetched, particularly the Eulalia interludes. But it is highly probable that Laurie was cross-examined and detained when it was discovered from his passport that he had been in Morocco in March

1936, at precisely the place and time Franco was mustering his rebel army. It is perfectly credible that he was summoned by name from his comrades in the barrack square for interrogation, as he recounts, since the Party hierarchy had been alerted by Wilma to look out for him and to send him home. Dr McLoughlin discovered that a similar band of eight newly-arrived British volunteers were detained at Figueras and then sent home because the group contained an epileptic, one man with tuberculosis and another so physically weak he 'looked like a wet bird'. Bob Doyle, who wrote the first report on Laurie, is now in his mid-eighties. He was captured soon afterwards, and spent the rest of the war imprisoned near Burgos, never imagining that what he wrote in 1937 would be exhumed from a Moscow vault sixty years later, to verify Laurie's presence. Dr McLoughlin has letters from the Salamanca and Barcelona archives stating that they have no records of any imprisonment of Laurie Lee. The death cell episodes must be imagined.

So Laurie's eye-witness story of the Spanish Civil War remains touching and vivid (as to atmosphere) and imaginative (as to hard fact). It must rest in the no man's land between history and invention. He had, when all was said and done, made the brave gesture, crossed the Pyrenees in a blizzard; and nobody denies that his book gave an almost cinematically vivid impression of what it felt like to be in Spain and under bombardment in the bloody winter of 1937 – the same kind of impression as that given in Ken Loach's 1996 film, *Land and Freedom*. 'Ill-fed and ill-armed, many of these young men died,' as he wrote. 'The survivors returned home to ignominy. But to me this seems to have been the last time that the young had a cause they could believe in and could fight from the heart.'[10] Why he should invent anything remains a mystery: his real story was a good one anyway.

In the year after his death, I learned not to dismiss any of Laurie's stories lightly. The girl from Buenos Aires who had taught Laurie to ask for a glass of water in Spanish might have sounded like a romantic fantasy, until the summer of 1998, when I came across the '*lección en castellano*' letter from Sufi Rogers. Days later, Kathy opened the door to a small moustachioed man from Buenos Aires.

It was Sufi's younger brother, back in Slad for a visit, who confirmed that the unlikely tale was entirely true.

Laurie's two women realized how much they had depended upon him. Kathy had devoted fifty years to Laurie. Now she was the keeper of the flame: presenting the Laurie Lee Memorial Cup at Sheepscombe Cricket Club, attending various Laurie Lee tributes and celebrations in Gloucestershire (including *¡No Pasarán!* – a performance of Spanish Civil War songs and poems by Stroud Football Poets). She and Jessy set about clearing out his Chelsea flat. Laurie had stipulated in his will that his three appointed trustees should sell the flat to help provide income. Jessy moved into Rose Cottage, efficiently refashioned it, and decided to deploy her highly vibrant personality in studying psychotherapy, since she had found analysis helpful in exploring the problems which she saw as rooted in her childhood.

A school-age reader had once written to ask Laurie: 'What frightens you in our modern world?'

'Ignorance, racism, nationalism and intolerance,' he replied. He was not a philosopher, he told the same child. 'The term "philosopher" suggests an academic and conscious theoretical mind at work. I am an observer. My reactions to life are intuitive rather than analytical.'

He had started out in life with so little – no money, small education, absolutely no connections, and parlous health. He had to survive entirely by his wits. But he was remarkably blessed, in his mother, in his artistic talents, in his wife, and in his friends. As Yasmin says, Laurie's orbit was an extremely magnetizing one. Charm is a gift, as he wrote, 'only given to give away, and the more used the more there is'. Everyone mentions how Laurie charmed and beguiled them; how he gave all his attentiveness, his listening absorption.

It was impossible not to love Laurie, when working on his life. I loved the fact that he turned his face to the sun, and became mahogany brown every summer. I loved his fine clear handwriting,

and the care he took over crafting his prose, in soft pencil on the backs of old radio scripts: 'I couldn't write on clean paper – it would seem too valuable. I'd get inhibited. As it is, I can turn over and it says, "Good morning, Mrs Dale, and how are you today?" and I feel comforted.'

He copied down into his 1954 diary a Lancashire dialect poem (anonymous) called 'Micky Thumps'. I longed to tell him that I too had copied down 'Micky Thumps' in my diary in 1962. Its last heart-wringing lines are:

Some stamped on his grave
Some spat on his grave
But I scraped my eyes out for my old friend Micky Thumps.[11]

I loved Laurie for according humour a proper place in his life by making a note of jokes:

– A notice in the grocer's: 'Please do not sit on the counters, as we are getting behind with our orders.'

– Edgar Allan Poe – otherwise known as the Chamber of Horrors.

– Bull to his herd: 'I love you for heifer and heifer.'

– 'Can you tell me the way to Rillington Place?' 'Sorry, I'm a strangler here myself.'

– Judging a poetry competition, finding dozens of poems from an old General, all about hooves ringing out on frosty roads: 'a slight case of Tallyhosis'.

– Why do they never say 'old', always 'elderly'? Elderly Tyme Dancing. Elderly King Cole was a merry elderly soul. The Elderly Bailey.

– The sound of the hoover: the dentist's drill of marriage.

– A succinct summing up of the life cycle: Sperms, germs, worms.

'I often make such good jokes asleep I wake myself up laughing,' Laurie wrote in his Dreams notebook. 'I like dreams. They give me special powers. I can talk foreign languages and commit crimes. I am possessed with the gift of argument. I have put many a bishop in his place and even corrected the Pope on a point of ritual.'

In his poem 'Night Speech', Laurie extols the powers bestowed by dreams:

This fur-lined hour
Makes princes of each wretch
whose day-bed wasted,
points each lax tongue
to daggered brightness,
says what we could not say.

He began invading my dreams too. In one, I drove Laurie in my car to his brother Jack's front door in Sydney, telling him: 'Laurie, we're going to see Jack' – and then woke with a start of disappointment. I suppose I longed to reunite them after their long estrangement, which persisted even when Jack's second wife Isabel died of cancer in 1985. 'A strange thing,' Jack told me wistfully, 'all these years gone by & so many of them wasted. We could have had such a wonderful relationship – we did for a few years, wrestling on the grass banks of the Slad valley – & it all came to such a wretched end. Alas now it is too late – like so many things – no way back, no recriminations, only sadness which will never go away.' Jack's will specifies that he will be cremated and his ashes scattered on Swift's Hill. 'Won't Laurie be mad when he looks across the valley from his beautiful grave in Slad churchyard, and there's me smoking away up there. Ashes Jack.'

Laurie proved a most addictive, obsessional character to live with. I began to have Laurie-like coincidental encounters. On the tiny Canary island of La Gomera, I was reading Laurie's poems when I looked up to see, at the next table, Brian Patten – whom I had just met when he read his poem at Laurie's memorial. We ended up joining in a wild New Year's Eve dancing party along with Spanish families, grandfathers, señoritas and children, in just the kind of scruffy *taberna* that Laurie liked.

Spain is still seething with Laurie's characters: a cadaverous Cervantes lookalike, playing a guitar in a square in Granada; a

woman dancing down the street with babe in arms; a circle of old men holding hands in the Plaza Mayor in Madrid; a raven-haired, blue-eyed *gitana* named Carmen, of startling grace and beauty, in the caves of Sacromonte; and everywhere dwarves and beggars and brazen-eyed waiters. Much has changed in Spain, but much remains as Laurie saw it.

In Laurie's second home, the Chelsea Arts Club, the poets and artists and hangers-on are still in the bar; his absence is almost palpable. Cars hurtle through the centre of Slad, and most of Laurie's contemporaries have gone, but in the Woolpack villagers convene round the fire; Annie's cottage is still there down its steep bank; and a hundred yards away his old friend Jack Eyers the dry-stone waller still keeps bees at the cottage in which he was born.

Exactly a year after Laurie's death, the village was taken over by television cameras again, for Adrian Bate's new version of *Cider with Rosie*. Laurie had stipulated to Bate, five years earlier, that he must not show a rose-tinted picture of village life but its darker side, and must reflect the multi-faceted character of Annie. After Laurie died, John Mortimer set to work on his screenplay and when Juliet Stevenson was cast as Laurie's mother, she read Annie's letters in preparation. Rose Cottage became the location for the pub. Cousin Charlie's grandson, John Light, played Phyllis's beau, Harold. Laurie's own voice, recorded on tape in 1988, was used for the narration, the film's ace card when it was shown at Christmas in 1998. *Cider with Rosie* remains among the twentieth-century classics which will endure in the next millennium. It is fixed in the canon. It is a catchphrase; frequently used by headline-writers and cartoonists (e.g. Two tramps drinking cider in a gutter: 'It all started with a girl named Rosie . . .' says one. Or a computer screen that reads 'Cyber With Rosie').

As Kathy, Jessy and I talked of Laurie over the kitchen table, we laughed about what he would say if he knew we were discussing and dissecting him. They said he would say: 'That's right – go on – tear me to pieces, you women. I'm off to the pub.'

A reader had once asked him how he saw women. He wrote:

'Submissives, dominators, predators, inspirers. Women are closer to the earth and to creation than men are. They are guardians of life and chroniclers of social history, and are of course men's supreme motivation for both physical and mental action.' Women were certainly his inspiration, his muses and mentors. In his last years he was planning to write another book, using his wartime journals,[12] which have many paragraphs marked by Laurie in red ink, and pieces of paper slipped between the pages indicating episodes he intended to relate. 'I still have much left to confess and celebrate,' Laurie had said in August 1992.

Laurie may have been, in his own words, 'a person of conceal-ment' but his entire opus consisted of fragments of autobiography: 'a celebration of living and an attempt to hoard its sensations'. He urged others always to take notes, especially if they travelled: 'There is nothing that preserves things so much as writing . . . And nothing obliterates the memory so much as not taking the trouble to make a record of it at the time. You do it in order to arrest time, and fix it in the mind, to perhaps cheat mortality to a point. I think that's as much as my writing aims to do, nothing more.'[13] As I sat in his study in Slad, on his leather swivel chair, gazing out on his view of Swift's Hill and the slanting shadows, I was grateful that Laurie, like all heart-and-soul writers, had hoarded his letters 'exhaling the heated breath of girls', and recorded the minutiae of his life so graphically. 'A day unremembered is like a soul unborn, worse than if it had never been,' as he wrote. 'What indeed was that summer if it is not recalled? That journey? That act of love? . . . Any bits of warm life preserved by the pen are trophies snatched from the dark . . .'

Appendix

Dear Mr Lee

Dear Mr Lee (Mr Smart says
it's rude to call you Laurie, but that's
how I think of you, having lived with you
really all year), Dear Mr Lee
(Laurie) I just want you to know
I used to hate English, and Mr Smart
is roughly my least favourite person,
and as for Shakespeare (we're doing him too)
I think he's a national disaster, with all those jokes
that Mr Smart has to explain why they're jokes,
and even then no one thinks they're funny,
And T. Hughes and P. Larkin and that lot
in our anthology, not exactly a laugh a minute,
pretty gloomy really, so that's why
I wanted to say Dear Laurie (sorry) your book's
the one that made up for the others, if you
could see my copy you'd know it's lived
with me, stained with Coke and Kit-kat
and when I had a cold, and I often
take you to bed with me to cheer me up
so Dear Laurie, I want to say sorry,
I didn't want to write a character-sketch
of your mother under headings, it seemed
wrong somehow when you'd made her so lovely,
and I didn't much like those questions
about *social welfare in the rural community*
and *the seasons as perceived by an adolescent*,
I didn't think you'd want your book

read that way, but bits of it I know by heart,
and I wish I had your uncles and your half-sisters
and lived in Slad, though Mr Smart says your view
of the class struggle is naïve and the examiners
won't be impressed by me knowing so much by heart,
they'll be looking for terse and cogent answers
to their questions, but I'm not much good at terse and cogent,
I'd just like to be like you, not mind about being poor,
see everything bright and strange, the way you do,
and I've got the next one out of the Public Library,
about Spain, and I asked Mum about learning
to play the fiddle, but Mr Smart says Spain isn't
like that any more, it's all Timeshare villas
and Torremolinos, and how old were you
when you became a poet? (Mr Smart says for anyone
with my punctuation to consider poetry as a career
is enough to make the angels weep.)
Dear Laurie, please don't feel guilty for
me failing the exam, it wasn't your fault,
it was mine, and Shakespeare's,
and maybe Mr Smart's, I still love *Cider*,
it hasn't made any difference.

U.A. FANTHORPE

Notes

1 | Annie Light of Sheepscombe

1. 'somewhat wildly': *Cider with Rosie*, 'Mother'.
2. 'ordinary poverty': ibid.
3. Critchley Bros: now Critchley Electrical Products of Brimscombe.
4. 'with rooks in the chimneys': *Cider with Rosie*, 'First Light'.
5. 'to better himself': Marjorie, interviewed in 'Vintage Cider' on Radio 4 in November 1984.
6. 'too honest, too natural': *Cider with Rosie*, 'Mother'.
7. 'appreciate books': Marjorie, 'Vintage Cider'.
8. 'the Rosie of the title': *Times Literary Supplement*, 20 November 1959.
9. 'mother like that': E.B. Mais, *Yorkshire Post*, 13 November 1959.
10. 'splendidly and richly mothered': Kate O'Brien, *Irish Times*, 28 December 1959.
11. 'and I wish for her own modest sake': letter from L.L. to Wilma Gregory, 14 June 1960.

2 | A Steep Cotswold Valley (1918–31)

1. 'herbaceous smugness of the English countryside': 'A Drink with a Witch', *Leader Magazine*, reproduced in *I Can't Stay Long*.
2. 'ordinary diseases like whooping cough': L.L. interviewed by John Cunningham, *Guardian*, 23 December 1971.
3. 'life was a glass-bottomed boat': *Daily Mail*, 1976.
4. The Bird and Tree essay competition was organized annually by the Royal Society for the Protection of Birds. Seventy years later L.L. confessed that he had never observed the dabchick and had made up the entire essay (*Daily Mail*, 22 January 1994).
5. 'a tunnel for my clockwork train': 'True Adventures of the Boy

Reader', *New York Times Book Review*, reproduced in *I Can't Stay Long*.

6. 'question my liberties': L.L. reminiscing in 1989 to Christopher Cook on Radio 3.
7. 'gave her a lot of silence': from 'Things I Wish I'd Known at Eighteen', interview with Frank Entwisle, *Sunday Express* magazine, 5 July 1981.
8. 'order the earth to bloom': L.L. writing about his garden in *Homes & Gardens*, June 1962.

3 | 'The well-loved stranger' (1932–4)

1. 'enveloped by love': 'Things I Wish I'd Known at Eighteen'.
2. 'never put it on paper': ibid.
3. 'taught me a few words of Spanish': L.L. interviewed by Christopher Eldon Lee, Radio 3, 2 July 1992.
4. 'If only I'd known': 'Things I Wish I'd Known at Eighteen'.
5. 'felt it all and suffered': ibid.
6. 'Marry, and settle down': *As I Walked Out One Midsummer Morning*, 'London Road'.

4 | Laurie Walks Out (1934–5)

1. 'a fluid young girl of sixteen': *As I Walked Out One Midsummer Morning*, 'London Road'.
2. Philip O'Connor, surrealist poet: his *Collected Poems 1936–66* were published by Jonathan Cape. He died in 1998.
3. 'the life of Reilly': L.L. in an *Evening Standard* article about his teenage years, December 1960.
4. The naval mutiny of Invergordon, Scapa Flow: in 1931 in the Firth of Cromarty, 12,000 ratings stalled fifteen ships for two days over pay rates imposed by the National Government that left them with 15s a week.
5. 'brown as an apostle': *As I Walked Out One Midsummer Morning*, 'London'.

6. Eric Coates (1886–1957): composer of many famous signature tunes including 'Knightsbridge', which introduced *In Town Tonight*; 'By the Sleepy Lagoon' (*Desert Island Discs*), 'Calling All Workers' (*Music While You Work*) and later, 'The Dam Busters March'.

7. 'He can't be my father': L.L. in conversation with Val Hennessy.

5 | 'Un vaso de agua' (1935–6)

1. 'held no memories for me': *As I Walked Out One Midsummer Morning*, 'Into Spain'.

2. 'voices that carried from hill to hill': *Daily Mail*, 12 February 1995.

3. John King: BBC film director, who made films of *As I Walked Out* and *A Rose for Winter*.

4. 'intimately shared with them': L.L. interviewed by Christopher Eldon Lee, Radio 3, 2 July 1992.

5. 'walked tall and talked tall': from L.L.'s foreword to *Light on a Dark Horse*, Roy Campbell's autobiography, first published 1951; repr. Hollis & Carter, 1969.

6. 'bizarre children': Michael Wishart in his autobiography, *High Diver*, Blond & Briggs, 1977.

7. 'easy to break in': Roy Campbell, *Light on a Dark Horse*.

8. 'gentleman with a park': ibid.

9. 'Weald Village post office': from *Vita*, the biography of V. Sackville-West by Victoria Glendinning, Weidenfeld & Nicolson, 1983.

10. 'like a firefly': *As I Walked Out One Midsummer Morning*, 'Toledo'.

11. 'drinking like a madman': Anna Campbell Lyle, in *Poetic Justice*, a memoir of her father, Typographeum, Francestown, New Hampshire, 1986.

12. 'one of my favourite names': L.L. to Val Hennessy, in the *Mail on Sunday*, 13 November 1988.

13. The township of Almuñécar has published a memorial journal. 'Almuñécar en la obra de Laurie Lee', an essay published in June 1998, was a collaboration between IES Antigua Sexi, the educational institute's geography and history faculty, and the municipality's department of culture.

14. 'possibly with a friend': there were two accounts of L.L.'s trip to Morocco in *A Moment of War*. 'I'd made a quick trip to Morocco with a French student from Arles . . . we'd spent most of our time in the rooms of small hotels, behind shutters, smoking hash', and 'my journey to Morocco had been solitary, innocent but damning'.

15. 'solid argument': Wilma's thesis was that feminists were mistaken to concentrate on higher education. Instead, women should try to gain a share in the control of industry – though as Rebecca West pointed out, Wilma did not explain how this was to be achieved 'by a sex almost entirely innocent of capital'.

16. 'off the menu': letters from H.G. Wells quoted in *The Young Rebecca, Writings of Rebecca West 1911–1917*, selected by Jane Marcus, Macmillan/Virago, 1982.

17. *Penguin New Writing*: the quarterly review containing examples of recent poetry and prose edited by John Lehmann and published by Penguin.

6 | A Hovel with Acreage (1936–7)

1. Padworth is still a small village tucked away off the A4, with charming Norman church, St John the Baptist, and ancient yew tree in the graveyard. Padworth House, whose last scion died in 1932, is now a college. Padworth has not been developed, thanks to its proximity to the Atomic Weapons Establishment at Aldermaston. No trace of Rosemary Cottage, the hovel with acreage, remains.

2. 'thin, hungry, and gorgeous': from Mavis Nicholson's TV interview 'Mavis Catches Up With . . .', 1989.

3. 'back of boys' motorbikes': Yasmin David in conversation with V.G.

4. 'treated me as a doll': Michael Wishart, *High Diver*.

5. 'moments of absent-mindedness': William Greaves, *Today*, 3 January 1987.

6. 'French dialect': *Two Women*.

7. 'like Jean Marais': Kitty Godley in conversation with V.G.

7 | A Winter of War (1937–8)

1. Constantino Dubac was a Communist from New York, whose last appointment in the International Brigades was as an operative in Servicio de Investigación Militar (SIM). He died in 1968.
2. 'He told Allen Andrews': L.L. interviewed in *Harper's Bazaar*, November 1961.
3. 'his Cotswold childhood': L.L. interviewed by Frank Entwisle in the *Evening Standard* series 'Heartwarmers', 6 April 1962.
4. 'on the same side': L.L. to Philip Oakes, *Sunday Times*, March 1977.
5. 'carried a gun, not a stretcher': ibid.
6. 'wounds of her absence': Michael Wishart, *High Diver*.

8 | Yasmin (1938–9)

1. 'helped D.H. Lawrence': Frieda, daughter of Baron von Richthofen, left three small children and a husband fourteen years older than herself to elope with D.H. Lawrence. His years of greatest creativity followed.

9 | The Green Caravan (1940–41)

1. 'speechless with dread and misery': Michael Wishart, *High Diver*.
2. In 1922 Vera Pragnall bought eight acres of land in West Sussex to form a bohemian commune, giving parcels of land to anyone who turned up in old buses, caravans, etc. She lived in Sanctuary Cottage, Sanctuary Lane, where there is now a statue of her, and lies buried (with the man she later married, a local property developer) in Washington parish cemetery. The commune disbanded in 1938, and during the Second World War the area was occupied by Canadian servicemen.
3. Jomo Kenyatta: the future president of Kenya had made his first visit to England in 1928, in his mid-thirties, to present a petition to the Colonial Office. He lived in England from 1932 until 1946, by which time he was a controversial figure. He was imprisoned in Kenya for

managing the Mau Mau secret society in 1953, and detained until 1961. He was prime minister of Kenya in 1963, became president on its independence and died in 1978.

4. 'friend of T.E. Lawrence': T.E. Lawrence had lived nearby at Clouds Hill; when he was killed in 1935 his funeral, attended by Churchill, was at Moreton's churchyard.

5. 'heart of a lion': Michael Wishart, *High Diver*.

10 | In Love and War (1941–2)

1. The Marchesa Luisa Casati: she refers to the poet Gabriele D'Annunzio (1863–1938), who won the MC and lived with Eleanora Duse.

2. Tambimuttu: known as Tambi, the pioneer hippie was a much-loved long-haired Sri Lankan literary guru who edited *Poetry London* from 1939 to 1947, publishing Dylan Thomas, Spender, MacNeice. After years in the US he returned to revive the magazine briefly in the 1970s as *Poetry London/Apple Magazine*. He died in London in 1983.

3. 'an operatic goddess of a woman': Nicolette Devas's description of Rosamond Lehmann in her memoirs, *Two Flamboyant Fathers*, Collins, 1966.

4. Rosamond Lehmann was the granddaughter of Robert Chambers, the *Chambers Dictionary* man, whose wife kept a Victorian literary salon, and the daughter of Rudolph Lehmann, classical scholar, fencer, oarsman, founder of *Granta*, Liberal MP, *Punch* editor.

5. 'as two complicated men can be': from Sean Day-Lewis's biography of his father, *C. Day-Lewis, An English Literary Life*, Weidenfeld & Nicolson, 1980.

11 | La Belle Dame Sans Merci (1943)

1. 'really caught up with': Lucian Freud, quoted in Lawrence Gowing, *Lucian Freud*, Thames & Hudson, 1982.

2. Laurie had recently stood godfather to the baby son of Sebastian and Elizabeth Leigh-Brown, whom he had met in Sussex.
3. Laurie still had Mavis's address in Australia in his address book in the 1960s.

12 | 'No One At Home' (1944–5)

1. 'Sat-Down-And-Wept': Elizabeth Smart's most famous work was her novel, *By Grand Central Station I Sat Down and Wept*, published in 1945 by Editions Poetry London.
2. 'had collected in their student days': Michael Wishart, *High Diver*.
3. The Hon. Wynne Alexander Hugh Godley (b. 1926), younger son of Lord Kilbracken, was professor of Applied Economics at Cambridge 1980–93.

13 | 'Warm thoughts of warm nights' (1946–7)

1. Odette Massigli: According to John Lehmann's biographer Adrian Wright, Madame Massigli, wife of the French ambassador, later became Lehmann's only female lover.
2. 'beginning to end': L.L. interviewed by Christopher Cook, Radio 3, 1989.
3. 'ambiguous protector': *Two Women*.
4. 'though not for ever': L.L. in conversation with Selina Hastings, 1996.

14 | Kathy Come Home (1948–9)

1. 'intimations of mischief': Sean Day-Lewis, *C. Day-Lewis*.
2. 'isolation even more': *Two Women*.
3. 'to betray both': L.L. in conversation with Selina Hastings, 1996.

15 | The Festival Jester (1950–54)

1. 'twice the size': *Two Women* (a story cited by the *Evening Standard* journalist Anne Sharpley years later as the only known instance of anyone actually being weighed on the scales at Victoria station).
2. 'bright and bragging and English': from Mary Banham and Bevis Hillier (eds.), *A Tonic to the Nation: The Festival of Britain 1951*, Thames & Hudson, 1976.
3. 'suffering ever since': Misha Black in *A Tonic to the Nation*.
4. Walham Green Empire: *Two Women*.
5. 'Beer was flowing, of course': G.S. Whittet in *A Tonic to the Nation*.
6. 'Festival English': 'A Few Words on Festival English' by Desmond Fitzgerald, in the *World Review*, June 1951.
7. 'fantastic cast of mind': Roy Fuller in *A Tonic to the Nation*.
8. 'Telemann concerto': Charles Plouviez in *A Tonic to the Nation*.
9. The contributors of exhibits were: Mr A.C. Wood, Commander J.D. Richard, RN, Mr L.A.V. Davoren, Mr Hugh Allen, Mrs A.A. Johnson, Mr Jack Hall and Mr P. Henniker-Heaton, Founder of the British Snail-Watching Society.
10. 'endless parties': Stephen Gardiner, *Frink*, HarperCollins, 1998.
11. Colquhoun and MacBryde: Robert Colquhoun (1914–62) and Robert MacBryde (1913–66), known as 'the Roberts', met at Glasgow School of Art and were inseparable companions. Their London studio became a writers' and artists' salon 1941–7.

16 | 'Write about your own life' (1955–8)

1. 'bloodiest as the latter undeniably is': from Kingsley Amis's correspondence with Robert Conquest, quoted in Eric Jacobs, *Kingsley Amis, a Biography*, Hodder & Stoughton, 1995.
2. Lady Mary Walker's house, and the home of the Brinton-Lee family, near La Línea, both remain much as they were in the 1950s.
3. Lewis Eyers: the Slad carrier.

4. Epstein's *Ecce Homo* was in Battersea Park in 1960, later removed to Coventry Cathedral.
5. 'weeping over long-lost friends': L.L. did not reveal to Sally that the long-lost friend was her mother, Rosamond Lehmann, who had fallen out with Enid Starkie over Enid's championing of Cecil Day-Lewis for the Oxford Poetry professorship, a job Day-Lewis had told Rosamond he could do only with her at his side. Rosamond sent L.L. Starkie's letters about this.
6. 'shaved him forthwith': from L.L.'s *Encounter* article, 'Ibiza High Fifties', reproduced in *I Can't Stay Long*.

17 | Back to Slad (1959)

1. Winifred Bryher's father was Sir John Reeves Ellerman, newspaper tycoon and shipping magnate. Bryher often wrote her novels in the person of a young man, and although in her twenties she formed an association with Hilda Doolittle which lasted until H.D.'s death in 1961, she also married, twice, to acquire the freedom of a married woman.
2. 'no less a person than Laurie Lee': *Stroud News*, 5 August 1959.
3. 'spread the gospel of the country to the world': *Bristol Evening Post*, September 1959.
4. Ann Elwell (*née* Glass) was a 'beautiful spy' recruited by MI5 at the age of eighteen. Matthew Smith left all his paintings and drawings to Mary Keene (including a Van Gogh and an Epstein sculpture) and the residue of his £173,948 to her in trust for life.

18 | Annus Mirabilis (1960)

1. 'a chill wind blew from the west': L.L. in *Evening Standard*, December 1960.
2. That year, Kathy's head was sculpted by Loris Rey and drawn by Edward Ardizzone.
3. Prince Ludwig of Hesse: As Ludwig Landgraf, Prince Ludwig published poems and translated texts and librettos for Benjamin Britten.

4. Gerald Brenan (1894–1986): poet, scholar, traveller, military man (winner of the MC and the Croix de Guerre) famous for *The Face of Spain* and *South from Granada*. His association with Spain began in 1919 when he settled in an Andalucian village. He married the American writer Elizabeth Gamel Woolsey, and when he returned to Spain for good in 1953, he became an object of literary pilgrimage.
5. The Stewarts of Gibraltar: John D. Stewart was a Northern Irish civil engineer employed by the Gibraltar government, who published a book called *Gibraltar the Keystone*. He died in 1996.
6. The Searles: John Searle was for thirty years editor of the *Gibraltar Chronicle*.
7. 'begging for church bread': from L.L.'s interview with Gordon Burn, *Radio Times*, 23 December 1971.
8. Dame Veronica Wedgwood, speaking about *Cider with Rosie* in 'Vintage Cider' on Radio 4 in November 1984.

20 | Laurie the Magician (1962–3)

1. 'inscrutable, dear boy': L.L. to Christopher Cook in Radio 3 interview, 1989.
2. 'when I returned home to my wife': Dannie Abse in his autobiography, *A Poet in the Family*, Hutchinson, 1974.
3. 'have a place on earth': L.L. in an article on his garden, *Homes & Gardens*, June 1962.
4. Cheltenham Festival panel to discuss autobiography: with L.L. were Elspeth Huxley, Alec Waugh and Danny Blanchflower.
5. 'a wistful fugitive': *Two Women*.
6. 'country recipes': Jeremy Sandford reporting for *Radio Times* on his 1962 interview with L.L. in Slad.
7. 'a mysterious act of fate': 'Relative Values', *Sunday Times* magazine, 9 March 1986.

21 | Jessy (1964–6)

1. 'which I've always wanted to do': 'Relative Values', 9 March 1986.
2. Ted Hughes wrote 'Full Moon and Little Frieda' about his daughter's first word: 'Moon! you cried suddenly. 'Moon! Moon!'
3. 'Kingsley Amis on the station bookstall': from Ian Jack's account of Lord Snowdon's picture session in the *Sunday Times* magazine, 14 February 1982.

22 | 'A wave through a dark window' (1967–9)

1. 'Popski', Col. V. Poliakoff, was a distinguished Polish-born army officer who made his name in the Second World War leading 'Popski's Private Army' in jeeps in the North African desert. Their courageous exploits led them to be regarded as the precursors of the SAS.
2. 'Gitano y Gitanas': published in *The Gypsies of Granada*, Athelnay Books, 1969.

23 | Dear Mr Lee . . . (1970–74)

1. The Flook luncheon, 8 May 1970: other guests included Frank Norman, Kenneth Allsop, Edna O'Brien, Joan Bakewell, Spike Milligan, the cartoonists Emmwood, Leslie Illingworth, Jon, Wally Fawkes, and George and Diana Melly.
2. 'What care I how kind she be?': George Wither (1588–1667), poet and satirist, imprisoned for his verses. No complete edition of his work has been published, but the poem referred to is in *Palgrave's Golden Treasury*.
3. Steanbridge House had by this time been restored to its former glory by Mr and Mrs David Naylor.
4. 'days filled with sun': Interview with Gordon Burn, *Radio Times*, 16–23 December 1971.

5. 'circling over cloud above Cheltenham': 'Concorde 002', *Telegraph* magazine, 4 February 1972, reproduced in *I Can't Stay Long*.
6. 'Dear Mr Lee': The poet Ursula Fanthorpe had been head of English at Cheltenham Ladies' College. 'Dear Mr Lee' is in her collection *A Watching Brief* (Peterloo Poets), and is reproduced here on page 523.

24 | I Can't Stay Long (1975–9)

1. 'mortally frightened': 'Books' page, *Daily Mail*, 21 April 1977.
2. 'A Village Christmas': *Reader's Digest*, December 1976.
3. *Sun*, 14 February 1979.
4. Hugh Thomas, *The Spanish Civil War*, Eyre & Spottiswoode, 1961, repr. Hamish Hamilton, 1977.

25 | Two Women (1980–83)

1. 'I do hope they see that': interview with L.L., *Wilts & Glos Standard*, 22 October 1983.
2. 'all over London': Angela Levin, *Mail on Sunday*, October 1983.

27 | Sans Everything (1986–90)

1. 'conferred immortality': in July 1977, Bevis Hillier's Generation Show for the Jubilee at the Corn Exchange, Brighton, included a list of books which had 'changed attitudes or epitomized them' since 1953, starting with Dr Spock's *Baby and Child Care*, Salinger's *The Catcher in the Rye*, Hoggart's *The Uses of Literacy* and Berne's *Games People Play*. Hillier appealed to *Sunday Times* readers for their own suggestions. As a result the year of 1959 included Burroughs's *The Naked Lunch*, Delaney's *A Taste of Honey*, Gombrich's *Art and Illusion*, Sillitoe's *The Loneliness of the Long Distance Runner*, Waterhouse's *Billy Liar*, Thomas's *The Establishment*, and *Cider with Rosie*.
2. '50 years ago': Peter Davalle in *The Times*, December 1987.

3. 'the La Roca apartment block': Val Hennessy, *Mail on Sunday*, 13 November 1988.

28 | The Last Book (1991)

1. Quotations from Bill Alexander and John Dunlop's critiques of *A Moment of War* come from the Spanish Civil War archives in the Imperial War Museum and the Marx Memorial Library.

29 | The Old Man of the Woolpack (1992–7)

1. 'rag-bag of mutilated texts': A.N. Wilson in the *Evening Standard*, January 1993.
2. The McGregor/Matthews room at New College is one of the most beautiful rooms in Oxford, on the top floor of the front quadrangle. Formerly known as the Wyatt library, it had been lined with deteriorating leather books which obscured the fine seventeenth-century windows overlooking the garden quad. The then Warden, Harvey McGregor QC, and Tom's widow Pam Matthews jointly paid the substantial cost of removing the books and restoring the room, now used for college meetings and concerts.

30 | Epilogue (1997–9)

1. 'blacking factory': Philip Oakes in conversation with V.G.
2. 'between myth and memoir': *The Times* obituary, 15 May 1997.
3. 'a person of concealment': *Daily Telegraph* obituary, 15 May 1997.
4. 'read like prose poetry': Jane Mack, letter to the *Guardian*, 17 May 1997.
5. 'a scrupulous historian could provide': Allan Massie in the *Daily Telegraph*, 1 January 1998.
6. 'a powerful fascination': Vernon Scannell in the *Guardian*, 1 January 1998.

7. 'quotidian lower-case truth': Ted Walker in a letter to V.G., February 1998.

8. 'safely dead, of course': Paul Burroughs, letter to the *Guardian*, 2 January 1998.

9. In February 1996, Dr McLoughlin had actually written to Penguin to tell them he had these documents pertaining to Laurie's arrival at the International Brigades HQ, which he would be glad to show to Laurie. But he received no reply.

10. 'fight from the heart': L.L. in *Evening Standard* article on his teenage years, December 1960.

11. 'Micky Thumps': the anonymous Lancashire ballad was included by C. Day-Lewis in *Poetry for You*, a book for schoolchildren on the enjoyment of poetry, published by Blackwell in 1944.

12. 'using his wartime journals': Clare Alexander of Penguin discussed another book with L.L. in 1995.

13. 'nothing more': L.L. to Mavis Nicholson in her television interview, *Mavis Catches Up With . . .*, 1989.

Bibliography

Works by Laurie Lee

Poetry

The Sun My Monument, The New Hogarth Library, 1944.

The Bloom of Candles, The Hogarth Press, 1947.

My Many-Coated Man, André Deutsch, 1955.

Pocket Poets, Vista Books, 1960.

15 Poems for William Shakespeare, Trustees and Guardians of Shakespeare's Birthplace, 1964.

Paintings and Drawings of Gypsies of Granada, Athelnay Books, 1969.

Pergamon Poets, Pergamon Press, 1970.

Selected Poems, André Deutsch, 1983.

Plays

Peasants' Priest, H.J. Goulden, Canterbury, 1947.

The Voyage of Magellan, John Lehmann, 1948.

I Call Me Adam (unpublished), 1959.

Prose

Land at War, HMSO, 1945.

(With Ralph Keene) *We Made a Film in Cyprus*, Longmans Green, 1947.

Vassos the Goatherd, Pilot Press, 1947.

A Rose for Winter, The Hogarth Press, 1955; Penguin 1971.

Cider with Rosie, The Hogarth Press, 1959; Penguin, 1962.

(With David Lambert) *Man Must Move: The Story of Transport*, Rathbone Books, 1960.

Atlantic Fairway, Cunard Line, 1962.

The Firstborn, The Hogarth Press, 1964.

As I Walked Out One Midsummer Morning, André Deutsch, 1969; Penguin, 1971.

The Wonderful World of Transport, Aldus Books, 1969.

I Can't Stay Long, André Deutsch, 1975; Penguin, 1977.

Two Women, André Deutsch, 1983.

Laurie Lee: A selection for use in schools, ed. Chris Buckton, Longman, 1985.

A Moment of War, Viking, 1991; Penguin, 1992.

Red Sky at Sunrise: omnibus edition of *Cider with Rosie, As I Walked Out One Midsummer Morning* and *A Moment of War*, Viking, 1992; Penguin Books, 1993.

To War in Spain, Penguin 60s, 1996.

Films

Malta VC, 1945.

Cyprus is an Island, 1946, Greenpark Productions.

A Tale in a Tea-cup, 1947, Greenpark Productions.

Journey into Spring, 1957, British Transport Films.

Books Consulted

Alexander, Bill, *British Volunteers for Liberty*, Lawrence & Wishart, 1982.

Angus, John, *With the International Brigade in Spain*, Department of Economics, Loughborough University, 1983.

Banham, Mary, and Hillier, Bevis (eds.), *A Tonic to the Nation: The Festival of Britain 1951*, Thames & Hudson, 1976.

Beevor, Antony, *The Spanish Civil War*, Orbis, 1982.

Brenan, Gerald, *Personal Record, 1920–1972*, Jonathan Cape, 1974.

Buchanan, Tom, *Britain and the Spanish Civil War*, Oxford University Press, 1996.

Campbell, Roy, *Light on a Dark Horse*, Hollis & Carter, 1951; reprinted 1969, with a foreword by Laurie Lee.

Carr, Raymond, *Spain 1808–1939*, Oxford University Press, 1966.

Courtauld, Simon, *Spanish Hours*, Libri Mundi, 1996.

Cross, Tom, *Artists & Bohemians: 100 Years with the Chelsea Arts Club*, Quiller Press, 1992.

Cunningham, Valentine, *Spanish Front: Writers on the Civil War*, Oxford University Press, 1986.

Cunningham, Valentine (ed.), *The Penguin Book of Spanish Civil War Verse*, Penguin, 1980.

Day-Lewis, Sean, *C. Day-Lewis, An English Literary Life*, Weidenfeld & Nicolson, 1980.

Devas, Nicolette, *Two Flamboyant Fathers*, Collins, 1966.

Fern, Jim, *Ferns in the Valley*, Millvale Publishing, Evesham, 1995.

Gallagher, Jock (ed.), *Laurie Lee, A Many-coated Man*, Viking, 1998.

Gardiner, Stephen, *Epstein*, Michael Joseph, 1992.

Gardiner, Stephen, *Frink*, HarperCollins, 1998.

Glendinning, Victoria, *Vita*, Weidenfeld & Nicolson, 1983.

Goodman, Celia (ed.), *Living with Koestler: Mamaine Koestler's Letters 1945–51*, Weidenfeld & Nicolson, 1985.

Gowing, Lawrence, *Lucian Freud*, Thames & Hudson, 1982.

Howson, Gerald, *Arms for Spain: The Untold Story of the Spanish Civil War*, John Murray, 1998.

Jacobs, Eric, *Kingsley Amis, a biography*, Hodder & Stoughton, 1995.

Kavanagh, P.J., *The Perfect Stranger*, Chatto & Windus, 1966.

Lyle, Anna Campbell, *Poetic Justice: a memoir of Roy Campbell*, Typographeum, Francestown, New Hampshire, 1986.

MacFarlane, Brian, *An Autobiography of British Cinema*, Methuen, 1997.

Mansell, Frank, *Cotswold Ballads*, with introduction by Laurie Lee, Wittantree press, Stroud, 1969; reprinted by R. Courtauld, Stroud, 1974.

Marcus, Jane, *The Young Rebecca. Writings of Rebecca West 1911–1917*, Macmillan/Virago, 1982.

Mitchell, David, *The Spanish Civil War*, Granada, 1982.

Mortimer, John, *Clinging to the Wreckage*, Weidenfeld & Nicolson, 1982.

Pritchett, V.S., *Marching Spain*, Ernest Benn, 1928.

Ray, Gordon N., *H.G. Wells and Rebecca West*, Macmillan, 1974.

Rust, William, *Britons in Spain*, Lawrence & Wishart, 1939.

Sebba, Anne, *Battling for News*, Hodder & Stoughton, 1994.

Thacker, Joy, *Whiteway Colony, The Social History of a Tolstoyan Community*, Sutton Publishing, Stroud, Glos., 1993.

Thomas, Hugh, *The Spanish Civil War*, Eyre & Spottiswoode, 1961; reprinted by Hamish Hamilton, 1977.

Tolley, A.T., *The Poetry of the Thirties*, Gollancz, 1975.

Walker, Ted, *In Spain*, Secker & Warburg, 1987.

Walker, Ted, *The Last of England*, Jonathan Cape, 1992.

Wishart, Michael, *High Diver*, Blond & Briggs, 1977.

Wright, Adrian, *John Lehmann, A Pagan Adventure*, Duckworth, 1998.

Index

Note: LL's own works appear directly under title; works by others under author's name

Friday Apr 17

A dis p...
of "P. of T" in Tribune
which is I think o...
humiliating things
said about one's ...
being accused of p...
Loona rang up at
her about it but
with laughter. Hou...
me I could only g...
to the film – discuss...
all day. Affectati...
more than anything
But increasingly
of many of my po...
good ones are c...

ng morning — review
cuses me of "affectation"
of the most
hat one can have
ing. Worse even than
had writing.
he Studio a I told
she just wared
it so dispirited
half my attention
an which went on
which I loathe
re in others!
feel the badness
in P of T. The
pletely destroyed by